Peddling Bicycles
to America

# Peddling Bicycles to America

*The Rise of an Industry*

Bruce D. Epperson

McFarland & Company, Inc., Publishers
*Jefferson, North Carolina, and London*

LIBRARY OF CONGRESS CATALOGUING-IN-PUBLICATION DATA

Epperson, Bruce D., 1957–
Peddling bicycles to America : the rise
of an industry / Bruce D. Epperson.

p.     cm.
Includes bibliographical references and index.

**ISBN 978-0-7864-4780-0**
softcover : 50# alkaline paper ∞

1. Bicycle industry — United States — History.
I. Title.

HD9993.B543U534   2010    338.4'76292272097309041—dc22    2010014903

British Library cataloguing data are available

©2010 Bruce D. Epperson. All rights reserved

*No part of this book may be reproduced or transmitted in any form
or by any means, electronic or mechanical, including photocopying
or recording, or by any information storage and retrieval system,
without permission in writing from the publisher.*

Front cover: C.W. Wilson Bicycle Co., Fergus Falls, Minnesota
(Minnesota Historical Society); illustration from Lallement's bicycle patent, 1866

Manufactured in the United States of America

*McFarland & Company, Inc., Publishers
Box 611, Jefferson, North Carolina 28640
www.mcfarlandpub.com*

For Nora

Strength and dignity are her clothing,
And she laughs at the time to come.

She opens her mouth with wisdom,
And the teachings of kindness are upon her tongue.

—Proverbs 31:25–6

# Table of Contents

*Preface and Acknowledgments* — 1
*Introduction: A Gala at the Allyn House* — 7

1. I Was Not a Bad Boy, Only Mischievous — 13
2. Colonel Pope Goes to Hartford — 24
3. The Great Patent Wars — 35
4. Building the Mass Market — 55
5. The Coming of the Safety Bicycle — 74
6. Reading, 'Riting, 'Rithmetic and Roads — 89
7. The Great Bicycle Boom — 105
8. The Motor Carriage — 129
9. Troubled Times — 149
10. The Bicycle Trust — 171
11. Picking Up the Pieces — 189
12. After Pope — 207
13. All Gone to Their Account — 229
14. The Long Road Home — 235

*Chapter Notes* — 247
*Bibliography* — 277
*Index* — 289

*Are there no calamities in history? Nothing tragic? May we never weep over the defeated...? Must we always desert the cause as soon as fortune forsakes it, and bind ourselves to the cause which is in the ascendant, and hurrah in the crowd that throw up their caps in honor of the conqueror?*

— Orestes Brownson

*Battles (as soldiers know, and newspaper editors do not) are usually fought, not as they ought to be fought, but as they can be fought; and while the literary man is laying down the law at his desk as to how many troops should be moved here, and what rivers should be crossed there, and where the cavalry should have been brought up, and when the flank should have been turned, the wretched man who has to do the work finds the matter settled for him by pestilence, want of shoes, empty stomachs, bad roads, heavy rains, hot suns, and a thousand other stern warriors who never show on paper.*

— Charles Kingsley,
*Westward Ho!*

# *Preface and Acknowledgments*

The foundation of this book was laid in 1988, when, as a college senior, I had run out of both time and money and dropped out with only my required fourth-year thesis remaining. The chair of the economics department at the University of Kansas, the noted economic historian Thomas Weiss, not only bent the more rigid rules of those days to allow me to submit mine by mail (a few years late), but agreed to act as my thesis advisor. Never able to settle on a specialty, I suddenly became an economic historian and promptly fell in love with that field precisely because it rewarded the generalist. For my topic, I attempted to verify the production numbers of the Great American Bicycle Boom of 1893 to 1900, and while I failed to pin down any conclusive figures, I established pretty convincingly that the stupendous numbers batted about over the previous three-quarters of a century were apocryphal. Shortly before this, a young technological historian, David Hounshell, had published a seminal book on the development of mass production in America, *From the American System to Mass Production*, which included a chapter on the production methods used by two large bicycle makers at the turn of the century, the Pope Manufacturing Company and the Western Wheel Works. This was the first book, at least in America, to cast a trained, objective eye on a subject that had previously been relegated to old bicycle enthusiasts and collectors (or, as they are referred to rather unflatteringly by academic scholars, "fetishists").

Despite my expectation that Hounshell's chapter would soon lead to a flowering of scholarly works on the technological and industrial history of the bicycle, the intervening decades have seen fewer than a single handful of books, almost all focusing on Europe. This book is thus the one that I thought someone else would have published a decade or more ago: an expansive, in-depth treatment of the issues raised and questions left unanswered in Hounshell's all-too-brief précis. It is not a book about bicycles; it is, rather, a book about how bicycles were made and how they were sold, especially before World War I. It follows the life and work of the most important figure of that period, Colonel Albert A. Pope of Boston and Hartford. Depending on how you define "bicycle," he either founded the American industry, or resurrected it after it had blundered into the production of boneshakers for two or three years, then rolled over and died for a decade. In either case, the bicycle industry we are familiar with today can trace its lineage directly to his work.

There has been a tendency to portray Colonel Pope as comprising the entire industry before the Great War, but this is not so. Pope was a larger-than-life, P.T. Barnum–type character, but except for his first two or three years in the trade, he probably never captured more than a third of the overall market, and during the great boom years of the 1890s, his factories were producing only about one out of every eight bicycles. There were equally big players, and the way they went about making and selling *their* bicycles was often very different from Pope's. Their story also deserves telling. However, unlike Pope, they usually did not relish the daily limelight, and thus far less is known about them. As far as possible, they are included here, as are the stories of factory employees, bicycle retailers, company field agents, wholesalers, and small-shop manufacturers.

\* \* \*

It is difficult to know where to begin with the thanks that needs to be given to those who have supported these efforts. First and foremost among the scholars, I must acknowledge the pathbreaking work of David Hounshell. Because of his attention to citation and documentation, he is cited here far less than he deserves, because he simply made it too easy to seek out and find the primary sources *he* used. Among the other members of the Society for the History of Technology (SHOT) who have lent me advice and support, discussions with Wiebie Bijker, Trevor Pinch, Philip Scranton and Steve Usselman have been encouraging and enlightening; Joe Schultz and David Lucsko at SHOT's journal, *Technology and Culture,* have been kind and patient editors; and John Staudenmaier, S.J., its editor-in-chief, courageously took the position that scholarly articles should be considered only on merit, not the affiliation of their author, thus opening *T&C*'s pages in 2000 for my first widely distributed article on bicycle building. A SHOT travel grant allowed me to present an earlier version of that paper at the 1997 annual conference in Pasadena.

One of the main problems with bicycle history as a scholarly discipline is that the field has been a stagnant backwater so long that nobody really appreciated how bad things had gotten. That started to change in 1990 when Englishman Nicholas Clayton organized the first International Cycle History Conference (ICHC), and three years later San Francisco publisher Rob van der Plas agreed to start printing and distributing each year's proceedings, seemingly always taking a loss. Through the ICHC, I have received support and assistance from Frank Berto, Carl and Clary Burgwardt, Thomas Burr, Nick Clayton, Pryor Dodge, David V. Herlihy, Hans-Erhard Lessing, Glen Norcliffe, Ross Petty, Andrew Ritchie, and Paul Rubenstein. Frank, Andrew, David, Ross, Paul and Nick all provided me with information I could not otherwise have gotten — some of it the most important in this book. Frank Berto was able to provide me with historic industry production figures prepared by the Schwinn company in the 1970s that was not intended for public consumption. Nick Clayton gave me his rare copy of A. E. Harrison's monumental work on the British bicycle industry at the turn of the century. Glen Norcliffe provided me with the year-by-year product summary of the Pope bicycle division that had been prepared for him by Ross Hill. (When I did my first presentation on Pope at the ICHC in 1999, I did not know that Glen had already been working on the topic for several years. He said nothing, and provided me with much valuable help. I'm sure it was mostly to keep me from feeling guilty that he made sure his 2001 book on Canadian bicycle history, *The Ride to Modernity,* was so well received.) Andrew Ritchie provided me with *Bearings* magazine's 1895–96 listing of every known bicycle maker, parts supplier and major jobber, which, until he showed it to me, I didn't know existed. David Herlihy gave me copies of depositions and affidavits from the earliest bicycle patent litigations that I doubt if even I, a lawyer, could have figured out how to get. Thomas Burr and Paul Rubenstein both gave me electronic copies of their bicycle-history-related dissertations. Carl read my paper on the great patent wars at an ICHC conference during a time when, as a starving law student, I simply didn't have the money to travel to Vienna.

It is a great tragedy that no American individual or institution was able or willing to find a home for the Burgwardt bicycle museum, which, as this is being written, is being containerized for shipment to an undisclosed, private, overseas home — the only destination willing and able to pay the $250,000 a year needed to house and maintain it. The collection itself, worth several million dollars, would probably have been entirely bequeathed had only a permanently endowed home for it been found.

Frank Berto was instrumental in securing generous financial support from the Shimano family that allowed me to travel to Osaka in 2000 to present my findings on the true dimensions of the great bicycle boom. It was there, at the 11th ICHC, that the collective decision was made for me that I would write this book. Well folks — here it is. I only hope it was worth the wait. Among other historians, Charles Meinert of the (American) Wheelmen provided invaluable information on Rollfast bicycles, American production data from the World War I era, and modern photos of the Columbia-Westfield factory.

One of the most interesting tales in the history of the writing of this book occurred in 2000. I was approached by Marjorie Prager, a historian and project manager for a consultant preparing a permanent exhibit on the history of New England enterprise for the Federal Reserve Bank of Boston. Through Marjorie, I worked in 2003 with one of the Boston Fed's economists, the delightful Phineas Baxandall, to estimate, as best we could, the Pope Manufacturing Company's investments and rates of return on capital, labor and material in the 1880s and 1890s. In the end, we had to admit we were largely guessing — systematic guessing, but still guessing. My wife and I finally had the chance to meet Marjorie and her husband, photographer Kevin Burke, over tempura in Cambridge. Kevin was researching a biography of Frederic Tudor, an eccentric Bostonian who made a fortune after the Civil War exporting ice to the tropics. Albert Pope, an automobile pioneer, had tried to talk the state of Massachusetts out of license plate No. 1, but the Tudor family beat him to it, causing, according to Kevin, much animosity. For my part, I could find nothing about it in Pope's papers (not surprising, when the Colonel lost at something, he usually denied anything ever happened), but Kevin did have a copy of an extraordinary letter: an admission by the treasurer of the great, but short-lived bicycle trust, the Colonel's cousin George Pope, that it was producing only about half the number of bicycles it publicly claimed. I will never, ever forget first laying eyes on that letter.

* * *

The list of archives, libraries and other related institutions that I visited over the almost twenty years of this project is astounding, and it boggles my mind that with but a single exception I was treated as a valued guest and respected scholar. Libraries and archives big and small, rich and poor, public, private and academic, asked only that I call, email or write a short time ahead to let them know what I was after. Only the library of one large, rich private university — a mere twenty miles from my front door — denied me access for lack of "adequate institutional affiliation."

In Hartford, the staff of the reading room of the Connecticut Historical Society made sure that the required permission of the Pope family to use the Pope scrapbook microfilms was in hand by the time I arrived. (This requirement has now, I understand, been relaxed.) Everett Wilkie (now at a different institution) even took me down into the basement to show me Mark Twain's Expert Columbia. The staff of the history and genealogy unit of the Connecticut State Library expedited my path through the state's somewhat cumbersome security clearance process so I would not expend the one day I had available there waiting. Dania Royce, librarian at Stowe-Day Library, cleared up my confusion over the location of the Harriet Beecher Stowe home that had been gradually swallowed up by the Hartford Cycle factory (she had two homes in Hartford) and filled me in as to the activities of architect George Keller and the Hartford Real Estate Improvement Association, which almost ended up building a Pullman-style model workers' village around the Pope factory.

In Massachusetts, Elizabeth Bouvier graciously granted me access to the cramped little garret that is the home of the archives division of the Massachusetts Supreme Judicial Court in downtown Boston so I could transcribe the will and codicil of Albert Pope. Susan Navarre at the Forrest Hills Cemetery located the Pope family columbarium at a time when seemingly nobody knew of its existence. (I gather it has since become something of a tourist stop for cycling buffs.) In the city of Newton, Edward English, Clerk of the Board of Alderman, went far beyond the scope of his duties to verify Pope's service as an alderman there. In Cohasset, Ellen M. Freda, who lived in what had formerly been Albert Pope's Lindermere stables, graciously dropped her weekend gardening to give me a tour of the place and later provided me with copies of historical surveys of the surviving Lindermere buildings. In Hull, the Reverend Father John G. Maheras showed me through what was once the Charles L. Pope Memorial Church. In Northampton, librarian Sherill Redmon of the Sophia Smith Collection at Smith College was very helpful in locating material relating to the Pope Memorial Dispensary within the archives of the New England Women's and Children's Hospital.

In New Jersey, Nydia Cruz of the Samuel C. Williams Library at the Stevens Institute of Technology in Hoboken (just down the street from the boyhood home of Frank Sinatra) helped me locate the somewhat obscure material in their Frederick W. Taylor collection related to Taylor's work spying on the Pope and Overman cycle factories. In Newark, James Lewis and the staff of the New Jersey Historical Society assisted in my efforts to locate material about the first days of the Electric Vehicle Company. As an aside, those interested in the technical history of the shaft-drive bicycle should note the extremely important technical evaluation of one brand of shaft-drive (The Tuttle) made by the engineering laboratory at Cornell University. Because the title of the report does not state exactly what the Cornell lab had been hired to test, it is not reflected in the cataloger's comments, and I stumbled across it purely by accident. It is filed under: "Report from R. C. Carpenter (Cornell Univ.) to H. Tuttle, 18 December 1899, William F. D. Crane Papers (MS 1092), Box 2, File 8 (5 pages)."

The staff of the reading room at the Ohio Historical Society in Columbus must be commended — they are under such tremendous financial constraints that they can open only three days a week, yet their assistance in pulling files from the Arthur Garford collection and photocopying for me on an assembly-line basis was phenomenal. (I wonder if they would have been so helpful had they realized that they were soon to be "outed" as the largest collection of historic material on the bicycle industry in America!) The reference staff at the main library at Ohio State University was able to make even OHS's closed days productive by pointing me to the large collection of microform cycling journals in their history of sport collection.

In Washington, James P. Roan, librarian at the Smithsonian's National Museum of American History, was extremely helpful in locating unpublished material, such as the guidebook to the "Golden Jubilee" antique automobile show in Hartford in 1950, written by Henry Cave, that contained many of the recollections of Hermann Cuntz about the sale of the Pope motor carriage division to the Electric Vehicle Company. Guardian of the NMAH transportation division's infamous "cage," the long-suffering Roger White still graciously gives a seemingly unending stream of bicycle researchers access to the Charles E. Pratt scrapbook, the Smithsonian's complete run of pre–World War I Columbia bicycle catalogs, and its bound copies of turn-of-the-century cycling journals. Roger always grumbles that this should be the Library of Congress's job, but knows that a majority of the call slips one submits in the LOC's reading room for pre–1910 bound bicycle journals will invariably come back as "unavailable," the result of decades of pilferage and inadequate staffing. In fact, based on my query to several institutions, the periodicals listserv of the American Library Association did a quick and informal survey of old cycling journals. The verdict: probably every pre–1910 bound cycling journal listed on the OCLC intercollegiate library catalog that is not held in a secure environment (such as a rare books room) is either lost, stolen or missing. Almost all of these are probably in one or another undisclosed private collection somewhere, a substantial sum of money having changed hands along the way. Librarian beware!

In Detroit, researcher Judith Kirsch and the staff of the Henry Ford assisted me most efficiently in tracking down material in the Frank Armstrong collection pertaining to the Electric Vehicle Company. I thank Mark Patrick, former curator of the National Automotive History Collection, for locating the deposition of George Pope among the thousands of pages of the Selden patent case record when I was unable to come up with the correct page numbers.

In Ottawa, at the Canadian National Museum of Science and Technology, Ada Adameck searched for me through the then still-uncataloged collection of bicycle history material that is now the Shields Collection.

Here in Florida, the Miami-Dade Main Public Library had a surprisingly large collection of 19th century general-interest journals, and the staff was always (and I mean always) willing to dig them out of basement storage for me. I also spent countless hours hogging the microfilm reader on the second floor while I went through year after year of the Boston and Hartford city directories, an unspeakably painful process that later proved amazingly valuable by making fruitful chance encounters with what would have otherwise been unfamiliar names. The downtown Fort Lauderdale branch of the Broward County Public Library was the source of such microform turn-of-the-century journals as *Iron Age* and *American Machinist,* as well as the early bicycle patent records. The staff there was kind enough to let me check out some normally non-circulating materials so I could take them to another library where a high-resolution digital scanner was located. The main library at Nova Southeastern University in Fort Lauderdale heartily welcomes independent scholars, and was the source of almost all the interlibrary loan material I received since 1994, as well as most of the digitally distributed journal articles, and, since 2002, census data and other genealogical material such as veteran's records, ship debarkation logs and passport applications. The Nova law library, which is likewise open to any lawyer or registered lay user, was the source for virtually all of the legal cases cited in this work, including the massive 900-plus-page case record of the 1886 *Pope v. Gormully* lawsuit. The Nova Southeastern library system was undoubtedly the single most important source of secondary material for this project and I am deeply indebted to the trustees, administrators and staff of that institution for their enlightened academic policies. The comparison between the young, vibrant and exciting Nova Southeastern in Fort Lauderdale and its old, tired and ossified competitor just down the highway, which refused me as "inadequately credentialed," is striking.

The real secret to the success of this book is that the author had his own professional research department. The problem is that it was composed of only one research librarian, who also had to walk the dogs, tend the garden, mend clothes, and, at times, put the author through school and nurse him back from the odd major illness and injury. I promised Nora for twenty years that when I wrote my book I would dedicate it to her, and it got to the point where she would roll her eyes and say, "The book, yeah, sure." Here it is, and it's yours. I hope you like it.

# Introduction: A Gala at the Allyn House

On a Thursday evening just before the Fourth of July weekend of 1903, a middle-aged, stocky man, not quite six feet tall, with a full beard and high forehead, stepped off a train onto the platform of Hartford's Union Station. It was crowded with well-wishers, as he had been away for almost four years and the entire city eagerly awaited his return.[1]

Twenty-seven years earlier, this man, Albert Augustus Pope of Boston, had similarly stepped off a southbound train and walked down this platform, but had then gone completely unnoticed until he reached the baggage car and claimed his odd cargo — an English high-wheeled bicycle — upon which he rode away after asking the directions to a local sewing machine factory. Nobody had ever seen such a thing or had the slightest idea what it was. They soon did, after Colonel Pope started paying the local Weed Sewing Machine Company a great deal of money to make his own brand of high-wheeler, the "Columbia," the first to be manufactured in America in any appreciable numbers. A decade later, Pope bought out Weed, and ten years after that Hartford's Park River was lined with five of his factories: two bicycle plants, a tire factory, a mill for making cold-drawn steel tube and an automobile factory. During the peak season, just after Christmas, almost two thousand men a day lined up to clock into one or the other of his plants. Samuel Colt's vast armory still claimed the west bank of the Connecticut River, and his widow Elizabeth still lived in "Armsmere," the grand mansion atop a hill overlooking the factory, but by the 1890s, Pope employed more workingmen. After the panic of 1893 devastated business at the armory and the town's other two major industrial employers, the toolmakers Pratt & Whitney and Billings & Spencer, Hartford's manufacturing solvency briefly rested squarely on the shoulders of the Colonel.

However, the new century had not been kind to the bicycle builders. The formerly lucrative trade descended into a tooth-and-claw battle for profits once chronic overproduction set in after 1896. The Gilded Age's smart set dropped the wheel with the sudden onset of Spanish-American War in the spring of 1898 and moved on to new, more genteel diversions. A year later, Pope, suffering personal and financial woes, sold out to an ill-conceived "bicycle trust," the American Bicycle Company, organized by sporting goods magnate A. G. Spalding. It failed in less than three years — barely enough time for Spalding to sell his interest and retire to California. Dominated by the Colonel's former foes from Chicago, the trust decided that the Columbia works were expendable, and by the time the American Bicycle Company rolled over and died like a sick mastodon in 1902, it employed fewer than 200 of Hartford's workers.

But those who counted the old man out were due for a rude shock. In a lightning, multimillion-dollar move, Pope swept up the securities of the dying trust and seized control. Three months before his appearance at Union Station, a federal court in Trenton had turned over formal control to him, and the first thing he subsequently did was ask the court to change the name back to that of his old Hartford-based firm, the Pope Manufacturing Company. The Colonel, who still lived by the sea outside Boston, had been avoiding Hartford almost since the day the trust took over, furious at the botch the new owners had made of things in his adopted hometown. "I foolishly went out of business," he told the men who came out to greet him. Now, after long years, he was back, and as one editor put it, he was breathing fire.[2]

After freshening up at the home of his son Harold, the Colonel rode, this time in an electric automobile, to the Allyn House Hotel and strolled into the ballroom to be feted by Connecticut's Governor Chamberlain, Hartford's Mayor Sullivan, a twenty-piece orchestra, a full chorus, and over a hundred guests. The nine-course meal required two hours, followed by eight speeches, including the Colonel's, and the presentation of a solid-silver loving cup. Long after midnight the weary participants staggered out of the gala.

If the late hours, the endless courses and the brimming glasses of wine had not dulled their ears too much, at least some of the guests must have left the Allyn House that morning troubled. "When men say to me, 'The bicycle business is dead and cannot be revived,' what do I care whether it can be revived or not?" Pope had thundered in his typically bombastic oratorical style. "Is there nothing else to do?"

This portrait, which appeared in an 1894 edition of the magazine *Cycling Life*, was drawn directly from the third of four official photographs Pope had taken over his thirty-year career as a bicycle manufacturer. They were widely distributed to newspapers and magazines, sent to fans who wrote asking for the Colonel's signature, and even reduced to the size of a large stamp and made into glass paperweights, now highly sought as collectibles (*Cycling Life*, February 22, 1894).

The bicycle business dead? Did he mean that? Could it really be true? The year before the trust was formed, its forty-five previously independent firms had made over 800,000 bicycles. Pope's two

# Introduction

Taken from the top of the Connecticut State House, this photograph looks east over downtown Hartford, towards the Connecticut River. The Pope factory is about a mile behind the photographer. The opposite view, from the factory to the State House, is on page 153. (Haines Photo Co., Library of Congress Call No. PAN US GEOG Conn. No. 7 [F size] [P&P]).

Hartford factories accounted for about 120,000 of these — the best, most expensive on the market, at prices up to $125 for a Columbia shaft-drive. In 1902, the trust turned out only 371,000 "wheels," with probably less than a tenth of these coming from the Columbia factory — the Hartford Cycle Company, Pope's other plant, having been shuttered two years before. The Colonel was now getting only about twenty dollars per bicycle on the wholesale market. That was still better than the others, the so-called independents. They were glad to get a paltry nine dollars in bulk sales on unbranded bicycles from the big regional distributors, called "jobbers," who put their own headbadges and decals on them.[3] Things would get far, far worse. In 1904, the Pope plants would make only 89,000 bicycles, and three years after that, no more than 50,000.

The great hope for the future, of course, was the automobile. Back in 1897, Pope's motor carriage division, under the direction of a brilliant young engineer named Hiram Percy Maxim, had been the first in America to produce and sell passenger automobiles in significant numbers. Fearful that this young enterprise would be driven into the ground by the bicycle trust, Pope sold it to a New York syndicate headed by William Whitney, the Metropolitan Traction magnate. Even at that early stage it had already made and sold some 300 autos, almost all electrics. But Whitney managed it poorly, and by 1903 most of the old Pope staff was drifting away from what was now called the Electric Vehicle Company. The company, or what was left of it, would soon become embroiled in controversy when it attempted to use a dubious 1895 patent over gasoline engines to create an automobile cartel that would make the fatal mistake of trying to shut down Henry Ford's latest venture.

In the meantime, the bicycle trust made several of its own attempts to put out an automobile, with varying degrees of success. An Indianapolis factory now produced a good electric car, the Waverley, and by mid–1903 had sold over 350 of them. A steam car and a gasoline model from Toledo were less successful, together accounting for about 200 units. After taking over, Pope told Toledo to drop the steam car and concentrate on a luxury gasoline model, while a former bicycle plant in Hagerstown, Maryland, was dusted off to make an inexpensive, no-frills gasoline model. The Colonel had already ordered the Hartford factory to speed the development of its own gasoline car. "The model is almost done," Pope announced to the Allyn House gathering.

But four cars in four different cities was stretching even the great man's resources thin. The Indianapolis plant was in good shape, running under the competent leadership of an old Pope hand, H. H. Rice. The Pope-Hartford auto project was being aided by the Colonel's nephew Harry, an MIT–trained engineer who had been working in his uncle's factories since 1888. But Harry was an increasingly unhappy man. After working on bicycles for over fifteen years, he helped Hiram Maxim develop a second generation of Columbia electric cars in 1898. When the Colonel sold the motor car division to Whitney's syndicate, Harry retired to his backyard gunsmithing shop, where he made superbly crafted rifle barrels sought by sportsmen around the world. He wanted his son Allen to join him and make it a full-scale family business, but he refused, Allen recalled, "very quickly." "I liked the work," Allen said, "but I didn't like being found fault with all the time." Orphaned as a young child and raised by various aunts, uncles and grandparents, Harry was brilliant, temperamental, and becoming increasingly eccentric. Desperately needing someone for the Pope-Hartford, the Colonel pressed him into the role of project engineer, even though Harry refused to give up his other job. "He used to be tired all the time," remembered Allen. "He was quick to anger."

Harry soon left when the J. P. Stevens firearms company bought out his gunsmithing shop; he moved his operation to Massachusetts and set it up as the company's custom-order department.[4] Another former Pope engineer, Henry Souther, also was pitching in as an independent consultant on the Hartford auto, but so far there was nobody to head up the redesign of the Pope-Toledo or the development of the inexpensive Pope-Tribune. In 1903 automotive engineers didn't grow on trees.

Some of the factories themselves were also in trouble. "My first love is this factory at Hartford. It bears my name," the Colonel told his audience at the hotel. "I shan't be satisfied until there is a man at every machine and every bench." But the Columbia plant was old. Originally a Sharps rifle factory, the core building, a four-story, 215-foot-by-45-foot brick mill, had been erected before the Civil War and expanded continuously since in a rabbit warren of extensions and sheds.[5] Completed automobiles would have to be lowered down an open-sided freight elevator to a small inner courtyard for test runs. In summer, fumes from the test yard permeated the factory.

The Toledo facility, on the other hand, was almost brand new, having been finished just before the bicycle trust took it over. But Toledo was a tough town, a place where "help had to be handled with silk gloves."[6] Pope's Hartford works had never had a strike, but Toledo would soon be convulsed by an unending series of labor actions that would last until the company finally gave up, suspended operations and sold the factory to Willys-Overland.[7] Many years later, it would become famous as the home of the Jeep, and would still have a reputation for hair-trigger labor relations.

This is how the Pope factory looked from Capitol Avenue between 1897 and 1916. The peaked-roof building in front of the smokestack is the original pre–Civil War Sharps Rifle factory. The Dept. of Tests building stands in front of it, to the viewer's left of the driveway. The light-colored building with the flag is the George Keller–designed headquarters building, erected in 1895. (Haines Photo. Co., Library of Congress Call No. PAN US GEOG Conn. No. 22 [E Size] [P&P]).

Some of the schemes the Colonel outlined that night had to make the guests blink, such as the new Columbia Cash Register. Pope had been making an inexpensive personal typewriter for years, but that operation never filled up more than a small corner of one factory, and since then Hartford had become the headquarters of Remington typewriter, Royal and Underwood, all producing the new high-speed QWERTY-keyboard models costing ten times as much as Pope's old "dial-and-strike" World typewriter. All three firms were working on a new generation of adding machines, cash registers, and other business products. A $500 automatic change-making cash register hardly looked like the way to get two thousand men back to work.

Pope's last announcement was the most startling. His oldest son, Albert Linder, the "little colonel," "Prince Albert," would take over as first vice president of the new firm. Albert Linder had briefly run operations in Hartford after the bicycle trust took over, but, disgusted with the cavalier treatment dished out by the Western men, he quit and became a stockbroker in New York. Asked by a reporter why he left, he replied, "Because trusts are bad things for the country," setting off a flurry of headlines.[8]

As a young man, Albert Linder had built up a rather checkered reputation, twice dropping out of prep school, living at home under a pseudonym, running a bicycle store, and spending a lot of his father's money on fast boats and yacht club bills. Starting in the mid–1890s, some of the men who had worked for the Pope organization for many years began to drift away, it was said, because they saw no future in the firm for anyone who was not the son or son-in-law of a Pope. George Day, "The Senator," whom Albert Pope had acquired along with the Weed Sewing Machine Company, and who had become his invaluable lieutenant for two decades, left shortly before the bicycle trust takeover to work for William Whitney at the Electric Vehicle Company. Day wasn't at the Allyn House, nor did he attend a much more intimate lunch the Colonel hosted for his men in New York a few months later.[9] In fact, Pope and Day were never again seen in the same room together. Only once did the Colonel try to explain why he sold out to the bicycle trust. "Some of my assistants thought they had enough money," he said. "They begged me and urged me to sell out to this great trust or combination ... I was overpersuaded."[10] When George Day died suddenly in 1907, the Colonel did not attend the funeral.

Many were surprised that young Albert would take the job. After leaving Hartford, he seemed happier as a stockbroker, out of his father's shadow and away from the bicycle business. Months earlier, the vice-presidency of the revamped Pope firm had been assigned to a long-time employee, Charles Walker, but shortly before the big Allyn House dinner the draft corporate bylaws were rewritten to include a second vice-presidential office. "It is the purpose, I believe, to have one of the vice presidents a figurehead more than anything else," a company insider wrote privately during the scramble.[11] Then came the dinner and Pope's announcement that the little colonel would come back.

A few of the Colonel's friends were genuinely worried that he wasn't moving the company in the direction it needed to go. As much as he believed in Pope, Ohioan Arthur Garford, the former "saddle king," who had steadfastly supported him during the years of the trust's brutal internecine warfare, realized that the new company was less an organization than a scattering of bits and pieces of the old trust, with fourteen factories flung across eight states, each making its own products and operating at various levels of efficiency.

"The whole thing resolves itself down to a question of good management throughout ALL of the companies and departments of the same, and I cannot say that at present a satisfactory condition prevails in some of these," Garford admitted.[12]

The dinner was intended to celebrate Hartford's new beginning. But as the guests walked out into the quiet pre-dawn morning of a Fourth of July weekend, some had to wonder if they were instead seeing the beginning of the end.

# 1

## I Was Not a Bad Boy, Only Mischievous

*He is besides a good fisherman of good stories, and is a good fisherman in improving the stories that he tells.*
— Charles E. Pratt, 1891[1]

*Aside from some things which he says of himself, his word can be accepted as true.*
— Arthur L. Garford, 1902[2]

One of Albert Pope's most carefully crafted works was his own life story. Pope enjoyed portraying himself as a character out of a Horatio Alger novel: a child of privilege, forced into the menial trades by the ill hand of fortune, able to overcome adversity through pluck and unflagging optimism. Although the tale is embellished — sometimes liberally embellished — it is essentially true.

Albert Augustus Pope was born in Boston on 20 May 1843, the fourth of eight children of Charles and Elizabeth Pope. Charles traced his American ancestry back five generations to John Pope, who immigrated from England in 1630 and helped found the town of Dorchester, just south of Boston, four years later.[3] Albert's grandfather Frederick and great-uncle William set up shop about 1790 in the lumber, shipping and real estate trades in what is still called the "Pope's Hill" neighborhood of Dorchester.[4] Nine years later, Frederick sailed to Maine, then a district of the Commonwealth of Massachusetts, to expand their lumber business. The gamble succeeded and the brothers soon become wealthy men. An orphaned nephew, also named William, joined the business in 1805 and remained with the firm for the rest of his life, traveling frequently between Massachusetts and Maine. Colonel William, as the nephew became known, took over the business when his uncles retired and passed it on to his seven sons, who split into Maine and Massachusetts clans and expanded the Pope enterprise into a bicoastal lumbering empire. The Pope and Talbot Lumber Company, still traded on the New York Stock Exchange, is a descendant of this family business, and even before the Civil War its San Francisco headquarters had become a home away from home for the Massachusetts and Maine Popes.

As Colonel William's family came to dominate the firm, the sons of the founders themselves either moved to Maine or remained in Dorchester and set themselves up as merchants and land developers, using their inheritances and contacts within the lumber and hardware trades to build careers without having to undergo the financial and personal risks of regular Massachusetts-to-Maine winter and spring sea travel. Albert's father Charles and uncle William remained Boston-based merchants all their lives. Charles and William were twins, born in Dorchester in 1814. Charles married twenty-two-year-old Elizabeth Bogman in 1834. Elizabeth was the oldest daughter of James and Parley Nelson Bogman of Providence. James Bogman was a sea captain, came from a family of seafaring men, and died at sea around 1820 when Elizabeth was only eight or nine. Parley was his third wife when they married in 1811. His first died two years after they were married. James then married Parley's sister Elizabeth, and after Elizabeth's untimely death he married Parley. James and Parley had four children, including Elizabeth and her sister Mary, who was four years younger.

Six years after Charles and Elizabeth married, William Pope wed Mary Bogman. A year later, in 1841, Charles started as a clerk at the shoe findings and hardware establishment of James Hall and J. W. Warren at 10 Dock Square in Boston.[5] There was a family connection of some type involved, as Moses Warren operated a hardware store next door at 9 Dock Square and Moses was married to Francis Bogman Warren, niece of the late Captain Bogman, and cousin to Elizabeth. Francis's brother, George Bogman, in partnership with James Vinal, soon bought out another hardware firm, at 7 Dock Square, that was doing business under the name Bell & Richards.[6] These family connections would intertwine the Popes with several second-generation Boston merchant families: the Talbots, Warrens, Beals and Vinals.

In 1845, two years after Albert was born, Charles was operating as feather merchant, sharing the Warren & Bogman quarters at 9 Dock Square and living on Pinkney Street in Beacon Hill. About this time, he purchased his first building lot in Brookline, where Moses Warren and his family already lived.[7] While he remained a feather merchant for only a couple of years, real estate appealed more, and he bought and sold an increasing number of properties in Brookline during the next six years, moving his family there in 1846. Meanwhile, William was finding success in the crockery business. After working as a clerk for four years, he was taken on as senior partner in the new crockery and glassware establishment of Pope & Waldron in 1845.

## *I Saw That Trouble Had Come*

The year 1850 was a prosperous one for the twins. Despite a net worth of $27,000— the equivalent of some $800,000 in today's dollars — Charles and William lived together in Brookline with their large and still-growing families. With a total of seventeen under one roof, it must have been a hectic household. Charles and Elizabeth had seven children, and William and Mary four. The household was affluent enough for two servants, Betty Burke and Bridget McDermot, both from Ireland.[8] However, harder times lay ahead. William and Mary soon lost three children in as many years. Young Mary died shortly before her fourth birthday, and their next two children, Warren and Annie, died in infancy. In addition, both brothers suffered significant financial reverses.

Charles was a fairly typical Boston-area real estate dealer of the period, buying and selling several dozen lots between 1845 and 1851. A dealer acted as a middleman between land speculators and building contractors. The speculator would buy anywhere between eight and forty acres, enough for 24 to 160 building lots. He would file a subdivision plat with the city and build the required streets and sidewalks, after which the city would lay the water and sewer lines. The speculator then sold small blocks of five or six lots to the real estate dealer, who, in turn, sold individual lots to builders and provided short-term construction loans. In some cases, dealers acted as straw men for speculators, putting their name on the deeds for an entire city block's worth of lots to reduce the speculator's risk of loss. It was a form of insurance, for which the dealer took a ten or twelve percent cut.

After six years of increasingly vigorous activity, Charles's land purchases suddenly stopped in June 1851. That November, he authorized an assignment for creditors, surrendering his remaining properties to a trustee for sale and the repayment of debts.[9] At about the same time, Pope & Waldron dropped out of the Boston commercial directory. In 1853 William Pope reappeared as a simple clerk at the crockery firm of John Collamore. While Albert Pope would in later years make frequent reference to his father's financial reverses, he never mentioned the double blow to his extended family caused by his uncle's misfortune.

The move was not without some advantages, however. At the Collamore store William met fellow employee Nelson Miles, a seventeen-year-old boy fresh off his parents' farm in rural western Massachusetts. William, in turn, introduced Miles to Albert and his son George. After earning the Congressional Medal of Honor in the Civil War, Miles would go on to a brilliant military career and become one of the few non–West Point officers to become commander-in-chief of the army.[10] Miles and the Pope cousins remained good friends for the remainder of their lives, and at various times would endure public ridicule to defend each other.

In April 1852 Albert hired himself out to a neighboring farmer as a plowboy after school and on weekends. Asked why he started work so young, Pope stated flatly that "my father failed when I was nine years of age—he had been a rich man, and I saw that trouble had come, the servants had gone, the horses had gone [and] we had moved into a little house."[11] Albert kept at his part-time plowman's job until the summer of 1856, when he started buying fruits and vegetables from his employer and other area farmers to sell door-to-door in Brookline. His business expanded over the next three seasons, eventually requiring him to buy his produce wholesale at the downtown Quincy Market and sell it from a rented horse and wagon.

Pope was not a stellar student. "I do not know that I ever studied in school in those days," he admitted. "My own son studied more in one year than I did in ten.... I was not a bad boy, only mischievous."[12] The family's run of misfortune continued into the spring of 1858 when Albert's older sister Mary died at the age of 17 of congenital heart disease. When school let out for the summer, Albert quit for good, ran his produce route for the summer, then started work for Andrew Harrington, a Brookline resident and wholesale produce merchant operating out of the Faneuil Hall Market. This lasted for only a few months before he hired on at the leather and shoefindings firm of Brooks & Mecuen on Blackstone Street in downtown Boston.[13] Although ostensibly a clerk, Pope recalled the job as that of an underpaid and overworked porter, earning four dollars a week to mix varnish, hoist bales and shovel snow from sidewalks. In later years, he rarely mentioned the firm by name and never had a good word to say about the four years he spent there.

By the summer of 1860, the pope family appeared to be on the road to recovery.

They were still living in Brookline, now in a modest home in a quiet neighborhood between a leather dealer and a carpenter.[14] Charles, a commercial merchant, owned the house, this one worth only four thousand dollars, and declared personal property valued at an additional $1,200. Older brother Charles Allen (everyone called him Allen) had left in 1852 to sail around Cape Horn for San Francisco and the California gold fields, after which he just kept going, traveling through China, Australia, India, Africa and Europe before returning in 1860 to marry Julia Anne Mellish. They settled down in nearby Worcester to raise a family.[15] Adelaide was teaching in the Brookline public schools. Despite Albert's later memory that "the servants had gone," the family's two loyal retainers, Betty and Bridget, were still with the household.

## The Popes Go to War

Like many young men his age, Pope was imbued with martial enthusiasm at the start of the Civil War in April 1861, blissfully unaware of the unmitigated carnage that would soon result as the new technologies of war wrought by the industrial revolution outpaced the ability of the generals on both sides to master them. The young Brooks & Mecuen clerk spent his spare time studying army regulations and drilling with a company of home guards. When President Lincoln called for 300,000 volunteers in the summer of 1862, Pope, barely 19, joined the Thirty-Fifth Regiment, Massachusetts Volunteers, as a second lieutenant, his youthful commission suggesting that the Pope family was contributing financial assistance toward the provisioning of the regiment.[16]

Six months later George, who had first joined the Forty-Fourth Massachusetts Infantry, transferred to the Fifty-Fourth Massachusetts Regiment as a captain. The Fifty-Fourth, better known as "Shaw's Regiment," was composed of white officers and black enlisted men. The posting was unpopular and dangerous, as Confederate soldiers boasted that they would rather kill the white officers of the Negro regiments than take them prisoner.[17]

Albert learned the brutal truth about modern warfare early. His most harrowing experiences were at the battles of Antietam, in September, a month after he enlisted, and at Fredericksburg the following December. At Antietam, Union General Burnside, not realizing Antietam Creek was fordable, ordered his men across a single-lane stone bridge and up the steep hill beyond it held by Confederate forces. At noon, the Thirty-Fifth started across the bridge. By nightfall, 214 of the regiment's 1013 men were dead, wounded or missing.[18] When the losses of both sides are included, it was the single bloodiest day in the history of American warfare. After becoming a wealthy man, Pope paid for the erection of a small granite memorial obelisk beside the stone bridge at the spot where the Thirty-Fifth was ordered to start its charge.

Three months later the regiment, whittled down by now to some 300 men by injury, disease, and various types of absenteeism, suffered in the Union defeat at Fredericksburg. Attacking a heavily fortified position without adequate artillery support, it took 63 casualties. Eight men, including commanding officer Sidney Williard, were killed. The officer ranks were now so thinned that Second Lieutenant Pope took command of five companies during the retreat march.[19] Although the Thirty-Fifth would see additional action over the next two and a half years, the bulk of its casualties were taken in just four months.

The war was not one long horror show, however. Stephen Goddard, a Hartford attorney who was given access to Albert's 276-page diary by the Pope family, said, "I found his Civil War diary remarkable in that this churchgoing, non-smoking, non-cussing young man, who sometimes came across as a bit of a prig, nevertheless spent a tremendous amount of time in the company of ladies, quite frequently overnight, it appears." Albert apparently harbored no grudges when it came to socializing with the fair sex, reporting once that "I met a young rebel lady at the house and went home with her to her own house."[20]

The war was more harrowing for George. At the assault of Fort Wagner in Charleston Harbor in July 1863, the Fifty-Fourth Colored Regiment suffered an astounding 259 killed or wounded, almost half its men. The fort was located on a point on the beach, and the Union generals marched the unit in formation right up the shoreline at dusk rather than wait until dark and infiltrate it along the dunes to Shaw's right. Later, the rumor spread that the Yankee generals wanted to see how close the Negroes would get to the fort and its artillery before they turned tail and ran. Shaw wisely had his officers dispense with their horses and lead the men on foot. When the shelling started, he ordered his men to break ranks and run toward the fort, scattering the troops without creating panic, then ordered them to turn toward the dunes when that proved inadequate to throw off the aim of the artillery. Fort Wagner was never captured during the war. Shaw was killed scaling its outer wall and was buried the next day along with two of his immediate subordinates and a hundred enlisted men in a trench grave. George Pope was shot in the leg and evacuated, but later returned to duty. During the war the Fifty-Fourth lost so many senior officers that George was promoted to major in 1864 and lieutenant colonel in 1865.[21]

In March 1863, Albert Pope, one of his regiment's few remaining original officers, was made a first lieutenant. On 1 April 1864, he was again promoted, this time to Captain, and put in command of Company I. A year later, on 9 April 1865, Lee surrendered to Grant at Appomattox Court House and Pope returned home to Brookline. In later years, some of Pope's rivals would cast aspirations on his use of the title "Colonel," claiming that he was never promoted to that rank or that the promotion was somehow illegitimate. Pope himself consistently reported that he was brevetted to the rank of major, then to lieutenant colonel, on a single day, 13 March 1865. This is also the date he gave to the census enumerator for the 1890 Special Census of Veterans. Brevet appointments were temporary or honorary field commissions that did not entitle the recipient to higher pay, benefits, or pension. The recordkeeping for brevet appointments was not handled in a systematic manner by the government. In Pope's case the evidence is mixed, but generally supports his claim.

In the closing days of the war, Union field units were requested to nominate regimental officers who had distinguished themselves in battle for honorary commissions. Although one regimental historian later dismissed the new regulation as something "we, at first, thought must be a joke," the historian stated that five officers of the Thirty-Fifth did receive the honor.[22] The *Official Army Register*, prepared by the Army's Adjutant General's Office in the summer of 1865, does not indicate Pope's promotion, although the report states that only information through 2 March 1865 is included.[23] (However, two other brevet appointments and one regular promotion awarded to officers in the Thirty-Fifth Regiment between the first and eighteenth of April 1865 are noted in it.) A later, 1869 report by the Adjutant General of the Commonwealth of Massachusetts, *Record of the Massachusetts Volunteers*, includes Pope's brevet appointment to lieutenant colonel, but does not specify the date.²⁴ Pope's army service record card lists his rank at the time he mustered out as captain, although it also contains a note that a field promotion was awarded, but does not state the date or grade.²⁵

In any event, for the rest of his life, Pope wished to be referred to as "Colonel" Pope. George received a full promotion to lieutenant colonel in July 1865 and was similarly referred to, even by Albert, as "Colonel George."²⁶

## Starting the Pope Manufacturing Company

Albert returned to Brooks & Mecuen to work for the princely sum of seven dollars a week. He stayed six weeks, then announced that he was leaving to start his own competing firm. The partners countered with an offer to raise his salary to ten dollars a week. "Many a man in business don't make ten dollars a week," they urged. "I'll make more than ten a week or I'll lose what I have," Pope retorted.²⁷ He took $900 in savings and hung out his shingle, "Albert A. Pope and Company, Shoefindings," at the family's space in Dock Square for a few months before moving to 15 Pearl Street. The sale of slipper decorations and shoemaker's supplies may not have been glamorous, but it was profitable. In his first year, Pope claims he made $8,000, and within four years, he was clearing $25,000 annually and had to hire on his younger brother Arthur as clerk.²⁸

Once he became a successful businessman, Albert Pope started underwriting several of his family's endeavors. His twin sisters, Emily and Caroline Augusta (she always called herself Augusta), deserve their own biography.²⁹ After graduating from Brookline High School, the twins entered Boston's New England Women's Medical College. The College was founded in 1848 by Samuel Gregory, but came of age in 1859 when it hired Marie Zakrzewska, a German immigrant midwife who earned her medical degree from the Western Reserve College (later Case Western Reserve). In 1856, Zakrzewska and Elizabeth Blackwell, another pioneering woman physician, started the New York Infirmary for Women and Children. Zakrzewska then moved to Boston at Gregory's behest, but stayed at the New England College for only three years before quitting in protest over Gregory's personal and professional conservatism. Taking most of her supporters and donors with her, Zakrzewska promptly started the New England Women's and Children's Hospital in Roxbury, which became a rock of stability in the often troubled south Boston community for the next century.

By the time the Pope sisters graduated from Gregory's New England College in 1870, it was widely considered an inferior institution, even among the limited number of legitimate medical schools that accepted women. Zakrzewska hired the Popes as interns and under her tutelage, sent them off to London and Paris to fill in the gaps left by Gregory's training.³⁰ This made for some interesting encounters, such as arriving in Paris just in time for the end of the Franco-Prussian war, the overthrow of the French Republic and the siege of Paris, which briefly trapped them in the City of Lights.³¹ They returned to Boston a year later and joined the all-female staff of the New England Hospital, where they remained for the next 40 years. The sisters gained national exposure in 1881 when they, along with fellow New England Hospital physician Emma Call, read a paper entitled "The Practice of Medicine by Women in the United States" before the annual meeting of the Social Science Association.³² The presentation made headlines and was soon expanded into a full-length book. Their survey of 430 women doctors concluded that there was no reason for an otherwise healthy female physician to suspend work for the duration of her menses, finding that "some unnecessary anxiety has been wasted on this point." Each of the twins' two-year medical education cost between six and seven hundred dollars, and their graduate studies in Europe probably a similar amount. Albert paid for it.[33] The Colonel's youngest brother Louis started at Harvard in 1869, but had to withdraw after his first year because of illness. A year later, he resumed his studies at Brown and graduated in 1874, then went on to Newton Theological Seminary and became a Baptist minister. Albert paid for his schooling as well.[34]

The year 1871 was a hectic but happy one for the Popes. Scattered across the Boston suburbs and even the world, the family was reuniting in a new neighborhood dredged from the mud of Boston Harbor. Back from Europe, Emily and Augusta hung out their joint shingle above a new home and office at 80 Chandler Street in Boston's South Back Bay. Just around the corner was the new railroad station, where they caught the interurban down Columbus Avenue to the Women's and Children's Hospital four miles away. They were joined by their elder sister Adelaide, who retired from her teaching job in Brookline to help care for niece and nephew Luella and Harry Pope, the children of oldest brother Allen.

Allen's wife Julia and their daughter Ada died within days of each other from diphtheria four years before, in 1867, and the surviving children were orphaned when Allen was struck and killed by a Boston and Providence Railroad train in November 1868.[35] A Pope family legend has it that the long tails of Allen's Prince Albert coat caught under the wheels of the train, dragging him under. The truth is more somber. Prince Albert coats were not in fashion in 1868 except as evening formalwear, and Allen was struck early in the morning on a weekday. There is no death notice or newspaper article about the accident, and family genealogist Charles H. Pope's usually loquacious 1888 history of the Dorchester Popes is similarly tight-lipped. Given the location of the B&PRR tracks on top of a narrow levee in the middle of a vast mud flat that would later become the west Back Bay, it is likely that Allen, despondent over the death of his wife and daughter, committed suicide.

The three sisters, Adelaide, Augusta and Emily, never married, and together they formed the nucleus of an extended Pope household that lasted for almost half a century. They were joined by their parents and brother Louis, who had been living in Newton and attending school while the twins were in Europe. Albert likewise moved into the smart new red-brick townhouse, but only for a few months. He had his own plans, and they included Abby Linder, daughter of George Linder, a successful Newton businessman, and his wife, Matilda. Abby lived up to the example of the strong, independent women typical of the Pope family, and she later listed women's suffrage as her greatest area of interest outside the home.[36] The two were married in Newton in September 1871. Rather than move Abby into town, he decided to commute and bought a large Queen Anne house with matching carriage house and gazebo on the north side of Washington Street, opposite Waverley Avenue, in Newton Corner. Matilda Linder, soon widowed, lived only four doors down. A servant for Abby and a coachman, Patrick Condon, made suburban life a little easier. Ten months later, their first son, Albert Linder, was born and a daughter, Mary, followed in 1874 but lived only three months. Margaret, born in 1876, was hale and hearty, as was Harold, who followed in 1879.[37]

In addition to the shoefindings business, Albert was becoming a significant real estate man in his own right. In 1870, the massive filling of the Back Bay was about half completed and the Commonwealth of Massachusetts was regularly selling building lots at auction. Ultimately, about 730 different residences and apartment buildings were built. Of these, 44 were designed by an architect named "Fred Pope," including one 12-unit apartment building, a second 6-unit structure, and the Copley Square Hotel.[38] Fred Pope pulled his own building permits for most jobs, indicating that he was acting both as general contractor and architect, a practice frowned upon by the Boston Society of Architects.

In fact, "Fred Pope" was a rather shadowy cousin of Albert's named Frederic R. Pope, and other than the facts that he was born in 1838 and was financially in debt to Albert for most of his adult life, very little is known about him.[39] After a couple of modest partnerships with other developers, Fred Pope suddenly became, in 1870, a major Back Bay builder. In 1871 alone he had 17 homes under construction, a huge number for the time. (As a comparison, the historian Sam Bass Warner found that the largest residential developer of the Boston suburbs averaged fewer than 12 homes a year between 1872 and 1901.[40]) Between 1890 and 1892 he designed, and was contractor for, the 114-room Copley Square Hotel. The land under it was owned by a Pope family trust managed by Albert's father Charles that sold $100 shares to raise the money for construction. While Fred Pope may have been the architect of record, it is unlikely that he actually drew up the plans for most of his projects. Architectural historian Bainbridge Bunting believes that the bland and repetitive style of his townhouses indicates they were actually designed by the contractors who built them. Fred Pope was not listed as a consulting architect in the Boston commercial directory during this period, and he never owned a home; he was always a boarder or renter. He dropped out of the directory completely after 1892. He was probably never anything more than a straw man for Albert and Charles, and possibly other members of the Pope family. There is nothing to explain why Albert and Charles needed a front man for their Back Bay projects. The Commonwealth relied on open auctions to sell lots and there were few, if any, improprieties during the process. It is possible that Charles's reputation was still clouded from his 1851 bankruptcy. In any event, there is little doubt that from 1870 to the early 1890s, Charles and Albert were major Back Bay real estate players.

Albert's growing business empire was not without its trials and tribulations. In 1872, most of downtown Boston burned down in a massive 35-hour conflagration. Justifiably proud of their brick and stone commercial center, Bostonians had been confident that they needn't fear the same type of horrific fire that destroyed much of central Chicago a year earlier; however, the city's French-style mansard roofs, framed in wood and used as attics to store old records, outdated furniture and other junk, proved its Achilles' heel, as the fire jumped from building to building along the rooflines. Over 800 structures were wiped out.[41] Albert A. Pope & Company, along with hundreds of other businesses, was forced to operate out of a series of makeshift quarters until finding a permanent home at 45 High Street in 1874. A year later, Pope claimed that he lost significant money in a friend's bad business deal. He does not name the errant partner, but it was probably John A. S. Graves, a businessman from Marblehead. Soon after moving to High Street, Pope turned his company over to younger brother Arthur and joined Graves and E. L. Howard in a new firm, Graves & Company, that made and sold ruffling, trimming and other premanufactured clothing accessories. Within a year, Graves & Company was gone and John Graves was pushing small wares out of a back-street cubbyhole.[42] However, Albert returned to his namesake firm and carried on, earning some $24,000 the next year.

The Graves & Company fling suggests that Pope was either getting bored with shoe trimmings, or more likely, never cared much for the business in the first place. He never spoke of his experience at Brooks & Mecuen with anything but loathing, and even his recollections of his ten years at Albert A. Pope & Company were limited to the amount of money he took in and the profits he made. It appears that for Pope, shoes were only a means to an end. Soon after parting from Graves, Pope branched out again. There are slightly different versions of the start of the Pope Manufacturing Company, depending on who is telling the story. Most generally agree, but occasionally they conflict on details, particularly exact dates. This shouldn't be surprising, as many participants were relating events that occurred years, even decades, earlier.

George Bidwell, who later became Pope's first Superintendent of Agencies, recalled that the Colonel and his cousin Edward started out making a hand-held cigarette-rolling machine in a small factory at 87 Summer Street. "This was in 1874–75," he remembered.[43] Cigarettes were new, and there was only one pre-made brand, the "Sweet Caporal," so the simple little machine, run by hand and carried in a pocket, proved popular. "The business was not so picayune as it might seem," recalled Bidwell. "It was a profitable business and the firm made plenty of money, enough to branch out and take on another line."

This "other line" was the firm's biggest pre-bicycle product, the "Pope's Target Air Pistol." Nephew Harry Pope recounted that in October 1874, the Colonel purchased the rights to an advanced air pistol invented by Henry M. Quackenbush of Herkimer, New York. Born in 1847, Quackenbush apprenticed at the Remington Arms Company and began a career as a prolific inventor while still in his teens. His first patent was for an extension ladder, which he sold for $500. During the great velocipede boom, Quackenbush purchased a velocipede manufacturing license from the owner of the all-controlling Lallement patent, Calvin Witty of New York, but in the end made only six or eight boneshakers before the boom collapsed.[44] In 1871 he patented a spring-driven air pistol, and a year later, he began selling his "Target" air pistol, a much-improved version that had the air chamber below the barrel instead of surrounding it.

In the fall of 1874, Pope and Quackenbush signed an agreement under which Pope took over the Target name and supported Quackenbush's venture. Soon after entering into the contract, Quackenbush applied for a reissue of the Target pistol's patent, assigning all rights to Pope. He also moved out of the cramped barn he had been using as a factory into a new two-story plant in Herkimer and added a foot-powered scroll saw to his catalog offerings.[45] The following February, Quackenbush filed another patent, this time for air gun darts and their construction. He built four delicate, complex automatic dart-making machines and sold one to Pope.[46] In January 1876 Pope received two patents in his own name covering improvements to the basic design of the Target.[47]

However, a dispute developed sometime in late 1875 or early 1876 over the dart-making machine, which Pope's men apparently could not get working right. Pope stopped making royalty payments, and, according to Harry Pope, Quackenbush sued in March 1876.[48] Pope and Quackenbush settled a few weeks later with Pope returning all the patent rights in both the Target Air Pistol and the dart-making machine. As in most business disputes, there was probably more at stake than either party was willing to admit in public. At least one of the other dart-making machines worked successfully for a century, until 1993, when it was retired by the Benjamin Air Rifle Company after producing almost two million darts. A few days after Quackenbush filed the paperwork to reclaim ownership of the Target patent, he filed another patent for an even better spring gun action that formed the basis of his Number 1 Air Rifle. Introduced in late 1876, the Number 1 revolutionized the gun industry, and it is essentially the same action that all single-stroke-cocking air guns have used ever since. Quackenbush sold thousands before the patent ran out, earning a modest fortune. By yielding his patents and failing to get half the rights to the Number 1, Pope missed out on the payoff from his and Quackenbush's two-year partnership, a mistake he later estimated cost him $100,000.[49] From that point on the Colonel began to exhibit a level of sophistication in patent matters that was exceeded only by his ruthlessness and tenacity.

The *Boston City Directory* first lists the Pope Manufacturing Company in mid-1876 at 45 High Street, the by-now well-established address of Albert A. Pope & Company. A year later, the firm is on Summer Street, at the cigarette machine quarters. It was located on the third floor of an office building, and a 1907 company history described the place as "nothing better than a loft with a sort of half-story garrett overhead." This attic later became known as "The Hospital" because it was where all the bent, broken and worn-out bicycles were sent. Bidwell recalled that they used the back of the downstairs loft as a riding school (with the windows protected with railings and the pillars wrapped in pads) and the front as an office and showroom.[50] While suitable for an air-pistol store, a third-story location obviously left something to be desired when it came to lugging around fifty-pound high-wheelers, and the company moved to a ground-floor storefront in late 1880 or early 1881. Although Pope may have gotten burned by Quackenbush, he continued to carry his air pistols, and one eyewitness to the early days specifically recalled that after Pope became interested in bicycles he "carried them in his air pistol store in Boston." The firm featured an engraving of an air gun on the company letterhead as late as 1880.[51]

Charles Gross, a Hartford lawyer, recalled his first meeting with the Colonel in March 1877. After a business meeting in Gross's office, three of the participants came back in and one of them asked, given the fact that Gross was already doing business with them, what was the lowest price he would charge to draw up Connecticut incorporation papers? Gross replied that he would charge half the usual fee. The three men pooled the money in their wallets and, after concluding that they would have enough left over for the train back to Boston, agreed to Gross's offer.[52] The three were Albert, Edward, and Charles Pope, and Gross promptly drew up articles of incorporation for the Pope Manufacturing Company, in business to:

> make, manufacture and sell and to license others to make, manufacture and sell air pistols and guns, darning machines, amateur lathes, cigarette rollers and other patented articles and to own, sell and deal in patents and patent rights for the manufacture thereof.[53]

The lathe was also a product of Quackenbush's factory, but no trace of a darning machine has turned up. A total of one thousand shares were issued, of which Albert received 595, Charles 400 and Edward five. The fact that Charles was issued so many shares and Edward so few strongly suggests that Charles helped put up money to start the company. Albert later stated that he invested $3,300 of his own money in the new firm.[54] If the shares were issued proportionately to their investment, Charles added an additional $2,200, for a total capitalization of $5,500. This belies the Pope family legend that after his failure in 1852 Charles was a broken, dependent man living off his son's beneficence. To the contrary, Albert's father appears to have been an active backer of his son's biggest venture. That a Boston-based company was incorporating in Connecticut was not unusual. Massachusetts still required all business incorporations to be approved by the state legislature, a holdover from colonial days, while Connecticut had instituted the more modern practice of simply requiring all new corporations to file the appropriate papers with the secretary of state and designate an approved in-state agent.

Pope's first advertisement for imported bicycles appeared on 16 March 1878, but the Colonel later claimed that he sold his first imported bicycle a month earlier. That may have been an exaggeration, as another Boston firm, Cunningham, Heath & Company, argued at the time that they, not Pope, were the first to import bicycles for sale, a claim Pope fought, although the evidence favored (and still favors) Cunningham. Until Albert turned over the shoefindings company to Arthur and took up station at 87 Summer Street full-time in 1887, cousin Edward was responsible for running things at the new company.

Edward and his brother George were the last two surviving children of Albert's uncle William. Although William Pope was by now an established and prosperous crockery merchant, his home life was as tragic as his business life was successful. Five of his seven children died in childhood and his wife Mary herself passed away in 1867. Although he remarried in 1871, that marriage lasted for only five years until William himself passed away in July 1876.[55] Newspaper and magazine articles often mistook Edward and George for the Colonel's brothers, and in almost every sense they were, having grown up together, shared the same house, and suffered the same grief. However, in several other ways, they were strikingly different. Albert was a big, burly, outgoing man, described in a private letter later written by a long-time employee as "a master showman." Edward was slight, thin and long of face. George was taller, of medium build and prematurely balding. Both were quieter, more methodical, less flamboyant. However, neither could be described as delicate: George had served hard duty during the war and been badly wounded; Edward was reportedly the best, fastest and most tenacious wheelman of the three, and it is probably his enthusiastic embrace of the new sport that ultimately led the Colonel to plunge into the bicycle importing business. At the time, both brothers were in the lumber business. George was with Hall & Company, a Montreal firm, and spent each summer in Quebec and the winters in Boston. Edward worked in the wholesale wool business for a few years, then became a stockbroker around 1870. That apparently did not work out, and in 1873 he started at the lumberyard of Shepard, Hall & Company. He didn't mind being outdoors, but knew there wasn't much future in the job, so he was more than eager to cast his lot with Albert in the new venture.

As if he weren't busy enough, Albert Pope was elected to a two-year term as Alderman to the Newton common council in November 1875.[56] Representing the City, Pope traveled to the Philadelphia Centennial Exhibition the following summer. While others ogled at the giant Corliss steam engine in the Machinery Hall, Pope's eye was caught by a small exhibition of English bicycles:

> They attracted my attention to such an extent that I paid many visits to this exhibit, studying carefully both the general plan and the details of construction, and wondering if any but trained gymnasts could master so strange and apparently unsteady a mount.[57]

Strange? Unsteady? Perhaps. But this handful of bicycles would soon change the Colonel's life to an extent even his flamboyant imagination probably couldn't envision.

# 2

## Colonel Pope Goes to Hartford

*No man appreciates profit more than the Colonel.*
— Arthur L. Garford, 1902[1]

The five high-wheeled, or "Ordinary," bicycles that Alderman Pope examined in Philadelphia had been imported by a Baltimore firm, Timms & Lawford, expressly for the Exposition. They were Ariels, made by Haynes & Jefferis under license from James K. Starley and William Hillman. In 1870 Starley created a sensation in England with his first Ariel, which incorporated improvements in wheel tensioning that allowed him to make his front wheels larger than 40 inches without twisting into the shape of a potato chip. A few years later, he improved the Ariel by introducing a "tangent-spoke" wheel that effectively permitted him to build a front wheel of unlimited size.[2] To prove his point, one of the Philadelphia machines had an 84-inch front wheel. It was absurdly impractical, but it did demonstrate the strength of Starley's latest development.

This display of Ariels was a fitting irony, as the first, brief flowering of the bicycle had occurred in America, not Europe, a full decade earlier. After a brief cultivation, it had flared into an unreal brilliance in one brief riot of commercial color in the spring of 1869, only to die by the time the first snows of winter fell. From a technical standpoint, the evolutionary paths of the bicycle in the United States and Europe couldn't be more different. All three of the primary advances in bicycle design, the velocipede, the high-wheeled Ordinary and the safety bicycle, matured in Europe and were transmitted to America only after a period of technical gestation. In Europe, the bicycle remained a commercially viable product more or less continuously from 1867 to 1900, but in the United States it passed through two distinct stages. The first was that brief, intense "bone-shaker" boom of 1868 and 1869, followed by a decade of commercial, technical and social abandonment. By the time the bicycle, now evolved into the Ordinary, was reintroduced in 1877, few Americans could even remember its predecessor, except perhaps as a dim memory. However, for men like Pope, who chose to make cycling a business, the memory of the great velocipede boom and its explosive growth and utter collapse left an indelible impression. "We remembered the old velocipede, and how quickly that went out of existence," Pope told a reporter in 1880, "I knew how much money was lost in its manufacture."[3]

While the velocipede boom was (and still is) usually dismissed as a historical aberration, the subsequent rebirth and development of the American bicycle industry a decade later cannot be understood without taking a backward look at it. The Colonel dedicated a decade of his life to making sure it never happened again.

## The Great Velocipede Boom

While America learned of the velocipede from Europe, the first fully functional velocipede was probably built in Ansonia, Connecticut. It was made in 1865 by a Frenchman, Pierre Lallement, using the wheels he had saved from an earlier machine he had assembled in Paris in the summer of 1863. At that time, he was twenty years old and working as a machinist in the shop of one Strohmeyer (or, possibly, Strohmeier or Stromaier), a maker of carts and baby-buggies. Lallement claims he thought of adding foot-driven pedals and cranks to the front wheel of an existing device known as a draisiane, also known as the velocipede, hobby-horse, or dandy-horse (depending on the country), after seeing a pedal-powered, rear-driven child's tricycle.[4]

Experimenters had been developing various human-powered, wheeled vehicles over the years, but about 1814 Baron Karl von Drais, a forestmaster working for the Grand Duchy of Baden, popularized a two-wheeled bicycle-like device that the rider powered by pushing directly against the ground with the feet. The draisiane was moderately popular for a decade or so in Germany, France and England, then quietly died out, only to experience brief, mild resurgences every few decades. Lallement later stated that his first Paris prototype was "no good," either because its geometry was wrong, based on the draisiane's function as a walking machine, or because it was too flexible or crudely made. It worked well enough, however, to satisfy the reason Lallement built it: to determine if one could balance, steer, and pedal the thing simultaneously. After he was finished with it, Lallement removed its wheels, junked the frame and started building a revised version.[5]

Work progressed slowly and he had not yet completed the new velocipede when he left for America in July 1865. He soon found work in a machine shop in Ansonia, Connecticut, and during his spare time completed the second machine. In the summer of 1883 cycling journalist Karl Kron interviewed one of Lallement's former co-workers who

> recalled him as a pleasant young fellow, whose good nature made him popular among the other workmen.... He did not impress them at all as a possible inventor, even prospectively; and as for his two-wheeled hobby-horse, by whose contortions upon the street, when working hours were over, he caused them to laugh, they never suspected that it contained any idea worth patenting, or that he himself thought he had discovered anything important when he put it together.[6]

The following summer Lallement visited New Haven, Connecticut, and showed off his invention by riding it around the public green. Although reportedly arrested, he did attract the attention of a local resident, James Carroll, who, in return for a half-ownership, advanced him the money to file for a patent on his machine that was approved on 20 November 1866.[7] However, attracting a manufacturer was more difficult and in early 1868 Lallement gave up and returned to Paris. To his surprise he discovered that the velocipede had become something of a mechanical celebrity during his absence. Back in 1863, Lallement made no attempt to hide his original experiments at Strohmeyer's cart-making shop, and they had attracted the attention of a man named René Oliviér. Rene and his two brothers, Marius and Aimé, were the sons of a prominent industrialist from Lyon.⁸ At that time, René and Aimé were students at the Ecole Centrale from which Marius had already graduated. René and a classmate, George de la Bouglise, hatched a plan to produce their own pedal velocipede using a malleable cast iron frame. At the time, malleable cast iron was not thought tough enough for such purposes, but it held out the promise of relatively fast, low-labor production as compared to the alternative: wrought iron. René Oliviér and Bouglise then approached a struggling Parisian blacksmithing firm run by Pierre Michaux to produce a handful of malleable cast iron prototypes in July 1865.⁹ René, Aimé, and George Bouglise tried testing them on a five-hundred-mile run from Paris to Avignon, but the prototypes eventually failed and they switched to wooden-framed backup models. The Oliviérs kept at it, however, and by early 1867 had a marketable product. They contracted the work out to Michaux's firm, advancing him the money he needed to expand his shop.

By this time a handful of other mechanics had begun experimenting with variations on Lallement's idea, and in 1867 a few machines were exhibited at the Paris Universal Exposition. In 1868, the year Lallement returned home, several firms, led by the Oliviérs and Michaux (under Michaux's headbadge), started making them in substantial quantities. By this time the Oliviers had apparently given up on malleable cast iron and turned to the tougher, but harder to forge, wrought iron. The Michaux shop lacked the large-scale capacity to forge wrought iron, so in 1868 the Oliviers arranged for most of their frames to be made at the Pastre shipbuilding foundry in Marseille, near the Oliviér family estate, then shipped to the factory in Paris for painting and assembly. In 1869 the Oliviérs, who now owned seventy percent of the firm, eased Michaux out, although they kept the name. There is a legend that Lallement was employed at the Michaux works after his return to France. This is not the case, although he did own a bicycle store in Paris, which he started in 1869 using the proceeds of the sale of his American patent.

Interest spread back to America through the Hanlon brothers, a troupe of gymnasts who toured the United States in the summer of 1868 featuring acrobatic velocipede riding in a stage act they performed. That winter, the fad of velocipede riding caught on with a vengeance, first in New York, then in several college towns along the East Coast. Virtually all velocipede riding occurred on indoor rinks where riders could take lessons and rent machines. The Hanlons ran the largest one in New York, with 25 velocipedes. The typical velocipede rented for 40 to 60 cents per hour, and Kron reported that while few rinks in New York would rent for outdoor riding, the standard fee for such use was 15 cents for 15 minutes. George Bidwell discovered that the rink in Buffalo would not even consider outdoor rental: "I remember asking the manager of the Buffalo school if I could take a machine out on the streets. I was met with a curt refusal and told that they were not intended for street use."[10]

The Hanlons introduced their own brand of velocipede, made for them by Calvin Witty, an established New York carriage maker. It incorporated several improvements contained in a patent the Hanlons filed in July 1868 and quickly became one of the best-selling American brands.[11] While most riders rented, the dedicated and wealthy young man with $75 to $125 to burn could buy an imported Michaux machine or one made by the rapidly growing number of American firms. The velocipede craze grew to the point that *Harper's Weekly* for 3 January 1869 depicted the old year as Father Time trundling off stage in a wheelbarrow, while on the other side of the stage, the infant New Year astride a velocipede burst through a tissue-paper hoop held by a lithesome young woman.

But by the winter of 1869, it was all over. Used velocipedes could be bought for $20 or less and many were simply scrapped. The new velocipede emporiums reverted back into dance halls, ice skating rinks and barns. Karl Kron, one of the few cyclists to participate in both the velocipede boom and the early years of the Ordinary a decade later, observed that only in America did the "boneshaker days have such a wildly impetuous beginning; but on the other hand have such a sudden and ignominious ending."[12]

Kron claimed that when velocipedists ventured out of their indoor rinks in the spring of 1869, they found their mounts all but impossible to use on the road. Having bought a second-hand model of one of the most popular velocipedes, he found that the farthest he could ride it was two miles, and "I presented it to a twelve-year-old boy." Nevertheless, he believed the velocipede's technical shortcomings were only a secondary problem. In his opinion, the main reason it failed was that it was legislated off the road, or, to be more precise, off the sidewalk. Kron referred to all his outdoor riding as "sidewalk riding" or "taking a spin of the sidewalk," and he had his favorite stretches of sidepath, all apparently paved with cement. Riding on the dirt or cobblestone roads of the period never occurred to him. Writing in May 1869, Kron exclaimed: "As for velocipedes, we can only tell, what we never expected to have to tell, of their dying days. Alas, poor Yorick! A dire pronouncement of the City fathers ... has sent you to an untimely grave."[13]

Bicycle historian David Herlihy maintains that much of the collapse can be blamed on the velocipede rink owners themselves. They often rented the cheapest, poorest quality velocipedes, neglected to maintain both premises and machines, and as the craze started to subside, turned to exploitive stunts such as crowded races, novelty shows or risqué female acrobats. "In sum," he concludes, "velocipede rinks epitomized the short sighted 'get-rich-quick' mentality which seems to have permeated the movement."[14]

Another reason, one that all contemporary observers appear to agree upon, was chaos over patent rights. After producing less than a hundred bicycles for the Hanlon brothers, Calvin Witty was approached by someone representing a New Haven carriage-fittings firm that employed James Carroll, owner of half-rights to Lallement's patent. It is unclear whether this was an offer to sell or a threat to sue, but within a few weeks Witty purchased Carroll's half and started tracking down Lallement. He found him in Paris and bought the other half of the patent, then negotiated an agreement with Stephen W. Smith of New York, who held the rights to a second patent that may have demonstrated prior art on some critical features of Lallement's. Together, the two men worked to levy retroactive royalties on Witty's competitors. Charles Pratt, later Pope's patent lawyer, believed that excessive patent royalties, which made velocipedes too expensive, were the primary cause of the velocipede's demise.

Pratt's judgment can be questioned as biased. He did, after all, make his career defending Pope's patents. However, both Pope and George Bidwell later noted that vastly better machines, with wire-spoke wheels, rubber tires, improved pedals and superior steering heads, were just around the corner in 1869. In fact, Bidwell's father bought him one of these second-generation velocipedes — a British import — which he used as basic transport for many years. But the continued refinement of the velocipede in America was halted when prices started to spiral out of control as the result of Witty's royalty demands. Many of the improvements to the velocipede that culminated in the French and English development of the high-wheeled Ordinary were actually of American origin, but were never used at home because there was no longer a market for them.[15] Together, these various factors led to the death of the pricey fad by the end of the year. As one participant noted, "the American carriage makers all dropped the veloce in a hurry, with a feeling of contempt for their own folly in having interrupted their proper business in behalf of such a deceptive toy"[16]

Although the craze quickly passed in America, development continued in Europe. By 1870, makers were using front wheels as large as 40 inches in an effort to increase speed. Experiments were tried with a 50-inch front wheel, but these were unsuccessful due to the weight penalty imposed by the wood-spoke carriage-style wheels then available. In late 1869 Eugene Meyer of Paris developed a wheel using thin wire spokes, a technology he adapted from waterwheels. By 1870, Meyer et Cie was building bicycles with 48-inch front wheels. Two Britons, James Starley and William Hillman, created a method of maintaining uniform spoke tension, facilitating their development in 1871 of the first true high-wheeled, or Ordinary, bicycle. As the Franco-Prussian War devastated the French economy, the center of bicycle production shifted west to the sewing machine manufacturing region around Coventry, England.[17] These were the bicycles exhibited at the Philadelphia Exposition, catching the Colonel's eye.

## *The First Columbias*

After seeing his first bicycles, Pope went home to Newton—and didn't do anything. In later years, he glossed over the fact that it took fourteen months for him to act on his new discovery. The summer after the exposition, Pope hosted an English houseguest, John Harrington, during his extended stay in the states. Harrington was an experienced cyclist, a bicycle businessman, and a principal behind the British "Arab" bicycle. Harrington contracted with a local machinist (legend says it was William S. Atwell, later a Pope employee) to custom-build an Ordinary. The job required three months and the princely sum of $313. After it was delivered in August 1877, Harrington taught his host how to mount, dismount and ride the high-wheeled machine.[18]

Meanwhile, the commercial potential of bicycles was starting to attract others. Timms & Lawford met only mediocre success selling the Philadelphia Exposition bicycles, but an English expatriate architect living in Boston, Frank Weston, talked his friend Arthur Cunningham into entering the bicycle importing business with him in the summer of 1877. The two recruited Harold Williams and Sidney Heath to joining them. The new Boston firm of Cunningham, Heath & Co. received its first order of English "Challenge" bicycles in November. Weston chose to remain a silent partner and started a new magazine, the *American Bicycle Journal,* that overtly promoted cycling and covertly boosted the interests of Cunningham, Heath.[19] A handful of other Boston enthusiasts imported bicycles for their own use. A young lawyer, Alfred Chandler, received his Singer Challenge in May, and he and the Colonel occasionally entered into impromptu races over the summer, with Pope on horseback.[20]

Although he was still carrying Quackenbush's air pistol, without the patent rights Pope realized he could never be more than a glorified retail agent. Left stranded without a gadget of his own to exploit, the possibilities of the bicycle were starting to look interesting. Pope claimed he ordered some through Harrington when Harrington returned to

England about August 1877, but that the shipment was delayed. Pope did definitely send an order to Coventry's Bayliss, Thomas and Company for eight of their "Duplex Excelsior" bicycles later that fall, and these arrived in January 1878.[21] After examining them, Pope decided to plunge into the importing business, with his first display ad appearing in *Bicycling World* in mid–March. Although the Pope firm offered to order "any make at reasonable prices," he featured the Duplex Excelsior in his ads and no other brand is mentioned in later accounts of his employees or customers.

Two months later, Weston formed the nation's first bicycle club, the Boston Bicycle Club, with essentially the same agenda as his irregular journal.[22] Over the next decade bicycling clubs and journals typically acted as partisans for one commercial interest or another. Although Edward Pope was a founding member of the Boston Bicycle Club, the Massachusetts Bicycle Club, chartered just days later, was the "Pope" club, with leadership prominently featuring Pope family members and company employees.

Pope brought two things to the infant bicycle industry that his competitor lacked: boldness and money. Looking back on his association with Cunningham & Heath (later Cunningham & Co.), Weston rued that "the head of the firm, poor Arthur Cunningham, was very conservative, the imported bicycles were slow in arriving, and more business energy, confidence and pluck were sadly needed." Despite his long association with the Colonel's first competitor, that "confidence and pluck" was provided only "in the spring of 1878 [when] Albert A. Pope embarked in the bicycle business."[23] He had money, and he was willing to spend it. Pope initially sank over $3,000 of his own funds into the Pope Manufacturing Company, the equivalent of about $125,000 in today's money.[24] By the spring of 1878 Pope had probably ordered somewhere around 50 English bicycles, an additional $4,000 investment at the traditional 20 percent dealer's discount. And he had even bigger plans. Not content to simply import bicycles, he wanted to manufacture them.

Although the Colonel never explained why he decided to expand into manufacturing, the economics were compelling. For each $90 British Ordinary, Pope was probably paying about $50 wholesale at the manufacturer's dock in England. Freight added five dollars, and the thirty-five percent Morrill Act tariff (on carriages) came to $17.50, a total cost of $72.50. That allowed him a gross profit of $17.50 on each sale, less advertising, office expenses and other overhead.

Charles Pratt later estimated that Pope built his early bicycles for $68.25 each. Although labor cost more, the biggest difference was a steep drop in import tariffs: an American bicycle required only about $6.50 in duties for raw material (mostly steel), a savings of $11.[25] Pope could build his own bicycles a little over four dollars cheaper and could price them about ten dollars higher because of the novelty factor, thus earning a profit of about $32.75 each — a tidy sum for 1878.

It is unlikely that Pope was the first to make an American Ordinary. An Englishman, R. H. Hodgson, probably produced a small number of bicycles at a Newton, Massachusetts, shop as early as 1878. However, no significant numbers were made until after Hodgson sold out in 1880. One A. M. Gooch was also apparently making a small number of bicycles in Newton, but his operation was described as "almost unknown ... practically a repair shop."[26] It is undisputed that Pope was the first to venture into manufacturing on anything approaching a commercial scale. However, lacking a factory of his own, he needed someone willing to take on the job of building them.

In May 1878 Pope stepped down from a southbound New Haven Railroad day coach onto the platform at Hartford. He quickly walked back to the baggage compartment to fetch the valuable cargo he brought along with him — a 56-inch Duplex Excelsior bicycle. Ignoring the stares of men and the shouts of boys, he asked where he could find the offices of the Weed Sewing Machine Company. Directed downtown to 239 Main, he discovered when he got there that this was only the firm's retail store and was correctly pointed to the factory on the north side of Capitol Avenue a mile west. Back again in the saddle, a winded and rapidly dwindling knot of small boys running after him, Pope arrived at the factory within a few minutes and was met at the front steps by George A. Fairfield, Weed's president.[27]

The doorway where Fairfield stood was virtually dead center of America's high-technology manufacturing region, the Silicon Valley of its day: the Connecticut River Valley. Its birthplace was Springfield, Massachusetts, 25 miles north, where, in 1794, the federal government established the Springfield Armory. After a checkered start, it was put under the command of Colonel Roswell Lee in 1815. Within a year he implemented two concurrent strategies: the standardization of interchangeable parts and the use of specialized machinery to make them.[28] An ardent student of Lee's methods was a Connecticut armsmaker, Samuel Colt. In 1848 Colt took over a former textile mill in Hartford. Although he used it to make guns, his real product was gun factories.[29] He built two, starting from the inside out, developing entirely new and novel machine tools. The first was shipped to London in 1852. The British were so impressed with its combination of interchangeable parts, complex die forgings and specialized machine tools that they coined Colt's methods "The American System." In 1855 Colt opened his second factory on the banks of the Connecticut River just south of downtown Hartford. Colt's Armory served as a training ground for two generations of men who would develop precision machinery in the Valley: Francis Pratt, Amos Whitney, Christopher Spencer, Charles Billings, George Fairfield and others. Many firms, recognizing the wealth of manpower and talent, moved there, including the Weed Sewing Machine Company.

In 1854, T. E. Weed patented an improved thread controller for sewing machines. His Weed Sewing Machine was manufactured in Nashua, New Hampshire, and St. Johns, New Brunswick, before a revamped company bearing his name was incorporated in West Winstead, Connecticut, in 1863. In July 1865 the firm moved to Hartford and rented the top two floors of the Pratt & Whitney tool factory.[30] The Weed Sewing Machine made a name for itself when it received a gold medal at the 1867 Paris Exhibition for its simplicity of construction and ease of operation. Sometime between 1869 and 1871 the firm moved south across the Park River and rented part of a Sharps Rifle Manufacturing Company building, built in 1852 to assemble the successful Sharps breech-loading rifle. When Sharps moved to Bridgeport in 1875, Weed bought the building. Although the company carried Weed's name and the machines used his patented thread controller, the man himself had not been associated with the firm since before the move to Hartford, and the primary responsibility for both design and construction of the firm's line of four sewing machines fell to Fairfield. In addition to sewing machines, the company made steel and iron forgings for agricultural equipment and, under contract, sewing machines for other firms.[31]

Pope may have been referred to Weed by Charles Pratt, or he may have heard of the firm from his previous visits to Hartford. One of the Weed models, the "General Favorite," was widely used in the shoe industry to sew leather, so it is possible that he knew about the firm from his shoefindings company. George Bidwell later speculated that Pope went to a sewing machine company because several of the better English makes were manufactured by such firms, and Weed advertised its machines as constructed of interchangeable parts, an attractive advantage for an entrepreneur who was moving up from smaller goods like cigarette rolling machines and air pistols.[32] Once settled in Fairfield's office, Pope requested that Weed build fifty bicycles for him. Rather than design a new product from scratch, Pope proposed that Fairfield simply copy the Duplex Excelsior he had brought from Boston. Fairfield demurred. Even with a prototype to work from, the magnitude of the job appeared formidable. However, the sewing machine business was in a slump, and the firm needed the money. Fairfield soon wired Boston accepting the assignment.[33]

As it turned out, his concern was not without justification. The bicycle's open head, which joined the forks to the handlebars and backbone, required a sequence of five forging dies, some of which were among the largest and most elaborate in use, costing over $500 to make. The finishing die broke on the eleventh stroke and had to be rebuilt. It proved impossible to roll wheel rims into the required U-shape, so the first year's bicycles featured V-shaped rims made out of angle iron scrounged in the nearby town of Windsor Locks. A special glue had to be developed to hold the solid rubber tires to the odd rims. All told, Weed had to produce 77 unique new parts, including bolts, nuts, spokes and pins.[34] Only the rubber tires were bought from an outside supplier.

Despite such travails, the bicycles were completed by September. Even before they were finished, Pope settled on a logo: "Colonel Pope decided that his wheel should be named 'Columbia,'" recalled George Bidwell. "About that time there was much talk of holding a Columbian Exposition some place in America in 1892, preferably New York, and the name seemed appropriate."[35] Pope sold 92 bicycles in 1878–50 Columbias and 42 imports, although some of the Weed-built machines were kept by the Pope firm for use in its training rinks. The rate of production increased slowly. Karl Kron bought serial number 234 in May 1879, and the last of the exact Duplex Excelsior copies, serial number 1091, was built late that year, suggesting that 1879 production was about a thousand units. The demand for Columbias at first greatly exceeded Weed's ability to make them. Bidwell ordered 75 for his customers in 1878, but had to talk them into taking Duplex Excelsiors, as Pope couldn't deliver the Hartford-made bicycles fast enough. Pope didn't even advertise the new bicycles until January 1879, but continued to heavily promote imports. Kron's order was promised in ten days, but took eight weeks to deliver.[36]

Fairfield's difficult job was made easier by Weed's new office manager, a young man by the name of George Herbert Day. Born in 1851 in Brooklyn, Connecticut, Day attended Hobart College for a year but had to drop out due to illness. In October 1870 he moved to Hartford and started work at the Charter Oak Life Insurance Company. His big break came in 1877, the year before Pope arrived, when he married Katherine Beach, daughter of J. Watson Beach, a Weed director.[37] Soon, he started as a clerk at Weed. While his father-in-law helped get him the job, there is no doubt that he rose through ranks through sheer ability. Day was made corporate secretary in early 1879. When George Fairfield left in July 1881 to start a new firm, Beach stepped in as president. Four years later, Day became treasurer and general manager. When Beach died in 1887, Day replaced him as president.

Early on, Day became Colonel Pope's invaluable right-hand man in Hartford. He

The biggest and most prestigious get-together for cyclists in the 1870s and 1880s was the annual fall race meet in Springfield, Massachusetts. Colonel Pope chose the 1879 tournament to unveil his new Columbia bicycle after a long summer of struggle to get the first fifty ready (created by Milton Bradley and Co. Library of Congress Call No. PGA-Bradley-Springfield [D Size] [P&P]).

was later referred to by his fellow bicycle executives as "The Senator," and was described by one of his assistants simply as "diplomat."[38] Day was as charming and tactful as Colonel Pope was bombastic. Even his refusal was reported to be a pleasant experience: "He always dismissed them so courteously that they were invariably glad they had called on him, and were sure that they had at least met a man of sympathy and a gentleman." Pope would frequently remind an audience, "I am a merchant through and through. I could not make a bicycle if my life depended on it."[39] For most of his career, Day was the man who got those bicycles built.

By 1880 the men at Weed grew confident that the bicycle business was for real. George Fairfield even took up the sport, pedaling around Boston in September 1879 in the nation's first organized two-day tour.[40] The firm began to re-engineer their product. The odd head-adjustment spring of the Duplex Excelsior was changed to a more standard arrangement. An improved seat spring was introduced. More dramatically, a new deluxe model, the "Special Columbia," was introduced. It featured a closed, Stanley-style head, the latest trend in English ordinaries, and a built-in ball bearing unit for the front wheel. Fairfield had begun work on the Special as early as the winter of 1878–79, but getting the forging die for the new head and the ball bearing unit right required another 16 months. The dies used to form the head, rear fork, wheel rims and other parts were so unique that the company patented them. The original model, now rechristened the "Standard Columbia," was redesigned so that it also could accept the ball bearing unit, but on the Standard it was a ten-dollar option. A 48-inch Standard without ball bearings or nickel plate cost $87.50. A Special Columbia of the same size and with full nickel plate (including rims) cost $132.50. Both weighed about forty-one pounds.[41]

However, not all of the action was taking place in Hartford. Almost from the minute that Fairfield accepted Pope's offer to build the first batch of 50 bicycles, the men had heard rumors of subpoenas, lawyers, depositions and all manner of talk relating to patents, claims and litigation. The older men could only shake their heads and groan, having lived through it once already. In 1846, Elias Howe of Cambridge, Massachusetts, received a patent relating to his work developing a machine for sewing cloth. It proved to be the basic patent common to all modern sewing machines. Unsuccessful in finding a financial backer, Howe left for England, but returned two years later, discouraged and virtually penniless. Meanwhile, other inventors in the United States had patented various other important features, leading to improved sewing machines by I. M. Singer & Company, Wheeler & Wilson, Grover & Baker, and others. In 1854, Howe sued Singer for patent infringement and won. The other manufacturers were forced to capitulate. Howe demanded a royalty of $25 per sewing machine. That this proportionately huge tariff crippled the sewing machine market mattered little to Howe, who wanted to produce his own machine and undercut the prices of the others. In short, he wanted a monopoly.[42]

George Day was Albert Pope's right-hand man in Hartford between 1878 and 1899. While Pope directed his firm's marketing and financial efforts from its Boston headquarters, Day supervised the development and manufacturing of bicycles from out of the former Weed Sewing Machine Co. factory. He broke from Pope to concentrate on the automobile business, but was soon forced into an early retirement by heart disease. Called "the Senator" by his fellow bicycle executives, he was warmly regarded even by Pope's many enemies (*Cycling Life,* February 22, 1894, author's photograph).

But without the newer features developed by the other firms, Howe's machine was a dud, and the others refused to share their patents with Howe unless he relented. Deadlock resulted, and fewer than 4,000 sewing machines were made in America in 1855. Orlando Potter of the Grover & Baker company proposed that all the disputants pool their patents, effectively locking out any new players. Without a significant patent to contribute, any prospective sewing machine maker would face putative royalty fees. That combination, which included the Weed Sewing Machine Company, proved highly effective until the last of the basic patents expired in 1877, the year before Pope showed up with his bicycle. By then American firms were producing close to a half-million sewing machines a year. As the Weed factory completed its second year's batch of bicycles, it was starting to look like history was going to repeat itself, threatening not only the new Columbia, but the entire infant American bicycle industry.

# 3

## The Great Patent Wars

*For a decade afterward came the wonderful battles of bicycle patents. All along Pope extended this department, and practically was in the position of a Czar.... Pope was largely hated and the Columbia was called the monopoly machine.*
— *Bicycling World*, 1902[1]

Starting in 1879, Pope plunged the bicycle industry into ten years of protracted and bloody legal warfare that destroyed many firms, almost wiped out his own, and could well have strangled the entire cycling industry while it still lay in the cradle. Many observers, both then and now, believed that the Colonel's ultimate goal was to monopolize the business. Pope and his lieutenants loudly dissented, arguing that their actions brought stability and mutual prosperity to what otherwise would have been commercial anarchy. While he did much to rationalize bicycle technology, there is no doubt that Pope was driven by self-interest, and his actions often stretched ethical and legal boundaries, even by the no-holds-barred standards of the Gilded Age. Closed court records, including Pope's letters to some of his most bitter rivals, makes clear that by the summer of 1883 the Colonel was attempting to create a tightly run oligopoly comprising of four major bicycle makers and a half-dozen smaller import houses.

The war was lengthy and sometimes convoluted. It is easiest to think of it as two distinct battles in a broad strategic campaign. The first, from 1878 to 1881, was fought over the control of Lallement's 1866 patent for the front-wheel drive bicycle. The second, starting in the spring of 1883, began as a reaction to an obscure Ohio court case concerning whale oil lamps that wound up, to everyone's surprise, in the Supreme Court and threatened to wipe out the supremacy of Lallement's patent. Pope's men were forced to buy up scores of secondary patents and resorted to the most arcane and deceptive business practices imaginable to maintain their cartel. Although their initial goal was to shore up the beleaguered Lallement patent, Pope's lieutenants discovered that if they played their cards right, they could give it an enforceable life beyond the normal 17-year patent tenure. Manipulating American contract law, they came very close to giving Lallement's patent perpetual existence, and had they succeeded they may well have re-written this nation's patent laws. As it was, Pope was defeated only by the United States Supreme Court and a handful of adversaries who vowed a fight to the finish.

## We Presume You Want to Upset Lallement's Patent

In 1879, Pope bought Lallement's basic bicycle patent, which had been divided at birth between the Frenchman and his American sponsor, James Carroll. The Pope Manufacturing Company's official 1907 history, *An Industrial Achievement*, offered the official account of how it came about:

> The company encountered a serious difficulty in the shape of a valuable patent in the hands of Richardson & McKee, of Boston. As this was one of the rare blanket patents it was impossible to successfully manufacture machines unless under a proper license..., Although Richardson & McKee managed the entire patent they owned outright only a half of it, and the other half was held by the Montpelier Manufacturing Company, in Vermont.... Numerous conferences were held with Richardson & McKee, resulting in the sale by that house to the Pope Manufacturing Company of one-half their interest, that is, one quarter of the patent. There is no doubt that in selling this fractional share, Richardson & McKee intended to take the considerable amount paid them and with it purchase the half interest held by the Montpelier Company, so that they would still control the situation.
>
> No sooner had the transaction been closed with Richardson & McKee, than Colonel Pope took the first train to Montpelier, arriving there twenty-four hours before the letter of those who had thought to outwit him.... A meeting of the directors of the Montpelier Manufacturing Company was immediately called in the parlor of one of the local hotels, and here he laid before them his proposition.... [They then] sold him outright their half of the patent.... Richardson & McKee realized at once their situation and the futility of any contest, they came into line and sold to the Pope interests their remaining share of the patents.'[2]

The story is basically true, but as usual, exaggerates the Colonel's personal exploits and ignores the valuable contributions of others. The basic bicycle patent in the United States was Lallement's 1866 "Improvement in Velocipedes" (Figure 1). In it, Lallement discussed the ability to balance on two wheels in great depth.[3] Indeed, this discovery was central to the concept of the bicycle. In 1863, while still in Paris, Lallement found that he could maintain his balance while turning the pedals with his feet and changing direction with the handlebars. However revolutionary, this was a discovery, not an invention, so it couldn't be patented. Thus, Lallement's official claims language asserted only that he had invented a vehicle with two wheels in tandem, with pedals and a guiding arm, or handlebar. By implication, the claim to the guiding arm gave him rights over the idea of a pivoting front wheel. It was simple, but enough to establish the basic patent covering a front-wheel drive bicycle. Or was it?

Seven years earlier, in 1862, Philip W. Mackenzie of Jersey City had patented an "Improvement in Cantering Propellers," a wheeled horse simulator.[4] The front legs of Mackenzie's hobby-horse were attached to cranks, which in turn drove the two front wheels (Figure 2). By pitching the front of the horse up and down, the rider turned the cranks and propelled the thing forward. The whole thing had very little to do with a bicycle, but it was a rolling device powered by cranks attached to wheels, making it legally relevant to Lallement's subsequent invention.

Two years later, Mackenzie filed another patent for a variation of his hobby-horse. His earlier design required a frame within which the horse rocked up and down. This time, he eliminated the frame by changing the cranks so that the rider's feet rested in stirrups bolted directly onto them (Figure 3). Like his earlier Cantering Propeller, both cranks went in the same direction, requiring the rider to thrust both feet forward together. Also like the first version, the rider pulled up on the horse's head with his hands at the same time as he pushed down with his feet, then leaned forward to push the horse down

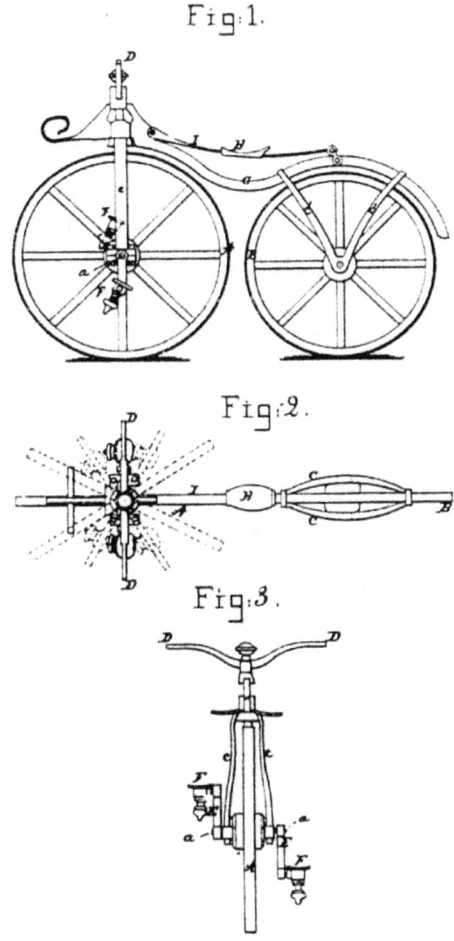

Pierre Lallement was awarded patent number 59,915, generally regarded as the world's first bicycle patent, which he shared with his American partner, James Carroll, about a year after he immigrated to the United States from France. The photograph shows Lallement's patent number 59,915 as it was reissued by the patent office in 1877 in reissue number 7,972.

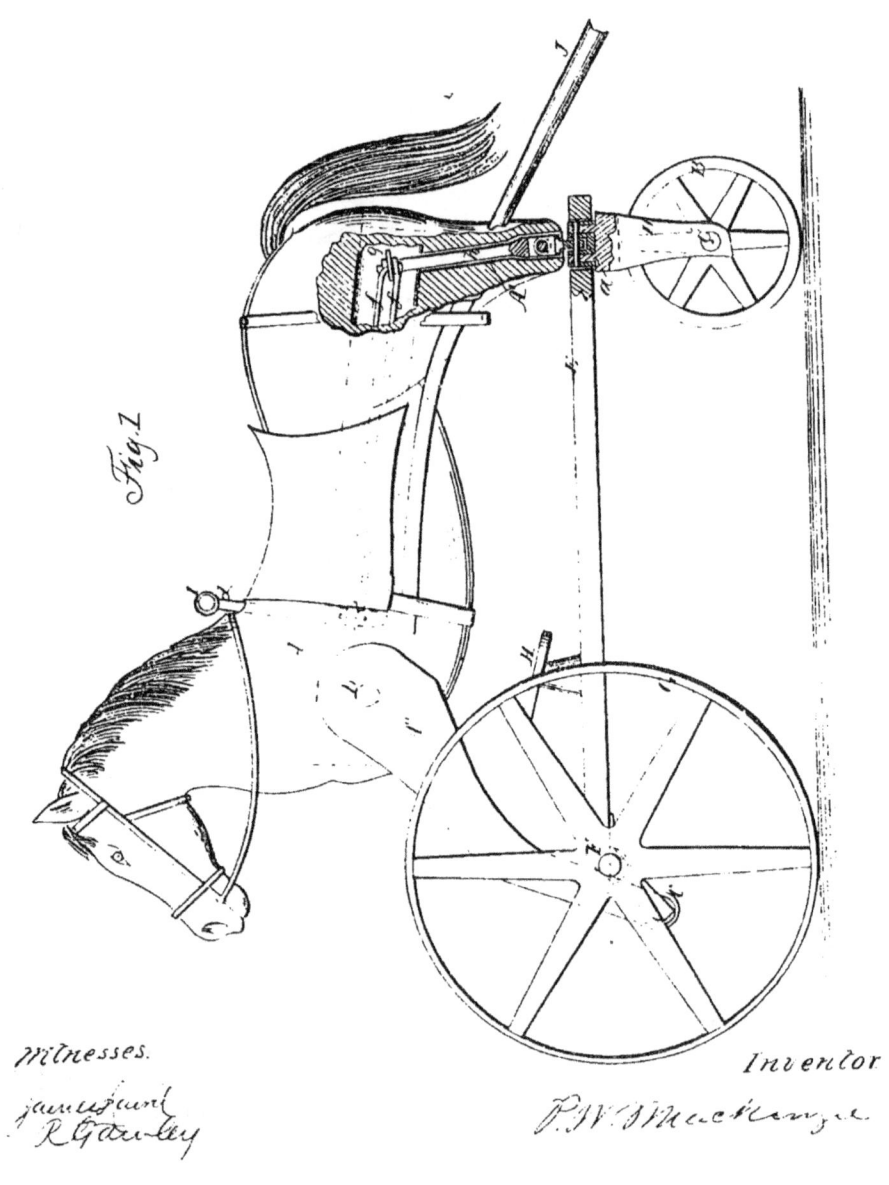

Although it bears little resemblance to a bicycle, the use of a crank to transfer the up-and-down motion of the horse's head into a circular rotation to drive the front wheels of this horse-riding simulator threatened to invalidate one of the most important parts of Lallement's velocipede patent.

## 3. The Great Patent Wars

Velocipede.

No. 41,310.  Patented Jan. 19, 1864

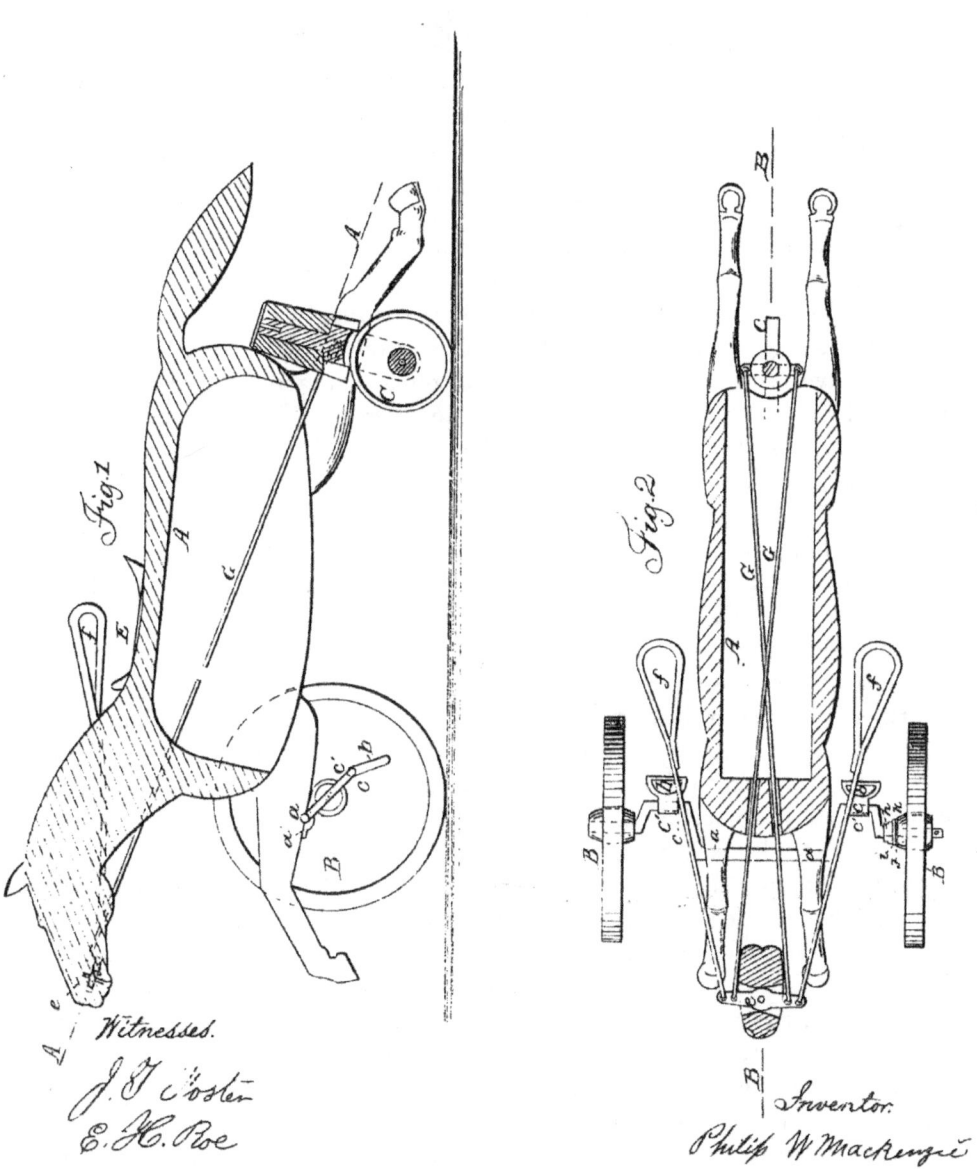

A slightly later version of Mackenzie's hobby-horse, this variant now has cranks directly powered by the rider's feet using stirrups that closely resemble bicycle pedals. However, both cranks still go in the same direction, so the rider still pushes forward with both feet at the same time, making the horse-head bob up and down.

while pulling his feet up. The claims language identified it as "a velocipede constructed with cranks having foot-rests ... adapted to receive the rider's feet," allowing Mackenzie to assert that he was the first to think up the idea of driving a wheeled vehicle using a foot-driven crank assembly. This concept was implied, but not explicitly stated, by Lallement. Both of Mackenzie's patents were assigned to Stephen W. Smith, a New York manufacturer of furniture and hobby-horses, along with a third, similar patent filed in 1863.[5]

Further muddying the waters, in March 1865, Harvey A. Reynolds of New York patented his own version of a horse simulator (Figure 4). The body of Reynolds's hobby-horse didn't bob up and down. Instead, the rider's feet rested on two cranks arranged opposite each other, like Lallement's velocipede. The rider turned his feet in a circular motion, driving the two front wheels.[6] Because Reynolds was astute enough to include the opposed, foot-driven crank within the claims language, his patent had even more potential than Mackenzie's to upset the priority of Lallement's patent, issued a year and a half later. The Mackenzie patents, in turn, posed a threat of "prior art" to the Reynolds patent. Reynolds did not immediately sell his patent.

All these arcane patent arguments suddenly became vital when the velocipede boom took off in 1868. As the Hanlon velocipede became popular, Calvin Witty, the successful New York carriage maker who manufactured it for the family of acrobats, started paying patent lawyers to examine the legal state of the art. At about this time, Witty was approached by a New Haven carriage maker who claimed his employee owned half the rights to the velocipede. The employee was James Carroll, Lallement's original partner. Witty snapped up his half-interest in January 1869.[7] Within a month, Witty's expert in Paris, David H. Brandon, managed to track down Lallement in a working-class district of the city, and buy his half of the patent for Witty. The price paid is subject to dispute: Karl Kron says Lallement received only about $2,000; Witty claimed his total cost to search out and buy both halves of the patent ran to $10,000.[8]

Meanwhile, Smith, who owned the Mackenzie patents, had gone even farther and had the 1862 patent reissued. At the time, the federal patent office permitted reissues as a way of correcting defects in an existing patent. The reissue replaced the original patent, but did not extend its 17-year lifespan. The practice was controversial because patent lawyers frequently tried to slip in language broadening the patent's scope or including claims contained in someone else's subsequent invention under the guise of a "correction." Smith used the 1869 reissue to significantly alter Mackenzie's original language away from a narrow focus on hobby-horse propulsion toward a broad coverage of any type of steerable wheeled vehicle powered by the feet using a crank.[9]

While the reissue wound its way through the patent bureaucracy, Smith and Witty sued each other over the Lallement and Mackenzie patents. Instead of fighting it out, they settled out of court and combined forces, demanding royalties of ten to twenty dollars per unit from both importers and manufacturers. The velocipede craze was rapidly dying by this time, and their demands convinced many firms to pull out of the business, further deflating the fad. Exactly how much money the two made is unclear. Witty claims he earned over $25,000 in December 1869 alone, and bicycle historian David Herlihy believes he turned down a $75,000 offer for the Lallement patent at the peak of the fad. After Smith died in 1874 his wife sold off the Mackenzie patents to her husband's former lawyer, Charles Durgin, who in turn sold them in the spring of 1876 to the Montpelier Manufacturing Company, a Vermont maker of baby carriages, sleds, hobby-horses and other toys.[10]

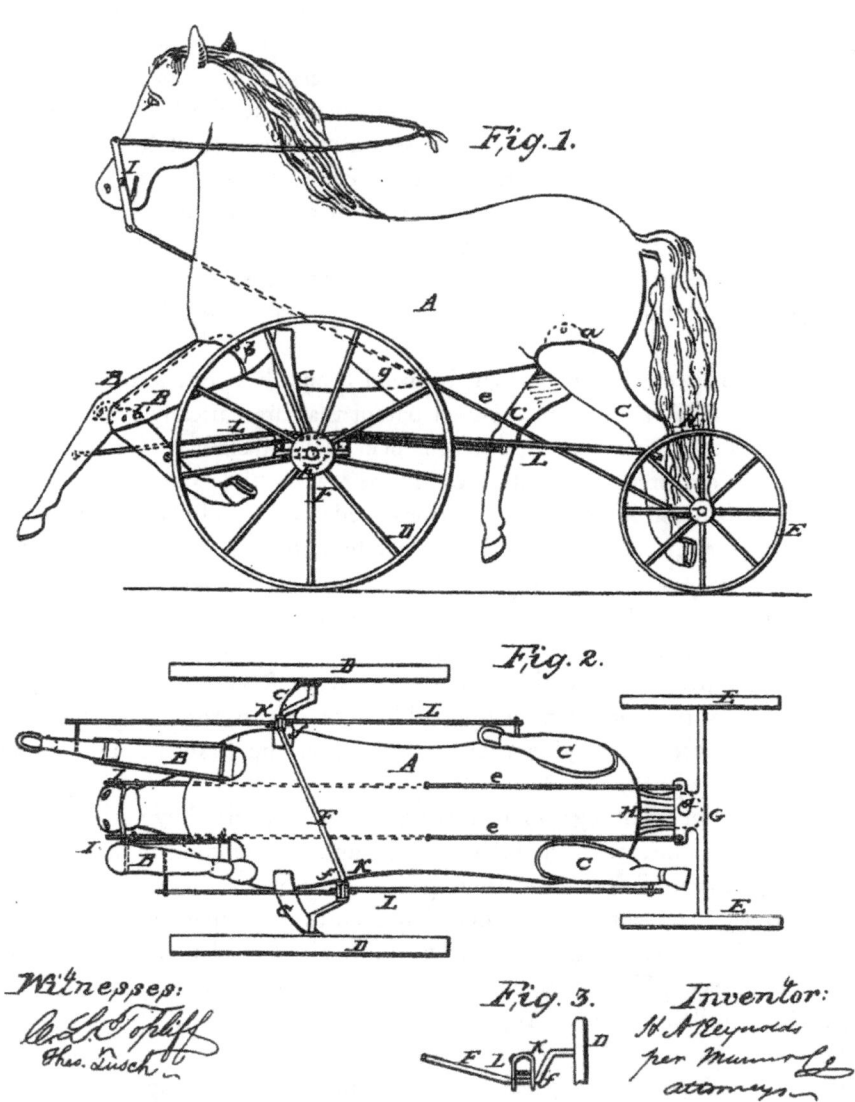

Reynolds's take on a horse-simulator may not have looked much like a bicycle, but because he jettisoned the idea of a bobbing head, it worked virtually the same: the rider turned opposing pedals in a circular motion. The pedals, in turn, were attached to cranks that spun a horizontal axle powering the driving wheels. Had the rider steered the driving wheel instead of the two rear wheels, it would have totally pre-empted Lallement. Coming after the two Mackenzie patents, but before Lallement's, it was probably the only one of the three with a real chance to knock out the Frenchman's 1866 claims.

With the American velocipede business dead, all four patents lay idle. However, as Americans began to show some interest in the high-wheeled bicycle after the 1876 world's fair, their owners started to pull them out of various drawers and dust them off. In July 1877 the Montpelier firm reissued Mackenzie's 1864 patent, changing its claims language in a way similar to that earlier done by Smith to Mackenzie's 1862 patent.[11] Calvin Witty sold the Lallement patent to a Boston firm, Richardson & McKee. Henry M. Richardson and George McKee made children's carriages, baby buggies and other light vehicles. About this time, they were joined by a relative of George's named Joseph McKee. Joseph was also a partner in a New York firm, McKee & Harrington, also a maker of carriages and carts. It is likely that the Colonel was acquainted with the Boston firm, as his old shoefindings company shared the same address as Richardson & McKee, 6 Merrimac, for several months in 1875 after the Great Boston Fire. Once he learned of the sale, Pope sought out exclusive use rights, but discovered, to the apparent consternation of both him and Richardson & McKee, that Cunningham & Company had already bought an option for its exclusive use from Witty prior to the sale. However, Cunningham allowed the option to expire, permitting Richardson & McKee to sell non-exclusive licenses to both firms.[12]

The rush for licenses apparently galvanized Richardson & McKee. They immediately applied for a reissue of the Lallement patent that dramatically expanded its claims language. From the original's simple one-sentence, 34-word claim grew a convoluted, five-claim, 600-word monster.[13] Richardson & McKee rewrote the patent with the knowledge that the Mackenzie and Reynolds applications predated it, and placed Lallement's foot-powered, crank-driven, bar-guided device squarely within the context of a pivoted frame with a front wheel set in a rotating fork turned by a handlebar. The whole thing was clearly an effort to save the patent from prior art claims.

Three days after the Lallement reissue was approved, Richardson & McKee bought three more velocipede patents, this time from Harvey Reynolds, including his crucial March 1865 patent that included the opposable, foot-driven, rotating cranks. Following the now-routine practice, they rewrote its description and claims, heavily emphasizing the priority of the cranks.[14]

After sixteen years of legal maneuvering, the Mackenzie, Reynolds and Lallement patents were now so interconnected that only a manufacturer controlling the whole bundle could be sure that he was not infringing on at least one of them. On 15 January 1878 Richardson & McKee and the Montpelier Manufacturing Company entered into an agreement pooling the rights to eight patents, including all of the Lallement, Mackenzie and Reynolds documents. The jigsaw puzzle was now complete. Richardson & McKee and Montpelier controlled the patent rights to the bicycle.[15]

Pope was in a bind. By early 1879, Richardson & McKee were squeezing him for royalties of $27.50 per bicycle.[16] Just as George Fairfield was gearing up for volume production, it looked like no one in America would be able to compete with the British. Charles Edward Pratt was the man Pope turned to in order to sort out the mess. Born in Vassalborough, Maine, on 13 March 1845, the son of a Quaker minister, Pratt graduated from Haverford College in Pennsylvania in 1870 and apprenticed at the Boston law firm of Jones & Otis. He was admitted to the Suffolk County Bar in 1871 and the United States Bar in 1872. Although he started out as a general practitioner, he soon specialized in patents. He learned to ride in the winter of 1877–78 at Cunningham, Heath's cycle rink, and helped smooth out a small customs dispute when Cunningham's first shipment of bicycles arrived in November 1877. Soon after, he switched his allegiance to Pope.[17]

In April 1878 he wrote David Brandon in Paris asking about French bicycle patents prior to 1866. Brandon replied "We presume that your object is to find a previous patent in order to upset Lallement's U.S. Patent."[18] Brandon was correct. If Pratt could prove that the U.S. patent examiner had approved Lallement's application in ignorance of a preceding foreign patent or a demonstration of prior art, he could invalidate the patent. However, the information Brandon could locate was of little assistance. Unable to break the patent pool, Pope instead opened his checkbook. In March 1879 Richardson & McKee sold half of their rights in the eight patents — a quarter of the total — to Pope. They sold only the rights as applied to bicycles, keeping everything related to baby buggies, hobbyhorses and children's vehicular toys. Although the agreement was dated 19 March, the full text of the agreement that the assignee is required to submit to the patent office (the so-called "liber document") was not sent until 21 April, suggesting that the two parties may have been tweaking the exact language of the document for a month after entering into their initial agreement.

The next day, 22 April, the directors of the Montpelier company agreed to sell all rights to their half-interest in the patents. Interestingly, Montpelier didn't sell to the Pope Manufacturing Company, but to Charles Pope, the Colonel's father, who subsequently conveyed his interest to the firm. A subsequent agreement the following August refining the terms of the sale was also sold to Charles.[19] Although the official history, with Albert racing through the night to cinch the deal, makes for good reading, the patent office ledgers suggest that in reality, Albert carefully crafted an agreement with Richardson & McKee in Boston, while Charles spent several days, possibly weeks, in Vermont negotiating with Montpelier. Once the Boston agreement was finalized, Albert wired his father in Vermont, who closed the other half of the purchase. Here again, the facts dispute the family legend that Charles was a broken man after his 1851 bankruptcy. To the contrary, he appears to have been a major participant in one of the biggest deals in the company's history. Six days after Montpelier agreed to sell, Richardson & McKee capitulated and sold their remaining interests, without limitations, to Pope.

Why did they agree to sell? Both Richardson & McKee and Montpelier entered into subsequent contracts over the next several months refining the terms of the original sale. Based on their language, they were done at the behest of the sellers, particularly Montpelier. They indemnified the sellers from the costs of existing and future patent litigation.[20] Although the official story, that Richardson & McKee initially sold because they thought they could use the money to buy Montpelier's share, is probably true, it is likely that the Vermont company found itself involved in unwanted and expensive patent suits, and Pope's offer allowed them to make a tidy profit, extract themselves from Richardson & McKee's speculative litigation and quietly return to their manufacturing business.

## The Only Fatality

Once in possession of the patents, Pope moved quickly. Pratt notified every bicycle maker and importer they could either pay royalties or get out of the business. A month later the Western Toy Company of Chicago was granted a license to make children's bicycles and that fall the St. Nicholas Toy Company was issued similar permission. Western soon upgraded its license to permit it to make inexpensive adult bicycles with front wheels up to 50 inches in diameter. In March 1880, Thomas B. Jeffery of Chicago received permission to make bicycles with front wheels up to 42 inches.[21] In purely monetary terms, these first licenses were not particularly onerous. The St. Nicholas agreement required royalties of one dollar for every bicycle with a front wheel under 42 inches and two dollars for every larger machine. Jeffery's license stipulated a fee of 40 cents for each bicycle under 32 inches, and a dollar for each bicycle with a front wheel between 32 and 42 inches.[22]

Their non-monetary covenants, on the other hand, were highly invasive. St. Nicholas could only make bicycles with wooden wheels. Every month, the firm had to provide Pope with a written report containing the number of bicycles sold and the name and address of each purchaser. If they tried to dispute the validity of any Pope patent or question Pope's rightful title to it, regardless of whether it was part of the license agreement, their license would be voided. The Jeffery license was similar. Pope claimed these covenants rationalized the industry. He boasted that he extended the same terms to his oldest rival, Cunningham & Co., that he did to anyone else, and claimed his intervention actually saved Cunningham at a time its owners were seriously considering abandoning the business.[23] However Pope's "salvation" came at a high price. By 1883 Pope's men were running the company with George Pope, Albert's cousin, acting as corporate secretary, and another cousin, Walter Pope, running a cyclometer-making business out of the Cunningham building. Pope had "saved" the firm by turning it into his importing house. In 1886 the Colonel quietly buried his oldest competitor and moved on to newer victims.

Others chose to fight back. In September 1880, McKee & Harrington, the New York carriage firm run by Joseph McKee and Charles F. Harrington, bought out the factory of R. H. Hodgson, an Englishman who had been making small numbers of his "Velocity" and "Newton Challenge" bicycles in Massachusetts. With a splash of publicity, they introduced their "Union" bicycle, the second American-made Ordinary produced in appreciable numbers. They had also developed a unique machine for forming the much-desired U-profile wheel rims and were offering these for sale, along with semi-finished rims, tires, and spokes. The partners didn't even bother applying for a license, maintaining that the Pope patents were invalid because one Monsieur Varrecke (or Varrecka), a Belgian acrobat, had toured New York and Philadelphia in 1863 featuring a velocipede in his act, thereby wiping out all the later American patents through a public display of prior art. The Varrecke story had been kicking around for several years, and the sketchy evidence to support it was probably passed from George to Joseph McKee.[24]

Pope promptly sued, claiming infringement of the Lallement and Reynolds patents.[25] A couple of months later, he got an injunction prohibiting the manufacture or sale of the Union without a license. McKee & Harrington slightly modified its design, twice appealed the injunction and kept on making bicycles. In the summer of 1882 a New York judge threw out the second appeal and found McKee & Harrington in contempt for ignoring the injunction. A full trial on the infringement suit was docketed. Meanwhile, somebody tracked down Pierre Lallement, who by this time was living back in America, in Brooklyn. He had used the money from selling his half of the patent to start a bicycle shop near the Champs-Elysees in the spring of 1869. However, it went under, his marriage fell apart, and he returned to America in mid–1879, possibly at the behest of Richardson & McKee.[26] Lallement provided a deposition, but before the trial could start, the parties agreed to a settlement. Pope had sought $2,000 in back royalties but agreed to take $300. McKee & Harrington received a license for the 100 or so bicycles then in various stages of manufacture and agreed to withdraw from the business.

After the case was over, Pratt tracked Lallement down in Brooklyn, wrote up his life story and persuaded the Colonel to give him a job. He worked as a machinist in the Boston store for three years, and in December 1885, appeared at an indoor race meet sponsored by the Massachusetts Bicycle Club. Between races, he circled the track on his original 1866 boneshaker, accompanied by William Rowe, Columbia's crack racing star, on an Ordinary. This was just about the last anyone saw of Lallement. He soon left Pope's employment, apparently began drinking heavily and fell deeply into debt. He died penniless and forgotten on 11 August 1891, buried in Mt. Benedict cemetery without a headstone at the charity of the Boston diocese. While many claim to have been wounded in the great patent wars, he was the only known fatality.[27]

## Cordial Hatreds

Soon after their settlement, McKee & Harrington issued a statement explaining that they still believed the Colonel's patents were worthless, but they wanted to get back to their baby carriage business, and the toil and expense of fighting Pope, who seemed willing to spend unlimited amounts of money litigating, simply wasn't worth it. A few months later, Tom Jeffery placed an advertisement in *Bicycling World* offering to sell the transcript of the Pope-McKee & Harrington lawsuit to anyone who was interested and stated he would supply information damaging to the credibility of the Lallement patent.[28]

A native of Devon, England, Thomas Buckland immigrated to America in 1863, where he changed his last name to Jeffery (his mother's maiden name) and started manufacturing telescopes, microscopes and other scientific instruments. He later added a lucrative side business making patent models for aspiring inventors. He built and repaired velocipedes during the boom of 1868–69, but like everyone else washed his hands of the business once Witty started in on his royalty threats and the market crashed. Excited by the growing British cycling trade he saw during a visit home in 1878, he decided he wanted to get in on the ground floor, and bought one of Pope's first manufacturing licenses.[29] He later expanded into the production of bicycle accessories and repair parts.

After reviewing the patents on which his 1880 license was based, Jeffery concluded that "they were worthless and if contested would not be worth the paper they were written on," and by the time the McKee & Harrington case was settled, he had stopped making his license payments. Pope sued, and he agreed to pay $142.17 for permission to finish up the bicycles then under construction. He then sold the business for $2,000 to an old friend, R. Philip Gormully, an outgoing, natural-born salesman who had earned a small fortune in architectural sheet metal work such as cornices and decorative tin roofing. As a sideline, Gormully had begun importing British Ordinaries the year before. After buying Jeffery's business, he retained his friend as foreman and carried on much as before, just under a new name.

Gormully first wrote Charles Pratt in late 1882 to ask about a license for this firm. "They, in reply, seemed anxious for me to take out a license," he recalled later, so anxious that they paid "the whole of my expenses to visit them in Boston." At the meeting, Gormully agreed to pay $500 for an interim license and told Pratt that he would get back to him on his offer of a long-term arrangement. "They claimed that they were in a very awkward position in allowing me to make bicycles without a license," Gormully remembered. "They were willing to make most any terms."[30]

Others got rougher treatment. In 1880, George Pressey invented a radical new bicycle called the Star. It looked like a backwards Ordinary, with the large wheel in back and a steerable, small front wheel. It was far more sophisticated than that, however, because the rear wheel was driven by a belt-and-clutch system adjustable for different conditions. It could be pedaled in short strokes or even thrust forward by pressing on both pedals simultaneously. Pressey contracted with the H. B. Smith Machine Co. of New Jersey in January, 1881 to build them. He grew discouraged with Smith's workmanship and asked the Pope company to take over manufacturing. In early 1882 the Colonel notified Pressey that he would have nothing to do with the Star, but would gladly sue the Smith firm if it didn't take out a license. Pressey hurried back to New Jersey to rebuild his relationship with Smith, a partnership that would, by the end of the decade, make both men wealthy.

Although Pressey was convinced that Pope's men "apparently mean business," Smith assured him that the Star violated none of Pope's patents, and the firm apparently escaped unscathed.[31]

And still others gave back as good as they got. Albert H. Overman's career contained many interesting parallels to Pope's.[32] After earning a modest fortune in Chicago, he moved to Hartford in 1881 and formed the Overman Wheel Company, both because several of his investors were executives at the city's Traveler's Insurance Company and because he planned to contract with Colt's Armory for his production. After manufacturing at Colt's for a year, he moved to Chicopee, Massachusetts, a Springfield suburb, and contracted out to the Ames Manufacturing Company.[33] To avoid Pope's patent monopoly, Overman built an adult tricycle, then becoming a popular item in England. The Victor was well made and beautifully finished in English baked enamel. The Colonel hadn't yet figured out how to bake enamel without melting the frame brazing, so he offered only an uninspiring matte paint or nickel plating, a twenty-dollar option. The Victor was a hit and Pope had to scramble to introduce his own tricycle, a copy of the English BSA National, the following year.

Perhaps because of this irritation, per-

Albert H. Overman earned a modest fortune selling bookbinding supplies in Chicago before moving to Hartford in 1881 to make bicycles and tricycles. Pope and Overman, according to most witnesses, "cordially hated each other." Overman suggested that Pope had faked his Civil War record. Pope, in turn, told acquaintances that Overman had been a bookmaker back in Chicago. After a dispute with his distributor, Spalding Bros., in 1894 over unsold bicycles Overman's firm went downhill and closed in 1897. He then became an automaker, mining engineer and farmer (*Bicycling World*, December 12, 1902, author's photograph).

haps because of the decision to locate in "his" backyard, the rivalry between the two men quickly grew personal as well as professional. Overman, like Pope, insisted on being called "Colonel," but he came by the title through a regular army commission, and frequently cast aspirations on Pope's brevet appointment. Pope, in turn, privately told friends that before entering the bicycle business Overman had been a bookmaker. In fact, he was a bookbinder and stationery wholesaler; Pope's quip was a clever but slanderous double entendre. "For five years thereafter these two colonels were engaged in a rivalry that was often bitter," recalled one cycling journal:

> If one flew the largest flag in New England over his factory, as Pope once did, the other immediately corralled the flag market and went him a few yards better. If one endowed a Hartford church with a $5,000 contribution, as Pope once did, the other immediately went him $5,000 better. And so it went on, all through five years of strife. Both men cordially hated each other.[34]

Pope's biggest headaches, however, were still in the courtroom. In 1877, a Connecticut court handed down a decision in an otherwise obscure patent case, *Miller v. Bridgeport Brass Co.*, concerning, of all things, an improved wick-holder for whale-oil lamps.[35] Its inventor, Joshua Ambrose, intended to patent a lamp that would burn without a glass chimney. It didn't work very well, and was soon forgotten. However, thirteen years later, the lamp-making firm of Edmund Miller & Co. discovered that the Ambrose wick-holder made a perfect explosion-proof gasoline lamp. They acquired Ambrose's patent and had it reissued with a new, second claim incorporating the explosion-proof feature. A competitor, Bridgeport Brass, sued, claiming that reissues could only be sought to correct errors, not to add newer, broader claims. The court agreed with Bridgeport, and to Colonel Pope's eternal regret, the Miller Company appealed to the U.S. Supreme Court.

The Supreme Court has never liked patent cases, then or now. They are complicated, boring, tedious, and often make the unfortunate justice picked to write the opinion look foolish. At least one justice has suggested that if the Constitution did not require the high court to hear them, they would long ago have been banished to the obscurity of some administrative tribunal.[36] Unable to make patent cases go away, the justices have often taken out their frustrations on the patents themselves. In October 1881, the Supreme Court rendered its decision in *Miller*. "Nothing but a clear mistake" was sufficient grounds to seek a reissue. That was not new law. The court, however, didn't stop there, finding that "the claim of a specific device or combination, and an omission to claim other devices or combinations apparent on the face of the patent, are in law, a dedication to the public which is not claimed." That is, if a patent contains a certain inherent feature (i.e., the ability to burn gasoline without risk of explosion) and this feature is not contained in the claims language, it cannot later be claimed by the applicant, or by anyone else, because it has been released to the public. The court continued: "It [the failure to assert a claim] is a declaration that that which is not claimed is either not the patentee's invention, or, if his, he dedicates it to the public."[37]

In other words, when the holder of a patent surrenders it for reissue, he admits that it is defective and needs correcting. If his application broadens its claims without demonstrating clear error, he also admits that the original patent actually contained those claims all along, but that he forgot to include them.[38] Because the original patent didn't mention them, they were waived by omission and released. Therefore, he can't assert ownership now because they belong to the public. Moreover, if anyone can show that the original patent really was the first demonstration of the disputed claim, nobody who filed for the same feature after the original patent can assert ownership either, because the original patent demonstrates prior art. The only way a subsequent patent holder can protect his interest is to prove that the earlier patent does not contain that feature. That's not a terrible burden — unless the earlier patent-holder filed his own reissue in an attempt to nullify the other's reissue, and neither application demonstrated clear error. This is, of course, exactly what happened in the bicycle patents. As a result, every one of the reissued Lallement, Mackenzie and Reynolds patents became essentially worthless.

On 5 March 1883, a week after Philip Gormully returned from his Pope-paid trip to Boston, an Ohio court, in *Pope v. Marqua*, voided a Pope patent agreement, ruling that because the *Miller* case invalidated Pope's patents, Charles Pratt's threats to sue any unlicensed infringers amounted to a fraudulent inducement to enter a contract. "I notice you have lately lost a suit in Ohio," wrote Gormully to Pratt a week later, his letter dripping with sarcasm, "Does it amount to anything?" Soon thereafter, the St. Nicholas Toy Company stopped sending its monthly reports and royalty payments to Boston.[39]

Scrambling to cover his now-exposed flank, the Colonel suddenly discovered the fine art of diplomacy. He wrote the next letter himself. Revealing the poorly kept secret that the St. Nicholas and Western licenses restricted them to low-end bicycles, he said that "They each have their field, and we have ours, and there is an intermediate field," and explained that "it is this intermediate field we want you to take." By working together, Pope believed that "you can do better and make more money in that field than you will by competing with the others directly." "With four strong concerns," he noted, "and a hold on a trade already worked up for two or three years, we could control the business substantially over the whole field of American manufacture, even after the patents have expired."[40]

Pope had pulled back the stick and offered a carrot — and what a carrot! By this time the Lallement patent had only six months left to run anyway, and anyone else would have thrown in the towel — but not Pope. His response to *Miller* was an even grander plan to extend his control beyond the life of the Lallement-era patents. Gormully rose to the bait. A month later he wrote Pratt that "I am willing to give the appearance of your controlling me ... [and] to make this arrangement for our mutual benefit and to continue the business as a monopoly." However, the Chicago businessman wanted a better deal. "I am still willing to keep a combination to keep others out," said Gormully, "but [I] am unwilling to give you all the profit ... but if you will make a reduction in royalties I should be willing to make this arrangement." Flexing a little muscle of his own, he asked Pratt to "save a lawsuit which would be expensive to me and to you, but [which] I am morally certain and sure I should win in the end." To back up his threat, Gormully informed Pratt that "I have a friend who is now on his way to Paris," with a mission to "obtain in Paris information regarding the machine used by Michaux and others prior to 1867 that will upset all vital claims."[41]

Pratt responded with an additional perk. Since 1880, Weed had been building a less-expensive boy's model for Pope, the Mustang, in sizes up to 46 inches. Pratt now offered to turn this market over to Gormully by canceling the Mustang, letting Gormully build a new boys bicycle, and sell it through Cunningham's store, promising that "we think we should be amongst your best customers." To clear the field for Gormully's new boy's Ordinary, "We should probably stop making Mustangs altogether and sell your goods. The

Cunningham Co. is one of our chief licensees, and we think it probable that they would handle the line of goods you will make."[42]

Pope apparently made good on at least some of the offer. A decade later a visitor to Philip Gormully's office spotted a portrait of Pope, framed with his contract to sell Gormully & Jeffery's "American Ideal" bicycle. At the top of the portrait, someone had written "our first agent."[43]

Meanwhile, Pratt was buying up every patent even remotely applicable to bicycles. After the Richardson & McKee-Montpelier purchase, Pratt had acquired only a handful of patents, and the men at the Weed factory had generated another dozen or so, mostly to protect the design of forging dies.[44] But starting in late 1882 and early 1883, he went on a buying spree, snapping up patents Tom Jeffery thought "were simply a junk shop." In one case, Pratt used an illiterate sign-painter working at the Weed factory as a strawman purchaser to hide his identity. The lucky painter earned a quick profit of $200 on a patent worth $500.[45] By the time Philip Gormully agreed to a licensing contract in the middle of 1883, Pratt could throw 39 patents into the deal.

There were actually two contracts. The first was a clean-up agreement that allowed Gormully to finish the bicycles then in production and the second was a permanent license to make bicycles up to 50 inches with a maximum price capped at 80 percent of that for the Columbia. Gormully paid an up-front fee of one thousand dollars and a ten-dollar-per-bicycle royalty. "The money [was] paid for the privilege of not being molested in our business," explained Thomas Jeffery bitterly.[46] Gormully had deliberately blurred his business relationship with his childhood friend during the negotiations, but once the contract was signed he made Jeffery a partner in the new firm of Gormully & Jeffery, selling him a half-interest for $5,000. Partnership hardly stilled either Tom Jeffery's loathing for both Pratt and Pope or his habit of letting the world know in no uncertain terms what he thought of them, and in November 1883, he took out another half-page ad in *Bicycling World* bashing the Pope patent catalog. Pratt, apoplectic, wrote Gormully:

> We understand Mr. Jeffery to be an employee of yours [and] you are responsible for him as you are for any other agent and employee of yours and it is neither according to the letter nor the spirit of our agreements with you that he should be constantly endeavoring, as he does, to impair the public respect for our patent rights ... as long as our title to the inventions covered by our patents is actually sustained under the laws, we and our licensees have the full benefit of it, no matter what the private opinions of individuals may be.[47]

Gormully undoubtedly had a good laugh as he handed the letter over for filing.

## *An Artfully Constructed Snare*

Although Pratt had finally talked Gormully & Jeffery into joining the combination, A. H. Overman quit when Pope wouldn't let him use his latest ball-bearing patents in the Overman tricycle. Overman went ahead anyway and Pratt sued him in the fall of 1884 for $50,000. When Gormully wrote Pratt in October that "I see by the late publications that the Overman Co. are going to bring out a line of bicycles next March," the Boston lawyer's lip curled in disgust: "Overman Company making bicycles for sale in March next?— are you so childlike as to believe everything that is published?"

On the first of March, 1885, the cycling journals oohhed and aahhed over the new Overman "Victor" bicycle. Finished in their unmatchable British enamel, the new machine offered several innovations even Pope's premier "Special Columbia" lacked, and was priced $7.50 less. Its introduction completely overshadowed Pope's unveiling of his new Hartford-built tricycle. Pope sued Overman a second time over the bicycle, placing a $73,000 attachment on the 500 machines that the Ames Manufacturing Company, Overman's supplier, was just then finishing, effectively blocking their shipment. Overman countersued and hired former Massachusetts governor B. F. Butler as his lawyer.[48]

That fall, Albert Pope visited Gormully in Chicago and the two took a leisurely drive in an open brougham through the city's parks, trying to thrash out their differences. Gormully had reluctantly agreed to an extension of the original contract the previous December that lasted until April 1886. It kept the existing royalties mostly intact, but allowed Gormully & Jeffery to make the American Ideal in sizes up to 52 inches. That agreement had been loaded, however, with a host of irritating little conditions, such as making them advertise in a new cycling magazine, *The Wheelman*. When a draft of the agreement crossed his desk with *The Wheelman* requirement, Gormully red-penciled it, writing Pratt that "I think it beyond the province and arbitrary." Pratt put it back in with a smirky reply: "You remark ... that it is beyond our province and arbitrary. Perhaps it is from your point of view, but it isn't from ours — if we grant a license at all we have the right to name the terms upon which we grant it." Pratt neglected to inform Gormully that *The Wheelman* was his personal pet project. A lavish and extravagant waste, it eventually cost Pope thousands. When later asked why he fought Pope at such great expense, Gormully once remarked, "I didn't share his taste in literature."[49]

As they rode through Chicago's parks Gormully told Pope that "I saw no reason for continuing any longer with them, as I did not know of any patents that they owned that would be of use to me." The Lallement patent expired the next year and Tom Jeffery had managed work-arounds for all the patents Pope had bought since 1882. They were already preparing the tooling for a high-grade bicycle to compete with the Columbias, to be introduced in the spring of 1886. When Gormully mentioned in passing that he was preparing to convert Gormully & Jeffery from a partnership to a corporation, Pope excitedly offered to buy into the new enterprise.[50] Horrified, Gormully hurriedly found his own Chicago backers.

Over the winter, the Pope-Overman war grew even more bitter. Neither side was backing down, and the money flowed like machine oil. In a breach of the unofficial rules of engagement to date, Pope named Ames as a party to the suit and tried to attach their machinery and real estate. Up to this point, the antagonists had treated their respective manufacturing contractors as neutral non-combatants. Even if Pope's claim was valid, Overman replied, there was no way he could have been damaged to even one-tenth of the amount of the attachment. The monopolist, Overman complained, was now trying to intimidate honest workmen. Privately, J. T. Ames admitted that the cost of the suit was dragging down production of their new bicycle.[51] In Hartford, Pratt was resorting to increasingly Byzantine legal maneuvers, such as playing a shell game with the Pope Manufacturing Company's corporate residency by surrendering its charter in Connecticut and reincorporating in Maine to dodge a court order, then refiling within weeks back in Connecticut.[52]

Springfield, Massachusetts, was the scene of the East's largest summer cycling fair, assembled around its annual race meet. Neither Pope nor Overman spent much time watching the racing, however. Conferring first through intermediaries and then face-to-face, in June the two announced that they had agreed to terms resolving the patent conflict. The same time that Pope and Overman were haggling over the "Treaty of Springfield," Gormully & Jeffery introduced the American Champion, their challenger to the Columbia. To Gormully's surprise, "I received a number of threatening letters both from the Pope Manufacturing Company and the Overman Wheel Company, from which I inferred that they wished to bulldoze me into taking licenses from both of them." Unknown to Gormully, the Treaty of Springfield required Pope to now actively enforce the same Overman-held patents he had just been trying to invalidate. A deeper mystery was why both firms were demanding that he pay royalties on patents that had clearly expired. The whole thing was ludicrous.[53]

Gormully & Jeffery had deliberately waited until after the expiration date of the Pope contract to introduce the American Champion. Its features were covered in a series of independent patents that they had acquired or invented themselves since 1882. This had been a sticking point back in 1884, the same time as *The Wheelman* spat. That license allowed them to use 15 Pope patents, all of which expired in or before April 1886. In return, Gormully & Jeffery promised not to use another 65 Pope patents or to use any similar feature, even if they had independent patents. For example, Gormully & Jeffery were prohibited from using hollow metallic rims, even though Tom Jeffery had come up with his own version of a hollow rim.

Pratt had originally wanted a ten-year license agreement. Gormully wrote back arguing that he wasn't about to sign a ten-year license for patents that expired in two years, especially when the license prohibited him from using his own patents in the meantime. Pratt responded soothingly that, "You should not be so much afraid of our wishing or trying to cripple you."

Hardly reassured, Gormully asked Pratt, "In my last letter I asked you to simply extend the present contract I have with you to allow me to make larger sizes.... Why not do that?" Pratt refused without really explaining why all the "unnecessary verbage" was necessary. Gormully wrote Pratt once again just before he signed the revised agreement seeking reassurance: "This license is to terminate, if I wish so, on the 1st of March, 1886, or sooner."[54]

After being sued by the new Treaty of Springfield allies, Gormully made a last attempt to peacefully sort out the problem. Colonel Pope asked him to attend a conference in Boston "to form an alliance for the general good of the business." When he arrived, he was surprised to find Overman in attendance. Attempting to smooth over his lieutenants' strong-arm demands for renewed royalty payments, Pope asked Gormully to "chip in" to a fund to support the business. "They wished to extort money from me" was the way Gormully remembered it. Having already paid Pope about $27,000 in fees and royalties, Gormully finally had enough. He told the participants he would get back to them after he returned from Europe and left. Before sailing, he sent Pope a draft agreement offering a lump-sum payment of a thousand dollars, five dollars for each American Champion, and two-fifty for each American Ideal. While he was away Pope's lawyers filed suit in Federal district court.[55]

By the time the case wound its way through the system to the U.S. Supreme Court, the *Pope v. Gormully* record was over 500 pages long, including testimony and documents. A glimpse into a typical day in the life of a lawsuit is this exchange between Tom Jeffery and L. L. Coburn, one of Pope's lawyers, during a deposition in August 1887. We join them *ten days* into the deposition (the most time normally allowed for a deposition today is *eight hours*). They are discussing how the rear wheel ball bearing unit of Gormully & Jeffery's American Champion differs from that in the Columbia. Coburn has just shown a cut-open model of the American Champion's rear hub to Jeffery:

> MR. JEFFERY: I refuse to have this model used as an exhibit or in any other way at this time.
> MR. COBURN: I picked up this model from the table where there were several of your models, did I not?
> MR. JEFFERY: I think not.
> MR. COBURN: Where did I get it, do you think?
> MR. JEFFERY: I do not know. I left it in a box containing my private papers.
> MR. COBURN: Don't you know that you are trying to prevaricate now, and don't you remember you have sworn to tell the truth?
> MR. OFFIELD (Jeffery's lawyer): I object as insulting to the witness.
> MR. JEFFERY: I refuse to answer any question implying a manifest insult.
> MR. COBURN: Don't you know that I haven't gotten up from this chair since I began to ask you questions this morning, and that you are sitting a few feet from me, facing me, and have been since I commenced asking questions this morning?
> MR. JEFFERY: I admit that, but you had ample opportunity to place the model in your pocket before adjourning [last night], and as I did not see that model between the time of adjournment and the time you produced as an illustration it is quite likely you did.
> MR. COBURN: You are willing to swear, are you, that you are of the opinion that I took that model last night after adjournment, carried it in my pocket, and produced it therefrom this morning when I asked my question instead of taking it from the table beside me where there are several of your small models and exhibits? And has not that ball-bearing model been lying around the room here just as common as the others during the entire time you have been testifying?
> MR. JEFFERY: I cannot form an opinion about the matter, for the last time I saw it before it was in your hands was as I have stated, and its production by you looks a little suspicious. I did not know and did not see the model lying on the table today, as you say you did.
> MR. OFFIELD: If it is of the slightest importance as to the exact point and locality that this model was picked up by Mr. Coburn, then he is respectfully requested to locate that point in the record and it will be unhesitatingly admitted as a fact. Mr. Coburn is requested to proceed with his legitimate cross examination.[56]

And so it went, on and on and on. After four and a half years, everyone finally gathered in a Chicago courtroom on a cold winter's day in 1888 for oral arguments. Pratt was not an Illinois attorney, so he watched as Edmund Wetmore explained his handiwork. What Mr. Pratt had prepared, Wetmore claimed, was not merely a license, but a contract. True, it did give Gormully & Jeffery a license to use fifteen Pope patents, a license that ended by mutual consent in April 1886. However, the end of the license did not terminate the contract, nor did it discharge Mr. Gormully from its remaining obligations. In exchange for a fourteen-month license, Mr. Gormully had agreed to abide by the residual terms of the contract in perpetuity, including his promise not to use any feature covered by 65 specified Pope patents, and his promise to never contest the validity of those patents. The contract did not prohibit Gormully & Jeffery from infringing on the claims of the 65 patents. Instead, it said that he could not use the *features* contained in those patents. Even though Tom Jeffery had developed his own, completely different, version of a hollow front fork, Gormully & Jeffery still breached the contract by using it because Pope had a patent on one. If Gormully & Jeffery fought this clause, they breached the agreement again, because it also prohibited objections based on features, not specific patent claims.

Wetmore dismissed Pratt's reassuring letters, explaining that "[Gormully] is not a lawyer, and in the negotiations of the terms of this contract of December 1, 1884, did not consult a lawyer."[57]

What Gormully thought Pratt had meant, or even what Pratt had led him to believe, was immaterial; Gormully was out of his league, Pratt had outmaneuvered him, he was stuck, how he got out of it was his problem. Gormully's attorney responded that his client's interpretation of the document was a "natural conclusion that any unsuspecting man, not a lawyer, would have drawn." In the end, the court agreed, calling the contract, when read in conjunction with Pratt's vague and misleading correspondence "an artfully constructed snare to bind [Mr. Gormully] in a manner which he did not contemplate at the time he became a party to it." The district judge warned that he would not allow the law to be used to "encourage parties holding such patents to invent or devise schemes by which to obtain admissions, directly or indirectly, of the validity of their patents."[58] Pratt's clever license was invalidated by the court.

To add insult to injury, the district judge then reviewed each of the patents in the agreement, invalidating them all. Gormully & Jeffery had infringed nothing. The next day, the *American Athlete and Cycle Trades Review* apologized to its readers for its late delivery, breathlessly explaining that "we have delayed the printing of the *Athlete* in order to publish a full report of the decision of the Illinois court." After a lengthy synopsis, the editors concluded that "this means that the days of the monopoly in the manufacture of high-grade cycles are numbered, and as a consequence bicycles are bound to come down in price ... this will be good news to all lovers of the sport."[59]

Even in the face of this stinging rebuke, Pope appealed. The Colonel appeared to relish courtroom warfare. In deploying his lawyers and experts, it was almost as if he was reliving the thrill and danger of the Civil War, only this time, he got to play the general. George Bidwell, on the other hand, thought it was just plain stubborness: "The Colonel was like that — never willing to admit that he had been bested in any argument."[60] The U.S. Supreme Court split the appeal into four parts, argued before the justices concurrently in March, 1892. Everyone focused on *Pope Manufacturing Co. v. Gormully*, concerning the licensing contract. The other three cases debated the validity of the patents. On 4 April Justice Brown delivered the Court's opinion. "It is rarely that this court is called upon to consider so unique a contract," began Brown, "and we have found some difficulty in assigning it to a proper place among legal obligations." Pope and his lawyers must have taken a deep breath. Justice Brown continued: "We are clearly of the opinion that it does not belong to that class of contracts, the specific performance of which a court of equity can be called upon to enforce." Legal scholarship of that era held that the power of contract was virtually absolute, and that the government could step in only to stop fraud or duress. Although the justices found Pratt's cleverly worded contract "unusual and oppressive," Brown almost apologetically concluded that "we are not satisfied that his [Gormully's] assent to this contact was obtained by any fraud or misrepresentation." In this narrow sense, the Supreme Court overruled the lower court.

However, while the Supreme Court may have lacked the power to invalidate the contract, it could refuse to enforce it. "From time immemorial it has been the recognized duty of courts to exercise a discretion to refuse their aid in the enforcement of unconscionable, oppressive or iniquitous contracts," explained Justice Brown. "We are clearly of the opinion that it is of such a character that the plaintiff has no right to call upon a court of equity to give it the relief it has sought."[61] That is, nothing in the law prevented the nine justices from simply looking in the other direction as Gormully & Jeffery walked away from the contract.

Having dealt with the core issue, Justice Brown quickly ran through the individual patent disputes: Veeder's Patent of 1882, not infringed by reason of limitation of previous patents; Moran's Patent of 1881, not infringed as it does not involve a valid invention; Latta's Patent of 1885, not infringed as the patent is void for want of novelty; Shire's Patent of 1879 and Kirkpatricks' Patent of 1877, not infringed as the Gormully & Jeffrey's design is materially different from that indicated in the patents, and so on down the list. Pope was utterly routed. There was no infringement, in most cases because the patents themselves were faulty. Pope was barred from using his patent catalog to control his licensees. The scope of any future patent license would be limited to the four corners of that patent. Lallement's patent was now, once and for all, as dead as he.

Pope and Pratt had studied the history of Orlando Potter's sewing machine patent pool, formed in 1856 and successful until 1877. Indeed, it would be hard for them to ignore: the Weed Sewing Machine Company was a participant.[62] However, Pope and Pratt failed to learn the fundamental lesson of Potter's example: a successful patent pool required both carrots and sticks. In the sewing machine combine, all the participants brought valuable patents to the table — about thirty were needed to build a competitive sewing machine in 1856. In return, each received a share of royalties proportional to the value of its patents and was permitted full access to the others. If a firm chose to not contribute, it could still access the technology, but only by paying full royalties and running the risk that its license could be revoked.

Pope tried to impose his pool unilaterally. At first, he had no choice — it was Richardson & McKee and Montpelier that assembled the first effective bicycle patent pool, and he could either buy the entire catalog or capitulate. Pope outmaneuvered them by playing on Montpelier's fear of endless, draining litigation. However, Pope's thinking from that point became incremental, not strategic. He relied too heavily on the Lallement-era patents until *Miller v. Bridgeport Brass* knocked the underpinnings out of their overinflated reissue claims. The hodgepodge of patents Pratt then collected were, as Tom Jeffery accurately described it, "a junk shop." The attempt to give them perpetual force through the "license-contract" system was a desperate contrivance that depended on endless infusions of the Colonel's cash for legal maneuvers. Years after the case was over, R. Philip Gormully estimated both sides together spent about a half-million dollars fighting it.[63] Potter's sewing machine pool never attempted to regulate prices, business practices or the products of its members. It concentrated solely on the administration and enforcement of patents. This was a warning signal that Pope and Pratt should have listened to.

The Gormully lawsuit was Charles Pratt's last big project for the Colonel. Never a robust man, he had been forced to curtail his riding after 1885 because of ill health. He now began a quiet withdrawal from the company. He died in Roxbury in 1898 at age 53. One journalist recalled him as "heavily spectacled, yet with an all-seeing eye. Pratt sat quietly at the head of the patent department, and made and unmade the destinies of ambitious importers and manufacturers.... After Pope, Pratt may be said to have been the most important factor ever known to cycling."[64]

The great patent wars were over. It was time to build bicycles.

# 4

# *Building the Mass Market*

*I could not make a bicycle if my life depended on it, but I know how to sell them.*
— Albert A. Pope, 1903[1]

In the mid–1970s an urban historian asked seventy-five-year-old Judith Levine about some of her earliest memories of life in Manhattan's lower east side, a notorious turn-of-the-century slum. When she was four, she remembered being run down by "a well dressed man, a bicycle man," no doubt a suburban-dwelling clerk on his way to nearby Wall Street. "Instead of helping he yelled at me for playing in the street.... I never saw him before or since." After three-quarters of a century, she still seethed at the memory.[2] When Pope sold his first Columbias, the average middle-class urbanite took fewer than a hundred trips a year by any means other than walking.[3] Not long after the street urchin went down, one early automobile pioneer admitted that the technology to build the first cars had been available twenty years earlier, but it didn't occur to anybody to use it before 1895 "because the bicycle had not yet come in numbers and had not directed men's minds to the possibilities of independent, long-distance travel."[4]

The spidery Ordinary was hardly a tool of social equality. A high-wheeler easily cost a hundred and twenty dollars — three months' wages for the skilled machinists who built them, an entire winter's toil for a common laborer. This didn't change until the mid–1890s when brutal competition, new manufacturing techniques and standardized components dropped the price of no-frills safeties to a price even the workingman could afford. In 1896, over five thousand men and women rode to work in downtown Chicago, a figure that doubled within two years. In a small city like Harrisburg, Pennsylvania, on a clear fall weekday in 1898, over twice as many cyclists as streetcar passengers passed through a downtown intersection. As late as 1915 the Pope company was urging potential customers not to throw their nickels into a coinbox, but to ride to work: "Trolley car? In 6 months you have spent $30.00 and have nothing to show for it. Buy a good Pope Bicycle. At the end of six months you can have your rides and have the Bicycle, too!"[5]

The story of this revolution — from the bicycle as a stable-mate to the horse, a playtoy of the rich, to the liberator of everyman — is the story of the Pope Manufacturing Company in its second decade. The allure and popularity of the bicycle did not just happen. It was a deliberately crafted and stage-managed creation, and the Colonel was its impresario. At first he surrounded the high-wheeled Ordinary with such a cachet of elegance and haughty sophistication that it still reverberates today, a century later. When the producers of the British cult 1970s television show *The Prisoner* wanted to portray a hallucinogenic island prison masquerading as a quaint seaside resort, they chose the Ordinary as the logo for the anonymous "village." It fit. Then, as technology and management pulled volume up and drove costs down, Pope was able to bottle this cachet like some exotic perfume and sell it to the middle class, then *hoi polloi*. The popularity of the bicycle in America was not preordained. It was a carefully crafted, thoroughly engineered artifact. This is the story of how the Colonel pulled it off.

## *A Plaything for the Elite*

At first, Pope's new diversion hardly took the country by storm. Bicycles were expensive and cyclists formed an economic and social elite. Although the first Columbias, at $90 each, were far less than the $128 Pope charged for his best imported Duplex Excelsior, they were never intended for the blue-collar man. The first cyclists were overwhelmingly young, affluent and male. When the Boston Bicycle Club formed in February 1878, its 25 founding members comprised six merchants, four salesmen, four college students, three lawyers, three clerks, two corporate officers, and one architect, literateur and physician.[6] There was not a single workingman among the group. Organized upon military lines, the early bicycle clubs offered their members a chance to escape their typically sedentary lives and participate in an activity hearkening back to the rigors and romance of the recent Civil War with only a modicum of its lethal potential.

Riding the Ordinary was difficult and occasionally dangerous. On his first try, Karl Kron broke his elbow, noting, with no small irony, that the resulting doctor bill exactly equaled the price of his new Columbia. Over the 6,175 miles Kron logged in his first four years, various headers, falls and crashes required a substantial list of repairs: bent crank (234 miles); another bent crank (673 miles); bent handlebar (907 miles); broken handlebar (1,350 miles); broken seat spring, requiring shipment back to the factory (1,480 miles); broken head (2,222 miles); broken backbone, fixed at Pope's flagship Boston store (2,993 miles); and a second broken head (4,872 miles). By the end, Kron was hard-pressed to identify an original part still left on his machine.[7]

In 1884, Hartford's most famous resident, Samuel Clemens, better known as the author Mark Twain, walked the few blocks from his home to the Weed factory and bought a 50-inch Columbia. As was the custom, he purchased twelve hours of riding lessons along with his machine, but paid extra to have "the Expert" come to the privacy of his back yard instead of taking classes downtown at the riding hall. His private journal suggests why: "The old forms of profanity were of no real use in learning the bicycle. They are pale & inadequate. What we need is something stronger, something with more color — something lurid."[8] Twain may never have mastered the Ordinary. Two years later, he walked into E. I. Horsman's store in New York City to look over a tricycle.

At first, mass production was the farthest thing from the minds of the bicycle makers. Although Weed's production of Columbias initially lagged behind demand, the main concern at Hartford was whether the sport would last long enough to pay for the tooling. George Bidwell visited Hartford in August 1879 and found George Fairfield "scared to death that the factory had caught up with their orders." Entering the plant, Bidwell

## 4. Building the Mass Market

The Massachusetts Bicycle Club was established in Boston in 1879 as the "Pope" bicycle club, and listed many Pope family members and early employees on its membership rolls. Here, in this 1884 indoor group portrait, the Colonel, as usual, stands front and center (No. 11) with long-time employees Charles F. Joy (No. 3) sitting in the front, to the viewer's left, and Charles M. Cox (No. 22) behind Pope, to the viewer's right.

found "wheels and frames were hanging all over the place," and Fairfield was afraid they would never sell. "I braced him up all I could," he recalled, "and said that they would soon dispose of all they had hanging around and would be behind in orders. While my talk was wishful thinking, that is the way it turned out."[9]

Production increased from about 1,200 bicycles in 1880 to a little over 5,000 in 1888, with employment varying between 250 and 350.[10] In January 1879 the *American Bicycling Journal* listed every known cyclist in the United States. There were 242 entries. The League of American Wheelmen formed at a bicycling meet in Newport, Rhode Island, in May 1880 with 133 cyclists. By September, 527 had signed up and paid the one-dollar annual membership fee. Although its rolls were probably skewed somewhat toward the wealthier and more urban cyclist, the growth of the League is good indicator of the increased interest in the sport during its early years: two thousand members in 1883, five thousand in 1885, eight thousand in 1886.[11]

The number of *bicycles* actually grew much more slowly than the number of *cyclists*. Bicycles tended to be relatively long-lived and cyclists somewhat ephemeral. Of the first 1878 batch of Columbias, most were still in service over a decade later, faithfully plugging away until rendered obsolete by the safety.[12] On the other hand, in any given year almost half the league's membership was new, indicating that cyclists drifted in and out of the sport fairly frequently. The typical Ordinary served several owners during its life. A good estimate is that the domestic production of adult Ordinaries grew from about 4,000 in 1882 to around 9,000 in 1887.

Given this lull, it is an opportune time to break from the chronological narrative to examine how Pope and his men sought to build and maintain a market for their machines — one that would turn into a truly mass market after the coming of the safety bicycle.

## *Advertising!*

Pope was crazy about publicity. Sam McClure, a Pope employee who later became editor and publisher of the famous *McClure's Magazine,* recalled that "It was a maxim of Colonel Pope's that 'some advertising was better than others, but all advertising was good.'" After working for him many years, another employee said that Pope possessed a "master showman's mind." Asked what were the three essentials of selling bicycles, Pope responded:

> "Advertising!"
> What was the second essential, then?
> "Big advertising!"
> And the third? The reply came in a thundering tone:
> "Bigger advertising!"[13]

Although he relished notoriety for its own sake, Pope's extroversion was a calculated part of his patent and manufacturing strategies. In opting for interchangeable parts, Pope had committed himself to much higher start-up costs than had his bicycles been hand-fitted, as was the universal British practice in 1878. His large patent investments also added to this front-end expense. To achieve profitability, these costs had to be amortized over a larger number of units than was feasible given the size of the market in the late 1870s. To succeed, Pope had to sell not just Columbias, but cycling itself.[14]

This he did with obvious glee. Pope preferred to locate ads on the back cover of a magazine, and ran full-page spreads in the summer and half-page ads in the winter. When his Boston store moved from 87 Summer to 597 Washington Street in 1881, the new building was big enough to take up multiple street addresses. The company ran ads offering free posters, lithographs, calendars and other ephemera by mail. Advertisements in different magazines, of different sizes or placed in different locations within journals contained different street addresses. The responses were recorded and compared to test the effectiveness of various strategies. "For several years, we kept this account and it satisfied us finally that the best and highest priced mediums were the ones for us to stick to," noted one company official. Even McClure, while attending far-off Knox College in tiny Galesburg, Illinois, remembered that "Every boy in the West knew the Pope Manufacturing Company ... the Pope advertisements [were] everywhere."[15] Looking back on the early days, one reporter recalled that "Pope kept the daily press supplied with matter. He was a great believer in that idea, and he flooded every paper in the country with bicycle stuff. The bicycle was a new thing, and little was known about it. The editors were hungry for news; they wanted either serious stuff or humorous stuff. Pope gave them all kinds, and billions of words were printed about the bicycle."[16]

Pope supplied the press with more than clippings. He courted journalists through interviews, lavish presentations, and carefully stage-managed acts of philanthropy. One wag noted that "whether it was charity ... or [a] good work of any kind, there was always an advertisement closely shadowing the act." One favorite promotional tool was the excursion train from New York or Boston organized to take journalists to factory tours in Hartford. During the trip, the scribes could ogle at such luminaries as General Miles or John Jacob Astor and dine on baked shad roe, spring lamb and strawberries with cream.[17] Although not much of a drinker himself, Pope knew journalists well enough to provide "a large punch bowl."

Pope sometimes needed to call in a favor from one of his friendly journalists, as his no-holds-barred patent policy sometimes opened him to a surprising level of animosity. "Throughout his entire career, Pope became a greatly hated man," recalled one cycling journal.[18] The cycling press was highly politicized and rife with conflict. Frank Weston, one of the founders of Cunningham, Heath & Co., remained a silent partner in that firm because he also ran a magazine, *The American Bicycling Journal,* that started in December 1877, a month after Cunningham opened its doors.[19] It is unlikely that Weston intended any conflict of interest, but the cycling community at the time was so small that anyone who tried to earn a living within it had to have his fingers in a number of different pies. In 1879 Weston sold the magazine to Charles Pratt and Edward C. "Ned" Hodges, who changed its title to *Bicycling World*. It was an unlikely partnership. By this time Pratt was becoming a Pope lawyer, and Hodges, a banker by trade, was one of Cunningham's partners. Their interests soon diverged even farther when Hodges invested in the Overman Wheel Company, eventually becoming its vice-president in 1886.[20]

In late 1881, Pope started taking a lot of heat from the cycling press, including *Bicycling World,* for demanding that individual cyclists who had imported bicycles for their own use pay the ten dollar Lallement royalty fee. Pratt, under orders from the Colonel, sued a couple of them, settling for ten dollars and an apology in each case.[21] Pope asked Pratt to tone down *Bicycling World*'s sniping, but Hodges, who paid the bills, simply demoted Pratt to contributing editor and continued on. The following summer, the Pope firm ran a full-page ad announcing a "literary and artistic competition" with two Columbias as prizes, one for the best article, the other for best drawing, all entries to be sent to Mr. Pratt at *Bicycling World*.

About this time, McClure, fresh out of Knox College with a journalism B.A. in his pocket, had, in a fit of desperation, bluffed his way into Pope's outer office to ask for a job. Two months before, he had talked the Colonel into paying five dollars for an ad in a college project, "The History of Western College Journalism," which McClure published just as he was graduating.[22] To his shock, he not only got an interview, but the Colonel put him to work at his cycling rink teaching new customers how to ride. McClure forgot to mention that he had never ridden a bicycle, but managed to muddle through and was soon put in charge of the cycling rink at the flagship Boston store. A few weeks later, Pope called McClure back in and told him to edit a new cycling magazine he was putting together to be called *The Wheelman*. McClure cautioned him that any new magazine needed a stockpile of articles before starting and asked if he had one yet. Pope replied that he had already seen to this and that McClure should consult with Mr. Pratt. However, for the opening issue Pope wanted something special.

Pratt, a prolific author, had written "A Wheel Around the Hub," describing a two-day tour around Boston held by the Massachusetts Bicycle Club. Published in the upscale *Scribner's Monthly* in 1880, it was one of the first cycling stories to appear in the popular press. Pope wanted to reprint the article. McClure suggested that he save time and money by simply buying the printing plates from *Scribner's* instead of having the article reset. The Colonel thought this was a good idea and sent him to New York, where he bought the plates for $300. With the finished plates — and their 31 etched drawings — in hand, McClure realized that "it would certainly be absurd" to have almost forty pages of *The Wheelman* in one format and the rest in another, so he simply used the *Scribner's* layout for the entire magazine. When the first number of *The Wheelman* appeared, McClure recalled many years later, it looked just like *Scribner's*, "somewhat to the astonishment of the publishers of the latter magazine, who had not intended to sell me their idea of make-up along with the plates."[23]

In the October 1882 debut issue of *The Wheelman*, "Wheel Around the Hub" was accompanied by several of the articles and illustrations submitted to the *Bicycling World* competition, much to the annoyance of Ned Hodges. He was even angrier when Pope announced that due to its outrageous editorial policy, he would be withdrawing his advertising from *Bicycling World* forthwith and instead spending his hard-earned dollars at that smart new magazine run by Mr. McClure. Looking back, Karl Kron speculated that Pope had been planning the magazine for some time, but the fortuitous appearance of McClure on his doorstep advanced his schedule by several months.

Working at *The Wheelman* was hectic and not particularly remunerative. McClure lived with his brother John and a friend in "one room somewhere in Boston." The long hours and bad housing took their toll. That December, he fell ill and his roommates finally had to tell the Colonel that he could not work. Pope asked his sisters to make a house call and they found him "well advanced in typhoid." Pope paid for his hospitalization. When he emerged three weeks later he was weak and depressed, so George Pope rewarded him with a membership to the Massachusetts Bicycle Club and a key to its clubrooms in the basement of the Lafayette Hotel.[24]

*The Wheelman* was lavish, heavily illustrated — and a money loser. In its eighteen-month life, Pope poured thousands into the project. Kron noted that "of the usual monthly edition of 10,000, quite as many copies were given to libraries, reading rooms, hotels, barber shops and other resorts as were sold to subscribers. In other words, the magazine was an elaborate illustrated advertisement — an enormously expensive trade circular." After 15 issues, Pope managed to unload it onto *Outing* magazine, owned by W. B. Howland. A new corporation was set up to run the combined magazine, awkwardly titled *Outing and The Wheelman*. Howland, Pratt and McClure were to run the publication by committee. McClure was willing to cede authority over business matters to Howland, but not its editorial content, and he quit to take a job in New York. The Colonel did not take the news well. "*The Wheelman* goes to press with the expectation that you need to remain with this Co.," he wrote the day after learning of the resignation. When it became apparent that McClure couldn't be blustered into staying, he demanded that McClure return his ownership rights in the new Wheelman Corporation and give back the "loaned" bicycle he had been using. McClure's reply was apparently less than civil: "A message comes back from you just now that you will bring it in when you get around to it," Pope fumed. "This is a very discourteous message.... I shall expect the bicycle will be returned tomorrow and am very sorry that it was necessary for me to write this."[25]

Neither man held a grudge, and within a couple of months, the two had made up. "Just as I am writing this, John has come in," wrote the Colonel, passing on to Sam a greeting from his brother, who remained a loyal Pope man. Pratt also remained a friend for his few remaining years. "[I] note with pleasure your contentment and success in present work," he wrote soon after McClure and his wife arrived in New York.[26] Pratt stayed on as editor, but turned over most day-to-day management to Howland. In the summer of 1885 Howland left to take over the *Cambridge Tribune*, and the firm was sold to a syndicate supposedly headed by Teddy Roosevelt, which moved it to New York, renamed it *Outing*, and continued it as a general outdoor adventure magazine.[27] McClure went on to start his own monthly, which became famous when *McClure's* published Ida Tarbell's scathing biography of Standard Oil president John D. Rockefeller in 1905.

*The Wheelman* acted as a magnet, drawing talented young men with promotional schemes into the Pope orbit. Thomas Stevens, like McClure, was a young man with ambition who was made by the Colonel. Born in England, he immigrated to the United States at 18 to help work his brother's farm near Kansas City.[28] In April 1884 he decided, without ever having ridden a bicycle, to cycle across the country from San Francisco to New York, and bought a Standard Columbia from Pope's San Francisco agent.

In June, he sent a long letter to *The Wheelman* from Omaha about his adventures over the Sierra Nevadas and Great Plains. The article appeared just after *The Wheelman* and *Outing* merged. McClure called Pope's attention to the plucky farmer. Stevens told a Chicago reporter he planned to push on to New York, but shortly before reaching the city he applied for membership in the League of American Wheelmen and somewhere between Cleveland and Buffalo announced that he would finish in Boston, after which he would continue on to England after "two or three weeks" in an attempt to be the first to circle the globe by bicycle.

He stayed in Boston seven weeks, and, as Karl Kron wrote: "Col. Pope then presented him with a nickeled Expert in exchange for the old machine, but made no further motion to encourage a continuance of the enterprise." Kron, who knew better, was covering for Stevens. The League of American Wheelmen, mimicking the British Cyclists Touring Club, maintained a "simon pure" approach to amateur standing, prohibiting anyone who competed for money, or pursued bicycling "as a means of livelihood."[29] Stevens was dawdling in Boston because he was writing a 38,000-word narrative of his transcontinental trip for serialization in *Outing*. Pope had neatly dodged the L.A.W. amateur requirements by making Stevens a professional author. Before his return from the around-the-world trip, Kron revealed that Pope had "commissioned him as a regular correspondent to complete the journey," and "like all such correspondents, he is presumably allowed his expenses and a sum for each printed publication." Kron said that Stevens had left the manuscript covering the trans–American part of his trip in London so it could be published as a free-standing book "in case he gets killed."[30] Stevens returned to San Francisco in January 1886, and his articles ran in *Outing* for three straight years. Scribner's published *Around the World on a Bicycle* in two volumes in 1887 and 1888.

The "nickeled Expert" that Pope gave Stevens wasn't one; it was a custom built experimental model made out of British cold-drawn steel tubing normally used for shotgun barrels. It used swaged (double-butted) spokes tapered in the middle, and hollow fork blades. It weighed about 12 pounds less than a normal Expert's 42 pounds, was about twice as strong, and cost a thousand dollars to make.[31] Because L.A.W. regulations prohibited even the contribution of a free bicycle, the Pope front office downplayed the donation, claiming it was an exchange for Stevens's worn transcontinental machine. Upon his return, Stevens told a newspaper reporter that "I am not engaged in advertising any particular make of bicycle, simply using that which I have."[32]

Alas, it was to no avail. Upon his return, the L.A.W. refused to renew his membership, charging him with professionalism. Although *Outing* sprung to Stevens's defense, Charles Pratt was ill and no longer active in the organization, and the league refused to back down. It hardly mattered, as *Around the World on a Bicycle* became a best-seller and Stevens was launched on a new career as a professional explorer. A horseback trip across Russia led to a new book, *Through Russia on a Mustang*, and in 1895 the *New York World* sent him to Africa to search for the lost Henry Morgan Stanley, of Stanley and Livingstone fame. Stevens's good fortune held on, as he found the British explorer alive and well. In 1895 Stevens married and settled in London, becoming the business manager of the Garrick Theatre.

Stevens's trip opened a frenzied half-decade of round-the-world cycling exploits. The era drew to a tragic close in May 1894, when Frank Lenz, a 25-year-old American sponsored by the Overman Wheel Company and *Outing*, started up Turkey's Deli Baba pass. He failed to reach his arranged checkpoint on the other side at Erzerum, 50 miles east.[33] Six months later, Lenz's family and *Outing* sent W. L. Sachtleben, an English cyclist who had recently completed his own global circumnavigation, to look for him. Sachtleben found pieces of bicycle tire being used to pad the saddle girth of a Kurdish horse. Half a bicycle bell lay in the dust of the Deli Baba with what looked like a bullet hole through it. A cyclist in Constantinople had been told by a soldier that Kurds shot Lenz, thinking that his nickel-plated bicycle was made of solid silver. Lenz's body was never found, and the grand era of bicycle exploration died with him. The cycle magazines turned to the increasingly professionalized sport of bicycle racing.

The tension between Pope the patron and Pope the monopolist resulted in a curious love/hate relationship with the press. While constantly wining, dining and flattering journalists, he could also snap out:

> There is not an industry in the country, large or small, that has as many trade papers as the cycling trade. There are altogether too many. It seems as though when any man or boy, who thinks that he can write, gets out of a job and has no money, he feels called on to start a cycling paper.... The thing must be stopped.... Something will probably be done in the matter.[34]

So sometimes the Colonel tried to circumvent the press entirely by appealing directly to the public through the use of contests and promotions, many of them targeting specific audiences. The *Bicycling World* contest that provided the material for the early issues of *The Wheelman* had been preceded by an earlier contest for the best essay by a clergyman on the theme of "bicycle use by ministers." The winning article by S. L. Gracy and a rather amazing fourteen additional entries also made their way into various copies of *The Wheelman*. A similar contest for physicians generated even more entries, several of which were reprinted together in a "medical symposium" that appeared in 1883.[35]

Although the obvious purpose of these contests was to use the entries as an inexpensive source of material for *The Wheelman*, the annual catalogs, and advertisements, they sometimes veered off in Quixotian directions as the Colonel tilted at one or the other of his personal windmills. He once invited school teachers to send in the best example of any "misstatement of fact which may appear in any school book."³⁶ The winner, of course, would receive a new Columbia. The office was so deluged with entries that six bicycles were eventually given away. The winner: *Butler's Elementary Geography*, which asked students "What strait connects the Caribbean Sea to the Atlantic Ocean?" Pope claimed the book made three errors on this single question. The given answer, the Florida Straight, was wrong (it connects the Atlantic and the Gulf of Mexico); none of the book's maps labeled the Florida Straight; and in actuality over 30 narrows, passages and straights connect the Caribbean to the Atlantic. After it was over, one editor asked, "Isn't it just possible that the Colonel is getting to be peculiar?"

At other times, the results could be impressive. A nationwide poster contest generated more than 400 entries. Several were so good that they were packaged into a traveling exhibit that toured several major cities. The *New York Times* art critic noted archly that "It takes one with an art education of the most recent type to find in the first prize poster all that the Boston critics found deserving in it," but this time the Colonel had the last laugh. Winner Maxfield Parrish went on to become one of the most famous American illustrators of the period, and an original print of his Pope poster is worth a small fortune.³⁷ On another occasion, Pope donated a $100 prize to the annual Waldorf doll show, hosted by New York's Waldorf Astoria Hotel, for the best doll dressed in women's cycling garb. The doll show, a charity benefit, was a major New York society event. The contest both promoted women's cycling and gave Pope valuable insight into what the wealthy and fashionable set considered appropriate dress for female cyclists.³⁸

By the early years of the twentieth century, the Pope Manufacturing Company had a fully self-contained publicity department, with offices, composing room and print shop. The company printed its own advertising material and offered printing and compositing services to its local agents. The publicity department also ran its own clipping service, reviewing hundreds of newspapers and magazines to create scrapbooks of articles about the company and the Pope family. By then, the department was managed by Robert Winkley, who had served as Pope's private secretary for over a decade before being given the post in 1903. A measure of the esteem that Pope held for both Winkley and the publicity department can be measured by his decision to include Winkley in his will, the only non-family company employee made a beneficiary.³⁹

## *Developing a National Marketing System*

Industrial historians have been skeptical about Pope's distribution and sales system. David Hounshell concludes that "Pope seems to have integrated in every direction except forward into marketing. Unlike Singer with sewing machines and Ford with automobiles, the Pope Manufacturing Company did not establish retail stores to market its products." Glen Norcliffe agrees, but notes that "Pope's system clearly had its merits. At a time when he was undercapitalized, he did not have to invest in a chain of stores."⁴⁰ On the other hand, Charles Pratt, reviewing the highlights of the firm's first decade, listed its system of dealers and agents as one of its four principal accomplishments. "These agencies have been like the downward rooting branches of the banyan tree, forming so many trees themselves, but still a part of the original growth, and secure in their life because of the sap from their parent stem."⁴¹

Why this dramatic disparity? Two reasons. First, retail distribution changed far more extensively during the twentieth century than did manufacturing, particularly in America, where most bicycle technology was imported. Second, bicycle historians have usually focused on the manufacturers themselves, glossing over the roots of Pratt's banyan tree, the sole proprietorships and small partnerships that distributed, sold and serviced bicycles and accessories. These networks were far more complex and fine-grained than usually portrayed.

Most historians assume that Pope entered the bicycle business from day one intending to become a major manufacturer. There is no evidence to support this, and it appears to read history backwards, using a result to prove intent. Pope saw his first bicycle at the Philadelphia Centennial Exposition in the summer of 1876, but didn't even learn to ride one for another year. His first order for imported bicycles comprised only eight machines, and the first Weed contract was only for 50 units. Given the start-up costs for dies and raw material, Pope probably couldn't hope to make a profit on that small a batch. He was thinking incrementally, preferring to take a predictable loss rather than run the risk of a factory full of dead stock.[42] Nor did George Fairfield and George Day drop everything to rush into the new venture—the Weed company continued to build sewing machines into the 1890s. In an 1880 *Scientific American* article, the firm described its sewing machine manufacturing in great detail, discussing bicycle production in only a few concluding paragraphs.[43]

Pope's agency network was not a non-system, as Hounshell suggests, nor was it merely an afterthought, as Norcliffe concludes. On the other hand, it was a long ways from the carefully nurtured, all-for-one-and-one-for-all fraternity of which Pratt boasted. Pope needed agents, but he also saw them as a threat. The relationship was similar to that of a far-flung colonial network. The secret was to cede each outpost enough autonomy and profit to keep it motivated while making sure it stayed too weak and impoverished to stir up any kind of trouble. Many of the young men who hired on as entry-level executives at the major cyclemakers found themselves thrown into a kind of foreign service, slogging interminably through swamps, jungles, and across trackless plains to Podunk towns to flatter, bribe, cajole, and (if necessary) threaten the sullen, devious, ungrateful and occasionally crazy agent who, it seemed, always demanded more each season while delivering less. Elmer Pratt, who later became a manager at the Grand Rapids Cycle Company, was one of the earliest of these traveling men. At first, Grand Rapids didn't have more than a dozen true retailers with storefronts. "The maker sold his bicycles through what is now termed the curbstone agent," he recalled. These were "rider agents—young men who clerked in stores, banks, etc." Factory terms were harsh. No demonstrator bicycles, no cash discounts, twenty-five percent down. Pratt remembered that "even catalogs were billed to the agent." However, such stringency wasn't motivated by greed. "Even under these conditions," he noted, "makers found much difficulty in making a profit. Such were the trade conditions."[44] The eager young factory drummers came and went, always a little harder and wiser, occasionally angry, sometimes determined to knock off their own little piece of the action.

The sewing machine business taught Pope how to do it. In the early 1850s Singer sold exclusive marketing territories to "jobbers," who, in turn, sold sewing machines to dealers, or, less often, directly to customers.[45] Jobbing was essentially a financing tool for the manufacturer—he recovered his up-front costs selling territories, then maintained cash flow by selling product to the jobber, leaving it to him to "push" the goods.

However, by 1856 Singer gave up on this system, bought back the territories and went to direct purchase, making many sales through installment credit. While Fairfield and George Day were impressed by Singer's ouster of the jobbers, they found time-payments equally objectionable, and Weed went one step further, selling directly to customers strictly for cash on delivery (C.O.D.). Pope followed, selling straight to customers who ordered out of increasingly detailed and lavish catalogs.

Such a plan would have been impossible ten years before, but the development of railway express and their C.O.D. service allowed packages and crates to be swiftly and economically shipped great distances with no risk. It was the perfect mode for shipping relatively light, compact and valuable crated items. Like Weed, Pope unified his system by offering bicycles at the same price regardless of whether they were bought at the Boston store, the Hartford factory or shipped anywhere east of Chicago. Karl Kron, for example, ordered his new Columbia at the Summer Street store in Boston, but had it shipped to him crated at Washington Square in New York City. However, Pope did use retail sellers almost from the start. Elliot Mason in Yonkers and George Bidwell of Buffalo were two of the first. Their contrasting careers illustrate the types of stores the firm relied upon: the company "branch house" and the independent agent.

Like Pope, George Bidwell saw his first Ordinary at the 1876 Philadelphia Exposition, but unlike the Colonel, he had also participated in the previous velocipede craze. Spying one of Pope's early Duplex Excelsior ads, he bought one and was soon exciting "more interest than a Barnum & Bailey Circus parade."[46] He figured that if he was going to provide entertainment, he might as well make money out of it. He sent a letter to Boston that was answered by the Colonel himself "who told me all about his new Columbia machine, soon to be turned out, which would surpass any foreign wheel." Bidwell replied that he would "take orders for 75 bicycles, receiving a down payment on each." However, he proved to be too good a salesman, as "I had sold three times as many bicycles as Col. Pope could turn out. I was then faced with the problem of inducing my clients to take Duplex Excelsior machines instead."[47]

Impressed by this display of talent, Pope hired him as his first Superintendent of Agencies. He spent the next couple of years on the road, traveling with a crated Columbia and a trunk full of literature. While he did spend his fair share of time in public squares "really putting on an act," more effort was spent showing new agents how to set up bicycles, run schools, and rent riding halls. Bidwell began a tradition of active field supervision. The firm not only kept a superintendent of agencies for the next twenty years, but also sent out most of the other company executives on long field trips as the number of agencies expanded. In 1890, Albert Pope started a second bicycle factory, the Hartford Cycle Company, to produce a mid-priced bicycle, recruiting cousin George away from his job in the lumber industry in Montreal to run it. A long-time Weed employee, David J. Post, was made company secretary and Albert's nephew Harry become superintendent. Post soon found that much of his time between January and April was spent on the road meeting and recruiting agents. The work could be wearying. "[I] have been absent from the City for five weeks," Post wrote a colleague.[48]

One of Post's field inspections resulted in an unusually frank assessment of what George and Albert Pope wanted in an agent: "[I] think he will stick to list price if anybody would though he was rather slow [to pay] and his capital limited."[49] It's important that an agent can pay his bills, of course, and nice if he has a little money in the bank, but he must always, always hold the price line. The Pope agency agreement contained 13 conditions, but only one was given in italics:

> *4. Agents are required to sign a contract agreeing to sell our good strictly at retail list price, which affords protection to them and to us. To prevent cutting of prices, and that our agencies may be conducted on business principles, we make it a point to remove agents who violate the spirit of their agreement with us.*[50]

This was not only the central tenant of the Pope agency network, it was the key to the entire Pope plan for the bicycle industry. As Pratt once explained, this, not customer service, not sales ability, not knowledge of the local market, not brand loyalty, was the foundation of the agency system: "It causes the various machines to hold their value when they had become the property of the riders, and prevents the business from being cut up and collapsing."[51]

Most of Pope's competitors continued to use the traditional jobber system. The Western Wheel Works (makers of the Crescent) relied on the Redhead, Norton & Lathrop Company of Des Moines to represent them, just as they did back when they were toymakers. Redhead printed its own dealer price and discount sheet, maintained its own accounts and issued its own credit. After Western moved into high-grade adult bicycles, one local agent accused the jobber of refusing warranty returns and of putting Crescent headbadges and decals on cheap, no-name bicycles.[52] It was exactly such "rough trade" that Pope sought to avoid.

Aside from holding the price line, Pope appeared to enforce few franchise-style requirements, and the quality and dedication of agents varied greatly. Although the Colonel recommended that dealers establish a repair shop, the company did not mandate even this basic service. Some dealers simply shipped bicycles back to the factory for anything beyond the most routine repair.[53] It seemed that if Pope had his wish, there would be no independent agents at all. All the way back in 1884 Julius Wilcox, the Colonel's friend and Charles Pratt's partner at *Bicycling World*, wrote that "If everyone who can possibly be led to think that he wants a bicycle would only order directly from the maker or importer, retail prices could be somewhat lower ... when the public gets fully convinced that they want bicycles, and fully decided as to which one they want, they can leave out the retailer."[54]

For Pope, no issue was more contentious than that of dealer markups. The price of an 1888 Expert Columbia, 50 inch, half-nickel finish, for a customer in Evanston, Illinois, was $130. However, that customer could buy his bicycle in one of three ways. First, he could purchase it from the local agent in Evanston. The cyclist paid the agent $130, the agent gave the factory $104, and the factory paid for shipping — roughly six dollars.[55] Alternatively, the customer could travel to downtown Chicago and buy it at the Columbia branch house, paying the same $130. In this case the factory made its $104, plus the $26 the agent would otherwise have pocketed, because the factory owned the branch house. The freight to the branch house, also six dollars, would have been paid by the factory. If the customer ordered directly from the Hartford, he paid $130 *and* the freight to his front door. Here, the factory reaped its profits, the agent's commission, and saved both the cost of freight and the expenses of the branch house. Pope made more than twice as much profit on a direct-to-customer sale as on an agency sale.[56]

The factory clearly came out best when the customer ordered direct. The primary purpose of the Pope distribution system was to eliminate the jobber and only secondarily to maximize sales. When George Pope suggested that the firm make Columbias and Hartfords more competitive in the West by paying the freight costs of dealer shipments beyond Chicago, the Colonel refused. "The Colonel rules that it is best for us to retain the same rules as last year, that is, we pay freight to Chicago," George wrote David Post, and in a rare display of ill humor, he vented his frustration: "If we are ever going West for a market the sooner our name is known there, the better. We shall have to do the best we can."[57]

The Colonel was unyielding as to margins. The early patent licenses even limited the discounts other manufacturers could offer, as Phillip Gormully discovered to his dismay: "I am prepared to make a license with you if you will somewhat conform to my ideas about the matters of discounts ... large dealers ... say they must have 35 per cent as an inducement to sell."[58] Pratt's response was swift and brisque: "We cannot agree ... our experience teaches us ... that large discounts are given away or divided by agents and dealers."[59] Pope had only to look over at the Western Wheel Works. Back in 1881, when it was still the Western Toy Company, a company bookkeeper named R. Lindsay Coleman asked the firm's easygoing, big-hearted owner, Louis Schoeninger, if he could hit the road to try pushing the company's lagging sales. He was so successful that he left Western and, along with his brother, started a jobbing house, R.L. & T.C. Coleman Co., to handle Western's goods on the east coast. As Western moved from toys into kids' bicycles, then full-size adult machines, the brothers made a fortune. They did so well, in fact, that they eventually teamed up with Schoeninger's plant manager, Otto Unzicker, to get rid of the original owner.[60] The Colonel was not a man who relished the thought of waking up one morning to find himself the employee of one of his former underlings.

But even given the pitiful wages of the period, a 20-percent markup was insufficient to keep a storefront retailer going, and when word of Pope's machinations began to trickle out after the Gormully & Jeffery suit, the backlash began. An agent in Burlington, Vermont, George Gunn, wrote George Pope "and sent us a stock order contingent upon a 25 percent discount." George replied that "we would be very glad to continue our business with him, which had been very satisfactory, but we could not give him over 20 percent." He regretted the likely loss of Gunn, as "he is to open a store this year and go more deeply into the business than before," and wrote David Post that "we think a number of agents will begin to argue as [Gunn] has."[61]

Although Colonel Pope publicly denounced the itinerant "curbstone" dealer, who bought one bicycle at wholesale for himself and a couple for his friends, it appears that he and George knew that low margins were inhibiting the growth of small, but full-service, agencies in real storefront shops. Agents began to take action. Some started shopping around for better margins — and often found them, as some newer cyclemakers would entice agents with introductory discounts of up to 40 or 50 percent.[62] A few agents took more drastic action — they sued:

> [We] sold one hundred and fifty-seven bicycles ... upon which the Pope Manufacturing Company allowed ... only twenty percent discount of gross sales, while falsely and fraudulently representing ... that twenty percent discount was the highest and best rate allowed its agents for sales of bicycles, whereas the highest and best rate of discount allowed by said Pope Manufacturing Company to its agents in said years was twenty-five percent.[63]

It was true: Pope drew up a second, secret price list for a handful of favored dealers, starting in early 1893.[64] It worked as long as the demand for Columbias and Hartfords exceeded supply, but it was a house of cards that collapsed when the market slumped and dealers, free to pick and choose from a venerable bazaar of overstocked and cash-starved bicycle makers, reached under their shop aprons and pulled out the knives sharpened by years of resentments and perceived slights.

We saw the path George Bidwell took from agent to superintendent of agencies, and the role he played in expanding Pope's retail system. However, it is also worthwhile to look at the career of another original Columbia agent, Elliot Mason. In the fall of 1879, Mason established himself in Yonkers, New York, as an agent for Cunningham, Heath & Co. He added the new Columbia as soon as he could start getting them.[65] In 1881, Colonel Pope brought George Bidwell in from the road and arranged for him to start work for E. I. Horsman's big sporting goods store in lower Manhattan. Horsman was opening a bicycle department and had been awarded a Columbia agency. Mason, in turn, replaced Bidwell as superintendent of agencies. About this time, Mason's brother opened a shop in mid-town Manhattan a mile or so north of Horsman's. A year later, Elliot returned to New York to open a new Pope branch house downtown on Warren Street only a block or two from Horsman's store. The Colonel then cancelled Horsman's franchise and transferred it to Bidwell so he could open his own store uptown. As a result, Pope's branch house had all of lower Manhattan to itself, while Mason's brother and Bidwell split the uptown business on the south edge of Central Park. Warren Street would become the firm's longest lived establishment, surviving over a decade into the twentieth century.

Two years after Elliot Mason's branch house opened, the company expanded into Chicago, then San Francisco, Buffalo and Providence. Eventually, the firm opened 16 branch houses. Unlike independent agencies, the front office meticulously controlled every facet of their management. In Detroit, George Day himself dropped by one winter, "and was not satisfied with the condition of the business." He ordered his sales manager, J. F. Cox, to investigate and Cox found that the "stock was in bad shape as to classification and arrangement; he [the store manager] had not taken an inventory" and that "although he had been asked for a report of the condition of the business ... it was not done."[66]

Cox wanted the manager fired, but George Pope, knowing he had been hurriedly promoted from salesman when his predecessor unexpectedly quit, and was simply in over his head, moved him back down to salesman and transferred in another branch manager. The work was demanding, but financially rewarding. A manager earned $1,500 a year, a senior salesman (probably doubling as an assistant manager) made $1,200 and a salesman about $700. At the same time, clerks, managers and foremen back at the factory were pulling in about $875 a year and an adult male shophand made around $550.[67]

The Gilded Age was the golden era of the American bicycle shop. All the major manufacturers established branch houses similar to Pope's. In most major cities brightly lit dealerships with garish window displays clustered near each other in "Great White Ways" along major boulevards: Columbus Avenue in Boston, Arch Street in Philadelphia, Wabash in Chicago. In Europe, the du Cros family, owners of the Dunlop tire company, reorganized the John Griffins Cycle Company in an attempt to create an international chain of cycle agencies.[68] The concept was simple, but brilliant: organize dealerships around the most frequently replaced part, the tire, not around any given make of bicycle. After all, a client may only need a bicycle every few years, but could wear through a set of pneumatic tires in a couple of months. John Griffins Cycles sold several brands of bicycles (the selection varied over the years), but all carried Dunlop tires.

The Ferodowill Brothers Cycle Company of St. Paul, Minnesota, was a typical Midwestern bicycle shop for the early 1890s. It was larger than average, and apparently well-stocked, but was located well away from downtown. Within a few years one of the brothers, Joseph, would move the business to much larger quarters in the heart of the city (The Minnesota Historical Society, St. Paul, Minnesota).

Alas, the future was not so rosy in the United States. Outside of the Great White Ways, even the branch houses were no picnic. One warm April Sunday in New Orleans, Mrs. Emily Williams and her fourteen-year-old daughter Florence were walking down the street when they were pursued by two men, who grabbed and held them. When the police arrived, they identified themselves as the proprietors of the local Pope branch house and said that the Williamses had previously "committed the felonious and infamous offense of grand larceny of two bicycles," and that they were acting upon instructions from headquarters when they chased down and captured the pair. Mrs. Williams and Florence spent the night in jail "in a malicious and cruel manner," until their minister bailed them out the next morning. Unfortunately for the Pope company, the two were discovered to be "persons of good moral character and reputation, professed Christians, members of the Baptist church, and in full enjoyment of their Christian faith," and completely innocent of the theft. They promptly sued for $10,000. The firm settled out of court.[69]

By 1902 the American luxury cycle shop was a thing of the past, and even before World War I many bicycles were already being sold in hard-good stores such as Goodyear, Firestone, John Deere, and Western Auto. Between the wars, a typical bicycle shop frequently had a dirt floor, a bench vise and a chest of hand tools. In the early 1950s, an enterprising young Californian named George Gardiner bought a hobby and bicycle shop in Van Nuys, outside Los Angeles.[70] Throwing out everything but the bicycles, he renovated the interior to create a clean, bright, open shopping environment. His bicycle

One-half of the former Ferodowill Brothers Cycle Co. moved into the storefront on the viewer's left about 1898, renaming the firm "Joseph H. Ferodowill, Cycle Mechanician." By the time this photograph was taken in 1903, Joseph's shop had moved into both storefronts and offered a wide range of services, including a full machine shop, custom-made bicycles (advertised on the street-level sign behind the bicycle to the viewer's right) and even automobile repairs. By 1905 the Ferodowill business had moved again, probably to a more garage-like facility that could better accommodate automobile work (photographer: Flashlighters. The Minnesota Historical Society, St. Paul, Minnesota).

supplier, Schwinn, noticed the steady increase in sales. In 1961, another Southern California Schwinn dealer, Helen Throckmorton, built a custom-designed free-standing store featuring modern lines and floor-to-ceiling windows. Two years later, Schwinn underwrote Gardiner's construction of a new store in Northridge, Illinois, outside Chicago, where the company's factory was located. Combining Throckmorton's architecture with Gardiner's interior layout, Schwinn created a model store, strong-arming its adoption by retailers through a carrot-and-stick approach combining generous financing with threats to drop recalcitrant outlets. After 50 years, the branch house had returned.

## *Defending Cyclists' Rights*

Most towns and cities reacted to the appearance of the velocipede by restricting its use, particularly on sidewalks and in parks. Because sidewalks were more frequently paved than the adjoining roadways and were free of horse manure, they were preferred by cyclists, as were the promenades within many urban parks. When the Ordinary made its appearance a decade later, the old velocipede laws were dusted off and used to ban them. A few cities interpreted their sidewalk laws to exclude bicycles from the entire roadway.[71]

In addition, the bicycle's novelty made its status as property unclear, which complicated the prosecution of bicycle thieves. Another form of abuse faced by the early cyclists was harassment and assault from teamsters and footmen who claimed that the sight and sound of bicycles frightened their horses. While this may have been true in isolated rural areas, urban horses were acclimatized to the noise and congestion of city street life. Urban clashes were more frequently real or perceived class conflicts. The pioneering cyclists were generally affluent and native-born, while teamsters were working-class first- or second-generation immigrants. A successful teamster was not a timid man; road, loading dock and parking space were all limited in the crowded city, and strong vocal chords and quick fists made the difference between a quick heave onto a dock or a long and exhausting portage down the street. Cyclists expected to be deferred to by their social inferiors on the street as they were in everyday life, while teamsters saw cyclists as effete dandies trying to dance around the edges of a street fight they didn't understand and couldn't protect themselves from.[72]

Legal troubles came early. In October 1878, Pope sent bicycle racer Will Pittman and one of the first Weed-built Columbias to New York City to introduce the good people of Gotham to cycling. The good people of Gotham promptly arrested Pittman for riding in Union Square. Pope bailed him out and paid for his legal defense. That experience galvanized the Colonel, who began to systematize his legal efforts beyond the occasional assistance he had been providing to local friends and clubmates.[73] He coordinated the effort through Charles Pratt. Starting in 1878, Pratt spent an increasing amount of time on cycling matters, including Pope's patent work, the writing and editing of cycling articles and books, and the management of the Boston and Massachusetts bicycle clubs, with the Colonel paying an ever-larger share of his income. In 1881, Pratt moved his offices into the Boston headquarters and became a full-time employee.

Pratt sat on the Boston common council and served as its president in 1881 and 1882, and from this base rescinded its exclusionary regulations. Cyclists in other cities were not as successful, notably New York, where in October 1879, the Board of Park Commissioners banned bicycles from Central Park and Riverside Drive Parkway.[74] Subsequently, it became great sport for younger and more impetuous cyclists to slip in late at night past sleeping Central Park gatekeepers and take moonlight rides on Frederick Law Olmstead's bridal paths. Their older, more established colleagues chose a daytime strategy, petitioning the park commission to let them back in. The matter was referred to a special committee, which reported favorably on the matter in June 1881, but the park commission declined to act.[75]

On the morning of 2 July, three volunteers from different New York cycling clubs rode into Central Park at 110th Street and were arrested. It was a staged event; they were cheered on by a multitude of their clubmates and the Colonel had already retained their lawyers. Arrangements for the arrest and transport of the offenders had been negotiated with a sympathetic precinct police captain. They were assessed a five dollar fine and refused to pay, demanding incarceration. The lawyers served previously prepared writs of habius corpus. It was Saturday, so normally no hearing would be available until Monday, but these were gentlemen and local residents, so they were paroled by the officer on duty after a brief ceremonial detention. It was a wonderful spectacle, but tragically, to no avail. President Garfield was shot by an assassin that afternoon and lay in a coma. The three cyclists quietly filed a civil suit against the commissioners the following week. In typical legal fashion, the case dragged on for a year until Judge Lawrence decided that "the power conferred ... upon the commissioners is very broad and comprehensive ... and no court would, in my opinion, be justified in setting aside a provision made by [them]."[76]

Partially as the result of the cycling bans in New York and other cities (including, for a short while, Hartford), representatives from 31 local clubs gathered at a cyclist's meet in Newport, Rhode Island to form a new national organization, the League of American Wheelmen, with Charles Pratt as president.[77] The League held its first annual meeting in New York in May 1883. The local clubs applied for a permit to allow a parade of wheelmen in the park. It was quickly granted. A month after the meet, the park commissioners voted to allow L.A.W. members in Central Park between midnight and 9 A.M., and on Riverside Drive except between 3 and 7 P.M. Members were to be identified through a lapel pin, although wearing a club uniform turned out to be the usual way. For all practical purposes, Riverside Drive restrictions ended (except for "furious" riding, which everyone thought reasonable), and it would prove to be the city's most popular cycling ground for the next quarter-century.

After three years of the limited Central Park policy, the cyclists decided to take on all restrictions. In a series of interviews by the New York Bicycle Club (N.Y.B.C.), one aldermanic candidate, Henry R. Beekman, announced that he would support complete equality between bicycling and equestrian rules if the N.Y.B.C would openly support his candidacy. They did, and Beekman won by ten thousand votes. Beekman carried out his promise, but was stymied by City regulations that restricted authority to the park board. In the time-honored tradition of New York reformers whose efforts are blocked by the city's Byzantine bureaucracy and utterly corrupt Tammany Hall administration, the cyclists tried an end run through the state capitol. The wheelmen proposed a law that defined a bicycle as a carriage and prohibited local regulations specific to cycles. The bill passed and went to Governor David Hill. City Mayor Abram Hewitt stamped his foot and demanded that Hill veto it. Hewitt, the son of a bankrupt cabinetmaker, earned his fortune by making friends with Edward Cooper (son of merchant prince Peter Cooper), then marrying his sister. He had been elected through the graces of a fragile coalition of the City's business elite and Tammany Hall, both terrified of the leading candidate, neo-socialist Henry George. The prissy, bigoted, stupid, and utterly incompetent Hewitt promptly alienated Tammany Hall, the business elite, the state legislature and the governor all at the same time — a political record that may never be equaled. The L.A.W. told Hill it would help him in the next election and (more importantly) wouldn't help Hewitt, and the Governor whisked the new law off his desk before the ink on his signature could dry. The roads of Central Park were at last open to cyclists. The entire campaign, from start to finish, cost Pope eight thousand dollars — the equivalent of $120,000 in today's money.[78]

By this time, Pope's main interest had shifted from legal rights to the promotion of better roads. The Supreme Court of Kansas, in *Swift v. City of Topeka*, had held the bicycle was a vehicle and should be regulated in a manner appropriate to other road users. The ruling was well written, highly influential and soon incorporated into most of the standard treatises on municipal law, helping doing away with the worst of the remaining velocipede ordinances.[79]

When Albert Pope put his first Columbias on the road, most Americans would have found the very idea that a man could remain upright on a machine with two in-line wheels preposterous. Some very early cyclists reported that they were actually mistaken for demons gliding down the road a few feet off the ground. Less then a decade later, even a preschooler deep in the slums of the lower east side knew what a bicyclist was: a rich, imperious Wall Streeter with neither the time nor the inclination to leave way for a ghetto girl. In a mere handful of years, Pope's propaganda machine created two distinct images for the bicycle — images that resonate to this day. The first is that of the high-wheeled Ordinary: dangerous, elegant, fast. More than 130 years later it continues to define the haughty, purposeless elegance of a bygone era. Many wanted it; only a few could afford it; even fewer had the prowess to tame it. When the technological leap to the safety bicycle made cycling physically accessible to everybody but the very poor and the elderly, the nation fell over itself in its rush to grasp a piece of that allure, igniting cycling's great golden era of the 1890s.

But Albert Pope's proselytizing had a second, even more enduring effect on the American landscape. Urban historian Clay McShane describes it as an "increased taste for high-speed, street-using transportation." He observes that by 1899 most city dwellers began to see wagons, streetcars, bicycles, and even the odd car and truck, in vaguely favorable terms. "This represented a dramatic shift," McShane says, "from the prohibitions on mechanical vehicles that had prevailed in the 1880s." While the former street urchin may still, eighty years later, have resented being knocked down in the middle of her game, most onlookers of our century, rich and poor alike, would ask the same question as her nemesis, the 1891 cyclist:

"Little girl, whatever are you doing playing in the street?"

# 5

## *The Coming of the Safety Bicycle*

*When I don't have to give a man instructions—only general directions—well, that is what we mean by saying a man is a Pope man.*
— Albert A. Pope, 1903[1]

In March 1892 Albert Pope was a man on top of the world. Literally, on top of the world. Well, so it seemed from the third floor balcony of the former Asa Potter mansion, perched atop a hill 150 feet above Massachusetts Bay, overlooking the Jerusalem Road, the old coast route between Hull and Cohasset. Under the watchful eyes of its gables and turrets, the 48-acre estate spread down the hill, across the road, and out to the Black Rocks a quarter-mile offshore. It included a stable, kennel, animal hospital, carriage house, a clubhouse for the bowling pitch and tennis courts, and three guest cottages.[2] And now, it all belonged to the Colonel.

Twenty miles southeast of Boston, Cohasset was a sleepy seaside port that, with the arrival of the New Haven railroad, had become a summertime suburb, Boston's version of Long Island's North Shore. It was a close, comfortable place. Pope's neighbors, the Henry M. Whitneys, were old friends, and the two estates shared a common driveway. Turning off the Jerusalem Road, the driveway curved gently as it wound its way around the hill's steep rise. At the top, Pope's driveway branched left, Whitney's to the right. While Pope's place had the top of the hill, Whitney, with flatter land to work with, had built his own golf course out the back door. From the bottom of the driveway, it was three miles to the left to the Hingham train depot and five miles, in the other direction, to Cohasset. Pope named the place "Lindermere" in honor of his wife's family, the Linders of Newton.[3] Pope called it his home for the rest of his life, and when the time came, he chose to die there.

The purchase of Lindermere was in many ways the capstone of Pope's career. Although he was on the verge of his greatest financial success, the Cohasset estate was the only truly large personal luxury he bought for himself. Was he a rich man? Maybe, he replied, but "not as compared with New York men."[4] Pope loved horses, but had no personal rail car; he kept a sloop, but it was no America's Cup yacht; he treasured his collection of nautical and cycling art and books, but built no private library or museum. Lindermere was his one great gift to himself, the one outward sign that he had arrived.

Built by Boston banker Asa Potter about 1887, this was Albert Pope's primary residence from 1892 until his death in 1909. Today, it holds ten condominiums, although it is well preserved. The most noticeable alteration from Pope's day is the replacement of the shake-shingle siding on the second floor with stucco, which is less prone to dry-rot and far more fire-resistant.

## *You Old Skunk!*

In 1882 the American bicycle industry was composed of seven significant firms. The Weed factory employed 350 hands, paid an annual wage bill of $166,650 and did about $500,000 in bicycle sales.[5] That output, which included accessories and parts, suggests an annual production of about 3,000 machines. The bicycle business was not yet a growth industry. Six years later, in 1888, the firm made 5,112 bicycles, followed by 6,752 in 1889, the first full year a low-wheeled safety was offered. Two separate sources state that about 250 men then worked at Hartford, earning annual wages of around $150,000. The 1890 Census of Manufacturers, taken in the summer of 1889, found that the entire domestic bicycle industry employed 1,925 employees, who earned wages of $1.1 million, and made $2.56 million in product, or somewhere around 20,500 bicycles.[6] Thus, Pope's employment accounted for about 16 percent of the total industry, although he was making about a third of its bicycles.

What kind of money was Pope earning? In 1882, Charles Pratt calculated the average $90 Ordinary cost a manufacturer $76.75 to make, including such indirect costs as advertising and freight, and that Pope was making a profit of between twelve and fifteen

This was the entry to Lindermere's livery compound. Passing under the entryway and into the courtyard beyond, the stables for the horses were to the viewer's left and the cattle stalls and dog kennels were to the viewer's right. (The piggery was about a quarter-mile farther from the manor house.) The graceful turned-down ends of its now-shingled roof help recall what this building looked like in Pope's day; like many of Lindermere's accessory structures, it originally had a thatched roof. Today, as is true of most of the estate buildings, it has been divided into residential condominiums.

dollars per bicycle.[7] Although others accused Pratt and Pope of overstating their costs, this was probably an honest estimate. The science of cost accounting was rudimentary and there was no standard method for allocating indirect costs such as the depreciation of machinery, management, research and development, and advertising. "No man knew at that time what a machine could be built for," said one bicycle factory foreman in 1881. At the H. B. Smith Machine Company, where the Star bicycle was made, George Pressey, the Star's inventor, calculated that each $120 bicycle cost $33 to make, while Smith himself placed the average cost of each machine, including overhead and indirect expenses, at $90.[8]

When the Pope firm sold directly to its customers, it also earned a retail margin of about thirteen dollars, yielding a total profit of $26 to $30. With the introduction of the Special and Expert Columbias in 1881 and 1883, a $90 Ordinary was at the low end of the price range. The Special was $110, and the same size Expert with full nickel plating was $140.[9] Using a conservative estimate of 4,000 bicycles in 1885, this would have meant a profit, net of advertising, freight, and front office costs, of about $120,000. Add to this another $30,000 per year from the sale of accessories, repairs and lessons, and perhaps another $10,000 from patent royalties (after considerable legal bills). Grand total: $160,000 per year profit.

In addition, Albert Pope maintained business interests outside the bicycle industry.[10] He managed a family trust that owned the land under the Copley Square Hotel. An 1889 loan made to the Semitropic Land and Water Company of San Bernadino, California, from sister Emily Pope was actually one of his investments. Even if he wasn't rich by the standards of the New York elite, he was becoming a very wealthy man. When Albert took leave of his family in 1871 to move with his bride Abby out to Newton, he was following a well-followed trail. At the time of the American revolution, Boston was a thin peninsula measuring less than a square mile in area. At one spot, near the present Union Park, the peninsula was barely wider than Washington Street, the only road between Boston and Roxbury. Only after the Civil War did developers start to fill the swampy mill pond that is now the Back Bay. Albert and Abby moved to Newton partially because there wasn't room in the City.

But it was a different story out in the suburbs around the big Queen Anne house. Albert Linder was born in July 1872 and Mary Linder in April 1874. Unfortunately, like her namesake aunt, Mary did not live long; she died three months after birth. Margaret Roberts was born in May 1876, Harold Linder in November 1879 and Charles Linder in November 1881.[11] After the Massachusetts Bicycle Club was formed in January 1879, the Newton house served as a frequent rest stop on weekend rides. The Colonel, Edward and Arthur were all charter members of the club, and by 1880 nephew Harry was racing under their colors.[12]

Harry was still living with his grandparents and aunts in town. He graduated from the School of Mechanical Arts at the Massachusetts Institute of Technology in 1881. MIT hadn't yet moved to Cambridge and was still located in the Back Bay, a five-minute walk from Chandler Street. Harry's uncle Louis (Albert's youngest brother) was away attending Brown University. After graduating from Jamaica Plain High School, Louis had entered Harvard in 1869, but had not found it to his liking.[13] Harvard was then a very different place from what it is today. Not very bright young men showed up each fall after spending four to six usually horrible years at a boarding school. Being legacies, Harvard accepted them without scrutiny and they spent their undergraduate years skipping classes, entertaining constantly and paying for a few hurried tutoring sessions in the closing weeks of each semester. Intellectual brilliance and artistic creativity counted for less than manners, breeding and athletic ability.

Louis, like the entire Pope family, was a Baptist, the religion of New England's working classes. After switching to Brown University (formerly Rhode Island College, a Baptist school), he graduated and entered Newton Theological Seminary, where he earned his doctorate in 1877. After working for Newton Theological and ministering in Rhode Island, he and his family moved to Maine in 1889, where he led a Baptist congregation and ran the local Columbia agency. "I knew you would like Louis," wrote George Pope after learning a co-worker had dropped in for a sales call, "everyone does."[14] MIT, where Harry attended, was also no Harvard. It opened its doors in 1865 to provide "scientific studies and practical exercises" for engineers, chemists, architects and builders. Although a private school, it was designated the state's land grant college under the Morrill Act, the same legislation that created the great flagship public universities of the midwest. It was coeducational from the day it opened. After graduating, Harry spent a year in Denver helping to set up its Columbia agency, returned to work as a machinist in the Boston store, then moved to Hartford to start as a draftsman at Weed in 1884.[15]

However, what was good enough for Louis and Harry wasn't good enough for Albert Linder, the Colonel's oldest. Taking his primary education at King's Boarding School, Albert Linder enrolled in 1888 at one of Harvard's favorite prep schools, Phillips Exeter. The editor of *American Wheelman* later gave this version of young Albert's misadventures:

> Albert L. Pope was attending college in New Hampshire, and got into disgrace through being a party to sneaking several bottles of wine into his room with other lads. The stern professor got onto the racket and called all the boys before him that were implicated in the deal. All hands, with the exception of young Pope, denied all knowledge of the wine, but [Albert Linder] truthfully spoke up: "Yes, I paid for the wine, and took it to my room." The liars were excused, but Albert Pope, Jr. fired, and he went home and as truthfully told his father all about the scrape. Colonel Pope soon called on the stern professor, and said something like this: "You old skunk, you retain liars and fire truthful boys, who dare to tell the truth, from your so-called college."[16]

The story is an utter fabrication. There is no record of Albert Linder Pope attending any college in New Hampshire. The archives of Phillips Exeter Academy show that he did enroll twice at the school. He entered as a freshman in September 1888, but left before the end of the term. He re-entered in September 1890 as a junior in the school's English course, reserved for those not yet fluent in Latin or Greek. Again, he withdrew before the end of the term. There are no records of disciplinary proceedings, although limited records indicate he earned poor marks in his classes. He is not mentioned in the school newspaper and is not listed as a member of any athletic club, even the bicycle club that started in 1890. It appears a story of florid disgrace was more interesting than one of simple academic failure.[17] After returning home, the Colonel added him to the sales staff at the Boston store. Never again did he attempt to send his sons down the path of Boston's Episcopal elite; from then on they attended Peekskill Military Institute and, in next-oldest son Harold's case, MIT.[18]

Even with a houseful of children, the Colonel's increasing business activity required more of his time in the city. The days he had to travel to Hartford were worse: he had to take the West End horsecar all the way downtown, then walk to the Boston and Providence Railroad station by the Public Garden and catch a train to Connecticut. So in 1885, Pope bought a townhouse at 378 Commonwealth. Designed by Peabody, Sterns, 378 Commonwealth was the left half of a four-story, red-sandstone duplex. Its building permit was issued to the Park Entrance Land Company, a development firm organized by Pope's future Cohasset neighbor, Henry M. Whitney. [19]

Whitney was a good man to know. After getting rich in the same Maine–Boston shipping trade in which the Popes made their fortune, Whitney speculated in Brookline real estate and started the West End Street Railway between Brookline and downtown. In 1886 Whitney electrified his railway, extended the line and threw open outer Brookline to large-scale residential development. The Popes and the Whitneys frequently attended each other's social events and it was probably Whitney who told Pope that his Cohasset neighbor, Asa Potter, was selling his estate.[20] In gilded age Boston, business was done through trusted friends and relatives.

From 378 Commonwealth, it was just a short walk down Massachusetts Avenue to either the Massachusetts Avenue or Back Bay train stations. And soon, it would be even easier to get together with the rest of the family, as Pope built a townhouse at 163 Newbury, in the heart of Back Bay, for the Pope clan. Augusta, Emily, Adelaide and father Charles moved there in 1886. Sadly, Elizabeth Bogman Pope, Albert's mother, died in February 1885 before the new house was finished. Albert and Abby had one more present for the family. On 23 March 1887 their youngest son was born, six years after his next oldest brother, Charles. Abby was 36 at the time. In 1887, this was cause for serious concern. Delivery was at the New England Women's and Children's Hospital, and the prognosis may not have been good, as they named the child simply "Linder Pope." All turned out well, however, and both mother and child were soon discharged.

Albert's father Charles was now 73. After the purchase of the Lallement patents in 1879, Charles does not appear to have been active again in the Pope Manufacturing Company, and he retired as a real estate broker in 1883. He died in 1888, two years after his move to Newbury Street.[21] His funeral was held at the townhouse on a Sunday afternoon and he was buried at Forest Hills Cemetery, halfway between Dorchester, the town of his birth, and Brookline, where his career was made.

Charles Pope has typically been portrayed as a broken, destitute man after his 1850 failure. While forthright about his shortcomings, his son was less than candid about the important role he played in the creation and survival of the Pope Manufacturing Company. During the incorporation, Charles was virtually a co-owner, controlling 40 percent of its shares, and he played a vital role in securing the early bicycle patents. In addition, he mentored his son in the assembly of a real estate empire that would last through the 1920s. Yet Albert Pope never publicly recognized his father's accomplishments. When the Colonel built a columbarium in Forest Hills to hold his family's ashes shortly before his own death, he ordered it built with two vertical columns of ash niches. His remains, of course, rest atop the column on the left, with his wife and children beneath him. But at the head of the column to the right is a simple brass plaque that reads:

Charles Pope<br>
Aug. 12 1814–Feb. 24 1888

In death, Albert Pope was able to acknowledge his father as an equal—something he apparently could not bring himself to do during his lifetime.

## What the Hell Would We Strike About?

In both Boston and Hartford, the growth of the company now required Pope to reach out beyond the narrow confines of his family and early cycling companions to recruit from a new cadre of educated young men. Years before Pope arrived, Weed president George Fairfield had worked his way up from shop hand to inside contractor at Colt's. An inside contractor was more than just a foreman—the company actually contracted with them to produce parts of a specific quality at a specific price. It was up to the contractor to hire and pay his men, set working conditions for his department, and guarantee that the job got done. The contractor paid himself a daily wage and kept any profits that resulted. If he underbid the contract or suffered unexpected problems, he personally suffered the loss.

Inside contracting was a mainstay at Colt's and at the Winchester Repeating Arms

Company until the First World War. In Hartford, Pratt & Whitney also used this system, as did Singer Sewing Machine in New Jersey and Brown & Sharpe in Rhode Island. Although popular with older firm owners because it minimized "indirect" management and office costs, it was unpopular with younger, more formally trained managers because it made quality and cost control difficult.[22]

In his history of the Pope firm, David Hounshell believes that the Weed Company was using inside contracting through 1899. I disagree. While there is no definitive statement either way, circumstantial evidence points to direct labor hiring. A. H. Overman flatly stated in 1891 that he did not use the contract system because he wanted the Overman Wheel Company to retain total control over employment. In 1883 the H. B. Smith Machine Co. was definitely using inside contractors to manufacture hubs and production tooling, and was probably continuing to do so as late as 1888.[23] In his study of England's Raleigh Cycle Company, Paul Rosen concludes that management discontinued outside contracting well before the turn of the century, putting their foremen on weekly wages, because of frequent objections to the labor practices foremen used when left to their own discretion.

Management at Weed likewise sought to exercise greater control over the floor after Fairfield left in 1881. His dual role as president and supervisor was split. John Knous was made superintendent and J. Watson Beach assumed the presidency. Beach was approaching retirement, and his authority actually passed to George Day. At the time Pope first asked Weed to build his bicycles the firm had only two front-office men who were not shop managers (like Fairfield) or directors (such as Beach and Day). They were bookkeeper Frank E. Belden and auditor E. W. House. By early 1883, clerk David Post was added, and in 1885 Harry Pope started. His presence indicated a new role for the front office: engineering. Harry provided the kind of technical expertise that Fairfield and Knous had, but without the day-to-day responsibility for directing production. Fairfield and Knous learned their trade working at Colt's, but Harry had gained it in the classroom and model shops of MIT.

In Boston, Albert and Edward Pope still largely ran the whole show. Charles F. Joy, who served with George Pope as an officer in Shaw's regiment during the war and was an early cycling companion of Edward's, hired on in 1880 and was promoted to superintendent three years later, overseeing the machine shop and repair depot at the Boston store.[24] About 1884, the Popes hired Arthur E. Pattison as a clerk in the Boston office. Pattison's contact was probably through George Day. Raised in Bethel, Connecticut, Pattison graduated from Hartford's Trinity College and lived for a year in a house in Hartford belonging to Day before moving to Boston.

The contrast between the traditional Fairfield and the young, well-educated Day was striking. It was a rough trade inside Colt's: Samuel Colt was a salesman, and for the most part he left the factory to the 31 inside contractors, who ran things as they saw fit. By working their men like dogs while cutting back piece rates, they made themselves rich. Raleigh found that the arrangement often led to kickbacks.

Day used a different method: industrial paternalism. New England textile manufacturers had a tradition of preferring the carrot over the stick. Increasingly violent labor management by the railroads and steel mills frightened the middle class and angered their legislators, who enacted protective state laws. Progressive managers responded with what George Pope later described as "a keener sense of social responsibility."[25] In 1888, Weed hired Hartford architect George Keller to design 24 rowhouses along a short cul-de-sac across Capitol Avenue from the factory, soon named Columbia Street. The plans were personally approved by Day, and proved to be wildly popular. "Everyone admires the row of cottages," Keller wrote his wife. "It is sort of a surprise to Hartford." Many of the homes were leased to Weed employees and their families, although two were used to house the firm's unmarried managers.[26] Not quite sure what to do with this embarrassment of riches, Weed sold the development and some Keller-designed duplexes in an adjacent neighborhood to a new nonprofit corporation, the Hartford Real Estate Improvement Company, run by George Day. It built a second development of 12 units next to Columbia Street on Park Terrace in 1895. Although architecturally different, they proved equally popular. The Improvement Company continued to build additional duplexes for several decades. After George Day's death in 1907 his widow Katherine Beach Day took his place on the company's board.

Designed by the noted Hartford architect George Keller, this graceful townhouse was built about 1895 by the Hartford Real Estate Improvement Company, a nonprofit entity run by George Day. Located in a row of about ten homes on Park Terrace, just south of Pope's factory, this was one of Day's last attempts to create a model community for bicycle workers. Like the homes on the adjacent Columbia Street, many of the units actually ended up in the hands of foremen, managers and other high-ranking company employees. Hayden Eames, who helped build Pope's two cold-drawn steel tube factories, lived here from 1895 to 1901. Today, Park Terrace, Columbia Street, and the adjacent George H. Day Memorial Playground make up the George Keller Historical District.

The Columbia Street and Park Terrace projects appear to have been inspired by two English workers' housing projects, Port Sunlight, built by the Lever Brothers' firm for their employees at the Sunlight Soap Works, and the Cadbury Brothers' development in Bourneville. The architecture, especially in Columbia Street, is particularly reminiscent of Port Sunlight; it is still possible today to stand in the middle of Columbia Street, facing away from the old Pope factory, and easily imagine that one is in a quiet English village. Keller's work was simply outstanding; both Columbia Street and Park Terrace are now located within a historic district, are exquisitely maintained and comprise an oasis of stately serenity in what has become a deeply distressed urban core. Keller himself lived with his family in 24 Park Terrace for over 40 years.

When a new wing was added to the factory in 1893, several employee amenities were added, including a locker and washroom on the ground floor, a library, and a cafeteria. Hot meals, sandwiches, coffee, desserts, and fruit were available at a small cost.[27] The reason for such generosity? Many saloons of the era offered a free lunch with the price of a drink. Few men stopped at one, and the thought of a drunken worker careening between foundry forges and drive belts was enough to give any employer the shivers. Also, the saloon food was often so bad that it sent employees home sick. Pope covered his bet twice over: he bought up the land surrounding the Weed factory and permitted only residential and factory uses, keeping the nearest saloon blocks from the front gate.

Pope engaged in several other forms of corporate welfare. The sheltered bicycle parking and lunch-time riding grounds were obvious ideas, but Pope's Military Band and Pope's Orchestra, with uniforms supplied by the firm, were just as popular. More substantially, the Mutual Benefit Association was an optional perk that cost each member a dollar a month but paid a disabled employee six dollars a week for six months and provided a fifty-dollar life insurance policy.[28]

This level of involvement with employee welfare strongly suggests that the Hartford employees, both before and after Pope bought out the Weed company in 1890, were directly employed and that inside contracting was not used. After all, a primary feature of the inside contracting system was the loyalty of the individual worker to the contractor, who had the absolute power to hire, fire and change wages. One additional factor suggests that inside contracting was shunned. Albert Pope was inordinately fond of motivational slogans, and apparently sincerely believed them. "Men, not things" and "all for one — one for all" were two of his favorites. Articles mention that he was so fond of such slogans that he had the publicity department print up motto cards that he inserted into each employee's pay envelope. How well these literary tidbits were received is open to speculation, but the point is that the workers were receiving their pay envelopes directly from the company, a procedure inconsistent with the use of inside contractors, who zealously guarded the details of their labor costs.[29]

The issue of inside contracting aside, one may still ask, "Why all the generosity?" Most employers used these practices to stave off government intervention and keep unions away.[30] However, the Pope company doesn't conform well to the historical pattern. Most paternalistic firms had a largely female work force, and welfare programs that succeeded at places such as Heinz and National Cash Register floundered at predominantly male factories such as Weed-Pope. A better analogy is found at England's Raleigh. Although it initiated corporate welfare several years after Pope, it faced nearly identical problems. It required a large number of highly skilled machinists. Located in small Nottingham,

Raleigh faced stiff competition for a limited labor pool. Its wages were barely competitive, especially compared to non-cycle firms, and because of the seasonality of the bicycle trade, the factory regularly oscillated between intense overtime and layoffs.[31] Raleigh's paternalism was an attempt to keep quality workers in an environment where it was difficult, if not impossible, to outbid rivals straight through the payroll window.

Wage competitiveness was clearly a problem in the American bicycle industry.[32] In 1889, the average wage for all American skilled and unskilled operatives over 16 was $498 per year. Within the bicycle industry, it was a little higher at $530. In Connecticut bicycle factories, it was higher yet, $550. But for Connecticut operatives, carriage- and wagon-making paid much better; they earned an average of $643 per year. Despite their lower-paid workers, bicycle makers were getting squeezed. For each $100 in final product turned out, the typical American wagonmaker paid $35.09 in wages, but bicycle manufacturers paid $43.05. While machinists, toolmakers and skilled foundry men could get more money outside the bicycle industry, bicycle makers couldn't afford to raise their salaries.

Bicycle-making was an intensely seasonal industry, making it even less attractive. In 1897, employment at Pope's factories varied during the year between 2000 to 3,400 hands. Nationally, employment in the bicycle industry in 1898–1899 oscillated between a low of 10,157 in August and a high of 22,671 in March, a 220-percent disparity. During a typical May, George Pope could write David Post that "everywhere we can put on a man we are putting him on," but an August visitor could also comment that the plant was "in the depth of the summer slack season, and [I] saw only a few hands at work on odds and ends of left-over jobs."[33]

With annual layoffs almost inevitable and limited means to outbid other employers for his best men, Day and the Colonel used corporate welfare to benefit faithful employees who would return every fall and put in long hours between Christmas and Easter. "Help had to be 'handled with silk gloves' even when paid top dollars, as they had only to choose where they would work," explained one foreman. It was a sound strategy, as the Hartford plant never experienced a strike in all the years that bicycles were made there. "What the hell would we have a strike for?" replied a Hartford shop hand when asked if there had ever been a walkout.[34]

## They Want It Light

When Pope built the first 50 Columbias in 1878, Fairfield simply copied Pope's favorite English bicycle, the Duplex Excelsior. However, other alternatives were available. As early as 1869, two Frenchmen, Hazard and Barberon, had patented a gearing system for front-drive bicycles that, in theory, could be used to reduce the diameter of the driving wheel without sacrificing speed. In 1877, James Starley of the Coventry Machinists Company (surely one of the most prolific innovators in the history of cycling) developed the Salvo tricycle.[35] It was the first cycle to make practical use of a chain drive system.

Starley had the advantage of James Slater's 1864 invention, the "bowl" or bushing chain. Slater's chain used cross-pins covered by free-rolling cylindrical bushings that dramatically reduced friction as the chain passed over a sprocket. In 1880, Hans Reynold improved on this by making the rollers fully independent of the bushings that connected adjacent chain links. His brush-roller chain is still in use in essentially unchanged form. With the development of variable gearing and an efficient chain drive, it was no longer necessary to use a large drive wheel or to mount the pedals and cranks on the driving wheel's axis. Theoretically, it would have been possible to develop the low-wheeled safety bicycle at about the same time as the Ordinary was introduced into America. However, for over a decade, bicycle makers integrated these elements only incrementally into the existing high-wheeler, usually by gearing up the drive ratio so a smaller front wheel could be used, or by offsetting the cranks down and to the rear of the front wheel's axle, placing the rider's seat (and the center of gravity) to the rear, making headers more difficult.

Although most of these experiments were carried out in Europe, Americans were well aware of these attempts to produce a safer and more efficient bicycle. Julius Wilcox, a pioneer cyclist and writer, was an enthusiastic follower of the new trend and wrote frequently about it in American cycling journals.[36] In general, the "safety Ordinary" or "improved Ordinary" used gears or lever systems to move the pedals behind the front wheel axle, allowing the saddle to be moved back and the angle of the front forks to be pushed forward. Starting in 1886, Pope offered its own geared safety Ordinary, and the following year Overman and Gormully & Jeffery followed suit.

More radical alternatives were tried, sometimes quite successfully. In 1882, the H. B. Smith Manufacturing Company of New Jersey introduced the "American Star," which looked like a high-wheeled Ordinary turned backward, with a small wheel in front turned via a long steering shaft and the large rear wheel driven by levers pulling canvas straps attached to its hub. They were not uncommon. Racing champion Arthur Zimmerman started his career on a Star, and Karl Kron spent two days in Maine touring with a Star rider. He noted that it was superior when coasting downhill, but had to be carefully ridden uphill because it tended to do a "backwards header," lifting the front wheel off the ground if pedaled too hard.[37]

However, these improved Ordinaries were soon rendered obsolete. In September 1885, the British firm of Starley and Sutton introduced its "Rover" safety bicycle, designed by John Kemp Starley, James Starley's nephew. The first Rover, using a 36-inch front wheel borrowed from the firm's tricycle and indirect steering through bridle rods, was not a technical or commercial success. A second version, introduced a month later, was vastly improved. It had almost equal-sized wheels and direct steering made possible by sloping the head tube back and sweeping the handlebars toward the rider. The following February, the definitive version was introduced with equal-sized wheels and an almost fully triangulated frame.[38] By March 1886 this final production version was being imported into the United States.

George Bidwell saw his first Rover at a League of American Wheelmen meeting in August. It was "a revolution in the industry," and after trying it he realized "the old high wheel was doomed." Bidwell pleaded with the Colonel to start development of his own safety: "But he only looked at me in a patronizing way as much as if to say poor boy, it is too bad you haven't had the experience of us older men ... you youngsters are carried away by every new toy that comes along.'" After working for Pope for a decade, Bidwell broke ranks over the safety. "I began negotiation with the Rudge Co. [in England] to sell the safety. When I returned to New York I could think of nothing else but what I had seen at Martha's Vineyard. From that day on I never ordered another high wheel from Pope."[39]

Overman responded first. While the Victor Safety was offered in his 1887 catalog, it wasn't available until late summer, leaving the peak sales season open for Bidwell and the other importers. However, it was a well-designed bicycle that featured a unique sprung front fork to reduce the vibrations caused by the safety's smaller front wheel and America's inferior roads. Pope and Gormully & Jeffery responded a year later with less innovative designs. Pope's Veloce lacked a suspension and weighed in at 51 pounds, 15 pounds more than his best road Ordinary.[40] Gormully & Jeffery's safety was even less impressive, based on a "C" shaped frame from France's J. Depard Paroy. The Veloce was buried on page 22 of the spring 1888 catalog, with no options or accessories listed. The Colonel was either unenthused, or, very much more likely, the men in Hartford were scrambling right up to the printer's deadline to figure out what it was going to look like, how it would work, and how much it was going to cost.

Even with these less than innovative designs, the American safety swept the high-wheeler off the table. Arthur Pattison admitted that Ordinaries accounted for only twenty percent of Columbia sales in 1889 and ten percent in 1890.[41] Pope's safety wasn't available until June, after that year's peak season was already over. From 1888 to 1891, the Pope Company sold 34,652 bicycles. Of these, 7,303 were Ordinaries and 27,303 were safeties. About four thousand of the Ordinaries were sold in 1888, before the Veloce was readily available. That means only about 3,000 high-wheelers were sold after cyclists had a real choice between the two.[42] For years afterward, the firm continued to advertise Ordinaries as "old friends," but while we now know that stories of cyclists throwing their high bicycles into junk piles are apocryphal, and that many wheelmen faithfully continued to use the high-wheeler, sales did quickly die.[43]

In 1890, the English Rudge firm improved Starley's design by lengthening its wheelbase and connecting the seat lug directly to the crank hanger by a straight tube, creating the now-familiar diamond frame. Because its primary frame tubes were stressed only in tension and compression (along their length), they could be made out of much thinner tubing. The three big American firms, Pope, Gormully & Jeffery and Overman, all adopted the diamond frame in 1892. It revolutionized bicycle construction. Between 1888 and 1891 Pope's engineers were able to reduce the weight of the Columbia safety by a mere three pounds, from 51 to 48 pounds. However, within two years of the fully triangulated frame, the Columbia's weight was down to 28 pounds, and by 1896 another six pounds had been shed. Frame tubing was now everything. The thin-walled, high-strength tubes now needed were more like shotgun barrels than the relatively thick and heavy backbones of the Ordinary. Asked in an unguarded moment, "What is the most imperative demand the people are making upon the manufacturers of bicycles right now?" a Pope spokesman replied, "Just what it is in religion — they want it light."[44]

## Cycles Will Form a Good Barricade Against a Mob

Not all of the Colonel's grand schemes went according to plan. In 1891, Pope gave ten Columbia safeties to the Connecticut National Guard to experiment with during their summer maneuvers. The following year, the Connecticut Guard organized a cycling unit of four officers and 36 enlisted men. Despite hopes that the bicycle could replace traditional cavalry, the consensus among the young officers who worked with the unit over the course of two summers was that this was not going to happen. "The cyclist as a combatant is nothing more than a mounted infantryman, who must get off his steel horse to fight," they observed. The special advantage of the cavalry "lies mainly in the momentum of its shock, owing to the speed and solidarity at moment of contact." Based upon their experience, they were forced to conclude that "the cyclist can develop the necessary speed on favorable ground, but solidarity and stability he does not have."[45]

This doesn't mean the Guard found their Columbias worthless. By walking and leaning on the machine, it was much easier to ford a rushing river with a heavy backpack. A bicycle left in a trail made a great trap for horses; their hooves and legs became entangled in the spokes. Heavily oiled, they could be stored indefinitely, out of sight, underwater in a lake or river, where they were actually less vulnerable to rust than when left outdoors. By wrapping the top tube in a blanket and raising the handlebar all the way, a wounded man could be draped over the top and transported much farther and faster than if carried. One lieutenant wrote that it proved "of the greatest value as a mount for scouts, orderlies, dispatch bearers, signalmen, engineers, [and] topographers," concluding that "Service with technical troops of this kind seems to me to be [its] true province."

Another early adopter was the District of Columbia National Guard. In 1892, General Albert Ordway of the District Guard wrote *The Cycle-Infantry Drill Regulations*, and Pope paid to have it printed by the thousands in a 70-page booklet.[46] However, the young Connecticut turks who actually lived with their bikes out in the field weren't very impressed. "General Ordway ... has compiled a rather elaborate set of regulations for bicycle drill, but these efforts seem to have wholly in view street and other parade performances and are of little practical utility," they noted dryly.[47]

Ordway was thinking about more than parades and funeral processions, however. He was responsible for the protection of Washington, and the year after he wrote his manual, the city was invaded by Coxley's Army, five hundred jobless Civil War veterans demanding benefits and relief. His manual included a section on "Street Riot Duty" that instructed field officers to "assume a defensive position against attack in one direction, form the company into line, facing that direction, and ground, invert or stack cycles. The cycles will form a troublesome barricade against assault by the mob."[48]

Ordway also advised that "riots may be prevented by breaking up mobs," but again the young field officers cautioned that the general had better try war-gaming that tactic first. "Cyclists are inferior to the cavalry in street warfare for quelling riots and dispersing mobs, lacking the moral effect of the flashing of the sabers and the clatter of the horses' feet." When the Connecticut Guard wrote its own manual, it recommended that during civil unrest, the advantage of the bicycle was not power, but stealth, and that "couriers serving in cities during riots can perform their duties in citizen's dress." [49] Indeed, this appeared to be exactly how they were used during mining strikes in Colorado in 1894 and Illinois in 1895.

Although the most systematic test of military cycling was the Connecticut National Guard's 1891–92 trials, the regular army undertook several splashy, if essentially pointless, projects. Colonel Pope's good friend General Nelson Miles organized a relay of citizen-cyclists to carry a goodwill message from his headquarters in Chicago to New York in May 1892, and in 1894 cyclists organized the delivery of a message from Washington to Denver by relay.[50] The army used its own ranks to mount a serious effort in 1896 when a Captain Abercrombie and three of his enlisted men traveled from Omaha to Chicago and back in 13 days (not counting a layover in Chicago), averaging 88 miles a day, mostly along railway lines.[51]

The big show, however, was in the summer of 1897, when the 25th Infantry Bicycle Corps left Fort Missoula, Montana, for St. Louis. Ostensibly under the overall command of General Miles, the unit was actually the responsibility of two white officers, Lieutenant James A. Moss and Assistant Surgeon J. M. Kennedy, and was manned by twenty black enlisted men.[52] Despite the fact that they were traversing the same terrain that Thomas Stevens had found, twenty years before, to be among the most difficult of his transcontinental ride, the unit rolled into St. Louis thirty-four days later having lost only one cyclist to injury.

The following spring, Lieutenant Moss and his unit were sent to undertake urban anti-riot duty in the Spanish-American War. The unit was disbanded soon after returning. This was the last active bicycle unit in the United States Army. As for Pope, he had long since bowed out of the military contracting game. Stung over criticism of his close relationship with Pope, General Miles recommended to the House Committee on Military Affairs that the federal government manufacture its own bicycles, just as it made its own guns at federal arsenals. That hurt. Also, field trials revealed that pneumatic tires had trouble handling off-road conditions, and recommended that an Overman non-pressurized cushion tire, called the "Arch Tire," be used instead.[53] Pope asked Overman to let him license the Arch Tire in 1891 for use on his proposed Columbia Military Special, but Overman refused. Pope tried to break the patent. He failed. By the time James Moss led the Twenty-Fifth out of Fort Missoula, the army was being supplied with Spalding bicycles using an improved version of the Arch Tire.

## The Public Are in the Dark

On 20 June 1890, Albert Pope crossed the line from merchant to industrialist when he purchased the Weed Sewing Machine Company for $300,000. Six months before, Weed's directors had approved a new 10-year contract with the Pope Manufacturing Company and authorized an increase in capital from $240,000 to $300,000. The $60,000 in new stock was sold to the Colonel. In January 1891, George Pope wrote David Post that "the Weed Company is no more": It had been purchased outright by Albert Pope. Technically, George was wrong, as the Weed Sewing Machine Company continued to exist, but only as a wholly owned subsidiary of the Pope Manufacturing Company, with its own stock and board of directors.[54]

At the parent Pope company, the Colonel, Edward Pope and Arthur Pattison retained their positions as president, treasurer and secretary, respectively. All three continued to work in the Boston office, with the Colonel heading to Hartford at least one day a week. George Day filled the newly created position of vice president and manager of the Hartford works. At the subsidiary Weed company, the Colonel replaced Day as president, who stepped down to become treasurer. Frank Belden, the former Weed secretary, accepted an offer to work at Colt's armory, and A. P. Day (no known relation to George), a bookkeeper at Weed since 1885, replaced him.[55]

Actually, the Weed plant was the Colonel's *second* bicycle factory. In November 1889, the same month he bought his initial one-fifth interest in Weed, he incorporated the Hartford Cycle Company with a modest capitalization of $25,000 and a small factory at 75–77 Commerce near the west bank of the Connecticut River. Pope issued David Post, who had been an aide to George Day since 1883, ten shares of stock and appointed him treasurer. Harry Pope likewise received a small number of shares and was also named a director.[56] More importantly, Harry became plant superintendent and put his MIT training to use setting up the new factory. The Colonel's Hartford lawyer, Charles E. Gross, became the third director, but he was just keeping the seat warm until a permanent president could be found. In the early summer of 1890 George Pope, Edward's brother and Albert's cousin, quit his job in Montreal in the lumber business to take over the new company. This was the second time he worked for the Colonel, having previously undertaken the rather unrewarding task of killing off Cunningham & Company in 1883.

Now discretion was again required. Colonel Pope's hated rival, A. H. Overman, was rumored to be developing a moderate-priced bicycle to capture the mass market. (In fact, the truth was even more awful: Overman was teaming up with sporting goods magnate A. G. Spalding to manufacture a moderate priced bicycle, the Credenda, for Spalding to sell in his Chicago and New York stores and through his mail-order catalog.) This presented two problems for the Colonel. First, he was loath to water down the glittering name of the Columbia with a second-tier line. Second, the 1886 "Treaty of Springfield" only gave Pope permission to use Overman's patents for ball bearings in the Columbia. Using them on another brand would breach the contract.[57]

So the Colonel created the Hartford Cycle Company as a separate, ostensibly autonomous, firm with its own factory, management and separate agency network. "The Hartford Cycle is another organization," Albert Pope cautioned David Post before George arrived in town, "of which the public are in the dark as to ownership." Of course, it was absurd to think that the ruse would work for long, and when Overman found out, there was hell to pay. "Overman is very likely now to turn his undivided attention and undivided wrath towards our company and we may expect any day to hear from him in some shape," sighed George. He was right: Overman quickly sued in a Connecticut court.[58] Like many of the Pope-Overman battles, this turned out to be a tempest in a teapot, as Overman had bigger things to worry about, such as the Credendas for Spalding: "I hear that the Lamb Knitting Co. [Overman's supplier] will not get out over 2000 altogether on their contract of 8000 for Overman" snickered George.[59]

George had almost identical problems. In charge less than five months, he discovered to his chagrin that "one thing is very apparent to me and that is our capacity is too limited for 2,500 machines [a year]. I have asked for a price on the whole of our building including the use of engine and boiler. With this we can make a good factory."[60] True to his word, within a few weeks the Hartford Cycle president was shopping around the city for new quarters. On the other side of town, George Day and his men huddled over plans for a new wing to the Columbia factory. In Boston, Albert and Edward walked around a nine thousand square foot lot on Columbus Avenue that would make a splendid headquarters building. It was an auspicious time. Like the rumbling of a distant thunderstorm, it was difficult to tell which direction the storm was coming from. The breeze had yet to switch directions, the cool, damp-smelling wind yet to rise. However, it was clear that something was coming. But what was it and from where? With the perspective of a century, we call that then still-distant storm "The Golden Era of Cycling." Much, much earlier, only a decade after it passed, its survivors referred to it among themselves simply as "the boom."

# 6

# Reading, 'Riting 'Rithmetic and Roads

> *Always alive to the opportunity of getting a word in edgewise in favor of his pet hobby, the vigorous advocate of good roads accompanies his pamphlet with a letter requesting us to advocate the extension of the fundamentals of the common school education by the addition of a fourth R, so that they should embrace Reading, 'Riting, 'Rithmetic and Roads. We print the suggestion, though we fail to see the slightest appropriateness in doing so.*
>
> —The Manufacturer and Builder, 1893[1]

Aside from his career as an industrialist, Albert Pope's most enduring fame came as a pioneer in the American good roads movement. When he imported his first bicycles in 1878, American highways were among the worst in the industrialized world. Federal highway funding was considered tantamount to socialism, and even the states shied away from direct involvement in construction or maintenance, delegating the job to townships or counties. By the time Pope passed away in 1909, Congress had created a Bureau of Public Roads, and seven years later authorized the first Federal Aid Road Act. By then, almost every state had already set up a road commissioner's office or a state highway department to centralize the construction and repair of major roads, and most had established some sort of supporting funding system.[2]

The only political office Pope ever held was a two-year term on the Newton Common Council in 1876–77. Late in life he claimed that he had often been urged to run for office, but always refused because it would require him to turn his back on friends and associates.[3] However, the Colonel's record within the good roads movement suggests that he may have tried to use it as a populist springboard to national office. While his primary interest was no doubt rooted in a deep-seated loyalty to the cycling fraternity, the national prominence of his good friend General Miles may have inspired him to seek the same type of power Miles enjoyed as Chief of Staff of the Army in the form of a national "highway czar." It appears that the very limited authority Congress initially chose to give to the Bureau of Public Roads (at first called the Office of Road Inquiry of the Department of Agriculture) at the time it was created in 1893 dissuaded Pope from entering government service.

## *Hypocrisy, Humbug, Shilly-Shally and Downright Lying*

One of the primary reasons behind the League of American Wheelmen was the need to overturn bicycle bans and other forms of discrimination.[4] The league was essentially a club of clubs, comprised of local bicycle organizations who maintained their own charters, uniforms, and headquarters. In its early years, the state divisions were its most important units. Each was semi-autonomous, headed by a chief consul, who oversaw a governing assembly of districts and local consuls. The local consuls were typically local club officers who themselves wielded considerable influence over state and national affairs. At the national level, the president and two vice-presidents comprised an Executive Committee, with ultimate authority vested in a National Board of Officers made up of representatives from among the state consuls, national officers and members of the standing committees.

The two most powerful of the standing committees were the Committee of Rights and Privileges, which oversaw legal affairs, and the Racing Committee, formed in 1882. The issue of racing was particularly contentious. At first, the league tried to follow a strict "Simon Pure" policy of amateurism, mirroring the English tradition. Under the rules, no member should receive any compensation for racing, teaching or coaching, and anyone who received anything of value, or who participated in any race with a non-amateur, should be expelled. Complicating matters was an exception clause allowing members who were employees of bicycle firms to retain their amateur status.[5] At the time the league was formed, races were considered "exhibitions," and racers often came from the ranks of factory hands. Asked about a $200 bookkeeping entry for "racingmen," one company officer responded that "I guess a certain number of these young men who worked in the bicycle department were also racing men ... there were some pretty prominent riders who worked in the department."[6] In addition to their regular wages, these "salesmen" demanded premiums for winning races and extra travel stipends. "We always objected to these expenses that were not really traveling expenses," explained a manager, "but our riders were never satisfied unless they were allowed ... they would not race, as a general thing [or] they might enter a race and not try to win."[7] When questioned about a five dollar company expenditure for wine at the 1883 Rochester summer races, a race team manager admitted that it was given to the judges because "the other judges were riders of the other machines and prejudiced in favor of the other machines, and five dollars was expended by Mr. Hall in wine as, you see, to soften their prejudices."

"Did it have the desired effect?"

"It did, yes sir."[8]

In 1885 the L.A.W. Racing Committee passed a rule requiring contestants to receive a sign-off from at least one committee official for each event. The manufacturers and trade journals objected, not only because it interfered with business, but because it completed the process of politicizing the Racing Committee, with members representing various makers either sanctimoniously denying racing permits to others' "professionals" or looking the other way as they signed off on permits for riders they knew were taking payments from patrons.[9]

In an attempt to stop the madness, the Chairman of the Racing Committee, Arthur Bassett, proposed at the 1885 L.A.W. convention that the word "amateur" be removed as a condition of league membership. His suggestion was greeted with "a thunderous No!"

and a demand that the Racing Committee initiate an investigation. It uncovered evidence that virtually every prominent American racer was receiving some form of sponsorship. The following February the committee issued its report and a list of offending racers, specifically recommending that 28 be expelled, and several more be refused entry into that June's Springfield race meet, the highlight of the American season. Most of the invited English cracks threatened to stay home if the situation was not quickly resolved.

In May, the promoter of the Springfield meet and representatives of the Lynn and Newton clubs, who also sponsored big race meets, met in Boston to found the American Cyclists' Union, a breakaway group organized for the purpose of sanctioning racing under "international" standards. Karl Kron explained to his readers that winning a race:

> has advertising value to the maker of the cycle upon which it is won. This fact renders extremely difficult the maintenance of any rule which tries to class in separate social grades the racers for glory and the racers for gain; and the attempts to maintain it cause a great deal of bitterness and acrimony to be displayed in public, and an endless amount of hypocrisy, humbug, shilly-shally, sophistry, treachery, deceit, and downright lying to prevail in private.[10]

After 1886, amateurs were required to submit affidavits attesting to their status, although even the chairman of the L.A.W Racing Committee admitted that riders could "produce unlimited strange and mighty oaths" attesting to the fact that the rider "never, no never, did, could, would, had, or might receive one penny from any person or persons, directly or indirectly, as a result of his riding."[11] This rigidity was one reason why record setting and touring became a favored method for American makers to demonstrate their mounts.

But even this seemingly more innocuous alternative fell prey to the cutthroat realities of the bicycle market. The builders of the Star bicycle hired A. A. McCurdy to break the world's 24-hour record, secretly paying him $150 upon his success. Colonel Pope hired his own man and soon broke that record. The Star people offered McCurdy $250 if he would take the trophy back. McCurdy failed the first time, earning nothing (but costing the firm $115 in expenses, to their great annoyance), but he succeeded at a second attempt a few weeks later. Pope tried several times to top it, but as the Ordinary era wound down in 1888 the Star still held the record.[12]

The never-ending racing imbroglio revealed two other stresses pulling at the rapidly growing league. The first was the growing imbalance between its members' sectional and national interests. When it was formed, the league was almost entirely composed of members and clubs from the northeast. In 1881, sixty percent of the membership came from just two states, New York and Massachusetts, but at the L.A.W.'s peak in 1897, only 38 percent came from there, with the midwest (especially Ohio and Illinois) contributing a proportionately larger share. With much of the league's administrative structure decentralized into state divisions, it was easy for national issues, such as racing, to be turned into sectional disputes, and the editor of the Illinois division's magazine accused the Racing Committee of making the amateurism debate "a sectional fight between the East and the West."[13]

The second divisive force was the proletarianization of bicycling. As new-wheel prices fell and a market for second-hand machines developed, clerks and tradesmen, then common laborers, took up cycling. Some L.A.W. members believed that this democratization was chasing away the gentlemen who had established the sport. Canadian bicycle historian Glen Norcliffe has documented the declining social prestige of the Montreal

Bicycle Club between 1885 and 1895 by tracing the gradual conversion of the names on its annual group portrait from Anglophone to Francophone.[14] In many cases, the new proletarians were unable or unwilling to afford the trappings of the original elite clubs. By 1889 both the Boston and Massachusetts Bicycle clubs, the first and second oldest in America, were bankrupt. For the latter, the end was particularly bitter. After sharing a clubhouse with the Boston club for several years, the Massachusetts group rented space in the basement of the Lafayette Hotel while a custom-built clubhouse was finished at 152 Newbury. In 1885, the three-story townhouse was the most luxurious in the world. On a cold January day four years later, its furnishings were sold on the front steps and the keys turned over to the Boston Art Club. Although both clubs would be resurrected in coming years, they would eschew such luxuries as clubhouses, holding meetings in local hotels and members' homes.[15] In other cases, long-standing racial and ethnic animosities between different groups of working-class cyclists themselves created stress as clubs expanded and broadened.

In the face of such divisive forces, the league needed a unifying issue. The road-ban fights were winding down as a growing number of state supreme courts recognized the bicycle as a legitimate road-going vehicle. By the late 1880s the Committee on Rights and Privileges turned its attention to securing reduced baggage rates for cyclists traveling on railroads and the local taxation of cyclists. Important issues, certainly, but lacking the resonance of a "do not enter" sign.

The good roads campaign fit the bill perfectly. It was an issue that all cyclists could agree on, but was compatible with a decentralized power structure where each state division could define its own particular needs. In Michigan, for example, wheelman Louis Bates had been lobbying since 1881 for a revised state law that would allow townships to collect at least part of their road taxes in cash. At that time, Michigan permitted only municipalities to assess monetary taxes — rural jurisdictions could collect their road tax only in the form of two day's labor or one day of labor plus the use of a plow and team. Townships couldn't even pay for a part-time road inspector, let alone buy the new specialized road-making equipment then entering the market. In New York, Pope man George Bidwell sought funds to permit his L.A.W. state counsel to prosecute negligent or corrupt county road supervisors.[16]

The good roads movement also held the promise of closing the gap between middle class city cyclists and rural farmers who blamed their crushing poverty on urban elites and modern technology. In Massachusetts, at least one state legislator withdrew his support from an 1889 bill creating a state highway commission simply because it was sponsored by the state L.A.W. division.[17] In the late 1880s the two surest ways to kill any transportation legislation in a midwestern capitol was to get it labeled a "railroad bill" or a "bicycle bill."

Some members used the goods roads movement to change the league's own policies, starting on the state level. Horatio S. Earle was appointed chairman of the Michigan division's good roads committee despite the fact that he was not a cyclist. Instead, he worked as a sales executive for an agricultural implement firm that made road-making equipment. Before 1890, this would have been impossible. Under the league's constitution, any applicant for membership had to be a wheelman. It was amended specifically to allow good-roads advocates to join. When he ran for election as Michigan's chief consul, Earle proposed to eliminate the state racing committee entirely and replace it with a good roads body. "There is no more sense in the L.A.W. running bicycle races than the poultry association staging cock fights or the dairy association, bull fights," he argued.[18] After he won, the division withdrew entirely from the regulation of racing.

At its national convention in June 1888 the league voted to create a National Committee for Highway Improvement. At first, the committee simply enhanced the work that divisions in Massachusetts, New York, Michigan, New Jersey and local clubs in Boston, Philadelphia and New York City were already doing. But in 1889, the Executive Committee drafted uniform legislation it introduced in nine states calling for the creation of a state highway commission, optional cash taxation in rural areas, and the development of highway surveys and plans. It was crushed in every state. "The farmers must bear the expense while bicyclists and pleasure-riding citizens will reap the larger benefits," complained the Michigan Grange.[19] "Give the farmer a fair price for his product and he will get to market all right without the aid of fancy roads and theoretical road makers," wrote one farmer.[20]

The league realized it was in trouble. "We must concentrate first on education, then agitation, and finally legislation," said President James Dunn. To make this happen, the league opened a Road Improvement Bureau in 1891 to distribute pamphlets and articles on good roads. By 1900 it had given out five million items, at a cost of $200,000, many marked as Department of Agriculture circulars. In 1892 the league started a monthly magazine, *Good Roads*. It cost twenty thousand dollars to get it up and running, of which six thousand was donated by the Colonel.[21]

Between 1892 and 1895, when *Good Roads* was merged into the *L.A.W. Bulletin*, circulation peaked at 75,000. Each league member was entitled to a free copy, but many asked to have their copy sent to a government official, library or Grange hall. The larger clubs bought multiple subscriptions for similar distribution. The league also made arrangements with press associations in New York, Chicago and Louisville to rent out its printing plates at nominal cost for use by newspapers and magazines. These were all tried and true techniques that the Pope firm had perfected in its decade of selling bicycles.

## Butter and Cheese Were the Only Questions

Although nobody realized it at first, a workable solution to the roads problem required a large reallocation of money from cities to rural areas. Farmers demanded the right to pay their road tax in labor because they lived a largely cashless lifestyle. A small farmer and his family consumed or bartered as much as half their annual production. A farmer who had to borrow money for equipment, land or seed, would likely turn a cash profit at year's end only in extraordinarily bountiful times. Excess cash was used to retire debt or buy more land, not sit in a bank somewhere. Every cash dollar demanded of the farmer was the equivalent of two or three dollars in crops or land.

Better roads benefited the farmer who sold proportionally more of his output and consumed less, and therefore needed to haul more to the railhead. Those were the big railroad-backed farmers. The call for good roads fueled farmers' fear that the railroads and big-city food processors, such as Heinz and Armour, would soon cut them out entirely and set up their own corporate farms. "I captivated the farmers completely," reported one wheelman who spoke to a Grange meeting, "talked Good Roads, got the privilege of reading an essay on the subject, but they could not find time to devote any attention to

Road Improvement; butter and cheese were the only questions."[22] Farm prices slumped badly after the panic of 1893, and the good roads movement increasingly became a touchstone for a variety of rural-urban schisms. One rural newspaper editor complained that "farmers pay all the tax they can under the very low prices of all farm products and the gold standard."[23]

The only way to bring the two sides together was through a system of state-aid road funding that transferred money from city to township. To secure the allegiance of rural farmers, urban cyclists would have to promise to pay the bill. This was initially a difficult position for the wheelmen to accept. The first mass-distribution brochure the league produced was Isaac B. Potter's *Gospel of Good Roads*, in 1891. Potter laid the blame for bad roads squarely on the farmer, portraying him as an ignorant rube and a Luddite fearful of any technological advance. It wasn't until 1898 that the league formally endorsed state-aid when it published Otto Dorner's *Must the Farmer Pay for Good Roads?*, openly advocating redistributive state highway programs to benefit farmers. Over half a million copies of the 41-page booklet were supplied to the Department of Agriculture, which mailed it out as *Circular Number 31*. By necessity, the farmer-cyclist alliance strategy relied on the league's state organizations, bypassing the national headquarters. The debacle of the 1889–90 legislative push demonstrated that the league had no hope of drafting a single uniform bill for nationwide acceptance. The process was slow, incremental and uncertain. By 1906 only twenty states had taken any steps to either establish some type of centralized statewide highway authority or develop a state aid funding system.

Slow, incremental and uncertain was not the Colonel's style, and almost from the start, he struck out on his own. In October 1889, speaking before the annual meeting of the National Carriage Builders Association, he proposed the creation of a national highway commission. Under his initial outline, the commission would be modest in scope, limited to compiling and distributing information on the condition of roads and recommending methods of road construction. But unlike the league, Pope stressed *national* action, however restrained, and he particularly focused on the need for some sort of centralized finance and oversight authority, which he justified before the Syracuse Board of Trade in 1890. "Road building is, and I fear may always be, too much dependant upon politics," he complained. "There are too many men today in public office responsible for the care of millions, and the expenditure of hundreds of thousands, whom we would never dream of electing as directors in any bank or mercantile corporation."[24] To prevent such waste, road work had to be done "under the eye of a special and competent engineer" who would be "watched and guided" by a citizen superintendent or "Citizen's Committee, or who you will, to make sure that your money is spent in the right direction."

As his model, Pope took the Roads Improvement Association (R.I.A.) of London, an agency charged with the "guidance of all authorities having control of roads" in the metropolitan area. Membership on the R.I.A. board came from the peerage and the city's professional classes. The Colonel similarly proposed a national highway commission "composed of your active and intelligent businessmen." Pope closed his remarks with the fable of the belling of the cat, noting that "It is one thing to propose, another to execute. Who will lead?" Although he left the question unanswered, he apparently had someone in mind. Himself.

Although his goals were outwardly modest, the Colonel was serious, and he ordered the printing of thousands of copies of these two speeches, which he mailed to newspaper editors, congressmen and prominent Americans.[25] These were the earliest of what would grow to almost a dozen such mass-distributed publications. Pope also donated $6,000 to the Massachusetts Institute of Technology to develop a department of highway engineering and endow a chair to head it.[26] Although Vanderbilt and the Case School (later Case Western Reserve) had established summer courses in road building, the MIT program was probably the first full program in roadway engineering in America.

He did not criticize the league's efforts or even contrast his own program to that being taken by the L.A.W., but it was clearly different. At this point, the league was still pulling together the various efforts of its state divisions and introducing the unsuccessful state highway acts. Pope had no public comment on this, but Isaac Potter and Charles Dodge, editor of *Outing*, both argued against it, maintaining that in 1890, it was still too early for the wheelmen to take such a high-profile political role.[27] On the other hand, the Colonel was fed up by the near-anarchy of the racing committee and the league's reluctance to act on his 1886 request to relieve him of some of the financial burden of providing legal aid to cyclists fallen victim to unjust laws or inequitable acts or assaults.[28]

The league disappointed him again in 1891 when President Dunn and Potter put Pope's national highway commission idea before the membership at the summer convention. Although Dunn favored a freestanding information bureau outside the Department of Agriculture and Potter wanted a federal road-building agency, both agreed with the Colonel that any successful bill required cooperation with farm-state legislators, and they put aside their pet projects to help promote Pope's concept, which had a better chance in the grain belt. At an earlier meeting of the league's national assembly, Potter had urged the L.A.W. to support the national Farmer's Alliance on upcoming crop-price support legislation in return for the Alliance's help on the national highway commission bill. The cyclists considered, then rejected, the request.[29]

Meanwhile, Pope had started working with General Roy Stone, a Civil War veteran and civil engineer out of New York. The two were introduced in 1890 by George Bidwell. Stone, who earned his engineering degree at West Point, came out of the French School of the Polytechnicians, a man of *Ponts et Chaussees*— roads and bridges. Stone believed the federal government should be directly involved in roads, just as it had in the dredging of rivers, the digging of canals, and the construction of great harbors. However, the proposal Stone took to Washington in May 1892 with Pope's blessing was considerably more modest. A national highway commission would function for two years. It would tabulate information, prepare an exhibit at the 1893 World's Columbian Exposition in Chicago, create, and draw up a national highways plan. At the end of two years a final report and estimates as to the cost and effectiveness of a permanent committee would be prepared. Of its fifteen commissioners, five would be citizens selected by the president.

The measure was introduced into Congress by Representative Philip Post of Illinois and Senator Charles Manderson of Nebraska in June while thousands of cyclists milled around town during the L.A.W.'s annual convention. The wheelmen soon went home, but Stone and league President Dunn stayed behind to lobby for the bill. It passed in the Senate once everyone agreed that no appropriation would be involved, effectively foisting the problem off on the lower chamber. To the surprise of most, House debate was entirely along North-South lines, ignoring the urban-rural split that lay at the heart of the issue. On the last day of the congressional session, Speaker of the House Charles Crisp refused to recognize the measure and it died when he gaveled the session to a close.

The end was not a surprise to Dunn, who, in a letter, admitted that "we have reason to believe that Crisp is not favorable to us."[30]

Crisp was the senior congressman from Georgia. When the wheelmen had been in town for their convention they had soundly defeated a measure proposed by Louisville member "Colonel" William Watts to amend the league constitution to restrict membership to whites. Appalled, *Bicycling World* editorialized that "we want every member and every dollar that is to be had. A black gentleman is infinitely superior to a white hoodlum."[31] Unorganized and unprepared, the "Color Bar" delegates were apparently genuinely shocked that anyone would object to such an obvious and patently sensible suggestion and let their congressmen know they had been slighted before they left town. Although Dunn and Roy may have pulled in the Republican farm states like Ohio, Nebraska and Kansas, any mention of the L.A.W. in Dixie instantly became pure poison.

The problem had started back in the fall of 1891 when the Mercury Wheel Club of Wilmington, Delaware, an all-black, upper-middle class L.A.W. member club, sponsored a 10-mile road race and sent the results, as per L.A.W. protocol, to *Wheel and Cycle Trades Review* for posting. There was apparently some sort of complaint, as the following spring, Sterling Elliot, then of the Massachusetts state division, wrote an editorial in the *L.A.W. Bulletin* explaining that African Americans were permitted under L.A.W. rules, acknowledging that there were black members, and stating that he believed that the rule should remain in its current form. A month later, in a column, the *Bulletin*'s editors noted that they had received many letters in response to Elliot's editorial, most in opposition.[32]

After the Washington, D.C., convention, Watts went back to Kentucky and immediately got a color bar inserted into the Kentucky state L.A.W. constitution. Six months later, he renewed the national constitutional amendment proposal at the league's national assembly. Watts and a member of the executive committee almost came to blows over Watts's repeated reference to "niggers" and "animals."[33] A narrow majority of the delegates —108 to 101— voted to approve the measure, but constitutional amendments required a two-thirds majority. At the 1894 convention in Philadelphia the Southerners were organized and the issue made it all the way to a floor vote before going down. The 1895 convention was in Louisville and "Negro Exclusion" was the headline issue. Watts read a letter sent by Frederick Scott of the Union Cycle Club, the largest black cycling club in the South (25 members), advocating the measure. It passed, 127 to 54, and the Massachusetts and New York delegations immediately withdrew.

Contacted later by a reporter, Frederick Scott was found to be a "pleasant and intelligent man" who explained that neither he nor his club could be admitted to the league in any Southern state anyway, and that Watts explained to him that the failure of the measure would be a detriment to the cyclists of Kentucky. "Mr. Scott is one of the few who do not care to force themselves where they are not wanted," explained the reporter. In 1894, about 190 African American men were lynched in the ten Southern states, plus Missouri and Texas. The number can only be approximated because so many went unrecorded by local law enforcement agencies or courts, who were often conspirators or participants.[34]

In a bitter irony, Colonel Watts's concerns proved to be well founded. After the dramatic fall in bicycle prices in 1897, one large Chicago manufacturer (probably the Western Wheel works, known for their good, inexpensive, no-frills bicycles) noticed a huge fall in sales in the Deep South and sent one of their department managers to New Orleans to investigate conditions. "It sounds odd to say it," reported the man upon his return, "[but] the Negro has killed the bicycle business in the south." With the easy availability of bicycles, corner groceries and hardware stores began carrying them. Banned from bicycle and sporting goods stores, blacks could now buy them from a familiar retailer within their own neighborhoods on a cash-and-carry basis (and for a fortunate few, even on time payments). Previously, their only option had been to put themselves at the mercy of a traveling drummer who took their orders, then might or might not deliver. But, discovered the Chicago man, "as soon as the Negro took to sporting a wheel, just that soon did the fad cease among the southern whites.... In New Orleans, in Birmingham and Nashville the business began to drop off perceptively."[35] Working-class white Southerners were so bigoted that they wouldn't even ride in the same roadways as their black counterparts.

Although nobody could have realized it at the time, the Louisville convention was the beginning of the end for the L.A.W. Dunn's successor, Sterling Elliott, soon boasted that the league wasn't even a bicycle club any more: "The League of American Wheelmen is fast getting to be a political party whose demands are equal rights and road improvement, and whose platform is made of broken rock and gravel."[36] That idea did not sit well with many community leaders, especially in the west. The *Cincinnati Commercial Gazette* cautioned that "there seems to be a desire on the part of some to drag the League into politics on the question of roads improvement. This is a mistake." Even John Wells, editor of *American Athlete*, warned that "though the membership is large and influential, the League would be but a small factor in the political working out of the end to be gained."[37] Wells recommended that the L.A.W. limit itself to coalition-building with carriage-builders and other transport interests.

The color bar, regional antagonisms, and near-daily embarrassments over racing issues, including revelations over fixes, fake amateurs, deliberate take-downs, and smear campaigns in the racing committee, continued to darken Elliot's overweening political ambitions. "Some of the greatest political parties have made mistakes," he said, trying to sweep the issues under the rug, "It cannot be expected that an organization comprised chiefly of young men should be entirely free from error."[38] While still financially flush, the league was flying apart from its own centripetal force as various social classes, sectional groups, business interests, and others spun off in their own directions. Horatio Earle, who had progressed from state consul to Michigan Highway Commissioner, wrote in his diary, "My candid estimation is that the L.A.W. is to grow smaller and smaller each year until there will be no divisions, probably only a secretary paid and he too will have other business."[39] Membership peaked on 21 January 1898 at 103,298. The following June, a *New York Times* headline announced: "Steady Decline in the League of American Wheelmen Membership Still Unchecked." In only six months, membership had fallen over ten percent, to about 90,000. By August it had shrunk to 81,300. It fell below the 50,000 mark in the Spring of 1900. By 1905 it was essentially dead, an old-timer's club for former Ordinary riders run off of Abbott Bassett's kitchen table.[40]

The moment Crisp's gavel fell in August 1892, it was apparent to Pope that the good-roads movement was going to have to cut loose the L.A.W. if it wanted federal action. Roy Stone and the Colonel organized a separate National League for Good Roads and convened an organizing convention in Chicago for the fall. This convention would, many years later, become the source of bitter acrimony between Stone and Pope, two strong men with stout egos. Nebraska Senator Manderson and Illinois Congressman Post, the two heroes of the failed highway commission bill, were the keynote speakers. Isaac Potter, that stalwart L.A.W. man, was given one last moment in the spotlight. Although he later worked to bridge the gap between cyclists and farmers, the sarcastic language of *The Gospel of Good Roads* couldn't be forgiven, so both the pamphlet and its author were best forgotten. Potter continued to work for good roads, but through the L.A.W., not the new Good Roads League, in which he held no office.[41]

Manderson was elected president of the new organization and Stone was named vice-president and treasurer. The ten-man board of directors included Clem Studebaker of the famous carriage-building family, and railroad men Leland Stanford and August Belmont. Philip Armour represented corporate agriculture. Pope men held three of the ten seats: the Colonel himself, Charles Burdett and George Wetmore. Wetmore had been Pope's trial lawyer in the 1886 *Pope v. Gormully* case, and Burdett, also a patent lawyer, was heavily involved in Pope's pneumatic tire and steel tube work. The resolutions committee proposed Pope's three goals: a national highway commission; a federal roads department; a world's fair exhibit.[42]

Pope's most intense work on good roads was done during this period from fall 1892 to spring 1893. At Manderson's urging, the roads league scheduled another convention just four months later, in January 1893, to coincide with the annual meeting of the National Board of Trade and the start of the new congressional session. The convention proposed that the commission be funded at $15,000, that six citizens be selected to serve on it without salary, and that $50,000 be allocated for the world's fair exhibition. Meanwhile, Pope printed up thousands of copies of a "monster petition" that he intended to present to Congress, calling for the commission, the world's fair exhibit, and a more permanent traveling exhibit of roadmaking techniques and machinery.

After talking it over, the House Agriculture Committee responded by authorizing the Department of Agriculture $10,000 for a roads office. Pope was decidedly unsatisfied with this compromise and wanted a completely separate bill prepared, bypassing the agriculture committee, and planned to use his petition to bludgeon the committee into permitting this bypass. Stone blanched at this naked show of force and urged Pope to delay presentation of the petition until after the House had considered the Agriculture Appropriation Act. President Harrison, having already lost the 1892 election, was leaving office on March 4th and badly wanted the appropriation measure approved before leaving for home. Pope let Stone know he would not tolerate dissent: "There have been attributed to you certain remarks derogatory of the great movement throughout the country for the purpose of founding at Washington a Road Department," he lectured. "Col. Burdett, a member of the Executive Committee, states that the matter was never brought before a meeting of the League, and whatever has been published was simply ... your individual opinion." His letter closed with an undisguised threat: "It is a serious mistake for the League for Good Roads to oppose the wishes of the people who are most deeply interested."[43]

However, Congressman Post quickly dissuaded Stone of Pope's separate-bill strategy, warning that it "stands a poor chance." Stone turned to his friends in the Senate. He asked Henry Alvord of the Association of American Agricultural Colleges and Experiment Stations to meet with a group of Senators, including Manderson. Alvord reported that they "had a conference and decided that it was more discreet to save the appr'n of $10nd, as it stood, than to attract attention to it by an amendment, & run the risk of a debate & losing all." Manderson himself was doubtful about anything beyond the agriculture appropriation. "Not only is Senate business great," reported the Senate clerk, to whom Manderson had forwarded Stone's appeal, "but the pressure for economy and cutting down are even greater." Stone finally talked Pope into accepting the bird in the hand, convincing him to delay the petition until after the agriculture appropriation was voted on. It was quietly approved and moved on to the president's desk. But the sharp language of Pope's letter had understandably wounded Stone, and from that point onward the relationship between the two men soured.[44]

President Harrison signed the appropriation bill in April, the day before his term ended and he turned the White House over to the new president, Grover Cleveland. In October, when the new fiscal year started, the Agriculture Department likewise had a new secretary, Nebraska's J. Sterling Morton. Morton approved of the roads bureau, but given the deep agricultural depression that followed the panic of 1893, he was forced to be a ruthless economizer, capping the salaries of women employees and questioning the expenditure of horse feed at extension stations.[45] Over the summer, Morton had hired Roy Stone as the road bureau's first director. Morton ordered that the agency, to be called the Office of Road Inquiry, be run on a shoe-string budget: "It is not expected that there will be any considerable force of clerical help, and, aside from your salary, no considerable expenditure." Stone's first task would be correspondingly modest: a report on state road finance laws.[46]

Above all else, Morton warned, the Office would stay out of the road-building business. "The actual expense in the construction of these highways is to be borne by the localities and States," he wrote. "This Department is to form no part of any plan, scheme, or organization, or to be a party to it in any way." He summed up what he termed the ORI's "restrictions": "The Department is to furnish information."[47] It seems improbable that the Secretary would take aboard the head of the nation's most influential good roads organization, then expect him to limit himself to the role of research correspondent. Indeed, the minute Stone found out he was hired, he closed up the New York headquarters of the Good Road League and moved it, files, furniture and all, to the Department of Agriculture building where he and stenographer Robert Grubbs became the Office of Road Inquiry. It is possible that Morton foresaw the subsidization of the ORI by the League of American Wheelmen that began after 1896 and tacitly looked the other way. Another possibility is that Morton was willing to run the risk of placing the politically volatile Stone in his organization because he wanted to do battle with Postmaster Wilson Bissell over the introduction of Rural Free Delivery, which Bissell opposed, but that both Morton's farmers and Stone's cyclists badly wanted. On the other hand, Morton may simply have thought he could stage-manage the General and the Wheelmen, but such naiveté seems unlikely.

In December, Pope presented his "monster petition" to Congress, calling for a National Highway Commission and a highway exhibit at the Chicago World's Fair. It reportedly contained 150,000 signatures. The fairground's permanent buildings had already opened and the start of the fair itself was only six months away. Nevertheless, Pope argued that "there is ample time to erect a suitable building."[48] Congress referred the petition to the Committee on the World's Columbian Exposition, which quickly approved it, although it is uncertain whether it actually approved an expenditure of government funds or merely accepted a $6,000 donation that Pope had previously offered to construct the pavilion.

After being received by Congress, Colonel Pope's "Monster Petition" for good roads sat in the basement of the Capitol for over forty years until 1937 when it was moved to the National Archives. Here (viewers L-R) Frank McCallister of the National Archives, Edwin Halsey, the Secretary of State, and Sen. Kenneth McKeller look it over before the move. It has been exhibited several times since, most recently in 2008–09 (photograph by Harris & Ewing for the National Archives. Library of Congress Call No. LC-H22 D 1389 [P&P]).

While a transportation pavilion was built, it featured no demonstration road, and, having visited the Exhibition two weeks after it opened, Senator Manderson wrote Roy Stone that it wasn't really missed. "Any money expended there in an Exhibit of roads— bad or improved—would be money wasted," he explained. "There is so much to be seen more interesting and more attractive ... that a good roads exhibit would be lost and unseen. The Exposition grounds themselves are an object lesson in good roads. When it rains mud is shoe deep."[49]

## Treat This as Confidential

For the first couple of years Stone stuck to his mandate and turned out reports. By begging for labor and materials, he even managed to get a demonstration road built at an Atlanta agricultural exposition in 1895. It was all of 150 feet long. While it was a tremendous victory for the roads advocates to get Stone into the office, it did pose the problem of what to do about the politics. Banned into neutrality by Secretary Morton's watchful gaze, Stone turned to his only available option, the L.A.W. The ORI survived from year to year only as a line item in the Agriculture Department budget. Every year Morton cut the allocation back, the league published the new figure, the members howled, and some of the cuts were restored.[50] It was the height of the bicycle boom and, at least for a little while, cyclists still had some clout left, especially within their respective state divisions.

In 1895, Sterling Elliot came to Stone with a problem he was having with the league's monthly magazine, the *Bulletin*. The Post Office would not grant it lower, second-class postage rates because members received it free while non-members were charged a subscription. It was an old problem. In the mid–1880s the L.A.W. had tried to solve it by contracting with a commercial bicycle journal to have the *Bulletin* added as an insert. Members got the magazine and the insert both free, while the magazine's non-member subscribers continued to get the magazine without the insert.[51] Needless to say, other journals were unhappy and a scandal erupted when the magazine's editor was caught steering advertisers away from the *Bulletin* and toward his own publication. The league had gone back to printing its own *Bulletin*, but at first-class rates postage cost more than producing the magazine. Elliot proposed that the league merge the *Bulletin* and *Good Roads*. Because nobody paid for *Good Roads*, the combined magazines might get second-class privileges. Elliot had written the Postmaster General, but received no reply. Could General Stone help? Stone wrote to an assistant postmaster general and got the needed information. The plan was acceptable to the Post Office, but some sections of the league constitution would have to be modified to make it legal. Grateful, Elliott handwrote at the bottom of his letter of thanks, "Your reward will come later."[52]

The idea of using the L.A.W. to write and print circulars for the ORI in exchange for using its federal government franking privileges was probably an outgrowth of these postage woes. The first half of the bargain, in which the league started supplying the printed material used by ORI, more or less became official policy after the agency's budget was cut in 1896. Like all government offices, it had trouble getting material printed cheaply by the Government Printing Office, and the league often saved money by piggybacking its printing jobs off the phenomenally large contracts the bicycle makers used for catalogs and trade circulars. Sterling Elliott explained to Stone that "We can certainly be of great assistance to each other," if only "we could agree upon certain things which should be printed."[53]

The next step, getting the ORI to mass-distribute the material through the mails using its postal privileges, was apparently the idea of Otto Dorner, secretary of the Wisconsin Good Roads League, who wrote Stone in November 1896 asking if he would use the Department of Agriculture mailroom to send out materials that his group had published.[54] A year later, Dorner, now chairman of the L.A.W.'s National Good Roads Committee, proposed that the league pay the costs of writing and printing a 41-page pamphlet, *Must the Farmer Pay for Good Roads?*, targeted directly at farmers. In return for thousands of free copies, the ORI would mail the document out as a government publication. Written in the margin of Dorner's letter was the admonition: "Plse. Treat this confidental as far as the public is concerned."[55] When Dorner's booklet arrived at the league's offices from the printers, it already had "Office of Road Inquiry Circular No. 31" printed on the cover.

How did the league and Stone pull the wool over Morton's eyes? They didn't. Back in 1891, John Wanamaker, President Harrison's Postmaster General, had asked for $10,000 to develop an experimental Rural Free Delivery program. It could be argued that Wanamaker, scion of the Philadelphia and New York department store family, had a slight conflict of interest in the matter, but the idea was immensely popular with farm organizations. But before it could be implemented, Harrison was out, Grover Cleveland was in, and Bissell, the new Postmaster General, quashed it, even after Congress doubled, then tripled, the appropriation for the experimental program. Bissell believed that RFD would give "certain big eastern merchants" (i.e., Wanamaker) too much of an advantage over local shopkeepers.

Both the Wheelmen and the Office of Road Inquiry realized that this was an issue that could bridge the interests of cyclists and farmers, so they pushed hard for the idea. In 1895, Bissell stepped down and was replaced by William Wilson. Wilson was skeptical of RFD's practicality, but knew that Congress had given his department an explicit order and he wasn't about to risk his head over something he didn't feel very strongly about. As it turned out, the test was a smashing success and by mid–1897 over 40 pilot routes were in place.[56] Congress and Wilson's office were deluged with requests for new routes. To prevent chaos, the Post Office developed a procedure requiring applicants to petition their congressmen for service. The Post Office then sent an inspector to survey the route. There were two requirements: a minimum of one hundred persons along a fourteen- to sixteen-mile loop, and a route with roads passable during every month of the year. Suddenly, farmers had a reason to worry about the quality of the roads in front of their house. At the same time, Stone revived an old idea that states be allowed to use loans from Post Office Savings Banks to finance road improvements.[57] Previously cool to the idea, the Post Office now thought that it looked like a good way to promote RFD and make some money in the process. Like it or not, the Post Office was now in the roads business, and free postage for Dorner's new brochure suddenly looked like a sound investment for both the Post Office and the Agriculture Department. Along with free printing, the league threw in a 300,000-name mailing list.

## Passing the Torch

Having gotten rid of President Harrison in 1892, big business found itself even more horrified by Grover Cleveland, and convinced that a low tariff caused the great panic of

1893, threw him out as soon as possible and turned to the master architect of protective tariffs, William McKinley, in 1896. When McKinley's Secretary of Agriculture, James Wilson, took office in March 1897, his liberalized rules for the ORI spelled the end of wheelmen influence. Although the ORI budget didn't see a dramatic increase until after 1898, Stone could at least spend money directly on the construction of experimental "object lesson" roads, and these increasingly became the focus of his office.

In June 1898 Stone took a leave of absence to serve under General Miles in the Spanish-American War. He helped secure Cuba and took part in the invasion of Puerto Rico, leading a small advance force of 75 men who surveyed routes, strung telegraph lines and opened impassible roads for the following main force. He returned in January 1899, but without his previous vigor. His assistant, Maurice Eldridge, later told a federal pension board that after the war "he often complained of stomach trouble, from which he never fully recovered." Eldridge told the board "I am convinced that he contracted a disease of the stomach in the tropics which ultimately caused his death."[58]

Stone resigned in October 1899, and after getting some of his strength back, reinvigorated the National League of Good Roads by working with the rapidly growing automobile clubs of New York, Philadelphia and Boston. In an April 1903 speech to the Good Roads League, Stone referred to Pope as merely one of three "great leaders" of the good roads movement (Isaac Potter and Iowa's Judge Thayer were the others), and claimed that he had to offer to pay the costs of the Chicago organizing convention before he could convince the other national leaders to go forward. "They had little faith, however, in a national convention," Stone said, and the convention was organized "with fear and trembling" until they became convinced by the reaction of the Chicago newspapers "which gave columns and pages to the proceedings" because of the tie to the following year's world's fair. The implication was clear: Pope only offered to contribute to the conference once he realized what a publicity bonanza it had become. Otherwise, the Colonel would have been perfectly happy to let him foot the bill on his meager Civil War pension.[59]

Pope sat out the 1903 convention and had little to say about good roads until after Stone's illness forced him into complete retirement in 1904. After Stone died in 1905 his widow sought reinstatement of his Civil War pension death benefits, which he had been forced to waive when he volunteered for action in Cuba. Although many of his colleagues came to her defense, Pope remained quiet. The friction between Albert Pope and Roy Stone ultimately reduced the credit both men deserved. Pope, if not a visionary, was at least thinking broadly at a time when others were mired in tactics. His belief that the bicycle could revolutionize transportation was not a marketing artifice. In 1895 he spoke to a reporter from *Scribner's Monthly*. It was supposed to be anonymous, but there was no mistaking who this bicycle manufacturer, "a shrewd Yankee," was:

> I really believe that between electric cars in cities and the bicycle in the country, the value of horseflesh will drop to almost nothing within twenty years. The time is fast coming when a good, serviceable bicycle machine will be sold for $50 or less. Already in every village and town the mechanic and factory hand goes to his work on his wheel, the postman takes his letters around in one; even the doctor and clergyman make their rounds on wheels. It is far more than recreation.[60]

This was six months before he started the motor carriage laboratory, and almost two years before he cut the Columbia's price from $125 to $100. The Colonel was already thinking beyond the carriage trade to a mass-market audience. But in a nation of small towns and villages (in 1900 America had fewer than 4,000 cities with a population over a thousand) he was never going to put a nation on wheels — his wheels — by concentrating on the boulevards of the big eastern cities.

There is no escaping the fact that Pope was galvanized by the idea of a national highway commission with appointed citizen commissioners. After the creation of the ORI, Pope increasingly distanced himself from the subject, at least until automobile interests stirred a renewed concern with federal funding between 1903 and 1907. However, Congress would not even commit itself to a rudimentary highway funding program until 1916. Pope's sharp letter to Roy Stone in January 1893, rebuking him for considering a compromise that would exclude the presidential commission, despite the many warnings from the House and Senate that holding fast would kill the entire plan, strongly suggests that Pope was motivated as much by the commission as by the prospect of a permanently staffed government agency. There is no letter, no speech, no diary in which Albert Pope openly expresses his desire to be one of the first federal highway commissioners. But the pattern of his involvement, especially between 1889 and 1893, seems to suggest that was his overriding goal. If so, he was bound to be disappointed, as the United States never did create a National Highway Commission. When President Eisenhower's council of economic advisors recommended the creation of a National Highway Authority in 1954 to build the proposed Interstate Highway System and take over the existing system of 2-lane federal highways, the idea got no farther than the Senate Public Works Committee. While the subsequent 1956 federal legislation did set up the famous highway trust fund, this was little more than a mechanism to ensure that future congresses would not steal the money raised through the act's sharply higher gasoline and excise taxes — the basic funding structure stayed the same as that put into place in 1916, and primary authority remained with the states, who turned to a private organization, the American Association of State Highway Officials, for guidance and expertise. The citizen-expert never became a part of the American road-building bureaucracy, which evolved along lines closer to the French system of polytechnicians familiar to Roy Stone.[61]

In 1954, Christy Borth, director of the Automobile Manufactures' Association, welcomed a young historian from Boston into his office for an interview. Borth was happy to talk to the young man, as he was himself an enthusiastic amateur transportation historian. In reply to the young scholar's questions he replied that yes, he was aware that some accounts said that the old bicyclists started the American highway movement, but that was wrong. Neither the Wheelmen nor any individual cyclist had any influence on the good-roads movement, which originated within the early automobile clubs. Americans had no interest in roads — they had no reason to — until after the introduction of the automobile. It was just that simple.[62]

# 7

# The Great Bicycle Boom

> *Hello from Los Angeles, in California.... The cyclists out here are thick as fleas, and those are mighty thick. We are all being eaten up alive with them and they are on everything, man, dog and bedclothes alike. The bicycle business in this country is going to be something enormous.*
>
> — Ed "On-the-Spot" Spooner, 1895[1]

In March 1892, the Colonel cut the ribbon on his palatial new Boston headquarters. The office building, located at the corner of Columbus Avenue and Morgan Street, had been designed by Peabody and Stearns, the architects of his Commonwealth Avenue townhouse. Five stories high, 105 feet wide and 185 feet deep, the Pope Building was faced in buff brick trimmed with limestone and terra-cotta.[2] The whole first floor, facing Columbus Avenue, was given over to plate glass windows, which wrapped back along Morgan Street to give passers-by a fish-bowl view into the new-bicycle showroom. Across the store's main aisle, to the right of the front entrance, was the second-hand bicycle and accessories department. The store management and clerks were located on a rear mezzanine overlooking the showroom. The second floor was given over to the corporate staff. The days when Edward Pope, the Colonel, and a couple of boys ran everything were gone, and Edward and Arthur Pattison looked out on a sea of 50 desks and rolling stools for the correspondents and filing clerks.

The Colonel's office on the second floor was paneled in oak and mahogany with a marble fireplace in the corner. Always fascinated by gadgets, his desk featured an electric keyboard to summon his subordinates from various points in the building, and two telephones — one connected to the local exchange, the other a direct line to the factory in Hartford. The third and fourth floors were still empty, while the fifth floor was given over to the riding school. The use of 22-inch rolled steel beams imported from England allowed a clear span across the entire floor, so the days when novice students stared panic-stricken at what looked like a forest of thinly padded pillars were over. In the half basement were the shipping and receiving departments and the repair shop. The repair shop was much more than a place to patch flat tires; it included a complete machine shop with the capability to undertake any job the factory could do.

Many bicycle histories give the impression that the great bicycle boom of the 1890s exploded immediately after the introduction of the safety bicycle, but that is not the case.

While the sale of low-wheeled safeties after 1888 grew significantly faster than did the sale of ordinaries after their production started in 1878, the boom really didn't take off until about 1893 or 1894. The early safeties cost even more than Ordinaries, both because they were genuinely expensive to make and because American makers could hide behind a wall of steep import tariffs. Four factors caused the great bicycle boom. The first is obvious: lots of people wanted bicycles. The Ordinary gave bicycling an aura of elite snobbery and dangerousness that many wanted and few could previously afford. Second, new technologies, mostly the diamond frame and the pneumatic tire, made it cheaper and easier to make bicycles by obviating the need for expensive vibration-control devices such as sprung forks or hammock saddles. Third, the price of vital raw materials started to come down, first for cold-drawn steel frame tubing, later for other parts such as hubs, bottom brackets and frame lugs. Mostly, this resulted from import substitution as American firms learned to make components that previously had to be imported. As a result, many firms were started, not to make bicycles, but to make parts or tools to sell to bicycle factories. Finally, factory owners in other industries, seeing the profits that could be made in bicycles, expanded into the bicycle business, mostly from the sewing machine, firearms and machine tool industries.

Between 1888 and 1895, most American wheelmakers used lowered production costs to increase profits rather than reduce prices, creating eye-popping profits. They could avoid dropping prices because of an increase in the tariff on imported bicycles brought about by the McKinley Act of 1891. However, the tariff also encouraged British investors to set up American bicycle factories rather than continue trying to export bicycles across the Atlantic. Also, the panic of 1893 hit the skilled metalworking trades especially hard—except for the bicycle factories. As a result, factory owners simply dropped what they were doing and rushed to convert their factories into bicycle plants, breaking the price dam wide open.

In 1890, Pope was still struggling to overcome his error in ignoring George Bidwell's 1888 recommendation to dive head-first into the low-wheeled safety. Production of the Veloce at the Columbia factory during the 1889–90 season was no more than ten thousand units. The capacity of the Hartford Cycle Company was even smaller. In 1891, its highest output was a mere 27 bicycles per day. George Pope started looking for a bigger factory and a new steam engine when he realized he couldn't make more than 2,500 wheels a season.[3] It may be surprising to learn that the capacity of a well stocked and staffed bicycle factory of the period was so low, but the Hartford Cycle Company was quite typical of most of the country's 22 wheelmakers. At a daily output of 25 bicycles the factory operated at its full potential only about 100 days per year. However, it frequently fell short of that target. The baking of enamel paint, for example, was a bottleneck, and an attempt to rush one lot melted the brazing of fenders and chainguards, an incident George Pope referred to as "the disaster in the ovens."[4]

The design of a season's wheel was locked in during the first week of October, when orders for purchased parts such as saddles and pedals were sent out.[5] The drop-forging of parts would slowly increase during October and November. Between Thanksgiving and Christmas, the factory shifted into high gear. Looking out over the factory floor one New Year's Eve, George remarked that "I have never seen anywhere near the quantity of parts.... The floor is fairly covered with them and the parts room is getting filled up."[6] Indeed, it was a lack of space that drove George to the new factory in 1891. George and

Harry initially wanted to expand into a building near the old plant, but decided to move when the large Board of Trade Building just down Capitol Avenue from the Columbia factory became available. The only major improvement needed was an enameling plant with new gas ovens that would not, hopefully, undo the day's work each evening.[7]

As the season grew nearer, the brazing of frames and assembly of complete bicycles started in early February, and by May both the Hartford and Pope factories were working at their "utmost capacity."[8] To George's shock, even with a new factory, production of the Hartfords was too slow: "Harry talks of a daily output of 40 machines. I hope it were so, but when the Pope Co. have tried in vain to average 100 daily, it hardly seems possible that we can strike a 40 gait."[9] George's admission is startling in two respects. First, it suggests that even at the new site, production was still only about 3,000 units a year. This is confirmed in a letter George sent to David Post in February 1892 indicating that the 600 orders received so far that year accounted for a fifth of the company's annual capacity. Second, George's letter states that capacity of the mighty Columbia factory was only 100 bicycles per day. Based on this letter and Pope's known 1890–91 production of 12,957 units, the Columbia factory probably made about 16,500 bicycles in 1892, for a combined production at both the Pope and Hartford works of about 19,500.

These numbers are far smaller than typically believed, even in those days. In 1898 Walter Wardrop, Secretary of the National Cycle Board of Trade, claimed that U.S. production in 1892 was 150,000 bicycles.[10] Either the Popes were dominating the American bicycle industry with thirteen percent of its total output, or the Wardrop numbers were wildly exaggerated. The latter is almost certainly the case. My estimate is that 60,700 bicycles were built in the United States that year. Also, some of this disparity came from imports. As Bidwell's story illustrates, it was not difficult for a successful agent to become a successful importer. That soon changed.

About the time Bidwell was getting rich on Pope's blunder, then-congressman William McKinley was preparing the gift of a lifetime for the cycle makers, or so they thought. When the first imported bicycles landed on the dock at Boston, Charles Pratt convinced the customs inspectors to levy the same tariff on them as a wagon or carriage, 35 percent. In 1882, the Colonel tried to talk the congressional tariff commission into lowering the tariff for bicycle steel from 45 percent to the same 35 percent.[11] Hoping to throw some sand in Pope's juggernaut, cycle importers responded with a petition to instead reduce the tariff on imported bicycles. The commission, not wanting to get caught in the middle, dropped the issue.

But by 1890 attitudes in Congress were changing. While European nations were giving each other low reciprocal tariff schedules, protectionists argued that America had its open western frontier. Given this difference, explained McKinley, the primary function of tariffs was not to raise revenue, but to erect a barrier to foreign goods that might discourage domestic development. Consequently, in 1891 Congress passed the McKinley Act, setting the most stringent tariff schedule in American history. The duties for bicycles, bicycle parts and raw material were equalized at 45 percent.

The effect was immediate and drastic. By 1894, European bicycle makers were effectively blocked out of the American market. Exports from England to the U.S. dropped by three-quarters from 1892 to 1894. In 1890, bicycles worth over $324,000 were shipped to America just from one city, Birmingham. In 1896, the American counsel in the city reported that he had received no requests for export licenses. Not one.[12]

However, the new tariff would prove to have a boomerang effect. An English bicycle manufacturer estimated that with freight, dock fees and insurance, his effective import duty was now about 60 percent. "A factory in America to save this duty is [now] an imperative," he observed, and he admitted to a reporter he had come to the States to locate one. "The factory we propose to build here will be along the same lines as the ones we have in Coventry," he explained. Henry Sweeting of the Sweeting Cycle Company also noted the trend, explaining that America "has only about 22 bicycle factories, all told, whereas England ... has over 580 ... there is an immense field in this county." England, with huge resources of liquid capital to invest, was looking to the colonies as a potentially lucrative place to invest in bicycle factories.[13]

Just as the bicycle industry started to look ripe to large-scale British investors, the panic of 1893 struck. After Wall Street's "Black Friday," 5 May 1893, the economy rapidly slid downhill, and by August, the *Commercial and Financial Chronicle* reported that: "Never before has there been such a sudden and striking cessation of industrial activity. Nor is any section of the country exempt from the paralysis."[14] *Bradstreet's* estimated that eight to nine hundred thousand Americans were thrown out of work by the Depression. The panic bottomed out just as wheelmakers were gearing up for their 1894 season production runs.[15] For any bicycle maker, the nightmare scenario was to commit to a specific production run in October, only to discover in March that there was no market. The second-worst situation was to under-guess that spring's demand and already be sold out by the time the first cycle was crated up for shipment in January.

Bicycle makers were not in the mass-production business. They were batch-makers, and the name of the game was to match October's estimate to April's market. Guess short, and you did okay, but your sales network would take a beating as your agents and customers, frustrated by their inability to get the wheels you tempted them with all winter, went elsewhere. Guess right on the money and you could become a very rich man. Guess long, and you slid toward bankruptcy with a warehouse full of obsolete wheels. It was a game of nerves. The previous season, George Pope told David Post in January that with just the early orders, "We can sell our output in the East this year," even though the factory hadn't yet crated up a single bicycle.[16]

The financial turmoil took its toll. At the end of January, 1893 orders for Hartford Cycles stood at 334, down from the 417 sold at the same time the year before.[17] The Hartford Cycle Company salesmen were encountering agents who wanted bigger discounts and more competitive prices. Unlike the past, when the company could choose between two or three applicants in each town who wanted the Hartford Cycle agency, dealers were now the ones shopping for the best bargain. "Marion is having a bad time," George Pope wrote David Post. "Both he and Fletcher are meeting a good deal of argument on the discount question from our agents." George was, quite frankly, frustrated: "Either some of the other manufacturers are satisfied with less profit than we are, or else they do not fully understand figuring the contingent expense and will find themselves out of the race in the course of a year or two."[18]

Even some of their oldest and most reliable agents were getting increasingly aggressive. Hughes, who trailed only the Pope company's own branch houses in the number of bicycles sold, grew so exasperated that he blew up at George and threatened to have it out with the Colonel himself:

> Hughes does not look at the matter of discounts in the right way ... we probably put more money into experimenting departments and into care of inspection than any other concern in the business. He does not give us credit for this, he admits that our goods are no better made than those of concerns that are giving 40 or 50 percent discounts. I certainly hope he will not go to the Colonel about discounts, for I know that he feels that he has made considerable concession already.[19]

Although the Colonel refused to break the price line, he knew better than to make a flat refusal. Hughes' Hartford Cycle orders started to specify no saddles or pedals, which he ordered separately from the main Columbia factory at special off-the-book prices.[20] Even Arthur Pattison at the Columbia factory was worried. "We know that we have got to make some exceptions to hold onto our best agents, but we must hold them," he warned.[21]

The newly formed Cycle Trades Association had organized its own trade show in January. It was no secret that the Colonel had a bug about cycle shows, and the Association hoped that by creating one big show, closed to the public, it could make the others go away. "Mr. Day and the Colonel both go out on Saturday night," said George Pope on the eve of the show. "They intend to have a number of salesmen in attendance, which I have recommended very strongly, for it will not do to have the dealers drifting about the shows, without us having plenty of force to keep track of them and see they do not stray away."[22] That's why Pope loathed the shows; he couldn't control them the way he could his stage-managed press extravaganzas, and during the shows his dealers, and probably his salesmen as well, got picked off by upstart rivals.

By the following summer, bicycle sales recovered and the industry shrugged off the panic. The rest of the economy was not so lucky. In fact, things were bad. One machine tool maker told *American Machinist* that business was "extremely dull, and the only thing keeping him going was orders from bicycle factories."[23] One cyclemaker recalled that "with general stagnation in practically every other manufacturing line, the bicycle industry had entered a state of unusual activity and prosperity." He found it "truly a peculiar situation ... abnormal both as to general business depression on one hand and personal poverty on one hand and particular prosperity and individual extravagance on the other." Factories that had been engaged in other lines of work or were closed down entirely quickly converted "for a part of the apparently enormous profits being realized."[24] Investors rushed in from everywhere: British cycle capitalists looking for a way around the McKinley tariff and home-grown factory owners wanting to become bicycle billionaires like Pope, Overman and Spalding. The *New York Herald* claimed that the average one hundred dollar bicycle actually cost $30.31 to make. "The bicycle has been discerned to be the most marketable commodity of the hour," reported one business editor.[25] The boom was on.

## The Pope Tube Company

With the demand for wheels rapidly swelling, manufacturers in both Europe and America began to compete for the limited supply of raw- and semi-finished products necessary to make them. The first problems began to crop up in high-strength frame tubing. The old Ordinary used what were essentially pipes, but the safety bicycle required the same type of extraordinarily thin, light and strong tubes as gun barrels. But a shotgun needed only three feet of tubing, so gun makers could afford to machine down billets — pierced, relatively thick cylinders of steel. Billets of high-strength steel (often called "high-speed" or "tool" steel, because it was developed for the cutting blades of lathes and milling machines) were available from Swedish sources, but a bicycle used up to 27 feet of tube, making it far too expensive to simply lathe down billets.[26]

In 1882, a British firm, the Credenda Cold Drawn Seamless Steel Company, perfected a process for making cold-drawn steel tubes by drawing billets through a matched die and mandrel. Typically, 15 or 16 draws were needed to turn a three-foot billet, two inches in diameter and one-eighth inch thick, into a 12- to 16-foot-long tube of 1.125-inch-diameter tube with walls only .028 inch thick. After each draw, the tube had to be baked, or annealed, for several hours in a special oven. The total time from billet to finished tube usually ran about three weeks. A German firm, the Mannesmann Company, had developed an alternative process in 1885 by winding sequential layers of thin steels bars in a spiral shape, then rolling to seal the seams. A British firm began producing Mannesmann tubing under license in 1887. However, Mannesmann tubes were even more expensive to make than drawn tubes and were highly prized by gunsmiths.[27]

The Pope company began experimenting with Credenda's cold-drawn seamless tubing in 1882 when it built a special high-wheeler for Thomas Stevens to use on his famous around-the-world tour.[28] As the popularity of the safety bicycle grew, seamless tubing became a scarce and valuable commodity on both sides of the Atlantic. David Post warned George Pope that Hartford Cycle agents in Washington, D.C., were pleading for samples of their new 1891 ladies' safety bicycle to show to prospective customers. In mid–January George replied that "we note what you say about sending a Ladies Safety to Washington, we only hope that we shall be able to do so, but are awful disappointed that none of our $9/16$ inch tubing is yet on the way." [29]

Two weeks later, the situation was growing worse, with George promising that they "will do all we can to get a Ladies Safety set up for you to use in Washington. If we do not get the $9/16$ inch tubing, we will see if we can turn down [i.e., lathe] some tubing of heavier gage to $9/16$ to set up one machine for you."[30] That solution failed, and with the passing of another week, George grew desperate. "Have nothing new to report," he wrote. "Am awful shaky about getting the Ladies Safety ready at the time we promised, but at any rate are doing all we possibly can. The *Umbria* [a cargo ship] was due in New York Saturday, but at 3 o'clock this afternoon the Pope Co. had received no invoice."[31]

The problem wasn't confined to America. Sir Frank Bowden, owner of the Raleigh Cycle Company, complained to his production director, R. M. Woodhead, that inadequate output was resulting in deteriorating relations with agents and customers, particularly the John Griffiths company, the Dunlop-owned chain of cycle agencies who operated a major depot in New York City that sold several major English brands. Trying valiantly to maintain the edge the English makers had built up from the belated response of U.S. firms to the Rover safety, John Griffiths was losing market share back to the Americans for lack of bicycles to sell. Woodhead responded that he couldn't build bicycles without tubes, and Raleigh's supplier, the Weldless Steel Tube Company, already owed them over a thousand feet of tube.[32] Once the large American firms realized the extent of the emerging bicycle boom, they rushed to Credenda and the Weldless Steel Tube Company with large, long-term contracts. With less access to ready cash, Raleigh faced a "tube famine." The firm cleared less than $18,000 from their American operations in 1892 and withdrew from the U.S. market the following August for over thirty years. Woodhead was fired in

October 1894, a victim of bad luck, inadequate capital and Bowden's tendency to personalize failure in his subordinates.[33]

Until the tube famine, American bicycle makers had little incentive to develop a domestic industry. The British makers imported Swedish steel billets as their raw material, and any prospective American tube maker would have to do the same. The tariff on billets and finished tubes was the same 45 percent, and transatlantic shipping costs for finished tubes were small relative to value. Thus, the price advantage accruing to a domestic drawing mill would be small, and if demand suddenly collapsed the potential investment loss on unused drawing benches and annealing ovens would be large. But when demand outran supply during the famine, the potential profits began to justify the risk.

Henry A. Lozier decided to take that risk. Before the safety came along, Lozier worked for the New Home Sewing Machine Company as their Ohio general agent. In 1887, he started selling bicycles on the side, and two years later joined forces with another sewing machine dealer, Joseph L. Yost, to form the Lozier & Yost Manufacturing Company to market the "Little Giant" line of juvenile bicycles. Noting the increased trade in seamless tubing, Lozier and Yost traveled to England in the summer of 1890 to learn more. Yost, disguised as an itinerant laborer, obtained work in a tube mill to gain technical information about the business.[34] The following January, they incorporated the Lozier-Yost Seamless Tube Company. It was quickly renamed the Shelby Steel Tube Company when the town of Shelby, Ohio, induced them to build a mill at the behest of Colonel D. L. Cockley, a local merchant who became the third major underwriter in the new venture. The first tubes were drawn in July 1891. The new seamless tube industry was inextricably linked to the bicycle industry. In late 1891, Lozier bought out Yost's half of the Little Giant business and, using his Shelby profits, organized the Lozier Manufacturing Company of Toledo to manufacture the "Cleveland" bicycle and a second firm, H. A. Lozier and Company, to market it. Within two years Lozier was one of the "big four" major American bicycle makers, alongside Pope, Overman, and Gormully & Jeffery.[35]

Albert Pope was one of the initial stockholders in the Shelby Steel Tube Company, but from the start was interested in the construction of his own plant. In the summer of 1891 Pope traveled to England and the trade press speculated that the purpose of his visit was to meet with either Credenda or the Weldless Steel Tube Co. to seek a license to build his own tubing. In June 1892, George Day announced that the Pope Manufacturing Company had purchased the farm of George Bartholomew, a former Weed company director, on the southwest edge of Hartford, and several adjoining parcels, 110 acres altogether. On eight acres at the corner of Park and Laurel the firm immediately started construction of a new steel tube plant. Other parcels of land on the banks of the Park River were reserved for future factory buildings. However, most of the land was platted for the construction of some 416 homes. This would be the first phase of a massive residential development that would ultimately contain some 1,200 homes, but groundbreaking would have to wait until after the pressing need for additional factory capacity was satisfied.[36]

The tube plant was finished in early September. However, Colonel Pope hedged his bet twice over. First, rather than build a broad, one-story mill, the new factory at 1 Laurel Street was designed along the lines of a standard, two-story general factory. The entire second story couldn't be used for tube making due to the weight and strain of the drawbenches. The tube factory was an experiment; the building was designed so if things didn't work out it could be used for something else or sold.[37] Second, Pope retained his ownership in the Shelby Tube Steel Company, and internal memos indicate that he was taking an active role in the management of the firm as late as mid–1893, almost a year after Laurel Street was completed. Moreover, he purchased a large block of stock from Captain Cockley, and was rumored to be negotiating with another director, W. E. Miller, to purchase his interest. In late 1894, two of Shelby's eight director seats were filled by Albert Pope and George Day.[38]

Nevertheless, Pope's men were optimistic: although never a separate organization, everyone in the firm kept referring to the new plant as "The Pope Tube Company." The project was responsible for the recruitment of two of the most important men in the firm's history. The first was Harold Hayden Eames. Hayden Eames was born on 19 December 1863 in Shanghai, China, the son of the American counsel in that city. He returned with his family to America in 1870 and eight years later, at age 15, entered the U.S. Naval Academy.[39] Graduating near the top of his class, Eames became an ordinance expert, and after serving at sea was assigned as an inspector at the Pratt & Whitney and Colt factories in Hartford, and the United States Projectile Company in nearby Lynn, Massachusetts. At American Projectile, he made the acquaintance of the company's young, MIT-trained superintendent, Hiram Percy Maxim, the son of Hiram S. Maxim, of Maxim machine gun fame (or infamy).

It is not clear how Eames came to the attention of George Day and the Popes. The most likely connection was Frank Belden, Weed's former corporate secretary. A year or so after Pope bought the Weed company, Belden went to work at Colt's, where he helped get bicycle production started for George Bidwell. In late 1892 or early 1893, Eames resigned from the navy and joined the Pope company to supervise the installation of the tube plant, then manage its operation. Maxim painted this description of the man who would later become his boss and brother-in-law:

> Hayden Eames was an intensely interesting character.... He was a great reader, remembered everything he read, and had the most amazing vocabulary ever bestowed upon mortal man. His emotions were just barely under control all the time. To hold himself in leash required a superhuman effort day and night. He was profane to a degree, but intellectually and poetically so; never was he vulgar. When he lost his grip on his emotions he would launch forth into an epic of profanity that was nothing short of inspiring. Many times have I listened to one of his profane perorations with the same enraptured feeling which I enjoy when listening to great music.[40]

Almost from the first day he walked in the factory, Hayden Eames became George Day's invaluable right-hand man, and would remain so for most of the rest of Day's life.

While a capable engineer and a superlative manager, Eames was no scientist and both he and Day agreed that devising new methods of drawing frame tubing would be of little advantage without knowing more about the material they were working with. Consequently, in 1893, Day hired Henry Souther to manage a new "Department of Tests." Souther was the second vital Pope employee to come on board during the early 1890s.

He was 27 at the time. Born in Boston, he graduated from MIT in 1887 with a degree in chemical engineering. During his summer breaks he worked at the Pennsylvania Steel Company, and after graduating traveled to Germany to further study steelmaking. He may have been the unnamed young man that George Pope mentioned in a letter hiring temporarily in September 1891 to assist Harry Pope with the move into the new factory.[41] In 1893 Day recruited him for the main factory. Souther, in turn, hired another young engineer, Hermann F. Cuntz, as a chemist. Cuntz recalls being put to work on the development of cushion and pneumatic tires. He stayed only about a year, until the fall of 1894, when he left for the New York area (either to finish his engineering degree at Stevens Institute or attend law school, it is unclear) but returned in early 1896 to participate in the company's first motor-car research.[42]

While Eames worked on methods to manufacture seamless tubing, Souther set to work studying the properties of the steel used in the tubing the company imported from England and in the semi-finished billets available from steel suppliers around the world. Soon after his hiring at Pope's, the company built a free-standing testing laboratory on the grassy lawn in front of the Columbia factory.[43] Souther was provided with an engineer's fantasyland of machines to shake, slam, stretch, twist and pull bicycles and their components to an untimely end.

He was particularly proud of his Emery Hydraulic Testing Machine, which could measure the force required to break a bicycle frame apart (sixty-five to seventy-nine thousand pounds, depending on the tubing and frame configuration used), or could find the breaking point of a single human hair (fifteen ounces). The Emory testing machine had a unique and somewhat checkered history.[44] Around 1870, architects and engineers began hectoring the big steel companies to test the properties of Bessemer process steel to see if it was adequate for use in fireproof buildings. The firms were uninterested; they could sell all the Bessemer steel they could churn out for railroad track rail. The architects turned to Congress, who authorized the money to conduct a series of tests overseen by a civilian test board at the Army arsenal in Watertown, Massachusetts. The test board contracted with the brothers Albert and Charles Emery to custom-build a testing machine. It was a marvelously crafted device that could test materials up to 30 feet long with failure strengths ranging between four ounces and 755,000 pounds. Unfortunately, it was also a house-sized monster that required four years to build and depleted the entire authorization before any actual work could be done. Watertown Arsenal, however, appreciated the gift, even if it was rather unwieldy and a bit of overkill given their needs. The Pope machine was a miniature copy of the Watertown Emery built by the William Sellers Company of Philadelphia. Limited to a ten-foot draw and a 100,000-pound pull, it still took up the space of a small living room. The Watertown and Pope machines were apparently the only Emery machines ever built, and the Pope machine continued to be used by various owners until sometime in the 1960s.[45]

Souther's work revealed that the high-strength "fifty carbon" tool steel used in most English frame tubing, which was supposed to have a one-half percent carbon content, actually had widely varying carbon compositions averaging around .35 percent. The lower carbon content reduced the steel's strength to about ninety percent of its stated value.[46] To eliminate such variability, Pope started to order its billets from a single Swedish source and accepted shipments only after a sample had been sent to Souther's laboratory for testing.

In 1894, the Colonel committed himself to the construction of a big permanent tube plant on Hamilton Street to replace the experimental works at 1 Laurel Street. Originally, the plant was to be a cooperative venture with the German Mannesmann Tube Company. Pope still held his interest in the Shelby Tube Steel Company, along with H. A. Lozier and a third man, William E. Miller. There had been a fourth big block of stock, owned by the president and works manager, Captain Cockley, but Cockley, disgusted with infighting between Miller and Lozier, wanted to sell. Pope bought him out and put

George Day on the board to play referee between Lozier and Miller. Cockley stayed on as superintendent, and Pope made Miller an open offer for his share of the company.[47]

In early 1894, Lozier brought to America a young British engineer named Ralph Stiefel, who worked for the English Mannesmann company. Stiefel told Lozier that he had an idea for a rotary billet piercer that would create a new, third way to make cold-

The Hamilton Street Tube factory was built in 1896. At the time, it was one of the most innovative industrial buildings in the country. Where most factories were still patterned after the blocky, vertical mill structures of the previous century, this horizontal, single-story plant featured a very early saw-tooth glass skylight roof, built by the Berlin Iron Bridge Company of East Berlin, Connecticut. Its unique iron roof trusses allowed interior spans of almost fifty feet between pillars. The building is still in active use today as a factory.

drawn steel tubes. The Kellogg process used at both Shelby and Pope required Swedish billets, imported with a 45 percent tariff, although the Mannesmann process, which rolled overlapping spiral-wound bars, could use American-made steel.

Cycle makers were hoping that a revision to the McKinley Act tariff rates scheduled for 1897 would reduce rates for semi-finished specialty steels. However, the Dingley Act tariff provisions first introduced in Congressional committee in 1894 kept both the 45 percent *ad valorum* tariff duty and the existing McKinley Act requirement that tariffs must be based on the greater of either the market or invoice price of the imported shipment.[48] If the market price of bicycle tubing dropped because of a slump in bicycle demand, tube makers still had to pay the invoice price on the paperwork that came over in the ship with the billets. On the other hand, if scarcity drove up prices, the customs agents ignored the paperwork and assessed the tariff based on the new, higher market price, even though that's not what the recipient actually paid for the billets. The only way out was to use American steel as the raw product for tubes. The Mannesmann system had this capability, but the process itself was monopolized by the German company. Stiefel's process promised to replace billets with solid rods as the raw material, and high-carbon steel was available in this format from a few American mills.

While Shelby worked on developing the Stiefel process, Pope used the threat of a new process to pressure the Mannesmann Company to work with him on establishing the new plant on Hamilton Street. The German process had the additional advantage that it could be used to make steam boiler tubes in sizes up to a foot in diameter, so Hamilton Street's products would have a far wider audience than just wheelmakers.[49]

The Germans agreed to set up a new American firm, the Pope-Mannesmann Company, with a capitalization of $750,000. Pope would provide the land, factory and his coterie of experts. The Germans would provide the equipment and money. Meanwhile, Miller had agreed to sell his Shelby stock to Pope. The Colonel looked to be the czar of steel tube, with ownership in two firms that controlled two different ways of making steel tubes, with the third method, Stefel's rotary-piercing mill, under development. If Stiefel's process worked, Pope would be the only man in the bicycle game to have a hand in both ways of making tubes that used tariff-free, American steel. The sale of stock in the new Pope-Mannesmann company was scheduled for noon, 21 September 1894 at the Hartford Board of Trade.

The day before the big sale, William Miller announced that he had purchased the Ellwood Shafting and Tube Company of Ellwood, Pennsylvania, was changing its name to the Ellwood Weldless Tube Company, and had appointed a young Englishman, Ralph Stiefel, as its works manager. Construction would commence the next month on a new type of tube mill that used American steel. Miller had taken Pope's money, his expert, and his as-yet-unpatented rotary-piercing process and started his own new company. The Mannesmann stock sale was postponed, and a month later the German company backed out of the project.[50] If he wanted an American-steel tube mill, the Colonel would have to go it alone. He did.

Souther discovered that a five-percent nickel steel alloy manufactured by the Bethlehem Steel Company promised to make excellent frame tubing. The problem was that Bethlehem had developed it for armoring warships and it only came in plate form. Eames, adapting a method first used by the U.S. Projectile Company in Brooklyn, developed a 13-step process for cupping the plates into the shape of a bowl, then a beer mug, and finally into a four-foot-long billet suitable for the tube-drawing benches.[51] Tests confirmed that after drawing, the new "Pioneer" nickel steel tubing was significantly stiffer and about 25 percent stronger than current carbon-steel tubing. However, its real advantage was that it was more resistant to denting than carbon steel, so it could be made thinner and lighter.

To make it, Pope built the most advanced seamless steel tube factory in the world.[52] Unlike Laurel Street, it was a single-story, purpose-built facility. The main floor measured about 350 by 160 feet, with a separate management wing and freestanding powerplant. The boiler drove twin hydraulic systems that used high-pressure water to drive the drawing benches. These replaced the inefficient and dangerous chain-draw benches in use elsewhere. On the old benches, the tubes were pulled through the die and mandrel by gripping tongs attached to chains. If the tongs slipped or the tube broke, the chains would whip back, sometimes disastrously. In the Hamilton Street plant, the tongs were attached to the head of a hydraulic piston running in a long cylinder. The pressure was

The large horizontal cylinders are water-driven hydraulic pistons used to power the drawing benches that, over the course of almost twenty passes, stretched a four-foot tubular steel billet into a twenty-two foot length of one-inch bicycle tubing. In the foreground is a pit that provided access to the tunnel through which the pressurized water was piped from a separate powerhouse a hundred feet beyond the far factory wall ("An American Bicycle Manufactory," *Engineering* [UK], July 16, 1897).

regulated on both the positive and negative pressure side of the piston. If a tube slipped out of its grip, the piston could only fly a few inches before rebounding against the water on the negative pressure side of the pull. The system also cut the power losses normally attributable to belts and shafting in half.

The old Laurel Street factory did not go idle. The Hartford Typewriter Company, another one of the Colonel's pet projects, was located on the second floor.[53] Patented in 1886, the "World" typewriter didn't use a keyboard; instead, the operator turned a wheel to line up the desired letter under a window and pressed a striking key to type. It was apparently an attempt to create a low-priced typewriter that would not infringe on the Sholes-Remington keyboard typewriter. It came in two versions that cost $10 and $15, compared to $125 for an office-quality Remington No. 6. The World was manufactured until about 1900 and enough were made that they are, a century later, not terribly scarce.

The first floor was given over to a mysterious project that seemed to take up more

This machine, one of only two in the country, was a smaller version of one developed for the Watertown Arsenal under a Congressional grant to develop fire-resistant building beams. Built by the William Sellers Company, of Philadelphia, it was located in a small building called the "Department of Tests" built for it in 1895 on the front lawn of the Columbia factory. It could either pull or push with a steadily increasing force or in cycles of varying stress. Although it was moved to another site in Hartford about 1910 when its building was razed to make way for a plant expansion, it is believed to have been in use until the late 1960s or early 1970s. (Source: *Columbia Bicycle Catalog for 1897*).

and more of the attention of the front office. The tube works, with its groaning draw benches, was one thing, but this sounded like the Colonel was experimenting with some sort of rapid-fire rifle. The machinists on the second floor would be going about their business assembling typewriters when they would be assaulted by the most unearthly noise, like the gunfire of an entire light artillery battalion. It would last for a few seconds, then stop. It was rumored that the experimenter, Hiram Maxim, had came over from the American Projectile company, and that his father had gotten rich in England inventing something called a "machine gun." A year or so after the tube works moved out, George Day offered Hartford Typewriter the chance to move to a corner of the main factory and John Fairfield, the company's superintendent (and George's son), gratefully accepted. One evening, as he was moving his office belongings, John saw Hiram Maxim and an assistant ride off down Park Street in a noisy little cart that had no horse, and by the looks of it, no cranks or pedals for the riders—it appeared to be powered by some sort of motor.

## *The Hartford Rubber Works*

The invention and early development of the pneumatic tire is a somewhat complex story that, due to the interaction of law and technology, varies somewhat depending upon which side of the Atlantic you are concerned with. John B. Dunlop, an Edinburgh veterinarian, invented an inflatable air tire in 1888 and, with the aid of a Dublin businessman, Harvey du Cros, formed a syndicate to exploit it in late 1889. Dunlop's original patent contained some technical shortcomings, so du Cros purchased two additional inventions, one by Welch in 1890 for an improved method of attaching the tire to the rim by means of two wire beads in each edge, and a valve patented by Woods a year later. Together, these gave form to the Dunlop "two-part" or "wired-on" tire with an outer casing and a separate inner tube.[54]

Dunlop's patent was soon invalidated because of a similar 1845 patent by Robert Thompson. However, because of du Cros's timely acquisition of the supporting patents, the Dunlop Tire Company still held a monopoly on the two-part tire/tube combination. In 1892, two Americans, Brown and Stillman, filed a U.S. patent on the wired-on tire concept. It was quickly purchased by the du Cros-Dunlop organization, who decided against licensing production out to any American firm. Given transportation and tariff costs, the Dunlop configuration was, for all intents and purposes, unavailable in the United States unless included as original equipment on an imported English bicycle.

In 1891 and 1892, the irrepressible Thomas B. Jeffery, the inventive half of Gormully & Jeffery, developed an alternative to the Dunlop. Unlike its U-shaped outer casing, the casing of the "G&J" tire went all the way around the inner tube, although it was split along its inner circumference. Two "wings," or clinchers, slipped into slots in the rim, holding the inner slot closed and affixing the tire to the rim. Because the sides of the Dunlop rim were required to laterally resist the outward air pressure of the inflated tire, the rim had to be made of steel and rolled to an exact shape. While the G&J also required its own matching rim, it was of a simpler shape and could be made of steel or wood. Jeffery patented the new idea, and contracted with the B. F. Goodrich tire company to produce it.

A year earlier, A. H. Overman had introduced his improved "Arch" cushion tire, a U-shaped affair that also fit into matching channels on the rim. Unlike the pneumatic tire, it didn't need inflating, but like the Dunlop and the G&J, it didn't have to be glued onto the rim. Both the solid tire of the Ordinary and most of the first-generation cushion tires for safeties required glue, which sometimes cracked or dried out, loosening the tire.[55]

Pope's tire supplier during the high-wheeler days was a local firm, the Hartford Rubber Works, founded in 1881 by John W. Gray to make shoes, belts, and other molded rubber products. As tire technology grew more complex with the introduction of cushion tires, the firm's inexperience started to show, as George Pope complained: "Gray, I know, has been badly equipped to get out the cushion [tires], in fact he had to learn how ... his experimenting put him behind on all his orders and he probably is shoving out a few at a time...."[56]

By early 1892, Pope was in a bind. As had been the case with the safety bicycle, the firm was caught flat-footed without a workable product to offer. Harry Goodman, an engineer, recalled just how far they were behind in 1890. The company couldn't buy a set of English pneumatics as an aftermarket item, so they simply imported a Dunlop-shod bicycle. When it was uncrated someone left it standing against a steam pipe. "As a result, the heat did its work and the front tire exploded with a bang, and we had but one tire remaining, and that one was deflated." They didn't know how to inflate a bicycle tire, so Goodman recounted that "we carried the bicycle to an adjoining factory, where there was a compressed air pump. We had no idea how much pressure the tire would stand, and the powerful pump inflated it so quickly that the tremendous pressure blew the tire to pieces before we knew where we were at."[57]

The Colonel tried to talk Overman into selling him his Arch cushion tire, but to nobody's surprise Overman turned him down flat. Goodrich's production of G&Js was fully committed to Gormully & Jeffery. In desperation, Pope turned to a tire developed in England by I. W. Boothroyd and patented in America with a few small improvements by P. W. Tillinghast. Boothroyd's "hose pipe" was virtually identical to today's racing tubular tire. The outer casing completely surrounded the inner tube and was sewn together on the inner, or rim, side. It had to be glued to the rim to stay in place. If punctured, the only permanent way of fixing it was to remove it from the rim, unsew the casing, locate the puncture on the inner tube and patch it with a hot iron, then replace and resew the casing, hopefully without repuncturing the inner tube in the process.[58] From a technical standpoint, the hose pipe was awful, "a glorified piece of endless garden hose with a valve in it," rued Frank Schwinn in 1942.[59]

This was a lesson the men at Pope's slowly and painfully discovered during 1892. "Rice [Charles Rice, one of the firms "inventors," or engineers] has made a very ingenious addition to the plug for repairing, which distends it on the inside of the tire, making it impossible for it to work outwards," wrote George Pope in January.[60] Plugging the tire with a small brass button was an idea born of desperation that George Day thought up sometime in late 1891. "Personally, I think that the design that Mr. Rice has gotten up ... is preferable to this and much cheaper," said Colonel George.[61] However, the early trials of Rice's plug, which required its own little self-contained toolkit, were a failure when left in the hands of the average cyclist. "The use of plugs has been abandoned," the firm admitted to *The American Athlete* in early 1893.[62] Its replacement was an injectable solvent designed to partially dissolve the rubber on the inside of the tire, essentially melting it over the puncture. That didn't work either, except for the smallest and cleanest of puncture wounds. The final solution was to make the whole thing the agents' problem. In case of puncture, Columbia and Hartford agents were told that they would have to repair the tire free of charge. If it burst, the agent must supply a new one out of stock, but the factory would replace it for free.[63] Nobody, of course, consulted the agents first.

The problem never really went away. By 1894 the best the factory could offer was a method using an injection of gum and solution. The owner, with a syringe, injected a mysterious "repairing solution" into the tire, let it stand for a few moments, then injected pre-liquefied gum rubber into the hole and hoped for the best. For field repairs, the factory recommended injecting only the repairing solution followed by a liberal wrapping of the outside of the tire with a special repair tape that was removed after the ride for the permanent repair.[64] In reality, even the two-injection method was a field-fix to get the Columbia rider to the nearest agent who provided a permanent repair or replaced the tire, an obligation that begin to chafe the locals when the Colonel cut prices and profits after the boom ebbed. Incredibly, the Tillinghast tire would ultimately outlive the Pope Manufacturing Company and became the standard American bicycle tire until the 1930s. U.S. Rubber held a monopoly on bicycle tire production after World War I, and it deemed the hose pipe the most profitable, to the rage and exasperation of Frank Schwinn. "The tires more than all the rest had held down the popularity of the bicycle" throughout the first twenty-five years of the century, he recalled.[65]

In early 1892, David Post began to report rumors that the Pope company had secretly acquired the Hartford Rubber Works. George assured him this was not the case: "All it amounts to is that [Pope's] are a very large customer and naturally Gray will give them all the advantage possible to hold their trade." He explained that the Colonel had gone so far as to ask competitors to work up sample products, "but in no case have they held up to Gray's goods."[66]

However, in June 1892, John Gray died, and the Colonel snapped up the Rubber Works from his heirs. Charles Rice, who had done most of the development work on the pneumatic tire, moved over from the Columbia factory to take over as superintendent. However, this was a temporary arrangement, as the following year another young man, Lewis D. Parker, was brought in as treasurer and works manager.[67]

A year later, both Overman and the Western Wheel Works began offering pneumatics. Overman featured its own proprietary brand and Western offered the Morgan & Wright tire. Both required gluing onto the rim, but once detached the inner tube could be pulled out of the casing either through a slit (Morgan & Wright) or a flap (Overman). The Overman bicycle itself featured a hinged flap built into the rim, so in the event of a flat, the lucky Victor owner merely had to open the rim's "manhole," pull up the casing flap, pull out the inner tube and patch it.[68]

Morgan & Wright was an independent maker whose product was available to any manufacturer. In 1895 Dunlop began to offer their two-piece tire to any American cycle maker and Gormully & Jeffery gave B. F. Goodrich permission to sell the G&J on the open market at about the same time. There were now three different rim standards: the "standard" glued-on rim that could accept the Tillinghast, Overman (sans manhole) or Morgan & Wright; the G&J clincher rim and tire, and the Dunlop wire-bead rim and tire, which became known as the "continental" setup. By 1900, the standard rim, with a Morgan & Wright tire, was the most popular combination, followed by the pricey (but vastly superior) continental configuration.[69]

The pneumatic tire greatly simplified the job of the cycle manufacturers. The relatively wide, low-pressure pneumatic tire could absorb much of the roadway vibration that formerly required spring forks or other shock-absorbing systems. In 1893 Overman introduced a lightweight "Victor Racer" that omitted the firm's famous spring fork; by 1894 the legendary innovation was gone entirely. The 1892 Columbia Century and Century Road Racer came with pneumatics and omitted their jointed sprung fork. Only the Columbia Light Roadster touring bicycle came with cushion tires and a sprung fork; after 1893 it was gone as well.

## *We Must Get Off Ten Pounds*

The same rapidly rising production volume that required the Colonel and his men to do whatever was needed to guarantee reliable supplies of raw and semi-finished material — even building their own factories and inventing their own tires and steel tube — also led them to re-think some of their most cherished and heavily guarded production processes. The use of drop-forged frame lugs was one example. From the first article describing bicycle production at Weed, the company boasted of its skill in the armory practice of die forging and precision machining. On the old Ordinary, the head was undoubtedly the single most important component. One forging connected the front forks, the handlebar, steering shaft and backbone. In 1881, Henry Russell, a Weed toolmaker, patented an ingenious set of stamping dies that enabled the firm to create an entire head out of a single solid piece of steel while requiring only seven press operations and three reheatings.[70]

However, as industrial journalist and editor Fred H. Colvin recalled, "The head and crank hangars of the safety were forgings that had to be machined to sheet-metal thinness — which meant cutting away about 80 percent of the original metal."[71] Machining away that much material defeated the whole purpose of armory practice. The obvious answer to the problem of making sheet-metal-thin parts was to use sheet metal. Starting with rolls of sheet steel, stamping presses could cut, bend and form the material. *American Machinist* author Horace Arnold claimed that Chicago's Western Wheel Works was using stamped crank hangars, frame lugs, fork heads and other parts as early as 1890; however Western's 1892 catalog boasted that its bicycles were "made of imported seamless steel tubing and steel drop forgings," and it is more likely that Western began using these components as they became available from outside suppliers in 1894 or 1895.[72] In Birmingham, Willard Mattox reported that English makers had actually tried to develop sheet steel stampings *before* the Americans, but had not been successful. "American makers did what English makers gave up in disgust — they learned how to make pressed work out of cold rolled steel, and succeeded in turning out an article just as strong and just as light," he wrote.[73]

In doing so, the Americans also learned to use a relatively new technology, electric resistance welders (arc welders) to close the seams of the stamped parts, an application for which it was particularly well suited. The Pope company had bought a Thompson Electric Welder in the late 1880s to weld the seams of metal wheel rims. It experimented with welding frame tubes together, with poor results. Like Pope, Western continued to braze its frames. Only the frame joining lugs were welded; the frames themselves continued to be assembled through brazing.[74] Techniques varied from firm to firm; Gormully

& Jeffery, for example, swaged one end the top and down tubes of the main frame triangle into cylindrical sleeves that acted like frame lugs. The head tube was inserted into these sleeves and brazed, a very simple and lightweight solution.

Although cycling journalists were quick to point out that such techniques had the potential to lower the cost of bicycles, the manufacturers themselves were more interested in other advantages. The first was weight. Over the course of a decade, Pope had lowered the weight of his lightest Ordinary from about 48 to 37 pounds. His first safety, the 1888 Veloce, weighed in at 51 pounds; by 1891 he had shaved off only three pounds. "Whatever else we do in '92" thundered George Pope, "we MUST get off 10 lbs. weight. If we don't capture that class, someone else will." George didn't get his wish for the Hartford until 1895. Only during the previous year had the Columbia Veloce finally been reduced to a lighter weight than the Columbia Light Roadster Ordinary it had replaced a half a decade before.[75] Pressed lugs could also be enameled without additional machining, and, unlike castings, were ready to use. "Sheet steel stampings," reported Mattox, "are practically ready to be assembled into the bicycle when they are bought, whereas English [forged] fittings are still in a crude, unfinished state. The bicycle maker using stampings does not need a costly plant for finishing his parts."[76]

An alternative for wheelmakers who wanted to continue producing as much of their bicycles in-house as possible was to choose from an increasing array of machine tools designed especially to make bicycle parts. By the mid–1890s tool makers Brown & Sharpe, Pratt & Whitney, Rudolphe & Krummel, E. W. Bliss and Garvin & Co. offered specialty machines to drill rims, grind bearing cones and cups, make hubs, shape wooden rims, and bend and taper fork blades. Rudolphe & Krummel was started by two employees of the E. W. Bliss company who learned that the Sterling Bicycle Company wanted a way to speed up the drilling of spoke holes. They invented their first automatic rim driller in 1892, and by 1895 had perfected it to the point where it would accept either 26- or 28-inch rims without resetting, would countersink the grommet holes used in wood rims, and drill the hole for the air valve in one operation. All the operator had to do was load the rim in the machine and remove it when finished. Pratt & Whitney offered a fully complete turnkey bicycle factory on demand. All the customer needed to provide was the building and the staff— Pratt & Whitney would do the rest. The factory could be pumping out bicycles in less than a month.[77]

After taking a grand tour of North American bicycle factories during the winter of 1895–96, *American Machinist*'s Horace Arnold wrote that he was having difficulty explaining all that he had seen. "I cannot inform anyone how bicycles are constructed," he admitted; "there is no machine in my knowledge which makes a bicycle, and only a very few machines which make all or even one single least part of a bicycle." In the past, metalworking shops, even the early bicycle factories, had been composed of general-purpose equipment: lathes, grinders, drill presses, and so on. A really well-established factory might have its own foundry and enameling shop. Similarly, factory buildings were the usual general-purpose two- or three-story brick mill-style structures, suitable for making everything from babycribs to coffins. But now, bicycles were fast becoming a big, specialized business, and the factories were evolving into integrated units. "An entire cycle factory," marveled Arnold, "its owners, patents, capital, superintendents, foremen, workmen, buildings and tools, all constitute one machine for the manufacture of the complete bicycle."

On the other hand, he was equally amazed by the diversity he found. "Shops are based on entirely different methods," he wrote; "the ideas practiced by one are entirely ignored by others, and each thinks his own the best." Some of this diversity he ascribed to manufacturing traditions: "Establishments, like the 'Warwick,' were found to be based entirely on the armory practice; some, like the 'Western Wheel,' on the German locksmith foundation, and others, like the 'St. Nicholas,' have worked on lines wholly their own." Other differences resulted from regional, even national, characteristics. He explained that the Warwick and the Columbia "embody the New England armory and sewing machine factory practice," while in the new immigrant capital of Chicago, the solution to most problems at the Western Wheel Works was "put everything on the punching press and run it on regular German locksmithing lines, with regular beer at 9:30 AM daily."[78]

Size wasn't the issue. Some "little shops" he inspected "buy all the parts at the lowest possible price, assemble them with cheap labor, put on a gaudy finish that will last until the low-priced wheel is sold, and change the name every season," while others, such as Iver Johnson, turned out a few jewel-like bicycles each year. Even in the biggest factories, production techniques ranged from the crude to the cutting-edge: "Take brazing, for instance. Brazing tools run all the way from mud ovens fired with soft coal ... a purgatory of smoke and flame, with streams of sweat running down the forms of the half-naked workmen ... to hardly visible pencils of gas and air flame so perfectly burning that hardly a flame can be seen."[79]

Although he didn't know it, Arnold was describing a rapidly passing era in the American bicycle industry. Shelby frame tubing, Morgan & Wright tires, Matthews-stamped frame lugs; all were accelerating a trend in the industry toward standardized parts purchased from outside suppliers. By 1895, the Shelby Steel Tube Company had moved beyond the production of raw tubing into pre-cut frame tube sets and finished components such as handlebars and seatposts. Cycle firms were overjoyed to let others worry about the headaches of making such troublesome parts, and by the 1890s the task was indeed a monumental headache. "There are so many standards that there is no standard," reported one cycling journal, "the supply house man knows all about it after he has been trying for a season to sell the small dealer and the small builder what they ask for." W. E. Kelly of the Kelly Handle Bar Co. said that he stocked 43 different handlebar stems, not counting the metric sizes needed to repair foreign cycles. Another supply house kept 24 different sizes and types of seat clusters (the frame lug just under the saddle, used to join the top and seat tubes to the seat stays and seat post) and 64 varieties of crank hangar brackets.[80] But slowly, through sheer economies of scale, as reflected in sharply lower prices for a few high-production variants, the partmakers imposed their idea of order.

In 1892, Arthur Garford, a Cleveland bank manager, developed a new leather saddle that was so superior to anything else available that most bicycle manufacturers gave up trying to make their own and switched to his. By specializing only on saddles, Garford made them better, and for less money, than even the Colonel. By 1896, Pope no longer offered a "factory issue" saddle, and the following year every Columbia and Hartford came equipped with Garford's "Calvary" as standard equipment.[81] The Indianapolis Chain and Stamping Co. provided either block or roller chains by the foot or the pound. Chain making was a slow and tedious operation. "There are no chains made which are a very close job," Horace Arnold observed, "the chains are in some cases so crooked that the next operation is straightening with a mallet."[82] If the customer wanted, Indianapolis

Chain could deliver their product pre-cut. All the customer needed to do was specify the length needed in links. In 1898, probably the most important single blow for standardization was struck — the Morrow coaster brake. Originally, safeties used the same type of brake as the Ordinary — a spoon-shaped plate pressing against the top of the front tire controlled by a lever on the handlebar. This worked fine for solid tires, but a good, hard application of the brake against a pneumatic would tear it to shreds or cause it to burst from heat. In 1897 most cyclists relied on the same braking method as their forebearers did twenty years earlier: by backpedaling, since the rear hub of the safety was fixed — it couldn't coast.

Pope and Lozier had both tried a variation on the rear band brake, in which squeezing the brake lever tightened a band around a drum attached to the rear hub. It was heavy and ineffective. The Morrow worked well, allowed freewheeling, and weighed little more than a fixed rear hub. However, it required bicycle makers to use standardized rear frame tips (today called dropouts), a set spacing between those tips, and standardized chains and sprockets. Most makers were more than happy to comply.

By the time of the 1899 Census of Manufacturers, almost a third of the total output of the American cycle industry was in the form of "other products," chiefly chains, spokes, saddles and handlebars. "In the beginning of the industry the larger establishments made nearly all the different parts of the bicycle they required," noted the census bureau's analyst, "but of late factories have more and more specialized their output, and now even some of the largest bicycle manufacturers merely buy the majority of the different parts and assemble them."[83] One almost invisible component was the shiny little spherical ball bearings used all over the safety bicycle. A coaster brake alone used over a hundred balls, and the average safety contained more than 300. *American Machinist*'s Horace Arnold reported that no cycle firm he knew of made their own balls because "the manufacture of solid, hard perfectly round steel balls presents many difficulties and requires capital, experience and extremely elaborate and well contrived machinery."[84]

Back in the Ordinary days, Pope's did make their own ball bearings, turning them one at a time from rod stock on a lathe. It was tedious and expensive, and ball bearing units for a Standard Columbia cost ten dollars extra. By 1895 the factory either bought them in boxes of 1000 or churned them out on fully automated machines. They actually shifted fairly often between making their own and buying them from suppliers, a situation that led to one of the more bizarre incidents in an industry already famous for its eccentricities.

## *Spy vs. Spy: Industrial Espionage*

Depending on whom you ask, Frederick W. Taylor was either one of the most important figures in the history of business management or the greatest proponent of modern slavery since the Emancipation Proclamation. Management guru Peter Drucker cut his teeth on Taylorism, which he considered the most important contribution America made "to Western thought since the Federalist Papers." The labor economist Harry Braverman, on the other hand, considered Taylor's work "a blueprint for the deskilling of labor."[85]

Taylor was born in Philadelphia in 1856, the son of a wealthy lawyer. He attended Phillips Exeter from 1872 to 1874, a little more than a decade before Albert Linder's brief and unsuccessful career there.[86] Taylor matriculated at Harvard, but soon dropped out, preferring to work as an apprentice machinist. Once a journeyman, he started at the Midvale Steel Works in Philadelphia, working his way up to chief engineer in 1884. At Midvale, as in most machine shops, the machinists were paid by the piece. If they worked hard, they could make a lot of money, but inevitably, management would reward such enthusiasm by "busting back" the piece rate. Management and labor existed in a sort of uneasy truce; the machinists would "soldier," working at modest speed and hiding their true capabilities, and the owners would pay an adequate but uncharitable piece rate. Management didn't possess the journeyman's skills in metalwork, such as which tool to use, how fast to run a lathe, how much to cut on each stroke, and so on. On the other hand, the machinists didn't know what each piece was worth, in monetary terms, to the owners and thus couldn't predict what it would be worth for them to speed up or slow down their work. Every machine shop was a shotgun marriage of skilled laborers and small, struggling owners.

Taylor thought he could put the two together. Using mirrors and stopwatches, he measured each separate motion a machinist used to make a given part. Putting these "time and motion" studies together, he could, without stepping foot on the shop floor, predict how long a worker should take to do a given job, and determine exactly the optimal procedure he should follow. Taylor was an idealist who thought he had found the solution to both soldiering and low pay, but the owners refused to pay higher rates for harder, better work and the machinists ignored his instruction cards, deliberately breaking tools when he ordered detailed procedures followed to the letter. One morning at Midvale, a 200-pound chunk of steel fell from an overhead gantry, barely missing him. Neither the laborers nor the foremen on the gantry saw anything. Taylor decided it was time to move on.[87]

Earlier, an official of the Simonds Rolling Ball Company had written Taylor asking about a forging patent Taylor had taken out. Simonds was owned by George F. Simonds, who had invented a new automatic machine for making ball bearings. Starting with ordinary steel rod stock, his machine could churn out 18,000 ball bearings a day.[88] Taylor was so impressed that he let the firm use his patents for free and agreed to sell Simonds stock to his friends and business associates. Within six months he had peddled off about a hundred thousand dollars in stock, and George Simonds asked him to join the board of directors and help get the firm's out-of-control costs in order.

Taylor worked off-and-on as a consultant for George Simonds until November 1894 when Simonds fell off a train in Scranton, Kansas, and was run over.[89] Although the firm's superintendent, George Weymouth, was an able administrator and familiar with the bicycle industry, he didn't know the technical side of the business and Simond's death left Taylor as the only man who knew the ball-forming method in detail. Alfred Bowditch, Simond's president, asked Taylor to go to work for the firm full-time.

Bowditch's grand scheme for the firm included an industrial combination of ball-bearing manufacturers, and he put Taylor in charge of the project. Three days before the conspirators met in New York's Murray Hill Hotel in April 1895, Taylor outlined to George Weymouth his plans, modeled along the lines of Andrew Carnegie's steel rail combination. "We all want higher prices for the balls we sell," he explained, "even though we may not be able to sell any more." The secret was to drive out any potential new firms. "We do not want any additional competition." The key to any form of collusive activity was secrecy: "It is highly desirable to keep the fact quiet, if possible, that there is any such combination whatsoever."⁹⁰ Taylor was either deluding himself or his employers. The machines Simonds used to make balls only cost about $650 and could be moved by two or three men using a hand cart.⁹¹ The real purpose of the ball trust was probably to harass a former Simonds superintendent, John Grant, who left to go to work for the Cleveland Screw Machine Company, showing them how to make ball bearings. Grant and Taylor loathed each other. "He was with our company under contract and our company refused to renew their contract with him," wrote Taylor. "He is a highly UNTRUTHFUL man." Grant reciprocated, strangling Taylor's infant ball trust in the cradle by threatening to start his own competing combination.⁹²

Taylor turned to espionage. During the next three years Taylor used a motley collection of professional investigators, disgruntled ex-employees, desperate job-seekers and amateur opportunists as spies to infiltrate at least five different firms, including both the Pope and Overman bicycle factories. Taylor's first spy was a young engineer named Newcomb Carlton. Carlton wanted a membership in the prestigious American Society of Mechanical Engineers (ASME) and needed a reference. Taylor said he'd help if Carlton would do a little work for him. He had Carlton go around to Simonds's three competitors posing as the representative of a "big bicycle-related capitalist" from Boston who was interested in buying a ball-bearing company. Two of the firms, the Excelsior Ball Company and Grant's Cleveland Screw Machine Corporation, told him to get lost, but the third, the Hathorn Fancy Forging Company of Bangor, Maine, was in money trouble and took the bait.

George Hathorn tried to work out a deal, but Carlton dithered around until he got what he really came for, samples of unfinished balls right off the rolling machine, which conclusively proved that Hathorn was not using the Simonds process. Carlton told George Hathorn that his employer had a sudden change of plans, and as Carlton reported: "Mr. Hathorn has written me one or two savage letters, but I find that the lying I have done lately has hardened me beyond any ordinary form of reproach."⁹³ Carlton went on to become president of Western Union, and never did have much to say about how he got into ASME.

At the same time Carlton was insinuating he was on a mission from Colonel Pope in order to pry information out of awed suppliers, Taylor was busy infiltrating the big man's factories. In early July, Taylor hired a laborer named W. A. Willard to get into the Columbia plant to try to get samples of Pope's ball bearings. "Well this is the worst job of getting what you want that could be," wrote Williard, "but I think I shall fix them in the end and that is what I am here for." Williard worked a week in the factory and quit, but then met an employee who worked in the ball-bearing room and gave him the information he wanted. Williard promptly got down to business with Taylor. "I have struck it sure but I shall have to go a little further to get positive evidence. You will have to send me a little money for I shall have to put out same." Taylor's notebook indicates a fifty dollar check was sent to Hartford the next day.⁹⁴

The mere fact that Taylor knew Pope was making his own balls was something of a coup. About this time, *American Machinist*'s Horace Arnold came through on a visit, and marveled that even though the Pope firm bought their balls "in boxes of 1,000 each from the factory, all solid, perfectly hard and perfectly round," it still ran each lot across a roundness table and sorted them, using gauges, into bins. He was taken aback about the sanguinity by which the factory shrugged at a surprisingly high rejection rate for what was supposed to be pre-inspected balls. In fact, these "purchased parts" were made in a small building in the back of the factory, packed into Simonds and Excelsior boxes, and trundled up to the front of the factory for a dog-and-pony show for the magazine.[95]

Pope was no greenhorn when it came to industrial espionage. He formed the Hartford Cycle Company back in 1890 because of information he received from an Overman employee that the firm was gearing up to produce a second, less expensive line of bicycles. Even before George Pope arrived in town, David Post told the Colonel that the informant had asked for a job at Pope's. "I should not object to the Hartford Co. hiring anyone that had left the Overmans' employ," the Colonel responded, "we should not think it advisable for our firm to do it, but the Hartford Cycle is another organization, of which the public are in the dark as to ownership."[96]

Willard's informant was Ernest Kendall, who had sharpened and repaired the dies for Pope's ball-making rolling machine for three years. Kendall then left Pope's to go to work for the League Cycle Company, who was developing a shaft-drive bicycle in Hartford. The League bicycle was a jewel, but a temperamental one. In practice, the shaft-drive mechanism was easily knocked out of alignment, and its bevel gears required machining to almost unheard of precision. The company ran out of money after three years and the receivers let the Colonel's men go through the books. League's employees hoped that Pope would save the firm, but true to form, he bought the bevel-drive patents and threw the rest away. Out of work and with little hope of returning to Pope's, Kendall sold out to Taylor. Two drafts of Kendall's testimony still exist; both are almost illegible due to the corrections and additions entered in Taylor's handwriting. The only recognizable contribution of Ernest Kendall is the signature at the bottom. In January, Simonds sued the Pope firm, and five months later, Pope's lawyers agreed to a settlement whereby the company paid Simonds a flat $600 per year for one machine and two dollars a day for each day a second machine was in use, and pledged not to sell balls to anyone else.[97] After leaving Hartford, Willard moved on to Chicopee Falls to find out if Overman was violating the Simonds patents. He couldn't get into the factory, but was able to get rough samples, probably by again bribing employees.[98] They seemed to indicate that Overman was not using the Simonds method.

Bowditch remained suspicious, so Taylor sent H. S. Shadbolt, a Chicago private detective, to Chicopee Falls in May 1897. For someone who claimed to be a specialist in patent and mechanical matters, Shadbolt was extraordinarily inept. At an earlier job in upstate New York, he smashed his foot by dropping a mill on it and ended up "hobbling around with an old boot and cane." At the end of his first week at that job he was forced to admit that "I got my discharge last night. When I drew my pay I was informed that my services were no longer required ... maybe they thought I was asking too many questions."[99] Like Willard, the hapless Shadbolt couldn't get hired on at the Overman works, so Taylor had him rent rooms over a saloon and spend a great deal of time drinking with the Overman employees, something he apparently was quite good at.[100]

Meanwhile, Taylor hired an expert witness, Coleman Sellers, to research the patent history of ball bearings. Sellers quickly discovered that he was going to need the help of the Pope Manufacturing Company, since they were using ball bearings in 1878, before anyone else in the bicycle business. Needless to say, the Colonel was not one to quickly forget a former courtroom adversary. "Mr. Pope has proved a difficult man to see" rued Taylor. As usual, George Day played diplomat, smoothing the way for Taylor's inquiries.

"I have had some interesting correspondence with the gentlemen connected with the Pope Manfg. Company," reported Sellers. They probably thought Sellers's information very interesting as well; two years later, when they suddenly broke their contract with Simonds, the patent department asserted that these conversations gave them grounds to do so.[101]

Up in Chicopee Falls, after a few hangovers, Shadbolt had became familiar enough with a couple of Overman Wheel foremen to talk them into letting him wander into the factory on some pretext, get "lost" trying to find his friends and drift into the ball-making room.[102] Before he was thrown out, he got a good enough look at the machinery to verify that Overman was using the Simonds process. Taylor sent this information off to Bowditch and waited to be contacted by Simonds's lawyers. Just before Christmas 1897, Taylor picked up a Boston morning paper and discovered that there would be no lawsuit — the Overman Wheel Company was bankrupt. The "big five" wheelmakers had very suddenly become the "big four." A few months later, Alfred Bowditch informed Taylor that Simonds was closing down their ball-making operation. "The ball business," he wrote, "is pretty well played out."[103] The great bicycle boom had taken a header.

# 8

## *The Motor Carriage*

*The worst casualty was the Pope Manufacturing Company. Here was a concern which had done some pioneering work with highway vehicles ... but which lost the opportunity because its officials allowed themselves to be tempted by an alluring get-rich-quick scheme. No other explanation is sufficient to account for the Pope catastrophe.*
— John B. Rae, *Business History Review*, 1955[1]

*Even if [they] had opted in 1897 to use internal combustion-powered vehicles, its ultimate fate would not likely have been different.*
— David Kirsch and Gijs Mom,
*Business History Review*, 2002[2]

Herb Alden was getting used to loud, strange noises coming from his boss's workshop. One would think that in a place like the American Projectile Company, that kind of thing would be normal, but quite the opposite was true. Explosions, machine-gun-like bursts, and other cacophonies in a munitions factory were very hard on the nerves and heavily discouraged. At least Hiram Maxim, Alden's supervisor, had learned to confine his experiments to nighttime, after the production crews had gone home.

Hiram Percy Maxim was the son of the brilliant, eccentric Hiram S. Maxim, inventor of the Maxim Machine Gun. In 1881, while his son was still in prep school, the elder Maxim abandoned his wife and children, moved to England and started a new family without bothering to get a divorce. Young Hiram never spoke to his father again. After graduating from MIT in 1886, he worked around for a couple of years before settling in, at age 23, as American Projectile's plant superintendent. There he came to know Hayden Eames, the naval ordnance inspector assigned to American, who, in 1893, left to go to work for Pope.[3]

Riding a bicycle one night from Salem home to Lynn, Maxim envisioned a compact, powerful motor that would propel him over the lonely county roads.[4] Amazingly, he claimed that he was unaware of the fairly sophisticated work on internal combustion engines then going on in Germany and France, and the less advanced efforts in his own country. By exploding atomized drops of gasoline in different shaped empty brass artillery shells, he was able to sketch out the basic layout for a small, three-piston motor that he spent over a year building and getting to run. He installed it in a well-used Columbia tricycle in the fall of 1894 and rode it once for about two hundred feet before its front wheel collapsed. He realized the thing had to have a clutch and spent the winter bench-testing the motor while he built one.

That May, Maxim visited Eames in Hartford and told him about the tricycle. Eames was skeptical, asserting that "the success of the bicycle was due to the physical exercise involved," but arranged a meeting with George Day, who asked Maxim to keep him posted. Maxim returned to Lynn, fixed the tricycle and re-installed the motor, although it appears that he never tried to repeat his sojourn of the prior year. When the work was done, he wrote Day, who sent Henry Souther up to Lynn to look it over. The motor turned over on the second try and Souther was duly impressed. Two weeks later Day offered Maxim a job, and he moved to Hartford in July 1895.

Maxim's new motor carriage laboratory was installed at the Laurel Street factory with Maxim reporting to Eames. His first job was to install the three-cylinder Lynn motor in the "Crawford Runabout," a prototype lightweight horse carriage the Pope firm had experimented with but never put into production. Its standard wooden piano-box body hid a sophisticated steel tube frame, ball bearing wheels, and pneumatic tires. It made a perfect platform for an experimental horseless carriage, and in only a month Maxim had it up and running. Although the motor lacked an effective cooling system, it was soon reliable for jaunts up to a mile or so.

Hiram Percy Maxim was only 25 when he started working at the Pope Motor Carriage Division in 1895, and before that he had been plant superintendent at the American Projectile Company for more than two years. By the time this photograph was taken in 1914, he had already made a fortune selling the "Maxim Silencer," the ominous-looking cylinder every movie hoodlum is seen screwing onto the front of their pistol before making a hit (Photographer unknown. Library of Congress, Washington, D.C., LC-USZ62-98479).

By October, Maxim had enough confidence in the Crawford to demonstrate it to his bosses, and at this point the story becomes a little cloudy. He later claimed that both he and Eames "were staunch advocates of the gasoline-engine." While they acknowledged that steam and electric batteries were, at least in 1895, "a more quiet, docile and reliable motive power," both "firmly believed the gasoline engine had qualities which would beat both steam and electricity in the end."[5] But he recalled that George Day was appalled by the thing. "He acted as though he was standing beside a ton of naked dynamite," Maxim wrote several years later. "It trembled and rattled and clattered, spat oil fire, smoke, and smell." The expression on Day's face as he watched the Crawford idle was so open that Maxim claimed he could read his mind: "so this is the new horseless carriage we have been reading about! By any stretch of the imagination can it be made to appear that anybody would buy such a monstrosity?"[6] The opinion that mattered, however, was the Colonel's, and his reaction is widely disputed. Hermann Cuntz's memory was that Pope said, "You cannot get people to sit over an explosion."[7] Maxim, who chauffeured him on his ride, had a very different impression, recalling that "his reaction was completely different [from Day's]." Maxim believed that "Pope was not so much interested in the performance or appearance of this first carriage," but was more interested in understanding its long-run business potential: "The Colonel assumed ultimate perfection, given sufficient time. Mr. Day could not picture the possibility of perfecting such a terrible contraption."[8]

Maxim said Eames ordered him to begin developing an electric automobile very soon after his arrival in Hartford as a "stop gap" until the gasoline motor could be perfected. Over Thanksgiving weekend, a month after the Crawford demonstration, Maxim went to Chicago to officiate in a horseless-carriage race sponsored by the *Chicago Times-Herald*.[9] Although several gasoline autos were entered, Maxim chose to ride on an electric vehicle entered by two Philadelphians, Henry Morris and Pedro Salom, called the "Electrobat." Despite the strange name, it was well built and quite refined, being the second-generation vehicle in Morris and Salom's development program. They had built Electrobat I in the summer of 1894, and the Chicago race was the first extensive trial of Electrobat II.

It snowed heavily the night before the race and only six vehicles made it to the starting line. Due to the added resistance of the slush, Morris, who was driving, decided that he could not make it all the way, and he turned off course at the eleven-mile mark and returned to the garage downtown. Only two cars finished, both gasoline-powered. In spite of this, Maxim claims that he left Chicago with the impression that Eames' stop-gap idea "was not half bad," as "only courageous men well equipped with tools, knowledge, and spare parts" were suitable customers for the gasoline car in its then-current state.[10]

Maxim returned to Hartford and started work on both an electric vehicle and a second-generation gasoline prototype. The electric car was ready the following April and worked well, although it proved somewhat fragile and needed a lot of road testing. Soon thereafter, Maxim rolled out the new gasoline vehicle, powered by a sophisticated, supercharged two-cycle motor called a pump-scavenging engine. It was a disaster and had to be abandoned within a couple of months. By the end of 1896, Pope set a target date of May 1897 for the commercial introduction of the Columbia Electric Motor Carriage.

## *A Parasitical Growth on the Automobile Industry?*

In subsequent years, Maxim's motor carriage laboratory would be the spark that ignited a firestorm of historical controversy. After introducing the Columbia Electric Carriage in the spring of 1897, Pope manufactured several hundred cars over the next two years. In 1899 he spun off the motor carriage division into a separate firm, the Columbia & Electric Vehicle Company and sold a half-interest in it to the Electric Vehicle Company (EVC), owned by a syndicate headed by William C. Whitney, the brother of his Cohasset neighbor Henry Whitney. The EVC already owned the Electric Storage Battery Company (later known as Exide) and Morris and Salom's former company, now converted into a New York electric taxi operation called the Electric Carriage & Wagon Company. Whitney's plan was that Hartford would build electric taxis, buses and delivery wagons, Exide would provide the batteries, and the Electric Vehicle Company would set up transportation franchises similar to Electric Carriage & Wagon in other major American and European cities.

In mid–1900 Pope sold his remaining half interest in the Columbia & Electric Vehicle Company to Whitney, who folded it into the Electric Vehicle Company, leaving only the parent EVC and one subsidiary, Exide. EVC managed everything, Hartford made the vehicles, and Exide supplied the batteries. The taxi franchises were each separate firms, and the Colonel held an interest in the Boston franchise, the New England Vehicle Transportation Company. The local taxi operations were unsuccessful, and in 1901 headquarters moved from New York to Hartford and the company once again focused on the manufacture and sales of electric (and by now gasoline) cars to individuals.

In the process of splitting off the motor carriage division from the bicycle works, Pope purchased a controversial patent from a lawyer and inventor named George Selden that Selden claimed to be the basic patent covering all internal combustion engines. After the taxi scheme went under, EVC attempted to exploit the patent much like Pope and Charles Pratt had earlier done with Lallement's patent. Under the direction of George Day, several leading automobile makers created a cartel, the Association of Licensed Automobile Manufacturers (ALAM) to enforce it. Henry Ford, after two failures, was just then getting his third venture, the Ford Motor Company, off the ground. Ford did not take out a license and was sued by the ALAM. After a long and bitter court fight, Ford won, and both the EVC and ALAM essentially went out of business. Ford had somewhat more success. The idea of an electric automobile company attempting to profit from the basic patent on the internal combustion engine was considered outrageous at the time, and the controversy has never died away.

In 1954, historian Allan Nevins wrote what was then considered the definite biography of Henry Ford.[11] One of Nevins's researchers was a young doctoral student named William Greenleaf, who wrote his dissertation on the Selden patent suit the same year his professor's book came out. Both were highly sympathetic to Ford and excoriated the EVC, the ALAM and anyone connected with them. In general, their explanation for the Selden patent controversy was that a group of inept businessmen chose a blatantly bad technology — the electric automobile — and when it proved a bust they tried to suppress the progress of the "right" technology using a patent monopoly. A year later, automotive historian John Rae, relying heavily on Greenleaf's graduate work, wrote a seminal article on the EVC in which he condemned it as "a parasitical growth on the automobile industry."[12] In 1961, Greenleaf published his dissertation as a book entitled *Monopoly on Wheels*.[13]

The Selden patent controversy has engendered its fair share of bitterness, anger, guilt, and an overwhelming desire to let old skeletons remain in the closet. In 1936, Hermann Cuntz wrote a friend that he had always believed that the ALAM was a "combination of manufacturers in an industry without restraint of trade," and that the organization had done far more good than harm during its brief life, mostly in the areas of materials research and parts standardization.[14] The following year, Hiram Maxim, in his memoirs, made a palpable effort to distance himself from the enterprise, noting only that "the scheme was a very broad one," and professing ignorance as to the true nature of the firm: "whether it was intended to develop profits out of earned dividends, or by unloading the stock on the public, I will not venture to guess."[15]

Although Maxim dedicated *Horseless Carriage Days* to his former boss, Hayden Eames, he neglected to mention that they were brothers-in-law, having married the sisters Claire and Josephine Hamilton, daughters of former Maryland governor Joseph Hamilton.[16] With so much retroactive damage control at work, it is worth digging a little deeper into the story of the ill-starred Pope motor carriage division.

## *My Storage-Battery Friends from Philadelphia*

By the time Maxim visited Eames in Hartford in May 1895, the Colonel had already developed a vigorous interest in motor vehicles. In 1891, he sent some of his men to investigate an electric automobile that an inventor near Boston had reportedly developed. (In 1896 or 1897 Hermann Cuntz was asked to re-locate the machine if it still existed. It did. He found it in storage in the town of Putnam.) In 1892, the Western Wheel Works designed and built "several hundred" electric tricycles for use at the 1893 Chicago's World Fair. The tricycles had two chair-like wicker seats with a tiller and small wheel in front. The battery was suspended under the seat and apparently drove only one of the two rear wheels. The overall appearance was more along the lines of a side-by-side wheelchair than a carriage, but it was reportedly good for 14 miles per charge. They were rented to fair-goers who didn't want to walk by a concessionaire, who shared profits with the fair. In January 1895, an anonymous bicycle magnate — probably Pope — told a reporter from *Scribner's Magazine* that "between electric cars in the cities and the bicycle in the country, the value of horseflesh will drop to almost nothing within twenty years."[17] The mere mention of an automobile in early 1895 appears incredibly prescient, but only because automobile historians in America, unlike Europe, have stridently ignored public transit as a source of automotive technology. In fact, the evolution of the automobile, especially the electric vehicle, has as much to do with the streetcar as the gasoline motor. In both Europe and America some of the earliest interest in the electric vehicle came out of the streetcar industry, including that of Albert Pope.

In 1888 Pope's friend and soon-to-be Cohasset neighbor Henry Whitney pieced together the fifteen different trolley lines serving the Boston area and merged them into a single holding company, the West End Street Railway Company.[18] In secret, Whitney's plan was even more audacious: he and a group of associates (who may have included Pope) had bought up huge tracts of land beyond the end of the line in Brookline, near Chestnut Hill Reservoir. If the West End line could be motorized, doubling its speed, those farms would suddenly become developable land, vastly increasing their value. Whitney turned to a protégé of Thomas Edison named Frank Sprague, who was building one of the first electric trolley systems in Richmond, Virginia. Whitney and his chief engineer toured the Richmond system and were impressed, but told Sprague that they were leaning toward a cable-car system. Given the narrow, congested streets in downtown Boston they feared that an overhead electric grid could not handle a long line of stalled trolleys suddenly getting underway after a traffic jam without blowing out the system. That night, after the Richmond system shut down, Sprague lined up 22 cars nose-to-tail for Whitney and started each as fast as the car ahead allowed. Their headlights dimmed, but nothing blew. Whitney bought the Sprague system, and the run to Chestnut Hill Reservoir was the first line upgraded and extended.

But by 1892, only part of the system had been converted, and Whitney, looking to spread out the backbreaking costs of electrification, wanted a way to retrofit existing streetcars so they wouldn't have to be scrapped. Installing battery-powered electric motors looked promising. The West End had actually installed two battery-powered lines, but by 1898 had replaced them with regular overhead wires.[19]

A more complete trial of battery-powered trolleys was underway in New York City, where Henry Whitney's brother William was integrating the various traction lines into his Metropolitan Traction Company. Metropolitan initially used underground cables, but soon switched to overhead electric. However, the owners of some isolated lines fought Whitney's overtures, and to prevent takeover, sought to block the installation of either underground cables or overhead electric lines. Battery-power, while not a long-term solution, was a promising tactical weapon, vastly superior to the other alternative Metropolitan was testing, compressed air.

In late 1894 Morris and Salom were hard at work on Electrobat I. Pedro Salom designed the battery system, having spent much of the previous decade working on battery-powered European streetcars. In fact, they were assisted by Salom's part-time employer, the Electric Storage Battery Company. It is against this background that Albert Pope made his comment at the January 1895 New York Cycle Show about electric vehicles in the city and bicycles in the country, suggesting that he may have been an investor in the rapidly growing Electric Storage Battery Company, along with William C. Whitney, who would ultimately sink over a million dollars into Exide.[20]

Returning to Maxim's memoirs, it is apparent that there are some unexplained gaps. Before coming to the American Projectile Company in 1892, he had spent several years working at the Sun Electric Company and the Jenny Electric Company. American Projectile was a subsidiary of the Thompson-Houston Electric Company, which later became part of General Electric. Thompson-Houston was the firm that supplied the electrical running equipment to Henry Whitney's West End streetcars and many other traction concerns. It was involved in munitions because of its experience in electric arc welding, and it was pioneering its use in making less expensive artillery shells. After leaving the Laurel Street factory in 1907, he went into business making his own electric automobile.[21] He was, in fact, quite an accomplished electrical engineer.

Had Albert Pope been purely interested in an internal combustion engine, he could have found an expert much closer to home. In 1891, a Hartford firm, the National Machine Company, built 30 small, high-speed Daimler gas engines for the Steinway Company.[22] Steinway licensed the design for use in small boats it was building in an attempt to diversify beyond pianos. Fred Law, a Hartford machinist, supervised the project. Law later went to work for the League Cycle Company, the chainless bicycle developer, and after it failed he moved to the Hartford Cycle Company in late 1894 or early 1895. The management at Pope's knew of his exceptional skill, and they moved him to the motor carriage laboratory almost as soon as Maxim arrived, where he became the man who actually built Maxim's experimental engines. If Maxim was as ignorant of gasoline engine development as he claims, Fred Law probably knew more than he did in early 1895. Yet, Pope and Day hired Maxim instead of using a man they already had on the payroll.

Maxim says that he did not begin work on his first electric carriage until he returned from the *Chicago Times-Herald* race over Thanksgiving weekend. Up to that point, he claims, "I had been working tooth and nail for a long time trying to get something that would run," and he dates his first meeting with the Eddy Electric and Manufacturing Company, who made Pope's electric motors, in early 1896. However, when he arrived in Chicago for the race, he met "my storage battery friends from Philadelphia, Messrs. Morris and Salom," and he was appointed to referee "my friend Mr. Morris' Electrobat." Finally, when the motor carriage division opened its doors for business in May 1897, accepting orders for the Mark III electric runabout, it announced that all Columbia Electrics would come equipped with Exide batteries.[23] Maxim's 1937 claim that he knew all along that the gasoline engine would prevail, and was turned away only by Day's fussiness, starts to sound a little self-serving.

This is not to say that it is completely false. In a private letter written in 1915, Henry Souther remarked that "it was very difficult for the engineering force to get the management to believe that anyone could be persuaded to buy a motor car with a hot, smelly, greasy, engine," which sounds much like Maxim's account.[24] Speaking in 1907, Hayden Eames asserted that "the electric vehicle first appealed to me almost by accident," and that initially "there was no intention of making electric vehicles at all." His explanation of this decision, however, contains some interesting technical details:

> The decision was that pending the development of a practical gasoline car, we would support ourselves with the sale of electric vehicles.... Hour after hour I studied with Mr. Maxim trying to devise some scheme by which the speed of the gas engine could be varied by five or six percent without a change of gear or a total loss of torque.[25]

This description simply does not match Maxim's Crawford runabout. First, the Crawford only had one forward gear. But even with this handicap, after Maxim rigged a crude engine cooling system, the little three-cylinder motor would carry two men up a hill on Park Street just east of the factory and over a steep railway bridge on Laurel Street to the north. "I was intoxicated to observe the way that little engine would settle down and pull," boasted Maxim.[26] On the other hand, the problem that Eames describes does sound very much like that afflicting a poorly designed high-speed two-cycle engine, such as the pump-scavaging Mark II motor Maxim built to replace the Crawford, the one he had to abandon after much trial and tribulation.

The Mark II was scrapped in late 1896, about the time George Day gave the green light for the Mark I electric, completed in April and secretly test run at night, to be shown to anyone outside the factory. It would have been a logical time to decide which unit to continue with. Eames' 1907 memory was sound, but if read after looking through Maxim's 1937 book, it seems to take on a different meaning. A decision was made, but it was probably a very specific production commitment, not a development initiative, and it was likely made in late 1896, after the Mark I electric worked and the Mark II failed, not in the summer of 1895 when Maxim first showed Day the Crawford carriage. It is probably true that the gasoline motor did worry Day, but a motor that was smelly, noisy, greasy and that utterly failed to work was an unlikely candidate in anyone's book.

It is far more likely that Maxim was hired in the summer of 1895 with the full intent of developing an electric automobile, that he was capable and experienced in this field, and that he knew this when he moved from Lynn to Hartford. While he was encouraged to experiment with the gasoline motor, and sincerely believed in its future, his claim that he was diverted from this pursuit only after starting work rings hollow. It was likely a selective memory born of a desire to "have been there first" embarrassment over the failure of his pump-scavaging brainstorm, a late-life desire to put as much distance as possible between himself and the Selden patent fiasco (and his ambiguous role within it), and, given Hayden Eames's 1907 account, a little disingenuousness on the part of the Colonel and George Day as well.

## Bad Technology Is Forgivable, but This Is Un-American

On 13 May 1897, Hayden Eames lined up the first Mark III electric carriages in the cavernous space of the Laurel Street plant. Over the winter, the steel tube division had moved to the new factory on Hamilton Street, and except for the typewriter company on the top floor, the building belonged to the motor carriage division. Special Pullman cars brought celebrities such as John Jacob Astor, Henry L. Higginson and, all the way from Chicago, Nelson Miles. Reporters from *Electrical World*, Horseless Age, *American Machinist*, *Iron Age*, *Motor World*, even *Scientific American* and the British journal *Engineering* attended. Hermann Cuntz was assigned the unenviable job of handling Horseless Age's irascible editor, E. P. Ingersoll, which he managed by keeping Ingersoll's glass of punch continually filled, "which had its amusing phases," he later recalled.[27] Despite a steady spring drizzle, Eames let the guests take a ride outside, or they could stay dry and have a member of the staff take them on a more sedate circle around the plant. The front office was filled to overflowing with food and a bar. "Eames staged it with the cooperating 'master showman's' mind of Col. A. A. Pope," Cuntz said.

Meanwhile, Maxim's friends Morris and Salom had been keeping busy in Philadelphia. A few months after the Chicago race, Pedro Salom gave a lecture at the Franklin Institute. Where others envisioned making and selling electric cars, Salom believed that reliable service required more. Vehicles should not be "broadcast over the country" unless "proper arrangements have been made for their intelligent care and maintenance." An operating company should be set up, "a building in a suitable central locality" acquired, and "the vehicles can then be operated either on a lease or rental plan, very similar to the manner in which a livery stable is at present conducted."[28] Such a scheme required more money than the two men had available, so they sold out to Isaac Rice and Exide, who reorganized the firm as the Electric Carriage & Wagon (EC&W) Company. The company soon moved into a central station in mid-town Manhattan and put twelve electric hansoms and a small surrey to work. Although it advertised itself as a taxicab company, it was essentially operating as a car-rental operation with a driver provided. Business wasn't bad; in June, a month after Pope's big gala, they rang up 632 calls, carrying 1,580 passengers 4,603 miles. The firm was already at its financial break-even point.

Things were less clear in Hartford. In the summer of 1897 the motor carriage division opened a service station in Newport and rented out Columbias, suggesting that they were thinking along the lines of EC&W, but they also retained export broker Hart O. Berg to sell both cars and foreign manufacturing rights. In mid–1897, Berlin's Ad. Altman & Company took out a license, building Columbia cars, buses and trucks until 1902. Additional licenses were issued in France, Belgium, and Austria.[29]

It is hard to determine exactly how many cars were built and where they went. In 1947 Cuntz guessed that from May 1897 to the summer of 1899, when Pope sold the motor carriage division, it made about 600 vehicles, of which half were exported to Europe. However, that figure probably includes an inexpensive gasoline delivery tricycle designed by Maxim and built at the Hartford Cycle Company. David Kirsch estimates that the division produced about 50 cars in 1897 and another 540 in 1898 and 1899, with 500 of these being electrics and 200 exported to Europe, including 80 to France. Gijs Mom believes that up to Janauary 1900, all manufacturers in the U.S., sold between 440 and 650 electric vehicles to private customers. Plant size and production in Hartford increased sharply after the April 1899 merger, but even then, an internal letter indicates that the firm could not meet a twelve-month production schedule of 1,600 units. Taking all this evidence together suggests a pre-split-off figure of about 350 (not including the delivery tricycles), with half of these exported.[30]

There are very few accounts of activities at the motor carriage division between May 1897 and April 1899. Maxim dismisses the development of the electric vehicle as a "body-design problem" that the firm solved by turning to an outside designer, William Atwood. Again, Maxim is being disingenuous. Motor speed on the first electrics, including the Columbia, was controlled through a technique known as voltage switching, in which more battery cells were thrown on-line as speed was increased. However, cells discharged at different rates, and the cross-flow generated compensation currents that eventually burned cells out or could actually arc across the battery bay as two cells short-circuited.[31] The cure was to use motor switching, in which pushing the speed lever forward either kicked in a second motor or, in a single motor, activated additional windings. The idea was first thought of in America for use in streetcars, but except for Pope, it was only applied to autos in Europe prior to 1900.

A visitor to the plant in late 1899 noted "a great many motors of different makes," lying around, having been tried and either discarded or destroyed during testing. Some Columbias used battery control and others used motor-switching, and the second-generation Mark III featured a unique split rear axle that allowed the installation of either one or two driving motors, making two-motor speed control possible.[32] The firm had a small motor unit available for dual-motor use in the Mark III, but preferred the single motor, apparently because it was more efficient and easier to cool if subject to constant overload. Maxim's memoirs notwithstanding, there was some hard work going into the electrics.

Instead, most of Maxim's memories of 1897 and 1898 are focused on a fairly trivial project called the Mark VII gasoline tricycle. In late 1896, shortly after giving up on the pump-scavaging Mark II, the Colonel summoned him to his office and:

> asked me if I could build a small gasoline-tricycle package-carrier that would be suitable for merchants use in making deliveries.... Something simple, light, not an elegant carriage ... it should be a cycle and not a wagon or carriage and the gasoline-motor should make it possible to carry greater loads and run at higher speeds than a boy could on a foot-pedaled tricycle."[33]

After some normal bugs, it worked well, and was manufactured in 1898 up the street at the Hartford Cycle works. Maxim hardly mentions Harry Pope, Hartford's superintendent, but Cuntz says that Harry started spending most of his time at the motor carriage division almost as soon as it opened. He recalled standing in the factory yard in 1896 and watching Harry roll a DeDion-Bouton gasoline tricycle trying to turn it into the gate too fast. A letter from George Pope written in December 1894 suggests that Harry may not have been working at the Hartford Cycle Company on a full-time basis, and while the city directory lists Harry as the Hartford Cycle superintendent in July 1895, he has no occupation at all the following year. In the summer of 1897 he is simply listed as being "at Pope's," and in July 1898 his entry states that he is a mechanical expert at the motor carriage division. "The cycle trade doesn't worry him much now," commented *Cycle Age* in mid–1899, "for he is deeply immersed in motor vehicles." [34]

Harry was growing bored and restless with the bicycle business, and his obsessive perfectionism was becoming a liability. An enthusiastic marksman, he started turning out his own rifle barrels in 1887, and by 1893 began a part-time business as a gunsmith in a barn-like shed behind his house. He soon built up a reputation as one of America's premier custom riflemakers. He frankly admitted to one of his customers that he would take up gunmaking full-time except that it was "folly to take a job unless there was a fair prospect of a fair profit." His son Allen, who helped him make rifle barrels, says that he "took it out on me if I did anything improperly." When Harry offered to set him up as his partner in business about 1901, he refused because "I didn't like being found fault with all the time."[35] Disappointed, Harry sold half the business to J. P. Stevens Firearms in nearby Springfield. The quality of Stevens's work didn't meet his exacting standards and in disgust he sold out completely and moved to California. He opened the doors of his San Francisco shop the day before the big 1906 earthquake. The quake spared the shop, but the resulting fire didn't and he lost everything he brought with him. He moved to Philadelphia and briefly went to work with a maker of telescopic gun sights until a group of affluent customers and supporters set him up in a new shop in New Jersey. He continued as an independent gunsmith, frequently complaining that his customers didn't appreciate him and wouldn't pay their bills, and he sometimes wrote friends that he was impoverished to the point of hunger. But when he died in 1950, his family found hundreds, perhaps thousands, of unopened letters from customers, and it appears that at one point he simply stopped opening his mail. He may have suffered from the same mental illness that precipitated his father's untimely death when he was a boy.

It is possible that the Mark VII tricycle was a way of keeping Harry involved in the Hartford Cycle Company. It is also likely that the company was in financial trouble and needed work that would absorb unused capacity. The mid-priced bicycle market had become saturated with products in the $35 to $65 price range, especially from Chicago, and lacking the Columbia cachet, the Hartford brand was taking a beating. When the Colonel sold out to the American Bicycle Company trust in September 1899, the Hartford Cycle Company was immediately closed and its factory sold.

Another interesting aspect of the Mark VII was its intended use. Although the firm did plan to eventually sell them directly to merchants, Pope wanted to use it for the first couple of years to establish package delivery agencies in Boston and Washington. In fact, at the time the EVC was formed in mid–1899, a spokesman for William Whitney said that the firm hoped to capture a big share of the urban freight market by undercutting express package rates and offering rapid door-to-door service. When Pope's Boston-based operation, the New England Vehicle Transportation Company, opened in May 1899, it not only rented out cabs and hansoms, but it also delivered orders for the big downtown department stores and distributed "hot" editions of the newspapers.[36]

If Pope had the package-express plan in late 1897 and Whitney had the same notion in 1899, where did the idea originate? Did Pope tell Maxim to begin work on the package delivery tricycle in anticipation of a Pope-Whitney merger, still a year and a half down the road, or did Whitney expand his electric taxicab scheme into package delivery to accommodate Pope's plans? Probably the latter. Subsequent events over the winter of 1897–98, when a blizzard paralyzed horse-drawn cabs in New York but left the EC&W's hansoms unfazed, probably lit the spark behind the big EVC expansion. However, the package delivery service should not be overlooked, because it provides important clues to the subsequent Pope-Whitney negotiations. First, it suggests that Pope's role went beyond that of mere supplier. Second, it indicates that by 1899 the Colonel still had not crystallized in his own mind the strategy he would use to exploit his lead position in the nascent automobile industry.

As historians Gijs Mom and David Kirsch point out, in his 1950s eulogy for the

Pope motor carriage division, John B. Rae is able to lament its merely "mistaken" choice of technology (electricity over internal combustion) because he made the "right" choice to sell individual cars to the public, but he excoriates the Electric Vehicle Company because it retained control of the automobiles, selling transport services such as vehicle leasing or taxi rides. Bad technology is forgivable, but collectivization, apparently, is un–American and parasitic.

However, Pope may not have been as wedded to a pure sales strategy as Rae gave him credit for. At exactly the same time that Isaac Rice was setting up his "central station" in mid-town Manhattan, Pope sent Eugene Russell to Newport to get his own service station up and running. It was operated as a satellite of the firm's Boston operation, and the cars apparently were sent back to Boston at the end of the summer. An advance payment of $150 bought 600 miles per month. Unlike EC&W's New York City operation, Pope's customers could hire with or without a driver, and most apparently chose to drive themselves. Newport residents wouldn't be caught dead in the converted horse barn; a team of drivers fanned out in the morning to deliver freshly charged cars. Customers lived up to Newport's reputation for fast living, and cars were driven into barns, through bonfires and down stairs.[37] On the other hand, malice was probably not the problem; the most frequent call for emergency service was from drivers who forgot to insert the safety plug, a bright-red cap about the size of child's fist that had to be plugged into a socket in the middle of the dash. Just because they were rich didn't necessarily mean they were bright.

## *We Get the Million Dollars!*

Back in New York, the success of the first twelve cabs led Isaac Rice to move operations to a former indoor cycling rink, the old Michaux Club, on lower Broadway. The scale of the new operation was mind-boggling. The upper floor could hold 100 cabs. Most of the lower floor was taken up by a charging floor for 200 battery units, each weighing 1,250 pounds. The facility was designed to pull a battery unit out of a cab and replace it in two minutes. The cab backed into one of two charging docks where it was grabbed by a series of hydraulic rams that lifted it up and positioned it horizontally and vertically with the loading table on the dock. The battery was rolled out of the cab and onto the table, where it was moved to the side. Meanwhile, an operator in an overhead crane grabbed a fresh battery unit from one of the charging stations and set it down on the loading table, where it was rolled four or five feet to the side, directly behind the waiting cab. A separate, horizontal ram pushed the battery unit into the cab where it automatically plugged itself in. The dock man closed the doors of the cab's battery chest, released the dock rams, and the driver pulled out. Meanwhile, the crane operator "flew" the spent battery unit back to the waiting charging station. One observer noted that "the manipulation resembles more than anything else the handling of steel billets in the reheating furnaces of rolling mills."[38]

However, Rice was having trouble filling his vast new headquarters. Morris and Salom had designed a second-generation cab for EVC, but by October 1898 only 20 were up and running. These had been built from components provided by suppliers, and rushed through as soon as the blueprints were ready in order to test them on the streets of New York. This limited tryout was not enough, and George Herbert Condict, EVC's chief engineer, later admitted that "none of the vehicles was right."[39] So that corrections would not slow down the construction of the newer cabs too much, they were built in batches of 50 that went unfinished until January, 1899. The separate batches and a series of field modifications to the older units left EVC with a hodgepodge of rolling equipment. Not even the battery packs were standardized.

Business was still good. A blizzard in January, 1899 paralyzed horse-drawn traffic, but the heavy cabs cut through the slush with little trouble and were, as one journal put it, "literally coining money." The company began designing a third-generation cab that would hopefully bring some order out of the engineering chaos. At the same time, the firm announced that it would soon expand into Philadelphia. Then all hell broke loose. On 21 February a New York Electric Vehicle Transportation Company was incorporated, with a huge capital fund of $25 million. Although President Rice shrugged it off as a mere reorganization and enlargement of the current firm, rumors tied it to William Whitney's Metropolitan Traction Company, and it appears that Whitney had already bought up most or all of Rice's ownership in both EVC and Exide at a considerable profit to Rice, who stayed on as EVC president. What appeared to trigger it all was a persistent rumor Henry Lawson was back in town to create an automobile trust.[40] Lawson! The mere mention of the name was enough to raise the hair of any honest man in the wheel business.

Englishman Henry John Lawson started out as an inventor who filed several bicycle-related British patents in the last half of the 1870s, including one for an early chain-drive, rear-wheel powered bicycle that became derisively known as the "crocodile." It was far from perfect, and soon died. Lawson turned from inventing to speculation. His specialty was convincing the owners of small, closely held cycle manufacturers to incorporate. British corporation law was meant to be used by large enterprises and was burdensome and expensive. Most of his targets were far too small to afford it or benefit from it. For his services, Lawson raked in outrageous fees that typically left him in control of the firms that "hired" him.[41] After 1898, he linked up with an even more notorious cycle promoter, E. Terah Hooley, a former Nottingham lace manufacturer who turned to financial speculation after inheriting $165,000 from his mother.[42] Hooley attracted investors to his shaky stock schemes by bribing prominent (but often broke) lords, dukes, and viscounts to sit as directors of the enterprises, including the former Lord Mayor of London. He made his first big score in the bicycle industry by taking over the Humber Cycle Company in 1895, and flush with victory, decided he could manage the vast company, too. He was a horrible administrator and promptly ran Humber into the ground. He then bought the Dunlop tire company for three million pounds and sold it again within a year, clearing two million, but leaving the firm so burdened with debt it needed World War I to recover. He was forced into bankruptcy, hid his assets in his wife's name, evaded creditors, and dodged the British prohibition on doing business as an undischarged bankrupt by acting through straw men, principally Lawson. Eventually, Lawson would serve a year in prison for misrepresentation and Hooley would serve three for fraud.

That would be much later, however. In early 1899, Lawson arrived in New York representing the Anglo-American Rapid Vehicle Company, a British syndicate, to meet with the Studebaker Brothers (who provided the wooden bodies for EVC's cabs) and W. W. Gibbs, former president of Exide, about setting up an electric taxi and trucking firm in New York. The rumor was that Anglo-American also wanted EVC.[43] In a lightning move to counter Lawson, EVC reorganized in late February, increased its capitalization to 12 million dollars, and announced plans to expand into Boston, Philadelphia, Chicago, Paris and London. Hermann Cuntz later recalled that EVC first approached the Pope company immediately after the end of the Spanish-American War seeking a bid for 200 cabs. This would have made it late 1898 or early 1899, when EVC was drawing up plans for its third-generation cabs. Cuntz believed that one reason William Whitney approached Pope was because Whitney, a former Navy Secretary, knew Hayden Eames, a former naval officer. Although possible, that is unlikely. In the early 1890s Secretary Whitney was already a wealthy and connected Wall Street lawyer, but Eames was merely a lieutenant, the son of humble foreign missionaries. On the other hand, Albert Pope and Whitney probably already knew each other. The Colonel and William Whitney's brother Henry were, of course, next-door neighbors in Cohasset, and William Whitney had been chief counsel for the City of New York during the 1882 Central Park bicycle ban case that Charles Pratt and Pope fought together. Finally, William Whitney's wife and brother-in-law (law partner, Henry Dimock), were from the same family as Dr. Susan Dimock, a colleague of the Colonel's physician sisters, Emily and Augusta, at the New England Women's and Children's Hospital before her untimely death in a shipwreck in 1875.[44] The Dimocks were major contributors to the New England Hospital, which, by this time, Emily was running.

Cuntz recalled that the merger of the Pope and Whitney interests was consummated at a meeting in Hartford in April 1899, where five representatives of the New York syndicate, including Whitney, met with George and Albert Pope, George Day, Hayden Eames and patent administrator Felton Parker. The Colonel and Whitney had already met alone in New York on 6 April, and on 26 April, at another New York meeting, the new Columbia Automobile Company selected a board of directors and started operations, so the big Hartford meeting fell somewhere between, probably on the twelfth.[45]

The deal was certainly big. The assets of the motor carriage division were worth a million dollars, as was the Electric Vehicle Company. A Whitney syndicate would inject another million in cash for operating funds. After the tense meeting was over, Eames burst into Cuntz's office and shouted, "We get our million dollars! We go full speed ahead!" The EVC immediately expanded its existing local transportation franchises in New York, Boston and Philadelphia and added new ones in Chicago, Washington, D.C., and Atlantic City. To supply them, the New York headquarters ordered 4,200 vehicles from Hartford within a month or two after the merger.[46]

Once again, there are some glaring discrepancies between various accounts. Both Cuntz and Maxim agree that the main reason EVC approached Pope about building 200 cabs was because, as Cuntz put it, "They could find no one to take a contract for so many." The assertion that only the Pope firm could, in early 1899, make cars in significant quantities has become the accepted wisdom, repeated by John B. Rae, William Greenleaf, James Flink and even the otherwise iconoclastic David Kirsch and Gijs Mom. However, it is not true, and is flatly contradicted by the fact that the production run of the 200 third-generation Morris and Salom cabs were not built in Hartford, but by EVC itself, following its original January 1899 plan, in its shop on 42nd Street in New York.[47] The motors were bought from Westinghouse and the bodies from Studebaker. They were built in one large batch that was completed in December 1899. The 42nd Street plant was modest in size, with only 12 lathes, 2 screw machines, 12 drill presses, 7 milling machines (including a specialized gear shaper and another crank shaper) and six bench grinders. In February 1900 it was dismantled and moved to Hartford. To get the local taxi franchises by until those third-generation cabs arrived, the existing cabs in New York were distributed around. By November 1899, 40 had been sent to Boston, Philadelphia and Chicago.[48]

Curiously, there appears to have been no pressing need for the 200 new cabs. Drawing up plans for an Atlantic City franchise, the general manager there reported that the season would start in February "and there is nothing in the way of vehicles available for that place except Mark XII Runabout, Mark XII Victoria and hansom cabs and broughams."[49] The Mark XII series was Hartford's lightest and smallest electric cars; they were intended for sale to private users. The "hansoms and broughams" were the second-generation EVC cabs, and it appears there were plenty of these to go around. In January 1900, a reporter from *Electrical World* paid a visit to the Hartford works. The manufacturing of cabs was never mentioned. The factory crew spent a great deal of time showing off new personal-use electric cars, including the updated Mark III and the new, smaller Mark XII, as well as a new electric truck, the Mark XI, which could be used as a delivery wagon, fire truck or omnibus. In his report from Atlantic City, the New Jersey general agent reported that "I would recommend that we secure omnibuses, if possible ... [although] the earliest date that the list from Hartford shows we could obtain eight-passenger omnibuses is March, and I do not believe that we can rely upon their delivery at that time." Similarly, he noted that in Newark "there is a field there for delivery wagons, as soon as we can obtain them, but I can not see where we are likely to obtain vehicles of this type before March or April at the earliest."[50]

Dutch historian Gijs Mom has debunked the myth that the EVC received some 2,000 electric cabs between 1899 and 1901. His research indicates that the total EVC fleet was around 850. However, even Mom assumes that most of this fleet was hansom and brougham cabs, which is doubtful. In January 1901 the Boston franchise had 250 vehicles, including cabs, delivery vans and cycles, and omnibuses. It reported that its cab fleet averaged 726 miles a day. If the Boston cabs were averaging the same 18.5 miles per day that the Atlantic City units were logging, Boston had only about 40 electric cabs, about the same number as the previous year.[51] Like Newark and Atlantic City, the big growth in Boston was in omnibuses. In 1897, Henry Whitney's streetcar empire was taken over by the Boston Transit Authority, or BTA. It immediately started implementing one of Whitney's original ideas, a subway tunnel under Tremont Street between Scollay Square and downtown. When it was done, the BTA replaced the surface trolleys with buses, contracting the service out to the local EVC franchise.

The other principal area of growth was selling owner-operated automobiles. The attention of the EVC Executive Committee in late 1899 appeared to be more drawn to sales than cab operations. Each local operating agency paid a franchise fee of two and a half percent of gross revenues to the home office in New York, with the exception of vehicle sales, which were assessed ten percent. But because "it was desirable to facilitate the sale of vehicles" the committee waived the ten-percent fee for most sales, making vehicle sales more lucrative than cab, bus or delivery services.[52]

It appears that the EVC itself was fully capable of manufacturing the third-generation cabs that it needed in early 1899, and that the 200 cabs it made at 42nd Street were sufficient to supply its local franchises through the end of 1900. However, it did badly need trucks and buses, for which Hartford's Mark XI truck chassis fit the bill perfectly, but the Mark XI didn't exist until late 1899, more than six months after the merger.[53] Also, rather than slow down the production of small automobiles intended for sale to individual owners to make room for cabs or buses, EVC encouraged its franchises to act as sales agents, with some degree of success. All this begs the question: why the great merger? If looked at strictly from automotive perspective, as most historians have done, these factors make the hurried approach of the Whitney syndicate appear irrational or, as Maxim hints, based on ulterior motives. However, if the bicycle side is also considered, a very different picture emerges — one that makes Albert Pope the suitor and Electric Vehicle Company the object of affection.

## Colonel Pope Does Love His Automobile

Various schemes for eliminating competition within the bicycle industry had been kicking around since 1896. In November of that year Charles F. Smith of the Indiana Bicycle Company had tried to put together a combination of western cyclemakers, but the plan fell apart when R. L. Coleman of the Western Wheel Works pulled out. A year later, a New Jersey company was actually formed to administer a patent pool for shaft-drive bicycles, but with the general collapse in prices, a $125 bicycle was such an exotic oddity that nobody paid any attention. In 1899 Arthur Garford of the Garford Saddle Company, who had worked with Charles Smith on the unsuccessful 1896 combination, tried to put together a trust of saddle and parts makers, with some success. A. G. Spalding, the sporting goods magnate, moved in with big-money backers and even bigger plans, and by March the groundwork for an industry-wide cycle trust were well advanced. The news broke on 16 March and neither Spalding nor the Colonel denied the story.[54]

But in April, the Colonel threatened to kill the deal because Spalding wanted all the subsidiaries included, and Pope would throw in only the two cycle factories and the Hartford Rubber Works. "While he does not love the Columbia less," noted one Hartford editor, "Colonel Pope does love his automobile the more." Throughout the spring, Pope still held out and Spalding admitted in early June that "I find the strain I have been in for the last three or four months in shaping up this bicycle matter is having its natural effect."[55] Two days later George Pope told a reporter that there was no news. Late Friday, 9 June, Pope told reporters in New York that he and Spalding had made a deal. Early the following Monday morning, Pope's lawyer appeared in the office of the Hartford City Clerk to transfer the deed of the Laurel Street factory to the Columbia & Electric Vehicle Company.[56] Although the Colonel may have reached a deal with Whitney in April, he waited until after he had reached a second deal with Spalding before taking the irrevocable step of physically transferring ownership in the motor carriage factory to EVC.

The Colonel has typically been portrayed as the passive party in the Electric Vehicle Company story. In fact, his role was much more active, and it is not impossible that he, not Whitney, was the initiator of the merger. The EVC was not driven by necessity to Hartford to build their third-generation taxicabs — they were already preparing to make the units themselves in New York. If the claim that "Hartford was the only place" is questionable, then why would the Colonel part with a motor carriage division "he views almost affectionately"? Given the timing of events on the bicycle side, the logical answer was to keep it out of the bicycle trust. Although Pope fully expected to play a leading role in the trust, the direct sale of the various cycle factories was optioned to

A. G. Spalding, who in turn planned to sell them to the yet-to-be-created trust. If something went wrong during the interim, all control could be lost. This very nearly happened in August when Spalding couldn't raise enough money for the cash buyouts and had to turn to financier Charles R. Flint for help. Flint extracted a high price to save the deal, demanding a $300,000 fee and the sale of the bicycle trust's tire factories to his rubber trust. The same fate could easily have befallen the motor carriage division. Pope knew the financing of the bicycle trust was thin and that the Flint bail-out was a bad deal, but his authority was limited and some of the other major players, especially Coleman, didn't trust him.[57]

Had the bicycle deal not gone through, the timing of the deed sale on the Laurel Street factory suggests that Pope may have pulled out of the Whitney merger. Greenleaf, the author of *Monopoly on Wheels*, expresses puzzlement over the rapid mutation of the EVC corporate structure around the time of the sale. The motor carriage division was spun off as its own corporation, the Columbia Automobile Company, on 18 April. On 3 May the Hartford factory, the 42nd Street shops in New York and Exide Battery were merged into the Columbia & Electric Vehicle Company, headquartered in Hartford. It wasn't until 20 June, eleven days after Pope and Spalding's deal, and nine days after Pope sold the Laurel Street factory to the Columbia & Electric Vehicle Company, that everything, including the local operating companies, was consolidated into a single firm, Whitney's EVC, in New York.[58]

Again, the Spalding deal is the critical clue. Had the bicycle trust fallen through, the Colonel would have kept the Columbia & Electric Vehicle Company and would have supplied William Whitney as an independent entity. It also explains why EVC continued to use the 42nd Street shop in New York after April 1899. Had the bicycle trust fallen through, the construction of the 200 cabs would have continued uninterrupted and the New York headquarters would have had the freedom to order more from Hartford or go somewhere else. The entire arrangement was a perfect triangulation. The bicycle trust could have fallen through or the Electric Vehicle Company merger could have collapsed. The failure of one would not force Pope into any action on the other, and allowed him to pull out of either without breaking up his empire. Only after both deals were set would he need to risk loss of control. The triangle only worked if Whitney could be brought in to hold up one corner. It is thus possible that the Colonel approached him first, not the other way around.

## The Selden Patent

One question that remains is why, if Pope was so attached to his motor carriage factory, he sold out completely to Whitney in June 1900.[59] The answer requires a review of the infamous Selden patent controversy. It is the main reason the Pope motor carriage division and the Electric Vehicle Company have stayed in the history books. George Selden was a patent lawyer and inventor living in Rochester, New York. In 1876, he saw an early two-cycle gasoline stationary motor at the Philadelphia World's Fair. Using this as a base, he designed a motor with a power-to-weight ratio of 90 pounds per horsepower, a fairly respectable figure for the time. In 1879 he applied for a patent "broadly covering a road vehicle propelled by a liquid hydrocarbon engine." Realizing it could never be commercially developed during the standard 17-year patent term, he used a series of corrections and amendments to delay its issuance for over 15 years.[60] By 1895, knowledge of Selden's application was fairly widespread, with a general consensus that it had been filed too early, was too crude, and contained claims too broad to be accepted. However, its patent examiner was a former naval engineer who had experimented with two-cycle motors for marine propulsion, and he believed that Selden's claims were tenable and approved the patent in late 1895.

Hermann Cuntz and Hiram Maxim shared rooms on Columbia Street and Cuntz would sit around the dinner table in the evening telling everyone that the Selden patent would cut the ground out from under the work the motor carriage division was doing on gasoline vehicles. Maxim thought he was nuts, arguing that Selden's vehicle could never run, and didn't even have a clutch. Cuntz countered that it was the claims language that mattered, not the specifications of the vehicle in the drawings. Cuntz had an even harder time convincing Eames and Day. "He was treated with scant sympathy," recalled Maxim. "None of them knew what to do." In hindsight, Maxim realized that Cuntz's explanation was simply "too awful to be believable."[61]

A couple of years earlier, William Whitney had taken a major loss on an investment in a papermill because of patent problems, so at the April 1899 meeting in Hartford one of the specific things he wanted to know was whether any patents posed a threat.[62] Eames rushed across the hall to Cuntz's office, where Cuntz provided him with three sheets for gas, electric and steam autos, each sheet providing a brief list of patents that could prove controlling. There were no basic patents for steam cars, the Pope firm already controlled everything for electrics, and there was only one item listed for gasoline autos: the Selden patent.

After consulting with Colonel Pope and Whitney, Eames rushed back across the hall to ask Cuntz if he knew the status of Selden's patent. Cuntz replied that he had been keeping track of it. Selden had been shopping it around but had found no takers so far. However, there was a rumor that a syndicate of five "financial parasites" was hoping to pool $250,000 to buy control of the patent as a speculative investment.[63] At this point the story starts to break down. Cuntz says he got his information from Philip T. Dodge, a lawyer and industrialist in New York who had briefly helped Selden with his patent application. However, back in 1892, Dodge had become president of the Merganthaler Linotype Company upon the recommendation of its managing director, William Whitney, and for many years the two worked closely together to help Merganthaler overcome potentially crippling patent litigation and become the dominant typesetting-machine maker in the world.[64] If Dodge was the source of information on Selden, it is very unlikely that Whitney had to find out through Cuntz. Whitney probably knew all about Selden even before he stepped off the train in Hartford.

A few weeks after the big meeting, Eames visited Selden and Selden then came to Hartford to look over the Pope factories and sign a series of short-term option contracts while the Pope forces further investigated the validity of his patent. On 4 November, Selden agreed to a long-term license that promised an annual fee of $5,000, fifteen dollars for every gasoline vehicle built, and an up-front payment of $10,000.[65] It would take a lot of cars to add up to the $250,000 that Cuntz claimed the New York financiers were offering, and even the ten thousand wasn't certain. The contract required only a ten percent down payment, with the balance due on 1 January 1900. Electric Carriage & Vehicle could walk away from the contract without obligation by simply refusing to make the January payment.

By December Spalding's bicycle trust was up and running under the name American Bicycle Company. Spalding himself had retired, taking his considerable promoter's fee and profits with him, and the Colonel had been rebuffed in his efforts to succeed him as president. But as chairman of the finance committee he worked closely with the trust's treasurer, Arthur Garford, the former saddle czar. On 29 December, Garford, in New York, wrote Pope in Boston asking what action Pope was taking "in regard to the gasoline carriage which you saw in New York a short time since, and which your expert from Hartford later on examined?" Garford wrote he was being pressed by "parties interested here in New York" who believed it "of considerable importance ... that they receive some indication of your intention, as other parties are seeking to secure control of it."[66] The next day, Pope replied that "I wanted to do something definite when I was in New York, but the others thought better to delay ... I made a suggestion by which the thing could be financed, but it was rejected, and I do not know what to do."[67] The following day the Colonel called Eames in Hartford and told him to send the $9,000 to Selden to close the contract.[68] It appears that the "two" parties dueling over the Selden patent were actually the two halves of the Pope empire — the Electric Vehicle Company and the American Bicycle Company!

While Whitney was assembling the EVC, Charles Flint, the savior and nemesis of the American Bicycle Company, was also looking into the possibility of creating a "lead cab trust," and it was probably his crowd that formed the "parasites" that Cuntz thought were trying buy the patent.[69] Far from learning it from Cuntz, however, Whitney likely prodded Cuntz's investigation because he knew what Flint was up to, and he knew it would light a fire under the Pope company executives when they found out. When Flint and the American Bicycle Company directors waffled, Pope ordered Eames to go forward. If this is correct, it means that the Colonel would have been perfectly happy to have had the bicycle trust own the Selden patent. By this time, Pope had cast his lot with the bicycle trust, leaving the former motor carriage division to Day and Eames, and would soon sell his half interest in it to Whitney. While he did continue to sit on EVC's board of directors through 1903, Pope did not take an active role in management, focusing instead on his local Boston franchise, the New England Electric Vehicle Transportation Company. By mid–1900, Flint had been nullified as a factor in the electric auto industry. Arthur Garford wrote a friend that "I guess Flint is out of it all right ... the Whitney crowd pretty well controls the electrical situation.... I was told that Flint would not dare interfere if Whitney called him off."[70]

After acquiring the patent, the EVC set out in mid–1900 to make money off it, suing two small firms for royalties. They agreed to settle.[71] Late that year, George Day — a chain smoker extraordinaire — suffered a heart attack, the first of several that would eventually lead to his premature death in 1907. In his absence, a managerial turf war ensued, and in the mess Eames, Maxim, Fred Law and several others fled. Day returned in 1901 to straighten things out, firing the troublemakers. Maxim returned, but Eames was lost for good, as were Fred Law and others.

The third company EVC attacked, the Winton Motor Carriage Company, fought back and the litigation promised to drag on for years. With his experience in the great bicycle patent wars, Day knew that the name of the game was to ask for modest royalties, avoid final court decisions, and create a community of interests through reciprocal license agreements. In August 1902 he asked the EVC board for permission to approach the other automakers with the idea of creating a trade association to administer the Selden patent. They agreed. He then went to George Selden and cut a secret deal whereby he and Selden would split Selden's share of the royalties.[72] He did not tell this to the EVC board.

Meeting principally with Henry Joy of Packard and Frederic Smith of Oldsmobile, Day crafted a new organization, the Association of Licensed Automobile Manufacturers, or ALAM. Joy and Smith drove a hard bargain, and the new arrangement effectively shut EVC out of control over the patent. The association, not EVC, would decide who would get a license, who would be sued, and if a given suit would be settled or fought. The ALAM would collect a 1.25 percent royalty from every licensed maker of gasoline automobiles. Only forty percent of this would go to EVC, with another twenty to Selden (actually, ten to Selden, ten to Day), and 40 percent to ALAM.

Selden's share was roughly half the rate he received from the original EVC contract, but now, he was paid for every licensed auto, not just EVC's cars. EVC got only one of five seats on the ALAM board and Selden received no representation at all. George Day resigned from EVC to take over the helm of the new association and was replaced by his assistant, Milton Budlong, a former manager of the Columbia Cycle branch store in Chicago, whom Day had recruited in 1899.

By 1904 some 30 carmakers had joined the ALAM. Henry Ford applied for a license, but was rebuffed. Exactly why is disputed. Nevins and Greenleaf maintain that it was because Ford planned to enter the low-cost auto market that Smith's Oldsmobile firm had already staked out. Others suggest that the always-secretive Ford refused to enter into the reciprocal patent agreements required by the association. Hermann Cuntz met with Ford occasionally during this period, and he claims that Day asked him to pass along an offer to Ford to buy a half interest in his company. Cuntz did not bring it up with Ford "because I understood Ford was not selling, but attempting to acquire all the stock of his friends, in order to make the company a family affair." This was, in fact, the case. Ford pressed on with his plans, and the ALAM sued him in 1903, winning in district court in 1909. Thomas Jeffery, recalling his own bitter patent battles, gave Ford $10,000 to finance his appeal. (He and his son were developing their own auto, the Rambler, and likewise refused to join the ALAM, but unlike Ford made no effort to contest the association. He ignored the ALAM and it ignored him.) Jeffery had learned his lesson in 1886 and advised Ford that "It is easier to fight a patent than break a contract."[73] In 1911, the appeals court ruled that the Selden patent only applied to two-cycle engines. Ford had won.

EVC had given up all pretense of being a manufacturer four years earlier. Its sole remaining asset was the Selden patent. When Day died in 1907 most of the confidence and leadership in the ALAM went with him. The organization passed out of existence the year after losing to Ford. It did, however, leave a lasting contribution to the automobile industry. Its engineering laboratory, run under the direction of former Pope man Henry Souther, was turned over to the Society of Automobile Engineers. In the ensuing years, the SAE lab would develop hundreds of innovations to improve the performance, efficiency and safety of the automobile. Hermann Cuntz always insisted that that it was the ALAM's goal to standardize, not monopolize, the auto industry, and many historians now agree that Nevins, Greenleaf and Rae may have exaggerated the ALAM's coercive intent.

Shortly before his death in 1938, Hiram Maxim told a story. He was talking with

Albert Pope in 1895, soon after starting at the motor carriage division. Suddenly, out of nowhere, the older man blurted out, "Maxim, I believe this horseless-carriage business will be one of the big businesses of the future!" After finishing the tale, the elderly Maxim, by then wealthy and successful in his own right, sighed that "one of my great regrets is that Colonel Albert A. Pope, the father of good roads in the United States, could not have lived to see his predictions come true a thousandfold."[74]

# 9

## *Troubled Times*

> *Albert Linder Pope, son of the famous head of the Pope Manufacturing Company, desires us to correct the statement that he is willing to let his honored Papa do all the work.... The "little colonel" says that he is earning his salary and can be found at his desk during business hours.*
> — American Wheelman, 1893[1]

It was a slow Thursday afternoon in the big flagship Columbia store on the ground floor of the Pope Building on Columbus Avenue. Not yet spring, March still held a grey and icy grip on Boston. John Costello, the manager of the used-bicycle department, busied himself dusting and straightening. The only customers since lunch had been two women looking for the riding school on the fifth floor. They had forgotten to bring the coupons for the free riding lessons they received with their new 1896 bicycles, but Mr. Richardson, the school manager, had straightened it out in a minute or two and the ladies were now happily careening around the rink with their instructor, the handsome young Mr. Chick, and five other women.[2]

As he bent over a bicycle by the front window, Costello thought he smelled a whiff of smoke and thought, "How odd." Once in a while a trace of some odor would come up from the repair shop in the basement, but it was in the rear of the building, behind the boiler room under the showrooms. Built in 1892, the Pope Building was only four years old, and used a blown-draft heating system that pulled fresh air from roof-top ducts. Even on the coldest day, Costello had never smelled anything from engineer Bill Troy's furnace. Costello walked to the back of the building. No odor. He turned around, and saw small puffs of smoke rising from around the base of the posts at the front of the store. He touched one. It singed his fingers. He ran into the corridor, shouting "Fire!" up the elevator shaft at the rear. On the top floor, Mr. Chick pulled the fire alarm. It rang at the central firehouse almost simultaneously with the automatic alarm in the basement. The time was 3:35 P.M.

On the mezzanine, Albert Linder sent his stenographer out of the building, and he and the chief bookkeeper, Mr. Davis, furiously gathered up the books and cash and put them in the massive fire safe in the rear. One floor above, the Colonel's office was dark, as he was on the train to Harford, but his private secretary, Robert Winkley, sent the office stenographer, Miss Hawes, out of the building and did the same with the boss's private records. On the ground floor, Alonso Peck, one of the very first Pope employees, now a new-bicycle salesman, realized that the only way out for the bicycle mechanics in the basement was up the rear stairwell. He and Lon Beers strapped on backpack fire extinguishers and started down the stairs. They emptied their extinguishers before reaching bottom and were forced back, coughing and gagging, to the ground floor.

This building at 221 Columbus Avenue in Boston's Back Bay served as the headquarters of the Pope Mfg. Co. from 1892 to 1895, and continued to house Col. Pope's personal offices until his death in 1909. The entire first floor was dedicated to the flagship Columbia bicycle store. The building was originally five stories high, and the first cornice-line is plainly visible two stories below the roof. When it was rebuilt after an 1896 fire, the top two levels were added. The roundels over the top-floor windows spell out "Pope." The building was renovated and converted into residential condominiums in the 1990s.

In the basement, the mechanics realized they were in trouble when the alarm started ringing. By then the stairwell was a cloud of smoke. The basement had small, high half-windows in the rear half of the building, but they were barred and nobody remembered where the keys to the grills were. They started hammering and sawing at them when a group of mechanics from the Union Bicycle Company across the street ran over with sledgehammers and wrecking bars and smashed in the windows, bars, frames and all.

The real hero of the day was the elevator boy, Joseph MacWaugh. When Costello cried out, MacWaugh was on his way up to the top floor to deliver the riding school coupons to Richardson. When he arrived, Richardson told him to wait for the customers, then calmly told the seven ladies they had to leave. The elevator could only carry five plus MacWaugh, so two women and the staff stayed. The two women decided to use the stairs, but had to duck below rolling smoke the last two flights. By the time they made the ground floor the stairs were impassable. MacWaugh, not knowing they were already out, returned to the top and retrieved the riding school staff. The elevator collapsed into the basement soon after they all ran out the front door.

The last two out of the building were Winkley and the building's janitor, William Aston, who was working on the fourth floor. Both were trapped on the second floor and had to be taken out by fire department ladders from the windows in the rear. Raising the ladders proved to be a tricky job. Electric lines ran along the rear alley and there was confusion over whether the power company had cut the current. Two firefighters were shocked and had to be treated on the scene, but did not need to be hospitalized. By the time hose ladders could be raised, all five floors were ablaze. A general alarm went in at 4:09, and every fire unit in central Boston rolled to the corner of Columbus Avenue and Morgan Street.

The fire made an eerie scene. More than 1,700 brand-new 1896 wheels were stored on the upper floors, waiting to be distributed around New England. As the ice-cold water hit their hot steel tubes, they shrieked and groaned in a gothic chorus. Pneumatic tires popped like firecrackers. The Youth's Companion Building was located just twelve feet north of the Pope Building, across a narrow alley. It housed a book and magazine publisher, and was filled with four floors of raw newsprint and printed material. Fortunately, it was a new building with steel fire shutters on the windows and its own fire-hose system. The printers aimed their hoses across the alley into the adjacent windows, left them there, closed the shutters, and ran. They probably saved the Pope Building.

By 6:30 there were no more flames and at 11:30 the firemen started to return to their stations. Edward Pope and Henry Hyde, the Colonel's personal lawyer, arrived sometime during the evening. Albert Linder made arrangements to stock a temporary store, which opened the next morning with 300 bicycles shipped on the overnight express train from Hartford.

In the morning, 221 Columbus was a sorry sight. Ironically, the building's high-tech heating system proved to be its undoing. The fire apparently started in a pile of discarded bicycle crates someone left piled against a wall in the boiler room. The oil-burning boiler was self-starting and self-regulating, and because the weather had been warm, it hadn't turned itself on for several days. Thursday was cold, and while Bill Troy checked the control panel on the front of the boiler room, he didn't go in because there was no need to stoke a fire, so he didn't find the trash.

The building's walls were still solid, and only the floor of the fifth story had burned through. The fire safes appeared intact, although the Colonel's display of bicycle-related art and the bicycle museum were destroyed. Lallement's 1866 velocipede; Harrington's $313 high-wheeler; Karl Kron's 10,000-mile "No. 234" Standard Columbia; Tom Stevens's around-the-world bicycle — all gone. Pope's exhibit at the 1893 Chicago World's Fair, the size of a small bungalow, had been stored on the third floor and was also lost. Fortunately the building was covered by insurance. The building itself was completely covered, but the contents were only insured for $73,000, about $100,000 short of the estimated loss of $175,000. The company had been using the place as a warehouse, but had neglected to adjust the insurance. The facts that there were fewer than twenty employees working in the place, and that the newest, swankest office building in Boston was being used mainly as a warehouse, were clues that something was amiss. The Pope Building was almost empty because the Colonel had moved company headquarters to Hartford the year before. The company didn't even own the Boston building anymore. Albert Pope had bought it for his personal portfolio and was renting space back to the firm.[3]

George Day had been urging the Colonel to unify operations in Hartford since 1892, when Pope bought the Bartholomew farm for the first tube factory and an expansion of the rubber works. In May 1894 Day announced that the board of directors had voted to move headquarters into a new office building to be built on the lawn in front of the Capitol Avenue factory. While the office staff would transfer to Hartford, the Colonel himself would not be moving, and his new office suite in Hartford would contain a small apartment to facilitate overnight visits.[4] George Keller, who designed the "Pope's Row" homes on Columbia Street and Park Terrace, drew up plans for the new building, which reflected the design of the Boston Pope Building, only smaller.

The week before Day announced the move, Albert Linder issued a press release stating that he had been appointed superintendent of the Pope Building. He was going to be the manager of the retail store, the riding school, the Colonel's private office suite, and three stories of empty space, at least until the building could be remodeled into rental offices.[5] Young Albert was an enigma. After dropping out of school for the last time in 1890, he later said that his father put him to work in the Hartford factory, although he never appeared in *Greer's Hartford Directory* during this period. Starting in July 1892 Albert Linder appears in the *Boston City Directory* under the pseudonym "Alexander L. Pope" as a boarder at the Pope family townhouse, and is listed as a clerk at the Pope Building. It would be easy to dismiss this as a directory error, but it continues for two years in a row until 1894, when he appears under his correct name.

The following year Albert Linder is listed as the manager of the downtown store, and still as a boarder with the family. Years later, the Colonel claimed that he paid his oldest son $1,500 a year to take over the Columbus Avenue store. There is a ring of truth in this, as $1,500 was the typical salary for the manager of a Pope branch house. But while $1,500 a year was nothing to turn your nose up about (it was double the salary for a skilled machinist in the Hartford factory), it is hard to see how young Albert could afford the sloop *Mystery*, the social life of a Commodore of the Hull Yacht Club, or two-month summer sailing excursions of that kind on money. Six months before the Pope Building burned, he traded the *Mystery* in for a full-fledged 50-foot racing yacht, the *Columbia*.[6]

Still, Albert Linder was only 23 at the time of the fire, and his mother Abby thought that a good marriage might settle him down. He announced his engagement at the debutante ball of his younger sister Margaret in December 1895.[7] The ball served double-duty.

On what is probably a spring day in 1905 (the summer awnings have not yet been installed), an unknown photographer took this shot of the Columbia factory from the roof of the Department of Tests building. The 1895 headquarters building is in the foreground to the viewer's left, with the 1897 east wing addition of the factory behind it. Beyond the plant, farther east, is the dome of the Connecticut Statehouse. George Day's innovative Columbia Street townhouses are out of camera range, slightly behind the photographer and to the viewer's right, across Capitol Avenue, the street in front of the factory.

Margaret was presented to Boston Brahmin society and the guests were introduced to young Albert's fiancée, Amy Jaynes, the daughter of a Newton businessman. Amy and Albert Linder were married in April, a month after the fire, and moved into the townhouse on Commonwealth Avenue. As the weather warmed up, Albert Linder announced he would be spending the summer out of town on board the *Columbia*.[8] If he felt left out, he was hiding it well.

## *It Is About the Silliest Idea!*

The headquarters relocation in December 1894 ushered in the most hectic two years of the bike boom. "The Boston Office force came down here last Thursday night," wrote George Pope as he sat in the darkened Hartford Cycle Company factory on New Year's Eve. "While there is some confusion on account of moving and the workmen not being all out of the building, I think that it has been very well managed and that all hands have gotten to work in a remarkably short space of time." As usual, George was being sanguine. A couple of weeks later, the Hartford YMCA hosted a dinner for the former Boston and Hartford staffs. The Boston men wore white ribbons, Hartford red. The Colonel spoke, as did YMCA President Thompson.[9] It was all rather awkward. A week before the Boston folks arrived, Edward Pope, the gentle, calm "E.W.," announced his retirement. "Why am I resigning?" he replied to a reporter's question. "Well, because I don't care to work so hard in the future as I have in the past. I do not need nor do I feel as if I should." True to his word, Edward retired to the life of a gentleman farmer and philanthropist. The Colonel named George to succeed his brother as the treasurer of the Pope company, and he now wore two hats, having kept his existing position as president of the Hartford Cycle Company.[10]

As soon as he came back from January's Chicago cycle show, David Post decided he too had enough. Pope's corporate secretary, Arthur Pattison, had taken the unusual step of writing him in mid–December to remind him that he must hold the line in the increasingly bitter battle to retain good agents. In his last letter to Post, George Pope is obviously responding to any angry blast from his young colleague: "The work you have done has been highly satisfactory and that you have quite a knack of clinching the agents.... I shall be glad to see you home again."[11] When he left, Post still owned ten shares of Pope Manufacturing Company stock that the Colonel had given him in 1890 to facilitate the incorporation of the Hartford Cycle Company. Post offered these back to Pope at par, $100 a share. Pope refused to pay that much, a rather strange rejection, as in the last stock sale, back in 1887, Charles Joy and the Colonel had bought twelve shares from the Colonel's brother Arthur for $227 a share. Post, hurt and angry, sold the shares to R. Lindsay Coleman, president of Western Wheel Works, who announced he would attend the next director's meeting in December. The Colonel had a fit: "It is about the silliest idea!" he exclaimed.[12]

The shares were bought back from Coleman at a considerable markup, and the embarrassment motivated the Colonel to undertake a long-overdue organizational cleanup. Maine allowed domestic corporations to own the stock of other corporations if they were in a related line of business, a provision the Colonel needed, so the Pope firm again "moved" there. The Weed Sewing Machine Company was terminated, and the Hartford Rubber Works Company and the Hartford Cycle Company became wholly owned subsidiaries of the Maine parent.[13] The little blocks of shares that various employees had held as they warmed directors' seats for family members over the years were purchased or exchanged for shares of the holding company, and the organizational chart, which had been repeatedly erased and re-written into an unrecognizable smear during the patent wars and the go-for-broke early 1890s, was cleaned up. E. W. and David Post were not the only old-timers to take advantage of the move to make their goodbyes. Charles Joy, who had started with the Colonel and Edward in 1880 as a bookkeeper and who had worked himself up to superintendent of headquarters operations, decided to stay in Boston and accepted a buy-out. L. S. Dow, manager of the sales department, did make the move, but only remained a year before quitting and moving to New York.[14]

Two of the seventy clerks, stenographers, bookkeepers, correspondents and managers transferred to Hartford were Charles and Wilbur Walker, the sons of an engraver from the Boston suburb of Chelsea. Charles began working for the Colonel as a messenger in

1885 when he was eighteen. Company lore had it that he started without pay, and skeptics said there was something a little too "pushing" in both brothers, a little too fawning. Wilbur started a couple of years after his brother, and by the time of the move Charles was chief of the order department and Wilbur was a bookkeeper. Within three years they had moved into modest, but substantial, side-by-side homes on Hartford's fashionable west side. Albert Linder would eventually live across the street from them. The personnel confusion caused by the move was not without its bright side, if you happened to have the right connections. By mid–1896 Jennie, John and William Pattison, the children of corporate secretary Arthur Pattison, were all working for one or the other of the Pope companies, as was George Day's daughter Helen, and Charles Gillette, who would soon marry George Pope's daughter Marion.[15]

One victim of the press for time and attention was the Colonel's model workers' village. The land for the Laurel Street factory, the Hamilton Street Tube Plant and the expansion of the Hartford Rubber Works came from the 1892 purchase of the Bartholomew Farm southwest of town. In addition to the farm itself, Pope bought four smaller sites for a total of 110 acres. The three factories used only 24 of these acres, and at the time he bought the Bartholomew place he ultimately hoped to build as many as 1,200 new homes in his own idyllic workers' village. Early plans called for the initial development of 200 homes in what would eventually be a 416-unit project.[16] However, cracks soon started to develop in the scheme. The original blueprints followed the upscale Columbia Street model, with leased townhouses, parks, roundabouts and other amenities. A revised 1893 plan was much plainer, with more typical rectangular blocks, detached homes, and fifty-by-one-hundred-foot lots.

In the end, it all came to naught. At the same press reception in which he announced that the Boston headquarters would be moved to Connecticut, George Day explained that the Bartholomew farm would be donated to the city for a park. There were several reasons for the cancellation, some stated, some not. First, the Colonel and Day apparently could not get the financial support they wanted out of the city. The proposed development required the realignment of several roads and the construction of two bridges, and while Hartford could not come up with money for that much infrastructure, in exchange for the park it did promise to build the roads and sewers necessary to service the industrial area on the west side of the Park River where the new tube plant and the Hartford Rubber Works were located. The city would also build a bridge for Hamilton Street across the Park River, bringing all the Pope factories within easy cycling distance of each other. The Colonel kept a few acres on the south edge of the new park for a small residential subdivision. For decades, the Pope family argued that the agreement included a property tax waiver, a position the City of Hartford disagreed with.[17]

Second, the mood of the country was hardening, and utopian housing schemes were no longer in favor, especially after the notorious Pullman strike. A local strike at the Pullman railroad car shops outside Chicago exploded into violence, largely because the workers were concentrated in one huge company town where everything was owned by the employer. The strike went nationwide when the American Railway Union refused to handle the Pullman "Palace Cars" the company leased to most major railroads. The federal Attorney General rashly dispatched troops to break up the strike over the objection of the Illinois governor. The troops mobilized, the workers burned the palace cars, the troops attacked the workers, and the police and local militia went after the troops. Over twenty died, 2,000 rail cars burned, and Chicago became an occupied city under the military grip of General Miles, who had commanded the troops at the bloody strikebreaking.[18] A government review board later questioned the wisdom of maintaining self-contained company towns, especially when the leases were tied to continued employment and a layoff meant simultaneous homelessness.

Two years earlier, the Colonel had delivered a Sunday afternoon lecture on "Economic and Social Problems" at the Boston YMCA, where he told the audience that "Everyone should sympathize with the workingman." He reasoned that the "better his wages the more he has to purchase" from local merchants and the manufacturers. Most importantly, "to improve the condition of the workingman, you must become employers ... [you must] become a capitalist yourself."[19] Pope probably still believed this, but he was no class warrior and he was certainly not anxious to get caught in a political crossfire between his associates and friends such as Nelson Miles.

At this, he probably didn't succeed. George Day's philanthropic drive originated from his wife, the vivacious and equally driven Katherine Beach Day. After George's untimely death in 1907, she took over the Hartford Real Estate Improvement Company and continued to build innovative alternative housing, albeit on a much smaller scale than Columbia Street or Park Terrace, until the mid–1920s. She helped found the Hartford chapter of the National Association for the Advancement of Colored People, and worked to overturn Connecticut's Comstock law prohibiting the sale or distribution of contraceptives to any person, married or single.[20] On the other hand, George Pope started moving to the right after the Pullman uprising, becoming active in the virulently anti-labor National Association of Manufacturers (NAM). A decade later, he led the Pope company into a long, bitter strike at a plant in Toledo. The workers and the company had no real substantive dispute; the object of the strike, backed by a national employers' association, was simply to break the back of the Machinists' union in Toledo, a stalwart labor town. The company prevailed, but the victory was so pyrrhic that George ultimately had to sell the plant. However, he used the victory as a springboard to the presidency of the NAM and into national prominence as an anti-union advocate. George Day and George Pope were the most influential Pope managers actually living and working on a daily basis in Hartford, and their growing political schism must have placed a strain on front-office relations.

The development of Pope Park proved problematic. While the promised improvements to Hamilton Street were mostly built, and the city hired Frederic Law Olmstead's landscape architecture firm in 1904 to create a master plan, many of its important features were never implemented, and the park evolved in fits and starts as a workable, if somewhat inefficiently laid out, recreational area. In the late 1950s its eastern edge, bordering the Park River and containing much of its inherent natural beauty, was wiped out to make room for an interstate highway, and the river itself was turned into a canal and an underground conduit. In 2001, Hartford hired a team of consultants to explore ways to salvage as much as possible of the old Olmstead plan, and since then progress has been steady but slow as the cash-starved city tries to find ways to finance the reconstruction.

## *A Little Less "Hurrah!"*

In the summer of 1895, George Keller, Pope's Hartford architect, tried to get a new Columbia out of George Day, but admitted that he "would not let me have a new bicycle as they have orders away ahead for all they can make."[21] At the Hartford Cycle factory, George Pope was burning the midnight oil, writing that "we are running until 10 o'clock" and that he was trying to decide if they wanted "to run all night after the New York Show." He wanted to avoid this, however, because "I believe that the night gang will produce one-third less than a day gang, so that it makes the direct labor for night work very much more expensive and cannot be excused except to get anybody out of a hole."[22]

Years later, Edward admitted that 1895 was the Pope firm's "greatest financial year." Testifying before a Congressional committee in 1901, George Pope agreed that "the business had been very profitable up to 1895."[23] The entire industry was in a fever, even in the most unlikely places. "The cyclists out here are as thick as fleas, and those are mighty thick," reported Ed "On the Spot" Spooner from Los Angeles.[24] After finishing up the last of his 1895 bicycles, Robert Keating of the Keating Wheel Works sat down and wrote his principal backer, Arthur Garford:

> The factory closes next Saturday night, as the water is drawn off from the canal for ten days. I shall take inventory, clean up machinery, and rearrange the factory for the biggest manufacturer's fight in '96 that a concern ever had. I can tell you that the outlook is beautiful and if we don't have well-filled pocket-books at the end of '96 it will be our own fault.[25]

Cycle firms were trading for outlandish prices. Garford was approached by a broker who offered him the Royal Cycle Works, which had defaulted on a bank loan. The little company had produced all of 1,540 wheels in its short life. The asking price: $36,000.[26] Scaled up, that made the Columbia works worth five million dollars. Garford passed.

As the Colonel and George Pope walked the factory aisles late each evening, exhorting the men to keep up the pace and ribbing them about all the good things their wives and girlfriends would be expecting with the fat paychecks, they must have wanted to scream, as every shiny new Columbia and Hartford going out the door was selling twenty-five dollars too cheaply. In a rare moment of doubt, the Colonel had blinked, and now he was paying for it. Back in March 1894, A. G. Spalding & Brothers had sent a circular to all the agents carrying Overman's "Victor" bicycle, offering to sell them wholesale lots of Spalding's "Credenda" brand bicycles at a giveaway price. It was no secret that Overman made the Credenda for Spalding's sporting-goods empire, and the circular explained that Spalding had taken delivery of a thousand with the understanding that Overman would take them back if they didn't sell, but he then refused.[27] Claiming they had no alternative, Spalding Brothers was offering them to Overman's dealers below cost. Overman exploded. He responded with his own letter to the dealers explaining that Spalding was required to take forty percent of Overman's 1893 production, but had virtually stopped taking deliveries in mid-summer. Overman told the agents that Spalding had then requested he take back the bicycles and issue a $54,000 refund. Overman implied that Spalding was having money troubles and couldn't pay for the bicycles. He warned that any dealer buying one of the cut-rate Credendas would be breaching his agency agreement. He then released the "confidential" letter to the press.

Spalding retorted that he returned the bicycles only because they were defective. "The circular is malicious," he complained. "Why! I bolstered up the Overman Wheel Co. for more than one year by advancing [him] money," he shouted. It turned out that Overman didn't make the Credenda himself, but subcontracted the work out to the Lamb Knitting Machine Company across town. He apparently forgot that Spalding Brothers

The Wilson Bicycle Company of Fergus Falls, Minnesota, was a typical regional jobber of the era, selling Columbia and Leader brand bicycles, wholesaling cycles and accessories throughout the upper Midwest, and manufacturing its own private-label bicycle, probably under contract to one of the established cycle factories back east (The Minnesota Historical Society, St. Paul, Minnesota).

already ran many of their own factories, and Spalding simply came down to Chicopee Falls and bought the Lamb company out from under Overman's nose.[28] Overman lost 40 percent of his sales, and worse, he now had no agents past Chicago, as Spalding Brothers had been his exclusive retailer in the west.

Amidst this high-profile controversy, and fearing a weak market, Pope decided to act. In October 1894, he announced that he was slashing the price of the Columbia from $125 to $100. In Chicago, Thomas Jeffery released a terse statement saying only that "we are not influenced by any other maker," but Curtis Space of Ames & Frost expressed the prevailing sentiment when he told a reporter that "of course, if Colonel Pope can sell Columbias for $100 we cannot hope to sell Imperials at a higher price." After asking around, a trade reporter concluded that the cut had been a strategic error, as it was likely that in 1895 "as many sales could have been made at the old price as at the new one, whereas now one-quarter more wheels must be sold."[29] He was right — that's exactly what happened, only Pope didn't have one-quarter more wheels to sell. If he had held the price line, Pope would have sold exactly the same number of bicycles, but would have earned twenty-five dollars more for each one.

Another victim of the confusion was the Cycles Trades Association. When it looked like grim times were on the horizon, Chairman Pope breathed fire, declaring war on year-long cycle warranties, trade shows, bicycling journals, English bicycles and seemingly everything else. As a result, by the time he stepped down in favor of A. G. Spalding in 1895, there was growing dissatisfaction with his presidency because many felt that other than bluster, "Pope had done nothing." However, Spalding, the former baseball star, league-winning manager and team owner, quickly discovered that cycling was not a team sport, but one composed of rugged, sometimes eccentric, individualists. "The bicycle trade is a jealous trade," predicted one editor at the start of his term. He was proved right within only a few months. "Spalding did not get the generous support he was lavishly promised," recalled another journalist. He compared the situation to that at the League of American Wheelmen where "the president ... has for the past decade been 'put up' and 'knocked down' with amusing and unprofitable periodicity."[30] Arthur Garford growled that "what we need in the cycle business at the present time is a little less of the 'hurrah!' idea and a little more good solid business sense." A year later, the association couldn't even find someone to volunteer for its presidency. "After every argument and possible means of persuasion had been employed," R. L. Coleman took the job after agreeing to overhaul the management of the organization's front office.[31]

As 1896 approached, *Iron Age*, the magazine for hardware dealers, advised its readers that "the possibility of an overproduction of machines in 1896 is seriously considered by some of the older manufacturers" and warned that "the market may be largely oversupplied, with a resultant break and demoralization in prices." The editors recommended that hardware dealers not hurry their pre-season orders just because some manufacturers ran out last year.[32] The cycle magazines, of course, hooted that down, loudly asserting that 1896 would be the year to end all years, but even *Scribner's* began wondering how long it could last, musing that "the market seems bound to be flooded," but it too had to admit that "there is no inclination at this writing that point has been reached."[33] In fact, over six thousand small shops and depots had set themselves up to "buy a few parts and put together a few bicycles during the winter," explained George Pope. "They went into it expecting to make up their machines and sell them and get their money back in two or three months."[34] There were over two hundred in Connecticut alone, and another six hundred in Massachusetts. A typical one had already been a bicycle repair depot for two to four years, had $1,100 in capital, and one or two employees plus the proprietor. It bought about $900 in prefabricated parts, virtually no raw materials, and turned out less than 140 bicycles a year.[35] A sales representative for a maker of sundries remembered visiting a Chicago store when a well dressed older gentleman bought a bicycle and asked to be taught to ride. Two months later, after recruiting a lawyer and a groceryman to join his project, he had started a bicycle company, bought parts and material on credit from jobbers, and had a wheel on the street. The old man was still the only one of the three who could ride, recalled the drummer with a shake of his head, adding that "they did not even know who made the Rambler, the Victor, the Columbia or any of the old makes."[36]

Not everyone decried them. "It is a well known fact that local builders who purchase all parts have made serious inroads upon the sales of goods made by manufacturers who continued to force business on a basis of fictional values," editorialized *Cycle Age and Trade Review*. Parts suppliers reported them to be generally good customers who ordered in sensible quantities and paid cash. With the availability of high-quality purchased parts "it is possible to build as good a bicycle in the small shop as in the large."

A local builder could custom-tailor a wheel to a customer's specifications. Most importantly, their advertising, unlike the razzle-dazzle of the major firms, "comprises nothing but the good word of the riders who use the machines." However, cautioned the journal, the advantages of the local builder are lost if he succumbs to hubris and convinces himself that he can "bid for something a little more ambitious than merely local trading." With the distrust of the big firms fading, prices falling, and buyers becoming less sophisticated "practically all that the small builder has to fall back upon" warned the editor, "is personal acquaintance and village pride, and these cannot be expanded to suit the builder's ambition."[37]

It was a bad omen when most of the bicycle industry's leadership almost burned up in January at the Madison Square Garden Cycle Show. The Peerless Cycle Company hoped to attract attention with a giant electric "Peerless" sign suspended fifty feet above their booth. A little after eight on Friday night, the letter "P" sputtered a few times, and as 5,000 watched, slowly caught fire and burned. "A vast cloud of smoke arose," wrote a reporter, "but there was no crazy individual to shout 'Fire!' and stampede the crowd." Garden employees appeared "from all directions," lowered the now-dark (but still smoldering) sign and quickly hustled it outside, where, fortunately, it was raining heavily.[38]

Unfortunately, it continued to rain heavily all spring, especially out west. Agents, over-booked in anticipation of the same shortages that dogged 1895, started to cut orders.[39]

**Roadside amenities for cyclists were popular during the late 1890s. Most were existing enterprises with a bicycle rack and a new sign added, and after the boom faded in 1900 the vast majority moved on to the latest fad. This concession stand beside a popular summertime recreation ground in then-suburban Minneapolis must have been, by 1910, one of the last holdouts (The Minnesota Historical Society, St. Paul, Minnesota).**

Jobbers, who had firm orders that didn't permit cancellations, started making side deals with agents. Factory salesmen who hadn't booked a single sale in some smaller western cities stepped off the train to find themselves awash in their firm's latest models. In New York, crates of outgoing bicycles piled up at the customs house. In May alone, over 5,000 cycles were shipped overseas. Exports doubled in just three months. Half went to the United Kingdom, in spite of the cold shoulder they received. "There is apparently a general distrust of American machines," the vice counsel in Dublin reported. "Nearly every detail on the machine is adversely criticized."[40] The lack of fenders, the inability to attach a gearcase, and the use of wooden rims, all of which made the bicycles incompatible with England's wet weather, were cited by the vice counsel. But what really drove the Brits to distraction were those Tillinghast "hosepipe" tires.

In England, many bicycles were not sold and serviced through independent agencies, but through large chains of company depots, run by tire makers. The largest operation was the John Griffins Company, owned by Dunlop. The American hosepipe was developed to avoid paying patent royalties, including Dunlop's, and when the English first encountered the single-tube they were justifiably appalled. The Americans had made the despicable garden hose work mostly by putting the onus on agents to fix or replace them, something the corporate-owned English shops weren't about to do. Soon, "Our British friends refused to touch anything Yankee," reported one trade journalist, who found that American bicycles "earned an opprobrium equal to the sneer once attached to 'made in Germany.'"[41]

In Boston, Pope continued to believe that the disruption was only temporary. A number of new, makeshift factories set up with borrowed money were running late in getting their products out, facing past due loans, and thus had to "push machines on the market at any price to meet obligations," he told *Iron Age*.[42] Nevertheless, he had to admit, "These machines are finding a ready sale." But it wasn't temporary. By July, entire lots of bicycles were auctioned off in Chicago, Boston, and New York. Waves of bicycles that experts could identify as having come from major firms, but lacking headbadges, trim paint, or serial numbers, washed out of Illinois, Ohio, and Indiana. Wild rumors that the Japanese were preparing to dump thousands of $10 wheels on the docks of San Francisco made headlines in both the cycle trade magazines and regular newspapers.[43] As the first snow fell, marking the end of the 1896 season, over a third of all the bicycles manufactured that year were still unsold. Most were left partially unassembled in factories. Nationwide, 1896 sales were no higher than the year before.[44]

In their rush to sell, the factories forgot about the careful selection of agents, letters of recommendation, Dun & Bradstreet's ratings and written oaths to hold prices. The ability to sell bicycles in a town or city was almost entirely dependent on whether you had an agent there, and the more, the better, at least for the manufacturer. When the Keating Wheel Company lost all 17 of its agents in New Hampshire in a single year, sales dropped from 290 to 15 wheels.[45] One bitter agent complained that "agencies ... were placed in barber shops, drug stores, book stores, clothing stores, dry goods stores and four or five with boys who had no office but in their hats."[46]

Agents were pressured from all sides. The Cycle Trades Association ordered warranties cut to six months, then ninety days. Agents were told to fix flats, pay freight, and repair hurriedly assembled bicycles. "The maker seems to suffer from a nervous fear that he will be asked to part with a cone or nut that perhaps cost a fraction of a penny without due cause," complained an agent. Terms were reduced to cash. "I can telegraph for a $500 boiler or steam engine and have it shipped at once on an open account easier than I can get a 25 cent repair part out of some of the bicycle firms," complained one Minnesota agent. Protected markets were shrunk, then forgotten. Some long-timers simply threw in the towel. One, who had "sold wheels from the time of the old Ordinary," determined that "the present profit on wheels is not sufficient ... [and] we decided at the close of last season to sell the wheels on hand and discontinue further sale."[47]

Others were less sanguine:

> I must confess that I take particular pleasure in the woes of the bicycle builder this season in his effort to place his product with legitimate dealers.... The manufacturers, and they alone, are to blame for the present demoralization.... The mills of the gods grind slowly, but they have made fairly good time with the Bicycle manufacturer.[48]

The 1897 season started ominously. In February, the manager of the Garford Saddle Company wrote that "Business is assuming a very peculiar attitude." He warned Garford that "manufacturers are sending in little orders of from one to 25 or 50 saddles, where last year we were shipping in thousands."[49] Saddles, unlike other parts, could be used interchangeably on any year's bicycle, and manufacturers were stripping saddles from their unsold 1896 bicycles to send out on 1897 units. In Boston, the Colonel received a letter from financier Henry Lee Higginson. "Values shift & machinery helps them to shift — downwards," he wrote in his typically disjointed prose. "Yours is bound & milked a splendid one — your factory — down as *well*." Higginson was the head of Boston's biggest merchant bank and the scion of one of its bluest of blue-blood families, and was, if not a friend, then an advisor to both the Colonel and especially George, who he greatly admired for his duty with Shaw's Colored Regiment.[50] Higginson advised the Colonel to "sell your business, factory & all for a great price, invest most of it safely & with the rest take hold of mining." Although risky, "no legislature, no city council meddles with good mines." He closed with an ominous reminder: "We are no longer young."[51]

Mines, especially gold mines, were the get-rich-quick fad of the day. Although the Colonel too would eventually fall for this rich man's conceit, this was not the time: "I am no longer young, but I am not as old as some," he retorted. "I have had many opportunities to sell out my business, but have declined them all.... I want my business to hand down to my sons."[52]

The buzzards were not only circling the Columbia factory, but the Garford saddle works in Ohio as well. Less than a week after Higginson wrote Pope, Vinton Sears, a Boston stock and bond broker, warned Arthur Garford that "parties who are well posted on the industrial and cycle business in England" had called him to "say a 'slump' is coming in the cycle business." Sears advised Garford that "it would not be bad judgment for you to sell out at the height of this season's business."[53]

## *This Is a Cash Proposition*

Garford wasn't going to wait around for the buzzards to land. John D. Rockefeller had a trust. So did Carnegie, and Frick. That's what was needed: a trust, a bicycle trust. Rockefeller's Standard Oil Company, formed in 1882, was the first. It was a vertical combination, joining together oil production, transportation, refining and retailing. On the other hand, the typical Gilded Age trust was a horizontal combination, and acted a little more brutally: select an industry, combine its firms, eliminate competition, set high prices, cut back production and close the surplus factories that resulted.

Arthur Lovett Garford was born in 1885 in Elyria, Ohio, the son of a landscape contractor. He graduated high school in 1875 and left for Cleveland to work as a clerk in an importing house. In 1880 he returned to Elyria to take a job as bookkeeper at Elyria's largest bank. In 1881, he was promoted to cashier, essentially making him floor manager — the highest non-partnership position in the firm. In 1888, while still cashier, he bought a patent for a bicycle saddle from its inventor, George Hazard. Garford asked a big Washington patent lawyer, Marcus Hopkins, to look it over, and Hopkins advised Garford that it was "the best bicycle saddle now in existence," and if he moved quickly he "could probably monopolize a great part of the saddle business." Garford followed his advice, and by the middle of the bicycle boom he was churning out 400,000 seats a year. Younger than most of the big bicycle magnates, Garford played no games and showed no favorites, and as a result was liked and trusted by them all. Many sought him out for his knowledge of banking and finance.[54]

In November 1896 Charles F. Smith reported to Garford that "I saw the Sterling people & found they were just as willing to sell as any of us."[55] "Us" was Smith's Indiana Bicycle Company (makers of the Waverley) and his tire factory, the Indianapolis Rubber Company, and Garford's two companies, the Garford Manufacturing Company, the saddle firm, and the Keating Wheel Company, a bicycle factory. Also included were Sterling, the Monarch Cycle Company, the Albany Manufacturing Company, A. Featherstone & Company and the Western Wheel Works, all cyclemakers.[56]

Initially, Smith and Garford had hoped each owner would sell for securities, but quickly discovered that "some money would have to be paid them instead of bonds." However, the owners were eager to sell, as Smith discovered when he met with J. W. Kiser of Monarch: "He made the remark that he would like to get out of business and would sell at net inventory."[57] As the plan evolved, Smith switched to a full-cash buyout. The two men would then float bonds to pay themselves back and take a promoter's profit on top. The bonds, in turn, would be repaid by either selling the factories off at a profit or continuing to operate them. "We can make for ourselves the profits to be acquired by consolidation," asserted Smith, "if [we] found customers [we] can deliver [the factories] without trouble or we can keep them & operate [them] if we wish." Smith proposed that he and Garford "divide the profits equally."[58]

What Smith was outlining was a third type of trust — a liquidation trust. What the wheelmakers needed was a way to sell out on a wholesale basis. Merge a bunch of factories together and sell one big issue of stocks and bonds for the whole group. After touting the new combination from the rivers to the hills, the sellers dump their securities and move on. If the bicycle market recovers, the new owners can jointly burn through the unassembled bicycles and the stockpiled raw material built up during the go-go years. If, on the other hand, the market doesn't pick up, the combination sells off the factories one-by-one and retires the bonds using the proceeds. As for the unfortunate stockholders who bought from the owners in the expectation that the new business would be a success? Well, business is all about risk, isn't it?

Based on his conversation with Kiser, Smith apparently believed that each firm's inventory of sellable bicycles, unassembled machines, and stored raw material would form the bedrock price below which no owner would sell. He used inventories as a proxy for

Arthur Garford, shown here on the viewer's left shaking hands with California Governor Hiram Johnson, was an Ohio bank manager who made it rich during the great bicycle boom of the mid–1890s by becoming the American "saddle king." In one year, Garford's factories churned out more than a half-million bicycle seats to supply the needs of the big manufacturers. Younger than most of the cycle magnates, this discreet and personable Midwesterner was nevertheless liked and respected by all the bicycle magnates, who frequently turned to him for advice on financial and banking matters (George G. Bain Collection, Library of Congress, Washington, D.C.).

each firm's outstanding debt load, showing his plan hinged on an assumption that the owners would be happy to wash their hands of the bicycle business for the cash sunk into it. Smith apparently believed that his fellow owners were sticking it out only because they couldn't afford to leave.

Even under this rosy scenario, he and Garford estimated that they would need to float about $12 million in securities, double even the most optimistic capital valuation of the factories ($6.6 million). The scheme was a classic illustration of a heavily watered corporation. If they sold off the plants, only $6.6 million in hard assets would back up the $12 million in securities. If liquidated, this was only enough to pay back the bondholders and the preferred stockholders, leaving the common stockholders exposed. In practice, letting go of that much real estate and machinery would flood the market, so the two would do well to raise the $3.5 million necessary to pay off the bondholders, who under law were considered secured creditors. In other words, all the stock was junk. The only way a stockholder could avoid a wipeout was hope the bicycle market stayed strong and the factories earned money. Even then, the demand for dividends would soon bleed the company white unless sales and profits increased exponentially. For example, the target companies together earned $971,000 a year during the peak of the bicycle boom. After the merger, the face value of the stock and bond dividends was $955,000, and if the firm missed its $210,000 annual bond premium, it would fall into receivership.[59]

Smith's figures omitted the Western Wheel Works. Sometime after Smith's meeting with R. L. Coleman, Coleman started demanding a series of impossible conditions. Garford continued trying to put the deal together throughout the spring of 1897, but weary and disgusted with the drawn-out negotiations, he gave up by mid-year. The Smith-Garford plan would have one lasting impact — it formed the basic blueprint for the 1899 American Bicycle Company, the Great Bicycle Trust.[60]

## Charley

There was no real season in 1897. With a backlog of 300,000 unfinished and unsold bicycles sitting in factories, nobody pre-ordered. Five million dollars' worth of bicycles, more than 83,000 bicycles, were sent overseas before the summer was half over, a figure five times higher than for all of 1896. In Berlin, the *Klein Journal* reported "phenomenal" imports of American bicycles. "The bicycle industry is in a bad way just now in America, on account of overproduction and the cutting of prices," it explained.[61] Ominously, the Columbia catalog was issued without prices, which were contained in a separate, laid-in sheet that could be changed on a moment's notice.

The Colonel's only respite from the daily grind of bad news was the reopening of the rebuilt Pope Building.[62] The Colonel ordered an additional two floors to be added on top of the original five levels of the burnt building. The new structure retained the cornice line of the existing façade, simply piling two new floors on top. As you stand on the Commonwealth Avenue sidewalk and look up at it, the unusual dimensions create the odd optical illusion that the building is leaning out over you in a gradual curve, as if to reprove you for having nothing better to do than stand there on the street gawking up at it. One part of the 1894 structure that was significantly redesigned was the rear basement. The repair shop, where six mechanics almost perished, now opened to Stanhope Street in the back. The repair shop and the delivery department each had their own doors, and the repair shop had real windows. True, the view out on Stanhope, which was really an alley, was nothing to get excited about, but it was better than the dungeon windows. There was even a self-service air hose for cyclists to use to pump up their tires.

In April, the company put out the greatest advertising bonanza in the history of cycling, a 42-page spread entitled "The Marvels of Bicycle Making," in the March issue of *McClure's*. The only obvious ads were on the inside covers; the remainder was a tour of the Columbia and Hartford factories, the Hamilton Street tube plant and the Hartford Rubber Works. S. S. McClure had started *McClure's* in 1893, ten years after leaving *The Wheelman*. In the summer of 1895, *McClure's* was caught up in a newsstand price war with *Cosmopolitan*, and losing a thousand dollars a month. McClure called upon the Colonel at Lindermere and asked for help. Pope advanced him $5,000 "against future advertising."[63] Now it was the publisher's turn to help. The spread became famous, but it didn't move bicycles.

As sales stagnated, uncompleted bicycles from previous years accumulated like unmelted snow. At the Keating Wheel Company, Robert Keating told Arthur Garford that he thought the factory had about 4,750 unassembled 1896 models left over. By the time the 1897 season ended, the firm had put together 7,000 of the old units and still had another thousand to go. Out of 9,306 bicycles sold that season, Keating could sell only 2,321 at a retail price of $100.[64] The next fall, the company had both 1897 and 1898 models stockpiled.

A group of Canadian cycle manufacturers went to Ottawa to complain that the Americans were using forced labor. "A very great proportion of the imported wheels sold in this country were the product of convict labor," complained the delegation. "That was the secret of their cheapness."[65] The Canadian wheelmakers were assured that the Crown's law against convict labor would be strictly enforced, and Royal customs officials were put on the alert. It made no difference; prices continued to slide. "Importation was practically undiminished by these precautions," reported the government. The reports of prisoners slaving away in foundries and over punch-presses were spurious.

Back in Boston, the Colonel gave fewer interviews, confining his remarks to good roads and fond memories of the early days. When pressed for a prognostication, he grumbled sourly that "I think there will be a good many less manufacturers." In Ohio, Arthur Garford agreed. "In my opinion it is going to be pretty slow.... I do not like the outlook."

In late June 1897 the Pope firms slashed the prices of all their bicycles, with the flagship models cut from $100 to $75. Many saw the move as the start of a campaign: "It means Colonel Pope is tired of the tactics of the small dealers and makers," they warned.[66] If that was the case, it was a scorched-earth strategy, devastating dealers and customers who had already bought 1897 bicycles. One customer, a Mrs. Pinkham, had purchased her bicycle in April on time payments. After the price cut, her outstanding balance was higher than the price of a new machine. Indignant, she refused to pay and tried to return the bicycle to the dealer, who turned her away. A court ordered her to continue payments. The Pope firm had a strict no-return policy towards its dealers, so any agent unfortunate enough to have already taken delivery of a full year's worth of stock had to sell them essentially at cost. The factory did offer some vaguely explained compensation for the reduction, but it involved rebates against future orders. Any agent bold enough to fight Hartford was on his own, and many agents simply joined the throng dumping wheels for whatever they could get.[67]

Three weeks after the big announcement, Albert Pope and A. G. Spalding sailed off to Europe. George Day, Harry Pope, Henry Souther, and Hayden Eames were already there looking over automobiles, but the fact that the Colonel and Spalding were taking William Redding, Pope's patent lawyer, raised a few eyebrows. "It is not the habit of either Colonel Pope or Mr. Spalding to start away on an expedition accompanied by an expert in patent matters," one New York newspaper noted. "Some move is to be made which will have direct bearing upon the cycle business throughout the world."[68] The trip did not move the world, but Pope did buy the rights to the French Metropole company's L'Acatène ("chainless") bevel gear system, which he combined with the League shaft-drive system he acquired in 1895. On the same trip, he purchased an alternative to the bevel gear system using angled roller bearings from a British concern.[69]

Pope and Spalding were laying the groundwork for later developments, but the Colonel was also escaping domestic unpleasantries. In August, the firm announced that Arthur E. Pattison, the company secretary, was stepping down, to be replaced by Albert Linder. It is unclear whether Pattison quit or was fired. He remained in Hartford without a job for a year before moving to Brooklyn to take a job with the A. E. Burt Shoe Company, suggesting he left on short notice. On the other hand, his daughter Jeanne continued to work as a stenographer in the front office for several years, and his son John worked his way up to manager of the sundries department before the bicycle trust decimated the staff in 1900, so relations between the firm and the Pattison family couldn't have been all that strained. In 1900, E.W. said that Pattison was "making a lot of money as a partner in the shoe and boot business."[70]

It was likely a combination of push and pull. As is true of any outsider in a family business when the sons start to come of age, Pattison probably realized that he would advance no higher, and that his loyalty and hard work would continue to be rewarded only as long as the patriarch stayed healthy and active. Pattison was also probably getting tired of spending his winters on the road, pleading and arguing and stroking agents who, after the June price cut, had no reason for loyalty. The same things had driven away David Post two years before. Finally, he may have just realized that the good times were over. He and the Colonel had both come out of the shoe and leather business, and while Pope may not have cared for the blandness of cowhide, people were always going to walk, and as long as they walked they needed shoes. Could the same be said for bicycles? And as for young Albert? Well, that was for the Colonel to decide — it was his company and his money.

Over the winter, German and Canadian cyclemakers demanded that their respective governments switch from *ad valorum* customs duties on American bicycles to flat rates. Both were attempts to cut off cheap bicycle dumping. Between 1897 and 1898, the increase in the number of bicycles imported into England increased by less than twenty percent, but the number of these bicycles that were immediately reshipped to other countries more than doubled.[71] In 1898, over a third of all bicycles shipped to England were re-exported. Such flipping made sense if the ultimate destination was other nations within the British Commonwealth, where trans-shipments were duty-free, but the vast majority of bicycles were reshipped to other European countries, and paid double tariffs, once in England and again at the final destination's port of entry.

This seemingly aberrant behavior was yet another tariff fluke. Prior to 1904, tariff rules permitted manufacturers to take a 99 percent "drawback," or refund, on any tariff previously paid on imported raw material, but only if it went into a finished product that was re-exported. At the front end of the boom many wheelmakers had guaranteed supplies of English tubing (or American tubes made of Swedish billets) by making massive, multi-year commitments. Both the tubes and the billets carried a 45 percent tariff at the time they were imported. These tubes were now piling up like snowdrifts in bicycle factories around the county. If a firm could stuff them into something resembling a bicycle, then get it on an outbound freighter, the company could apply for the drawback. Although they were usually woefully built and equipped, the epithet that the British subsequently placed on these bicycles — "gaspipe machines" — was a misnomer, as they were made out of some of the best cold-drawn seamless tubing any American firm would use for the next century.[72] It was a sign of how bad things had gotten when the best thing you could do with your bicycles was heave them off the east coast docks for a ten or eleven dollar tariff rebate.

Pope introduced his Columbia chainless bicycle in the fall. It cost $125, fifty dollars more than his best chain-drive cycle. Most of his major competitors followed suit, "although none of them, outside of Colonel Pope, appears anxious to place a chainless wheel on the market," noted one newspaper.[73] The chainless had a checkered history that is still largely undocumented. The bevel-gear version was invented twice, in 1893 in France by the Metropole firm and in 1892 in Springfield, Massachusetts, by S. A. Grant.[74] Grant assigned his patent rights to a new firm organized by a group of investors in Hartford, the League Cycle Company, who had their bicycle on the market by 1893.[75] The bevel gears had to be machined to exacting tolerances and it appears that League could not do the job in-house, contracting the job out to the Leland & Faulconer machine shop in Detroit, at that time acclaimed as the best precision machinists in the nation. (Henry M. Leland would go on to found the Cadillac Motor Company.)[76] It seems that League could not afford Leland & Faulconer's work and the firm folded in late 1894 or early 1895 and was bought up by Pope, who kept only the Grant patents and threw away the rest.

Industry insiders apparently believed that the Colonel would re-introduce League's chainless as soon as the bankruptcy paperwork was settled. In reply to a query from Arthur Garford, Pope engineer Charles E. Hawley wrote in late 1895 that there was "nothing new on the chainless," which led Garford to remind Hawley "do not neglect to send me the chainless as soon as you can."[77] The subsequent two-year delay seems to have resulted from both design and fabrication problems. Norman Clarke, who was president and owner of Pope's successor firm, the Columbia Manufacturing firm, had several Columbia shaft-drives and noted that they "always got out of adjustment ... they just did not stay in adjustment." The Metropole L'Acatène did not appear to share this problem, as the famous French cyclotourist Vélociode (Paul de Vivie) used one for nineteen years and when it was restored in the 1980s it was found to be in perfect condition, which may explain why Pope was anxious to acquire its rights.[78] In addition, the Colonel found the problem of fabricating the precise bevel gears as daunting as League had, spending, according to one account, $300,000 to develop the necessary machinery. In the end, Pope engineer Charles D. Rice came through with a fully automatic gear-cutting machine that required the operator only to load and unload a rough-cut blank. The machine cut one tooth at a time, requiring almost an hour for an entire gear, although the actual cutting time was only 31 seconds per unit.[79] Finally, there were very real questions as to whether the chainless actually justified the additional $50. A test by the engineering school at Cornell University found that in simulating a speed of 15 mph over a smooth road, a chainless bicycle delivered a mechanical efficiency of 95.6 percent, while a chainwheel cycle under the same conditions was 92.6 percent efficient, a differential of about one percent. The drop in friction from switching to a chainless bicycle was less than the advantage resulting from better gear selection.[80]

The 1898 season went up in flames with the battleship *Maine* in Havana harbor on 15 February. In April, *Cycle Age* frankly stated that "the business that was in sight a few weeks ago has not materialized ... it is the well-worn and exasperating 'war scare' that has cast its baneful influence." Two weeks later the United States blockaded Cuba and Spain declared war. By the time the Spanish-American War was over in August, the United States held Cuba, Puerto Rico and the Philippines. "Trade in bicycles is reported to be nearly at a standstill," noted the *New York Times* two weeks after the war started. "The influence of the members of the National Guard has been found to be of considerable importance. Probably the majority of them, or at least a large minority, are wheelmen." Garford estimated that 300,000 cyclists enlisted and "threw their wheels on the market at very low prices, not knowing when, if ever, they should again need them."[81]

A month before the *Maine* went to the bottom, Pope wrote Henry Higginson that "My sympathy is with the Cuban cause. I believe they will win."[82] The Pope Manufacturing Company guaranteed to hold the job of any employee volunteering for the military, and gave each volunteer a free $1,000 life insurance policy.[83] The army selected Nelson Miles to lead the regiments liberating Puerto Rico throughout May and June. The Colonel would have been proud, had he been reading the papers, but he probably was not.

On Tuesday evening, 19 April, Pope's wife Abby received an urgent telephone call at the Commonwealth Avenue townhouse.[84] It was the Peekskill Military Academy in upstate New York, where her son Charles had been a student since the fall of 1896. She had been informed on Monday that he wasn't feeling well and had been excused from chapel and parade, but now, the voice on the line said, it had grown serious and she was needed. She arrived the next morning. Charles was running a high temperature, probably either scarlet or typhoid fever. By early Thursday, he was having convulsions. Abby sent a telegram to Hartford, where the Colonel was working, and he caught the morning express. Charles Linder Pope died early in the afternoon of Thursday, 21 April 1898, at age 16. A student in Peekskill's scientific department, his grades were good and he expected to enter MIT in the spring of 1899. His father arrived about an hour after he passed away.

Forest Hills Cemetery is still one of the most beautiful places in Boston. At the turn of the century, Sundays were the busiest days of the week on the West End streetcar, when families traveled out to the end of the line to picnic there at the grave of a loved one. The Pope family columbarium — a mausoleum for cremated remains — had been built in 1896, a Greek revivalist temple built into the granite cliff under the police and firemen's memorial hill.[85] The imposing memorial carries a plain brass niche plate with Charles's date of birth and death. On the lawn in front of it Abby placed a small headstone bearing the single word "Charley."

The Colonel retreated to his hilltop estate in Cohasset. The Pope publicity machine ground on, generating facts and figures, photos and specifications, but the Colossus himself retreated into solitude. For months, there are no interviews, no direct quotes, none of the Colonel's bombast. As the summer of 1898 rolled past and the early snows fell, Robert Keating of the Keating Wheel Company again wrote to his sponsor, but with a different message. "I wish matters were so straightened around here that the bicycle business was out of the factory," he complained. Reviewing the end of the 1898 season, one cycling editor looked back and sighed, "Not again for a long time can we hope to reach the high water mark of 1895." It would take 77 years.[86]

# 10

## *The Bicycle Trust*

*The Colonel told me that in spite of losing millions ... to give you a check now for $15,000 would be like me paying for a cigar.*
— S. B. "Ely" Leonard, 1902[1]

*I am like you and many others of the A.B.C. with no money on hand and a good deal in debt.*
— Albert A. Pope, 1901[2]

The origins of the American Bicycle Company are murky. A 1914 history of the trust by Harvard professor Arthur Dewing claims that a Boston law firm, Alexander & Green, approached sporting goods magnate A. G. Spalding in the late summer of 1898 and suggested that he lead the promotion of a bicycle trust. The story is plausible, as Arthur Garford had tried to interest two of the firm's partners, the Alexander brothers, in his 1896–97 combine. Garford had since retooled his scheme into an effort to form a nationwide merger of saddlemakers. By January 1899 he had been working on the idea for several months with some success, and a few years later one of his lieutenants said that he believed the saddle combine was the nucleus around which the "big co." jelled. Throughout 1898, Garford and Spalding had been in court over the rights to the popular "Christy" saddle. When the two settled amicably in November, *Bicycling World* noted that given the industry's fractious history of patent litigation their mutually beneficial resolution "will come in the nature of a surprise to many." Spalding became yet another Garford supporter.[3]

Spalding contacted Garford about his merger plan in March 1899 and asked him to coordinate discussions with several cycle parts makers and assist in their appraisals.[4] Spalding told Garford that he intended to follow the strategy he and Smith had developed three years before. "You understand that this is a cash proposition and I will depend on you to get a cash option that will be attractive to the people identified."

At almost exactly the same time that Garford and Spalding met, the *Chicago Tribune* broke the story of Spalding's proposed bicycle trust, relayed the next day to a nationwide audience by the *New York Times*. Spalding didn't deny the talks, but implied that only a few large makers would be involved. Contacted in Boston, the Colonel announced that "I approve of the plan heartily."[5] Despite frequent references, both then and now, to "Pope's bicycle trust," there are few signs that he was participating in the early groundwork of the new company, let alone was its mastermind. There had been a flurry of headlines back in the summer of 1897 when Pope, Spalding and William Redding sailed together to Europe, but it appeared that the purpose of that trip had been to negotiate French patents related to shaft-drive bicycles, and it is likely that the Colonel himself had spent much of his time as a guest of French bicyclemaker Adolphe Clement, whom Pope had befriended in 1894 when Clement stopped in Hartford during a tour of American bicycle plants. Now, in the spring of 1899, he was just starting to get back on his feet.[6] At least in its early stages, the trust was the work of A. G. Spalding and the Alexander brothers.

Alexander & Green incorporated the trust under the name "American Bicycle Company" (A.B.C.) in New Jersey on 12 May. It is unclear exactly what Spalding's early plans were, and more than one observer said that he did not think the baseball man was well versed about the bicycle industry. Despite what he said to the *New York Times,* he told one cycle trades journal that he planned to include every bicycle maker with a capacity over 5,000 machines a year, which he believed to be about forty firms, but which the editors estimated at 102.[7] When R. L. Coleman learned of Spalding and Garford's efforts to create a massive combination, he not only pulled out his Western Wheel

Albert Goodwill Spalding was already in the twilight of a long and successful career in sports when he assembled the American Bicycle Company, the great "bicycle trust." Starting as a professional baseball player in 1871, he later worked his way up as captain, manager, president and finally owner of the Chicago White Stockings. In 1876, he and his brother Walter started a Chicago baseball-supply store that grew into an international sporting goods conglomerate. Spalding served only briefly as president of the bicycle trust, retiring to California in 1901, a year after the combination was organized. This photograph was taken in 1910, five years before his death (George G. Bain Collection, Library of Congress, Washington, D.C.).

Works, but started his own combination, the International Vehicle and Manufacturing Company, to compete with it. "Mr. Spalding has gathered so many people, including parts makers and others not included in the original proposition, as to make the whole scheme absurd," complained Coleman's lawyer, Frederick Stimson.[8] As was the case back in 1896, Coleman wanted cold, hard cash for his factory and believed that Spalding's overbroad scheme would never be able to raise it. Within a week, Coleman was mollified when Spalding promised him that the captive steel tube plants and tire factories that belonged to bicycle makers would not be included, and that their owners would be free to sell them off to the rumored steel tube and rubber trusts being formed in New York City. "Mr. Coleman might decide to limit the combination to six or eight concerns," stated attorney Stimson. Although peace now reigned — at least for the time being — the bicycle trust drama now played out as a very public melodrama on the pages of the *Commercial and Financial Chronicle* and the cycling tabloids.[9]

With the coming of spring, the Colonel started to shake himself out of his grief-stricken lethargy. He purchased an acre of land at West Corner, on the south shore of Straight's Pond about a quarter-mile from Lindermere, to build a small stone church in the memory of the lost Charles. Finished the following summer, it served as an ecumenical chapel during the Colonel's lifetime, then a Methodist church, and has, since about 2001, been owned by a Greek Orthodox congregation. Its location on Straight's Pond, a popular spot for locals to teach their children sailing, has led to a persistent legend that Charles drowned in the pond after falling from a sailboat. The truth is, if anything, even a little more eerie. At the time of his death, Charlie was attending school at Peekskill Military Academy along with his older brother Harold, who graduated later in 1898. Less than two weeks after Charlie died, a third student, Harold Whitehouse of Brooklyn, fell into the Hudson River, which ran adjacent to campus. Whitehouse, who couldn't swim, was almost drowned when Harold dove in, pulled him to shore and saved him.[10] Over the years, the two stories merged into a single gothic tale of Charles's death at the back door of the church that still bears his name.

The Colonel was also roused to action in the defense of his friend, the flamboyant General Nelson Miles, who was again in trouble. Malaria and typhoid fever had ravaged the American troops in Cuba and Puerto Rico during the Spanish-American War, killing far more than the Spanish. As part of the troops' provisioning, the big Chicago meatpackers had supplied canned beef that, instead of salted or smoked, was made resistant to the tropical climate with a new substance called "preservatine." It didn't work well, being, at best, no improvement over the traditional methods, and it tasted bad. Hundreds of field officers complained about this "embalmed" beef, and Miles, in an era when the nature of infectious diseases was not well understood, blamed it for the high rate of sickness and death. He leveled his charges in the newspapers upon his return, after which the meatpackers announced that they would give $100,000 to anyone who could prove the meat was tainted, a move Miles scoffed at as "pure bluff." After a preliminary investigation, the Army Inspector General Breckenridge advised that Miles's accusation should not be dismissed out of hand. An investigative court martial was convened. It concluded that no impropriety occurred, and rumors flew that Miles and Breckenridge would be disciplined. At this point, the Colonel stepped in, sending a telegram to Miles authorizing him to draw on his bank account to fund the investigation necessary "to prove that chemicals were used to embalm beef furnished our soldiers." At this point, Miles realized things were on the verge of spinning out of control and told a crowd of reporters assembled in the Waldorf-Astoria Hotel in New York that while "I appreciate his patriotism and have great respect for the public spirit which he displays," he had to admit that "I do not think it necessary to spend any such sums." Neither the beef packers nor Miles suffered any sanctions, and the matter slowly drifted away.[11]

By late May the options of over a hundred firms were extended to 1 August. Scores of smaller factory owners were summoned to Spalding's temporary quarters on the thirteenth floor of the Waldorf-Astoria Hotel, only to be kept waiting, some for days, while the underwriters decided if they were in or out. Rumors flew through the Waldorf's lobby that the combine had no intention of actually buying most of the optioned firms. "I, in common with fifty others, have simply been humbugged for the purpose of delaying my business so as to seriously hamper it for next season," complained one irate factory owner.[12]

Spalding winnowed out the also-rans at a meeting at the Waldorf over the weekend of June 21–23. *Cycle Age* published a list of twenty-five firms it said were in; the rest, it asserted, perhaps eighty companies, would be cut loose when their options lapsed.[13] The Colonel threatened to upset this applecart by holding out. The problems began in the spring, and centered around the disposition of the seamless tube, tire and motor carriage subsidiaries. In May, the Morgan & Wright tire company had been bought out by a new firm, the Rubber Goods Manufacturing Company, a holding company made up of seven firms making rubber belts, hoses and tires. The firm also wanted the Hartford Rubber Company. Similarly, the Shelby Tube Steel Company, partially owned by Pope, had combined with a couple of other bicycle tube makers and was interested in buying Pope's Hamilton Street works. Spalding had changed his mind a couple times as to whether he wanted such subsidiaries included in the bicycle trust, or to save money, sold off first.[14] By June those issues had been resolved.

The deal-breaker looked to be the motor carriage division, which Pope flatly refused to sell to the trust. Although the Pope-Whitney deal had been inked back in April and a new company incorporated, Pope hadn't actually sold the hard assets of the motor carriage division to it yet. In mid–June, George Pope announced that the Colonel and Spalding had reached a deal, and the next morning the Colonel's Hartford lawyer transferred the deed for the factory at 1 Laurel Street to the Columbia and Electric Vehicle Company.

Nine days later the Waldorf-Astoria meeting went forward as planned. *Cycle Age* was right: only about a third of the option holders were invited. As promised, Spalding offered each firm a straight cash buy-out. Pope's selling price was somewhere between four and five million dollars, which included the rubber works, but not the steel tube plant, which had been optioned to Shelby in May. However, to raise the necessary $80 million, the owners had to subscribe to $31 million of the new firm's stock, and they signed up for only $12 million, leaving the rest to be covered by the underwriters, who refused to subsidize the bicycle trust so deeply. This was a good barometer of the owners' attitudes. They saw the trust mainly as a chance to cut and run from the business and had neither confidence in the future of the cycling industry nor the ability of the combine to turn its fortunes around. In early July Spalding's wife Josie suddenly died at their summer home in New Jersey.[15] Temporarily leaderless, the trust started to fall apart.

## *The Finances Stagger These Fellows*

The near-collapse of the first plan introduced the next major player in the American Bicycle Company drama. Charles R. Flint was a true raconteur, an American version of Henry J. Lawson and Terah Hooley. He got his start in the lumber business, where he merged several small Canadian-American lumber companies into a cartel, the Export Lumber Company, to fix prices for ship-building lumber. George Pope knew Flint from those days, having managed the Montreal office of one of the lumber firms, Hall & Company, swallowed up by Export Lumber in 1889. When Export closed the Montreal office, George moved back to the States to take over the Hartford Cycle Company.[16]

Flint's latest scheme was the Rubber Goods Manufacturing Company, the "rubber trust" formed in May around Morgan & Wright. In July, the R.G.M.C. acquired Dunlop's North American operations. If Spalding's bicycle trust succeeded, it would control Pope's Hartford Rubber Works and three other tire factories, and would thus be self-sufficient in tires, throwing a wrench in Flint's plans to dominate the business.[17] When the bicycle trust's underwriters refused to guarantee the needed $68 million in securities, Spalding hurriedly arranged a second Waldorf meeting in July. He now offered the owners sixty percent cash and forty percent bonds. Coleman, Lozier, Waverley Cycle's Charles F. Smith, and Gormully & Jeffery rejected the new plan. At this point, accounts differ. Some say Flint was already working behind the scenes to sink Spalding's scheme. Others believe the dissension among the owners was now so deep that there was nothing left to sink.[18]

Flint himself later said that it was Spalding who approached Joseph Auerbach, Flint's lawyer, asking for help. Flint and Auerbach invited him and the underwriters to spend the night on Flint's yacht to work out a deal. George Young, one of the bankers, said he had to go home to get a nightshirt, but Flint assured him he had plenty on the boat.[19] The midnight deal they hammered out significantly reduced the scope of the trust. Forty million in stocks and bonds would be issued, half the size of the original. Each firm would be valued at 110 percent of its appraised worth, and each owner would receive 80 percent of this in stocks and thirty percent in either cash or twenty-year debenture bonds. Flint and his people would help guarantee the necessary financing and make some direct loans to the new company. In return, the A.B.C. promised not to sell tires outside of its own needs and to buy at least 90 percent of any outside tire purchases from Flint's rubber trust. Flint also demanded a fee of $300,000 in A.B.C. stock. After hearing this, Spalding complained that he didn't need a nightshirt, he needed a shroud.

Two weeks later, Colonel Pope sold the Hamilton Street tube mill to Shelby, who also bought another tube plant jointly owned by the Western Wheel Works, Gormully & Jeffery and the Indiana Bicycle Company. Like the motor carriage deal, the sale of the tube works probably contained a contingency clause that allowed the Colonel to bail out if the bicycle trust deal fell through. Pope was paid $740,000, a good deal if he took cash, not so good if he took stock, as Garford, another Shelby investor, later said that his shares lost three-quarters of their value between 1897 and 1901.[20]

The A.B.C. formally started operations in September, but for the first few months the factories continued to carry on as autonomous operations simply because there wasn't time to centralize things at the new Nassau Street headquarters in New York. "The concerns that are in the new company have gone about estimating and laying out their output for 1900 just as if nothing had happened," reported one magazine. George Pope agreed, admitting that he did not "fall in with the common belief that the A.B.C. will revolutionize the business," and acknowledging that "it would be eighteen months or possibly two years before all things would be working smoothly."[21]

The exception was the trust's finances, which were a mess. The reduction in capitalization left the new company with no working funds, and although each individual firm was supposed to have paid off its debts and closed its books before September 1, several owners took the opportunity to run up debts before transferring control, saddling the trust with unpaid bills. The forty smaller firms had total debts in the range of $200,000, the Pope Manufacturing Company still owed the Hartford Rubber Works $153,000, and the Western Wheel Works was mortgaged an eye-popping $340,000 to various banks.²² When the A.B.C.'s worried bankers asked treasurer Garford how much the unexpected debt would run, "I replied that it was impossible for me to give him any definite information ... that [while] I had made every effort to secure definite information on all these points from the constituent Companies now comprising the American Bicycle Company ... comparatively few had responded to my demands."

The depth of these worries was revealed in early October by the arrival of a messenger asking Garford to attend an emergency meeting with the underwriters across town. Arriving, he found them already huddling with Charles Flint. It was widely believed that the price of his cooperation was an agreement that the A.B.C. would let the tire factories in Hartford, Indianapolis and Peoria be sold to his rubber trust, just as the tube mills had been sold to Shelby. However, Flint either neglected to formalize or renew his option contracts, and in September, Spalding told Flint that the A.B.C. would not unilaterally agree to replace the expired options and would include the plants when it bought their parent cyclemakers. Flint, needless to say, was extraordinarily angry. "It is difficult to understand, unless Mr. Flint demanded an exorbitant price for his tires, what is to be gained by this latest move ... a first class row is imminent,"²³ wrote the *Cycle Age and Trade Review*."¹³

Once Garford arrived, Flint announced that a million and a quarter dollar's worth of securities had been repudiated by several subscribers, including one of the participants, George Black of the Black Manufacturing Company. Flint said the situation "was most certainly a most embarrassing one," and that the only way out of the problem was for the A.B.C. to sell the tire factories. Although Flint was throwing some sharp elbows, he was right: the A.B.C. was in deep money trouble. The cashout portion of each firm's purchase was scheduled for 26 October, nine days away. The debenture bonds had gone on sale in September. Spalding had hoped most of the owners would take their 30 percent cash/bond option in bonds, but almost none did, and the payout was going to be huge. Flint offered a million dollars in cash, spread out over five years and stock in the R.G.M.C. He also personally guaranteed a $500,000 loan and offered to negotiate another $250,000 loan through a bank he did business with.²⁴

The sale of the rubber plants themselves was pure chaos. In Hartford, nobody told the management what was happening. Lewis Parker, who had run the factory almost since Albert Pope bought it from the Gray family, was in New York either (depending on who you asked) meeting with Flint's managers or looking for independent investors to buy out the company. On 28 October, the A.B.C. fired Parker. His lieutenants quit in protest and most of the foremen followed them out the door.²⁵ Albert Linder Pope, who was managing the Columbia works, moved into Parker's office and the Colonel himself put in an appearance to calm the factory hands. The sale to Flint was announced the next morning, and a day after that everyone was rehired to their old jobs.

After postponing the cashout a few days, the owners got their money on the first of November. The Flint deal would be a thorn in the side of the Colonel for a decade. Two days before the payout, Pope wrote Garford that "I am sorry you did not get but one hundred thousand out of Flint. You must get one hundred a day until you get it all." Pope suggested that Garford pay the rubber trust for its tires in IOUs until it had worked up a balance of a million dollars, then let Flint worry about redeeming them.²⁶ But not even Flint's million could staunch the bleeding. Three days after the start of the twentieth century, Garford rued that "every day brings its particular demands upon this office, and arrangements to meet these demands must be made quickly or the situation will become serious and embarrassing." In February, outgoing cash exceeded revenues by an incredible $1.9 million.[27]

The Colonel, as the head of the finance committee, spent much of the winter pounding the pavements of Wall Street and the Boston financial district trying to get loans. It was a frustrating search. "I had the International on the string.... The President, Mr. John Graham, is my friend," wrote Pope to Garford in February. "He tried to get his Executive Committee to agree to open an account ... but we were such large borrowers, they would not do it." Pope summed up the problem: "The finances stagger these fellows."[28] Finally, the A.B.C. was forced to turn to its own directors for help. Pope, H. A. Lozier and R. L. Coleman each pledged a million dollars in loans to the trust. Contacted in Chicago, Philip Gormully emphatically stated that he wanted nothing further to do with the business. (Ill and in great pain, he died soon thereafter.) The three men would eventually pledge $2.2 million before the financial bleeding stopped during that disastrous first winter.[29]

However, if he was to shoulder the risk, the Colonel wanted more control. Three years earlier, Pope had told Henry Higginson that "I have generally made money in the businesses that I manage myself," and he felt no differently now. Everyone knew that Spalding planned to step down in mid–January and be replaced by a permanent president. Publicly, the Colonel said that he was not a candidate: "I am fifty-six years old. I have no desire to assume new responsibilities. I will not be president. Presidents can be hired and no man living can pay me a salary at my time of life."[30] Privately, he was pushing hard for the office. "The longer we wait before doing something, the worse it is," he wrote Garford. "The biggest banker here [in Boston] says, 'You have got to go to the head if you want to win. The head of the Company ought to be a man whose financial standing would bring money to any company.'"[31] Four days later, Arthur Garford received a hand-written "personal and confidential" letter from Robert Winkley, the Colonel's personal secretary. After beating around the bush for several pages, Winkley finally came to the point: "The consensus of opinion is that the present management is not strong enough.... The shot that comes most frequently is: 'Why is not the Colonel at the helm?'"[32]

On 24 January, the board of directors appointed R. L. Coleman president and Albert Pope chairman of the board. Arthur Garford remained treasurer. The animosity between the two former rivals was always just below the surface, and Garford often acted as mediator. However, even he eventually grew tired of Coleman's penchant for quick-fix solutions to financial problems. Where Pope preferred to work off long-term debt from revenues, Coleman wanted to avoid loans, even if it meant dismantling the company and selling off valuable assets. By spring, fifteen plants had already been closed, most of which were in rented facilities and could thus be quickly liquidated. "It is no secret that some of the companies did not own the buildings in which their plants were operated or the ground on which the building stood," noted *Cycle Age*. "The question for the financiers to consider is why the now defunct concerns were purchased at all."[33]

The trust continued shuttering plants through the summer, and several of these were old-line firms with long roots in their communities. In June, the Grand Rapids Cycle Company, maker of the Clipper, was closed down. "Good-bye to the Clipper — the trust has killed it," complained an observer bitterly. "Grand Rapids was proud of it, for it was built with care, on sound business principles which few factories could equal." Around town, it was rumored that the reason for the closing was that the Clipper chainless was proving to be a better bicycle than the Columbia and was outselling it, putting the Colonel's men in Hartford out on the street.[34]

The situation came to a head in August when Garford told the board that there was little hope of paying back the money the company still owed under the Pope, Coleman and Lozier promissory notes. The Colonel and Garford wanted to roll the loans over for another season, but Coleman insisted that the company sell off the 34,500 shares of Rubber Goods Manufacturing Association stock it had received from Charles Flint. Coleman talked the rest of the board into the idea, and the shares were quickly sold. Garford fumed that "it would have been far wiser to have carried a loan of a million and a half or two million dollars for another year than to have sacrificed from $200,000 to $300,000."[35] From that point forward, relations between the directors soured, with Garford complaining that Coleman's "dictatorial manner of handling things has cost him the respect and hearty support of nearly every officer of the Company." Garford knew that the "Western Men" still controlled things on the board, but admitted to a friend in Elyria, "I hope, however, that there will be a change in Presidents."[36] He began spending more of his weekends as the houseguest of the Colonel and Abby at Lindermere.[37]

For Spalding, stepping down from the A.B.C. presidency marked not only his retirement from the bicycle industry, but the end of a long and storied career. He soon married his long-time mistress, Elizabeth Churchill, and adopted their child, renaming him Albert Goodwill Spalding, Jr. Elizabeth was an ardent follower of the Raja Yoga Theosophist Katherine Tingley, who was then creating a model community at Point Loma, California, near San Diego. Spalding, his wife, their son, and his four children from his marriage to Josie, moved to California in 1901. He bought a large tract of land next to Tingley's "White City," where he built a mansion and nine-hole golf course. He was drafted as the Republican candidate for state senator in 1910 as a progressive, ran a reluctant campaign, and still narrowly lost. He died at Point Loma of a stroke in September 1915. He was elected to the Baseball Hall of Fame in Cooperstown in 1939.[38]

## There Must Be Something Wrong There

At the time the trust was formed, the promoters claimed that the constituent factories had produced some 841,000 bicycles during the 1898–99 season, about sixty percent of the nation's total output.[39] The Nassau Street headquarters told its managers to expect similar sales for the A.B.C.'s first full year. By March 1900, it was clear that the company was not going to meet that target. "The specifications we have received to date fall far short of 800,000," warned Herman Ely at the American Saddle Company. "It is going to be absolutely necessary that we lay off from 50 to 100 men." The fact that production that year was only around 550,000 bicycles was bad enough, but it turned out that some 150,000 left-over saddles were stashed at various factories. Reports from the field were not encouraging: "I can readily see from this part of the country that business has not been up to some former years," reported an Ohio-based manager. "Many dealers here report that business is poor; very few reporting an increase."[40] The trust was quick to respond with layoffs and plant closings. "Nearly a dozen cities have been deprived of industries and two or three thousand men have been thrown out of employment. The managers and heads of some of the factories have been discharged without an hour's notice," reported *Cycle Age*. "The closures, were, of course, designed to effect economies and clear the market which the trust considers undesirable, but the effect has been to throw nearly all the business formerly done into the hands of independent manufacturers, to their great advantage and the trust's discomfiture."[41]

Still, the news wasn't all bad. Garford told the Colonel that early reports on "the Lawson Gasoline Gyrascope" had proved to be "exceedingly encouraging." Mr. Coleman was delighted over the results, he reported, and it was the general feeling around headquarters that "they are on the right track in producing an automobile of a kind the public can afford."[42] By mid-year the A.B.C. was producing a steam-powered tricycle at the old Lozier factory in Toledo and an electric car at the former Indiana Cycle Company plant. The "Waverley" electric was also the brainchild of Coleman, who was working through Charles Flint to get the help of the Studebaker Brothers, who had made some of the bodies for the early Electric Vehicle Company taxicabs.[43] The Studebakers were interested in going into the new automobile business in a big way, and while their firm had the facilities to make bodies, wheels and axles, it needed someone to manufacture motors and batteries. However, the idea proved too risky for the A.B.C. and was eventually shelved.

Coleman's obsession with the automobile caused some anxiety among his fellow directors, as the trust was going to live or die by the wheel, and Coleman seemed to be increasingly detached and apathetic about the bicycle market. Similarly, Thomas Jeffery and his son Charles were experimenting with a gasoline car at the old Gormully & Jeffery factory in Chicago, and when the directors decided they only had enough money for one gasoline automobile project, the Jefferys packed up and moved to Kenosha, Wisconsin, buying the old Sterling factory from the A.B.C. for $65,000. They named their new car after Gormully & Jeffery's most famous bicycle: Rambler.[44] All this automobile exuberance goes a long way toward explaining why the Colonel took such care to sell off his motor carriage division before joining the trust. Old-time rivals like Coleman and Jeffery must have been salivating at the thought of getting their hands on Pope's motor carriage division, the biggest and best in the country; against their likes Day, Eames and Maxim wouldn't have had a chance. While the solution Pope chose may not have turned out to be the best, it was still better than the alternative. In the end, the only vehicle the A.B.C. actually put on the road in any appreciable numbers was the Waverley electric, built by former Pope man H. H. Rice.

As the bicycle bust deepened, the stocks and bonds of the A.B.C. tanked. Initially denied a place on the New York Stock Exchange trading board, the prices quoted by brokers and speculators were open to rumor, and more and more of Arthur Garford's mail was made up of once-eager investors now facing possible ruin, as one old friend lamented:

> I see by to-day's quotations that A.B.C. common is $9\frac{7}{8}$ and you know that I only have 109 shares in the savings bank as collateral for $1000. If it goes any lower they will no doubt ask me for additional security, and I haven't a thing in the world to give them.... I sometimes wish even for your sake that we had failed in bringing the saddle people together, which I believe resulted in the big. co.[45]

There has always been a lot of speculation about how much the A.B.C. was really worth. At the time it was formed, it had outstanding stock and bonds worth slightly less than $40 million and loans of about $3 million. Against this, management claimed assets of $45.4 million:

|  |  |
|---|---|
| $30 million | plants and equipment |
| $5.7 million | inventory |
| $4.4 million | accounts receivable |
| $5.3 million | cash and investments |

But at this time it filed a report with the Commonwealth of Massachusetts giving only $24.2 million in hard assets, with indications that some $4.9 million in plants and equipment were subject to accelerated depreciation (i.e., they were obsolete or almost worn out). In 1914, Arthur Dewing of the Harvard Business School estimated that the A.B.C. really had $14 million in solid assets: $5 million in plants and equipment, $5 million in cash and receivables and $4 million in inventories. Unknown to Dewing, at least a million dollars of the receivables were hopeless bad debts and three-quarters of the inventory was worthless, putting the best estimate of the true value of the bicycle trust somewhere around ten or eleven million dollars.[46]

As the numbers continued to crumble, so did Garford. "If I had known the magnitude and character of the work I should never have accepted the position," he confided. Worn out, homesick for Ohio and dispirited over losing the battle of the rubber trust stock, he submitted his resignation in August. Garford was one of the few exiting the company offering to leave voluntarily. When he bought up the factories, Spalding offered five-year employment contracts to their owners and general managers printed on pink paper. Some owners declined the "pink contracts," others signed, and the few who took the trouble to read them discovered that they were nothing more than option contracts for consulting services and demanded firm agreements. When the entire management of the Stearns Cycle Company, including A. C. Stearns, were fired *en bloc* they found that their employment agreements were nothing but the dreaded "pink contracts." "Having disposed of the smaller fry the trust is after bigger game ... whose positions were supposed to be as safe as the rock of Gibraltar," reported a cycle magazine.[47] Not even those who bargained for a better deal escaped the axe. George Thayer of the Plymouth Wood Rim Company put his employment agreement directly in his firm's sales contract to A.B.C, but still found himself out on the street when he discovered his employment agreement ended if the trust closed the factory, which it did in the fall of 1900. Others were demoted to dead-end jobs or reduced to uncompetitive wages.[48]

However, if nothing else, the Colonel was a superlative judge of lieutenants, and Garford was one man he was not about to let go. He quickly hatched a plan to keep the Ohioan in his orbit, solve the financial problems that the continued contraction in bicycle production was causing the semi-autonomous parts-making factories, and circumvent the power of R. L. Coleman and his westerners on the A.B.C. board. "Certain matters are being considered here at headquarters," confided Garford three days after his resignation was rejected, "that may change the whole character of handling our parts companies." Meanwhile, "there is very little new that I can say in relation to the A.B.C. Company," he grumbled, "I am continuing here practically under protest."[49]

At the Nassau Street headquarters the tension grew as the annual report for the fiscal year grew near. "I am anxious to get news," wrote Pope in mid–September. "Isn't there anything you can tell me confidentially?" Garford's reply was sobering. "We must disabuse our minds of any expectation they may now entertain of a large showing," he wrote. "If we are able to make up a statement that will show an operating profit ... we shall do all that I hope for. Our cash balance is nothing to brag of." When the report was released, it showed a net profit of $605,500 on sales of almost fourteen million dollars. However, over a million dollars of profit had come from selling the rubber trust stock. The bicycle factories themselves lost a half-million dollars. Even worse, after raising over three million dollars selling off factories and machinery, the company was still strapped for cash.[50]

Pope was flabbergasted. "It cannot be that with all the business they have done this year they have made no profit.... There must be something wrong there," he wrote Garford. The answer, replied Garford, lay in inflated inventories and accounts receivable that the A.B.C. had inherited from the constituent firms. Early in the year he had to write off over a half-million dollars in bad debts, and a later inventory shrinkage to adjust for inflated figures inherited from the constituent firms was along the same magnitude. While Garford took some heavy criticism from the executive committee, especially Coleman, for writing down the worth of the company, Garford confided to a friend that "personally, I believe it fairly represents the condition of the business."[51]

The new season started out just as badly as the old. The Colonel went to the National Cycle Show, but left on Friday, "as the attendance was so slim at the show that I did not think it worthwhile to stay."[52] Over a hundred makers had left the cycle trade since the trust was formed (21 shuttered by the A.B.C.), leaving an estimated 69 plants making over 1,000 units a year (each A.B.C. plant counted separately). Trade journals predicted a total market of about 600,000 cycles for the upcoming season, with the 14 remaining A.B.C. factories accounting for about two-thirds of these.[53] Meanwhile, Garford was preparing to move back to Ohio. In January, the executive committee agreed to his and Pope's plan to spin off the cycle parts companies into a new autonomous subsidiary, the Automobile & Cycle Parts Company, that Garford would run from his old saddle factory in Elyria. With a little distance between him and New York, Garford offered an unusually frank assessment of conditions at Nassau Street: "Col. Pope, R. L. Coleman, and substantially all of the large subscribers ... find themselves to-day possessors of a tremendous quantities [sic] of securities, which, at market prices, shows immense loss to them."[54]

The Colonel wasn't inclined to argue, writing Garford, now in Elyria, "I don't like the looks of things in New York." Despite vice-president George Pope's assertion that "we are not in the real estate business," thirteen plants had already been sold off, seven leased out, and six rented factories returned to their landlords. Perhaps Colonel George meant that they weren't very good at the real estate business. He was offering the old Fay factory in Elyria, worth $16,000, for ten thousand dollars. The A.B.C. rented out the former Milwaukee Manufacturing Company for a paltry $750 per year, and when it was damaged by fire, simply abandoned it.[55]

By mid–1901 it was apparent to all that the A.B.C. would take a loss when the books closed in October. The firm accelerated the process of dismembering itself. In the spring, the trust had paired the sales departments of the separate firms into six units, located at the Columbia, Cleveland, Crescent, Rambler, Monarch and Featherstone factories. These were not insubstantial operations. The Columbia sales department employed 52 men, only about half of which were salesmen. The rest were managers, correspondents and cashiers. The trust now cut these down to just three offices in New York, Chicago and San Francisco. To the anger of the Popes, the Chicago branch continued to be located at the old Western Wheel Works office, sparing many of Coleman's former men, while the Columbia office in Hartford was closed. Albert Linder, who had been managing both the Columbia sales department and the Hartford works, quit and moved to New York to become a stockbroker. Asked why he left, young Albert replied, "Because trusts are bad things for the country," creating a flurry of headlines in the cycle trades press. The Colonel did manage to save the New York retail store of Elliot Mason, but in Hartford, the trust closed the cafeteria and reading room in the Columbia factory; the men either had to walk through the late-fall slush home to lunch or sneak down Capitol Avenue to one of the downtown saloons. By then there were only about 125 men still working. It looked to be a long, depressing winter.[56]

Everybody was suffering. Warwick, probably the largest wheelmaker to stay out of the A.B.C., liquidated at the end of 1901. The J. P. Stevens Arms Company considered buying the closed Overman plant and putting it to work making cheap $15 and $20 bicycles, but decided there wasn't even a market for those. In Worcester, Massachusetts, the Worcester Cycle Company's factory was auctioned off on the courthouse steps for back taxes. There were no serious bidders and the city bought the $140,000 building for $22,500 to protect its tax lien. In New York City, the former "Cycle Row" on Warren Street was now a line of empty storefronts, with only Elliot Mason's place still open. Abbot Bassett, president of the League of American Wheelmen, counted only 10,754 wheelmen who bothered to sign up for 1901. In 1898, membership had been 103,293. Bassett would continue to run the L.A.W. as a nostalgic old-timer's club from off his kitchen table until 1924 when both he and the league died.[57]

## Hope in Great Chunks

"Every man has his hobby," Arthur Garford wrote a friend. "I entertain in mines and mining." He was not alone; many men of his generation looked to the mineral wealth of the American frontier as a path to instant fame and fortune. As he put it: "If one is looking for hope in chunks, he can find it in no field that offers it in more abundant quantities than mines." Eventually, Pope too caught the gold bug. "No man appreciates profit more than the Colonel," Garford confided. In the midst of the bicycle trust debacle, Pope's taste for the placer fields of the west led to one of the quirkiest and most amusing chapters of an already colorful life: The Town Built in a Day.[58]

The Colonel had been going west since the Civil War to visit relatives on the Pacific coast, who, like the Maine Popes, were active in the lumber and shipping trades. He ventured as far north as Alaska and as far south as Mexico, regularly visiting Seattle and San Francisco, where the Pope & Talbot Lumber Company kept offices. He was an investor in the Semitropic Land and Water Company, developers of the town of Rialto, California, in San Bernardino County, near where he had a cattle ranch.[59]

Pope started speculating in mines towards the end of the 1890s, buying into the Hot Pot near Central City, Colorado. However, the Colonel was a real estate man before he was a bicycle man, and he knew he could make a buck in Colorado as well as Boston. In March 1899 he hired the Pheonix Construction Company to build a two-story commercial building for him on land he had purchased in downtown Pueblo. As usual, rumors preceded him, and by the time he showed up in town the local newspapers had him erecting a magnificent auditorium and convention hall to rival the new one just finished in

Denver. "There is nothing unusual about the building, which is like other business blocks," a somewhat startled Pope told a reporter when his train pulled into town. "It will contain no hall." The rumor probably started because the new building was located next to the local opera house.[60]

In the spring of 1902, locals in Custer County, a remote mining region about fifty miles west of Pueblo, reported that surveyors from an outfit called the Boston Mining & Milling Company were laying out streets and platting lots on top of a hill in the middle of nowhere. The only thing close was the Bassick mine a mile or so to the northwest. On 25 April the railroad delivered sixteen carloads of lumber to the railhead in Westcliffe, ten miles away. The next day the Denver papers reported that Colonel Pope was the backer of the new town, to be called Custer City, which would be built in a single day, on 10 June, with dedication ceremonies to follow on the eleventh.[61]

The Colonel was only one of several partners. Despite its name, the Boston Mining & Milling Co., was actually a San Francisco–based outfit probably affiliated with Pope & Talbot. G. Henry Whitcomb of Worcester was another partner. A printer, he had invested heavily in Pueblo real estate and would later move on to become a real estate speculator in downtown Seattle. Both men were represented in Pueblo by Francis Meston of the Pueblo Trust, Deposit and Security Company.[62]

The newly created Custer Mining & Realty Company apparently cheated a little, as a correspondent to the *Denver Times* reported in early June that a crew had already erected the exterior walls for several homes. Nevertheless, several reporters, along with the Colonel, Colorado Governor Orman and General George Custer's widow watched as at least a hundred houses, a train depot, hotel, bank, newspaper office, assay office, and other commercial buildings were built on the appointed day. In a special demonstration, three houses were erected in ten minutes from prefabricated components. That evening a giant outdoor dance and fireworks display was held. The next day the Colonel caught a ride to his train and never returned. A year later, the Rio Grand Railroad had yet to extend the branch line in Westcliffe ten miles east to the new town. The last report of mining activity, in June 1903, stated that after 25 feet of digging and shoring a quartz vein only two inches wide had been found. By then, Pope and his partners had already bailed out, selling to a group of Boston speculators for $750,000. Custer City's lifespan was so brief that the *Atlas of Colorado Ghost Towns* incorrectly states that it never went beyond the planning stage.[63]

Although willing to dabble in mining himself, he was less than enthusiastic when he found out that Arthur Garford was investing heavily in Colorado claims. Although Garford called it a hobby, the Colonel knew that he was, if not exactly desperate, then certainly pushing his luck. "Since selling out to the A.B.C. Company I have met with several reverses," Garford admitted. "Tomorrow's operations in a mine may uncover treasures that will meet all of the living expenses of one's family besides furnishing luxuries."[64] Garford asked a friend, Ely Leonard, to visit Pope in February 1902 in Boston to solicit his interest in the "Cash" gold mine near Leadville. The cold winter was taking its toll on the Colonel; Leonard found him laid up in bed with gout. Pope passed on the Cash Mine: "Oh, the Colonel believes in you all right," Leonard wrote, "but doesn't think you are much of a miner." He was, however, eager to go into business with Garford in the bicycle and automobile industry, and made it clear that he was far from washed up:

The Colonel told me that in spite of losing millions in late adventures that he had a few millions left — he is on easy street for ready money and to give you now a check for $15,000 would be like me paying for a cigar. So if you can think of a proposition that would suit him and at the same time convince him that you would not lose your head in mines ... why, you would get the check.[65]

## *Things Look Pretty Stormy Around Bicycle Headquarters*

Back at Nassau Street, it appeared that the Colonel threw in the towel during the October 1901 annual meeting. In the weeks leading up to it, he tried to mount a proxy war, pocketing a little over six million votes, but needed almost nine to take control, and the western men were still solidly behind Coleman.[66] Two of the three vice-presidential offices, held by George Pope and Theodore Merceles, were eliminated in an apparent east-west compromise, but Coleman immediately appointed the hugely unpopular Merceles as his assistant. In addition, Otto Unzicker, Coleman's old partner at the Western Wheel Works, was added to the board of directors.[67] The Colonel decided to give Coleman the rope he needed to hang himself.

In December, Charles Flint was forced out of the Rubber Goods Manufacturing Company. He was reported to be badly squeezed on Wall Street, and both he and his brother Wallace were asked to leave. The contract between the rubber and bicycle trusts required the R.G.M.C. to pay the A.B.C. $200,000 each November from 1900 to 1905, a total of a million dollars. In return, the A.B.C. promised to buy 90 percent of its tires and rubber products from Flint's trust.[68] The R.G.M.C. came through with the November 1901 payment, but there was a lot of grumbling that the A.B.C. was shipping out stripped bicycles lacking tires and tubes, dumping them overseas to rot. If these bicycles, used to keep surplus factories going and puff up sales figures, were counted as part of total production, then 90 percent of the A.B.C.'s bicycles weren't going out the door with rubber trust tires on them. On the other hand, the bicycle trust wasn't buying tires from anyone else; it was just crating up incomplete wheels. The buyer was on his own when it came to getting the rubber parts. It was a legal loophole in the contract. Relations between the two trusts started to take a nosedive. Flint, for all the headaches he had caused, had a knack for twisting the arms of the bankers for loans to the bicycle trust, but now he was begging just to keep his own empire afloat. Coleman had relied upon Flint to shore up his presidency, and with his ally gone he apparently started casting around for a new line of work.

In April, the Colonel walked into a regularly scheduled meeting of the A.B.C. executive committee and quit. That afternoon, sales of the previously moribund A.B.C. stock went through the roof. During the next 35 days some two million dollars' worth of stock changed hands. "Not since the American Bicycle Company's securities were listed on the New York Stock Exchange have they displayed such strength and been so freely traded," noted *Bicycling World*. "Insiders profess to know of no reason." Pope played his cards close to his vest, not even revealing his plans to his friend Garford. "About the stock," he wrote in late April, "I do not know what to say. I am at sea as much as you are." The rumor mill said that the directors were selling their stock as fast as they could. Pope denied it; Coleman refused comment and Lozier privately admitted to the Colonel that he had sold out, not realizing that he was speaking to the buyer. Rumors also said that Coleman would retire as president in October, and that a Pope takeover was being backed by John

D. Rockefeller, the oil magnate. The cafeteria and reading room at the Hartford factory suddenly reopened with a free dinner for 600 Hartfordians.[69]

As the August board meeting approached, the issue boiled down to the interest payment on the bonds. The cash portion of each firm's purchase had been financed through a ten million dollar issue of 20-year debenture bonds requiring semi-annual interest payments of $250,000. They were draining the life out of the company, and after spending two years begging for loans and carving up the company to make each payment, Pope was ready to consider the alternative. "Things in general look pretty stormy around the bicycle headquarters," Arthur Garford wrote home from New York just before the board meeting.[70] The A.B.C. was well on its way to losing $800,000 that year. It assembled only 378,000 bicycles, less than half the pre-merger number, and bicycle operations showed a profit of $160,000 only because some 200,000 of those wheels were built from raw material and parts still left over from before 1899, and thus, for accounting purposes, didn't cost anything to manufacture except for labor and purchased parts.[71]

When they emerged, Coleman read from a prepared statement: "Interest on this

Arthur Garford served as treasurer of the American Bicycle Company from 1899 to 1902, then returned home to Ohio to take over the bicycle trust's parts-making subsidiary, the Federal Manufacturing Company, which he then acquired a year later upon the trust's collapse. After being involved in the automobile industry for a decade, he sold out to Studebaker in 1912 and became a full-time politician, running for Ohio governor and senator, losing both times. He is shown here, probably during his 1914 senate campaign, with Teddy Roosevelt (center) and James R. Garfield (viewer's left), Roosevelt's Secretary of the Interior from 1907 to 1909 (George G. Bain Collection, Library of Congress, Washington, D.C.).

company's debenture bonds, due this day, will not be paid at this time. Proceedings have been instituted looking to the appointment of receivers." Once back in Ohio, Garford exploded: "no one can regret more than I [this] radical and, to my mind, foolish action." Garford caught a train to Chicago to discuss a plan to inject some liquidity into the company and rapidly dismiss the receivers. "For this really valuable service I received condemnation and cussing in real cold chunks from Mr. Coleman, who mildly expressed himself that 'I was sticking my damned nose in other people's business,'" recounted Garford.[72] He hadn't yet realized that he was not part of a mere financial reshuffling, but was caught up in a full-blown corporate coup d 'état, a top-to-bottom Pope takeover.

Almost immediately after the meeting, the purge started. Headquarters announced that the recently relocated New York sales office would move back to Hartford. A. L. Atkins, a Pope man since the early Ordinary days, went to Chicago in October to head up the trust's bicycle operations, pushing out J. C. Matlack and J. E. Bromley, two of Coleman's westerners. Three days later, Pope shut down the Columbia factory in Hartford "for an indefinite period," claiming that the price of coal to run it was too high. By then, only about 125 workers were left. All its A.B.C.–hired managers and foremen were fired, and within a few weeks the factory reopened, restocked with old Pope men from before the buy-out.[73] Nassau street itself soon belonged to the Popes. "Col. Albert is here most of the time, Mr. Coleman only about half of the time," wrote an A.B.C. officeworker. The despised Merceles hadn't even been seen for three weeks and "I heard him tell one man that he would remain with the company only long enough to finish certain business." Merceles said that "he intended to have left over a year ago, but circumstances made it seem best for him to remain, which in other words means I suppose he could not otherwise obtain a salary of $6,000 anywhere else."[74]

Merceles was not the only one talking of greener pastures. "Mr. Coleman takes every opportunity to tell people he is getting out because he is tired of the business," an insider reported. Coleman soon left for the National Battery Company, makers of electric cells for automobiles.[75] By the end of the year, the Colonel rented out his Boston townhouse and moved to New York, where he and Abby took up residence at the Cambridge Hotel.

The reorganization plan called for a complete overhaul of the firm's financial organization. Each $1,000 A.B.C. debenture bond was worth 10 shares of new second preferred stock. The owners of the old preferred stock, worth $100 a share, had to turn it in and pay an additional nine dollars per share in cash to get one-half share of new common stock. For those who held the old common stock, the scheme worked the same except that each share of old stock was only worth one-quarter share of new common stock instead of one-half.[76] This slashed the total value of securities from $36 million to $20.5 million, and raised about $2.5 million in cash. The scheme overwhelmingly favored those who owned the old A.B.C. bonds. That meant Pope. Back when the trust was being formed, each owner was given the option of taking 30 percent of his buy-out price in cash or bonds. Everyone except Pope, Coleman, and Lozier took cash, and Pope bought the bonds of many other owners. When the Colonel loaned the A.B.C. almost a million dollars to tide it over its first winter, he accepted repayment in the form of bonds. As the value of common stock slumped to as little as three or four dollars in late 1901, Pope found he could take over control of the A.B.C. by vacuuming up the common stock, then keep control through the reorganization by converting the high-value bonds to stock. When he quit and walked out of the board meeting in April, he owned about 23 percent of the

A.B.C.'s stock (about 62,000 shares), and in the ensuing six weeks bought another 150,000 shares, mostly of common stock.[77]

But even for the Colonel, this move stretched him to the limit. The takeover needed backers, the foremost of which was a man named Colgate Hoyt. Born and raised in Cleveland, Hoyt was six years younger than the Colonel. A banker and stockbroker by trade, he worked his way up in the railroad business before starting his own firm about 1890. He had the good fortune to worship at Cleveland's Euclid Avenue Baptist Church, the center of John D. Rockefeller's social life. Although a meticulous manager of the Standard Oil Company, Rockefeller was far less careful with his personal fortune, and at Hoyt's urging had invested in several highly speculative ventures, few of which made any money. It is likely that some of these involved Pope family lumber holdings in the Puget Sound area near Seattle. Partially due to poor returns, and partially because Hoyt sometimes used Rockefeller's name to attract other investors — a major transgression to the obsessively private oilman — by the mid-1890s Rockefeller's family was trying to ease Hoyt out of his circle of business associates. However, as late as 1904 Hoyt, a friend of Arthur Garford's, was still sometimes working with the oilman, and businessmen interested in contacting Rockefeller would regularly approach him and his brother.[78] It is possible that a Pope family lumber or mining connection or Rockefeller's enthusiasm for cycling (he rode a Columbia) allowed Hoyt to talk the retired Standard Oil president into some type of participation in the new post–A.B.C. company. More likely, the talk of a Pope-Rockefeller connection was just one more example of Hoyt's propensity to drop his famous client's name to serve his own interests. To his credit, Hoyt remained one of Colonel Pope's staunchest supporters, serving as a director of the reorganized company until 1912 when the firm was well into its twilight period.

The requirement that stockholders had to inject new cash into the company while the bondholders got off free did not sit well with many of the former directors. "As you know, it is necessary to respond to an assessment of $9.00 per share if any stock rights in the new company are to be preserved," grumbled Arthur Garford. "I hardly think I shall pay the assessment on mine." He confessed that he wanted the money for something he thought more promising — gold mining! "To me there is really more value in selling the stock, even at present market prices, then there is in keeping it."[79]

In March, the receivers announced that the reorganized firm would be named the Pope Manufacturing Company. In New York, Robert Winkley, the Colonel's personal secretary, arrived to take over the Nassau Street offices until the bankruptcy court formally turned over control. When a reporter asked the Colonel when he was going to Hartford, he glared and replied, "When the Columbia factory is again the property of the Pope Manufacturing Company and not until then."[80]

In May 1903 the receivers turned the A.B.C. over to the new Pope firm, this time a New Jersey holding corporation. "Col. Albert seems to be in complete control and what he says seems to go," observed the office bookkeeper.[81] So far in 1903 the firm was averaging about $20 per wheel sold, nine dollars more than in 1902. In automobiles, 97 gasoline cars, 126 steam cars and 357 of the Waverley electrics had been sold through May, bringing in about $600,000. The only thing that caused any talk around the office was the scramble over the last-minute insertion of a second vice-president's office into the new bylaws. Everyone knew that Colonel Albert would be president and Colonel George would carry over as treasurer. Charles Walker had come up from Hartford with Winkley to straighten out the New York office, but soon returned to take over operations there, and he had been everyone's pick to become the new vice president, but nobody knew why the second vice-presidential office was being created. "It is the purpose, I believe, to have one of the Vice Presidents a figurehead more than anything else," speculated the bookkeeper, but nobody had any idea who the figurehead would be. In Ohio, Arthur Garford was cautious about the future: "I also feel fairly optimistic ... the whole thing resolves itself down to a question of good management throughout ... and I cannot say that at present a satisfactory condition prevails in some of these departments."[82]

Completing all the details of the handover took several months. Meanwhile, operations gradually shifted, department by department, from the receivers to the Pope Manufacturing Company. To avoid this legally necessary but psychologically unsatisfying state of affairs, the Fourth of July weekend was picked as the "official" turnover day. The ballroom of the Allyn House Hotel in Hartford was rented for a grand reception and banquet, banners and bunting were hung throughout the business district and around the capitol, and the return of Colonel Albert A. Pope after an absence of four years was heralded in all the local papers. In Ohio, Arthur Garford wrote to one of his associates that he needed to reschedule their meeting: "I am expecting now to attend the banquet on Thursday evening July 2nd tendered by the Business Men's Assn. of Hartford to Colonel Pope."[83] It promised to be quite a party.

# 11

## Picking Up the Pieces

*I have got to raise so much money.*
—Albert A. Pope, 1903[1]

The problem was what to do about Harold.

The Colonel, hoping to avoid Albert Linder's debacle at Phillips Exeter, sent both Harold and Charles to the Peekskill Military Academy in upstate New York. It seemed to work, as Harold graduated in 1898 and started at MIT. However, he quit after his first year, and the Colonel sent him to Hartford to work in the Columbia factory. That settled things until the A.B.C. took over, but Harold was soon at loggerheads with the new managers from Chicago. "Morgan does not care for him," complained the Colonel. "He knows too much." Things grew more complicated in 1901 when Harold married Clara Hinkley, daughter of Harold Hinkley, a wealthy Hartford businessman. Three years earlier, Harold's older sister Margaret had married Clara's brother Freeman Hinkley, so the Boston Popes and the Hartford Hinkleys were becoming pretty close, and the Colonel was reluctant to turn to in-laws for help. Instead, Pope sought out his friend Garford, now back running his old saddle factory in Elyria. "Won't you look things over, please," begged Pope, "and see what you can do with him?" Garford knew better than to get mixed up in the Colonel's family woes: "We have no opening suitable to his capabilities," he replied. "In fact we have no vacancies." Instead, Pope sent Harold off to the John T. Robinson Company in Hyde Park, Massachusetts, where a member of the family was underwriting the new Pope-Robinson automobile. Within three years, Harold was back, working as an assistant superintendent at the Columbia factory before taking over the Hagerstown, Maryland, plant, where the short-lived Pope-Tribune auto and low-end bicycles were made.[2] Almost everyone agreed that he was doing well.

Garford was still helping the Colonel and George Pope pull the revamped Pope Manufacturing Company out of the wreckage of the old bicycle trust. One crisis hanging over the entire bicycle industry was lingering overcapacity. Another was the growing muscle of the jobbers. In November 1902 Garford wrote to all the independent bicycle makers, inviting them to a meeting in Cleveland "to carefully discuss the subject of advancing the price of bicycles." Many firms begged off. "While I approve of any movement that would increase the selling price of bicycles," replied Homer Snyder of Rollfast,

These Pope-Toledos, lined up in front of the Hotel Wentworth in Portsmouth, New Hampshire, were donated by the factory for use to ferry delegates and other VIPs at Theodore Roosevelt's successful peace conference to end the Russo-Japanese War in August 1905 (Photographer unknown. Library of Congress Call No. LOT 2624 No. 38 [P&P]).

"I do not, however, believe that it will be possible to make any lasting agreement between the manufacturers." Snyder warned Garford that "my experience ... on this matter has been very unsatisfactory."[3]

Only ten makers showed up.[4] However, those in attendance agreed to form a new organization, the Bicycle Manufacturers' Association, to try to grapple with these problems, and they scheduled a two-day meeting at New York's Waldorf Astoria Hotel the following week. It was a disaster. On the opening day, a minimum price of ten dollars was proposed for stripped-down jobber bicycles and rejected as inadequate. After recessing for the evening, many of the delegates bolted from the room to telephone jobbers with offers of nine dollars per wheel. The following day, those present agreed to very little except to meet again in Cleveland the following week.[5]

In Cleveland, Colonel Pope showed up, as did representatives of sixteen of the independents. The Colonel opened the meeting by requesting that each of the firms secretly provide the organization's secretary, outside attorney Edwin Jackson, with the number of bicycles produced in 1902, and the number already sold for the upcoming year. During the 1901–02 season the members had made 530,000 bicycles, of which 245,800 were sold to jobbers. So far in the 1902–03 season, they had booked 266,250 sales, 196,700 to jobbers. The statistics must have been sobering to the group. If they insisted on a price war over cheap bicycles, Pope could bury them all with his production might. Within an hour they hammered out an agreement not to sell any more bicycles for less than nine dollars. "The price of wheels [to jobbers] has been fixed at $9.00 for the rest of the year," warned Jackson in a follow-up letter. "If any of them [jobbers] wish to buy any more than is now due them it will have to be at that price ... I shall now proceed to communicate with parties who were not present at our last meeting."[6]

But the Association never really had a chance. The A.B.C. had made 378,000 bicycles during the 1901–02 season, and privately, George Pope predicted a continued slide for the upcoming year down to about 300,000. Less than three months after the manufacturers' association was formed, the New York State Jobber's Association took over the National Cycle Trade Association and turned it into a national jobbers' association. At the first national convention of the revamped organization in the spring of 1903, Garford characterized the relationship between the two organizations as "fraternal commercialism," and the Colonel admitted to a packed audience of jobbers that the old A.B.C. "had done its share to demoralize the trade," but that under his direction "there would positively be a profit on every wheel sold." At the next year's annual meeting Fred Gilbert of the Pope company was the keynote speaker, discussing ways jobbers and manufacturers could stimulate interest in cycling.[7]

## The Bicycle Is a Necessity

In keeping with the best traditions of the firm, the first act of the new Pope Manufacturing Company, once it was given new life by the court in October 1903, was to sue somebody. In this case it was the Rubber Goods Manufacturing Company, Charles Flint's old rubber trust. The sale of the rubber factories that Flint had strong-armed the A.B.C. out of back in late 1899 required the R.G.M.C. to make annual cash payments of $200,000 for five years, provided the bicycle trust purchased 90 percent of its tires and inner tubes from the rubber trust. The R.G.M.C. made good on the agreement until November 1902, when it refused payments on the grounds that the A.B.C.'s insolvency voided the agreement. Because it contained no provision for assigning the contract from one company to another, the R.G.M.C. asserted that the new Pope firm wasn't entitled to the last two payments, and that the A.B.C. had already breached it by exporting stripped bicycles lacking tires. The Colonel's men countered that they were the legal heirs to the old A.B.C. and were required only to make 90 percent of their tire purchases (if any) from the R.G.M.C., not to guarantee that 90 percent of the bicycles shipped would be shod with R.G.M.C. tires. The case limped along for several years before it was finally settled out-of-court.[8]

"We have simply had to start all over again," rued new Eastern Division Manager Charles Walker. "The foundation was there, but the structure had been badly damaged."[9] For the firm's management, 1903 was one long game of musical chairs. Arthur L. Atkins had originally been a Pope man starting in the late 1880s who jumped ship to Coleman's Western Wheel Works about 1895 when the Crescent became a best-seller. He had lately been whiling away his time as the A.B.C.'s assistant superintendent at the Columbia factory, but the Colonel sent him back to Chicago to thin out Coleman's minions and take over the Crescent, Rambler and the now-empty Imperial bicycle factories. These became Pope's "Western Department," and carried on the medium-price, no-frills approach that the city had become famous for. Its Rambler, Monarch, Crescent and Imperial bicycles were priced at 85 percent of Hartford's Columbia and Cleveland, which became the premier models. Similarly, the Rambler (Gormully & Jeffery's old brand) motor bicycle used a 1¾ horsepower Thor motor purchased from a supplier, while the Columbia used a 2¼ hp engine made in-house.[10]

Atkins's Western Department signed up hardware dealers and department stores with the straightforward sales pitch that "a bicycle is a vehicle, pure and simple — the cheapest and easiest means of moving quickly, and therefore a necessity." What made the Pope product different was that "we shall spend immense sums of money in high class advertising to the ultimate profit of the dealer who handles our product." It was a business model the bicycle industry would stick to for the next thirty years, but nobody in the Pope organization seemed to realize the potential for problems quite like a reporter from *Bicycling World* did when he got Atkins to admit that "his department is an active competitor of the Hartford establishment."[11] Good, well-priced bicycles didn't worry Hartford so long as they believed the market for pricey flagship models would come back. If it didn't, the company would be forced to choose between the more efficient, but far-away, Chicago factories or the older, costlier plant at home.

Increasingly, dealers were turning away from bicycles altogether to move into the automobile business. "I cannot imagine any calling that would better fit a man to grapple with the perplexing problems of the automobile business than that of the cycle dealer, particularly if he has, as I have, been through it from the days of the Ordinary," said W. C. Rand of Detroit. While he was glad he made the switch, he cautioned others that "in the automobile business one cannot expect to find the fun of the rollicking old bicycle days.... The selling of automobiles is a business in which to be successful it is necessary to follow established principles."[12]

Charles Walker was running the Eastern Division, which made bicycles in parts of the Hartford and Hagerstown factories, and had exclusive use of the factory at Westfield, just west of Springfield, Massachusetts. It was actually a former Lozier plant, built during the great bicycle boom, to make the Cleveland bicycle. Rather than expand the crowded Toledo factory, H. A. Lozier built a new factory in 1896 in Thompsonville, Connecticut, about fifteen miles north of Hartford. With the bike boom in full swing, the demand for Clevelands outstripped Thompsonville, so Lozier turned right around and began construction of the Westfield facility, finished in February 1897. It was so big that the neighborhood around it became known as "Lozierville."[13] Westfield was arguably the best bicycle factory in the country — new, well designed, and well equipped. Within a couple of years, Walker moved bicycle work out of Hartford entirely, turning it over to the Pope-Hartford auto, and made all the pricey Columbias and Clevelands in Westfield, with the lower-cost models coming from Chicago and the cheap, no-name jobbers built in Hagerstown.[14]

It's not clear where Charles went after the A.B.C. closed the eastern regional office in 1902, but he probably transferred to the Colonel's personal staff in Boston. Meanwhile, his brother Wilbur went to work for the Hartford Woven Wire Mattress Company. After returning to the new Pope company, Wilbur became the Hartford office's credit manager. Despite these modest titles, the Walkers had become the power behind the throne, not just for bicycle production, but over all Pope operations. Largely, this was by default, as there was still nobody from the family in Hartford yet. The Colonel was again living in Boston after spending the A.B.C. years shuttling between New York in the winter and Cohasset in the summer. George Pope stayed in New York (he lived in Orange, New Jersey) until 1906. Albert Linder was still a junior partner in the New York stockbrokerage of Yates, Ritchie & Pope. As late as the summer of 1903 the little Colonel was talking to A. L. Garford about taking on his stock exchange account.[15] Garford apparently thought highly of his skills, and transferred his account that July, telling Albert Linder that "I should like to make a connection that will be of a lasting character, where I may depend on the best of treatment."[16]

Alas, he did not get his wish, as bad luck again dogged the Colonel's oldest son. Yates, Ritchie & Pope's seat on the New York Stock Exchange was owned by senior partner John W. Ritchie, who had bought it in 1901, shortly before Albert Linder joined. A couple of years later Ritchie got himself in trouble with the exchange for improperly executing sales. Instead of selling promptly upon the receipt of a client's order, he would wait until he accumulated several sell slips for the same firm, then offer the stock as a block for a better price, pocketing the difference. His game depended on the quick execution of a sale during small price dips, so the exchange first took away his floor telephone. Ritchie responded by standing just inside the glass doors of the member's lounge and giving signals to a runner on the floor. The exchange countered by installing frosted glass in the lounge doors. Ritchie moved outside to the sidewalk, sending messenger boys in to a bank of phones just inside a side door. The exchange finally had enough, expelled him and sold his seat. He was only the seventh member evicted since Revolutionary War days. Albert Linder, seeing the writing on the wall, or, more accurately, the doors, quit the firm in October 1904, about the time the exchange installed the frosted glass. Ritchie was sacked three months later, just in time for Christmas, which he complained was "unexpected" and "unfair." Like it not, the young Colonel was back in the family business full time. He soon returned to Hartford.[17]

Albert Linder, vice-president of the parent Pope Manufacturing Company, also ran its subsidiary, the Pope Motor Car Company. The Waverley factory, making its electrics in Indianapolis under the competent direction of H. H. Rice, mostly well ran itself without a great deal of attention from headquarters. (H. H. shouldn't be confused with engineer Charles D. Rice. H. H. worked his way up through Pope's branch house system, becoming manager of the Providence store in 1897, and managed to keep it open in spite of the A.B.C.'s cost-cutting onslaught. He was still running it when the Colonel sent him to Indianapolis).[18] This was also true of Hagerstown, making the inexpensive single-cylinder Pope-Tribune under Harold's management. However, even his best efforts couldn't make up for the unfortunate truth that the Tribune was merely an average-to-good entry in a highly crowded market for $850 autos, and it sold poorly. Often quiet, much of the factory's work was taken up producing cheap bicycles and stamping out parts for the other auto plants.

Arthur Garford ran the fourth Pope division, the Federal Manufacturing Company, which made auto and bicycle parts, and was setting up a plant for turning out high-grade sheet steel for stamping out auto parts. However, by 1904 Garford was becoming disillusioned with the Pope family way of doing business. "The parts business cannot be successfully run as an adjunct to the Pope Mfg. Co.," he wrote a friend. "The old Colonel and his cohorts," he grumbled, "have done altogether too much talking," and this "created much prejudice."[19] Many in the industry still harbored old grievances against "monopoly Pope," and when he let it out that Federal Mfg., was a part of his empire, they sent their orders elsewhere. "We were only able to command such orders as people were compelled to give us in order to protect themselves," complained Garford. He knew the Colossus was faltering, and fear alone could no longer be relied upon as a reliable marketing weapon. He convinced the Colonel to sell him the division, some of which he parceled off, the rest he consolidated in Elyria and Cleveland. Almost immediately, he announced that he was abandoning the bicycle business to focus on supplying automobile firms.[20] Garford was through with bicycles.

The Hartford factory introduced its first automobiles, the Model A (runabout) and B (tonneau, both sharing the same undercarriage) at the New York Automobile Show in January 1904. In July, the company sent two Model A's overland from Hartford to the world's fair in St. Louis. One was driven by Harold Pope, the other was piloted by Marion Gillette, George Pope's daughter, and her husband Howard. Howard had lots of time on his hands, as the Gillette Brothers sporting goods store, Hartford's largest bicycle dealership, had gone under in late 1902 when it couldn't pay its bills to the bicycle trust.[21] Although the cars made it to St. Louis without trouble, the A/B, a ten-horsepower, single-cylinder design, was already dated, and by the end of 1904 the factory was selling them at a deep discount to make room for its replacement, the Model D. The Model D was the first Pope-Hartford designed by the firm's new engineering department. Herb Alden, who Hiram Maxim had originally brought with him to Hartford from the American Projective Company in 1895, moved from the Electric Vehicle plant on Laurel Street to the Columbia factory in early 1904 along with Lindley D. Hubbell, who had started as a draftsman at the Columbia factory in 1894 and shifted to Electric Vehicle when Pope sold it. Hubbell, Alden, and Henry Souther, working as a consultant from his own firm, the Henry Souther Engineering Company, formed the core of the Pope-Hartford engineering unit.[22]

Although the Colonel was no fan of either bicycle or automobile competitions, his oldest son had already spent a great deal of the family money racing sailboats, and young Albert took an immediate interest in this side of the new business, entering two Pope-Toledos in the first Vanderbilt Cup races in October 1904. This was a tad surprising, as Vanderbilt's racing contests, staged over the public streets of Long Island, had already gained a reputation for maiming and killing both participants and spectators, and the Pope firm was already tangled up in one racing-related lawsuit. In September 1903, a Pope Waverley was racing a Baker electric at a horse track in Cleveland when the contest grew a little over-spirited. The cars collided and the Baker crashed through a board fence on the outside of the track and into the crowd, running over a spectator who sued both Baker and Pope. Fortunately for Pope, their half of the suit was later dismissed when it was discovered that the Waverley had been entered by a private owner with no affiliation to the factory. Nothing similar happened in the Long Island races, and Pope's lead driver, Herb Lytle, finished third in the Vanderbilt Cup behind two French autos, but the following year, both Pope-Toledos dropped out after crashes.[23]

In 1906, Albert Linder found himself in the middle of one of the first great controversies of Vanderbilt Cup racing. Qualification for the main race was determined in a series of shorter elimination heats. In the middle of one of these, the Pope-Toledo driven by Lytle shredded a tire, breaking a gear shift linkage. The car was stuck in a narrow place in the circuit, so the team towed it off the course with a rope to a nearby garage for repairs, then returned it to the same spot to resume the contest. Lytle did well enough to bump a Frayer-Miller out of the big race, so its owner, Miller, protested the tow. Young Albert admitted to what happened, arguing that it would have been too unsafe to fix the car where it stopped. The rules made no exception for safety, so the Pope-Toledo was disqualified. Albert was applauded for his honesty and Miller was given the cold shoulder by the Vanderbilts after the hearing. But a week later, just before the big race, Albert showed up before the rules committee with evidence that others, including the Frayer-Miller, had similarly been towed during elimination races. The committee, obviously wishing the young man would have quit while he still looked good, cleared their throats and declared that the designated time for appeals had lapsed. That year's Vanderbilt Cup race was a bloodbath, with both dead participants and spectators, and various local governments banned the race until Vanderbilt completed his own private racecourse, which later became the right-of-way for the Long Island Expressway. Racing resumed in 1908.[24]

Autos were not the only form of racing the firm moved back into. The original Pope company had never been as large a supporter of bicycle racing as many of the western makers, probably because the brutal internecine warfare over the control of the sport posed a threat to the Colonel's interest in building a good-roads coalition. But by the spring of 1904, the L.A.W. was no longer the good roads juggernaut it had been a decade before, and the company announced that it would be sponsoring three international teams: a Rambler squad headed by German sprinter Walter Rutt; a Columbia/Cleveland team with American Bobby Walthour and Swedes Iver Lawson and Eddie Root; and a Tribune team captained by Californian Floyd McFarland. It was probably the best lineup money could buy. Walthour was half of a pair that won the 1903 Madison Square Garden six-day, and Root had just won the first of his four Madison Square sixes when Pope's men signed him up. Six-days weren't Walthour's specialty, though. Motorpaced races, in which each competitor was led by a motorcycle to speeds of up to 60 mph on high-banked tracks were his thing. He broke one or the other of his collarbones 46 times, fractured 32 ribs, and was once prematurely taken to the Paris morgue.[25] He stayed healthy in 1904, however, and cleaned up, winning virtually every motorpace contest he entered on the lucrative European circuit.

Lawson also justified his sponsor's confidence in him by winning that summer's world professional sprint championship in London, but it was a close thing that he was able to compete at all. Earlier in the year, he had been racing in Australia against Marshall W. "Major" Taylor, America's first great black sports champion, when Taylor crashed. The League of Victorian Wheelmen charged Lawson with knocking Taylor down and imposed a three year suspension that, under the rules of the International Cyclists' Union, applied worldwide. Lawson appealed, and a board of inquiry reduced the charge to careless riding and assessed a three-month suspension, which Lawson did not contest. He sailed home with McFarland, who himself had a long history of clashing with Taylor.

Taylor claimed McFarland was a rube and a bigot, but the feud resulted as much from McFarland's exasperation with Taylor's carefully cultivated choir-boy image and a series of previous sanctioning-body disputes as with McFarland's racial antipathy. To make a long story short, McFarland felt Taylor had a history of scabbing against the riders' unofficial union. Taylor, being black, believed he had never been let into the union and thus always had to fend for himself. In any case, McFarland was no rube. He was bright, had a high school diploma, and was an articulate speaker. He did, however, have a penchant for fighting. While riding in Tribune colors that summer at the national championships in Newark, he got into a brawl with a competitor, reportedly one of "a number of fistic encounters between the contestants" that day, according to the *New York Times*. Spectators started to join in "and the services of the police had to be called."[26] In Australia, McFarland had picked a fight with Bull Williams, a local professional boxer. The six-foot-four McFarland put Williams on his back. McFarland retired in 1911 to

McFarland, a track racing specialist, turned professional in 1896. Intelligent, aggressive and entrepreneurial, he was running his own racing team and organizing races at age 20 while still racing. The American Bicycle Company hired him in 1900 to both manage their team and race. He is best known for his bitter rivalry with America's first black world champion in any sport, Marshall W. Taylor. Taylor accused McFarland of bigotry, but historians still debate how much of their mutual animosity was due to race and how much resulted from clashing personalities and egos. After retiring in 1906, McFarland became a race promoter, dying in 1915 after a brawl with one of his own concessionaires (George G. Bain Collection, Library of Congress, Washington, D.C.)

become a bike race promoter. In 1915 he got into another fight with a concessionaire, David Lantenberg, over the location of some posters Lantenberg was screwing onto a wall. Lantenberg, who stood all of five-four and weighed 120 pounds, still had the screwdriver in his hand when McFarland took a swing at him. He missed. Lantenberg didn't, and the blade went five inches into McFarland's skull. He died a few hours later. Lantenberg was charged in the death, but acquitted.[27]

Although bicycle racing was wildly popular, it was also considered a lowbrow sport along the same lines as boxing or cockfighting. "A less intelligent form of amusement was never devised," thundered the *New York Times*, "nor is there nowadays any general interest in bicycling sufficient to explain the huge attendance."[28] However, Pope's men were to prove the *Times* man wrong on that last point, at least for one final time. On the first Sunday in May, 1904 Lon Peck (who, during the Pope Building fire, had been one of the men who ran down the burning stairs with a fire extinguisher trying to free the bicycle mechanics trapped in the basement) organized a cyclist's gathering and ride at Chestnut Hill Reservoir, a traditional meeting point for cyclists since Ordinary days just outside Boston. Two and a half thousand wheelmen showed up, many on their old high-wheelers.[29]

Alfred Chandler, America's first cyclist, who the Colonel used to race on horseback, was there with a high-wheeler. Billy Atwell, the builder of the very first "313 dollar" bicycle for Colonel Pope and John Harrington back in the summer of 1877, showed up in a frock coat and high hat. E.W. Pope came to ride, as did Papa Weston, the last survivor of the old Cunningham firm since Ned Hodges died the previous December.[30] With so many of the old-timers gone, past rivalries were laughed away. Massachusetts and Boston clubmen, *Bicycling World* and *American Cycling Journal* contributors, diehard Columbia and Victor advocates, fell into each others' arms and laughed and cried and hoisted huge mugs of hot coffee spiked from hip flasks into the cool spring air in honor of the departed. The Colonel (for yet another winter, gimped with gout) and General Miles showed up in a motorcar and oversaw the distribution of box lunches and 150 gallons of coffee. Afterward, all 2,500 gathered on the gentle slope of the reservoir's earthen dam while Chickering of Boston snapped a group portrait.

Later that summer, the Century Road Club tried it in New York City. Another 2,500 were expected. Maybe seven hundred showed up. "As you know," Albert Linder explained rather weakly, "the bicycle business in this country has been rather in the hollow of a wave."[31]

In fact, after more than six years of decline, the bicycle industry finally bottomed out in 1904, when only 257,000 wheels were manufactured, 89,000 by the five Pope factories.[32] Financially, 1895 had been the most lucrative year, but it is likely that either 1897, 1898 or 1899 was the year of largest production, with somewhere between 1.2 and 1.6 million bicycles made. It is very difficult to be precise, for a variety of reasons. First, production years did not correspond to the calendar year. Production typically started in

Pope's Hartford operation had a bicycle club from its earliest days, even when the factory was still the Weed Sewing Machine Company. Here, the members have gathered in front of the George Keller-designed headquarters building, built in 1895. The third bicycle from the viewer's left is a Columbia shaft-drive (The Connecticut Historical Society, Hartford, Connecticut).

October and extended, in a good year, as late as June or July. In 1898 or 1899, on the other hand, the large makers were probably furloughing workers as early as March. Second, with massive quantities of bicycles dumped overseas to rust on docks or in warehouses between 1897 and 1901, there is a big difference between a bicycle "produced" in the U.S. during this period and one "consumed" in America. As many as a million bicycles were "manufactured" during this four or five year period, only to be quickly exported and never see the outside of a packing crate. Third, by 1899 the availability of purchased parts was so widespread that thousands of bicycle shops and repair depots were assembling small batches of bicycles to sell themselves in small wholesale lots to neighborhood hardware or department stores. Such "shop bicycles" probably accounted for about a third of all bicycles produced in 1898–99, about 500,000 out of a total of around 1.6 million. Except for one or two well-organized jobbers, nobody in 1904 was attempting to build their own off-brand, small-batch bicycles — not when cheap, no-name wheels were available from all the major bicycle firms.[33]

Was there anything resembling a market for bicycles after 1902? Yes. As R. G. Betts, editor of *Bicycling World*, told the *New York Times*, "The bicycle is no more likely to pass than is the sewing machine or piano." He explained that cycling "no longer represents a silly craze," but had become "a staple means of health, pleasure and transportation," and that "it should be viewed in that light."[34] To keep things in perspective, even in the dismal year of 1904, more bicycles were sold than during 1893 or in any previous year. Up

William Knight, age 15 (on the viewer's left), and his pal Charles Halla, 14, on their way to work at Pope's Westfield, Massachusetts plant, sometime before the first World War (Photographer: Lewis Hine. Library of Congress Call No. DIG-nclc 05104.)

to 1907, the Minneapolis city engineer counted over 1,200 bicycles a day between April and September on the downtown streets of his city. On some days, bicycles accounted for as much as a fifth of daily traffic. As late as 1910, summertime counts in that city were higher for bicycles than for autos. While these numbers were much smaller than during the golden decade, when the City of Chicago counted a little over 5,000 cyclists entering its downtown in one day in 1896 and 10,700 in 1898, the 1907 rider was likely to be a workaday commuter, a clerk or entry-level manager just trying to make ends meet. The *Sporting Goods Dealer* talked about "the crowds awheel, whose course is set during the rush hour of the morning towards the business center, and again in the evening as they seek the home," and Norman Clarke, president of the Columbia Manufacturing Company from 1955 to 1974, recalled that "there was a market from 1920 to 1933 for a functional transportation bike for factory workers." In the 1920s he remembered seeing large parking sheds for employee bicycles and "300 to 500 employees coming to work on bikes." The level of thefts reported to urban police departments also predictably rose and fell with the utility use of bicycles by the middle and working classes. In Detroit, annual reported thefts peaked at 645 in 1902–1903, then dropped to 350 by 1907–08. In Minneapolis, 1,036 bicycles were stolen in 1905; this number also fell, to 719 by 1911. What happened to the commuters? Clarke unhesitatingly answers: "The Model T. The cheap automobile."[35]

One clear fact emerges from this haze of statistics, however: no matter how fast the bicycle market was shrinking, the bicycle trust, and the revamped Pope company after that, was withdrawing even faster. In the summer of 1899, on the eve of the trust's formation, its forty-four or forty-five factories (depending on who was doing the counting) produced 871,000 bicycles out of a nationwide total of 1.6 million. In 1904, the (probably) four remaining Pope bicycle plants produced 89,000 of the country's total of 257,000 bicycles.[36] Five years later, during the 1908–09 season, with only one remaining plant (Westfield) the Pope company was making only about 50,000 bicycles, even though the American market as a whole was about the same size in 1909 as it had been in 1904.[37] At its start, the trust was making 54 percent of all the bicycles in the country. Two years after picking up the pieces, Pope was producing only 34 percent. A half-decade later, that share was down to a little over 21 percent. The plain truth was that Pope was walking away from the bicycle business.

The money was, of course, going into automobiles. A riskier, more expensive start-up enterprise could hardly be imagined. Of the roughly 116 firms entering the American automobile business before 1902, none survived to 1944, except as a vestigial piece of some other company. About 1,100 firms entered the automobile business between 1902 and 1927. Only 181 of these ever produced a single auto, and of these, only 44 remained in business in 1944 — most as part of a larger conglomerate such as General Motors, Chrysler or American Motors.[38] Those that did manage some form of survival followed a strategy directly opposite that of Pope. Where the Colonel sought to produce all parts in-house (at least for the Toledo and Hartford models; while the same claim was made for the Tribune, it is unlikely), firms such as Ford relied almost exclusively on off-the-shelf parts provided by suppliers. While Ford demanded cash on delivery for his cars, he bought his parts on 90-day credit and often paid late. This allowed him to collect payment on his purchased parts before he paid his bills on them.

Unlike most American firms, British bicycle makers diversified into the motor indus-

The Roach Bicycle Shop of Minneapolis had a fairly well-equipped repair shop for the era, with a heavy-duty drill press, grinder and what appears to be a table-top band saw visible. While they were still powered through a shaft-and-belt system, it was driven by an electric motor (the control box is on the wall, about five feet in front of the mechanic). However, by the looks of the mechanic, the place could use a better heating stove (The Minnesota Historical Society, St. Paul, Minnesota).

try cautiously and incrementally. Henry Sturmey (of Sturmey-Archer 3-speed fame) asked Raleigh in 1898 to make motorcycles and light automobiles, but Raleigh directors refused because they did not want to be distracted from bicycles. Raleigh stayed out of the business until 1902–03, when it briefly flirted with motorcycles and three-wheeled cyclecars. Only two years later managing director Frank Bowden pulled the firm out of the business until after World War I.[39] Humber stayed with it, introducing its 5-hp Humberette light car in 1900 and steadily introducing larger and more powerful models. Triumph brought out a motorcycle in 1902 and was selling a thousand a year by 1907. Rover moved into motorcycles in 1903, did not find success, withdrew, and returned in 1906 with a 6-hp light car. Two years later, it brought out a 1¼ horsepower motor that could be retrofitted to a bicycle, and in 1910 reintroduced motorcycles.[40]

What these efforts all shared was a thorough grounding in the bicycle industry. Product and production technologies evolved from existing processes, starting by inserting a purchased Minerva or De Dion motor into a modified bicycle frame, followed by the introduction of an integrated motorcycle, then the development of a light automobile or cyclecar. The timing and pace of development was usually determined by the profitability (or lack thereof) in the cycle industry. For many firms, such as Humber, Singer, Riley, Swift and Enfield, the trick was to keep cyclemaking as profitable as possible to cover the long and gradual process of moving into motor vehicles. For others, notably the conservative, Starley-family-dominated Rover, diversity was a reluctant decision, mandated by unstable annual profitability from bicycles.[41]

In America, the very early history of the motorcycle seemed to suggest that several firms would follow the same path. The Orient Cycle Company introduced a motor bicycle called the Orient-Aster in the spring of 1899. A year later, Marsh and Waltham followed suit. Both the Orient and the Marsh used European-made, De Dion–type engines wedged into minimally altered bicycle frames. Three years earlier, Hiram Maxim had developed a package-delivery tricycle for the Hartford Cycle Co., using a simple, rugged one-cylinder motor with a hot-tube ignition plug heated by a pilot lamp. Maxim gleefully tested several prototypes to destruction in 1897 and as a result, the motor for the resulting Mark VII was probably the most efficient and reliable small engine in the country when production started in 1898, and with the addition of a magneto and spark plug it would have made a formidable motorcycle or light car engine.

The Colonel was apparently less than enthusiastic about the idea of introducing a shaft-drive bicycle. Although he snapped up the League Cycle Company's patent for it in 1894, and as early as fall 1895, Arthur Garford was writing friends at the Columbia factory asking when he could have one, the Pope firm did not introduce a chainless bicycle until 1897, nor did it bring out its own coaster brake until 1899, or a two-speed rear hub until 1901.[42] Rumors repeatedly cropped up in 1899 that the real reason for these pricey developments was that Pope wanted them for a motorcycle he would introduce in the spring of 1900. Either the rumors were premature or the development program was killed by the trust. Company officials told reporters that the A.B.C. would introduce a Chicago-built motorcycle in the fall of 1900, but no machine appeared and many thought the announcement was a ploy to scare away the Waltham Manufacturing Company, a cyclemaker who had refused to enter the trust, from bringing out their own motorcycle, which they did anyway in mid–1900 to great success.[43]

When the bicycle trust finally introduced a motorcycle in March 1902, it was a relatively conservative 2¼ horsepower, chain-drive, single-gear design, with frame and motor manufactured at Hartford.[44] Overall, the machine was not as advanced as the "American Indian" that Oscar Hendee had shown at the London Cycle Show the previous December.[45] The A.B.C. motorcycle was initially sold with as many as seven different headbadges, including Columbia, Cleveland, Rambler, Imperial and Crescent. Later, when Pope took over, he kept the machine, but dropped everything but the Columbia and Cleveland names. He had the Western Department develop a lower-cost motor bicycle using a 1¾-hp Thor motor purchased from the Aurora Automatic Machinery Company of Aurora, Illinois. By this time (1904) the Thor had become the American equivalent of the Minerva, being used by many different manufacturers who lacked the capacity to develop their own power plant. According to Indian motorcycle historian Harry Sucher, the Aurora Automatic Machinery Company was hired by Indian in 1901 to make their first motors, and the Thor was a derivative of this first-generation engine.

It appears that in 1906, the same year that Indian introduced a twin-cylinder model (selling about 1,700 of them), Pope quietly pulled out of the motorcycle market to concentrate on automobiles.[46] It wasn't for lack of demand. Fred Randall, the Indian agent in Boston, reported that "they have gone daft over motor bicycles." While his agency out in suburban Chelsea was selling regular bicycles "to beat the band," he doubted that he was selling one a week at his "bicycle row" store in town on Commonwealth Avenue, just down the street from the Pope Building. On the other hand, he had orders for over 50 Indian motorcycles "and had he been able to promise deliveries," he said that he could have sold "three times as many."[47] More likely, Pope, like most of the old bicycle magnates, was simply not interested in the motorcycle. "I doubt very much whether there will be any extensive sale for motor cycles," wrote Arthur Garford back when he was still treasurer of the bicycle trust, "A bicycle is such that to attach a motor is all out of harmony with its purpose and legitimate requirements and will never be popular with the public."[48] This was a reflection of their class bias. As a historian of the Detroit auto industry notes of that city's industrial pioneers: "As prosperity came their way [they] thought that the whole world grew more prosperous with them.... They built their cars for themselves instead of for the public."[49] But the whole world wasn't like them. The market for mid- and high-priced autos was saturated from the start, and competition was fierce. Yet, Pope was doing surprisingly well. The Pope-Toledo, selling for between $2,800 and $5,000, sold 569 units during the fiscal year ending 1 August 1904, and about 550 the following year.[50] Then came the strike.

## A Contest of Strength and Endurance

The year 1906 started out with bad omens. Early in the year the company finally had to admit that the Colonel's pet project, the Columbia mechanical cashier, was not going to succeed. They simply could not get enough customers to shell out $500 for what amounted to a glorified cash register. The firm admitted to a $16,000 write-off on the project; the actual losses were probably somewhere between fifty and a hundred thousand. On 18 April, the company's new western headquarters was wiped out by the great San Francisco earthquake. With so many of the Popes and their cousins the Talbots settled in San Francisco, the Colonel had decided to make an exception to his policy of shutting down branch stores and built a retail store and distribution depot for the Pacific and western states. The new building survived the earthquake, but not the resulting fire, and as in the Boston fire a decade before, hundreds of wheels were lost. This time they decided not to replace the facility.

Another victim of the earthquake was Harry Pope's new gunsmithing shop. He and the J. P. Stevens firearms company had never gotten along, and they parted ways in 1905. Harry left for the west coast and outfitted a new shop. "I had just got my shop ready, and started the power for the first time at three o'clock on the day preceding the disaster," he recalled. "I lost everything I had in San Francisco except the clothes on my back."[51] Broke and with no insurance, he moved to Los Angeles for nine months before accepting a job at a friend's rifle-scope factory in Philadelphia.

Things seemed to be going smoothly in Toledo, however. The plant was under the management of Albert E. Schaaf, who started out racing Ordinaries at age 14 in his home town of Buffalo. He gave up studying to be a lawyer to go to work for Gormully & Jeffery about 1888 and ran their Boston branch house for most of the 1890s, where he made the Colonel's acquaintance. He went to work for the A.B.C. in New York and after the collapse Pope hired him on and sent him to Toledo.[52] The Pope-Toledo's success as a racing car was bringing in a healthy run of orders, especially after the introduction of the 60-hp, 4-speed Model XIV touring car. But Toledo was a labor town, and even in bicycle days it had a reputation as a place where help "had to be handled with silk gloves." It had been the home of the International Union of Bicycle Workers, formed in 1896. With the decline in the bicycle business, its name changed in 1900 to the International

Association of Allied Metal Mechanics and soon thereafter it merged into the Brotherhood of Machinists.[53] The city's main newspaper, the *Toledo News-Bee*, was staunchly pro-union, and its mayor, Brand Whitlock, held to a neutral, middle-of-the-road policy that was variously interpreted as "refusing to provide adequate police protection" (by local factory owners), or "refusing to use the police department as a strike breaking factor" (by local labor leaders).[54]

The years 1904 and 1905 had been calm, but in June 1906 a local branch of the National Metal Trades Association (NMTA) was established in the city. The NMTA was founded in 1899 as an organization of business owners and managers who feared that the United States would suffer the same type of paralyzing general strike that effectively shut down all of England in 1897. The NMTA brokered two nationwide "treaties" with the Machinists' union in 1900 and 1901, but they both collapsed amid fundamental disagreements over wages and work hours.

In 1903 the NMTA transformed itself into a union-busting trade group with a national headquarters and local chapters in fifteen cities. While member firms pledged not to make active efforts to incite a strike, they also promised not to talk or settle with strikers. In the event of a strike, the affected firm would turn over all jurisdiction for negotiations and settlement to the NMTA who would, in turn, provide security officers and replacement workers.[55] NMTA "negotiators" presented a rigid, unvarying set of demands: rank and file strikers may return to work on the same employment terms as before without fear of retribution. All strike leaders will be fired. The factory will operate as an open shop and no union activities will be tolerated. No other conditions or agreements will be considered.

On the morning of 30 August 1906, about 238 of the 1,200 workers at the Pope-Toledo factory walked off the job. The company had discharged two machinists, one in early August, the other four days before the walkout. The plant's assistant manager told both a *Toledo Union-Bee* reporter and a state investigator that the men had been fired for talking about union matters during working hours. No other reason was offered. Representatives of the Ohio Board of Arbitration arrived the next day, but were informed by Pope managers that they would not "consider any request or proposition" for a settlement, as only NMTA officials were authorized to negotiate. The strikers, from several different unions, told the arbitrators they were willing to meet with company representatives as a group or through a committee. They said that while the firings may have precipitated the action, its root cause was the company's gradual squeezing out of union members in favor of non-union machinists.[56]

The NMTA quickly set up makeshift barracks on the factory grounds and imported replacement workers. The machinists' union acquired a blank employment contract indicating that each replacement worker was required to pay his own way to Toledo. Most had been deliberately recruited from distant sites and had to borrow travel money from the firm. The contract required them to reimburse the firm through payroll deductions from their first four paychecks. The contract warned that if they quit before this advance was paid off, their tools would be seized. It did, however, caution the employee that he was being hired into a strike zone, contradicting union claims that the replacements had no idea of what was going on before the NMTA dumped them on the streets of Toledo. The *Union-Bee* did report that several newly arrived men, after sizing up the situation, told their reporter that they did not want to stay in town and would not go to work if they had a choice.[57]

The strike dragged on, although violence was surprisingly light, mostly because Mayor Whitlock's police concentrated on keeping the parties separated and not on bullying one side or the other. The arbitrators returned in October and their services were again declined. "The strike had been on for four months," reported the arbitrators, "and there was apparently no change in attitude." They summed up the situation as "a contest of strength and endurance between the National Metal Trades Association and the International Association of Machinists."[58] Frustrated that the city police wouldn't break up the picket lines, the company sought a court order to command federal marshals to do the job, arguing that "picketing, though intended to be peaceable, and engaged in by no more than two or three at each station, necessarily results in violence or intimidation, and is itself intimidating." The case went to the courtroom of District Judge Taylor, who flatly refused, stating that "one of the forms of persuasion which, under proper circumstances, the law recognizes as permissible, is picketing." He warned that no violence or intimidation would be tolerated on either side, ordering away six men whom the company proved were prior malefactors, but there would be no Pullman-style showdown in Toledo.[59]

The strike continued until late February, and even then the cure proved worse than the disease. The terms of the settlement were at best unclear, many of the replacement workers were discharged on short notice to make room for former strikers, and some 59 returning union men were fired on their first day back, apparently to enforce an unwritten edict capping union membership in any given department at one-third of those working. A few workers reported that they had been given instructions to prepare machinery for dismantling and shipment to Hartford. After two weeks a thousand workers, both union members and non-members, walked out. By now the entire town was against the Popes. The strikers held parades with cheering crowds lining the streets. Picketers rarely went hungry or lacked for firewood to warm themselves, as the local citizenry kept them well stocked. Fewer than 100 men still manned the factory. After three more weeks, Mayor Whitlock stepped in and all but ordered general manager Schaaf to enter into arbitration, hinting that he would not drain Toledo's police budget dry simply to protect the Popes' property against the wrath of an entire city. Schaaf and the union quickly reached a compromise in which the company agreed not to discriminate against union workers and the union agreed not to interfere with company operations or do union business on company time. Union membership remained voluntary.[60]

Five months later, the Pope Manufacturing Company declared itself insolvent when it was unable to pay a bill for less than $4,500 to the McManus-Kelly Company of Toledo, an advertising firm. During the strike, the company had to cancel 186 firm orders for 1906 Pope-Toledos, and even before the second walkout in March, the *Toledo Blade* estimated the strike had cost the firm over a hundred thousand dollars.[61] Theodore McManus of the McManus-Kelly Company explained that "to say that the receivership was directly caused by the Toledo strike is unjust," but had to admit that "had there been no strike there need have been no receivership."[62] It is difficult to know why the Pope family insisted on such a hard line at that time and place after so many years of peaceful labor relations in Hartford, but the growing power of George Pope within the firm is the most likely explanation. When plant manager A. E. Schaaf heard of the receivership from a newspaper reporter, he replied, probably honestly: "This is certainly news to me." In November, three months after the receivership, the firm fired Schaaf, who unsuccessfully protested his dismissal. The local papers reported that the firing resulted less from dissatisfaction over his management than from internal conflict within the Pope family.[63]

In 1916, after taking over as president of the National Association of Manufacturers, George Pope told a reporter from the *New York Times* that "the country is suffering from an inflation of wages," and that he favored a nationwide version of the employers' union that had tried to break the machinists in Toledo, even though he could foresee "the grim conditions that would then prevail." "The ultimate result," he predicted, "will only be accomplished through the harsh processes of natural law." He admitted that such an employers' union would violate anti-trust laws, but justified the concept based on the Toledo strike nine years before. "The final result for all was most unsatisfactory," he complained, "conditions in the labor market became onerous and uncertain."[64] John Willys, who by then was making well over 50,000 cars a year in the same factory, would probably disagree.[65]

The receivers' balance sheet, when it was released in August 1907 was a shocker. Up to the time of the receivership, the company had claimed assets of $23.7 million. Now, it admitted that over $14 million of this had been allocated to goodwill—that is, the intangible value of the Pope name. A million in value had been apportioned to the motor car company above and beyond its hard assets—essentially another million chalked up to the allure of the Pope name. The Federal Manufacturing Company, the Columbia Steel Company and the Pope Mfg. Co., of California were collectively valued at $700,000, although they no longer did business or had any hard assets. The company did have plants and equipment worth about $2.7 million, inventory and materials it claimed were worth $1.7 million (but were probably only worth about $1.2 million, because much of the equipment at Hartford was worn out), and accounts receivable of around a million. Total: between four and five million dollars. Against this, it owed banks $1.3 million and suppliers another $425,000. It had $93,000 in the bank.[66] Actually, this was not a horrible financial position, unless one kept in mind that the shareholders held $23 million in stock and believed they should own something tangible to back it up. "Some water in the company," dryly noted the *New York Times*.[67] The Colonel, on the other hand, blamed the banks, and told the *Times* man that "the banks will get what is due them when the company gets ready to pay them."

In Toledo, local creditors appealed to the district court to remove Albert Linder as managing receiver, claiming that he was attempting to gut the Toledo plant for the benefit of Hartford. Once again rumors flew of machine tools being shipped out in the dead of night. The parent Pope Manufacturing Company sued its own automaking subsidiary for $788,000 in an attempt to get money tied up in bank accounts in Ohio transferred to Hartford or Boston. Finally, Judge Taylor (the same man who ruled against the company in the picketing case) ordered the appointment of a separate receiver to protect the interests of local creditors and instructed the company not to disassemble the plant. In early 1909, Richard Apperson of the Apperson Motorcar Company offered a million dollars for it, but he essentially wanted the city to subsidize his fledgling company by buying the factory from him, then lease it back at a nominal rent. The scheme fell through.[68]

John Willys was about to leave Elmira, New York, on a trip when he heard of the collapse of the Apperson deal. Willys started in the early 1890s as a bicycle agent, then moved into jobbing. About 1904 he added the Overland automobile to his line. During the panic of 1907 he learned that Overland was about to go under and propped up the firm by covering a couple of payrolls, then took it over the next year. He was on his way to New York City to raise funds for a plant expansion and switched tickets for Toledo, where he bought the Pope-Toledo plant for the bargain-basement price of $285,000 in late 1908. Many years later, this factory would become famous as the home of the Jeep.[69]

The Pope company retrenched into its Hartford and Westfield, Massachusetts, factories. The Waverley factory in Indianapolis was sold off intact to its manager, H. H. Rice; Garford bought an empty plant in Milwaukee; Hagerstown was sold empty to a casket-making company, and much of the rest was unloaded on liquidators.[70] Unlike the 1903 reorganization, this time the family was hit hard. The Colonel personally owned about 21 percent of the company's first preferred stock, 19 percent of the second preferred stock and 71 percent of the common stock, and the price the bankers demanded to rescue to company was the obliteration of the common stock. The company that emerged, the Pope Manufacturing Company of Connecticut, was capitalized at a modest $6.1 million dollars. If you had sold your bicycle company to the A.B.C. back in September 1899 and received a $1,000 debenture bond in lieu of the $910 in cash you could have chosen, and you had then held on to that paper through the two successive reorganizations, you would now own two shares of Pope common stock, currently trading at twelve dollars a share. The Colonel's ownership now comprised 18 percent of the preferred stock and 22 percent of the common stock.[71] For 1909 the firm hoped to make 400 autos and 50,000 bicycles. But by now, the Colonel was so ill and so tired he no longer cared.

# 12

## *After Pope*

The Colossus died at home, Lindermere-by-the-Sea, on the evening of 10 August 1909. He had been confined to his bed, very ill, for over a month, and the night before the family started to assemble in anticipation of his passing. When the time came, Abby was beside him, and Albert, Ralph and his three sisters, Emily, Augusta and Leonora, were in the room. Later, they did not wish to comment on the final hours. Daughter Margaret came soon after and Harold, working in Toledo, arrived on the night train. Pope's long-time physician, Dr. Oliver Howe, attended him throughout the day and signed the death certificate. The body was cremated and interred without ceremony in the family's columbarium in Forest Hills.[1]

There has been some speculation about what killed the Colonel. Dr. Howe entered "pneumonia" and "arteriosclerosis" on the death certificate, but several newspapers mentioned "a breaking down of the nervous system," and the next day's *Hartford Courant* reported that he died of locomotor ataxia, a progressive, degenerative disease of the lower spinal cord. Years later, it was established that there is no such disease — locomotor ataxia is, instead, a cluster of symptoms associated with the tertiary stage of syphilis. Rather than infect the brain, causing the horrifying mental breakdown then known as "paresis," in locomotor ataxia the syphilis bacteria slowly kills the nerve tissue of the lower spine, leading to a progressively rising semi-paralysis. Sufferers start to exhibit an awkward, stamping shuffle as they lose feeling in their feet, some become paraplegics, and most die of pneumonia as their heart and lungs begin to fail.

After I initially reported these findings in 1998, some members of the Pope family told another Albert Pope biographer, Stephen Goddard, that they disagreed with my theory, pointing out that both his son Ralph and grandson, Ralph Jr. suffered from Parkinson's disease, and they believed the Colonel may have as well.[2] This is plausible, as neuropathology was in its infancy in 1909 and the label "locomotor ataxia" was so broadly used that it was virtually a synonym for what we would today call "idiopathic" neurological disorders, those resulting from unknown or anomalous sources. Part of the reason I gave credence to the *Courant* story was that some press accounts from the last years of the Colonel's life talk of him being conveyed around at special events in an automobile or carriage because he could not walk due to an attack of "gout," which I thought to be a cover story for his growing paralysis.[3] However, private correspondence I later uncovered proved that Pope did, in fact, suffer from crippling wintertime gout as early as 1901 or 1902.

I am now of the opinion that this nervous disorder, whatever it was, did not disable the Colonel until the last year of his life, and that his symptoms do not suggest a diagnosis of either spinal syphilis or Parkinson's. Both are slowly wasting diseases, and my recent research convinces me that the Colonel was active in the daily management of the company through at least 1904, and probably all the way to the start of the August 1907 receivership. Parkinson's causes shaking and instability in the hands and arms and I can detect no degradation in his handwriting from 1883 to 1904 — it was awful when he was in his prime, and it was equally bad when he was old. (Thank goodness he was infatuated with the typewriter!) After a decade of investigation, I now take his obituaries at their word: He probably died of congestive cardiopneumonary failure resulting from old age, obesity, and great stress as he tried to save what remained of his empire. If Albert Pope did suffer from either Parkinson's disease or syphilis, they were not historically significant factors.

The Colonel had no funeral — not even a memorial service at the Charles Pope Memorial Church is mentioned in the press. In true Pope style, the Colonel's memorials, so to speak, came in the courtrooms of downtown Boston a little less than two years later. The cases were called *Pope v. Pope* and *Pope v. Hinkley*, but the labels were the unfortunate result of Massachusetts's somewhat antiquated probate laws, which required Albert, as trustee of his father's estate, to sue his mother and, in turn, that Abby sue her son-in-law Freeman Hinkley, another trustee. There was no actual dispute, just the need for clarification, and today there would only be a single case styled *In re Pope*, or *In the Matter of the Estate of Pope*.[4]

The Colonel had divided his wealth into two halves, a personal estate and his business empire. Abby received almost all of the personal estate, including Lindermere, the Commonwealth Avenue townhouse, the fine horses and carriages, the art and the books. Almost immediately, Abby sold Lindermere to Ernest G. Howes, a wealthy leather merchant.[5] The Colonel had made it a truly beautiful place, but it was also hugely expensive: in 1900, twenty-seven of Pope's nearest neighbors were estate retainers or their dependents, including gardeners, servants, cooks, hostlers, laborers, a house painter and a golf teacher.[6] Abby moved to Commonwealth Avenue, where she spent the rest of her days.

About four hundred shares of Pope company stock were turned over to the personal estate so they could be bequeathed as gifts. The Charles Pope Memorial Church received 80 shares, and about a dozen charitable causes were granted ten shares each, including the YMCA of Boston; the societies for the prevention of cruelty to children and to animals; Lincoln University; Brea College; the New England Home for Wanderers; the Massachusetts Order of the Loyal Legion; and the Boston Floating Hospital, a lifetime project of E.W.'s. James Quigley, his loyal coachman, and Alfred Cross, his head gardener, likewise received ten shares, as did each of Pope's nieces and nephews, Abby's sister and each of her children, George's daughter Marion and an old army buddy, William Meserve.

The rest was put into the Albert A. Pope Memorial Trust. It was what was called a *cestuis que* trust: it retained the corpus of the estate as its principal and distributed the income each year in the form of annuities to its designated beneficiaries. These included

Abby, the three sisters, the children, a niece (Harry's sister Ella) and Louis's widow. There was a problem, however. To pay all the annuities, the trust had to generate $65,500 in income, and by 1911 it wasn't making that much. The corpus of the trust, including the stock (about a quarter of the total outstanding shares of the Pope company), the Pope Building in Boston, and real estate in Hartford, Pueblo and California, couldn't generate even a tenth of the income the Pope Manufacturing Company by itself paid out in 1893. The question the trustees were forced to put before the court was: how should the money be divided? More specifically, did everyone get an equally reduced share, or did Abby have dower's rights, meaning she received her full $12,000 per year ahead of everyone else? The court instructed the trustees to give her dower's rights.

What was wrong with the trust? Assuming a six percent rate of return, an inability to earn $65,000 a year meant its principal may have been worth as little as $1.3 million. That couldn't be right, as the Pope Building alone was worth half that much. The key lay in article twelve of the Colonel's will, where he authorized the trustees to settle any claims or suits "the nature of these claims and my wishes in respect to them Mr. Winkley fully understands." Even as the Pope clan gathered in court to sort out Abby's problem, just down the hallway Winkley, the Colonel's former private secretary, was defending himself, and by extension, Pope himself, against accusations of fraudulent conduct.

Eleanor Ashley had owned some of the $100 bonds that Charles and Albert Pope sold in the late 1880s to raise money for the construction of the Copley Square Hotel. After the construction was done, the bonds, which essentially acted as a first mortgage, were held in a trust with three trustees: Charles Pope, Fred Pope (the architect and Albert's cousin) and a third trustee unnamed in the lawsuit.[7] The trust then leased the hotel to a man named Risteen, who operated it through his firm, the Copley Square Hotel Company. Charles Pope died in 1888 and the unnamed trustee resigned a couple of years later, so for over a decade Fred Pope had been the only trustee. That didn't matter much because Albert Pope owned about two-thirds of the bonds and Fred's main source of income was sponging off of his rich cousin, so he did what the Colonel told him to do.

Things stayed like this until 1907, when the Pope Manufacturing Company went into receivership again and the Colonel needed quick cash. He appointed Winkley to be the second trustee. The two trustees then fired the Copley Square Hotel Company, keeping the hotel supplies and furniture belonging to it, including Risteen's personal furniture, in his manager's apartment. They then defaulted on a paltry $50,000 second mortgage, forcing the hotel into a foreclosure sale, where it was sold at a steep loss. Although the Colonel probably made a quick $100,000 or so, the minority bondholders, including Mrs. Ashley, were forced to sacrifice their bonds for about a third less than they were actually worth. As if to rub salt in their wounds, the court discovered that the trustees had paid Albert Pope $5,300 to "rent" the hotel's furniture between the time it was taken from Risteen to when it was transferred to the new operating company even though it likely didn't belong to him.

Noting that Fred Pope and Winkley "were not well qualified" to run the hotel's land trust, Judge Bradley concluded that the only reason they were trustees was because of their "personal relations with Albert A. Pope," and that "it is only when these relations are understood that the unfortunate conduct of the trustees becomes intelligible." He determined that, "Albert A. Pope, having participated in their misconduct," and indeed, "virtually directed the sale," was liable for $104,000, plus interest, effective September

1907. Albert Pope the man having passed on, the estate was now liable for the judgment. Fully aware since Pope's death that there would probably be an adverse judgment, but not knowing how much it would be for (their strategy was to blame everything on the hapless Fred Pope, who was flat broke), the executors of the family estate could not fully invest its assets for fear they would need quick cash to pay Mrs. Ashley and her fellow victims. With this embarrassment behind them, the executors could now go on about their business. The Albert A. Pope Memorial Trust would continue successfully until 1941, the longest tenure allowed under Massachusetts law, after which its principal was distributed to the Colonel's many heirs.

## *Oh, No!*

At the 1911 Chicago Motorcycle and Bicycle Show, the Pope firm unveiled its new motorcycle, a 3-horsepower, single-cylinder model known as the Model H, selling for $175. A year later the Model K, better known as the "Pope Twin," was introduced. It was upgraded the following year to the Model L. With a displacement of about 61 cubic inches, the Model L was advertised as an official eight horsepower, but tests showed it could pull as many as fifteen, giving it a top speed of 65 mph. Although Westfield made the frame and engine, many of the other important components were purchased from outside suppliers, principally the Corbin Screw Company of New Britain, Connecticut, who provided the hubs, brake (singular) and chain. Corbin was a survivor from bicycle days, when they had gained a foothold with an innovative coaster brake design.[8]

Although the Pope motorcycle earned a long-lasting reputation for quality, and may have become the firm's most famous product, taking its place in private collections and museums alongside early Harley-Davidsons, Excelsiors and Indians, the company was again running behind technologically. By 1910, heavy twins already outsold light single-cylinders four-to-one. That year, Indian, in a plant about four miles from the Pope factory, offered eight different models based around four different motors, two single-cylinders and two twins. The larger, 4-hp single and the big 7-hp twin could be ordered with two-speed gearboxes and clutches. Within two years the smallest single and the smaller 5-hp twin were dropped as customers increasingly moved to heavier, more powerful machines. Excelsior, in Chicago, didn't even make light singles by 1912, specializing exclusively in big-valve twins. In 1910, Indian sold over 6,100 motorcycles and was building a new factory that would soon triple its output. In its best year, probably 1913, Pope never made more than 3,500 motorcycles.[9]

The bicycle industry stabilized after 1904, but it was a much smaller and poorer business. "There are but a few of us left," lamented Fred Finkenstandt of the National Cycle Manufacturing Company to a Congressional committee in 1908, "nineteen only, we believe, and few of those would still be in the business if they could find other lines which would keep their factories busy." E. J. Lonn of the Great Western Manufacturing Company agreed: "The present selling price of bicycles in the United States is very low," he rued, offering "only a small profit to the manufacturer at best."[10] The industry finally bottomed out in 1909 when only 234,000 bicycles were made. After moving all the name-brand bicycle production to Westfield in 1906 and selling off the Hagerstown plant in 1908, Pope's production dropped to a steady 50,000 or so per year. Including the plethora of private-label jobber models, Westfield was making over fifty different styles of bicycles. On New

Year's Eve, 1913, the factory threw every hand on the final assembly line so it could ship out 1,138 bicycles to get its total for the year over the magic 50,000 mark. "Trolley car or bicycle?" was its advertising push for 1915. "At 4 rides per day at 5 cents and 25 working days per month, you have spent $30.00 and have nothing to show for it! Buy a good Pope bicycle [and] at the end of 6 months have your rides and the bicycle too!"[11] Not exactly inspiring stuff.

American firms had been completely driven out of the export market. "English and German shops are now equipped with the most modern machinery—most of it of American makes," explained George Pope to the congressional trade committee. "With their cheap labor, they have been able to take all the export business," added Arthur Gendron of the Gendron Wheel Company. "We have [even] been driven out of the Japanese market, where we had a good trade," noted Fred Johnson of Iver Johnson. As a result, overcapacity was still a chronic problem: "To-day the productive capacity of American bicycle factories is probably double the actual output," estimated National's Finkenstandt.

Pope Manufacturing's bicycle operations responded fairly well to the shift in demand from luxury to utilitarian users. Although the firm still offered a $100 two-speed shaft-drive model, Columbia chain-drive roadsters and racers were available for half that. A Hartford-brand model was available at $30, and Fay and Ideal children's bikes could be

Postal Telegraph Company began widely using bicycle messengers during the mid–1890s, several years earlier than its bigger rival, Western Union. However, starting in 1920, Western Union bought as many as 5,000 specially-designed bicycles a year, selling them on the installment plan to its messengers. By 1930 half of all Western Union messengers were using cycles. This young man worked for Postal Telegraph in Birmingham, Alabama, about 1915. (photograph by Lewis Wickes Hine, Library of Congress Call No. Lot 7480 v.2, no. 1822 [P&P]).

bought for as little as $22.50. A heavy-duty "Pope Daily Service" delivery bike was offered at $40 and a "Messenger Special" for use by telegraph boys was available at $35.[12] A Washington, D.C., Western Union office used four Ordinaries for message deliveries as early as 1884, and in 1896 an Omaha branch was using fifteen safeties. By 1910 this segment of the market was big enough for the company to introduce a rugged, plain, relatively inexpensive bicycle intended for such use. In 1923 Western Union started buying them directly from the Westfield factory, reselling them to its delivery boys at cost on an installment plan. In 1929, five thousand of these bicycles cost Western Union $120,000, an average price of $24 each. As a perk, Westfield let Western Union managers buy Messenger Specials at the bulk price for their friends and relatives.[13]

But at other times, Albert Linder could be profoundly shortsighted. In 1909, the company shipped an assortment of bicycles to Wanamaker's, the giant New York and Philadelphia department store operation. Wanamaker's used them as demonstrators and, after trying them out and taking a few orders, returned them. Albert insisted that the bicycles were the property of Wanamaker's and that they should pay for them. The store's staff said they should be happy with the orders they received. Albert sued, and lost. Wanamaker's started looking elsewhere for their bicycles.[14]

Albert was spending far more time concentrating on the automobile. In fact, he had, as far as can be determined, no comment at all about either the bicycle industry or his own bicycle company any time after his father's death. He did, however, continue to keep the firm active in motor racing, substituting factory-modified Pope-Hartfords for the larger and more powerful Pope-Toledos that had previously carried the company's flag into competition. At the 1910 Vanderbilt Cup, two factory specials came in sixth and tenth. In early 1911, Bert Dingley, who had come in tenth in the Vanderbilt, won the Portola Road Race in Oakland, California, and the factory subsequently introduced a "Portola Roadster" with minimal bodywork, two wicker bucket seats, and a rear bench seat that could be removed to reveal a built-in rack for two spare tires. A few months later, two Pope-Hartfords raced in the first Indianapolis 500, coming in 22nd and 35th out of 40 starters.

Meanwhile, out in California, Dingley was creating one of the odder Pope legends. After winning the Portola in early 1911, he took his winning Pope-Hartford, which still bore some resemblance to a factory roadster, and modified it into a purpose-built racer he named "Baby Doll," using it to come in second in an unlimited race at Santa Monica, California in October. The factory didn't have a 6-cylinder motor available until 1912, but somehow Dingley's Baby Doll had an engine that measured around 340 cubic inches, so it was a long ways from the 1911 Pope-Hartford's 50-hp four-cylinder. Following the Santa Monica race, Dingley hotted up the motor even more and dropped it into a double-chain-drive Fiat 120 chassis, a creation that became known as the "Ono" (as in "Oh, no!"). The monstrous Ono lived up to its name when, a couple of years later, Dingley crashed it, nearly killing his riding mechanic and injuring himself so badly he had to end his racing career. The car was rebuilt and purchased in 1919 by a family in San Diego that reportedly still owns it. Now comes the weird part. There is an *identical* Ono in the Indianapolis Motor Speedway Museum. In 1958, auto historian Julian Goodell claimed that the Hartford factory built three copies of the Dingley machine and sold them to very rich and very brave enthusiasts. The claim is controversial, but highly plausible, the strongest argument against it being that no rationally managed automobile factory

Summertime excursions to the seaside resort of Savin Rock, Connecticut, near New Haven, were a Pope company tradition. In this photograph taken during the August 1905 trip, Albert Linder Pope sits front center, looking off to something on the viewer's right. To the viewer's right of him sits Arthur Wallace Pope, Colonel Pope's brother, and by this time a member of the firm's board of directors. To the viewer's right of Arthur sits George Pope. One row behind Albert Linder and one over to the viewer's left (in bow tie, leaning slightly over), is Wilbur Walker, and to the viewer's left of him is Charles Walker (The Connecticut Historical Society, Hartford, Connecticut).

experiencing deep financial trouble would spend that kind of money on three huge, Frankensteinian racing cars. But this is Albert Linder Pope we are talking about.[15]

## Ninety-one and a Half Cents on the Dollar

The Pope Manufacturing Company failed for the third and last time in August 1913. Up to early 1913, things seemed to be going along fairly well. In 1910, the company bought back the old Pope tube works plant (the second one, on Hamilton Street) to use for building car bodies and developing a new truck. That freed up the space Westfield needed to produce the motorcycle.[16] After the company sold the Toledo factory, Harold Pope had stayed on with the new owners for a year or so, helping Willys-Overland set up their new quarters, then had taken over as chief engineer at the Matheson Automobile Company in Wilkes-Barre, Pennsylvania. When his older brother told him he was needed in Hartford, he reluctantly took over as manager of the tube factory, now optimistically called the West Works. Some trucks and ambulances were sold, but the backbone of sales seemed to be about 400 cars and, as noted above, around 3,500 motorcycles and 50,000 bicycles a year. The company made a small profit and paid a small dividend each year, although it always looked to be somewhat short of cash. Then, two days before the Christmas of 1912, the firm suddenly surrendered their Connecticut charter and reincorporated in Massachusetts. In late February, Arthur W. Pope, the Colonel's brother, who still ran the leather and shoefindings company that had once been Albert A. Pope & Co., and who had been chairman of the Pope Manufacturing Company since 1910, filed for bankruptcy, claiming assets of $100,000 and liabilities three times that large. "Mr. Pope has been making heavy investments in outside companies and drawn from the firm of Arthur W. Pope & Co. to aid him," explained his attorney.[17] Nobody was quite sure where those "heavy investments" had gone.

After the Pope Manufacturing Company announced its receivership, the financial newspapers speculated that the Pope family and the Walker brothers had snapped up most of the stock and were now the owners. Three weeks later, the board voted to dissolve the company. Judge Joseph Tuttle, in Hartford, appointed George Pope as receiver. A group of bankers in Boston complained, and Judge Tuttle appointed two co-receivers from Massachusetts to protect their interests. In June, a lawyer representing a Boston-based syndicate offered to buy the company for $1.8 million, mostly in the form of stock and bonds of a new company the syndicate proposed to create.[18] The syndicate, which included David J. Post and one of Hiram Maxim's old assistants, Eugene Lobdell, undoubtedly represented Pope and Walker interests.[19] The judge rejected the offer out of hand, saying that he would not allow receivers to engage in financial speculation and would not force creditors to accept the securities of an unformed company to settle their debts. He instead proposed separate public sales of the Hartford and Westfield properties. George Pope objected, arguing that while the Westfield operation was profitable and would sell for a good price, the once-proud Columbia factory could only be sold as real estate and would probably only return about 30 percent of its book value. The Judge determined that if "the Connecticut property would be sacrificed" the creditors could be paid off "and there may be something [left] for the preferred stockholders."[20] He ordered the sale to go forward.

In January 1915 the Columbia factory and the George Keller–designed Pope headquarters building were auctioned off to Pratt & Whitney for $306,000, who announced that they intended to use it to make guns for the Chinese army. Ten days later, the old tube works, on Hamilton Street, was sold off for $80,000 to a New York maker of factory equipment, the Thomas F. Garvan Company. The sale of the Westfield factory was set for July. In June, Charles Walker filed for personal bankruptcy. The court announced that his New England Discount Company "and other concerns" were under federal investigation for unspecified offenses. In his bankruptcy filing several assets and liabilities were listed as "uncertain," drawing the attention of creditors and the attorney general. Walker quietly resigned as vice-president of Pope Manufacturing. A month later, the Westfield plant was sold to a new firm, the Westfield Manufacturing Company, for $725,000. The principals in the new company were Wilbur C. Walker and Stephen C. ("Scotty") Millett of an investment house, Millett, Roe and Hagen, representing the two parties who put up most of the money. George Pope, as receiver, was able to pay off the creditors "ninety one and a half cents on the dollar," and in September he was, to the appreciation and gratitude of the court and his fellow receivers, discharged by the judge. If the owner of a bicycle factory sold it to the bicycle trust in 1899 and received, as part of the purchase price, one of the A.B.C.'s $1,000 debenture bonds, then grimly held onto it down through the years, he would get back, for all his time and trouble and fourteen years' wait, a grand total of $18.30.

Colonel George retired to his home in Hartford and his service with the National Association of Manufacturers.[21] Harold left for Cleveland, where he briefly worked at the Ferro Machine & Foundry Company, then found a new profession in the burgeoning aircraft industry with Glenn Martin's new company.[22] For Albert Linder, the demise of

Two wings of the Columbia factory still stand, both newer additions built using fireproof technology. Pope sold the factory in 1915 to the Pratt & Whitney Tool Company, which used it until the late 1950s. In the 1970s it was purchased by the Aetna Life Insurance Company, which tore most of it down, but saved and renovated the two wings for use as offices. They have since been purchased by the State of Connecticut and are now used for state business. The lobby area contains a small display explaining the history of the facility.

the Pope company opened a new phase in his life — father and family man. His daughter Francis was born in 1913 and a son, William, followed in 1919. Albert took over the ailing Taplan Manufacturing Company, a maker of kitchen utensils in nearby New Britain, Connecticut, and the family stayed in the reserved but elegant home that Albert built in 1911 on West Hartford's Sycamore Road. Albert continued to take an interest in the auto industry, first with the National Automobile Chamber of Commerce, later with the Automobile Old Timer's Club. In 1947, Ralph Powers, a Connecticut automobile collector, opened a museum in Southington to exhibit the vehicles he had been assembling over the years. Shortly after opening day Powers approached an elderly man closely examining a 1912 Pope-Hartford and offered to explain the history of the car. The old man smiled, gently shook his head and replied, "You won't have to tell me about this one." It was Albert Linder, who died in Hartford a few years later.[23]

## *A Scandal in Westfield*

In the new company, Wilbur and Charles Walker ran the front office while Scotty Millett dealt with the bankers. To handle production, they hired John P. Fogarty as general manager. Fogarty had been a traveling salesman for Pope in the pre–A.B.C. years, and like most of the salesmen, he lost his job when the trust eliminated the Hartford sales office. The revamped Pope company hired him back in 1906 as a purchasing agent, and when it went under for good in 1913 he started work as a draftsman for the state highway commission. He came to the attention of the Walkers when, during the 1910s, he lived just around the corner from Charles and next door to Joseph F. Cox, who worked with Charles in Boston as one of the Colonel's office boys, moved to Hartford with him in 1895 when George Day transferred the company headquarters, then subsequently worked his way up to manager of the bicycle department. When the Walkers hired Fogarty in 1916, Fogarty asked Norman R. (Russell) Clarke to come work for him as his assistant. Clarke's story was much like Fogarty's: he hired on for a short while at the Electric Vehicle Company in 1906, then moved to Pope's, working as a clerk in the purchasing department. When he lost his job in 1913, he started in middle management at Firestone, moving his young family to Akron. His wife hated the gritty Ohio city, so when Fogarty called, he welcomed the chance to return East.[24]

The Walkers were strictly absentee owners. Wilbur had a suite of offices atop a Dodge dealership he and Charles (and perhaps Albert Linder Pope) owned in downtown Hartford, and Fogarty would come down from Westfield one day a month to talk strategy and finances. Norman Clarke, Russell's son, recalled that his father also made regular monthly trips to Walker's Hartford office suite, although Fogarty, not Walker, was his father's immediate superior. Norman accompanied his father on several of these trips starting in the early 1920s and never saw either Charles Walker or Scotty Millett at these meetings.[25]

According to Frank Schwinn, son of co-founder Ignatz Schwinn, the period between 1903 and 1925 was defined by "the almost complete standardization of all bicycle parts." Power within the industry began to flow away from bicycle makers toward the large parts firms, principally U.S. Rubber (tires), New Departure (hubs and coaster brakes); Diamond Chain (chain and cable); and Torrington (most other specialty parts). By 1923, wrote Schwinn, "the cycle manufacturer made only the frame set; that is, the frame, fork [and] cranks." The component makers took "virtual control of the bicycle industry," and while

John Fogarty worked briefly for the Pope company in the late 1890s as a salesman, but was furloughed by the bicycle trust along with most of the sales force after it took over the firm in 1899, then rehired in 1906 as a purchasing agent. Charles and Wilbur Walker promoted him to general manager after they bought the Pope bicycle factories in 1913. At the invitation of the Walkers, he invested heavily in the firm in 1930, only to be wiped out after the brothers stole the company's money. In late 1931 he resigned and moved to Florida. When he died suddenly in early 1932, most of his friends and co-workers believed he committed suicide (The Connecticut Historical Society, Hartford, Connecticut).

they "did much to hold the industry together by stimulating interest ... policing prices, [and] fostering trade associations," they left the industry with monotonous, unchanging, and relatively low-quality products. "The bicycle was so completely standardized that one bicycle looked, and was, almost exactly like another," Schwinn complained. "The manufacturers were asleep. The last thing they wanted was change." Norman Clarke agrees that annual model changes at the Westfield factory "at that time were mostly cosmetic. We didn't get into functional stuff until the mid-fifties."[26]

The Colonel's old dream of a long-lasting, stable oligopoly was being realized, but by the makers of components, not bicycles. "Check the record of failures among cycle manufacturers 1900–1930 against the same for parts makers," argued Schwinn. To a large extent, he was right. In 1903, Arthur Garford saw the industry as being made up of twenty significant bicycle makers, nine that were relatively unimportant, and three that would

After many failures, the Cycle Trades Association tried again in 1906, and this times succeeded for many decades. Its 8th Annual Convention was held near Los Angeles (probably Santa Monica) in the spring of 1914. John Fogarty sits front center in a light colored suit; Ignatz Schwinn stands at the top of the stairs (*George Loren Prince, Library of Congress Call No. PAN No. 54 [E Size] [P&P]*).

probably soon fail. In 1913, the industry was composed of only eleven makers, and by 1933 this was down to seven.[27] Frank Schwinn asserted that except for 1923–29, "the cycle industry did not do too well," but in a clear contradiction, in 1911 he and his father were able to put up half a million dollars in cash to purchase the Excelsior Supply Company, a motorcycle manufacturer. Six years later, they purchased the Henderson Motorcycle Company and by 1920 the Schwinn family was the third largest motorcycle manufacturer in the country after Indian and Harley-Davidson.[28] According to Norman Clarke, who had plenty of opportunity to observe his fellow company president, it was typical of Frank W. Schwinn, better known to his colleagues as Frank Sr., to overlook the good in favor of the bad. He was "a very sour, bitter and moody individual," recalled Clarke, "who always addressed Bicycle Manufacturers' Association meetings with a long harangue about parts makers and the policies of Sears, Montgomery Ward, and so on, all of which he despised." Frank Sr. was a man who "never smiled, always wore a black suit, was fervent in his belief in his company, and no one else."[29]

Another firm that took advantage of the open playing field left by the withdrawal of the A.B.C. and Pope from the bicycle market after 1902 was Rollfast, which was actually a symbiotic pairing of two separate firms, the H. P. Snyder Manufacturing Company and the D. P. Harris Hardware and Manufacturing Company. In 1895 Homer P. Snyder and a partner, Michael Fisher, began to produce bicycles. When the bike boom played out the firm floundered, and Fisher left in 1898. Although incorporated the following year, it was still too insignificant to be incorporated into the trust and endured a twilight existence until 1913 when Major Edward Teall, Snyder's son-in-law, left the army to join the firm, freeing up Snyder to launch a career in politics (he served as Congressman from New York for ten years.)

In 1916 Teall and Snyder reached an agreement with DeLancy P. Harris, whose D. P. Harris firm was probably the largest jobber of bicycles, roller skates, scooters and other wheel-goods in the country. Under their agreement, he became the exclusive seller of Snyder's bicycles, marketing them under the Rollfast name. "We never knew what the story was," says Norman Clarke. "After all, you don't sell just to one person year after year without some kind of connection.... Their only customer was D. P. Harris."

DeLancy Harris "was quite an aristocrat," noted an admiring Clarke, who called him "one of the founders of the [modern] cycle trades." Harris built up Rollfast the old-fashioned way: by hitting the road, week after week. "D. P. Harris," announced a trade magazine in 1916, "is starting out on one of his famous Rollfast trips." The Snyder company itself became invisible: its name was never mentioned in the cycle trades press, and Homer was rarely, if ever, seen at trade gatherings. Later, Bill Snyder, Homer's nephew, joined the firm, becoming president of H. P. Snyder after World War II. "Bill Snyder was a very close friend of mine," said Clarke with a laugh. "Even then, he would never tell me what the connection was."[30]

Like the Schwinns, Harrises, Snyders and Huffmans, the Walkers were becoming very wealthy. "They lived awful high," said Norman Clarke. "They had two of the biggest houses in West Hartford.... Wilbur Walker had a J-Class racing sloop and the *Thor*, a big 50-foot motor cruiser. He was building the largest house to be built in Madison, Connecticut, down on the shore." The brothers once again had side-by-side houses at 1810 and 1820 Albany Avenue in West Hartford. Charles Walker estimated the value of his place at $60,000, and Wilbur and his wife Mary had two live-in maids and a cook, even though the kids were grown and it was just the two of them at home. Wilbur's house in Madison was so large that it's now the home of the Madison Beach Yacht Club. He never had a chance to live in it.[31]

Throughout the 1920s Westfield Manufacturing had been earning gross profits of about $350,000 a year, most of which was passed through as dividends to its shareholders — primarily the Walker brothers and Scotty Millett. In 1929 they began a wholesale conversion of the firm's securities, retiring the preferred stock and replacing it with common stock, offering 12,000 new shares of common stock and so on.[32] Some of the stock was offered to employees. Russell Clarke bought forty shares for $4,000 and John Fogarty may have bought as many as 200. The Great Depression hit the bicycle industry just in time for the Christmas season of 1929. By this time, the production season had shifted around the demand of the holidays. Norman Clarke says that during this period "40 percent of all the bicycles that we made in a year were for Christmas." The factory would ramp up employment and production starting in late March, hit full stride in late April or early May, then produce at capacity until a week or two before Christmas. "A terrible time to let people go," rued Clarke. With the holidays knocked out, 1929 was essentially a ruin. Industry-wide production dropped from 348,000 in 1928 to 308,000 in 1929 and a low of 260,000 in 1932.[33]

"The Depression lifted earlier for the bicycle industry than it did for other things," notes Clarke. Nellie Coffman ran the Desert Inn in Palm Springs, where movie moguls and the occasional star sent their pampered daughters in the winter to keep them out of trouble. With the Depression on, Coffman had cut back on the horses in her livery stable and the girls started riding bicycles. They took a liking to them, Coffman later reported, because they could ride in shorts, swimming suits, or whatever they had on at the time instead of the sweltering Eastern riding gear. Returning home, they asked their folks for a bicycle, a cheap enough indulgence. When DeLancy Harris of Rollfast read in late March 1933 of three debutantes detained in San Diego for taking a nighttime spin on the beach in the nude, he put $250 in the pocket of his son George and sent him across the country to find out what was going on. George asked around, swallowed hard, and told his dad to send twenty-seven carloads of bicycles to California. In Little Falls, at the Snyder factory, Major Teall told DeLancy that he thought George had gone crazy. DeLancy thought not: Many of the California distributors had pre-paid.[34]

By 1934 sales were the highest since 1923, and two years later production topped the one million mark for the first time since 1898 or 1899. But the end of the Depression didn't come soon enough for Westfield, which hadn't suspended its stock dividends during the hard times. The end of the 1930–31 fiscal year was inexplicably stretched from August (where it had been since Pope days) to the end of the calendar year. John Fogarty unexpectedly quit in the fall of 1931 and moved to Clearwater, Florida. In March, he suddenly died at the Harrison Hotel. His doctor entered "organic heart disease" on the death certificate. The real reason was an overdose of barbiturates. Was it suicide? "Yes, that was the feeling at the time," responds Clarke. A September 1933 article in *Fortune* hinted darkly at this, but stopped short of saying so explicitly, probably fearing a libel suit. "My father was very active in trying to stop that, without success," says Clarke of the article, explaining that "he [Fogarty] lived just up the street."[35]

In July 1932, Wilbur Walker declared bankruptcy and asked the court to appoint him receiver, which it did. However, in September the judge summarily dismissed Walker and replaced him with Edward H. ("Ned") Broadwell, previously an executive at Fisk Rubber Company. DeLancy Harris offered $400,000, Torrington offered $315,000. The court and Broadwell accepted Torrington's offer, probably because the Westfield factory, like everyone else in the bicycle industry, bought so many of its parts from the Connecticut company, and thus owed it so much money, that it was the only way to settle the bankruptcy without liquidating Westfield or forcing Torrington to settle its debt for less than full value. Broadwell hired back Russell Clarke to take over as general manager. "There weren't really many executives, it wasn't a big company, and he knew the business," explains Norman Clarke. "Ned Broadwell didn't know anything about it."

The first thing Russell Clarke did was call Westfield's acting assistant manager, Jeffrey Kingsbury, into his office, the same office John Fogarty had used, and fire him. "Kingsbury got that job because he married Wilbur Walker's daughter," says Norman Clarke. "He fired him because he was no damn good. He was a playboy." The Kingsburys lived next door to the Clarkes, and Norman Clarke remembers watching as Walker's daughter and her husband slid progressively deeper into debt. "She owed everyone in town, but she was living the high life just the same." Wilbur Walker himself became "absolutely destitute. He had nothing," and died about 1937 when "he was hit by a car or something." His brother apparently retired, moving into the Wallingford Masonic Home from 1945 until his death in 1954. "At the end," Norman Clarke says of his father, "he hated them because they screwed him. They convinced him to buy stock when they were stealing it. The company went into bankruptcy because of them, so he didn't have a job. He wasn't being paid. And the Walkers, they were—well, they just screwed him."[36]

## *You Are Expendable*

Typically, Frank Schwinn, Sr., remembered the 1930s as a time of unrelieved misery. About 1925, such chain stores as Sears and Montgomery Ward, and tire stores like Firestone, Goodyear, and Western Auto, became the pre-eminent bicycle sellers in America. Schwinn claimed that the chains went so far as to make their own deals with the component makers, who dropped-shipped their parts to the bicycle factories for assembly. As a result, the typical bicycle maker was "reduced in most cases to building bicycles largely from his customer's parts on a cost-plus basis.... The parts maker sold more than half of his bicycle to his customer direct."[37] Independent jobbers and retailers suffered along with the manufacturers. But the worst — the very nadir of the industry, according to Schwinn — was the tires. In the ultimate irony, Pope's 1891 desperation-move acquisition, the Tillinghast single-tube tire, had become the near-universal standard for the bicycle industry. Produced in massive numbers by U.S. Rubber at the old Hartford Rubber Works, they were, as Schwinn later wrote, "just irreparable." You fixed them in 1930 the same way the Colonel intended for them to be fixed back in 1893 — by taking them to a bike shop:

> Have a repairman shoot some cement coated rubber band into the puncture, or work in a brass screw button, any of these agony prolongers at 25 to 50 cents per prolong, but they never worked and every puncture sold a new tire sooner or later, and mostly sooner. It was really better to have nice glass cut. That was just not repairable and you bought a new tire immediately.[38]

In 1931, Arnold, Schwinn & Co. liquidated its Excelsior-Henderson motorcycle operation. In 1942 Frank Sr. wrote that this was the defining moment in the company's history, because it forced the firm's managerial talent, which by now had become completely focused on the motorcycle, to move physically, mentally and emotionally into the bicycle business. They were appalled by everything they found. It was as if the bicycle industry had gone to sleep in 1903 and never woken up as the rest of the industrial world passed it by. They determined that the only way to survive was to create, then dominate, a top end for the market. Frank Sr. started with the tires. Nobody had ever liked the single-tube. "Ever since we have handled single tube tires, no matter what make, we have always had more or less trouble with them," reported a Columbus, Ohio, dealer in 1898. "My attempts at permanent repairs have not been at all pleasing," added a colleague from Wisconsin," The only way to do a satisfactory work to both my customers and myself is to cut them open and put in an inner tube." "Single tube tires would be a disgrace to all ordinary junk shops," chimed in a third. "Many tires have been put out which have blown out before riding twenty miles." "I follow the catalog equipment as near as possible to avoid delay in shipment," advised a fourth, with one exception: "Dunlop tires are used on all my Crescent wheels." [39] Now, after thirty years, Schwinn heeded the advice of this canny Georgia agent, and decided to switch to motorcycle-type tires, a wider, lower-pressure descendent of the old two-part Dunlop. U.S. Rubber refused to make them, so Schwinn turned to Germany's Continental Tire, who made up a shipment of non-metric prototypes. When Schwinn told U.S. Rubber that they could either gear up for his motorcycle-type tire or he would import all his rubber goods, they relented, running off a lot of 5,000 for his "folly" while Firestone arranged for matching rims. In 1933, Schwinn introduced the "Super Balloon Tire Bicycle," and two years later the Chicago firm was making a hundred thousand of them. Frank Sr. eventually pulled his bikes out of the chain stores entirely, relying on independent dealers and a network of dedicated, but independent, jobbers. [40]

Norman Clarke, by nature a far more optimistic individual, did not remember things being nearly so bad. His company made "at least some profit" every year after 1932. When he started in 1933, the factory employed about 800 during the peak season and produced about 800 bicycles a day. "It used to be a rule of thumb: one bike per man per shift." (That would change significantly after World War II. In 1976, Westfield produced 4,800 bicycles per shift with 900 people.) He agreed that the parts makers did sell components directly to the chain store customers, but claimed that this practice only allowed the major sellers "to partially determine costs" and thus improve their overall bargaining position.

However, Westfield was in a good position to resist because it made so many of its own parts, including frame tubes, forks, cranks, sprockets, and some rims and handlebars. Over time, this would expand to include pedals, spokes, all rims, all handlebars and stems by the 1960s. The decision whether to produce a part in-house or buy it was primarily determined by price and the available factory capacity. The only parts never considered for in-house manufacture were coaster brakes, saddles and tires. Clarke said Westfield pulled out of the chain stores in the late 1930s and believes that Schwinn did about this time as well. However, Clarke pointed to an important factor not mentioned by Frank Sr.— the decision of a new firm, Murray-Ohio, and a recently reorganized one, Huffman Manufacturing (the old White-Davis firm), to move strongly into the chain and department store market on the lower-price end.[41]

At Westfield, Clark recalled the introduction of the balloon-tired bicycle as only one of two significant developments during the pre–World War II era. The other was a decision by Sears in 1935 to move into high-quality bicycles. Sears hired "a hot-shot designer" by the name of Juan Raydolphus Morgansky, better known as John Morgan, to create three new bikes, the Elgin Bluebird, Skylark and Robin. Sears contracted with Westfield for their production, and building the custom tooling required almost a year. The first production prototypes were taken to the Sears Philadelphia headquarters to show to Lessing Rosewald, the company president. The trip was so important that Russell Clarke sent his son along to make sure nothing happened. Literally at the last minute, John Morgan decided to change the headlight design on one of the bikes, and Morgan and Norman Clarke swapped its chrome metal headlamp for a painted clay designer's model. The bikes were set up behind a curtain on a small stage in Rosewald's office. When he arrived and sat behind his desk, Morgan's design people pulled back the curtain. "Lots of oohs and aahs," recalls Clarke, breaking up. Rosewald, giving the bikes a look-over, "grabbed ahold of that clay model and squeezed it, and all this clay came out." That was an omen: The bikes were a bust. "I don't think we made 2,000 of the girl's bike, the Skylark, and I think we made about 4,000 of the Bluebird. The Robin we probably made about 25,000 of. That was a cheaper, lower-end model. The others were much too heavy, much too fancy, much too expensive."[42] But the money from building tools and starting production got Westfield through some lean years, and because the tooling could be adapted to other bikes, it allowed Westfield to battle Schwinn for the high-end cruiser market at minimal expense to itself.

During World War II, Westfield and Huffman were allowed to sell bikes to civilians, with Westfield allocated a maximum of 6,000 units a month and Huffman 4,000. Both were required to produce a standardized "victory" model, a rugged, no-frills, balloon-tired bike stripped of non-essentials such as fenders and chainguard. Clarke says that these were "surplus" bicycles: the war production board allocated Westfield an absolute limit of 25,000 bicycles a month for the military. If these were not needed, the overflow could be sold, up to six thousand.[43] Clarke tried to talk the war production board into accepting a lighter, more practical victory bicycle design, something more along the lines of an early 1900s Pope Messenger Special, but the board wanted a balloon-tired cruiser. However, as was true for all the bicycle makers, most of Westfield's capacity was turned over to war material. Its primary product was Bazooka rocket launchers and ammunition. "The Torrington president came to me and said, 'what's a bicycle company going to do during the war?'" recalls Clarke. "So during the war I got very active in Bazooka designing." Through better heat-treatment and engineering "we were selling these Bazooka rockets that were much better than the government designed for about half of what they first paid us when we first got going." The firm eventually made about eighteen million rockets, which were shipped to Ohio for charging with propellants and explosives. The factory did not require significant alteration for war production: "Oh, no, practically everything we had we could use." The end of the war brought everything to a screeching halt "just like that — we were called one morning at eleven o'clock: 'Cease all production.'"[44]

The firm was ready to make bicycles the day war production ended, but war restrictions remained in place for several months. Clarke recalls what happened:

> My father, one night ... it was after the war. But I happened to be there, he got a call from Harold Ickes — the father of the one that's now there — and he said he was going to be responsible for releasing the controls and for a certain consideration, he could see to it that Columbia got the right to go back to making bicycles ahead of our competitors. My father told him to go to hell.... I heard it, I was there.[45]

From January to September 1946 the American industry shipped 1.1 million bicycles. Clarke's memory that the business was strongly seasonal was borne out by Department of Commerce post-war recovery surveys, which indicated a low point in shipments in March at 97.4 thousand, with the high in August at 140.6 thousand, a difference of 44 percent. This is supported by Canadian government data, which indicated that hourly employees in 1934 reached a low of 222 in January and a high of 301 in July, a swelling of ranks of 35.6 percent. This continued to be true after the war, with 1955 employment ranging between 389 (January) and 524 (June), a seasonal increase of 34.7 percent.[46]

Clarke remembers the period from 1945 to 1965 as probably the hardest of his 40-year career. After World War II, the British economy was a shambles. Essentially bankrupt, its government informed the U.S. State Department that it could no longer afford to maintain troops in Greece and other central European nations to counter pro–Communist agitation. It was forced to devalue the pound in 1949 to stop runaway inflation. The Chancellor of Exchequer warned the Prime Minister that the country needed hard currency — U.S. and Canadian dollars — fast. In early 1953, Gabriel Hauge, President Eisenhower's economic advisor, summoned the members of the Bicycle Manufacturers Association.[47] Hauge told the group that England needed drastic relief. Its bicycle industry had been the world's largest before the war, and most of its cycle factories had escaped unharmed. Setting up a large-scale import market for the British motor industry would take too long and be too expensive, but a thriving bicycle sector could be put together in less than a year. "The President believes you can do other things," Hauge concluded. "You are expendable." The import duty on bicycles was cut from 30 to 7.5 percent. Sales by American firms dropped 50 percent in a single year.[48]

Some World War II veterans had brought home European lightweight 3-speed and 5-speed bicycles, sparking a brief cycle renaissance, particularly in the Midwest. They and their friends wanted more of them and turned up their noses at the American-made bicycles of the 50s, which they considered overpriced, heavy and badly designed. The only exception was Schwinn's Paramount, made by hand in Wisconsin but very expensive. The Eisenhower tariff ruling assured these enthusiasts that if they could find a dealer dedicated enough to carry the exotic European equipment, it would be available at a reasonable price. Schwinn executive Ray Burch later visited a dealer near Chicago, and, without announcing himself, asked to see a Schwinn 3-speed "English Racer." The dealer happily showed him the bike, but then took him across the store to a Raleigh, telling him that if he was after an English Racer, it was both lighter and less expensive. Burch pulled out his business card, informing the dealer that in addition to being lighter and cheaper, he knew full well that Raleighs paid a bigger dealer margin, but that he would not allow Schwinns to be used to pull customers into a store so it could sell another brand. He cancelled the store's franchise.

The BIA bitterly fought Eisenhower's low import tariff, and after a bruising round of hearings in 1954, the tariff commission voted 7–0 to raise the duty from 7.5 to 15 percent. Eisenhower had sixty days to reject or modify the board's recommendation. Sixty-four days later he knocked the tariff down from 15 to 11.25 percent. "We asked the attorneys in Washington," recalled Clarke, "can he do that? They said no, but nobody sues the President." It was October 1954. "You had to help England earn dollars. That's what they told us," says Clarke, shaking his head. "That was the beginning of the demise of the American bicycle industry."[49]

Industry executives soon realized that the only way to offset their shrinking slice of the market was to expand the entire pie by cultivating a thriving adult market. Clarke had no illusions about why they needed adults: "Volume! Good God!" In addition to size, the adult market also allowed the industry to escape its intensely seasonal production cycle. "Christmas became just another day, then. It wasn't the same. We didn't do 40 percent of our business for Christmas anymore." Westfield had never quit making a lightweight, geared adult bicycle, and in the early 1960s, Clarke was approached by one of his young engineers, Harold Maschin, who suggested they look into some new technology coming out of Europe. Maschin subscribed to several British and continental cycling magazines and read about a "10-speed gear, actually an 8-speed, which Huret was making in France." Derailleurs had been around for many years, but the Huret was an early entry in the market for a relatively simple-to-use, rugged, and cheap alternative to Sturmey-Archer's 3-, 4-, and 5-speed internal hub gears. Clarke bought several sets, which Maschin rebuilt into 10-speeds. Westfield built prototypes around them and "I kept them in my garage and let the neighbors ride them to see what happened." Unfamiliar with the exotic components, the neighbors blew up several derailleurs and through this crude, but effective testing program Columbia "found certain shortcomings we had to fix."[50] Columbia introduced its first 10-speed about 1962.

To build up the adult market, Clarke and Horace Huffman lobbied for bikeways, with Columbia actually paying for a Boston path near the Charles River in the mid–1960s. Clarke estimated that by 1965, a third of Westfield's total production of 650,000 was in the form of multi-geared bicycles: "3-speeds and 5-speeds, some 10-speeds." Between 1970 and 1972, the great bicycle boom hit, as domestic production increased from 4.9 million to 8.7 million, and total sales — domestics and imports — shot up from 6.9 million to 13.9 million.[51] *Fortune* magazine derided the American industry as one that had "plodded along in comfortable obscurity," and was avoided by "the more imaginative business minds." Its executives did no market research or ignored the little that was done and were unpleasantly surprised by the boom.[52] Clarke hotly disputed this. When asked if he thought the great bike boom "did just come out of nowhere," he replied "Oh no — we worked like hell for it. We worked on it all the time."[53]

Despite *Fortune*'s claim that the boom was a predictable outcome of the environmental movement, a 1987 analysis by economist Peter Kerr found that no single economic or demographic characteristic, including income, bicycle and gasoline prices, or the aging of baby boomers, adequately explained it. The most plausible explanation was made by former cycling journalist Frank Berto in 1999, when he posited that a combination of the baby boom demographic bulge and the hi-rise, banana-seat bicycle craze of the mid–1960s created a huge unfilled demand for adult bicycles about 1968.

Starting in 1963, Sting-Rays pushed out middleweight and lightweight 1- and 3-speeds as the bicycle of choice for teens. While the latter could be adapted for use by young adults, Sting-Rays were strictly kid's stuff, so as teens aged into young adults, they had to buy new bicycles if they wanted to keep riding. At the same time, these Sting-Ray boys and girls, members of the peak birth years of the post-war baby boom, moved into young adulthood in record numbers. Thus, they threw a double whammy on the industry: young adults were growing in record numbers, they wanted bicycles, and the bicycles they already had turned, like so many Cinderella carriages, into useless pumpkins.[54]

On other hand, many of the young, college-trained business managers who entered the bicycle industry seconded *Fortune*'s claims of mismanagement. Peter Davis, who later became Schwinn's director of corporate planning, recalled making a presentation to Frank Jr. of a sophisticated econometric model he had developed to predict spring and early summer sales. Schwinn responded that "all that matters is how many days of rain we get in April." Schwinn, who had become increasingly disengaged from the business after a 1974 heart attack, retired in 1979 and his nephew, Ed Schwinn, took over. There are strong disagreements about who is to blame for the ultimate downfall of the Schwinn firm, which fell into bankruptcy in 1992. Jack Ahern, vice president of manufacturing under Frank Jr., believed that both Frank Sr. and Jr. were to blame for not giving more control to talented outsiders such as general manager Bill Stoeffhaas, executive vice president for product design and manufacturing Al Fritz, and vice president for marketing Ray Burch. "The Schwinn family couldn't allow anyone to be top dog unless their name was Schwinn," Ahern concluded. Clarke, on the other hand, lays the blame squarely on Ed Schwinn. "Eddie Schwinn was nothing — he absolutely ruined the company."[55]

## A Broken-Down Bicycle Plant in a Broken-Down Town

Norman Clarke assumed the presidency of the Westfield firm in 1955 when his father, Russell, retired. At that point, Torrington had owned Westfield for 22 years. After buying it for $315,000, Torrington paid itself a stock dividend out of Westfield's treasury every year except the first. "They took many millions out of it," complained Clarke. In 1959 Torrington's headquarters factory in Connecticut suffered a long, very bitter, labor strike, which eventually forced it to adopt a company-supported pension fund for its employees. "The minute Torrington did it, it was obvious that our people were going to have to have it," said Clarke. Instead, Torrington executives summoned him to headquarters and told him that "We see no place for a broken-down bicycle plant in a broken-down business in a broken-down town in a broken-down state." Clarke was told that Westfield would be sold as soon as possible and the potential buyers approached so far all indicated that they would consider it only if they were free to move or liquidate the factory. Clarke asked only one question: "Do I have any rights?" The price was four million dollars, and the deal was probably one of the first leveraged buyouts in American corporate history. The first thing Clarke did was change the name of the firm to the Columbia Manufacturing Company because "Westfield didn't mean much to people in California, but Columbia did."[56] It was a risky move and Clarke remembers that "I needed all the help I could get." He got it.

Western Auto ran a nationwide chain of auto parts and tire stores which also sold hard goods, such as washing machines, lawn mowers—and bicycles. They were the largest seller of Raleigh bicycles in the country, but under their name, not Raleigh's. Throughout the 1950s, Raleigh had maintained a craftwork culture, leaving the low end of the market for its competitor, the British Cycle Corporation (BCC). But in 1957, Raleigh opened a large and expensive new Factory 3 in Nottingham and bought the bicycle division of another competitor, BSA. Both proved unnecessary as demand in Britain and the Commonwealth flattened. Three years later, Raleigh merged with Tube Investments, the parent corporation of BCC, to become TI-Raleigh. BCC was heavily involved in selling private-label bicycles to American mass merchandisers after the Eisenhower tariff reductions. To fill unused plant capacity, TI-Raleigh shifted much of its private-label work to the Raleigh factory, closing many BCC plants. In the early 1960s, Raleigh was shipping 800,000 bicycles a year to America, but only 60,000 were under the Raleigh or Carlton names, and it was selling some jobber bicycles at wholesale prices as low as $18.[57] As a result, the Nottingham plant was experiencing quality control problems on both the cheap bikes and its high-end units. It hired the consulting firm of Booz, Allen and Hamilton to help it sort out the problem. They recommended that Raleigh dump the North American private-label, mass-market segment and focus on its specialty bike-shop lines.[58]

About a year after buying the firm, Clarke was approached by Western Auto executives who told him that Raleigh had suddenly cancelled all their orders for lightweight bicycles. "Western Auto had catalogs out, prices out, everything ready for distribution, and Raleigh pulled out, just like that," recalls Clarke. Western Auto approached Schwinn asking for replacements, but after two decades of struggle, Frank Sr. had finally freed himself from both private labeling and the chain stores and wanted nothing more to do with either. He refused. They next turned to Columbia. Clarke was ecstatic: "I had just bought the company. I needed anything like that.... It gave us volume."[59] The problem was that Clarke knew about what Western Auto had been paying Raleigh for its English Racers, and he knew Columbia couldn't match that price because Raleigh owned Sturmey-Archer, who made the bikes' 3-speed hubs, and sold them to Raleigh for about half the wholesale market price. However, he could make it—just barely—if he could use Shimano hub gears. A year earlier, the brothers Keizo and Yoshi Shimano had come over from Seiki City, bringing with them a variety of samples which young Harold Maschin happily turned into scrap metal. He liked what he found. "We were familiar with Shimano's product, had been testing them for awhile. They were just as good," says Clarke. Appalled at the thought of using Japanese parts, the Western Auto men turned him down.

"Okay, a week goes by," remembers Clark. "Western Auto comes down with their executives. They said they had to have 175,000 units to fulfill their existing commitments. 'We'll buy them if you'll stand behind them,' they said. I said we would. I hopped on a plane the next day to Japan." Clarke had always done his own overseas buying. "If I went as president of my own company, I'd meet the president of the foreign parts companies. If Schwinn sent their purchasing manager, he'd meet with the sales manager. If Murray-Ohio sent a vice-president, he'd meet with a vice president. But I went myself.

I used to love it. I met some wonderful people." He also got better deals. "I'd negotiate with them, and we'd do very well. That lasted awhile, and then the rest of them caught on to what was happening."⁶⁰

In Japan, he was entertained, he says with a twinkle in his eye, "very fabulously." He not only stopped at Shimano's suburban Osaka factory (where he was greeted by a brass band), but bought some nine million dollars' worth of components from Araya, Honda, Maeda (SunTour) and Sugino. "Because I did it," says Clarke, "every one of the other eight [BMA members] went back the next year and started buying Japanese parts. In no time they were selling a hundred million dollars' worth of parts in this country."⁶¹

The Japanese products had a downside, however. Their component makers required advance letters of credit, so Columbia was constantly burdened with large, short-term loans. When Clarke approached the banks for a long-term loan to expand and update the factory, they turned him down because he was already at his credit limit. So in 1969 he sold the firm to Cleveland's Modern Tool and Design (MTD), then the nation's largest maker of lawn mowers. Clarke stayed on as a consultant for five years, then retired. "I was 62 years old. I'd been there for 41 years," he explained.⁶² Unlike Murray-Ohio, which had moved operations from Cleveland to Tennessee in the early 1960s, then had made steady expansions until the plant covered almost 1.5 million square feet in 1967, MTD made no major investments in Westfield, and during 1973, the last full year of the great bicycle boom, production hit only 600,000 units, a quarter of those turned out by industry-leading Murray (2.4 million) and second place Huffman (2.3 million), and less than half made by "specialty" producer Schwinn (1.47 million). In fact, Columbia's output was barely more than the imports brought in by the two largest foreign makers, Raleigh and Peugeot (460,000 and 175,000, respectively).⁶³

MTD invested none of its boom-year profits on human or physical capital, and during the subsequent post–1974 slump there was no money to rebuild or re-equip. This is not to say that investments in new American bicycle plants were a panacea: Huffy replaced its original Gilbert Avenue factory in Dayton with a new plant in Celina, Ohio, in 1955, opened a new factory in Azusa, California, in 1959, and purchased land for a third plant in Ponca City, Oklahoma, in 1980. However, after the sharp recession of 1980–82, Huffy closed Azusa and sold the Oklahoma land because it could not afford the overhead of excess capacity while waiting for the market to cycle back up. Similarly, Schwinn opened a new factory in Greenville, Mississippi, in 1981, only to find that it was bleeding money. The problem was that by the time it discovered this, Schwinn, unlike Huffy, had nothing to go back to: it had been forced to close its rickety, fire-prone, inaccessible urban Chicago factory in 1983. It solved the problem by pulling the plug on Greenville, halting all domestic production, in 1993.⁶⁴

In 1984 MTD demanded that employees take a ten percent cut in wages and a thirty percent cut in health insurance and pension benefits. The Machinists' union called a strike. "They had a very strong union," said Clarke. Although MTD eventually won, Columbia was mortally wounded, and in 1987 declared bankruptcy.⁶⁵ It was sold to its own employees, and continued making bicycles until 1991, when it abandoned the business and concentrated on its other main product, school furniture. "We started that in 1958," remembers Clarke. "There wasn't an awful lot of money in it." It was steady work, however, and it kept the firm's 200 employees going.

Huffy had a similar story. When losses mounted in the early 1990s, workers at the Celina plant agreed to take a 20 percent pay cut. In 1998 the union asked for a return of the 1995 cut. Lost in the wake of Horace Huffman's death, the company panicked, shuttered Celina, and contracted out the following year's production to Taiwan. In 1993, after closing its Mississippi factory, Schwinn declared bankruptcy and the family sold the company to the Scott Sports Group, a skiing products firm in Boulder, Colorado, who turned it into a marketing company for American-engineered, Chinese-built products. In 1995, they introduced a meticulously exact replica of Schwinn's famous Black Phantom, priced at $3,000.[66] It made it into that annual testament to capitalistic excess, the Neiman-Marcus Christmas catalog, and became something of a sensation. Columbia followed along in 1997, introducing a replica of its 1941 Columbia Superb cruiser. Columbia had previously had some success selling a couple of semi-replicas in the 1980s for about $400, but discontinued them in 1991 at the same time it discontinued its regular mass-market bicycles.[67] Columbia hoped to sell five to seven thousand of the Superb at a more modest $1,500, but quickly learned that Schwinn never really expected to make a profit from the Black Phantom; it was simply a wonderfully innovative marketing tool, and for this purpose the eyebrow-raising price was actually an advantage. The market for five-foot-long wall sculptures was limited, Columbia probably never sold more than a couple thousand Superbs and within a few years it was back to school desks.

In the end, the Scott Sports Group was prescient: the future of the American bicycle industry, at least for bicycles under a thousand dollars, lay with firms that designed them in the United States, contracted production to huge, highly flexible overseas (typically Chinese) factories, brokered their rapid shipment back to the U.S. by container ship, then marketed them without a great deal of concern about whether the client was a bike shop, a big-box sporting-goods retailer or a mega-discount store. Ironically, Scott couldn't make its own strategy work: Schwinn went under a second time in 2001 and was bought by mega-distributor Pacific Cycle, who uses it exclusively as a department-store brand, having completely abandoned its network of retail bicycle shops as too expensive to service. Huffy declared bankruptcy in 2004 and was reorganized as a distributor of sporting goods. Murray-Ohio was sold to a Swedish conglomerate in the mid–1990s and closed down its Tennessee plant in 1999. Brunswick, another sporting goods conglomerate, made one last attempt to start an American bicycle factory. Frames were fabricated using robots, then shipped to a maquiladora plant in northern Mexico for painting and assembly. That venture was also unsuccessful and Brunswick shut it down in 2001. In 1988, TI sold Raleigh-UK to Derby International, an investment group, who in turn sold it to a corporate liquidation specialist, Lexmark, in 2000. Its Sturmey-Archer division was sold to a Taiwanese component maker, SunRace, and by 2003 Lexmark had disposed of the Nottingham factory and was using the Raleigh logo as a licensing trademark.[68]

The land under the Columbia factory had been abused for over a century, the careless disposal of chrome-plating materials early in the century and the exigencies of World War II having taken their toll on the soil and groundwater. In 2008, Columbia, the Commonwealth of Massachusetts and the federal EPA agreed that the only economical way to deal with the problem was to raze the old bicycle factory, leaving only the relatively small, new building used for manufacturing school furniture. The Queen of Lozierville was the last of the grand old dames, and now it is no more.

# 13

## *All Gone to Their Account*

*Pope, Gormully, Jeffery, Coleman, Lozier and many others, pioneers of that great industry, all gone to their account. They were men of heroic mold, who in spite of the panicky conditions then prevailing, built up a mammoth industry that gave employment to tens of thousands of men who otherwise could have found no other market for their labor, and which at the same time furnished recreation and enjoyment for hundreds of thousands of individuals.*

— Arthur L. Garford, 1914[1]

- **Herbert Alden**, who came with Hiram Percy Maxim to the motor carriage division in 1895, was promoted to chief engineer at the Electric Vehicle Company after Maxim left. When EVC stopped making cars in Hartford about 1905, he worked briefly at Pope's, then went to the Timken Roller Bearing Company in Ohio as their chief engineer. He moved to Detroit in 1910 when the firm split off its automobile axle operation as a new firm, the Timken-Detroit Axle Company. He was appointed vice-president, later rising to president and part-owner. He retired about 1925 and died in 1950.[2]
- **Milton Budlong**, the Chicago-area Columbia bicycle salesman who became George Day's successor at the Electric Vehicle Company, later became sales manager for Packard and served as president of the National Association of Automobile Manufacturers. He died in 1941.[3]
- **Norman R. "Russell" Clarke,** who took over the Westfield factory after the Walker brothers were swept out in 1933–34, retired as president in 1955 and passed away in 1964. His son, **Norman Clarke,** who succeeded him as president, then owned the firm for almost ten years after a leveraged buyout, retired as president of the Columbia Mfg. Co. in 1974. He worked with the Bicycle Manufacturers' Association for three years to promote bicycle use, then moved full-time to his home on Cape Cod. He died in 2009.
- **R. L. Coleman** worked briefly for the National Battery Company after leaving the American Bicycle Company in 1902, then retired to the life of a gentleman farmer at his estate in Orange County, Virginia. He died about 1912.[4]
- For someone who provided so much information about the Selden patent affair, data on **Hermann Cuntz** himself has proved harder to come by. He remained with

the Electric Vehicle Company and its successor, the Columbia Motor Car Company, until its end in 1912. He then practiced as a patent attorney in Hartford until 1915, when he moved to New York, where he continued in law. He frequently answered authors' inquiries about the Selden patent, and in September 1947 wrote a lengthy, three-part article, "Hartford, Birthplace of Automobile Industry" for the *Hartford Times*. The date of his death is unknown, although he was corresponding with author William Greenleaf as late as 1954.

- In the years after his death from a heart attack in Daytona Beach, Florida, in 1907, **George H. Day's** widow Katherine Beach Day took his place as a director of the Hartford Real Estate Improvement Company, remaining in that position for many years. She also helped to found the Hartford chapter of the National Association for the Advancement of Colored People, and in conjunction with Margaret Sanger and Elizabeth Hepburn (mother of actress Katharine Hepburn) helped lead the effort of the Connecticut Birth Control League to overturn Connecticut's Comstock law prohibiting the sale or distribution of contraceptives to any person, married or single. Their son, George Jr., became a Connecticut Supreme Court justice.[5]

- **Hayden Eames** left the Electric Vehicle Company soon after it was split off from the Pope empire and went on to a notable career at Westinghouse and Studebaker before going to work for Charles R. Flint as an arms consultant. On a business trip for Flint to Russia in 1917, he was trapped by the Soviet revolution and had to make his way west across Siberia for 23 days on the last trans-Siberian train to run for a decade. During World War I he was commissioned a Lieutenant Colonel in the army, making him one of only a few Americans to serve as an officer in two different branches of the military. Hiram Maxim dedicated *Horseless Carriage Days* to him in 1936. He died in 1938.[6]

- **George A. Fairfield** left the Weed Sewing Machine Company in 1881 when his Hartford Machine Screw Company outgrew its borrowed quarters in a corner of the Weed plant and moved into its own sprawling factory next door. He retired in 1905, but stayed busy as secretary-treasurer of the Hartford Board of Trade. He died in 1908.[7]

- After being forced out as president of U. S. Rubber in 1901, **Charles R. Flint** kept busy in street railways and as an arms broker, selling warships to Japan and Russia. He retired in 1928, but growing bored, tried to make a comeback in 1930, but later complained that his services were in little demand, the swashbuckling days of American business having given way to an era of organization, systemization, and planning. He died in Washington, D.C., in 1934.[8]

- By 1904, **Arthur L. Garford** had grown disenchanted with both Albert Pope, who he called "The Old Colonel," and the bicycle business, and announced that his Federal Manufacturing Company would abandon bicycle parts entirely in favor of the automobile trade. In 1908 he merged Federal into Studebaker, and four years later left the motor industry for good when Studebaker sold Federal to Willys-Overland. He remained in Elyria the rest of his life, remaining active in politics. A Teddy Roosevelt man, he lost as the Progressive Party candidate for governor and senator in 1908 and 1912. He died at home in 1933.[9]

- After **R. Philip Gormully** died in August 1900 at only age 53, **Thomas B. Jeffery** was said to have blamed Colonel Pope for his death, attributing Gormully's broken health to the strain of the *Pope v. Gormully* suit. After selling Gormully & Jeffery to the bicycle trust, he went into the automobile business with his son Charles in the former Sterling bicycle factory in Kenosha, Wisconsin. Their Rambler was very successful, selling 1,350 units in 1903. Jeffery got his revenge, in a way, in 1907, supplying money and moral support to Henry Ford in his fight over the Selden patent at a time when things looked bleak, allowing Ford to fight back to ultimate victory three years later. Jeffery died while vacationing in Italy in 1910. After narrowly avoiding his own death in the sinking of the *Lusitania* in 1915, Charles decided to retire and sold out to Nash. After World War II, Nash-Rambler became part of American Motors.

- **Fred Law**, who built the thirty Steinway gas motors in 1890 and later joined the Pope motor carriage division, left in 1904 to start his own firm, the F. A. Law Machine Company, then returned again to the Pope factory to design automobiles. After Pope's folded, he became chief inspector at the Hamilton (later Hamilton-Standard) Propeller Company in Hartford. He died in the 1930s.
- **Henry A. Lozier** retired after selling his firms to the bicycle trust in 1899, and moved to Plattsburg, New York, where he became an art dealer and helped his son Edward start an automobile company, which survived until it was sold it to Locomobile in 1915. Henry died in 1903.[10]
- **Elliott Mason** continued to run his store on Warren Street in lower Manhattan, but with each passing year it became less and less a bicycle shop and more and more an auto repair garage. He died in 1911 at his home in New Jersey.
- After leaving the Electric Vehicle Company in 1907, **Hiram Maxim** briefly tried his hand at making his own electric automobile, then earned a vast fortune as the inventor and manufacturer of the Maxim Silencer, the ominous-looking cylinder every movie hoodlum is seen screwing on the front of his pistol. (The design was based on the principle of the automobile muffler.) He remained president of the Maxim Silent Firearms Company until his death in 1938.
- After selling the remnants of the Overman Wheel Company to the J. P. Stevens Arms Co. in 1899, **Albert H. Overman** started an automobile firm in Chicopee Falls, the Overman Automobile Company, in 1901. In 1904 he sold it to Locomobile. He then went on to a career as a hydraulic engineer, probably in mining, then retired to a farm in New Hampshire. He died sometime in the 1920s.
- **Abby Pope** continued to live at the Commonwealth Avenue townhouse for the rest of her life, traveling and working on behalf of women's suffrage. She died in 1929.[11]
- Something about the end of the Pope Manufacturing Company in 1913 seemed to free **Albert Linder Pope**. That year, when he was 40 and Amy was 36, their first child, a daughter, Francis, was born. He took over a struggling maker of kitchen utensils in nearby New Britain, the Taplin Manufacturing Company, and turned it around. Albert and Amy traveled extensively, and a son, William, was born in 1919 while the family was living in France. William eventually became vice president of Taplin. Albert died in Hartford in 1955.[12]
- After retiring from the Pope firm in 1896, **Edward W. Pope** lived on his farm near Lincoln, Massachusetts, and served on the boards of many Boston area charities, most notably the Floating Hospital. When his wife died he moved back into town

to be with his daughter and her husband, an Episcopal priest. He died in 1936 at age 91.[13]

- **Emily, Augusta and Adelaide Pope** lived out their days together at the home the Colonel built for them on Newberry Street. In 1922, Augusta fell ill and was left almost completely paralyzed, able to move only her eyes and the fingers of one hand, yet it was Emily who died first, in August 1930. Augusta died seven months later, in March 1931. Adelaide outlived all her brothers and sisters, dying in 1935. The book that Augusta and Emily wrote, along with fellow New England Hospital physician Emma Call, *The Practice of Medicine by Women in the United States* (1881), has been republished at least once since their deaths.[14]
- **George Pope** retired as a manufacturer after winding up the receivership of the Pope Manufacturing Co. in 1914, only to embark on a new career — conservative activist. In 1913 he was elected president of the National Association of Manufacturers, an anti-union, anti-government organization of big business leaders. In 1916, he advocated an "employers' union" to deal with labor unrest — in effect, a call for universal, organized resistance to the Sherman Anti-trust Act. He also denounced government aid programs. "When misfortune, accident, sickness, or old age lessen the power of the individual to provide for himself," he urged, "let us help him to help himself." He remained a partner of the Walker brothers in a Hartford-based auto supply business, the Walker & Barkman Manufacturing Co. He died in Hartford in 1918.[15]
- **Harold L. Pope's** professional career was as successful as his personal life was fractured. He stayed with Willys-Overland for a year or so after they bought Pope's Toledo motor car plant in 1909, then returned to Hartford to work for the family firm until its end in 1913. After working as chief engineer and factory manager under Henry Souther for the Ferro Machine & Foundry Co. in Cleveland for two years, he became an executive at the Martin, Wright-Martin and Wright aircraft firms in New Jersey and California until 1926, ending up as vice-president of Curtiss-Wright, followed by a stint as chief engineer at the refrigerator firm Kelvinator. Excited by the young aircraft industry, he joined a new aircraft firm, Crescent Aircraft, that pioneer transatlantic aviator Clarence Chamberlin was starting. Unfortunately, unknown to either Harold or Chamberlin, Crescent was a stock scam, and regulators shut it down in August 1929, just weeks before the stock exchange crashed. To weather out the storm, he settled in at the family's leather business, where he stayed until his retirement in 1937. He and his wife Clara separated in 1927, after the death of Harold's sister Margaret (they were sisters-in-law, as Margaret was married to Clara's brother Freeman Hinkley). He began a new family with a woman he could not marry because Clara would not grant a divorce unless he provided her with an irrevocable support trust, which he refused to do. Harold remained estranged from Clara and their children for the rest of his life. She died in 1956 and Harold passed away in California in 1961.[16]
- **Harry M. Pope's** last gunsmithing shop was located in a former Colgate factory building in Jersey City, just across the river from New York City, where he moved in 1908. He chronically complained of being simultaneously broke (sometimes to the point of starvation) and overworked, but his son Allen later said that Colgate didn't charge him rent, and that as far as money was concerned, Allen noticed only

that his father was "deeply disappointed" he could never afford a house in the country. Illness forced Harry to retire about the time America entered World War II, and he died in 1950. After his death, large bundles of mail were found in his incredibly cluttered shop and it appears that at some point, he simply stopped opening his mail, which may explain why he believed he wasn't getting paid.[17]

- **Margaret Roberts Pope Hinkley,** the Colonel's only grown daughter, died in 1927. Her husband, Freeman Hinkley, never remarried. He died in 1951.
- **Ralph L. Pope,** the Colonel's youngest son, went to work for one of the family's main businesses, the Northwestern Leather Co., in 1911. In 1925, he became president, and in 1931 succeeded Robert Winkley as managing trustee for the Albert A. Pope Estate until it was dissolved, as required by law, after 31 years in 1941. He died in 1968.[18]
- **Frank W. Schwinn, Sr.,** stayed in charge of his family's business right up to his end in 1963. In spite of his importance to the local economy, he was, as an individual, so low-key that his obituary in the *Chicago Tribune* ran to only 251 words. Although the ability of his son and successor, Frank W. Schwinn, Jr., to lead the firm became impaired after a major heart attack in 1974, he did not step down in favor of his nephew, Edward R. Schwinn, Jr., until 1979. He died in 1988.[19]
- **Henry Souther** left Pope's when it was taken over by the bicycle trust in 1899, but worked closely with both the Electric Vehicle Company factory and the second Pope firm as the head of his own consulting firm, the Henry Souther Company, and was Hartford's water commissioner. A trusted aide, H. B. Newell, subsequently ran the firm on a day-to-day basis while Souther worked as vice president of a Cleveland firm, the Ferro Machine & Foundry Co. (where he gave a job to Harold Pope) and in Philadelphia at the Standard Roller Bearing Company. He was commissioned an army aviation officer at the outbreak of World War I, but died suddenly in 1917 after an operation. His family and Newell continued the Henry Souther Engineering Company, which remained in Hartford until the mid–1970s, when it was sold.[20]
- **A. G. Spalding** retired after stepping down as A.B.C. president in 1899. He married his long-time mistress, Elizabeth Churchill, and adopted their child, renaming him Albert Goodwill Spalding, Jr. Elizabeth was an ardent follower of the Raja Yoga theosophist Katherine Tingley, who was then creating a model community at Point Loma, California, near San Diego. Spalding, his wife, their son, and his four children by his previous marriage to the late Josie Keith, moved there in 1901. He bought a large tract of land next to Tingley's "White City," and while Elizabeth sought spiritual enlightenment, he built a golf course. He reluctantly allowed himself to be drafted as a progressive-wing Republican candidate for senator in 1910, and while he could never really hide the fact that he would rather be playing golf, still lost by only a narrow margin. He died at Point Loma of a stroke in 1915. Former baseball player, manager and owner A. G. Spalding was selected to baseball's Hall of Fame in 1939.[21]
- After his misadventures in industrial spying and assembling ball bearing cartels, **Frederick W. Taylor** was hired by Bethlehem Steel in 1898, where he performed his famous pig-iron loading and shoveling experiments. Charles Schwab bought Bethlehem in 1901 and fired Taylor and his scientific management crew. In 1904,

Taylor started giving lectures on scientific management at Boxley, his home near Philadelphia, and with the assistance of journalist Morris Cooke, Taylor organized the lectures into a 1911 book, *Principles of Scientific Management*, which made him famous. He died in 1915. In 1923 a carefully stage-managed biography of him was published, after which about half of his papers were destroyed before the rest were donated to the Stevens Institute in 1949. It is not known if the Pope-Overman espionage material survived because the incident was so unusual, or because that particular job was so small relative to other similar projects that it was overlooked.[22]

- Despite Norman Clarke's conviction that **Wilbur C. Walker** died in ignominious poverty, all that can be verified is that he passed away in Connecticut sometime between 1935 and 1943. By this time, his son Charles had already graduated from Yale Law School, and he went on to become a wealthy and privileged member of Stamford society, but there is no mention after 1933 of Wilbur's oldest daughter, Gertrude Kingsbury, wife of the former Westfield plant manager. Wilbur's brother **Charles E. Walker** entered the Connecticut Masonic Home in Wallingford, near Hartford, in 1945, and died there in 1950.[23]
- **William C. Whitney** retired from active life in 1902 and died in New York City in 1904. His biographer, Mark Hirsch, believed that had he been in better heath in his late years and lived longer, he would have taken a more active interest in automobiles, buses and taxi services, and as a result the Electric Vehicle Company would have had a far better chance of succeeding.[24]
- **Robert L. Winkley**, the Colonel's loyal personal secretary, continued to serve him even in death as the managing trustee of the Albert A. Pope Estate until he retired in 1931. He died in New York City in 1938.[25]
- After selling off his velocipede patents in 1877, **Calvin Witty** stayed in carriage making, his firm already having become large and prosperous in that trade in the New York City area. He died in Brooklyn in 1903.

# 14

## *The Long Road Home*

> *The advent of the bicycle gave the first real impetus to the designing and building of machine tools for mass production ... but the locomotive, being a self-contained power plant on wheels ... composed of thousands of machined parts, had a far more extensive effect upon the growth of machine tools than had the bicycle.*
> — Fred Colvin, editor-in-chief,
> *American Machinist*, 1947[1]

Industrial historians have struggled to find the proper place for the Colonel and his contemporaries, largely because they have failed to grasp the fundamental nature of the bicycle industry itself. In his 1984 book *From the American System to Mass Production*, David Hounshell argued that cyclemakers formed a transitional way-station between American armory practice and twentieth-century mass production.[2] As we have seen, armory practice, also known as the "American System," born and bred in the armories of the Connecticut River valley, used advanced forging, precision machining and quality control systems such as "go/no-go" gauges to enable interchangeability and high output capacity while maintaining standards rivaling the best artisanal practice. However, Hounshell believed that prior to 1890, bicycle manufacturers had not yet learned to apply the lessons of gunmaking to larger, more diverse products that placed a greater emphasis on rapid, efficient assembly. It was easy to physically move one of Colt's pistols through the factory and once the forging, machining, gauging and polishing of its components was done, the job was virtually complete. Also, given their worth, guns were easy to stockpile in anticipation of future orders. Bicycles, however, were larger, more awkward to handle and store, and required more time and resources at the final assembly stage. When Chicago and Toledo manufacturers learned that a safety bicycle made of sheet-metal stampings functioned as well as one with forged parts, they freed themselves of the pressure to constantly improve their forging and machining techniques, and could then turn to the problems of rapid, efficient materiel control and final assembly. At this point the bicycle industry was, according to Hounshell, ready to hand off the evolutionary baton to the next generation of Detroit automakers.

A decade later, geographer Glen Norcliffe challenged this theory, asserting that "Pope's overall contribution to the system of mass production was of greater importance.... Pope has good claims to be ranked close to Ford and [Frederick W.] Taylor as a pioneer in the development of mass production."³ In particular, he pointed to Pope's growing vertical integration in buying out the Weed firm, his vigorous pursuit of patent rights, and his reliance on mass advertising. In fact, another business historian, Ross Petty, agues that it was Pope's use of mass marketing techniques to stimulate large-scale demand, more than his production methods, that uniquely identifies him as a seminal figure in the history of American manufacturing.⁴

I disagree with both interpretations. Instead, I believe that bicyclemakers were fundamentally batch builders, and probably continued to rely on batch building through the 1960s. As such, their strategic goal was not to maximize output or minimize cost. Indeed, as they learned in the second half of the 1890s, price competition and scale economies were fundamentally antagonistic to specialty manufacturing.⁵ Above all, batch builders tried to avoid accumulating either raw material or finished goods. It was imperative that they predict an appropriate batch size to meet their current demand; produce that batch on time, efficiently and well; and that they ship out each batch's final unit just in time to meet the last possible order that could be wrung from the market. "We do not care to order largely ahead of requirements, as it locks up too much capital," cautioned H. B. Smith, builder of the Star bicycle, in 1882, who recommended carrying only the minimum number of bicycles necessary to make up a "respectable" stock of inventory.⁶

Batch builders could be small, or as large as the biggest mass-producers, but they all had to know their customer base well enough to match supply to demand. In the batch game, advantage inherently goes to the smaller entrepreneur who knows his local market. Underestimate your batch size and you will create unfulfilled customers who will migrate to your competitors, and an unhappy sales force that will likely do the same. Overestimate, and you'll be stuck with inventory that must be stored, maintained, and quite probably sold at a loss or even scrapped. The farther away from local, personal knowledge the batch builder is, the more conservative he must be in estimating each production run, the more he must spend on advertising per unit, and the harder he must work on establishing and preserving a sales network.

It is my belief that many of the factors that historians such as Hounshell, Norcliffe, and Petty identify in the Gilded Age bicycle industry as prescient movements toward modern Taylorist/Fordist/Sloanist mass production were, instead, *ad hoc* remedies to the inherent inefficiencies of batch-building for a large, nationwide audience. While the collapse of the American bicycle boom after 1897 clearly originated from simple overproduction, the particular institutional mechanisms by which that productive deflation were carried out was largely preordained by these same forces.

It is necessary to define some basic terms.⁷ There are four broad approaches to manufacturing: custom, batch, bulk and mass. In custom work, an item is individually crafted to the specifications provided by a customer. In Pope's day, ships, steam turbines, and electrical generating equipment were almost entirely "one-off" creations. In batch building, goods are made in lots of various sizes, usually on the basis of accumulated orders. Batch building in the era of the safety bicycle was surprisingly widespread. Railroad locomotives, costume jewelry, book publishing, saddles, household furniture, and machine tools were typical examples. Bulk manufacturing, such as flour milling, linseed oil production, or oil refining, relies on relatively simple processes to produce large quantities of unvarying products. Mass production similarly involves a mass-flow strategy, but within a more elaborate technical and managerial structure. For example, Henry Ford was supposedly inspired to develop his moving assembly lines after seeing hogs moved through a packinghouse on overhead conveyors. It would be a mistake, however, to equate a Model T with a pork chop. Ford himself pointed out that a slaughterhouse was a disassembly factory, not an assembly plant. If the left front leg of a hog wasn't separated at the correct station, a butcher at the right front leg could step in, the tasks being essentially the same, where if left wheel assemblies quit arriving on the Model T final assembly line, no amount of right wheels could make up for them — the line would shut down.

There is a lesson there. The earliest of bulk producers — grain millers — had developed sophisticated material handling methods and machines by the 1780s. They had to — their product was so heavy, bulky and awkward that most of their costs came from simply moving it around. Colt's armory didn't need expensive conveyors, belts or chutes because their product was small and expensive per pound — not because it was unsophisticated. In a bicycle factory, once the frames were assembled and components began to be hung, the task of moving them about, working on them, and storing them expanded exponentially. Was the installation of a moving overhead conveyor, as occurred in Raleigh's Nottingham plant in 1931, at Huffman Manufacturing in 1939 or at the Columbia Manufacturing Company in the 1950s, a technological breakthrough, or simply an admission that bicycles were more like hogs than pistols?[8]

We must be careful. Whales swim in the ocean, but they are not fish. In 1937, Raleigh director A. E. Simpson complained at a board of directors meeting that "it is scarcely possible to see two consecutive machines of the same type passing along the conveyor." Indeed, Nottingham was producing fourteen different models that year — a number that actually increased to eighteen in a decade. It was not unusual in 1939 for those much-heralded conveyors to move through production runs of as small as fifty bicycles, an application that nullified their advantage.[9] And in the least likely of places, a 1985 children's book called *Bicycle Factory*, photographer Harold Roth magnificently illustrated the Columbia Manufacturing Company's overhead conveyor assembly line — and the mid–1890s Rudolphe & Krumel rim-driller used to supply it. Hand fed, with a capacity of but one rim at a time, it was apparently still the state of the art ninety years after it was made.[10] Probably the most illustrative example was that of Huffman, which had gone from producing 12 Huffys a day in 1934 to 200 in 1937 by selling cheap, reliable bikes to Firestone for sale in its tire stores. But in 1938 Firestone cancelled the contract because Huffman couldn't turn their spring and Christmas orders around fast enough — they lacked peak load capacity. So Horace Huffman installed a straight-line conveyerized assembly line, increased daily capacity, and regained the Firestone contract.[11] The new system wasn't needed to increase overall capacity — what Firestone wanted Huffman to do was act as their warehouse, storing bicycles for instant availability, at their expense and risk, until the tire giant needed them. Huffy could either pre-assemble these Firestone-branded bicycles, running the risk of dead stock if the tire company didn't need them, or cut down their final assembly lead time. They chose the latter. Huffy was weak because power had shifted away from the bicyclemakers, upstream to the partsmakers like U.S. Rubber, New Departure and Torrington, and downstream to the big buyers.

Relegating the bicycle industry to something less than Fordist/Sloanist magnificence should not be seen as a denigration; it should be viewed as a critique of narratives that equate mass production with such overarching sociological constructs as modernity or progress. When historians assess American manufacturing in the nineteenth century, they typically look for evidence to support an inexorable march toward complex mass production, but up to the late 1890s, specialty production "was substantial, expanding, and ubiquitous across the American manufacturing belt." Batch- and custom-builders were "consistently the nation's leading employers of skilled labor.... Their efforts were not simply labor-intensive or capital intensive, but instead featured a differentiated, productive meshing of skill and investment."[12] One batch builder of the era described his business as one of "sharp fluctuation of demand; impossibility of manufacturing in advance of orders; impracticality of mass production; necessity for employing specialists; high cost of the completed item and varying conditions under which it is sold and used."[13] This accurately describes conditions in the American bicycle industry, at least through about 1895, and probably much later.

## Annual Model Changes

Let us look at one of the American bicycle industry's most enduring myths: its supposed use of annual model changes to stimulate artificial demand. In fact, annual specification changes were already an established fact of life in the British industry when Pope and Cunningham started importing in the fall of 1878. In England, the first Stanley Club Exhibition was held in 1877 as a small show for members. It expanded into the Holborn Town Hall the following year and opened to the public in 1884.[14] For the next three decades it gave the public and the industry a preview of the upcoming year. As H. O. Duncan at the British magazine *Cyclist* noted, firms used "the dull wintry months" after September for "getting out and testing new models and improvements, and otherwise introducing modifications into the standard patterns ... which the experience and wear of a past season have pointed out as necessary." By the time the show rolled around in January or February, most makers had already produced "a large quantity of standard-pattern machines," which they stored away "to provide against delay in case of a big order and to otherwise insure speedy delivery in the full swing of the coming season." But as the Stanley Show became an increasingly popular mid-winter event, cyclemakers started to display special one-off machines made just for the show, with the unintended consequence that customers started to "buy no other cycles than those on the exact lines of these specially constructed machines." Factories were swamped with these last-minute bookings, "half of which orders will be lost, owing to the total impossibility of the firm to turn [these] machines out fast enough." By 1888 this had happened for two or three years in a row and Duncan complained that it had now become "a difficult matter to avoid." Duncan, an industry insider, overlooked the obvious solution that makers show self-restraint in favor of the more improbable remedy of forcing the Stanley Club to shut down its show.[15] Far from proving themselves capable manipulators of public tastes, the British makers had started out incorporating predictable and incremental technical changes pragmatically, when it was cheapest and easiest to do so during the winter, then had let a rather innocuous marketing gimmick get out of hand, throwing control of production scheduling and inventory management over to their customers.

Another source of information was Henry Sturmey's *Indispensable Bicyclist's Handbook*, likewise introduced in 1878. Issued annually, it was a detailed guide to all the bicycles manufactured the previous year in England; by 1880 these amounted to some 330 different models. The *Indispensable Handbook* proves that annual changes in the British industry resulted not from mere cosmetic variations, but from very real technological improvements. Fewer than half of all models in 1877 came with closed Stanley heads; the rest were the traditional open head (as was the original Standard Columbia). But by 1880, eighty-seven percent of all British machines came with Stanley heads. In 1877, only five percent of all models were equipped with ball bearings; by 1880 that percentage had increased to forty. Only a little more than ten percent of the offerings of 1877 had direct spokes; by 1880 well over two-thirds did.[16]

The Stanley show and *Sturmey's Indispensable Guide* were themselves unique and valuable innovations, especially important in keeping Americans appraised about the state of the art in bicycle technology. Any American importer foolish enough to order in such large quantities as to have inventory left over after the new models were introduced at the Stanley show could expect to sell his leftovers at a deep discount. It was only natural that when Americans began to make their own bicycles they would apply the same practices they followed as importers. For example, Colonel Pope did not contract for his first production run until spring, after he knew what the British would be offering, and he ordered a mere fifty units, a number he was sure he could sell. With sales for the firm, including both Columbias and imports, totaling 94 units in 1878, his order was a good, only slightly conservative, bet on an as-yet untested and high-risk market. When George Bidwell visited the factory less than a year later, he found "wheels and frames hanging up all over the place" and George Fairfield "scared to death" that they couldn't be sold.[17] Stock was the enemy, soaking up capital and killing cash flow. "There is, even now, a risk in the uncertainty of demand," observed Julius Wilcox, a *Bicycling World* editor, in 1884. "The risk of oversupply on one hand, or of a jam in the market and delay in supply on the other, must be paid for." The solution, added Wilcox, was to reduce the seasonality of the trade: "Whenever the public learn to prolong the term of use, and to crowd less of the year's trade into a 'season,' this trouble will be mollified."[18] The problem, of course, is that the only sure way to flatten the peak is to vary prices to encourage customers to buy outside of spring, and variable pricing was anathema to the Colonel, whose unshakable rule was that a Columbia "could be had ... at exactly the price, nothing less and nothing more," and that nothing must "jar the trade or cut the prices."[19]

Batch production was not an attempt to make each successive year's bicycle *appear* different, it was a way to deal with the often painful inevitability that they *would be* different. The specter of obsolescence continued through the early 1890s, as evidenced by George Pope's anguished (and entirely serious) cry that "whatever else we do in '92 we MUST get off 10 lbs weight," an astounding goal given that in another half-decade, ten pounds would be starting to approach half the weight of a top-line Hartford brand bicycle.[20] It is true that by the end of the 1890s this had changed, and that the bicycle had reached a period of technical quietude interrupted only by the Baroque irrelevance of the shaft-drive and the solidly practical coaster brake. *Scientific American*, for example, agonized over the "retrogressive heaviness" of post–1896 bicycles caused, primarily, by manufacturers switching from 18 tooth front sprockets to those with 30 teeth![21] Such stagnation would normally encourage a move towards mass-flow production, but building in discreet batches was still forced on bicycle builders by the residual expectations of the market. When the Keating Cycle Company guessed long on its 1897 batch and had to sell them the following year alongside their 1898 model, they could only get $30 for the '97s, even though they had originally sold for $100 the year before, and were little different from the '98s.[22] "Many of those who built bicycles to order this year," warned *Cycle Age* in 1898, "contemplate taking chances for next year by building during the winter in advance of orders. If they should fail to sell their product there will be business failures and demoralization."[23]

Annual model changes in the second half of the 1890s were not caused by makers trying to pull in customers, it was the opposite — it was the result of the market pushing them, often reluctantly, into the novelty game. Pope's 1896 Columbia was identical to the 1895 model, probably for the same reason Keating was selling "old" bicycles — inventory carryover. Although Pope held to his previous year's prices, sales suffered, and 1897 was the year of the "priceless" catalog and the infamous pre-season price cut to $75. Consumers had become so habituated to seeing real technological advances every spring that they continued to factor it into bicycle prices long after it had ceased being a substantive reality. Some savvy agents, such as Oscar Lear of Columbus, Ohio, turned this phenomenon to their advantage. "Lear has put in a stock of well made machines of 1898 model which he will sell this coming season as a medium grade," reported a trade journal. "Since there will be no great change in the make-up of bicycles generally, Mr. Lear considers this plan of buying ... a good solution of the problem of securing goods at a reduced price. He is now in New York, looking up new goods."[24]

Those firms not buried under stores of unsold stock could still drown in raw material. Reacting to a "tube famine" in 1894, American manufacturers monopolized the output of British tube mills by signing multi-year contracts that obligated them to take large minimum shipments for several years.[25] The fear of another "tube famine" in 1896 drove many mid-sized and large cyclemakers to do the same with the new American tube mills. But by 1897 both England and America tube mills had so much capacity that the market was saturated, and over-aggressive cyclemakers saw their factories turned into tube warehouses. "The tube mills are forcing us to take the tubing we have contracted for," admitted the manager of one anonymous factory (probably the Buffalo Cycle Co.) in mid–1899. "We have sufficient on hand to carry us for two years or more with our plant working at full capacity."[26] He also told the reporter that after the bust of 1898 he no longer had any illusion they would ever again work at full capacity.

Each annual batch *had* to give the appearance of improvement, and that made leftover stocks of raw material or unassembled bicycles nearly worthless. Continuing the production of annual batches despite technological stability was not some clever marketing strategy, but was, instead, evidence of an industry-wide, structural weakness. It is little wonder that when Arthur Garford and Charles Smith attempted to put their bicycle trust together in the fall of 1896, they equated the bedrock value of each firm to its inventory of raw material, unassembled bicycles and ready-to-ship wheels: a firm was worth only what could be sold *today*— tomorrow didn't matter. "He made the remark that he would like to get out of business and would sell at net inventory," Smith wrote Garford about a conversation he had with Sterling owner J. W. Kaiser in late 1896 as rumors of vast overproduction spread. Inventory amounted to a sunk cost if not used immediately. It became an unwanted fixture, like a steam engine in the basement that had become too small, too old or too worn out: not worth keeping, but too expensive to dig out and scrap.

Inventory problems could loom so large as to dominate technical considerations. In his chapter on the American bicycle industry, Hounshell stressed the development and dissemination of bicycle parts stamped from sheet steel, an innovation he traced to Chicago manufacturers familiar, not with New England armory practice, but German locksmithing and toymaking practices. However, English bicycle manufacturers unsuccessfully experimented with pressed-steel parts years before the technology was successfully applied in America. Even after it became the better alternative, English builders resolutely ignored it simply because they had overflowing bins of the old fittings:

> English makers tried to turn out an acceptable quality of sheet steel stampings some years ago, but partially failed and discarded them.... American makers did what English makers gave up in disgust — they learned how to make pressed work out of cold rolled steel, and succeeded in turning out an article just as strong and just as light ... [but] makers have stocked themselves heavily with fittings. They have an immense quantity of parts paid for, and which they must use up.[27]

## "Mass" Advertising?

The most straightforward way to avoid the twin evils of inventory carry-over and surplus raw material was to stay small, stick to a local market, and know it well. In 1901, George Pope dismissed small assemblers as "new people," amateurs with "no adequate capital ... pressed for money ... compelled to throw their machines on the market and get cash out of them." Except for defending a few high-quality, low-volume shops such as Iver Johnson and Pierce, bicycle historians have tended to accept his assessment uncritically.[28] In fact, small assemblers were early into the market, widespread, and diverse. They could be found not only on the lowest and highest rungs of the price/quality ladder, but everywhere in between. By the time of the great bicycle boom, the big firms *had* to resort to large-scale advertising to overcome the inherent disadvantages of their diseconomies of scale. Much of their money was spent, not in building up a brand loyalty, but simply to neutralize each other and to overcome the inherent distrust by which all the big firms were held, especially by cyclists outside the big cities. "Public demand is still better assured through the personal influence that floats out from the great number of small makers who are located in minor towns," noted one correspondent.[29]

At the same time the Colonel first asked Weed to build his bicycles (and perhaps even earlier), R. H. Hodgson was turning out small batches of his "Velocity" Ordinary in suburban Boston using imported castings and other English parts. In the mid–1880s, George Hughes of Wolverhampton, England was offering British-made bicycle fittings, including heads, bearing boxes and rear-wheel fork crowns, for sale to small American makers.[30] Charles Huntington of East Randolph, New York, started making small lots of bicycles in 1880. Nineteen years later, he was still at it — turning out a half-dozen wheels that season. With three lathes, two drill presses, two grinders, an enameling oven and a full blacksmithing shop, Huntington could make more, but chose not to. He stayed small because he believed in his local market. "If I buy a wheel in Chicago and it breaks down, I am without it for a week to a month. If I buy at home and anything happens, I can get hold of the builder quickly."[31]

"Isn't it about time to stop calling the people who make less than 1,000 bicycles assemblers?" complained the Latta brothers in upstate New York. "There is not one big maker who actually makes every part of his bicycle. They are therefore all assemblers." The Lattas, who averaged about 250 units a year, claimed that buying parts was actually better than making them yourself: "It is a fact that one can buy a better set of fittings of the different parts makers than have ever been made by any one concern."[32] Another small maker pointed to his ability to give the customer something approaching a custom-machine at the same cost and with little more effort than his standard model: "Many a rider of the repair-shop machine is extremely proud of his purchase because it possesses a few trifling features incorporated at his dictation."[33] Several told *Cycle Age* that while they did not build-to-order, they did let customers select their individual mount as it sat on the brazing jig or assembly stand, giving them the same pride of ownership as a custom job for less money. Amused by a huge ruckus in the trade magazines over attempts by the big manufacturers to shorten warranties to ninety days, the Latta brothers claimed their one-year guarantee cost them a mere 40 cents per bicycle.

Risking the wrath of the "mammoths" and the loss of their advertising, one or two cycle journals actually defended small builders: "Their facilities, being limited, only local buyers can be supplied; their advertising comprises nothing but the good words of riders who use the machines already built.... They have no waste stock on hand, no large amount of capital invested, and no squabbles with customers."[34] But one editor cautioned that success should not tempt a small shop into "going big." "Can the small builder obtain results if he must go outside of his immediate vicinity in order to sell his entire production?" he asked, answering with his own observation that "more disastrous attempts are recorded than profitable ventures." He advised small builders that the factor "which has balanced the scale to profit side" for the small shop in the 1890s was a "reputation for mechanical ability, which attracted that class of customers who had come to distrust the values offered by the large manufacturers," but closed with this dire warning: "Practically all that the small builder has to fall back upon ... is personal acquaintance and village pride, and these are factors which cannot be expanded to suit the builder's ambition...."[35]

Just what was "mass" advertising? After the collapse of the bicycle trust, lurid tales of profligacy hung over the debris: estimates of between four and nine million dollars a year spent in advertising by the "big five" during the 1890s, industry totals of $100 million spent between 1890 and 1896, and one assertion that a billion dollars was thrown out just in 1897![36] The real numbers are certainly much smaller. Pope described his advertising budget for 1878 as "a few hundred dollars," a magnitude consistent with the claim of the Monarch Cycle Company that it spent "a few thousand dollars" during its first year in business, 1893, when it sold 1,200 bicycles. Three years later, Monarch said it made 50,000 bicycles (39,000 probably being a better figure) and spent $125,000 on advertising. In an 1896 interview, Pope characterized his aggregate advertising expenditures for his first eight years in the business as "hundreds of thousands of dollars," not millions. "It was judicious advertising for the first ten years of bicycle making that prevented the few factories making them from going into the hands of the sheriff or a receiver," recalled one journalist.[37]

One reason the early bicycle makers could afford to be judicious was that the costs of mass advertising started dropping enormously just as the Ordinary made its first American appearance. National-circulation magazines such as *Scribner's* and *Harper's*, taking advantage of new printing technologies, drastically cut ad rates, especially for whole- or half-pages, which were cheap to set up.[38] When Frank Weston started the *American Bicycling Journal* in 1878, he charged $25 for a full page if you provided the plates, $13 for a half-page. A quarter-page ad in *The American Athlete and Cycle Trades Review* in 1893 cost only about $15. Most cycling books sold ads, and they were also inexpensive. A full page in Chris Wheeler's 1885 *Rhymes of the River Road* averaged $18, while the *Wheelman's Reference Book* of 1886, with a distribution guaranteed at five thousand by the Pope firm, cost $75 per page. Most English publications were even cheaper: *Cyclist* and *Wheeling Annual*, two competitors to Sturmey's *Indispensible Guide*, each asked $20 per page from American advertisers. In Canada, the Canadian Wheelmans' Association managed to get out its bi-monthly magazine, *Canadian Wheelman*, on $250 in annual ad revenues, as its total cost only ran to $600 a year. Although Charles Pratt claimed the Colonel lost $100,000 on *The Wheelman*, Karl Kron, who was in a position to know, said its fifteen issues actually cost "about a tenth of that," even though most were given away. Pope's 42-page 1897 advertising spectacular in *McClure's* magazine cost him only $5,000, money the Colonel had given Sam McClure two years earlier so he could survive a newsstand price war with *Cosmopolitan*.[39]

Similarly, the early costs of sponsoring racing teams and record-breaking events were smaller than one would expect. In 1883, C. H. Chickering, manager of the Star racing team, said the costs of setting, losing (to Pope), then defending the world's 24-hour record in 1884–85 were $515, plus track rental and the expenses of scorekeepers. Reimbursing the company's shop account for the absentee wages of factory hands who doubled as racing cracks cost $200, apparently for a month.[40]

Still, the marketing costs facing a small local builder who wanted to go nationwide were daunting. One journal editor estimated it would cost a local builder the equivalent of one-third to one-half his total material costs to expand into a regional or national market. "While the mammoth establishments perform excellent missionary work through the ordinary channels such as advertisements," he wrote, local assemblers "preach the cycle gospel in their own way, which, if it is not quite orthodox, is marvelously effective."[41] The Latta brothers asserted that it was the need for exorbitant advertising that gave the small builder his advantage in the "solid middle" market:

> The average small maker cannot compete in price with the cycles turned out by many of the big makers, and it is folly for him to attempt to do so. It is in good sound medium grade work that the small builder stands a chance and can actually undersell the big maker, as his savings in selling expenses are more than enough to offset his extra cost of manufacture.[42]

A reoccurring theme throughout the cycle trades press in the 1890s was the "wastefulness" or "inefficiency" of mass, nationwide advertising. In 1893, Gormully & Jeffery accused one magazine, *Sporting Life*, of using "blackmail tactics" to sell space. They said the journal had run news items criticizing one of its distributors "by name," with the comments disappearing once it started buying advertising. Gormully & Jeffery said the magazine tried the same thing directly on them, even though *Sporting Life* was "not a suitable medium to reach people who would buy our goods, its clientage being composed mostly of baseball people." They were amazed that "the simple loss of a $15 ad will produce such rancid humor as has been displayed."[43]

For a man who repeatedly boasted that he couldn't care less how much he spent "preaching the testament of cycling and the gospel of Columbia," the Colonel could be surprisingly conservative in his fiscal decision-making. In January 1892, he instructed cousin George to maintain the Hartford firm's existing policy of not paying for the shipping of bicycles to agents west of Chicago. "Another year he thinks it probable that we shall have to do more towards paying freight," George wrote an associate. "This year he feels very confident that we shall sell our product and therefore that it is not necessary."[44]

"Freights west" would have run a little over a thousand dollars that year. Although not necessary to sell the 1892 batch, wasn't it a worthwhile investment to help expand sales in 1893? No, because the Colonel was not so much worried about *if* people would buy his bicycles, he was concerned about *how* they bought them, and spending on advertising was part of his approach to this problem.

Like the sewing machine makers that preceded him, Pope had specific marketing problems upon starting out. His product was new, unusual, complex, and expensive. It required demonstration, instruction, and an unusually high amount of after-sale service. In short, it required face-to-face contact. The sewing machine people at Weed already knew this: even before the Civil War, their competitors at Singer had established a network of trained young women to demonstrate their product, followed later by a system of exclusive-territory independent agencies and a hire-purchase plan. But the agents were expensive, willful and obstinate.[45] During economic slumps, many installment buyers defaulted, and it was excessive repair costs that eventually led Singer, about 1872, to undertake the backbreaking effort of implementing interchangeable parts so the machines could be fixed in the field instead of having to be sent back to the factory. Eventually, the firm ended hire-purchase and bought back most of its territories.

When Weed started out a decade later, it learned from Singer, using interchangeable parts from day one and selling machines directly from the factory C.O.D.[46] Pope, in turn, adopted Weed's practices. Although he did use agents, his franchise terms and conditions were never generous and, with the exception of a few favored long-time loyalists, dealers were held at arm's length and rarely considered anything more than disposable commodities. After using them to build a local market, Pope anticipated switching to Weed's simpler and more lucrative direct sales strategy. In 1884 Julius Wilcox, a colleague of Charles Pratt, wrote that "If everyone who can possibly be led to think that he wants a bicycle would only order directly from the maker or importer, retail prices could be somewhat lower ... when the public gets fully convinced that they want bicycles, and fully decided as to which one they want, they can leave out the retailer."[47]

Ultimately, of course, this proved impossible, for a number of reasons. The promise of rapid, light freight from factory to doorstep outside of cities was not realized for another twenty years until the advent of Postal Rural Free Delivery; local shops quickly became far more proficient at service and repairs than the makers believed possible; but mostly because the manufacturers were never able to create a stable, long-lasting oligopoly extending down to the local level. By 1890, Charles Pratt realized that the threat to the big firms no longer came from the lack of control over local agents, but from the establishment of regional jobbers: "The job-lot era ... must undoubtedly come some time, [but] has so far been indicated by mild symptoms."[48] Jobbers actually resisted national brands, preferring their own private labels because they were more profitable. When jobbers, led by such early Pope agents as George Bidwell and George Rouse, entered the bicycle market after 1890, this was exactly the path they chose, and after the fall of the bicycle trust it was the jobbers who controlled pricing and distribution for almost half a century.[49]

## *Then, and Now*

We must also remember that the bicycle trust was remarkably ineffective in eliminating small makers. In fact, it was far more adept in wiping itself out. During the 1900 season, 165 large (over 10,000 units) and medium-sized (over 3,000 units) makers produced bicycles. A year later, only 69 were left. Of those who left the business, 21 (of its initial 43) were closed by the trust — all in only six months. Of these 21, about 12 were formerly large-size producers.[50] *Cycle Age* estimated that about 40 percent of all bicycles would come from independent (i.e., non-trust) makers, and of these, almost a third would come from firms making less than 5,000 bicycles, with 50,000 from very small shops each making fewer than a thousand units. "The bicycle business is a specialty manufacturing business," it concluded. "The fancies and demands of the riders are numerous and their dealers would find their requirements better met by a hundred makers."

Small and mid-sized firms were also the norm after the fall of the trust. In 1903, Arthur Garford identified 33 firms still in the business. By 1908, there were nineteen, and in 1914 thirteen plants had survived the worst days of the post-trust Depression. In 1946, the U.S. Commerce Department counted ten firms. It is unlikely that any company, including Pope, or its successor, Columbia, made more than 60,000 bicycles per year between 1917 and 1934, and no firm topped the million-unit mark until the early- to mid–1960s.

By and large, these firms continued to follow intensely seasonal production cycles. In 1946, aggregate monthly shipments for the American industry rose and fell by almost half between March and September, not even including the volatile Christmas season.[51] In Canada, the number of non-salaried (hourly) employees in 1955 swelled between January and June by 35 percent. Norman Clarke, president of the Columbia Manufacturing Company, estimated that between the 1920s and the mid–1960s, 40 percent of the firm's production was sold at retail during the Christmas season, and in a good year employment would vary from a low of 250 in January to a high of 900 in June or July.[52] That changed after about 1963 when many more adults started riding, and Peter Davis, later Schwinn's director of planning, recalls Frank Schwinn telling him in the 1970s that when it came to sales, "all that matters is how many days of rain we get in April."[53] In the second great bicycle boom, Schwinn deliberately capped output growth to 65 percent between 1968 and 1971. Mainly, they did this to maintain quality control, but it reflects a corporate culture more comfortable with consistency and incremental decisionmaking than rapid, explosive change. In their corporate biography of Schwinn, Judith Crown and Glen Coleman assert that American bicycle makers wore out their machinery attempting to keep up with the 1970s boom. Norman Clarke dismisses this, pointing out that not even World War II armsmaking adversely affected equipment: "It was good, heavy-duty machinery, it didn't take much of a beating."[54] It was simply that American manufacturers were equipped for annual batch sizes varying within a limited range, and the only way to stretch this envelope was to either add an additional shift or stretch the peak employment season. The latter was not usually an option because it resulted only in shipments that customers would refuse as too late. During the 1970s boom American makers discovered the same thing George Pope did almost a century earlier: "A night gang will produce one-third less than the day gang, so that it makes the direct labor for night work very much more expensive and cannot be excused except to get anyone out of a hole."[55]

In conclusion, it is futile to look to the American bicycle industry as a harbinger of the future or to deify its leaders as prophets. The industry was what is was, and its entrepreneurs did what they did because it had to be done to get through the season. While the American bicycle industry proved to be an exceptional training ground for the managers, technicians and skilled operatives who would later staff the automobile and aircraft industries, had it never existed, the firearms, sewing machine, and machine tool industries would have been fully capable of providing the necessary human capital required, with a delay of probably no more than a year or two. In the end, the American bicycle business did not define the technological or industrial trajectory of the Gilded Age; it was, instead, defined by it.

# Chapter Notes

## Introduction

1. Most of the information in this chapter is taken from "Welcome to Pope," *Hartford Courant*, 3 July 1903, as are all quotes, unless otherwise specified.
2. "Col. Pope Breathes Fire," *Bicycling World* 47, 7 (16 May 1903): 222.
3. 1898 production: Arthur Dewing, "The American Bicycle Company," in *Corporate Promotions and Reorganizations* (Cambridge: Harvard University Press, 1914), 249–68; 1902 production: letter from George Pope to Henry L. Higginson, 3 December 1902, 1902 General Correspondence, N-R, Henry L. Higginson Collection, Baker Library, Harvard; 1904 production: *Commercial and Financial Chronicle* 80 (14 January 1905): 160–61; twenty dollars per bicycle: letter from Arthur L. Patrick to Arthur L. Garford, 1 June 1903, Box 5, File 6, Arthur L. Garford Papers (MSS 6), Ohio Historical Society, Columbus; nine dollars per bicycle: letter from Arthur L. Garford to the members of the Bicycle Manufacturer's Association, 21 November 1902, Box 5, File 1, Arthur L. Garford Papers, OHS.
4. Gerald O. Kelver, *Respectfully Yours—H. M. Pope* (Fort Collins: Robinson Press, 1976), 113–14; Ray M. Smith, *The Story of Pope's Barrels* (Harrisburg, PA: Stackpole Books, 1960), 3–28.
5. Guy Hubbard, "Development of Machine Tools in New England, Part 11," *American Machinist* 60, 5 (31 January 1924): 171–73.
6. Hugh Dolnar, "Bicycle Tools, Part XVIII," *American Machinist* 19, 8 (20 February 1896): 206.
7. Donald G. Bahma, "The Pope-Toledo Strike, Part 1," *Northwest Ohio Quarterly* 35 (Summer 1963): 106–21; "The Pope-Toledo Strike, Part 2," *Northwest Ohio Quarterly* 35 (Autumn 1963): 172–87.
8. "All Sales Departments Go," *Bicycling World* 44, 1 (3 October 1901): 1.
9. "Dined by Col. Pope," *Bicycling World* 48, 17 (23 January 1904): 465.
10. "Horseshoe for Col. Pope," *Bicycling World* 48, 3 (17 October 1903): 61.
11. Letter from Arthur L. Patrick to Arthur L. Garford, 1 June 1903, Box 5, File 6, Arthur L. Garford Papers, OHS.
12. Letter from Arthur L. Garford to Arthur L. Patrick, 10 June 1903, Box 5, File 6, Arthur L. Garford Papers, OHS.

## Chapter 1

1. Charles E. Pratt, "A Sketch of American Cycling and Its Founder," *Outing* 18, 4 (July 1891): 348.
2. Letter from Arthur L. Garford to S. B. "Ely" Leonard, 7 February 1902, Box 4, File 5, Arthur L. Garford Papers (MSS 6), Ohio Historical Society, Columbus.
3. Charles H. Pope, *A History of the Dorchester Pope Family* (Boston: Charles H. Pope, 1888), 156–67; 201–17. At one time, Dorchester extended from south Boston halfway to Rhode Island.
4. Sam Bass Warner, *Streetcar Suburbs: The Process of Growth in Boston, 1879–1900* (Cambridge: Harvard University Press, 1978 [1962]), 71. There is a Pope's Hill Street on the northeast flank of the hill, by the bay.
5. This location is now a plaza just north of the 60 North State Street building in Boston's financial district.
6. Emily Wilder Leavitt, *A Genealogy of the Bogman Family* (No location [Boston]: Moses Conant Warren, 1890), 2–29; *Boston City Directory* (Boston: Sampson, Davenport and Co.) for the years 1841–50; Nancy S. Seasholes, *Gaining Ground: A History of Landmaking in Boston* (Cambridge: MIT Press, 2003), 20–26.
7. Stephen B. Goddard, *Colonel Albert Pope and His American Dream Machines* (Jefferson, NC: McFarland, 2000), 28–30.
8. *Sixth Census of the United States* [1850], *Schedule I, Population*: County of Norfolk, Town of Brookline, House 117, Family 158: page 72; Pope, *A History of the Dorchester Pope Family*, 215.
9. Goddard, *Colonel Albert Pope*, 30; *Boston City Directory*, 1851–53.
10. "Miles, Nelson Appleton," *Dictionary of American Biography*, Dumas Malone, ed. (New York: Charles Scribner's Sons, 1933).
11. "Horseshoe for Col. Pope," *Bicycling World* 48, 3 (17 October 1903): 61.
12. *Ibid.*, 61.
13. Death Certificate of Mary Elizabeth Pope, 4 March 1858. Massachusetts Secretary of State, Archives

Division. "Welcome to Pope," *Hartford Courant*, 3 July 1903; "Horseshoe for Col. Pope": 61; "Col. Pope Passes Away at Cohasset," *Boston Post*, 11 August 1909; *Boston City Directory*, 1859–63.

14. *Seventh Census of United States [1860]: Schedule I, Population*: County of Norfolk, City of Brookline, House 254, Family 335: page 54.

15. Leavitt, *A Genealogy of the Bogman Family*, 11.

16. Albert Pope enlisted on 22 August 1861: *1890 Census of Veterans*, State of Massachusetts, City of Boston, SD 67; ED 910; House 130; Family 230; Janet B. Hewett, *Supplement to the Official Records of the Union and Confederate Armies, Part II: Record of Events* (Wilmington: Broadfoot Publishing, 1996), XXIX, 148–81.

17. "Death Comes to Col. George Pope," *Hartford Courant*, 20 April 1918; "Recent Deaths: Colonel George Pope," *Boston Transcript*, 20 April 1918; *Official Army Register of the Volunteer Force of the United States Army for the Years 1861–65* (Washington, D.C.: U.S. Army, Adjutant General's Office, 1866): Part 8 (Colored Infantry), 313–14.

18. Hewett, *Supplement to the Official Records of the Union and Confederate Armies*, 148; "Colonel Pope's Generosity," *Bearings* 9, 24 (13 July 1894): 14.

19. Goddard, *Colonel Albert Pope*, 42; "Col. Pope Passes Away" (*Boston Post*); Hewett, *Supplement to the Official Records of the Union and Confederate Armies*, 148.

20. Electronic mail from Stephen B. Goddard to the author, 22 March 1999; Goddard, *Colonel Albert Pope*, 44.

21. *Official Army Register of the Volunteer Force of the United States Army for the Years 1861–65*, 313–14; "Death Comes to Col. George Pope," (*Hartford Courant*): 22.

22. Pope's claim: "Death Comes to Col. Albert A. Pope," *Boston Globe*, 11 August 1909; "a joke": Goddard, *Colonel Albert Pope*, 51. However, every biography of Albert Pope providing the specific date of his brevet appointment to lieutenant colonel lists 13 April 1865.

23. *Official Army Register of the Volunteer Force of the United States Army for the Years 1861–65*, 205–07. This last source does not include Albert Pope's brevet commission to lieutenant colonel, although the brevets of two other officers on 2 April 1865 are listed.

24. Adjutant General of Massachusetts, *Record of the Massachusetts Volunteers, 1861–1865* (Boston: Wright & Potter, 1898), 1: 734.

25. The information is accessible through ProQuest's Heritage database: http//persi. heritagequestonline.com.

26. *Official Army Register of the Volunteer Force of the United States Army*, 313.

27. "Welcome to Pope."

28. "Horseshoe for Col. Pope," 8. Other sources say Pope made a $9,600 profit his first year: "Col. Pope Passes Away at Cohasset."

29. Pope, *A History of the Dorchester Pope Family*, 254–59; "Dr. Augusta C. Pope [sic]," *New York Times*, 29 March 1931; "Dr. C. Augusta Pope," *Boston Globe*, 29 March 1931; Letter from Dr. Emily F. Pope to Dr. Margaret Noyes Kleinert, 11 January 1928, Box 9, Folder 34, New England Hospital Collection, Sophia Smith Collection, Smith College; Regina Markell Morantz-Sanchez, *Sympathy and Science: Women Physicians in American Medicine* (New York, 1985), 72–84; Virginia G. Drachman, *Hospital with a Heart: Women Doctors and the Paradox of Separatism at the New England Hospital, 1862–1969* (Ithaca, NY: Cornell University Press, 1984), 21–35, 105, 146. The New England Hospital closed in 1969, but carries on as a community medical center.

30. "Pope, Albert Augustus," *Appleton's Cyclopaedia of American Biography*, James Grant Wilson and John Fisk, eds. (New York: D. Appleton and Co., 1888). Although the entry is for the Colonel, it contains one of the few biographies of Emily and Augusta Pope. The sisters were extremely reticent and left few records, even within the archives of the New England Hospital located at Radcliff and Smith colleges.

31. Leavitt, *A Genealogy of the Bogman Family*, 13.

32. "Social Science Studies," *New York Times*, 8 September 1881; Emily F. Pope, C. Augusta Pope and Emma Call, *The Practice of Medicine by Women in the United States* (Boston: Wright & Potter, 1881).

33. "Col. Pope Passes Away at Cohasset"; Morantz-Sanchez, *Sympathy and Science*, 96.

34. "Rev. Louis A. Pope of Newburyport," *Boston Transcript*, 21 August 1903.

35. Family legend: Goddard, *Colonel Albert Pope*, 63; Allen's death: Pope, *A History of the Dorchester Pope Family*, 254–59; *Boston City Directory*, 1868–85; 1930–31; "Harry M. Pope, 89, Expert on Rifles," *New York Times*, 13 October 1950; *Copy of Record of Death: Charles Allen Pope*, Commonwealth of Massachusetts, Archives Division; Smith, *The Story of Pope's Barrels*, 3.

36. "Pope, Abby Linden [sic]," *The Biographical Cyclopaedia of American Women* (New York: Halvord Publishing, 1924). An engraving of the Popes' Newton home is included in "The Massachusetts Bicycle Club," *The Wheelman* 2, 3 (June 1883): 168.

37. *Tenth Census of the United States [1880], Schedule I, Population*: County of Middlesex, City of Newton, Ward 7, E.D. 479, House 217, Family 241.

38. Bainbridge Bunting, *Houses of Boston's Back Bay, 1840–1917* (Cambridge, MA: Belknap Press, 1967), Appendix 1.

39. *Ashley v. Winley*, 95 N.E. 932, 933 (Mass. 1911).

40. Warner, "Streetcar Suburbs," 126.

41. Sara E. Wermiel, *The Fireproof Building: Technology and Public Safety in the Nineteenth Century* (Baltimore: Johns Hopkins University Press, 2000), 4–6; 82–83.

42. *Boston City Directory*, 1872–76; "Horseshoe for Col. Pope": 61.

43. Carl F. Burgwardt, "A Landscape of Early Bicycle History: From the Lips of George R. Bidwell, an Extraordinary Pioneer Wheelman from Buffalo, N.Y.," *Cycle History 7: Proceedings of the 7th International Cycle History Conference*, ed. Rob van der Plas. (Osceola, WI: Motorbooks International, 1997), 89. An ad for Pope's "Harvard Cigarette Roller" is reproduced in James Zordich's "The A.B.C.'s of the Pope Manufacturing Company," *Horseless Carriage Gazette* (July–August 1984): 28.

44. W.H.B. Smith, *Smith's Standard Encyclopedia of Gas, Air and Spring Guns* (New York: Castle Books, 1957), 30–36; John Groenewold, *Quackenbush Guns* (Mundelein, IL: John Groenewold, 2000), 7–9. One of the Quackenbush boneshakers is in the Herkimer Co. (NY) Historical Society.

45. "Improvement in Air Pistols," Patent No. 156,890, 17 November 1874, to Henry M. Quackenbush of Herkimer, New York, assignor to Albert A. Pope of Boston.

46. Groenewold, *Quackenbush Guns*, 165–68.

47. These were patents 172,583 and 172,584 (both 25 January 1876).

48. Kelver, *Respectfully Yours, H. M. Pope*, 101. Harry was working in his uncle's air-gun shop at this time.

49. Groenewold, *Quackenbush Guns*, 80–82; "Horseshoe for Col. Pope": 62.

50. Quote taken from *An Industrial Achievement: The Pope Manufacturing Company* (Hartford: Pope Mfg. Co., 1907), 11; Albert S. Parsons, "The Massachusetts Bicycle Club," *The Wheelman* 2, 3 (June 1883): 163; Carl F. Burgwardt, *Buffalo's Bicycles* (Orchard Park, NY: Pedaling History Museum, 2001), 19.

51. *Boston City Directory*, 1875–78; Carried them in his air pistol store: "Albert A. Pope: His Place in History," *Bicycling World* 46, 12 (18 December 1902): 313. A letter written on Pope Manufacturing Company letterhead in 1880 features an engraving of the "Rifle" air pistol: Charles Pratt Scrapbook, Transportation Division, National Museum of American History, Smithsonian Institution, Washington, D.C.

52. "Horseshoe for Col. Pope," 61.

53. "Articles of Incorporation, Pope Manufacturing Company," Record Group #6:32, Box 4, Vol. 12, 224–26, History and Genealogy Division, Connecticut State Library, Hartford.

54. "Horseshoe for Col. Pope," 62.

55. First ad: *Bicycling World* 46, 12 (18 December 1902): 311; a month before: "Col. Pope Interviewed," *Bicycling World* (18 June 1897): 20–21; Edward and George: "Death Comes to Col. George Pope"; "Edward W. Pope Dead in Newton," *Boston Globe* (15 December 1936). Charles Pratt claimed that he and Edward took the first long-distance cycle tour in the country, from Boston to Portland in August 1879: Karl Kron [Lyman H. Bagg], *Ten Thousand Miles on a Bicycle* (New York: Karl Kron, 1887), 503; William Pope: Leavitt, *A Genealogy of the Bogman Family*, 16. Edward said he was a stockbroker: *Ninth Decennial Census of the United States [1870], Schedule 1, Population*: County of New York, Borough of Manhattan: sheet 40.

56. Pope was elected Alderman from Newton's Seventh Ward: Records of the Aldermanic Offices, City of Newton, Massachusetts.

57. Albert A. Pope, "The Bicycle Industry," *One Hundred Years of American Commerce*, ed. Chauncey M. Depew (New York: D.O. Haynes, 1895), I, 550.

## Chapter 2

1. Letter from Arthur L. Garford to S. B. Leonard, 7 February 1902, Box 4, File 3, Arthur L. Garford Papers (MSS 6), Ohio Historical Society, Columbus.

2. "Looking Backward Twenty-Five Years and Beyond," *Bicycling World* 58, 12 (18 December 1902): 303–05. A 60-inch ordinary is very high—about the largest even a tall man can use. A 50- to 58-inch is more typical.

3. *Bicycling World* 1, 14 (15 May 1880): 222.

4. David V. Herlihy, *Bicycle: The History* (New Haven: Yale University Press, 2004), 86–90. David V. Herlihy, "Who Invented the Bicycle?" *Cycle History: Proceedings of the 4th International Cycle History Conference*, ed. Rob van der Plas (San Francisco: Van der Plas Publications, 1994), 11–26. See Herlihy's book for numerous additional citations to earlier work. Charles E. Pratt, "Pierre Lallement and His Bicycle," *The Wheelman* 4, 2 (October 1883): 4–13.

5. "Deposition of Pierre Lallement, May 29, 1882," *Pope Manufacturing Company v. Joseph McKee and Charles D. Harrington*, U.S. Circuit Court, Southern District of New York, unpublished case record, at 362. Thanks to David Herlihy for this item.

6. Karl Kron [Lyman H. Bagg], *Ten Thousand Miles on a Bicycle* (New York: Karl Kron, 1887), 140–41.

7. Pratt, "Pierre Lallement and His Bicycle," 8; Letter from David Brandon to C. E. Pratt, 15 August 1878, Pratt Scrapbook, Transportation Division, National Museum of American History, Smithsonian Institution, Washington D.C.; A. G. Batchelder, "The Story of the Bicycle," *Harper's Weekly* 60 (11 April 1896): 359.

8. Herlihy, *Bicycle*, 86–95.

9. Pryor Dodge, *The Bicycle* (Paris: Flammarion, 1996), 39–42; Herlihy, *Bicycle*, 86–95.

10. Carl F. Burgwardt, "A Landscape of Early Bicycle History," *Cycle History: Proceedings of the 7th International Cycle History Conference*, ed. Rob van der Plas (San Francisco: Van der Plas Publications, 1997), 88.

11. David V. Herlihy, "The Velocipede Craze in Maine," *Maine History* 38, 3/4 (1999): 188–89; "Improvement in Velocipedes," Patent No. 86,834, 9 February 1869, to William Hanlon of New York.

12. Kron, *Ten Thousand Miles on a Bicycle*, 395–410.

13. *Ibid.*, 405.

14. Herlihy, "The Velocipede Craze in Maine," 204–05.

15. Charles E. Pratt, "A Sketch of American Bicycling and Its Founder," *Outing* 18, 4 (July 1891): 344; Burgwardt, "A Landscape of Early Bicycle History," 90; Albert A. Pope, "The American Bicycle Industry," *One Hundred Years of American Commerce*, ed. Chauncey M. Depew (New York: D.O. Haynes, 1895): II, 549–53.

16. Kron, *Ten Thousand Miles on a Bicycle*, 402.

17. Nick Clayton, "Who Invented the Penny-Farthing?" *Cycle History: Proceedings of the 7th International Cycle History Conference*, ed. Rob van der Plas (San Francisco: Van der Plas Publications, 1997), 31–40; Geoffrey Williamson, *Wheels Within Wheels: The Story of the Starleys of Coventry* (London: Goeffrey Bles, 1966), 49–50.

18. Over the years, Pope's story evolved several times. First, Harrington ordered and paid for the bicycle. Then, both men were jointly responsible. Finally, Pope claimed that "I had a bicycle constructed under the personal supervision of an English gentleman who was a guest at my house." (Pope, "The Bicycle Industry": II, 550). Both the earliest account of this story, probably written by Charles E. Pratt ("A Great American Manufacture," *Bicycling World* 2, 21 [1 April 1881]: 326) and the earliest account that quotes Albert Pope directly ("Col. Pope's Response to the Toast, 'The Wheel' at the L.O.W. Banquet," *The Wheelman* 1, 1 [October 1882]: 70) agree that Harrington was responsible for it. ("Filled with enthusiasm for the possibilities of the bicycle in this country, he [Harrington] caused one to be made, at an expense of over $300.") William S. Atwell was identified as the famous bicycle's maker well before the turn of the century ("Albert A. Pope: His Place in History," *Bicycling World* 46, 12 [18 December 1902]: 313). It was probably destroyed in an 1896 fire.

19. Timms & Lawford: "The Story of the Bicycle," 359; "The Industry: How It Grew Up," *Bicycling World* 46, 12 (18 December 1902): 325; Kron, *Ten Thousand Miles on a Bicycle*, 504; Pratt, "A Sketch of American Bicycling and Its Founder," 342–49. Cunningham, Heath &

Co.: "Looking Back Twenty-Five Years—and Beyond," *Bicycling World* 46, 12 (18 December 1902): 305; "Frank W. Weston: The Man and His Work," *Bicycling World* 46, 12 (18 December 1902): 309; "Col. Pope's Response to the Toast," 70.

20. "The History of the American Bicycle," *American Athlete* 7, 11 (20 March 1891): 240.

21. "Papa Weston Thumbs Back Numbers," *Bicycling World* 46, 12 (18 December 1902): 311; "History of the American Bicycle," 240. The story of Harrington's bicycle order being delayed didn't crop up until after Cunningham & Co. challenged the Colonel's claim that he was the first to import bicycles into the United States (*Bicycling World* 2, 4 [3 December 1880]: 6). In its December 1902 issue (p. 310) *Bicycling World* reproduces what they claim is the first Pope ad, dated 16 March 1878.

22. Bicycle journals and clubs: "Frank W. Weston: The Man and His Work," 309; "Papa Weston Thumbs Back Numbers," 311; Kron, *Ten Thousand Miles on a Bicycle*, 503–04; 654–72; Charles E. Pratt, "Our First Bicycle Club," *The Wheelman* 1, 6 (March, 1883): 401–12; Albert S. Parsons, "The Massachusetts Bicycle Club," *The Wheelman* 2, 3 (June 1883): 161–72.

23. "Papa Weston Thumbs Back Numbers," 311.

24. "Horseshoe for Col. Pope," *Bicycling World* 48, 3 (17 October 1903): 62.

25. Charles E. Pratt, "The Tariff Question," *The Wheelman* 1, 1 (October 1882): 60–69. Pratt's numbers were slightly different from mine because of the way he calculated maker's profit and domestic freight costs from factory to customer.

26. "The Industry: How It Grew Up," 325; "Albert A. Pope: His Place in History," 314.

27. "Welcome to Pope," *Hartford Courant*, 3 July 1903; Henry P. Woodward, "Manufacturers in Hartford," *Hartford in History* (Hartford: Board of Trade, 1889), 112–16.

28. Nathan Rosenberg, "Technological Change in the Machine Tool Industry, 1840–1910," *Journal of Economic History* 23 (1963): 414–43; David A. Hounshell, *From the American System to Mass Production, 1800–1832* (Baltimore: Johns Hopkins University Press, 1984), 17–29.

29. Hounshell, *From the American System to Mass Production*, 46–51. Ellsworth Grant, *Yankee Dreamers and Doers: The Story of Connecticut Manufacturing* (Hartford: Connecticut Historical Society, n.d. [1996?]), 192–201.

30. Frederick G. Bourne, "American Sewing Machines," *One Hundred Years of American Commerce*, ed. Chauncy M. Depew (New York: D.O. Haynes, 1895), II, 532; Guy Hubbard, "The Development of Machine Tools in New England," *American Machinist* 60, 5 (31 January 1924): 171–73; Woodward, "Manufacturers in Hartford": 112–16; Ellsworth, *Yankee Dreamers and Doers*, 250–56; *Accuracy for Seventy Years: Pratt and Whitney 1860–1930* (Hartford: Pratt and Whitney Co., n.d. [1930?]), 27. I appreciate the assistance of the legal staff of the current Pratt and Whitney Aeronautical Company, who have asked me to pass along the following historical note. The Pratt and Whitney tool company was formed in 1860. It made tools, industrial instruments and munitions. From 1914 to 1939 it owned the plant and grounds of the former Pope Manufacturing Company. In 1925 it allowed Frederick Rentschler to use part of its factory to build a prototype radial aircraft engine, the Wasp. It was an outstanding success and in 1929 Rentschler moved his firm to East Hartford and named it the Pratt and Whitney Aircraft Company. Nobody remembers why he did this, possibly gratitude, maybe to encourage investment by the owners of the tool company. The old tool company moved out to the suburbs in 1939 and went out of business in 1991. The present aeronautical company is now a part of United Technologies. Its archives contain no records of the old tool company, and are not open.

31. "The Manufacture of Sewing Machines," *Scientific American* 42, 12 (30 March 1880): 181.

32. Carl F. Burgwardt, *Buffalo's Bicycles* (Orchard Park: Pedaling History Museum, 2001), 19.

33. "Albert A. Pope: His Place in History," 314; "A Great American Manufacture," 326. The Duplex Excelsior clones are identifiable because of their head adjustment tension spring mechanism: G. Donald Adams, *Collecting and Restoring Antique Bicycles* (Orchard Park: Pedaling History Museum, 2nd ed., 1996), 61–70; electronic mail transmission from Nicholas Clayton, 10 September 2008.

34. "The Manufacture of Sewing Machines," 42; "The Bicycle Industry," *Hartford Courant*, April 2, 1899; "Bicycle Making," *Frank Leslie's Illustrated Monthly* 5 (1882): 641–42; "Bicycle Manufacture," *Iron Age* 27, 25 (June 23, 1881): 1; Hugh Dolnar, "Bicycle Tools IV: Steel Rims," *American Machinist* 18, 44 (11 November 1895): 910.

35. The 1892 Columbian Exposition ended up being held in Chicago. Burgwardt, "A Landscape of Early Bicycle History," 91; Pope, "The Bicycle Industry," 550. Bidwell implied that half (25) of the first lot of Weed-built bicycles were retained by the Pope company.

36. "The Industry: How It Grew Up," 325; Kron, *Ten Thousand Miles on a Bicycle*, 25–26; Burgwardt, "A Landscape of Early Bicycle History," 92. Bidwell recalls this as having occurred in spring 1879, but this could not be correct, as he clearly states that he expected a shipment of the *first* lot of Hartford bicycles, produced a year earlier.

37. "George H. Day Dead," *Hartford Courant*, 21 November 1907; "Mr. Day's Funeral," *Hartford Times*, 22 November 1907; "Day, George H.," *The Automobile Industry 1896–1920*, George S. May, ed. (New York, 1990).

38. "The Senator," *Automobile Magazine*, 5 (January 1903): 107; "Harold Hayden Eames," a manuscript prepared by Hermann F. Cuntz for Henry Cave, 12 October 1940, Box 3, File 1, Henry Cave Collection, National Automotive History Collection, Detroit Public Library.

39. "Col. Pope Breathes Fire," *Bicycling World* 47, 7 (16 May 1903): 222.

40. Andrew Ritchie, *King of the Road: An Illustrated History of the Bicycle* (Berkeley: Ten Speed Press, 1975), 83.

41. *Columbia Bicycle Catalog for 1880*; "A Great American Manufacture," 327.

42. "History of the Sewing Machine," *Atlantic Monthly* 19 (May 1897): 529–44; Frederick L. Lewton, "The Servant in the House: A Brief History of the Sewing Machine," *Annual Report of the Board of Regents of the Smithsonian Institution, 1929* (Washington, 1930): 559–83; Bourne, "American Sewing Machines," 525–39.

## Chapter 3

1. "Looking Backward Twenty-Five Years—and Beyond," *Bicycling World* 46, 12 (18 December 1902): 307.

2. *An Industrial Achievement* (Hartford: The Pope Mfg. Co., 1907), 11–13.

3. "Improvement in Velocipedes," Patent No. 59,915, 20 November 1866, to Pierre Lallement of Paris, France, Assignor to Himself and James Carroll, of New Haven; "Deposition of Pierre Lallement, 29 May 1882" in the case file of *Pope Manufacturing Company v. Joseph McKee and Charles Harrington* (Docket No. unk., S.D.N.Y. 1882).

4. "Improvement in Cantering Propellers," Patent No. 36,161, 12 August 1862, to P. W. Mackenzie of Jersey City, New Jersey.

5. "Improvement in Auto-Propelling Horses and Vehicles," Patent No. 41,310, 19 January 1864, to P. W. Mackenzie of Jersey City, New Jersey; *Digest of Patent Assignments*, National Archives, College Park, MD. Record Group NC-147, Vol. M-2, 219, 237; *New York City Directory*, May 1864–65; May 1865–66; May 1866–67; May 1867–68 and May 1868–69.

6. "Improvement in Velocipede Trotting or Pacing Horse," Patent No. 46,705, 7 March 1865, to Harvey A. Reynolds, of New York.

7. David V. Helihy, "The Velocipede Craze in Maine," *Maine History* 38, 3/4 (1999): 194. The original source of much of this information is the *Portland Eastern Argus*, 2 March 1869; "Deposition of Calvin Witty, 1 February 1881" in the case file of *Pope Manufacturing Company v. Joseph McKee and Charles Harrington* (Docket No. unk., S.D.N.Y., 1882).

8. Brandon conveyed his interest in the Lallement patent to Witty on 5 March 1869: *Digest of Patent Assignments*, L-2: 259, 261, 269; L-3: 4; Letter from C. B. Brandon to Charles E. Pratt, 15 August 1878, Charles Pratt Scrapbook, Transportation Division, National Museum of American History, Smithsonian Institution; "Deposition of Calvin Witty," *Pope Mfg. Co. v. McKee & Harrington;* Karl Kron [Lyman H. Bagg], *Ten Thousand Miles on A Bicycle* (New York: Karl Kron, 1887), 140.

9. "Improvement in Velocipedes," Patent No. 36,161, 12 August 1862, to Stephen W. Smith, of New York, Assignee of P. W. Mackenzie; Reissue No. 3,319, 2 March 1869.

10. Lallement patent royalties: "Deposition of Calvin Witty"; Herlihy, "The Velocipede Craze in Maine," 194. Sale to Durgin: *Digest of Patent Assignments*, M-7: 22; 265.

11. "Improvement in Velocipedes," Patent No. 41,310, 19 January 1864, to Montpelier Manufacturing Company, assignees of Philip W. Mackenzie. Reissue No. 7,818, 31 July 1877.

12. Witty sells Lallement patent: *Digest of Patent Assignments*, L-5: 108. George and Joseph McKee: *Boston City Directory* for the years 1869–1878; *New York City Directory* for the years 1868–1880. Pope seeks license: "Col. Pope Interviewed," *Bicycling World* 35, 14 (18 June 1897): 20; *An Industrial Achievement*, 13; *Digest of Patent Assignments*, L-5: 108.

13. "Improvement in Velocipedes," Patent No. 59,915, 20 November 1866, to Henry M. Richardson and George McKee, assignees of Pierre Lallement. Reissue No. 7,972, 27 November 1877.

14. "Improvement in Velocipedes," Patent No. 46,705, 7 March 1865, to Harvey A. Reynolds, assignor to Henry M. Richardson and George McKee. Reissue No. 8,252, 28 May 1878.

15. *Digest of Patent Assignments*, M-7: 138; L-5: 232. Although the indenture agreement between Richardson & McKee and Montpelier was made on 15 January 1878, it was not recorded until nearly a year later, on 6 January 6 1879. The dates are the same for the Mackenzie, Lallement and Reynolds patents. I am at a loss to explain this.

16. Charles E. Pratt, "A Sketch of American Bicycling and Its Founder," *Outing* 18, 4 (July 1891): 344.

17. "Catalog of the Large and Valuable Library of the Late Ch. Eadward Pratt, Esq.," in the Pratt Scrapbook, Transportation Division, National Museum of American History, Smithsonian Institution; *Boston Transcript* (22 August 1898); Kron, *Ten Thousand Miles on a Bicycle*, 503; Charles E. Pratt, "The Tariff Question," *The Wheelman* 1, 1 (October 1882): 60–69.

18. Letter from C. E. Brandon to Charles E. Pratt, 15 August 1878, Pratt Scrapbook, Transportation Division, National Museum of American History, Smithsonian Institution.

19. March license: *Digest of Patent Assignments*, M-9: 171, 191; L-3: 232. 22. April sale: *Digest of Patent Assignments*, M-9: 188. Conveyance from Charles Pope to Pope Mfg. Co.: *Digest of Patent Assignments*, M-9: 222.

20. *Digest of Patent Assignments*, M-9: 263; *Digest of Patent Assignments*, M-9: 222, 262, 263.

21. *Pope Manufacturing Co. v. Owsley*, 27 F. 100, 101 (N.D. Ill. 1886); "Col. Pope Interviewed," 20.

22. *Pope v. Owsley*, 27 F. 100, 101; "Letter from the Pope Manufacturing Company," *Bicycling World* 3, 2 (20 May 1881): 18–19; *Pope Manufacturing Co. v. R. Philip Gormully*, 144, U.S. 224, 226 (1892); *Pope Manufacturing Co. v. R. Philip Gormully*, Case Record No. 13,260, at 475 (hereafter, "*Pope v. Gormully* Case Record").

23. "Col. Pope's Response to the Toast, 'The Wheel,' at the L.O.W. Banquet." *The Wheelman*, 1, 1 (October 1882): 71. *Boston City Directory* (Boston: Sampson, Davenport and Co.) for the years 1884–85 and 1885–86. Cunningham allowed to go out of business: "The Industry: How It Grew Up," *Bicycling World* 46, 12 (18 December 1902): 330; Letter from Charles E. Pratt to R. Philip Gormully, 4 May 1883, *Pope v. Gormully* Case Record: 473–74.

24. "The Industry: How It Grew Up," 328; letter from George W. Pressey to the H.B. Smith Manufacturing Company, 11 January 1881, *Transcript of Witnesses, 23 January 1888, Pressey v. H. B. Smith Mfg. Co.*, 19 A. 618 (N.J. App. 1889): 124 (Hagley Museum and Library, Wilmington, Delaware) (hereafter, "*Pressey v. Smith* Case Record"); "Answer of Charles Koop," case record of *Pope Manufacturing Co. v. Koop*, Docket No. D-1814 (S.D.N.Y. 1881). Varrecke probably did tour the United States, but in 1869, as Calvin Witty identified several features of his velocipede in a lithograph made during the tour that were first invented in Witty's shop in 1869 and were based on the Hanlons' patent: "Deposition of Calvin Witty."

25. "Albert Pope: His Place in History," *Bicycling World* 46, 12 (18 December 1902): 316; "Velocipede Patent Litigation," *The Wheelman* 1, 2 (November 1882): 152; "Bicycle Litigation," *Iron Age* 29 (29 June 1882): 24; "Deposition of Pierre Lallement."

26. Lallement arrived in New York on the *Canada* on 17 July 1879. Electronic mail correspondence from David V. Herlihy to the author, 3 and 4 November 2008.

27. In 1992, historian David V. Herlihy raised the

money for Lallement's headstone. Charles E. Pratt, "Pierre Lallement and His Bicycle," *The Wheelman*, 3, 1 (October 1883): 4–13; David V. Herlihy, *Pierre Lallement and His Bicycle* (Boston: David V. Herlihy, 1992); Todd Balf, "The Great Debate," *Bicycling* 36, 5 (May 1998): 70–74; "The Industry: How It Grew Up," 330.

28. "The Industry: How it Grew Up," 328; "Albert A. Pope: His Place in History," 317.

29. Beverly Rae Kimes, "A Family in Kenosha: The Story of the Rambler and the Jeffery," *Automobile Quarterly* 16, 2 (1978): 130; "Gormully and Jeffery Mfg. Co.," *Bearings* 8, 21 (22 December 1893): 16; "Thomas B. Jeffery Dead," *Horseless Age* 25, 14 (6 April 1910): 521; "The Industry: How it Grew Up," 328; "Deposition of Philip Gormully," *Pope v. Gormully* Case Record: 391; miscellaneous, *Pope v. Gormully* Case Record: 279.

30. "Deposition of Philip Gormully," *Pope v. Gormully* Case Record: 391–93.

31. "Testimony of George W. Pressey," *Pressey v. Smith Case Record;* see also the case's published opinion: 19 A. 618 (N.J. App. 1889): 154–67.

32. *Greer's Hartford Directory* for the year 1882–83. Overman Wheel Company director G. Pierrepont Davis was the medical examiner at Traveler's, director Edward V. Preston was vice president and director Rodney Dennis was secretary; Vera Shlakman, *Economic History of A Small Town: A Study of Chicopee, Massachusetts* (New York: Octagon Books, 1934 [1969]), 327.

33. "The Overman Wheel Co.," *The National Magazine*, 17, 1 (November 1892): xxvii–xxxii.

34. "The Industry: How It Grew Up," 329.

35. *Miller v. Bridgeport Brass Co.*, 17 F.Cass. 309 (D.Conn. 1877).

36. Unable to make patent cases go away, the U.S. Supreme Court did the next best thing in 1984 by creating a special court, the Federal Circuit Court of Appeals for the Federal Circuit, to hear them, and since then has accepted only a bare handful of cases.

37. *Miller v. Bridgeport Brass*, 104 U.S. 350 (1881).

38. Two points: 1) I assume for simplicity that the reissue applicant is the original patentee. That need not always be the case. 2) To be precise, in *Miller*, the defendant asserted that the error needing correction was the original patent applicant's failure to make the original claims sufficiently broad. This was rejected. Subsequent cases made it clear that the "error" must be one that renders the device itself dysfunctional.

39. *Pope Manufacturing Co. v. Marqua*, 15 Fed. R. 400 (1883); Letter from R. Philip Gormully to Charles E. Pratt, 23 April 23, 1883, *Pope v. Gormully* Case Record: 283; *Pope v. Owlsley*, 27 F. 100, 103.

40. Letter from Albert A. Pope to R. Philip Gormully, 17 March 1883, *Pope v. Gormully* Case Record: 471.

41. Letter from R. Philip Gormully to Charles E. Pratt, 23 April 1883, *Pope v. Gormully* Case Record: 283.

42. Letter from Charles E. Pratt to R. Philip Gormully, 4 May 1883, *Pope v. Gormully* Case Record: 473.

43. "Gormully & Jeffery Mfg. Co.," 1.

44. *Columbia Cycle Catalogs for 1882 and 1883*. The Richardson & McKee/ Montpelier purchase contained about a dozen patents by Lallement, Mackenzie, Reynolds, the Hanlons, Witty, and a couple of carriage-wheel designs by John Buzzell. By 1882, Pratt had added another six or seven. The Hartford factory had generated fourteen, mostly for dies, but also for parts and accessories such as lanterns.

45. A junk shop: "Deposition of Thomas Jeffery," *Pope v. Gormully* Case Record: 350–51. Straw-man purchases: "Deposition of Charles E. Pratt," *Pope v. Gormully* Case Record: 54–56; Letter from Charles E. Pratt to Orrin E. Peters, 14 October 1882, *Pope v. Gormully* Case Record: 478–79.

46. *Pope v. Gormully* Case Record: 255–64; "Deposition of Thomas Jeffery," *Pope v. Gormully* Case Record: 351.

47. Letter from Charles E. Pratt to R. Philip Gormully, 7 December 1883, *Pope v. Gormully* Case Record: 483.

48. "Deposition of Charles E. Pratt," *Pope v. Gormully* Case Record: 51; "The Industry: How It Grew Up," 329; Letter from R. Philip Gormully to Charles E. Pratt, October 20, 1884, *Pope v. Gormully* Case Record: 475; Letter from Charles E. Pratt to R. Philip Gormully, October 24, 1884, *Pope v. Gormully* Case Record: 484; "A Family in Kenosha," 132.

49. Letter from R. Philip Gormully to Charles E. Pratt, October 29, 1884, *Pope v. Gormully* Case Record: 475; Letter, Charles E. Pratt to R. Philip Gormully, November 4, 1884, *Pope v. Gormully* Case Record: 484. "A Family In Kenosha," 132.

50. "Deposition of R. Philip Gormully," *Pope v. Gormully* Case Record: 389; 394.

51. "The Industry: How It Grew Up," 330; "The Overman Wheel Company to Its Friends," *Bicycling World* 12, 18 (5 March 1886): 1; "Deposition of Charles R. Pratt," *Pope v. Gormully* Case Record: 51–52; *Economic History of A Small Town*, 199.

52. The Pope Manufacturing Co. was originally incorporated in Connecticut. As late as March 1891 it was still incorporated there, *Pope Manufacturing Co. v. Clark*, 46 F. 768 (D. Conn. 1891), but by 7 April 1891 it was a Maine corporation, resulting in the dismissal of an Overman suit for lack of jurisdiction. *Overman Wheel Co. v. Pope Manufacturing Co.*,46 F. 577 (D. Conn. 1891). On 5 July it was back in Connecticut, resulting in another involuntary dismissal. *National Typewriter Co. v. Pope Manufacturing Co.*, 56 F. 849 (D.Mass. 1893).

53. "The Industry: How it Grew Up," 330; *Pope v. Clark*, 46 F. 768, 769; "Deposition of Philip Gormully," *Pope v. Gormully* Case Record: 399.

54. Letter from R. Philip Gormully to Charles E. Pratt, 20 October 1884, *Pope v. Gormully* Case Record: 474; Letter from Charles E. Pratt to R. Philip Gormully, 24 October 1884, *Pope v. Gormully* Case Record: 484; Letter from R. Philip Gormully to Charles E. Pratt, 29 October 1884, *Pope v. Gormully* Case Record: 475 Letter from R. Philip Gormully to Charles E. Pratt, 14 October 1884, *Pope v. Gormully* Case Record: 476–77.

55. "Deposition of Philip Gormully," *Pope v. Gormully* Case Record: 400; "Gormully's Proposed New License," *Pope v. Gormully* Case Record: 271–80. Pope's attorneys filed in federal court on 5 February 1887.

56. "Deposition of Thomas B. Jeffery," *Pope v. Gormully* Case Record: 353–54;

57. *Pope v. Gormully*, 34 F. 877, 878–80. *Pope v. Gormully*, 144 U.S. 224, appellee's brief at 16.

58. *Pope v. Gormully*, 34 F. 877, 884–85.

59. *American Athlete and Cycle Trades Review* 3, 5 (2 May 1888): 55.

60. Carl M. Burgwardt, *Buffalo's Bicycles* (Orchard Park, NY: Pedaling History Museum, 2001), 22.

61. *Pope v. Gormully*, 144 U.S. 224, 233.

62. Frederick G. Bourne, "American Sewing Machines," *One Hundred Years of American Commerce*, ed. Chauncey M. Depew (New York: D.O. Haynes, 1895): 530.
63. "Gormully and Jeffery Mfg. Co.," 1.
64. Kron, *Ten Thousand Miles on A Bicycle*, 503; "Projector of the L.A.W.," 7. "Albert Pope: His Place in History," 317.

## Chapter 4

1. "Col. Pope Breathes Fire," *Bicycling World* 47, 7 (16 May 1903): 222.
2. Cary Goodman, *Choosing Sides: Playground and Street Life on the Lower East Side* (New York: Schocken Books, 1979), xiii.
3. Clay McShane, *Down the Asphalt Path: The Automobile and the American City* (New York: Columbia University Press, 1994), 16.
4. Hiram Percy Maxim, *Horseless Carriage Days* (New York: Harper and Brothers, 1962 [1936]), 5.
5. Chicago: "Utilitarian Side of Cycling," *Cycle Age and Trade Review* 21 (22 September 1898): 602; Harrisburg: "Street Railways Lose Money," *Cycle Age and Trade Review* 20 (6 January 1898): 333; Good Pope Bicycle: Form Letter from Pope Manufacturing Co. to dealers, 23 March 1915, Soo Hardware Collection, Hagley Museum and Library, Wilmington, Delaware.
6. Charles E. Pratt, "Our First Bicycle Club," *The Wheelman* 1, 6 (March 1883): 402.
7. Karl Kron [Lyman H. Bagg], *Ten Thousand Miles on A Bicycle* (New York: Karl Kron, 1887), 27–40.
8. Mark Twain, "Taming the Bicycle," *Collected Tales, Sketches, Speeches & Essays, 1852–1890* (New York: Library of America, 1992): 892–99. Frederick Anderson (ed.), *Mark Twain's Notebooks and Journals, Volume III, 1883–1891* (Berkeley: University of California Press, 1979.), 55. Twain's Expert Columbia still exists; it is in the collection of the Connecticut Historical Society in Hartford. My thanks to Everett C. Wilkie, Jr., for letting me examine it. Twain's visit to Horsman's shop: *Notebooks and Journals, Volume III*: 256.
9. Carl F. Burgwardt, "A Landscape of Early Bicycle History," *Cycle History 7: Proceedings of the 7th International Cycle History Conference*, ed. Rob van der Plas (San Francisco: Van der Plas Publications, 1997), 92.
10. Bruce Epperson, "How Many Bikes: An Investigation Into the Quantification of Bicycling, 1878–1914," *Cycle History 11: Proceedings of the 11th International Cycle History Conference*, ed. Andrew Ritchie and Rob van der Plas (San Francisco: Van der Plas Publications, 2001), 32–42.
11. League membership: Sept. 1880—527; May 1881—1654; June 1881—1571;Oct. 1881—2103; May 1882 (est.)—1836; May 1883—2131; May 1884—4250; Dec. 1885—5176; May 1886—8463: Kron, *Ten Thousand Miles on a Bicycle*, 616–26.
12. "The Bicycle Industry," *Hartford Courant*, 2 April 1899, Pope Scrapbooks, Connecticut Historical Society, Hartford.
13. S. S. McClure, *My Autobiography* (New York: Frederick A. Stokes, 1914), 145. "Master Showman" is taken from a sketch of the life of Harold Hayden Eames prepared by Hermann F. Cuntz for Henry Cave, 12 October 1940, Box 3, File 1, Henry Cave Collection, National Automotive History Collection, Detroit Public Library; the quote is from "Col. Pope Breathes Fire," *Bicycling World* 47, 7 (16 May 1903): 222.

14. "A Great American Manufactory," *Bicycling World* 2, 21 (1 April 1881): 329.
15. "Albert A. Pope: His Place in History," *Bicycling World* 46, 12 (18 December 1902): 319; "Advertising the Columbia," *Profitable Advertising* 7, 8 (1897): 275–78; McClure, *My Autobiography*, 145.
16. "Albert A. Pope: His Place in History," 319.
17. *The Wheel* (21 May 1897); *American Cyclist* (15 April 1894), both Pope Scrapbooks, CHS; Hermann F. Cuntz, "Hartford the Birthplace of Automobile Industry," *Hartford Times*, October 16–18, 1947.
18. "Albert A. Pope: His Place in History," 319.
19. "Frank W. Weston: The Man and His Work," *Bicycling World* 46, 12 (18 December 1902): 309.
20. "Papa Weston Thumbs Back Numbers," *Bicycling World* 26, 12 (18 December 1902): 311; Kron, *Ten Thousand Miles on A Bicycle*, 503, "E. C. Hodges Dead, *Bicycling World* 48, 12 (19 December 1903): 310–11.
21. "Rights of Importation," *Bicycling World* 3, 2 (20 May 1881): 18. *The Wheelman* tale comes from three sources: Kron, *Ten Thousand Miles on a Bicycle*, 656–59; McClure, *My Autobiography*, 142–61; and "Albert A. Pope: His Place in History," 319.
22. Letter from Albert A. Pope to S. S. McClure, 24 May 1882, McClure Manuscript Collection 3 (incoming correspondence by alphabet), Manuscripts Department, Lilly Library, Indiana University.
23. Most versions of this story say that the original publication of Pratt's article was in *The Century*. However, it was actually *Scribner's*, which evolved into *Century* a few months later. Charles E. Pratt, "A Wheel Around the Hub," *Scribner's Monthly* 40, 4 (February 1880): 481–500.
24. McClure, *My Autobiography*, 150–55; letter from George Pope to S. S. McClure, 4 January 1883, McClure MS-3, Lilly Library, IU.
25. Letters from Albert A. Pope to S. S. McClure, 4 and 6 December 1883, McClure MS-3, Lilly Library, IU.
26. Letter from Albert A. Pope to S. S. McClure, 9 February 1884, letter from Charles E. Pratt to S. S. McClure, 9 January 1884, both McClure MS-3, Lilly Library, IU.
27. Kron, *Ten Thousand Miles on a Bicycle*, 657.
28. Thomas Stevens's story is taken from two main sources: Kron, *Ten Thousand Miles on a Bicycle*, 473–75, and Thomas Pauly's introduction to the reprint of: Thomas Stevens, *Around the World on a Bicycle* (Mechanicsburg, PA: Stackpole Books, 2001 [1887]), v–xv.
29. Edward Howland, "A Bicycle Era," *Harper's Monthly* 63 (July 1881): 282.
30. Kron, *Ten Thousand Miles on a Bicycle*, 474.
31. Andrew Millward, *Factors Contributing to the Sustained Success of the U.K. Cycle Industry, 1870–1939* (Doctoral thesis, University of Birmingham, October 1999): Section 1.2.3. Millward is citing *The Cycle Trader*, 15 July 1896.
32. *Around the World on a Bicycle*, ix. Pauly is citing the *San Francisco Chronicle*, 8 January 1887.
33. "Lenz's World Tour Awheel," *Outing* 29 (January 1897): 382–89; Robert A. Smith, *A Social History of the Bicycle* (New York: American Heritage Press, 1972), 131.
34. "Pope on the Trade Association," *Bearings* (26 January 1894), Pope Scrapbooks, CHS.
35. Kron, *Ten Thousand Miles on a Bicycle*, 658.

36. "Errors in School Books," *The Manufacturer and Builder* 25, 2 (February 1893): 41.
37. *New York Times*, 13 March 1896; "Parrish, Maxfield (Frederick)," the *Grove Dictionary of Art* (internet version: http://www.groveart.com). Entry revised 27 August 1999.
38. *Vogue (New York)*, (22 April 1897): 63.
39. *An Industrial Achievement* (Hartford: Pope Mfg. Co., 1907), 25–29; "Pope's Publicity Producer," *Bicycling World* 49, 11 (11 June 1904): 340. Winkley was also named an executor and trustee of Pope's estate: *Last Will and Testament of Albert A. Pope*, 16 June 1905 and codicil, 28 May, 1906. Docket S.J.C. 504, Archives of the Supreme Judicial Court of Massachusetts, Boston, Massachusetts. See also: *Ashley v. Winkley*, 95 N.E. 932 (Mass. 1911).
40. David A. Hounshell, *From the American System to Mass Production* (Baltimore: Johns Hopkins University Press, 1984), 203; Glen Norcliffe, "Popeism and Fordism: Examining the Roots of Mass Production," *Regional Studies* 31, 3 (1997): 276.
41. Pratt, "A Sketch of American Bicycling and Its Founder," 347. Pratt's list of Pope Co. accomplishments: 1) First to make significant capital investment in the business; 2) first to rationalize patent management and control; 3) first to develop an extensive system of agents; 4) single-handedly creating trust and confidence in the stability of the bicycle industry.
42. "Col. Pope's response to the Toast," 70.
43. The Manufacture of Sewing Machines," *Scientific American* 42, 12 (20 March 1880): 181.
44. "Lessons of Cycle History," *Cycle Age and Trade Review* 23 (21 September 1899): 518.
45. Hounshell, *From American System to Mass Production*, 89; Susan Strasser, *Satisfaction Guaranteed: The Making of the American Mass Market* (Washington: Smithsonian Institution Press, 1989), 60.
46. Burgwardt, "A Landscape of Early Bicycle History," 89. Bidwell recalled these events as having occurred in the spring of 1879, but given that he was relating events occurring 50 years earlier, a one-year discrepancy is understandable.
47. It appears that Pope kept about 25 of the first lot for use in his own cycle rinks: Burgwardt, "A Landscape of Early Bicycle History," 89. This corroborates information contained in "The Bicycle Industry," *Hartford Courant*, 2 April 1899, Pope Scrapbooks, CHS.
48. Letter from David J. Post to W. S. Warner, 1 March 1893, Pope/ Hartford Papers, History and Genealogy Division, Connecticut State Library, Hartford.
49. Letter from George Pope to David J. Post, 26 January 1891, Pope/Hartford Papers, CSL.
50. Letter from J. F. Cox to Ira Brink, with Circular Letter No. 36, 14 March 1895, Shields Collection, National Museum of Science and Technology, Ottawa, Canada.
51. Pratt, "A Sketch of American Bicycling and Its Founder," 348.
52. *Burr v. Redhead, Norton, Lathrop Co.*, 72 N.W. 1058, 1059 (Neb. 1897).
53. "Colonel Pope on the Bicycle Trade," *Iron Age* 40 (29 April 1897): 34; *Pope Mfg. Co. v. Welch*, 37 S.E. 20, 22 (S.C., 1900).
54. Julius Wilcox, "The Cost of It," *The Wheelman* 3, 5 (February 1884): 379–80.
55. Dealer markup: Letter from George Pope to David J. Post, 4 February 1892, Pope/Hartford Papers, CSL; Letter from J. F. Cox to Ira Brink, with Circular Letter No. 36, 14 March 1895, Shields Collection, Ottawa. Whether freight was charged: Letter from George Pope to David J. Post, 9 January 1892, 18 January 1892, Pope/Hartford papers, CSL. The value of freight charges was estimated from information in Strasser, *Satisfaction Guaranteed*, Chapter 3.

56.
| | Customer Cost | Factory's Profit | Dealer's Profit |
|---|---|---|---|
| Bought via agent | $130 | $27.25 | $26.00 |
| Bought via branch house (some goes to factory) | $130 | $40.25* | $13.00* |
| Bought factory direct | $136 | $59.25 | $0 |

*assumes that a branch house costs $13 per bicycle to operate, so only $13 of $26 is profit.*

57. Letters from George Pope to David J. Post, 9 January 1892 and 18 January 1892, Pope/Hartford Papers, CSL.
58. Letter from R. Phillip Gormully to Charles E. Pratt, 23 April 1883, *Pope Manufacturing Co. v. Gormully*, 144 U.S. 224, Case Record No. 13,260 at 282.
59. Letter from Charles E. Pratt to R. Phillip Gormully, 4 May 1883, *Pope v. Gormully Case Record*: 473–74.
60. "Historical Review of Prominent Companies," *Cycle Age and Trade Review* 19 (7 September 1899): 464; "The Industry: How It Grew Up," 327.
61. Twenty percent insufficient: Strasser, *Satisfaction Guaranteed*, 83. A storefront retailer needed a minimum 18 to 20 percent margin to clear any profit at all, assuming no shipping or set-up costs. Quote: Letter from George Pope to David J. Post, 4 February 1892, Pope/Hartford Papers, CSL.
62. Letter from George Post to David J. Post, 24 January 1893, Pope/ Hartford Papers, CSL.
63. *Pope v. Welch*, 37 S.E. 20, 21.
64. Letter from George Pope to David J. Post, 13 January 1893, Pope/Hartford Papers, CSL.
65. "Elliot Mason," *K-Grippy Gazette* (1 June 1892), Pope Scrapbooks, CHS. Burgwardt, "A Landscape of Early Bicycle History," 91; *Columbia Bicycle Catalog for 1881*, 16; "The Pioneers of the Retail Trade," *Bicycling World* 46, 12 (18 December 1902): 335–337.
66. *Teichner v. Pope Mfg. Co.*, 83 N.W. 1031, 1034 (Mich. 1900).
67. Shop salaries: *Teichner v. Pope Mfg. Co.*, 83 N.W. 1031; factory wages: Axel Josephsson, "Bicycles and Tricycles," *Twelfth Annual Census of the United States [1900]*, Manufacturers, Part 3: Special Reports, 336. The data is contained in Table 9.
68. Millward, *Factors Contributing to the Sustained Success of the UK Cycle Industry*: Section 2.3.2(4).
69. *Williams, et al. v. Pope Manufacturing Co.*, 27 So. 851 (La. 1900).
70. Judith Crown and Glenn Coleman, *No Hands: The Rise and Fall of the Schwinn Bicycle Company* (New York: Henry Holt, 1996), Chapter 4.

71. Ross D. Petty, "The Impact of the Sport of Bicycle Riding on Safety Law," *American Business Law Journal* 35, 2 (Winter 1998): 185–224.

72. McShane, *Down the Asphalt Path*, 118.

73. Pratt, "A Sketch of American Bicycling and Its Founder," 345; A. G. Batchelder, "The Story of the Bicycle," *Harper's Weekly* 60, 2051 (11 April 1896): 359; "Memoir" in *Catalog of the Large and Valuable Library of the Late Ch. Eadward Pratt, esq.*, Charles Pratt Scrapbook, Transportation Division, National Museum of American History, Smithsonian Institution, Washington, D.C.; Kron, *Ten Thousand Miles on a Bicycle*, 503–04.

74. *In re Wright et. al.*, 63 How. 345 (S.C.N.Y.C. 1882). There is a discrepancy in the dates of the adoption of the Central Park ordinance. Kron says it was 27 October 1879, but *In re Wright* states it was 7 July 1880. There were probably two ordinances, with the July 1880 version adding tricycles to the earlier prohibition on bicycles.

75. Information on the Central Park case of 1881–83 comes from three sources: Kron, *Ten Thousand Miles on a Bicycle*, 92–95; *In re Wright et. al.*, 63 How. 345 (S.C.N.Y.C. 1882); and *In re Wright, Foster & Walker*, 65 How. 119 (S.C.N.Y.C. 1883).

76. *In re Wright et. al.*, 63 How. 345.

77. Philip P. Mason, *The League of American Wheelmen and the Good-Roads Movement, 1880–1905* (Doctoral dissertation, University of Michigan, 1957), 37; Gregory C. Lisa, "Bicyclists and Bureaucrats: The League of American Wheelmen and the Public Choice Theory Applied," *Georgetown Law Review* 84 (1995): 379.

78. Pratt, "The L.A.W. and Legal Rights," *Outing* 7 (January 1886): 456; Pratt, "A Sketch of American Bicycling and its Founder": 345; Pope, "The American Bicycle Industry," 550; Kron, *Ten Thousand Miles on a Bicycle*, 94. The original source of the $8,000 figure may be a 72-page booklet written by Pratt and published by the Pope Manufacturing Company in April 1884 entitled *What and Why*. (See Kron, page 678.)

79. *Swift v. City of Topeka*, 23 P. 1075 (Kan. 1890); McShane, *Down the Asphalt Path*, 117.

## Chapter 5

1. "Welcome to Pope," *Hartford Courant*, 3 July 1903.

2. "Colonel Pope's Purchase," *Boston Post*, 4 April 1892; "Along the Jerusalem Road," *Boston Post*, 5 August 1894, both Pope Scrapbook, Connecticut Historical Society, Hartford; "Map of the Town of Cohasset from U. S. Coast and Geodetic Survey, 1894," George L. Davenport and Elizabeth O. Davenport, *Genealogies of the Families of Cohasset, Massachusetts* (Somersworth, NH: New England Press, 1984 [1909]). In 1991, David Wadsworth of the Cohasset Historical Commission prepared inventories of the surviving structures of the former Pope and Whitney estates, most of which have been converted to residences. I thank Ms. Ellen M. Freda, who lived in part of the renovated Pope stables in 2000, for providing me copies of several of the Wadsworth surveys.

3. "Pope, Abby Linden [sic]," *The Biographical Cyclopaedia of American Women*, Mabel Ward Cameron, ed. (New York: Halvord Publishing, 1924).

4. "Horseshoe for Col. Pope," *Bicycling World* 48, 3 (17 October 1903): 61–62.

5. Charles E. Pratt, "The Tariff Question," *The Wheelman* 1 (October 1882): 63–69. "A Plea For Fair Trade: Speech of Col. Albert A. Pope Before the Tariff Commission," *The Wheelman* 1 (October 1882) 60–63.

6. *Kirkpatrick v. Pope Manufacturing Company*, 64 F. 369, 374 (1894); Henry P. Woodward, "Manufacturers in Hartford," *Hartford in History* (Hartford: Board of Trade, 1889): 112–16; *Greer's Hartford Directory* for the year 1889-90; Bureau of the Census, *Tenth Census of the United States [1890]: Manufacturers*, III, 126–27. Only the value of output in dollars is given. To estimate number of bicycles produced. I assumed that 80 percent of output was for bicycles (the remainder being for parts and accessories), with an average factory value of $100 each.

7. Pratt, "The Tariff Question," 68.

8. No man knew: "Testimony of Carl Norcross," *Transcript of Witnesses, 23 January 1888, Pressey v. H. B. Smith Mfg. Co.*, 19 A. 618 (N.J. App. 1889), 74–77 (Hagley Museum and Library, Wilmington, Delaware) (hereafter *Pressey v. Smith* case record); Cost estimates: "Testimony of George W. Pressey," *Pressey v. Smith* case record: 154–67.

9. *Columbia Bicycle Catalog for 1883*, 21.

10. Stephen B. Goddard, *Colonel Albert Pope and His American Dream Machines* (Jefferson, NC: McFarland, 2000), 84; Copley Square Hotel: *Ashley v. Winkley*, 95 N.E. 932 (Mass. 1911); California loan: *Pierce v. Merrill*, 61 P. 64 (Calif. 1900).

11. Albert Linder: "Albert Linder Pope Dies, Pioneer in Auto Industry," *Hartford Courant*, 11 August 1955; "Albert Linder Pope Dies, Retired Industrialist," *Hartford Times*, 10 August 1955. Mary Linder: *Copy of Record of Death: Mary Linder Pope*, 1874, Vol. 266, Page 165, No. 77, Massachusetts Archives; Margaret Roberts: C. H. Pope, *A History of the Dorchester Pope Family, 1634–1888* (Boston: C.H. Pope, 1888), 256. Harold Linder: Pope, *A History of the Dorchester Pope Family*, 256; Charles Linder: *Boston Transcript*, 22 April 1898; *Boston Post*, 22 April 1898. All of these dates were verified in Emily Wilder Leavitt, *A Genealogy of the Bogman Family* (No location [Boston]: Moses Conant Warren, 1890), 2–29, and the dates of birth listed on the Pope family columbarium in Boston. Many thanks to Ms. Susan Navarre of Forest Hills Cemetery for locating the Pope family site and the cemetery's records relating to it.

12. "The Massachusetts Bicycle Club," *The Wheelman* 2, 3 (June 1883): 160–165.

13. "Harry M. Pope, 89, Expert on Rifles," *New York Times*, 13 October 1950; "Rev. Louis A. Pope of Newburyport," *Boston Transcript*, 21 August 1903; *A History of the Dorchester Pope Family*, 255.

14. Letter from George Pope to David J. Post, 15 May 1891, Pope/Hartford Papers, History and Genealogy Division, Connecticut State Library, Hartford.

15. *First Catalog of the Massachusetts Institute of Technology, 1865–66*, 3; Hugh David Graham and Nancy Diamond, *The Rise of American Research Universities* (Baltimore: Johns Hopkins University, 1997), 18, n24; "Harry M. Pope, 89, Expert on Rifles"; *Boston City Directory* (Boston: Sampson, Davenport and Co.) for the years 1881 through 1884; *Greer's Harford Directory*, 1883–84 through 1885–86.

16. *American Wheelman* (9 July 1892), Pope Scrapbooks, CHS.

17. Letter from Edouard L. Desrochers, Academy Archivist, Phillips Exeter Academy, to author, 17 January 2000; Letter from Philip N. Crowenwett, Special Collections Librarian, Dartmouth College Library, to author, 26 October 1999.

18. Pope, *A History of the Dorchester Pope Family*, 256; "Pope, Harold Linder," 51; *Boston Transcript*, 22 April 1898, *Boston Post*, 22 April 1898, both Pope Scrapbooks, CHS.

19. Bunting, *Houses of Boston's Back Bay*, 429; Goddard, *Col. Albert Pope*, 84.

20. Sam Bass Warner, *Streetcar Suburbs: The Process of Growth in Boston, 1870–1900* (Cambridge: Harvard University Press, 1978), 25–26, 125, 144–145; "Arthur Pope Married," *Boston News*, 26 October 1892; "Wedded in White Room," *Boston Herald*, 26 October 1892; "Miss Pope's Debut," *Boston Post*, 11 December 1895, all Pope Scrapbooks, CHS.

21. *Boston City Directory*, 1882–83 and 1883–84; *Boston Transcript*, 25 February 1888. Charles Pope's obituary is also the source of information on the death of Elizabeth Bogman Pope.

22. John Buttrick, "Inside the Contract System," *Journal of Economic History* 12, 3 (Summer 1952): 206; David Hounshell, *From the American System to Mass Production* (Baltimore: Johns Hopkins University Press, 1986), passim; "Victor Bicycles," *Scientific American* 64, 18 (2 May 1891): 1; Paul Rosen, *Framing Production: Technology, Culture and Change in the British Bicycle Industry* (Cambridge: MIT Press, 2002), 82–85; Ellsworth Grant, *Yankee Dreamers and Doers: The Story of Connecticut Manufacturing* (Hartford: Connecticut Historical Society, no date [c.1992]), 252; *Boston City Directory*, 1880–81 and 1881–82; *Greer's Hartford Directory*, 1881–82, 1885–86 and 1886–87.

23. "Testimony of William Kelly," *Pressey v. Smith* Case File, 43. 1 *Columbia Bicycle Catalog for 1883*, 21.

24. *Boston City Directory*, 1880–81 and 1881–82; "Massachusetts Bicycle Club in 1884," *Bicycling World* 46, 12 (12 December 1902): 316; *Greer's Hartford Directory*, 1877–78 through 1883–84; *Boston City Directory*, 1885–86 and 1889–90. I conclude that Pattison acted as Colonel Pope's personal secretary from the fact that he lived in one of the cottages at Lindermere during the summer. ("Along the Jerusalem Road," *Boston Post*, 5 August 1894, Pope Scrapbooks, CHS.) In later years this role was filled by Robert Winkley. "Pope's Publicity Producer," *Bicycling World* 49, 11 (11 June 1904): 340; Grant, *Yankee Dreamers and Doers*, 195; Rosen, *Framing Production*, 84; Buttrick, "Inside the Contract System": 214, n15.

25. Andrea Tone, *The Business of Benevolence: Industrial Paternalism in Progressive America* (Ithaca: Cornell University Press, 1997), 36. George Pope quote taken from U.S. Bureau of Labor Statistics, *Proceedings on the Conference on Social Insurance*, Bulletin 212 (1917), 850–54.

26. David F. Ransom, *George Keller, Architect* (Hartford: Stowe-Day Foundation, 1978), 179. Keller's quote is taken from a letter from Keller to his wife Mary dated 20 August 1889; *Greer's Hartford Directory*, 1908–1914; Edwin L. Shuey, *Factory People and Their Employees* (New York: Lentilhon & Co., 1900), 128–30.

27. Cleveland Moffett, *Marvels of Bicycle Making*. This brochure, assembled from what were originally inserts to four unspecified issues of *McClure's Magazine*, was published by the Pope Mfg. Co. in 1897. A copy is in the Warshaw Collection of Business Americana, Smithsonian Archives, National Museum of American History, Washington, D.C., in the vertical file *Bicycles*, Box 2, File 34; "Capital and Labor," Chester (PA) *Daily Local Irish*, 26 April 1894, Pope Scrapbooks, CHS.

28. Moffett, *Marvels of Bicycle Making*, unpaginated. The Pope Mutual Benefit Association, later a freestanding nonprofit corporation, continued in existence until the firm went under in 1914: *Greer's Hartford Directory*, 1910–11 through 1915–16.

29. "Col. Pope Breathes Fire," *Bicycling World* 47, 7 (16 May 1903): 222; *Stevens-Davis Co. v. Mather & Co.*, 230 Ill. App. 45, 83 (Ill. App. 1923); Buttrick, "Inside the Contract System," 210.

30. Tone, *The Business of Benevolence*, Chapter 1.

31. Roger Lloyd-Jones and M. J. Lewis, *Raleigh and the British Bicycle Industry: An Economic and Industrial History, 1870–1960* (Aldershot, UK: Ashgate, 2000), 73–74, 150–51.

32. *1890 Census of Manufacturers*, 126–29, 150–51. Bicycle industry data for Connecticut was combined with five other states, creating an aggregate of seven firms, but Pope's numbers so overwhelm those of the others that they can be all but ignored.

33. "Col. Pope Interviewed," *Bicycling World*, 16 June 1897, Pope Scrapbooks, CHS; *Twelfth Census of the United States [1900], Manufacturing Industries, Part 3: Special Reports, Bicycles and Tricycles*, by Axel Josephsson, 336–37. Letter from George Pope to David J. Post, 12 May 1891, Pope/Hartford Papers, CHS; Hugh Dolnar, "Bicycle Brazing," *American Machinist* 19 (19 November 1896): 1080.

34. Hugh Dolnar, "Bicycle Tools, Part XVIII," *American Machinist* 18 (27 February 1896): 231; Duncan B. Harrison, "Solves the Labor Problem," *Omaha World Herald*, 9 September 1895, Pope Scrapbook, CHS.

35. Frank Berto, et. al. *The Dancing Chain: The History and Development of the Derailleur Bicycle* (San Francisco: Van der Plas Publications, 2000), 15–20; Geoffrey Williamson, *Wheels Within Wheels: The Story of the Starleys of Coventry* (London: Geoffrey Bles, 1966), passim. While a useful biographical source, Williamson's work contains many technical errors.

36. "The Industry: How It Grew Up," *Bicycling World* 46, 12 (18 December 1902): 327.

37. "The Industry: How It Grew Up," 326; Jay Pridmore and Jim Hurd, *The American Bicycle* (Osceola: Motorbooks International, 1995), 106; Kron, *Ten Thousand Miles on A Bicycle*, 370–71.

38. *The Boneshaker* 6, 55 (1969), 106. Nick Clayton, "The Quest for Safety: What Took So Long?" *Cycle History 8: Proceedings of the 8th International Cycle History Conference*, ed. Nicholas Oddy and Rob van der Plas (San Francisco: Van der Plas Publications, 1998), 17.

39. Carl F. Burgwardt, "A Landscape of Early Cycle History," *Cycle History 7: Proceedings of the Seventh International Cycle History Conference*, ed. Rob van der Plas (San Francisco: Van der Plas Publications, 1997), 90. Bidwell states that the Martha's Vineyard meet was in August 1887, but Kron, in *Ten Thousand Miles on a Bicycle*, confirms that it was actually a year earlier.

40. Pridmore and Hurd, *The American Bicycle*, 32; G. Donald Adams, *Collecting and Restoring Antique Bicycles* (Orchard Park: Pedaling History Museum, 2nd ed., 1996), 126–33.

41. *American Athlete and Cycle Trades Review* 7, 1 (2 January 1891): 7.

42. Bruce Epperson, "How Many Bikes: An Investigation into the Quantification of Cycling, 1877–1914," *Cycle History 11: The Proceedings of the Eleventh International Cycle History Conference*, ed. Andrew Ritchie and Rob van der Plas (San Francisco: Van der Plas Publications, 2001), 42–50.

43. *American Athlete and Cycle Trades Review* 7, 1 (2 January 1891): 7. Photos from the early 1890s continue to show many ordinaries in use, and there were shops that specialized in the used ordinary trade. The L.A.W. held races just for them until 1894: "Racing Rules," *American Athlete and Cycle Trades Review* 11, 16 (21 April 1893): 356.

44. Archibald Sharp, *Bicycles and Tricycles: An Elementary Treatise on Their Design and Construction* (Cambridge: MIT Press, 1977 [1896]), 157. They want it light: "Capital and Labor."

45. Lt. Henry H. Whitney, "The Adaptation of the Bicycle to Military Uses," *Journal of the Military Services Institution of the United States* 17 (1895): 542–63.

46. Brig. Gen. Albert Ordway, *Cycle-Infantry Drill Regulations* (Boston: Pope Mfg. Co., 1892).

47. Lt. E.P. Lawton, "The Bicycle in Military Use," *Journal of the Military Services Institution of the United States* 21 (1897): 458–59.

48. Ordway, *Cycle-Infantry Drill Regulations*, 50.

49. Ordway, *Cycle-Infantry Drill Regulations*, 51; Whitney, "The Adaptation of the Bicycle to Military Uses," 555; Howard A. Giddings, *Manual for Cyclists for the Use of the Regular Army, Organized Militia, and Volunteer Troops of the United States* (Kansas City: n.p., 1898), 98.

50. Whitney, "The Adaptation of the Bicycle to Military Uses," 551.

51. Lawton, "The Bicycle in Military Use," 459.

52. James A. Moss, "Report of a Bicycle Trip from Fort Missoula, Montana, to St. Louis, Missouri," *Army and Navy Journal* 1 September, 1897: 3; John H. Nankivell (ed.) *History of the 25th Regiment United States Infantry From 1869 to 1926* (Denver, 1927), 45.

53. Whitney, "The Adaptation of the Bicycle to Military Uses," 562.

54. *Hartford Times*, 20 June 1890; *Hartford Times*, 9 November 1889, both Pope Scrapbooks, CHS; *Greer's Hartford Directory*, 1885–1886; Letter from George Pope to David J. Post, 12 January 1891, Pope/Hartford Papers, CSL.

55. *Hartford Times*, 9 November 1889, Pope Scrapbooks, CHS; *Greer's Hartford Directory*, 1889–90 through 1895–96.

56. *Greer's Hartford Directory*, 1890–July 1891. A receipt for Post's ten shares is contained in the Pope/Harford Papers, CSL.

57. Letters from George Pope to David J. Post 12, January 1891, 10 April 1891, 15 April 1891, 15 May 1891, 22 May 1891, all Pope/Hartford Papers, CSL.

58. The public are in the dark: Letter from Albert A. Pope to David J. Post, 24 July 1890, Pope/Hartford Papers, CSL. Undivided attention: Letter from Albert A. Pope to David J. Post, 15 May 1891, Pope/Hartford Papers, CSL; *American Athlete and Cycle Trades Review* 7, 17 (24 April 1891): 354.

59. Letter from George Pope to David J. Post, 22 May 1891, Pope/Hartford Papers, CSL.

60. Letter from George Pope to David J. Post, 18 April 1891, Pope/Hartford Papers, CSL.

## Chapter 6

1. "Errors in School Books," *The Manufacturer and Builder* 25, 2 (February 1893): 41.

2. Philip P. Mason. *The League of American Wheelmen and the Good-Roads Movement, 1880–1905* (Ph.D. dissertation, University of Michigan, 1957.) Most of the background on the good-roads movement and the role of cyclists in this chapter are based on Mason's dissertation, which is still the basic source of information on this topic.

3. Robert T. Capless, *Historical Compendium: City of Newton Legislative Branch, 1874–1997* (Unpublished Manuscript; Clerk of the Board of Aldermen of the City of Newton, n.d.). Many thanks to Newton Town Clerk Edward G. English for this valuable source.

4. Charles E. Pratt, "The L.A.W. and Legal Rights," *Outing* 7 (January 1886): 454–56; Ross D. Petty, "The Impact of the Sport of Bicycle Riding on Safety Law," *American Business Law Journal* 35, 2 (Winter 1998): 185–224; Gregory C. Lisa, "Bicyclists and Bureaucrats: The League of American Wheelmen and Public Choice Theory Applied," *Georgetown Law Review* 84 (1995): 373–98.

5. Thomas C. Burr, *Markets as Producers and Consumers: The French and U.S. National Markets, 1875–1910* (Ph.D. Dissertation, University of California at Davis, 2005), 87.

6. "Testimony of William S. Kelly," *Transcript of Witnesses*, 23 January 1888, *Pressey v. H. B. Smith Mfg. Co.*, 19 A. 618 (N.J. App. 1889), 49 (Hagley Museum and Library, Wilmington, Delaware) (hereafter "*Pressey v. Smith* Case File").

7. "Testimony of C. H. Chickering," *Pressey v. Smith* Case File, 517.

8. "Testimony of Bert Pressey," *Pressey v. Smith* Case File, 251.

9. Mason, *The League of American Wheelmen and the Good-Roads Movement*, 46. Karl Kron [Lyman Hotchkiss Bagg], *Ten Thousand Miles on a Bicycle* (New York: Karl Kron, 1887), 626.

10. Kron, *Ten Thousand Miles on a Bicycle*, 627.

11. George D. Gideon, "A Defense of the Two-Class System in Bicycle Racing," *Harper's Weekly* 39 (March 1895): 286.

12. "Testimony of William S. Kelly," *Pressey v. Smith* Case File, 549.

13. Letter from David J. Post to Sam A. Miles, 27 June 1891, Pope/Hartford Papers, Connecticut State Library, Hartford, Connecticut.

14. Mason, *The League of American Wheelmen and the Good-Roads Movement*, 47; Glen Norcliffe, *The Ride to Modernity: The Bicycle in Canada, 1869–1900* (Toronto: University of Toronto Press, 2001), 197.

15. "The Massachusetts Bicycle Club," *The Wheelman* 2, 3 (June, 1883): 161–72; *American Athlete and Cycle Trades Review* 4, 2 (2 January 1889): 109; *American Athlete and Cycle Trades Review* 7, 12 (27 March 1891): 231.

16. Mason, *The League of American Wheelmen and the Good-Roads Movement*, 69–71; 76.

17. *Ibid.*, 88–89.

18. Horatio Sawyer Earle, *The Autobiography of "By Gum" Earle* (Lansing: State Review Publishing, 1929), 42–48; League members had to be wheelmen: Sterling Elliott, "The League of American Wheelmen: Its Origin, Growth, and Prospects," *Harper's Weekly* 39 (March 1895): 284–86.

19. *Engineering News* 30 (December 1893): 30.
20. "The Editor's Table," *Good Roads* 1 (April 1892): 224.
21. "L.A.W. National Assembly," *Wheel and Cycling Trade Review* 6 (February 1891): 681; Mason, *The League of American Wheelmen and the Good-Roads Movement*, 108; *Wheel and Cycling Trade Review* 8, (December 1891): 525. The league contributed $6,000, and the following individuals donated additional funds: Albert Overman, $6,000, Albert Pope, $6,000, George Bidwell, $1,000, anonymous, $1,000.
22. Letter from H. S. Robinson to Roy Stone, Bureau of Public Roads Inquiry, 3 February 1893, Record Group 30.1.1, File 67 (Records of the Bureau of Public Roads), National Archives, Archives II Facility, College Park, MD. (Hereafter: 30.1.1/67 BPR Papers, Archives II).
23. Mason, *The League of American Wheelmen and the Good-Roads Movement*, 91, citing the *Michigan Farmer*, 13 March 1897.
24. Albert A. Pope, *The Relation of Good Street to the Prosperity of a City: An Address* (Boston: Pope Mfg. Co., 1892).
25. Albert A. Pope, *Highway Improvement: An Address* (Boston: Pope Mfg. Co., 1889).
26. "Instruction in Road Making," *New York Times*, 28 September 1890, 1; *Engineering* 24, 41 (11 October 1890): 311.
27. *Wheel and Cycling Trade Review*, 4 (February 1890): 520; *Outing* 16 (July 1890): 331–32.
28. Pratt, "The L.A.W. and Legal Rights," 454–56. Pratt cautioned that the league's failure to provide assistance "has occasioned more dissatisfaction and coldness towards the League amongst wheelmen than anything else," and that the legal victories to date were the result of "large contribution of funds for the litigation by one of the League's best friends." In April the L.A.W. capitulated and started to make limited funds available to the state divisions for the legal needs of both members and non-members.
29. Mason, *The League of American Wheelmen and the Good-Roads Movement*, 117; 126.
30. Letter from James Dunn to Roy Stone, 27 July 1892, RG30.1.2/2 BPR Papers, Archives II.
31. Andrew Ritchie, *Major Taylor: The Extraordinary Career of a Champion Bicycle Racer* (San Francisco: Bicycle Books, 1988), 38–39; citing *Bicycling World*, 3 June 1892.
32. *Wheel and Cycle Trades Review* (27 November 1891): 435; *Bicycling World and L.A.W. Bulletin* (3 June 1892): 1065; *Bicycling World and L.A.W. Bulletin* (8 July 1892): 1272.
33. "Meeting of the National Assembly," *American Athlete and Cycle Trades Review* 11, 8 (24 February 1893): 159.
34. Ritchie, *Major Taylor*, 38, citing *Bearings*, 9 March 1894.
35. "Killed by Negroes," *Cycle Age and Trade Review* 20 (23 November 1899): 107.
36. Elliott, "The League of American Wheelmen," 284.
37. *American Athlete and Cycle Trades Review* 5, 38 (22 November 1889): 576; "The League and Politics," *American Athlete and Cycle Trades Review* 5, 36 (8 November 1889): 547.
38. Elliott, "The League of American Wheelmen," 286.
39. Mason, *The League of American Wheelmen and the Good-Roads Movement*, 217.

40. "News of the Cyclers," *New York Times*, 5 June 1898; "Gossip of the Cyclers," *New York Times*, 28 August 1898; Mason, *The League of American Wheelmen and the Good-Roads Movement*, 217.
41. Mason, *The League of American Wheelmen and the Good-Roads Movement*, 127. At a convention in Washington four months later, Potter did not appear.
42. "Col. Burdett's Tragic End," *Bicycling World*, 44, 22 (27 February 1902): 564. (Burdett died in a New York hotel fire); Letter from Albert A. Pope to Roy Stone, 1 January 1893, RG30.1.2/80 BPR Papers, Archives II; Roy Stone, "The Necessity of Congressional Action in Road Improvement," *Office of Road Improvement Bulletin Number 25* (Washington: Government Printing Office, 1902), 23.
43. Richard F. Weingroff, *Portrait of a General: General Roy Stone* (Unpublished Manuscript, Federal Highway Administration, U.S. Department of Transportation, 2003), 39; Letter from Albert A. Pope to Roy Stone, 1 January 1893, RG30.1.2/80 BPR Papers, Archives II.
44. Rep. Phillip S. Post to Roy Stone, 28 January 1893, RG30.1.2/2 BPR Papers, Archives II; Undated note from Henry Alvord to Roy Stone, [ca. February 1893], RG30.1.2 Box 31 Papers, Archives II; Charles Johnson to Roy Stone, 24 February 1893, RG30.1.2/2 BPR Papers, Archives II. Stone commented about his relations with Pope in a 1903 speech, after he retired: Weingroff, *Portrait of a General*, 65.
45. Weingroff, *Portrait of a General*, 42; Letter from J. Sterling Morton to Roy Stone, date unknown [ca. October 1893], RG30.1.2/2 Box 66 BPR Papers, Archives II.
46. William Stull Holt, *The Bureau of Public Roads: Its History, Activities, and Organization* (Baltimore: Institute for Government Research Service, 1923), 7. Holt is quoting a letter from Morton to Stone dated 3 October 1893.
47. Weingroff, *Portrait of a General*, 43.
48. Pope, *The Movement for Better Roads*, 27.
49. Letter from Senator Charles S. Manderson to Roy Stone, 12 May 1893, RG30.1.2 Box 31 BPR Papers, Archives II.
50. Holt, *The Bureau of Public Roads*, 9. After $10,000 in funding in FY 1894 and 1895, the allocation was cut back to $8,000 for the rest of the decade before being increased to $14,000 in FY 1901.
51. Kron, *Ten Thousand Miles on a Bicycle*, 619.
52. Lisa, "Bicyclists and Bureaucrats," 373–398; Letter from Sterling Elliot to Roy Stone, 13 February 1895, RG30.1.2/2 BPR Papers, Archives II. The league did briefly combine *Good Roads* and the *Bulletin* into a single publication after 1895.
53. Letter from Sterling Elliott to Roy Stone, 19 February 1896, RG30.1.2/2 BPR Papers, Archives II.
54. Letter from Otto Dorner to Roy Stone, 1 November 1896, RG30.1.2/2 BPR Papers, Archives II.
55. Lisa, "Bicyclists and Bureaucrats," 393; Letter from Otto Dorner to Roy Stone, 22 September 1897, RG30.1.2/2 BPR Papers, Archives II.
56. Mason, *The League of American Wheelmen and the Good-Roads Movement*, 202.
57. Lisa, "Bicyclists and Bureaucrats," 395. Although the Department of Agriculture and the Post Office did not reach a formal agreement until 1906, they were working together on the RFD-roads issue as early as 1896: Mason, *The League of American Wheelmen and the Good-Roads Movement*, 207.

58. Weingroff, *Portrait of a General*, 65.
59. Weingroff, *Portrait of a General*, 62.
60. Philip G. Hubert, Jr., "The Wheel of To-Day," *Scribner's Magazine* 17, 6 (18 June 1895): 692–702.
61. Mark H. Rose, *Interstate: Express Highway Politics, 1939–1989* (Knoxville: University of Tennessee Press, 1990), 39–50.
62. Mason, *The League of American Wheelmen and the Good-Roads Movement*, 241.

## Chapter 7

1. Letter from F. Ed. Spooner, general manager, National Cycle News Bureau, to Arthur L. Garford, 14 November 1895, Box 1, File 4, Arthur Garford Collection (MSS 6), Ohio Historical Society, Columbus.
2. "The New Home of the Columbias," *Boston Post*, 17 March 1892.
3. Letter from George Pope to David J. Post, 21 January 1892, Pope/Hartford Papers, Archives and Genealogical Unit, Connecticut State Library, Hartford.
4. Letters from George Pope to David J. Post, 10 April 1892 (first letter this date) and 10 April 1892 (second letter this date), Pope/Hartford Papers, CSL.
5. Letter from Roger B. McMullen to Arthur L. Garford, 4 October 1895, Box 1, File 4, Arthur L. Garford Papers, OHS.
6. Letter from George Pope to David J. Post, 31 December 1894, Pope/Hartford Papers, CSL.
7. Letter from George Pope to David J. Post, 18 April 1891, Pope/Hartford Papers, CSL; "The Hartford Cycle Co.'s New Building," *American Athlete and Cycle Trades Review* 7, 23 (4 December 1891): 480.
8. Letter from George Pope to David J. Post, 15 May 1891, Pope/Hartford Papers, CSL.
9. Letter from George Pope to David J. Post, 21 January 1892, Pope/Hartford Papers, CSL.
10. Norman Leslie Dunham, *The Bicycle Era in America* (Ph.D. dissertation, Harvard University, 1957), *passim*. The original source of Wardrop's information is apparently a newspaper article, "With the Wheelmen," *Detroit Free Press* (3 April 1898).
11. Charles E. Pratt, "The Tariff Question," *The Wheelman* 1, 1 (October 1882): 64; "A Plea for Fair Trade: Speech of Col. Albert A. Pope Before the Tariff Commission," *The Wheelman* 1, 1 (October 1882): 63; Paul Wolman, *Most Favored Nation: The Republican Revisionists and U. S. Tariff Policy, 1897–1912* (Chapel Hill: University of North Carolina Press, 1992), 2.
12. Roger Lloyd-Jones and M. J. Lewis, *Raleigh and the British Bicycle Industry: An Economic and Industrial History, 1870–1960* (Aldershot: Ashgate, 2000), 60; George F. Parker, "American Bicycles in England," *North American Review* 163, 481 (December 1896): 688–95.
13. "A Big Manufacturing Deal," *American Athlete and Cycle Trades Review* 7, 22 (27 November 1891): 462.
14. Samuel Rezneck, "Unemployment, Unrest and Relief in the United States During the Depression of 1893–1897," *Journal of Political Economy*, 4 (August 1953): 324–45.
15. *Bradstreet's* 21 (12 August 1893): 502.
16. George Pope to David J. Post, 18 January 1892, George Pope to David J. Post, 22 January 1892, both Pope/Hartford Papers, CSL.
17. George Pope to David J. Post, 24 January 1893, Pope/Hartford Papers, CSL. For a complete and incisive discussion of batch building versus mass production, see Philip Scranton, *Endless Novelty: Specialty Production and American Industrialization, 1865–1925* (Princeton: Princeton University Press, 1997).
18. George Pope to David J. Post, 24 January 1893, Pope/Hartford Papers, CSL.
19. Hughes a major dealer: George Pope to David J. Post, 31 January 1893, Pope/Hartford Papers, CSL; quote from: George Pope to David J. Post, 24 January 1893, Pope/Hartford Papers, CSL.
20. George Pope to David J. Post, 26 January 1893, Pope/Hartford papers, CSL.
21. Arthur E. Pattison to David J. Post, 13 December 1894, Pope/Hartford Papers, CSL.
22. George Pope to David J. Post, 31 January 1893, Pope/Hartford Papers, CSL.
23. Hugh Dolnar, "Bicycle Tools, Pt. XVII," *American Machinist*, 19, 8 (February 27, 1896): 232.
24. This is from a fragment of a confidential report prepared by Arthur Garford for the directors of the Cleveland Machine Screw Company, August 1901. Box 7, File 7, Arthur L. Garford Papers, OHS.
25. One hundred dollar bicycle: Robert A. Smith, *The Social History of the Bicycle* (New York, American Heritage Press, 1972): 30. Smith is citing the *Minneapolis Tribune* of 12 June 1896. Most marketable commodity: "Point of View," *Scribner's Monthly*, 19, 6 (June 1896): 783.
26. P. J. Boore, *The Seamless Story* (Los Angeles: Commonwealth, 1951), 36–38; Victor Clark, *The History of Manufacturers in the United States* (Cleveland: Carnegie Institution, 1929), II, 347. The difference between "standard" and "specialty" or "high-speed" steel was sometimes as much a political or legal issue as a technical one: Wolman, *Most Favored Nation*, 161.
27. Boore, *The Seamless Story*, 38; Clark, *The History of Manufacturers in the United States*, 347. For an excellent description of the die-and-mandrel process (sometimes called the "Kellogg" process), see "An American Bicycle Manufactory," *Engineering* 64 (16 July 1897): 66.
28. Andrew Millward, *Factors Contributing to the Sustained Success of the U.K. Cycle Industry, 1870–1939* (Doctoral thesis, University of Birmingham, October 1999), Section 1.2.3. Millward is citing *The Cycle Trader*, 15 July 1896: 56.
29. George Pope to David J. Post, 12 January 1891, Pope/Hartford Papers, CSL.
30. George Pope to David J. Post, 26 January 1891, Pope/Hartford Papers, CSL.
31. George Pope to David J. Post, 2 February 1891, Pope/Hartford Papers, CSL.
32. Lloyd-Jones and Lewis, *Raleigh and the British Bicycle Industry*, 60–62.
33. Parker, "American Bicycles in England," 689; Lloyd-Jones and Lewis, *Raleigh and the British Bicycle Industry*, 60–62.
34. "H. A. Lozier Dead," *Bicycling World* 47, 9 (30 May 1903):1; Boore, *The Seamless Story*, 35–37. "Looking Backward Twenty Five Years and Beyond," *Bicycling World* 46, 12 (18 December 1902): 305. Some stories later said that it was Colonel Pope who infiltrated the British factory. This is impossible, as by the summer of 1890 Pope would have been instantly recognized. The Yost tale appears to have originated with an undated story in the *Pittsburgh Dispatch* that was cited in the *American Iron and Steel Association Bulletin* (20 November 1896): 257. The muddled story probably originated with Pope's visit to England in the summer of 1891 to

try to persuade either Credenda or the Weldless Steel Tube Company to set up an American plant for him. Because he was simultaneously a major investor in the Shelby tube factory, Pope would have had good reason to keep such a mission quiet. Boore, *The Seamless Story*, 35, citing *The Wheel*, 7 August 1891.

35. Boore, *The Seamless Story*, 43; "H. A. Lozier Dead," 1.

36. Boore, *The Seamless Story*, 36; "Another Enterprise: A Large Factory to Go Up," *Hartford Times*, 1 June 1892; "Booming Hartford," *New York Sporting Times* (25 June 1892); "Colonel Pope's Homes," *Hartford Post*, 22 May 1893; "Col. Pope's Plans for Homes for Workingmen Discussed," *Hartford Courant*, 25 June 1892, all Pope Scrapbooks, CHS.

37. "The Manufacture of Bicycle Tubing," *Iron Age* 54 (7 January 1897): 1.

38. "Suggestions for Shelby Tube Co. Management," [28 May 1893] Pope Letterbook, Vol. 1: 22, Connecticut Historical Society, Hartford; "D.L. Cockley Dead," *Bicycling World* 44, 14 (2 January 1902): 299; Boore, *The Seamless Story*, 43.

39. "Hayden Eames, 74, An Industrialist," *New York Times*, 25 November 1938; "Harold Hayden Eames," a biographical sketch prepared by Hermann F. Cuntz for Henry Cave, dated 12 October 1940. Box 3, File 1, Henry Cave Collection, National Automotive History Collection, Detroit Public Library.

40. Hiram Percy Maxim, *Horseless Carriage Days* (New York: Harper Brothers, 1936), 28.

41. Letter from George Pope to David J. Post, 25 May 1891, Pope/Hartford Papers, CSL.

42. Letter from Hermann F. Cuntz to Charles B. King, 11 August 1936, Charles B. King Collection, National Automotive History Collection, Detroit Public Library; *Greer's Hartford Directory* for the years 1894–95 and 1895–96.

43. "Testing the Parts of a Modern Bicycle," *Scientific American* 75 (11 July 1896): 1–6; "An American Bicycle Manufactory": 66; Leonard Waldo, "The American Bicycle: Its Theory and Practice of Construction," *Engineering* 64 (3 December 1897): 679.

44. "The Manufacture of Bicycle Tubing, Part 2," *Iron Age* 54 (14 January 1897): 1–5; Sara E. Wermiel, *The Fireproof Building: Technology and Public Safety in the Nineteenth-Century American City* (Baltimore: Johns Hopkins University Press, 2001), 151–52.

45. When the Columbia factory was sold to the American Bicycle Company in 1899, the Department of Tests building was leased to Henry Souther, who continued as an independent consultant. The "Department of Tests" building was torn down about 1912 to make room for a factory expansion and Souther (and apparently the Emery Machine) moved to a new building on Laurel Street, where the Henry Souther Company continued to do business until the late 1960s or early '70s, when it then moved out of town. Records of the Henry Souther Engineering Company, MS 9246, Archives Division, Connecticut State Library, Hartford, CT.

46. "An American Bicycle Manufactory," 66; "The Manufacture of Bicycle Tubing," 3.

47. "Suggestions for Shelby Tube Co. Management," May 28, 1893, Pope Letterbooks, CHS; "Colonel Cockley Dead," 299; Boore, *The Seamless Story*, 35–55.

48. Wolman, *Most Favored Nation*, 19, 63.

49. "Seamless Steel Tubes," *Hartford Daily*, 15 September 1894, Pope Scrapbooks, CHS.

50. "A New Corporation," *Hartford Courant*, 20 September 1894, Pope Scrapbooks, CHS; Boore, *The Seamless Story*, 44; *American Wheelman* (25 October 1894), Pope Scrapbooks, CHS.

51. "The Tube Mill of the United States Projectile Company," *Iron Age*, 59 (18 March 1897): 1–3. The U.S. Projectile process was still under development when Eames was a naval inspector in the early 1890s, and he probably saw it there.

52. "The Manufacture of Bicycle Tubing, Part 2," 1–5; Boore, *The Seamless Story*, 75; "Testing the Parts of the Modern Bicycle," 1, 23; "The Manufacture of Bicycle Tubing," 1–6; "An American Bicycle Manufactory," 66;"The American Bicycle: Its Theory and Practice of Construction," 679.

53. *Greer's Hartford Directory*, 1895–96. Donald R. Hoke, *Ingenious Yankees: The Rise of the American System of Manufacturers* (New York: Columbia University Press, 1990), 22–23, 27–28.

54. Arthur Roy Du Cros, *Wheels of Fortune* (London: Chapman & Hall, 1938), Chapter 2; Walter E. Burton, *The Story of Tire Beads and Tires* (New York: National-Standard Co., 1954), 9–16; 29.

55. G. Donald Adams, *Collecting and Restoring Antique Bicycles* (Orchard Park, NY: Pedaling History Museum, 2nd ed., 1996), 203.

56. *Greer's Hartford Directory*, 1882–83; Letter from George Pope to David J. Post, 4 March 1891, Pope/Hartford Papers, CSL.

57. "Pope's First Pneumatics," *Bicycling World*, 44, 15 (9 January 1902): 357.

58. "A Chat with E. W. Pope," *Wheel* (15 February 1900), Pope Scrapbooks, CHS; Cleveland Moffett, "A Visit to the Hartford Rubber Works." The latter is part of the *Marvels of Bicycle Making* booklet at the Warshaw Business Collection, Smithsonian Archives, National Museum of American History, Washington, D.C. Pardon W. Tillinghast patented his "single tube" tire in 1893 (Burton, *The Story of Tire Beads and Tires*, 124), but Pope employees and John Gray were working on the manufacture and repair of the tire as early as fall 1891.

59. Frank W. Schwinn, *1942 Personal Notes on the Bicycle Industry* (Unpublished manuscript, Bicycle Museum of America, 1993), 18. The Bicycle Museum of America in Chicago is no longer in operation.

60. Letter from George Pope to David J. Post, 12 January 1892, Pope/ Hartford Papers, CSL.

61. Letter from George Pope to David J. Post, 13 January 1892, Pope/ Hartford Papers, CSL.

62. "The Famous Hose-Pipe and a Method of Repairing Same," *American Athlete and Cycle Trades Review* 11, 11 (17 March 1893): 222.

63. Letter from George Pope to David J. Post, 9 January 1892, Pope/Hartford letters, CSL.

64. "The Famous Hose-Pipe," 222.

65. *1942 Personal Notes on the Bicycle Industry*, 18.

66. Letter from George Pope to David J. Post, 4 February 1892, Pope/ Hartford Papers, CSL.

67. "Colonel Pope Controls," *Hartford Courant*, 29 August 1892, Pope Scrapbooks, CHS; *Greer's Hartford Directory* for the years 1892–93 and 1893–94.

68. Burton, *The Story of Tires and Tire Beads*, 122; Adams, *Collecting and Restoring Antique Bicycles*, 144.

69. Burton, *The Story of Tires and Tire Beads*, 122–24. By 1897 the Hartford Rubber Works was manufacturing both the G&J and Dunlop tires under license: Moffett, *Marvels of Bicycle Making*, n.p.

70. "The Manufacture of Sewing Machines," *Scientific American* 42, 12 (20 March 1880): 181; "Die for Forging Bicycle-Head Blanks," United States Patent No. 350,981, 13 December 1881, to Henry T. Russell, of Hartford, Connecticut, Assignor to the Pope Mfg. Co.

71. Fred H. Colvin, *60 Years with Men and Machines* (New York: McGraw-Hill, 1947), 85.

72. Hugh Dolnar, "Cycle Stampings," *American Machinist* 19 (17 December 1896): 1163; the Western Wheel Works Catalog is reproduced in Jay Pridmore and Jim Hurd, *The American Bicycle* (Osceola: Motorbooks International, 1995), 58.

73. Willard S. Mattox, "American Bicycle Fittings and Machinery in England," *Iron Age* 62 (3 November 1898): 8.

74. Arnold, "Cycle Stampings," 1163; Hugh Dolnar, "Press and Die Work on Bicycles," *American Machinist* 19, 48 (26 November 1896): 1097; David A. Hounshell, *From American System to Mass Production, 1800–1932* (Baltimore: Johns Hopkins University Press, 1984), 200–01. Some who have not closely read Hounshell believe that he states that electric welding was used to assemble bicycle frames starting in the 1890s. This is erroneous. Hounshell correctly explains that welding was used to fabricate the stamped frame joining lugs and bottom bracket shells used to braze together bicycle frames, not to assemble the frames themselves.

75. Letter from George Pope to David J. Post, 4 March 1891, Pope/Hartford Papers, CSL; Columbia and Hartford Cycle Catalogs for 1889, 1891, 1893, 1895.

76. Mattox, "American Bicycle Fittings and Machinery in England," 8.

77. Hugh Dolnar, "Bicycle Tools XI," *American Machinist* 19, 1 (2 January 1896): 1.

78. Hugh Dolnar, "Bicycle Tools I," *American Machinist* 18, 40 (10 October 1895): 781–82; "Bicycle Tools XII," *American Machinist* 19, 2 (9 January 1896): 50–51.

79. Hugh Dolnar, "Bicycle Tools XII," *American Machinist* 19, 2 (9 January 1896): 50–51.

80. "Chaos of Cycle Dimensions," *Cycle Age and Trade Review* 21 (25 August 1898): 461.

81. "Garford, Arthur Lovett," *The Automobile Industry: 1896–1920*, George S. May, ed. (New York: Facts on File, 1990); Letter from Arthur L. Garford to Edwin Oliver, 2 November 1896, Box 1, File 5, Arthur L. Garford Papers, OHS; Columbia Bicycle Catalogs for 1896 and 1898.

82. Hugh Dolnar, "Bicycle Tools XXXI," *American Machinist* 19, 32 (24 September 1896): 896.

83. *Twelfth Census of the United States [1900], Manufacturing Industries, Part 3, Special Reports, Bicycle and Tricycles*, by Axel Josephson, 335.

84. Hugh Dolnar, "Bicycle Tools XXVI," *American Machinist* 19, 23 (25 June 1896): 617.

85. Harry Braverman, *Labor and Monopoly Capital* (New York: Monthly Review Press, 1974); Peter Drucker, *The Practice of Management* (New York: Perennial Library, 1986 [1954]).

86. Charles D. Wrege and Ronald G. Greenwood, *Frederick W. Taylor: The Father of Scientific Management* (Homewood, IL: Business One Irwin, 1991), 4.

87. Later in life, Taylor's views became sharply antilabor. "Pay workers too much," he wrote author Upton Sinclair in 1911, and they would "work irregularly and tend to become shiftless, extravagant and dissipated." Robert Kanigel, *The One Best Way: Frederick Winslow Taylor and the Enigma of Efficiency* (New York: Viking, 1997), 466. 200-pound chunk of metal: Kanigel, *The One Best Way*, 166.

88. "How Balls Are Made," *Bearings*, 9, 1 (2 February 1894): 4.

89. Charles D. Wrenge and Ronald Greenwood, "Frederick W. Taylor and Industrial Espionage, 1895–1897," *Business and Economic History: Papers Presented at the Thirty-Second Annual Meeting of the Business History Conference*, ed. Jeremy Atack (Champaign: University of Illinois Press, 1987), 184.

90. Letter from Frederick W. Taylor to George Weymouth, 20 April 1895, File 43, Frederick W. Taylor Collection, Stevens Institute, Hoboken.

91. *Simonds Rolling Machine Company v. Pope Manufacturing Company*, 62 N.E. 467, 468 (Mass. 1902).

92. Frederick W. Taylor to Coleman Sellers, 21 May 1897, File 43, FWT Collection, Stevens.

93. Newcomb Carlton to Frederick W. Taylor, November 22, 1895, File 41, FWT Collection, Stevens.

94. Letters from W. A. Willard to Frederick W. Taylor, July 3, 1895 (2 letters), FWT Collection, Stevens; Kanigel, *The One Best Way*, 287–88.

95. Hugh Dolnar, "Bicycle Tools XXVI," *American Machinist* 19, 23 (25 June 1896): 617–18. Pope and Simonds entered into a settlement agreement on 29 May 1896, but the *American Machinist* article suggests that the reporter was at the factory several weeks before the settlement. Moreover, in the settlement Pope agreed to pay a royalty to Simonds for the use of the existing ball-making machine in the factory, not to buy boxes of balls from Simonds. Affidavit of Ernest Kendall, 4 December 1895, File 41, FWT Collection, Stevens. "I worked for over two years in making dies for a rolling machine used in rolling bicycle balls.... The room in which I worked is situated adjoining the ball-rolling room.... The whole of the lower floor of a small building next to the Park River was used entirely for the ball bearing plant."

96. Letter from Albert A. Pope to David J. Post, 24 July 1890, Pope/Hartford Papers, CHS.

97. "Testimony of Ernest A.V. Kendall," 4 December 1895; "Affidavit of E.A.V. Kendall," 4 December 1895, File 43, FWT Taylor Collection, Stevens; *Simonds v. Pope*, 62 N.E. 467; Letter from Treasurer's Office, Simonds Rolling Machine Company to Frederick Taylor, 1 January 1896, File 43, FWT Collection, Stevens.

98. Letter from Frederick W. Taylor to Alfred Bowditch, 3 August 1898, File 43, FWT Collection, Stevens.

99. Letter from H.S. Shadbolt to Frederick W. Taylor, 22 September 1895, File 43, FWT Collection, Stevens.

100. Letter from Frederick Taylor to H.S. Shadbolt, 27 May 1897, File 43, FWT Collection, Stevens.

101. Letter from Coleman Sellers to Frederick W. Taylor, 12 May 1897; letter from Coleman Sellers to Frederick W. Taylor, 7 June 1897, letter from Frederick W. Taylor to Coleman Sellers, 19 May 1897, all File 43, FWT Collection, Stevens; *Simonds v. Pope*, 62 N.E. 467, 468.

102. Letter from H.S. Shadbolt to Frederick W. Taylor, 27 May 1897; letter from Frederick Taylor to H.S. Shadbolt, 28 May 1897, File 43 FWT Collection, Stevens.

103. Wrenge and Greenwood, "Frederick W. Taylor

and Industrial Espionage, 1895–1897," 191; Alfred Bowditch to Frederick W. Taylor, 14 June 1898, File 41, FWT Collection, Stevens. The "big five": Pope, Western, Overman, Gormully & Jeffery, and Lozier.

## Chapter 8

1. John B. Rae, "The Electric Vehicle Company: A Monopoly That Missed," *Business History Review* 29 (December 1955): 298–311.

2. David A. Kirsch and Gijs P. A. Mom, "Visions of Transportation: The EVC and the Transition from Service- to Product-Based Mobility," *Business History Review* 76, 1 (Spring 2002): 75–110.

3. Hiram Percy Maxim, *A Genius in the Family* (New York: Harper Brothers, 1936); "Maxim, Hiram Percy," *The Automobile Industry, 1890–1920*, George S. May, ed. (New York: Facts on File, 1990); Manuscript biography of Harold Hayden Eames by Hermann Cuntz, 12 October 1940, Henry Cave Collection, Box 3, File 1, National Automotive History Collection, Detroit Public Library.

4. Hiram Percy Maxim, *Horseless Carriage Days* (New York: Harper Brothers, 1938), 1.

5. Ibid., 94.

6. Ibid., 47–48.

7. Hermann Cuntz, "Hartford, the Birthplace of the Automobile, Part 1," *Hartford Times* (17 September 1947).

8. Maxim, *Horseless Carriage Days*, 48–49.

9. "The Chicago Motocycle Contest," *American Machinist* 18 (19 December 1895): 1009–1011; Maxim, *Horseless Carriage Days*, 51–55; Gijs Mom, *Electric Vehicle: Technology and Expectations in the Automobile Age* (Baltimore: Johns Hopkins University Press, 2004), 79; David A. Kirsch, *The Electric Vehicle and the Burden of History* (New Brunswick: Rutgers University Press, 2000), 34–35.

10. Maxim, *Horseless Carriage Days*, 54–55.

11. Allan Nevins, *Ford: The Man, the Times, and the Machine* (New York: Scribner's, 1954); William Greenleaf, *Monopoly on Wheels: Henry Ford and the Selden Automobile Patent* (Detroit: Wayne State University Press, 1961). Although the Selden patent dispute was recognized as a historical milestone as early as 1916 (see James Rood Doolittle, *The Romance of the Automobile Industry* [New York: Klebold Press, 1916]), Nevins and Greenleaf appear to be the first to claim that the use of the patent was a deliberate attempt to monopolize the early automobile industry.

12. Rae, "The Electric Vehicle Company."

13. Greenleaf, *Monopoly on Wheels*. To illustrate how all the various permutations of the Pope-EVC story eventually trace their way back to Nevins and Greenleaf, see Footnote 1 of Kirsch and Mom, "Visions of Transportation."

14. Letter from Hermann F. Cuntz to Charles B. King, 11 August 1936, Charles King Collection, National Automotive History Collection, Detroit Public Library.

15. Maxim, *Horseless Carriage Days*, 165.

16. "Hayden Eames, 74, an Industrialist," *New York Times* (25 November 1938); "Hiram Percy Maxim," 328.

17. "Electric Cycles at the World's Fair," *American Athlete and Cycle Trades Review* 10, 9 (19 August 1892): 135. The Putnam electric: letter from Hermann F. Cuntz to Charles B. King, 11 August 1936, King Collection, NAHC; Philip G. Hubert, "The Bicycle: The Wheel of To-Day," *Scribner's Magazine* 17, 6 (18 June 1895): 692–702. Pope was interviewed at the New York Cycle Show the previous January.

18. Louis P. Hagar, *History of the West End Street Railway Company* (Boston: Louis P. Hagar, 1892), 24; Brian J. Cudahy, *Cash, Tokens, and Transfers: A History of Mass Transit in America* (New York: Fordham University Press, 1990), 45–46.

19. Mark D. Hirsch, *William C. Whitney: Modern Warwick* (Hamden, CT: Archon, 1969 [1948]), 225, 442–44.

20. Kirsch, *The Electric Vehicle and the Burden of History*, 33; "A Powerful Storage Battery Combination," *Electrical Review* 25 (12 December 1894): 298; Hirsch, *William C. Whitney: Modern Warwick*, 440. Hirsch says Whitney's Exide investment was "in or about" 1896, and that it was about a million dollars in size, but the late 1894–early 1895 date makes more sense given the rapid escalation of the firm during this period, and is consistent with the information in the *Electrical Review* article.

21. John B. Rae, *American Automobile Manufacturers: The First Forty Years* (Philadelphia: Chilton, 1959), 71; *Automobile* 18, 18 (30 April 1908): 609.

22. Henry Cave, "Hartford, The Incubator of the Automobile Industry," *Old Timers News* 2, 2 (April 1944): 24–33; Henry Cave, "The Start of the U.S. Automobile Industry in Hartford, Connecticut," *Hartford's Golden Automobile Jubilee: An Exhibition of Early Model Cars, September 17, 1947*. Exhibit catalog in the library of the National Museum of American History, Smithsonian Exhibition, Washington D.C.

23. Maxim, *Horseless Carriage Days*, 51; Mom, *Electric Vehicle: Technology and Expectations in the Automobile Age*, 27.

24. Letter from Henry Souther to David Becroft, 10 December 1915, David Becroft Collection, National Automotive History Collection, Detroit Public Library.

25. "The Electric Wagon: Address Delivered by Hayden Eames Before the Association of Electric Vehicle Manufacturers," *Power Wagon* 2 (April 1907): 11–12.

26. Maxim, *Horseless Carriage Days*, 50.

27. Letter from Hermann F. Cuntz to Charles B. King, 11 August 1936. King Collection, NAHC.

28. Kirsch, *The Electric Vehicle and the Burden of History*, 35; "Electric Motor-Cab Service in New York, Parts I & II," *Electrical World* 30, 7 & 8 (14 August 1897): 183–186; (21 August 1897): 213–216; Hirsch, *William C. Whitney: Modern Warwick*, 440.

29. Mom, *Electric Vehicle: Technology and Expectations in the Automobile Age*, 22; Hermann Cuntz, *Story of the Selden Case and Hartford*. Manuscript dated 11 September 1940, Cave Collection, NAHC.

30. Hermann Cuntz, "Hartford, the Birthplace of the Automobile, Part 2," *Hartford Times*, 18 September 1947; Kirsch and Mom, "Visions of Transportation," Footnote 53; Mom, *Electric Vehicle: Technology and Expectations in the Automobile Age*, 322, footnote 37; Letter from W. H. Johnson to Electric Vehicle Company New York Office, 24 November 1899, Frank C. Armstrong Collection, Acc. 1750, Box 5, Folder 7 (New Jersey Electric Vehicle Transportation Co. Correspondence, 1899–1900) Benson Ford Research Center, Dearborn, Michigan.

31. Maxim, *Horseless Carriage Days*, 105. This is not to say that Maxim was not right: a contemporary account states that "Aside from providing accommoda-

tions for the batteries and controller, the carriage builders' ideas have been adhered to as much as possible. This is indeed a provision from a commercial point of view. The users of carriages and horses are a conservative class and scrupulously avoid anything that suggests a departure from the appearances to which they are accustomed": "The Manufacture of Electric Automobiles," *Electrical World and Engineer* 35, 2 (13 January 1900): 53–56; Mom, *Electric Vehicle: Technology and Expectations in the Automobile Age*, 18.

32. "The Manufacture of Electric Automobiles," *Electrical World and Engineer* 35, 2 (13 January 1900): 53–56.

33. Maxim, *Horseless Carriage Days*, 74.

34. Maxim, *Horseless Carriage Days*, 103; Cuntz, "Biography of Harold Hayden Eames," 2; Cuntz, "Hartford, the Birthplace of the Automobile"; *Greer's Hartford Directory* for years 1895–96 through 1898–99; letter from George Pope to David J. Post, 31 December 1894, Pope/Hartford Papers, History and Genealogy Division, Connecticut State Library, Hartford. George reported that a man named Carlisle had come over from the Columbia factory "practically as my lieutenant," and that he "will have general charge of pushing the work," a task formerly ascribed to Harry Pope. "Historical Review of the Prominent Companies," *Cycle Age and Trade Review* 23 (7 September 1899): 464.

35. Letter from Harry M. Pope to Mrs. W. F. Doyle, 4 July 1936, reproduced in Ray M. Smith, *The Story of Pope's Barrels* (Harrisburg: Stackpole Books, 1960), 25–26; letter from Harry M. Pope to William V. Lowe, 7 October 1895, reproduced in Gerald O. Kelver, *Respectfully Yours, H. M. Pope* (Fort Collins: Robinson Press, 1976), 16.

36. Maxim, *Horseless Carriage Days*, 74; Cuntz, "Hartford, the Birthplace of the Automobile"; Greenleaf, *Monopoly on Wheels*, 68. Greenleaf is citing articles in the *Detroit News-Tribune*, 4 June 1899, and the *Detroit Journal*, 7 August 1900. "Lead Cab Activity in Boston," *Horseless Age* 5, 17 (24 January 1900): 13; "Electric Automobiles in Boston," *Electrical World and Engineer* 35, 24 (16 June 1900): 895–96; "Electrical Automobiles in New England," *Electrical World and Engineer* 37, 5 (19 January 1901): 136–37.

37. Cuntz, "Biography of Harold Hayden Eames"; Kirsch, *The Electric Vehicle and the Burden of History*, 63.

38. "Central Station of the Electric Vehicle Company," *Horseless Age* 3 (September 1898): 9–17; "New York's Electric Cab Service," *American Electrician* 10, 9 (September 1898): 409–418; Kirsch, *The Electric Vehicle and the Burden of History*, 43.

39. Letter from George Herbert Condict to William F. D. Crane, October 11 1898, Box 1, File 2; letter from George Herbert Condict to W. H. Johnson (EVC New York), 27 November 1899, Box 2, File 8; Letter from George Herbert Condict to W. H. Johnson (EVC New York), 27 November 1899, Box 2, File 8, William F. D. Crane Collection (MS 1092), New Jersey Historical Society, Newark, NJ; W. H. Palmer, "The Storage Battery in the Commercial Operation of Electric Automotives," *Electrical World* 39 (12 April 1902): 646.

40. Kirsch, *The Electric Vehicle and the Burden of History*, 48; Cuntz, "Hartford, Birthplace of the Automobile, Part 2"; Mom, *Electric Vehicle: Technology and Expectations in the Automobile Age*, 85; "We Draw the Line," *Horseless Age* 5, 19 (7 February 1900): 9–13.

41. Geoffery Williamson, *Wheels Within Wheels: The Story of the Starleys of Coventry* (London: Geoffrey Bles, 1968), 116; Roger Lloyd-Jones and M.J. Lewis, *Raleigh and the British Bicycle Industry* (Aldershot: Aldgate, 2000), 26–31; A. E. Harrison, "Joint-Stock Company Flotation in the Cycle, Motor-Vehicle and Related Industries, 1882–1914," *Business History* 23, 3 (July 1981): 165–89.

42. "Mr. Hooley a Bankrupt," *New York Times*, 9 June 1898; "High Price for Influence," *New York Times*, 3 November 1898.

43. Mom, *Electric Vehicle: Technology and Expectations in the Automobile Age*, 85; "We Draw the Line," 9–13

44. Mark D. Hirsch, *William C. Whitney: Modern Warwick*, 17–25; Virginia G. Drachman, *Hospital with a Heart: Women Doctors and the Paradox of Separatism at the New England Hospital, 1862–1969* (Ithaca: Cornell University Press, 1984), Passim.

45. Cuntz, "Hartford the Birthplace of Automobile Industry, Part 2"; Memo from Albert A. Pope to William C. Whitney, 4 April 1899, Container 137, William C. Whitney Papers, Manuscripts Division, Library of Congress; "Will Manufacture Automobiles," *New York World Herald*, 27 April 1899, Pope Scrapbooks, CHS. In 1940, Cuntz recalled the date of the big Hartford meeting as 12 April: Cuntz, "The Story of the Selden Case and Hartford." This is consistent with Pope's filing of incorporation papers for the motor carriage division a week later: "Colonel Pope and Automobiles," *Electrical Review* (19 April 1899), Pope Scrapbooks, CHS.

46. Cuntz, "Hartford the Birthplace of Automobile Industry"; Cuntz, "The Story of the Selden Case and Hartford"; Minutes of Electric Vehicle Company Executive Committee, 25 July 1899, Box 1, File 6, Frank C. Armstrong Collection, Ford Center.

47. Letter from George Herbert Condict to W. H. Johnson (EVC New York), 27 November 1899, Box 2, File 8, William F. D. Crane Papers, NJHS.

48. The drafts of these contracts are in Box 2, File 3 (Westinghouse) and Box 2, File 4 (Studebaker) of the William F. D. Crane Papers, NJHS. "Tools in 42nd Street Shop on October 4th, 1899," Box 2, File 8, William F. D. Crane Papers, NJHS. "The Transfer of the 42nd Street Shop," Box 2, File 8, William F. D. Crane Papers, NJHS; "Minutes of Electric Vehicle Company Executive Committee, 26 December 1899," Box 1, File 6, Frank C. Armstrong Collection, Ford Center. Letter from George Herbert Condict to W. H. Johnson (EVC New York), 27 November 1899, Box 2, File 8, William F. D. Crane Papers, NJHS.

49. Letter from J. M. Hill to W. H. Johnson (EVC New York), 24 November 1899, Box 5, File 7, Frank C. Armstrong Collection, Ford Center.

50. "The Manufacture of Electric Automobiles," *Electrical World and Engineer* 35, 2 (13 January 1900): 53–56. Letter from J. M. Hill to W. H. Johnson (EVC New York), 24 November 1899, Box 5, File 7, Frank C. Armstrong Collection (MS 1750), Ford Center.

51. Mom, *Electric Vehicle: Technology and Expectations in the Automobile Age*, 89; Kirsch, *The Electric Vehicle and the Burden of History*, 69; "Electrical Automobiles in New England," 136.

52. Sam Bass Warner, *Streetcar Suburbs: The Process of Growth in Boston, 1870–1900* (Cambridge: Harvard University Press, 1978 [1962]), 25–28. The former West End was leased by the Boston Elevated Street Railway Company, a private company, who operated it under the supervision of the BTA, owner of the subway. Pope is

not listed as an officer in the New England Electric Vehicle Transportation Company, but his *Boston Globe* obituary discusses his involvement in the Tremont Street electric omnibuses. "Electrical Automobiles in New England," 136–137; "Death Comes to Col. Albert Pope," *Boston Globe*, 11 August 1909. Waiving ten percent fee: "Minutes of Electric Vehicle Company Executive Committee, 26 December 1899," Box 1, File 6, Frank C. Armstrong Collection, Ford Center.

53. In Maxim's book *Horseless Carriage Days*, he is shown demonstrating the new omnibus (Plate 24). He dates the photo 26 October 1899.

54. Letters from Charles F. Smith to Arthur L. Garford, 11 November 1896 and 22 November 1896, both Box 1, File 5, Arthur L. Garford Papers, OHS. "To Form a Bicycle Trust," *New York Times*, 17 March 1899; "The Combine Story" and "Chainless Wheel," *Dayton Times*, 27 October 1897; *Bearings*, 4 November 1897; all Pope Scrapbooks, CHS; Letter from A. B. Leonard to Arthur L. Garford, 1 May 1900, Box 2, File 4, Arthur L. Garford Papers, OHS. Arthur Dewing, "The American Bicycle Company," *Corporate Promotions and Reorganizations* (Cambridge: Harvard University Press, 1914), 250–51; Letter from A. G. Spalding to Arthur L. Garford, 24 March 1899, Box 1, File 12, Arthur L. Garford Papers, OHS; "A Big Bicycle Combine," *Seattle Post-Intelligencer*, 16 March 1899, Pope Scrapbooks, CHS.

55. "Affidavit of George Pope, 20 May 1901," *Report of the Industrial Commission on Trusts and Combinations* (Washington: Government Printing Office, 1904), XII, 689–90; "Cycle Pool May Fail," *New York Commericial*, 8 April 1899; *Hartford Post*, 16 April 1899, Pope Scrapbooks, CHS; Letter from A. G. Spalding to H. L. Higginson, 7 June 1899, File XII-6B (General Correspondence, R-S), H. L. Higginson Collection, Baker Library, Harvard Business School.

56. *Hartford Post*, 9 June 1899; "Automobile Transfer," *Hartford Post*, 12 June 1899, both Pope Scrapbooks, CHS.

57. "The Plan in Detail," *Cycle Age* 23, 12 (20 July 1899): 321; "Memo to File," 17 October 1899, Box 3, File 1, Arthur L. Garford Papers, OHS; Charles R. Flint, *Memories of an Active Life* (New York: G. P. Putnam's Sons, 1923), 268–69; Letter from Albert A. Pope to Arthur L. Garford, 11 November 1899; Letter from Albert A. Pope to Arthur L. Garford, 4 December 1899; Letter from Albert A. Pope to Arthur L. Garford, 30 December 1899, all Box 1, File 12, Arthur L. Garford Papers, OHS.

58. Greenleaf, *Monopoly on Wheels*, 110–112.

59. Memo from Thomas J. Regan to George H. Day, 19 June 1900, Container 114, William C. Whitney Papers, Library of Congress.

60. Rae, *American Automobile Manufacturers*, 72–73. Selden's patent was no. 549,160, issued 5 November 1895.

61. Cuntz, "Story of the Selden Case and Hartford"; Maxim, *Horseless Carriage Days*, 164.

62. Robert Kanigel, *The One Best Way: Frederick Winslow Taylor and the Enigma of Efficiency* (New York: Viking, 1997), 241–58. Proof that it is a small world: the manager of the Whitney paper mill was Frederick W. Taylor. When it went under in 1893, Taylor was forced into itinerant work, including industrial espionage against the Pope factory.

63. Cuntz, "Story of the Selden Case and Hartford"; Letter from Hermann F. Cuntz to Henry Cave, 4 May 1944, Cave Collection, NAHC.

64. Hirsch, *William Whitney: Modern Warwick*, 561.

65. "License Agreement Between George B. Selden and the Columbia & Electric Vehicle Company, November 4, 1899," *Electric Vehicle Company v. C.A. Duerr & Company*, Case Record 8566, Volume II, 435–450. The volume and page references are to the bound set of the Selden Case Record at the National Automotive History Collection at the Detroit Public Library.

66. Arthur L. Garford to Albert A. Pope, 29 December 1899, Box 1, File 12, Arthur L. Garford Papers, OHS.

67. Albert A. Pope to Arthur L. Garford, 30 December 1899, Box 1, File 12, Arthur L. Garford Papers, OHS.

68. Cuntz, "Hartford, Birthplace of the Automobile, Part 2." George Day was away in the Bahamas.

69. Letter from Arthur L. Garford to M. B. Johnson, 1 May 1900, Box 2, File 4, Arthur L. Garford Papers, OHS.

70. Letter from Arthur L. Garford to M. B. Johnson, 1 May 1900, Box 2, File 4, Arthur L. Garford Papers, OHS.

71. The subsequent account is taken from Greenleaf, *Monopoly on Wheels*, 77–93; Rae, *American Automobile Manufacturers: The First Forty Years*, 67–85; and George S. May, *A Most Unique Machine: The Michigan Origins of the American Automobile Industry* (Grand Rapids, MI: William B. Eerdmans Publishing, 1975), Chapter 9.

72. "Deposition of George B. Selden," *Electric Vehicle Company v. C.A. Duerr & Company*, Case Record 8566, Volume VI, 2871–74.

73. Beverly Rae Kimes, "A Family in Kenosha: The Story of the Rambler and the Jeffery," *Automobile Quarterly* 16, 2 (2nd Quarter, 1978): 130–145. R. Philip Gormully had died in August 1900 and reportedly Jeffery held Pope responsible for his untimely death because of the *Pope v. Gormully* litigation.

74. Maxim, *Horseless Carriage Days*, 173–74.

## Chapter 9

1. *American Wheelman* (30 December 1893), Pope Scrapbooks, Connecticut Historical Society, Hartford.

2. The story of the Pope Building fire is taken from: "Fire Loss, $275,000," *Boston Globe*, 13 March 1896; "Pope Building Not a Ruin," *Boston Transcript*, 13 March 1896.

3. *Boston Journal*, 6 June 1895, Pope Scrapbooks, CHS.

4. "Pope's New Structure," *Hartford Daily Times*, 26 May 1894; "New Building at Pope's," *Hartford Courant*, 26 May 1894; "Boston's Loss," *Boston Post*, 27 May 1894, all Pope Scrapbooks, CHS.

5. *American Cyclist*, 15 May 1894, Pope Scrapbooks, CHS.

6. The Colonel supposedly told young Albert's story to Charles Schwab over dinner. Overheard by a journalist, Pope confirmed it: "Death Comes to Col. Albert A. Pope," *Boston Globe*, 11 August 1909. Branch house salaries: *Teichner v. Pope Manufacturing Company*, 83 N.W. 1031 (Mich. 1900). Young Albert's sailing: "Albert L. Pope," *American Cyclist* (15 May 1894); *Boston Post*, 7 September 1894, *Boston House Journal* (3 August 1895), all Pope Scrapbooks, CHS.

7. "Miss Pope's Debut," *Boston Post*, 11 December 1895, Pope Scrapbooks, CHS.

8. *Boston Globe*, 16 May 1897, Pope Scrapbooks, CHS.

9. Letter from George Pope to David J. Post, 31 December 1894, Pope/Hartford Papers, History and Genealogy Division, Connecticut State Library, Hartford; *Hartford Telegram*, 31 January 1895, Pope Scrapbooks, CHS.

10. *Referee* (28 December 1894); "A Chat with E. W. Pope," *Wheel* (15 February 1900), both Pope Scrapbooks, CHS; "Edward W. Pope Dead in Newton," *Boston Globe*, 15 December 1936; *Who Was Who in America* (Chicago: Marquis, 1968), 759; *Bicycling World* (28 December 1894), "The Pope Mfg. Co.'s New Treasurer," *American Cyclist* (28 December 1894), Pope Scrapbooks, CHS.

11. Letter from George Pope to David J. Post, 31 December 1894, Pope/Hartford Papers, CSL.

12. *Referee* (17 October 1895); *New York Recorder*, 24 October 1895, both Pope Scrapbooks, CHS. Post left the Hartford Cycle Company to become vice-president of the Veeder Manufacturing Co., later Veeder-Root, a maker of pumps and other equipment, most famously gas pumps for service stations. The animosity apparently didn't last; in 1914 Post headed up an unsuccessful effort to save the bankrupt Pope firm from liquidation: *Commercial and Financial Chronicle* 98 (20 June 1914): 1923.

13. The best way to follow the reorganization is by comparing the information for each firm in the "corporations" section of *Greer's Hartford Directory* throughout the 1890s. Maine's holding company law: William G. Roy, *Socializing Capital: The Rise of the Large Industrial Corporation in America* (Princeton: Princeton University Press, 1977), 152.

14. *Boston City Directory* (Boston: Sampson, Davenport and Co.) for years 1878 through 1899; "A Chat with E. W. Pope"; *Greer's Hartford Directory* for years 1895–96 and 1896–97.

15. Seventy clerks: "New Building at Pope's"; the Walkers: *Boston City Directory*, 1885, 1886, 1890; "Horseshoe for Col. Pope," *Bicycling World*, 48, 3 (17 October 1903): 61; a little too pushing: "What Pope Is Doing," *Bicycling World*, 48, 11 (12 December 1903): 281. *Greer's Hartford Directory*, 1895–96 through 1899–00. Relatives working at Pope's: *Greer's Hartford Directory*.

16. "Booming Hartford," *New York Sporting Times*, 25 June 1892, "Colonel Pope's Homes," *Hartford Post*, 22 May 1893, *Hartford Courant*, 24 May 1892, all Pope Scrapbook, CHS.

17. *Hartford Courant*, 16 November 1894; "Hartford Happy," *Boston Journal*, 16 November 1894, "Gift of Col. Albert A. Pope," *Boston Herald*, 16 November 1894, all Pope Scrapbooks, CHS; *Pope et. al. v. Town and City of Hartford*, 74 A. 751 (Conn. 1909).

18. Samuel Reznek, "Unemployment, Unrest and Relief in the United States during the Depression of 1893–1897," *Journal of Political Economy* 4, 9 (August 1953): 324–45; *United States Strike Commission's Report on the Chicago Strike of June-July, 1894*, 53rd Congress, 3rd Session, Senate Executive Document No. 7 (Washington: Government Printing Office, 1895), 572ff.

19. *Boston Globe*, 28 March 1892, Pope Scrapbooks, CHS.

20. The Comstock law stayed on the books until 1965, when the U.S. Supreme Court held that married couples had a right to contraceptive aids in *Griswold v. Connecticut*, 381 U.S. 479 (1965). An analogous holding for unmarried persons followed seven years later in *Eisenstadt v. Baird*, 405 U.S. 438 (1972).

21. Letter from George Keller to Mary Keller, 9 August 1895, George Keller Collection, Stowe-Day Memorial Home, Hartford.

22. Letter from George Pope to David J. Post, 5 January 1895, Pope/Hartford Papers, CHS.

23. "A Chat with E. W. Pope"; "Affidavit of Mr. George Pope, May 20, 1901," *Report of the Industrial Commission on Trusts and Tariffs* (Washington: Government Printing Office, 1909), VII, 689.

24. Letter from F. Ed Spooner, National Cycle News Bureau, to Arthur L. Garford, 14 November 1895, Box 1, File 4, Arthur L. Garford Papers, OHS.

25. Letter from Robert M. Keating to Arthur L. Garford, 23 June 1895, Arthur L. Garford Papers, OHS.

26. Letter from Fred Colson to Arthur L. Garford, 20 August 1895, Box 1, File 3, Arthur L. Garford Papers, OHS.

27. "Overman-Spalding War," *Bearings*, 9, 7 (16 March 1894): 1–2; "Mr. Overman's Story," *Bearings*, 9, 9 (30 March 1894): 6; Vera Shlakman, *Economic History of a Factory Town* (New York: Octagon Books, 1969 [1934]), 200–02.

28. Peter Levine, *A. G. Spalding and the Rise of Baseball* (New York: Oxford University Press, 1985), 79–94.

29. "1895 Columbias $100!" *Bearings* 10, 13 (26 October 1894): 25; "New York Trade News," *Bearings* 10, 14 (2 November 1894): 34.

30. "American Bicycle Company," *Cycle Age and Trade Review* 23 (27 July 1899): 305; "The Board of Trade's Future," *Bearings*, 10 January 1896, Pope Scrapbooks, CHS.

31. Letter from Arthur L. Garford to Eugene Ward, 14 July 1897, Box 4, File 5, Arthur L. Garford Papers, OHS.

32. "Trade News," *Iron Age* 56 (10 October 1895): 11.

33. "Point of View," *Scribner's Monthly* 19, 6 (June 1896): 783–84.

34. "Affidavit of Mr. George Pope," 688–90.

35. *Twelfth Census of the United States [1900]: Manufacturing Industries*, Table 4: specified industries by state and territory (Bicycle and Tricycle Repairing) (Washington, Government Printing Office, 1904), 78–81.

36. "Retail Notes," *The Sporting Goods Dealer* (June 1900): 14.

37. "Local Builders' Risks," *Cycle Age and Trade Review* 21 (27 October 1898): 755; "Importance of the Assemblers," *Cycle Age and Trade Review* 23 (29 June 1899): 211.

38. "Fire at the Cycle Show," *New York Times* (24 January 1896): 6.

39. "The Bicycle Trade," *Iron Age*, 58 (9 July 1896): 68.

40. "Exports of American Cycles," *Iron Age* 58 (16 July 1896): 143; "American Bicycles Abroad," *Iron Age*, 58 (3 September 1896): 472.

41. Williard S. Mattox, "American Bicycle Fittings and Machinery in England," *Iron Age*, 62 (3 November 1898): 8.

42. "The Bicycle Market," *Iron Age*, 58 (9 July 1896): 90.

43. "The Bicycle Trade," 68; "The Bicycle Market," 90.

44. "Bicycles in the Hardware Trade," *Iron Age*, 59 (11 March 1897): 34; "The Bicycle Situation," *Iron Age*, 58 (1 October 1896): 655. How many bicycles were made that year, or any other, is highly conjectural. The traditional estimate for 1896 is 1,200,000 units, supposedly a figure taken from the National Cycle Board of Trade and

reported in a 1957 Harvard Ph.D. dissertation by Norman Leslie Dunham, *The Bicycle Era in America*. My own estimate, formulated in 2000 ("How Many Bikes: An Investigation into the Quantification of Bicycling, 1878–1914," *Cycle History 11: Proceedings of the Eleventh International Cycle History Conference*, ed. Andrew Ritchie and Rob van der Plas [San Francisco: Van der Plas Publications, 2001]: 49), was a production of 437,200 with exports of 23,590. "The Bicycle Situation" (which I uncovered after my 2000 paper), reported that the industry purchased enough material to produce about 1,000,000 bicycles in 1896, and of this, material for 300,000 was either not used, remained in the form of unassembled bicycles or was assembled into finished but unsold units. Generally, I find *Iron Age*, when it presents specifics, to be more reliable than the cycle trades press because it did not depend on cyclemakers for advertising. The same *Iron Age* article stated that the 1896 domestic figure was the same as the 1895 domestic market, about 650,000–675,000.

45. Letter and accompanying table from Arthur L. Patrick to Arthur L. Garford, 5 September 1898, Box 1, File 10, Arthur L. Garford Papers, OHS.

46. "Wild-Cat Agencies for Bicycles," *Iron Age* 59 (25 March 1897): 37.

47. "Trend of the Retail Trade," *Cycle Age and Trade Review* 20 (21 April 1898): 957; "Opinions of Dealers," *Cycle Age and Trade Review* 21 (1 September 1898): 498; "Bicycles in the Hardware Trade," 34.

48. "Wild-Cat Agencies for Bicycles," 37.

49. Letters from Fred N. Smith to Arthur L. Garford, 15 February 1897 and 27 March 1897, Arthur L. Garford Papers, OHS.

50. Lawrence W. Levine, *Highbrow, Lowbrow: The Emergence of Cultural Hierarchy in America* (Cambridge: Harvard University Press, 1988), 122–23.

51. Henry L. Higginson to Albert A. Pope, 31 March 1897, Higginson Collection, File XV-1, folder 165, Baker Library, Harvard Business School.

52. Letter from Albert A. Pope to Henry L. Higginson, 2 April 1897, Higginson Collection File XV-1, folder 165, Baker library, Harvard.

53. Letter from Vinton A. Sears to Arthur L. Garford, 9 April 1897, Box 1, File 6, Arthur L. Garford Papers, OHS.

54. "Garford, Arthur Lovett," *The Automobile Industry, 1896–1920*, George S. May, ed. (New York: Facts on File, 1990); *American Athlete and Cycle Trades Review* 7, 4 (28 November 1891): 4; Letter from Marcus S. Hopkins to Arthur L Garford, 5 January 1889, Box 1, File 1; letter from Arthur L. Garford to Edwin Oliver, 2 November 1896, Box 1, File 5, both Arthur L. Garford Papers, OHS.

55. Letter from Charles F. Smith to Arthur L. Garford, 11 November 1896, Box 1, File 5, Arthur L. Garford Papers, OHS.

56. Letter from Charles F. Smith to Arthur L. Garford, 22 November 1896, Box 1, File 5, Arthur L. Garford Papers, OHS.

57. Smith to Garford, 11 November; Smith to Garford, 22 November.

58. Smith to Garford, 22 November.

59. These figures are taken from an attachment to Charles F. Smith's letter to Arthur L. Garford of 22 November.

60. Letter from Vinson A. Sears to Arthur L. Garford, 9 April 1897, Box 1, File 7, Arthur L. Garford Papers, OHS.

61. "Exports of Bicycles and Bicycle Materials," *Iron Age* 59 (24 June 1897): 35; *Literary Digest* 15, 30 (30 November 1897): 896.

62. "Ideal Building," *Boston Evening Record*, 8 May 1897, Pope Scrapbooks, CHS.

63. Peter Lyon, *Success Story: The Life and Times of S. S. McClure* (New York: Charles Scribner's Sons, 1963), 131.

64. Letter from M. S. Gross to Arthur L. Garford, 6 May 1898; Letter from A. L. Patrick to Arthur L. Garford, 5 September 1898, both Box 1, File 9, Arthur Garford Papers, OHS.

65. "Canadian News: More Protection for the Bicycle Industry," *Iron Age*, 61 (3 February 1898): 17.

66. "Col. Pope Interviewed," *Bicycling World* (18 June 1897), Pope Scrapbooks, CHS; Letter from Arthur L. Garford to C. A. Weaver, 19 May 1897, Box 1, File 7, Arthur Garford Papers, OHS; *New York Herald*, 30 June 1897, Pope Scrapbooks, CHS.

67. Robert A. Smith, *A Social History of the Bicycle* (New York: American Heritage Press, 1972), 37; Letter from George Pope to David J. Post, 31 December 1894, Pope/Hartford Papers, CSL.

68. "Cyclemen Going Abroad," *New York Journal*, 19 July 1897, Pope Scrapbooks, CHS.

69. "A Big Bicycle Combine," *Seattle Post Intelligencer* (16 March 1899), Pope Scrapbooks, OHS.

70. "Goes Permanently to Hartford," *Bicycling World* (27 August 1897), Pope Scrapbooks, CHS; *Greer's Hartford Directory*, 1896–97 through 1900–01; "A Chat with E. W. Pope."

71. "German Bicycle Manufacturers and Their Desire for a Prohibitive Duty on Bicycles," *Iron Age* 61, (13 January 1898): 32; "Canadian News," 17; Roger Lloyd-Jones and M. J. Lewis, *Raleigh and the British Bicycle Industry: A Business and Economic History, 1870–1960* (Aldershot: Ashgate, 2000), 255.

72. Wolman, *Most Favored Nation*, 85–88; *Pope Mfg. Co. v. Rubber Goods Mfg. Co.*, 97, N.Y.S. 73, 76 (S.Ct. App. Div. 1 Dept. 1905).

73. "Chainless Wheel," *Dayton Times*, 27 October 1897; "The Combine Story: The Toledo End," *Bearings* (4 November 1897), Pope Scrapbooks, CHS.

74. "The Inventor's Opinion," *Bearings* (4 November 1897), Pope Scrapbooks, CHS; Frank Berto, *The Dancing Chain* (2nd ed.) (San Francisco, Van der Plas Publications, 2005), 69.

75. *Greer's Hartford Directory*, 1893–94.

76. James J. Flink, *America Adopts the Automobile*, 1895–1910 (Cambridge: MIT Press, 1970), 262

77. Letter from C. E. Hawley to Arthur L. Garford, 20–25 November 1895, Box 1, File 4, Arthur Garford Papers, OHS,

78. "Interview with Norman A. Clarke, 5 April 1998, North Chatham, MA" (unpublished manuscript), 35. Berto, *The Dancing Chain*, 69.

79. "The Making of a Bicycle," *The Sporting Goods Dealer* (July 1900): 5.

80. Letter from Prof. R. C. Carpenter, Cornell University, to R. C. Tuttle, Tuttle Chainless Bicycle Co., 18 December 1899, Box 2, File 8, William F. D. Crane Papers (MS 1092), New Jersey Historical Society, Newark, New Jersey.

81. "Mild War Scare," *Cycle Age and Trade Review* 20 (21 April 1898): 957; "Gossip of the Cyclers," *New York Times*, 1 May 1898, 16; undated address to the shareholders of the Cleveland Machine Screw Company [ca.

August 1901], Box 7, File 7, Arthur Garford Papers, OHS.
82. Letter from Albert A. Pope to Henry L. Higginson, 18 January 1898, File XII-5D, Baker Library, Harvard.
83. *The Wheel* 21, 12 (5 May 1898): 5.
84. "Death of Charles Linder Pope," *Boston Post*, 22 April 1898; *Boston Transcript*, Friday, 22 April 1898; "Death List of a Day," *New York Times*, 22 April 1898.
85. "Monument at Forest Hills Cemetery," *American Architect and Building News*, 60, 1049 (1 February 1896); Letter from Susan Navarre (Forest Hills Cemetery) to author, 3 November 1999.
86. Letter from R. M. Keating to Arthur L. Garford, 8 November 1899, Box 1, File 12, Arthur Garford Papers, OHS; "Outlook in Cycles," *Iron Age*, 62 (23 December 1898): 43; Frank Berto, "The Great American Bicycle Boom," *Cycle History 10: Proceedings of the 10th International Cycle History Conference*, ed. Hans-Erhard Lessing and Andrew Ritchie (San Francisco: Van der Plas Publications, 2000): 135. Sales of bicycles in 1973 were 15.21 million, or 1 bicycle for every 72 Americans. Sales in 1898 (not including units dumped overseas) were about 1.2 million, or about 1 in 52.

## Chapter 10

1. Letter from S. B. "Ely" Leonard to Arthur L. Garford, 5 February 1902, Box 4, File 5, Arthur L. Garford Papers (MSS 6), Ohio Historical Society, Columbus.
2. Letter from Albert A. Pope to Arthur L. Garford, 12 August 1901, Box 4, File 1, Arthur L. Garford Papers, OHS.
3. Arthur Dewing, "The American Bicycle Company," *Corporate Promotions and Reorganizations* (Cambridge: Harvard University Press, 1914), 249–68; interest of Alexander brothers in 1896–97 merger: letter from Vinson A. Sears to Arthur L. Garford, 9 April 1897, Box 1, File 7, Arthur Garford Papers, OHS, Columbus; saddlemaker's trust: letter from Arthur L. Garford to Arthur L. Patrick, 12 January 1899, Box 1, File 12; Letter from S.B. Leonard to Arthur L. Garford, 1 May 1900, Box 2, File 4, both Arthur L. Garford Papers, OHS; Garford-Spalding suit: "Settled Out of Court," *Bicycling World* 38, 6 (11 November 1898): 231.
4. Letter from A. G. Spalding to Arthur L. Garford, 24 March 1899, Box 1, File 12, Arthur L. Garford Papers, OHS.
5. "To Form a Bicycle Trust," *New York Times*, 17 March 1899; "More Concerning the Wheel Trust," *Buffalo Commercial*, 17 April 1899, Pope Scrapbooks, Connecticut Historical Society, Hartford.
6. "Memorial Church," *Boston Transcript*, 24 July 1899, Pope Scrapbooks, CHS.
7. "The Combine and Cycle Age," *Cycle Age and Trade Review* 23 (1 June 1899): 111–12.
8. "Two Bike Trusts Planned," *New York Morning World*, 11 May 1899, Pope Scrapbooks, CHS; *Commercial and Financial Chronicle* 68 (20 May 1899): 974; "Coleman Organizes New Combine," *Cycle Age and Trade Review* 23 (11 May 1899): 34–35.
9. "Combine Now Practically Assured," *Cycle Age and Trade Review* 23 (18 May 1899): 63–64.
10. "Saved Schoolmate from Drowning," *New York Times*, 8 May 1898.
11. New York Morning Telegraph, 1 February 1899, Pope Scrapbooks, CHS; "The Army Meat Scandal," *New York Times*, 1 February 1899.
12. "The Combine and Cycle Age," 112.
13. *Ibid*: 113. The list was quite good. All the named firms were ultimately included, and because several of the firms had multiple subsidiaries, *Cycle Age* got about 28 of the 43 or so plants right.
14. *Hartford Post*, 16 April 1899; *Hartford Post*, 12 June 1899; Pope Scrapbooks, CHS. The number of firms eventually forming the bicycle trust varies between 41 and 45, depending on who is doing the counting, and which firms should be considered divisions of the same company and which were actually separate entities. "Morgan & Wright Sell Out," *Cycle Age and Trade Review* 23 (11 May 1899): 35; "Combine Now Practically Assured," 63.
15. Waldorf meeting: *Bicycling World* 31, 15 (12 July 1899): 3; "Official Version of the A.B.C. Meeting," *Cycle Age and Trade Review* 23 (29 June 1899): 207–08. Death of Josie Keith Spalding: Peter Levine, *A.G. Spalding and the Rise of Baseball* (New York: Oxford University Press, 1985), 124–25.
16. Letters from George Pope to David J. Post, 3 October 1890 and 14 November 1890, Pope/Hartford Papers, CSL.
17. *Commercial and Financial Chronicle*, 69 (11 November 1899): 1015; (2 December 1899): 1150.
18. "The Plan in Detail," *Cycle Age* 23, 12 (20 July 1899): 1; "Bicycle Trust Is Still Alive," *Brooklyn Citizen*, 23 July 1899, Pope Scrapbooks, CHS.
19. Charles R. Flint, *Memories of an Active Life* (New York: G.P. Putnam's Sons, 1923), 268–69.
20. "Aggressiveness Will Rule," *Bicycling World* (3 August 1899), Pope Scrapbooks, CHS; *Commercial and Financial Chronicle*, 69 (5 August 1899): 286; P.J. Boore, *The Seamless Story* (Los Angeles: Commonwealth, 1951), 65–67; Letter from Arthur L. Garford to Jesse Stearns, 27 July 1901, Box 4, File 1, Arthur L. Garford Papers, OHS.
21. "Some Are Still Dissatisfied," *The Cycle Age and Trade Review* 23 (3 August 1899): 327.
22. Memo from Arthur L. Garford to file, 17 October 1899, Box 3, File 1 [this item is mistakenly filed as 17 October 1900]; Memo from H.E.L. [probably Ely Leonard] to Arthur L. Garford, 28 October 1899, Box 1, File 12; Letter from Arthur L. Garford to Albert A. Pope, 2 December 1899, Box 1, File 12; all Arthur Garford Papers, OHS.
23. "Personnel of Management of A.B.C.," *Cycle Age and Trade Review* 23 (7 September 1899): 463.
24. *Pope Mfg. Co. v. Rubber Goods Mfg. Co.*, 97 N.Y.S. 73 (Supp.Ct. 1905); "Money Paid to the Makers," *Wheel* (2 November 1899), Pope Scrapbooks, CHS; Memo from Arthur L. Garford to file, 17 October 1899, Box 3, File 1, Arthur Garford Papers, OHS.
25. "Manager at Pope's," *Hartford Courant*, 21 October 1899; *New Haven Ledger*, 28 October 1899; *New Haven Register*, 9 November 1899; "Flint Finally Gets Hartford Rubber Works," *New Haven Leader*, 9 November 1899, all Pope Scrapbooks, CHS.
26. Letter from Albert A. Pope to Arthur L. Garford, 29 November 1899; letter from Albert A. Pope to Arthur L. Garford, 4 December 1899, both Box 1, File 12, Arthur L. Garford Papers, OHS.
27. Arthur L. Garford to Albert A. Pope, 3 January 1900; Albert A. Pope to Arthur L. Garford, both Box 2, File 1, Arthur L. Garford Papers, OHS.

28. Letter from Albert A. Pope to Arthur L. Garford, 3 February 1900, Box 2, File 1, Arthur L. Garford Papers, OHS.
29. Letter from Arthur L. Garford to Albert A. Pope, 15 January 1900, Box 2, File 1, Arthur L. Garford Papers, OHS.
30. *Hartford Times*, 4 August 1899, Pope Scrapbooks, CHS.
31. Letter from Albert A. Pope to Arthur L. Garford, 30 December 1899, Box 1, File 12, Arthur L. Garford Papers, OHS.
32. Letter from Robert Winkley to Arthur L. Garford, 4 January 1900, Box 2, File 1, Arthur L. Garford Papers, OHS.
33. "Six Months of the Trust," *The Cycle Age and Trade Review* 25 (3 May 1900): 5.
34. "No More Clipper Bicycles," *The Cycle Age and Trade Review* 25 (28 June 1900): 219.
35. *Commercial and Financial Chronicle* 71 (25 August 1900): 891; letter from Arthur L. Garford to J.C. Hill, 30 August 1900, Box 2, File 10, Arthur L. Garford Papers, OHS.
36. Letter from Arthur L. Garford to J.C. Hill, 30 August 1900, Box 2, File 10, Arthur L. Garford Papers, OHS.
37. Letter from Arthur L. Garford to Albert A. Pope, 23 July 1900, Box 2, File 10, Arthur L. Garford Papers, OHS.
38. Levine, *A. G. Spalding and the Rise of Baseball*, 125–27.
39. A detailed analysis in *Cycle Age* in mid-1899 generally agrees with the 841,000 number (it estimated 668,000, but didn't include thirteen firms that were ultimately brought into the trust, bringing the total up to 828,000), but asserted that the A.B.C.'s production was only about 40 percent of the industry total. "Combine Cannot Control the Trade," *Cycle Age and Trade Review* 23 (8 June 1899): 137–39.
40. Letter from Herman Ely to H. J. Cassidy, 7 March 1900, Box 2, File 2, Arthur L. Garford Papers, OHS; Production of 550,000: estimated from figures provided on a sales statement attached to a letter from Herman Ely to Arthur L. Garford, 6 April 1900, Box 2, File 2, Arthur L. Garford Papers, OHS; 150,000 saddles stashed: letter from Arthur Garford to Herman Ely, 20 April 1900, Box 2, File 3, Arthur L. Garford Papers, OHS; Letter from J. A. Hunt to Arthur L. Garford, 17 July 1900, Box 2, File 8, Arthur L. Garford Papers, OHS. *Cycle Age* later asserted that the A.B.C. manufactured only 450,000 during the '99-00 season: "A.B.C. Men Silent," *Cycle Age and Trade Review* 26 (15 November 1900): 50.
41. "Six Months of the Trust," 5–6.
42. Letter from Arthur L. Garford to Albert A. Pope, 23 July 1900, Box 2, File 8, Arthur L. Garford Papers, OHS.
43. *Commercial and Financial Chronicle* 71 (25 August 1900): 891; Letter from Arthur L. Garford to M. Blake Johnson, 5 May 1900, Box 2, File 4, Arthur L. Garford Papers, OHS.
44. Beverly Rae Kimes, "A Family in Kenosha: The Story of the Rambler and the Jeffery," *Automobile Quarterly* 16, 2 (2nd Quarter, 1978): 130–45.
45. Letter from S.B. Leonard to Arthur L. Garford, 1 May 1900, Box 2, File 4, Arthur L. Garford Papers, OHS.
46. *Commercial and Financial Chronicle* 73 (12 October 1901): 782; Dewing, "The American Bicycle Company," 254–55.
47. "Came Like a Thunderbolt," *The Cycle Age and Trade Review* 25 (5 July 1900): 240.
48. "Sorry They Sold to Trust," *The Cycle Age and Trade Review* 26 (8 November 1900): 26.
49. Resignation letter of Arthur L. Garford, 18 August 1900, Box 2, File 2; "If I had known": Letter from Arthur L. Garford to A. Grasselli, 19 March 1900, Box 2, File 2; "certain matters": letter from Arthur L. Garford to J. A. Hunt, 21 August 1900, Box 2 File 8; "practically under protest": letter from Arthur L. Garford to Herman Ely, 17 September 1900, Box 2, File 10, all Arthur L. Garford Papers, OHS.
50. Letter from Albert A. Pope to Arthur L. Garford, 20 September 1900; letter from Arthur L. Garford to Albert L. Pope, 21 September 1900, both Box 2, File 10, Arthur Garford Papers, OHS; *Commercial and Financial Chronicle* 72 (16 March 1901): 536.
51. Letter from Albert A. Pope to Arthur L. Garford, 28 September 1900; letter from Arthur L. Garford to M.B. Johnson, 12 October 1900; letter from Arthur L. Garford to J. C. Hill, 13 October 1900, all Box 2, File 10, Arthur Garford Papers, OHS.
52. Letter from Albert A. Pope to Arthur L. Garford, 15 January 1901, Box 3, File 1, Arthur Garford Papers, OHS.
53. "Survival of the Fittest I," *The Cycle Age and Trade Review* 26 (1 November 1900): 1; "A.B.C. Men Silent," 50.
54. Untitled report from Arthur Garford to the shareholders of the Cleveland Machine Screw Co., August 1901, Box 7, File 7, Arthur L. Garford Papers, OHS.
55. Letter from Albert A. Pope to Arthur L. Garford, 22 September 1901, Box 4, File 2, letter from George Pope to Arthur L. Garford, 16 March 1901, Box 3, File 9, Arthur Garford Papers, OHS; *Commercial and Financial Chronicle* 72 (16 March 1901): 534–36; *American Bicycle Co. v. Hoyt*, 95 N.W. 92 (Wisc. 1903).
56. Letter from Arthur L. Patrick to Arthur L. Garford, 17 August 1901, Box 4, File 1, letter from Albert A. Pope to Arthur L. Garford, 22 September, 1901, Box 4, File 2, Arthur L. Garford Papers, OHS; "Group Photograph — Columbia Sales Department," *Columbia* 1, 8 (15 December 1900), unpaginated; *Bicycling World* 44, 4 (24 October 1901): 48; "All Sales Departments Go," *Bicycling World* 44, 1 (3 October 1901): 1; *American Machinist* 25 (2 October 1902): 1431.
57. "Warwick Still in Court," *Bicycling World*, 44, 13 (26 December 1901): 1; *Bicycling World* 44, 4 (24 October 1901): 48; Philip P. Mason, *The League of American Wheelmen and the Good Roads Movement, 1880–1905* (Ph.D. dissertation, University of Michigan, 1957), 63. The L.A.W. would be resurrected in 1934, only to die again in the late '50s. Born again in the bike boom of the early 1970s, it survives to this day as Bicycling USA.
58. Letter from Arthur L. Garford to S. B. Hunt, 7 February 1902, Box 4, File 7, Arthur Garford Papers, OHS.
59. *Boston Post*, 9 August 1892; *Boston Herald*, 28 August 1892; *Oakland Engineer*, 4 January 1893; "The Observant Citizen," *Boston Post*, 14 February 1893, all Pope Scrapbooks, CHS; *Pierce v. Merrill*, 61 P. 64 (Calif. 1900).
60. "Col Pope's New Building," *Denver Post*, 7 April 1899; "Not a Pope Auditorium," *Boston Transcript*, 31 March 1899, both Pope Scrapbooks, CHS.
61. The Custer City site is just south of the present

hamlet of Querida, about ten miles east of the town of Westcliffe on Highway 96.

62. "Boston Company Starts New Town in Custer County," *Denver Times* (25 April 1902); "Town to Rise in a Night," *Denver Times* (26 April 1902). For background information on the partners: *Matzger v. Arcade Bldg. and Realty Co.*, 141 P. 900 (Wash. 1914); *Hill v. Whitcomb et. al.*, 12 F.Cas. 182 (C.Ct. Mass. 1874); *Meston v. Davies et. al.* 36 S.W. 805 (Tex. Civ. App. 1896).

63. "Town Springs Up in a Day," *Denver Times* (10 June 1902); "City Christened," *Rocky Mountain News* (11 June 1902); "Dedication of Custer a Success," *Denver Times* (11 June 1902); "Syndicate Buys Town and Mines," *Denver Times* (4 April 1903); *Denver Times* (16 June 1903); *Atlas of Colorado Ghost Towns*, Vol. 1 (Denver, 1984), 57-58.

64. Letter from Arthur L. Garford to Albert A. Pope, 6 August 1901, Box 4 File 2; letter from Arthur L. Garford to S. B. Leonard, 2 February 1902, Box 4, File 3, both Arthur L Garford Papers, OHS.

65. Letter from S. B. Leonard to Arthur L. Garford, 5 February 1902, Box 4, File 3, Arthur L. Garford Papers, OHS.

66. Letter from Albert A. Pope to Arthur L. Garford, 22 September 1901, Box 4, File 2, Arthur L. Garford Papers, OHS.

67. "Executive Committee Cut Out," *Bicycling World*, 44, 2 (10 October 1901): 30.

68. *Bicycling World* 44, 13 (26 December 1901): 278; *Pope Mfg. Co. v. Rubber Goods Mfg. Co.*, 100 A.D. 353 (S.C.N.Y. 1905); *Pope Mfg. Co. v. Rubber Goods Mfg. Co.*, 110 A.D. 341 (S.C.N.Y. 1905).

69. *Bicycling World* 45, 10 (10 April 1902): 45; Letter from Albert A. Pope to Arthur L. Garford, 25 April 1902, Box 2, File 7, Arthur L. Garford Papers, OHS; *Bicycling World* 55, 5 (1 May 1902): 86; *New York Times*, 16 June 1902, 1; *Bicycling World* 45, 12 (19 June 1902): 325.

70. Arthur L. Garford to R. E. McMullen, 4 September 1902, Box 4, File 12, Arthur L. Garford Papers, OHS.

71. George Pope to Henry L. Higginson, 3 December 1902, Box 12, File 7B, Henry L. Higginson Papers, Baker Library, Harvard University.

72. "A.B.C. Affairs Come to a Climax," *Bicycling World* 55, 23 (4 September 1902): 580; Arthur L. Garford to Fraser Moffat, 24 September 1902, Box 4, File 12; Arthur L. Garford to Arthur L. Patrick, 1 November 1902, Box 5, File 1, both Arthur L. Garford Papers, OHS.

73. "Columbia Bicycle Works Closed, " *New York Times*, 27 September 1902; *Bicycling World* 45, 26 (25 September 1902): 637; "President Bromley Retires," *Bicycling World* 46, (2 October 1902): 1. Bromley was president of the Chicago-based American Cycle Manufacturing Co., the bicycle-making subsidiary of the A.B.C.

74. Arthur L. Patrick to Arthur L. Garford, December 12, 1902, Box 5, File 2, Arthur L. Garford Papers, OHS.

75. Arthur L. Patrick to Arthur L. Garford, February 25, 1903, Box 5, File 4, Arthur L. Garford Papers, OHS.

76. Dewing, "The American Bicycle Company," 249-68.

77. "Pope Gets Majority," *Bicycling World* 45, 5 (1 May 1902): 173. This is confirmed by the weekly records of A.B.C. stock transactions published in the *Commercial and Financial Chronicle*.

78. Ron Chernow, *Titan: The Life of John D. Rockefeller Sr.* (New York: Random House, 1988), 366-80; letter from Edgar Park to Arthur L. Garford, 29 August 1904, Box 7, File 5, Arthur L. Garford Papers, OHS.

79. Arthur L. Garford to H. E. Maslin, 11 December 1902, Box 5, File 2, Arthur L. Garford Papers, OHS.

80. "Exit ABC; Enter Pope," *Bicycling World*, 47, 5 (2 May 1903): 145; letter from Arthur L. Patrick to Arthur L. Garford, 2 April 1903, Box 5, File 6, Arthur L. Garford Papers, OHS; *Bicycling World*, 47 1 (4 April 1903): 11.

81. Letter from Arthur L. Patrick to Arthur L. Garford, 4 May 1903, Box 5, File 7, Arthur L. Garford Papers, OHS.

82. Arthur L. Garford to Arthur L. Patrick, June 10, 1903, Box 5, File 6, Arthur L. Garford Papers, OHS.

83. Arthur L. Garford to Edgar Park, 27 June 1903, Box 5, File 8, Arthur L. Garford Papers, OHS.

## Chapter 11

1. Letter from Albert A. Pope to Arthur L. Garford, 14 January 1903 [erroneously dated as 14 January 1902], Box 4, File 5, Arthur L. Garford Papers (MSS 6), Ohio Historical Society, Columbus.

2. Letter from Albert A. Pope to Arthur L. Garford, 23 December 1901; letter from Arthur L. Garford to Albert A. Pope, 26 December 1901, both Box 4, File 4, Arthur L. Garford Papers, OHS; "Harold Linder Pope," *National Cyclopedia of American Biography* (New York: Scribner's, 1958); *Greer's Hartford Directory* for 1904-05 and 1905-06.

3. Form letter from Arthur L. Garford to bicycle manufacturers, 4 November 1902; letter from Homer P. Snyder to Arthur L. Garford, 5 November 1902, both Box 5, File 1, Arthur L. Garford Papers, OHS.

4. Out of about thirty-two firms, twenty were invited, nine were not (they were primarily jobbers who contracted out for production), and three were believed to be withdrawing from business before the new season started: "List of Bicycle Manufacturers Invited to Attend Meeting of Nov'r. 8th per Mr. Garford"; "Minutes of November 8th, 1902 Meeting," both Box 5, File 1, Arthur L. Garford Papers, OHS.

5. "Association Not Formed," *Bicycling World* 46, 8 (20 November 1902): 174.

6. "Minutes of Adjourned Meeting of the Bicycle Manufacturers, Friday, Nov. 21st," "This Agreement" [i.e., proposed bylaws], 21 November 1902; "To the Members of the Bicycle Manufacturers Association" from E. E. Jackson of Park & Jackson, attorneys, 26 November 1902, all Box 5, File 1, Arthur L. Garford Papers , OHS.

7. "National Cycle Trade Association," *Cycle and Automobile Trade Journal* 7 (1 March 1903): 24; "The Jobbers' Programme," *Bicycling World* 49, 9 (28 May 1904): 279.

8. "Sues for $200,000 Rebate," *Bicycling World* 48, 3 (17 October 1903): 54; *Pope Mfg. Co. v. Rubber Goods Mfg. Co.*, 91 N.Y.S. 826 (N.Y. 1905); *Pope Mfg. Co. v. Rubber Goods Mfg. Co.*, 97 N.Y.S. 73 (N.Y. 1905).

9. "What Pope is Doing," *Bicycling World* 48, 11 (12 December 1903): 281.

10. "Bicycles of 1904," *Bicycling World* 49, 1 (2 April

1904): 25–34; "Motor Bicycles of 1904," *Bicycling World* 49, 1 (2 April 1904): 41–44.

11. Letter from Thomas E. Propst (Pope Mfg. Agency Dept.) to George W. Smith, 18 January 1904, File 36, Box 2, Warshaw Business History Collection, Smithsonian Archives Collection, National Museum of American History, Washington, D.C.; "Best in Four Years," *Bicycling World* 48, 17 (23 January 1904): 461.

12. "Cycle Dealers who are Handling Automobiles Successfully," *Cycle and Automobile Trade Journal* 8 (1 July 1903): 36.

13. Construction of Westfield factory: *Cleveland Bicycles Catalog for 1897*, Box 2, File 6, Warshaw Business Collection, Smithsonian Archives, National Museum of American History, Washington, D.C.; "Lozierville": transcript of author's interview with Norman A. Clarke, April 5, 1998, North Chatham, Massachusetts.

14. *An Industrial Achievement* (Hartford: The Pope Manufacturing Company, 1907), 16, 24.

15. Letter from Albert L. Pope to Arthur L. Garford, 14 July 1903, Box 5, File 7, Arthur L. Garford Papers, OHS.

16. Letter from Arthur L. Garford to Albert L. Pope, 22 July 1903, Box 5, File 10, Arthur L. Garford Papers, OHS.

17. "Told 'Round the Ticker," *New York Times*, 23 October 1904; "Exchange Expels Member: Unusual Punishment for J. W. Ritchie," *New York Times*, 21 December 1904.

18. *Bicycling World* 49, 5 (30 April 1904): 157.

19. Letter from Arthur L. Garford to Hart O. Berg, 6 October 1904, Box 7, File 5, Arthur Garford Papers, OHS.

20. *Commercial and Financial Chronicle* 80 (22 April 1905): 1482; (29 April 1905): 1734; (3 June 1905): 2348; "Quits the Cycle Trade," *Bicycling World* 49 (28 May 1904): 232.

21. Thomas F. Saal, "Pope-Hartford: Too Good to Fail," *Automobile Quarterly* 36, 1 (December, 1996): 93–109; "Gillettes Go Under," *Bicycling World* 46, 8 (20 November 1902): 45.

22. Henry Cave, "Hartford, The Incubator of the Automobile Industry," *Old Timers News* 2, 2 (April 1944): 24–33; *Greer's Hartford Directory*, 1902–03 through 1905–06.

23. Vanderbuilt races: Saal, "Pope-Hartford: Too Good to Fail": 102; Pope-Baker Race: *Turner v. Pope Motor Car Co.*, 86 N.E. 651 (Ohio Cir. 1908); "Automobile Notes of Interest," *New York Times*, 22 October 1905.

24. "Lytle's Car Barred from Big Auto Race," *New York Times*, 26 September 1906; "Auto Dispute Settled; Pope-Toledo Withdraws," *New York Times*, 4 October 1906.

25. "Pope's Decision Made," *Bicycling World* 49, 3 (16 April 1904): 107; Peter Joffre Nye, *The Six-Day Bicycle Races* (San Francisco: Van der Plas Publications, 2006), 45–78.

26. "Police Arrest Cyclists," *New York Times*, 5 July 1904; Andrew Ritchie, *Major Taylor: The Extraordinary Career of a Champion Bicycle Racer* (San Francisco: Bicycle Books, 1998), *passim*.

27. Peter Nye, *Hearts of Lions: The History of American Bicycle Racing* (New York: W. W. Norton, 1988), 81–83; 95–96.

28. "Hypnotized by the Thousands," *New York Times*, 10 December 1907.

29. "The Greatest Gathering of Cyclists Since Cycling Ceased to Be a Craze," *Bicycling World* 49, 6 (7 May 1904): 204–08.

30. "E. C. Hodges Dead," *Bicycling World* 48, 12 (19 December 1903): 310–11.

31. "Big Increase in Sales of Bicycles," *New York Times*, 12 June 1904.

32. *Census of Manufactures, 1905, Special Report: Bicycles and Tricycles*, by Robert Merriam (Washington, Government Printing Office, 1907); *Commercial and Financial Chronicle* 80 (14 January 1905): 160–61.

33. *Twelfth Census of the United States [1890], Manufacturing Industries, Part 3, Special Reports, Bicycles and Tricycles*, by Axel Josephsson. (Washington, Government Printing Office, 1894): Vol. 3, 325–39; "Affidavit of Mr. George Pope, 20 May 1901," *Report of the Industrial Commission on Trusts and Combination, 1902* (Washington, Government Printing Office, 1904): VII: 688–90.

34. R. G. Betts, "Revival in the Bicycle Trade," *New York Times*, 29 July 1907.

35. Thomas C. Burr, *Markets As Producers and Consumers: The French and U.S. National Bicycle Markets, 1875–1910* (Ph.D. dissertation, University of California at Davis, 2005), Chapters 6 and 7; Clay McShane, *Down the Asphalt Path: The Automobile and the American City* (New York: Columbia University Press, 1994), 41–50; *Sporting Goods Dealer* 9 (May 1900): 9; Letter from Norman A. Clarke to Bruce Epperson, 7 May 1997; "Interview With Norman A. Clarke," 21–22.

36. "Affidavit of Mr. George Pope," *Commercial and Financial Chronicle* 80 (14 January 1905): 160.

37. *Commercial and Financial Chronicle* 87 (22 August 1908): 483; *Thirteenth Census of the United States [1910], Manufacturing Industries, Part 3, Special Reports, "Bicycles, Motorcycles and Parts."*

38. Lawrence H. Seltzer, *A Financial History of the American Automobile Industry* (Boston: Houghton Mifflin, 1928), 19, 25, 26.

39. Andrew Millward, *Factors Contributing to the Sustained Success of the U.K. Cycle Industry, 1870–1939* (Doctoral dissertation, University of Birmingham, 1999), sections 2.3.1 and 2.3.2; Roger Lloyd-Jones and M. J. Lewis, *Raleigh and the British Cycle Industry: An Economic and Business History, 1870–1960* (Aldershot: Ashgate, 2000), 38–40; 88–92; Paul Rosen, *Framing Production: Technology, Culture, and Change in the British Bicycle Industry* (Cambridge: MIT Press, 2002), *passim*.

40. James Foreman-Peck, "Diversification and the Growth of the Firm: The Rover Company to 1914," *Business History* 25, 2 (July 1983): 179–92; A.E. Harrison, "Joint Stock Company Flotation in the Cycle, Motor-Vehicle and Related Industries, 1882–1914," *Business History* 23, 3 (July 1981): 165–89; A.E. Harrison, "The Competitiveness of the British Cycle Industry, 1890–1914," *Economic History Review* 22, 2 (August 1969): 287–303.

41. Foreman-Peck, "Diversification and the Growth of the Firm," 180–81; Harrison, "The Competitiveness of the British Cycle Industry," 302–03.

42. Letter from C. E. Hawley, Pope Manufacturing Co., to Arthur L. Garford, 20 November 1895, Box 1, File 4, Arthur L. Garford Papers, OHS.

43. "Timely Trade Topics," *The Sporting Goods Dealer* (July 1900): 16–17; "Is Making Motor Bicycles," *Cycle Age and Trade Review* 25 (5 July 1900).

44. Harry V. Sucher, *The Iron Redskin* (Newbury Park: Haynes Publishing, 1988 [1977]), 17.

45. "British Motor Cycles," *Bicycling World* 44, 11 (12 December 1901): 233; "A.B.C.'s Motocycle," *Bicycling World* 23, 6 (6 March 1902): 597.

46. "Motor Bicycles of 1904," *Bicycling World* 49, 1 (2 April 1904): 44–48; Sucher, *The Iron Redskin*, 18–22.

47. "Boston the Hotbed," *Bicycling World* 45, 9 (20 May 1902): 253.

48. Arthur L. Garford to J. A. Hunt, 13 August 1900, Box 2, File 8, Arthur Garford Papers, OHS.

49. Donald Davis, *Conspicuous Production: Automobiles and Elites in Detroit, 1899–1933* (Philadelphia: Temple University Press, 1988), 5–10.

50. *Commercial and Financial Chronicle* 80 (14 January 1905): 160; 83 (29 December 1906): 1589.

51. Ray M. Smith, *The Story of Pope's Barrels* (Harrisburg: Stackpole Books, 1960), 43–44.

52. Carl F. Burgwardt, *The Story of Buffalo's Bicycles* (Orchard Park, NY: Pedaling History Bicycle Museum, 2001), 56–59.

53. Hugh Dolnar, "Bicycle Tools, Pt. XVIII," *American Machinist* 19, 8 (27 February 1896): 231–33; James Smith, *Seventh Biennial Report of the Bureau of Labor Statistics of the State of Colorado, 1899–1900* (Denver: State of Colorado, 1901), 354.

54. Donald G. Bahna, "The Pope Toledo Strike of 1907: Part I," *Northwest Ohio Quarterly* 35 (Summer 1963): 106–21; "Part II," *Northwest Ohio Quarterly* 35 (Autumn 1963): 172–87.

55. Bahna, "The Pope Toledo Strike, Part I," 106–21; William Franklin Willoughby, "Employers' Associations for Dealing with Labor in the United States," *Quarterly Journal of Economics* 20, 1 (November 1905): 110–50.

56. Ohio State Board of Arbitration, *Fourteenth Annual Report to the Governor of the State of Ohio for the Year Ending December 31, 1906* (Columbus: F. J. Hess, state printer, 1907), 36–40; *Toledo Union-Bee*, 30 August 1906.

57. Bahna, "The Pope Toledo Strike, Part I," 112–13.

58. Ohio State Board of Arbitration, *Fourteenth Annual Report*, 38.

59. *Pope Motor Car Company v. Keegan*, 150 F. 148 (N.D. Ohio 1906).

60. Bahna, "The Pope Toledo Strike of 1907: Part II," 175–180.

61. "Strike Costly to Pope's," *Toledo Blade*, 25 February 1907.

62. *Toledo News-Bee*, 17 August 1907.

63. News to me: *Toledo News-Bee*, 15 August 1907; internal conflict: *Toledo Blade*, 11 November 1907.

64. "Colonel George Pope Wants Employers' Union," *New York Times*, 13 August 1916.

65. Seltzer, *A Financial History of the American Automobile Industry*, 57.

66. *Commercial and Financial Chronicle* 85 (17 August 1907): 403.

67. "Big Pope Concern in Receiver's Hands," *New York Times*, 15 August 1907.

68. Bahna, "The Pope Toledo Strike of 1907: Part II," 175–80.

69. John B. Rae, *American Automobile Manufacturers: The First Forty Years* (Philadelphia: Chilton, 1959), 48–49. The Jeep was actually developed in the late 1930s by Bantam, but most of those used in World War II were made by Willys and Ford. Jeep continued to use the Toledo plant until the early 1990s.

70. *Commercial and Financial Chronicle* 87 (10 October 1908): 952; (19 December 1908): 1608.

71. Dewing, "The American Bicycle Company," 260–268; *Pope v. Hinkley*, 905 N.E. 798 (S.J.C. Mass., 1911), unpublished material.

## Chapter 12

1. "Death Comes to Col. Albert A. Pope," *Boston Globe*, 11 August 1909; "Col. A. A. Pope Passes Away at Cohasset," *Boston Post*, 11 August 1909; "Col. Albert A. Pope Dies of Pneumonia," *Hartford Courant*, 11 August 1909; "The Bicycle Age Was a Great Age," *Hartford Courant*, 12 August 1909; "Col. A. A. Pope Dies at Summer Home," *New York Times*, 11 August 1909: 3.

2. Bruce Epperson, "Failed Colossus: Albert A. Pope and the Pope Manufacturing Company, 1876–1900," *Cycle History 9: Proceedings of the 9th International Cycle History Conference*, ed. Glen Norcliffe and Rob van der Plas (San Francisco: Van der Plas Publications, 1999): 93–112.

3. *See*, for example, "The Greatest Gathering of Cyclists," *Bicycling World* 49, 6 (7 May 1904): 204–08; private correspondence discussing gout: letter from A. B. Leonard to Arthur L. Garford, 5 February 1902, Box 4, File 3, Arthur L. Garford Papers (MSS 6), Ohio Historical Society, Columbus.

4. *Pope v. Pope*, 95 N.E. 864 (Mass. 1911); *Pope v. Hinkley*, 95 N.E. 798 (Mass. 1911). The text of Pope's will, dated 16 June 1905, and a codicil, dated 28 May 1906, are filed under the Massachusetts Supreme Judicial Court designator for *Pope v. Hinkley*, 209 Mass. 323 (S.J.C. Mass. 1911), docket number S.J.C. 504.

5. Molly Hochkeppel, "English Country Feeling on Howe Road," *Quincy Patriot Ledger*, 31 October 1991.

6. *Twelfth Census of the United States* [1900]. Schedule I, Population: Norfolk County, E.D. 1829, page 22.

7. *Ashley v. Winkley*, 95 N.E. 932 (Mass. 1911).

8. "New Pope Motor Cycle" (advertising flyer, 30 January 1911), "A confidential letter to our dealers" (advertising flyer, 5 October 1912), both Box 2, File 36, Warshaw Business History Collection, Smithsonian Archives Collection, Museum of American History, Washington, D.C.; Pope motorcycle: Smith Hempstone Oliver and Donald H. Berkebile, *The Smithsonian Collection of Automobiles and Motorcycles* (Washington, D.C.: Smithsonian Institution Press, 1968),119–121; "The Coaster Brake," *Bicycling World* 49, 1 (2 April 1904): 35–37.

9. Indian and Excelsior: Harry V. Sucher, *The Iron Redskin* (Newbury Park, CA: Haynes Publishing), 49–60; Pope: *Commercial and Financial Chronicle* 101 (28 August 1915): 698.

10. *Tariff Hearings Before the House Committee on Ways and Means, 1908–1909, Vol. III, Paragraph 193 (Bicycles)* (Washington, D.C.: Government Printing Office, 1909), 2718–2725. 60th Congress, 2nd Session, Document No. 1505.

11. Industry statistics: *Census of Manufacturers, 1905: Special Reports: Bicycles and Tricycles*, by Robert Merriam (Bulletin No. 66), (Washington, D.C.: Government Printing Office), 289–296; *Twelfth Census of the United States [1910]: Manufacturing Industries, Part 3, Special Reports: Bicycles, Motorcycles and Parts* (Washington, D.C.: Government Printing Office, 1913), 825–828; *Census of Manufacturers, 1914: Special Reports: Motorcycles and Parts*, by Harry B. Cohen (Washington, D.C.: Government Printing Office), II, 749–753. Pope statis-

tics: *Commercial and Financial Chronicle* 87 (8 August 1908): 351; *Commercial and Financial Chronicle* 99 (2 July 1914): 274; Westfield situation and advertising: "Letter from the Pope Mfg. Co. to Pope Bicycle Dealers," 11 June 1914; "The Pope Mfg. Co. to Our Bicycle Dealers," 23 March 1915, both in files of Soo Hardware (Michigan); Hagley Museum and Library, Wilmington Delaware.

12. "Pope Manufacturing Confidential Price Sheet and Terms to Dealers," 1 September 1912, Box 2, File 36, Warshaw Business History Collection, Smithsonian Archives, NMAH.

13. Ross Petty, "The Bicycle as a Communications Medium: A Comparison of Bicycle Use by the U.S. Postal Service and Western Union Telegraph Company," *Cycle History 16: Proceedings of the 16th International Cycle history Conference*, ed. Andrew Ritchie (San Francisco: Van der Plas Publications, 2006): 147–59; Gregory J. Downey, *Telegraph Messenger Boys: Labor, Technology and Geography, 1850–1950* (New York: Routledge, 2002), 73–77.

14. *Pope v. Fairchild*, 133 A. 886 (N.Y.S. 1909).

15. Thomas F. Saal, "Pope Hartford: Too Good to Fail?" *Automobile Quarterly* 36, 1 (December, 1996): 93–109.

16. *Commercial and Financial Chronicle* 91 (1 October 1910): 868.

17. *Commercial and Financial Chronicle* 96 (4 January 1913): 65; "A. W. Pope & Co. to Assign," *New York Times*, 26 February 1913.

18. *Commercial and Financial Chronicle* 97 (11 October 1913): 937; "Pope Manufacturing Goes Into a Receivership," *Wall Street Journal*, 29 August 1913; "Receiver for the Pope Mfg. Co.," *New York Times*, 29 October 1913.

19. In David Post's case, evidence that time does heal all wounds. It probably didn't hurt that Post had become very wealthy and successful as vice-president of the Veeder Mfg. Co. of Hartford.

20. *Commercial and Financial Chronicle* 98 (20 June 1914): 1923; (27 June 1914): 1997; *Commercial and Financial Chronicle* 99 (11 July 1914).

21. "Business Troubles," *New York Times*, 3 June 1915; *Commercial and Financial Chronicle* 99 (1 August 1914): 347; *Commercial and Financial Chronicle* 101 (28 August 1915): 698; (11 September 1915): 850.

22. "Pope, Harold Linder," *National Cyclopedia of American Biography* (New York: Scribner's, 1958).

23. "98 Model Prized by Auto Museum in Connecticut for 'New' Features," *New York Times*, 18 August 1947.

24. "Interview with Norman A. Clarke, April 5, 1998, North Chatham, MA," 33–34. This interview was transcribed by the author in 1998–99 from audiotape. The original tapes are on deposit at the American Bicycling Museum, New Bremen, OH. Fogarty, Walker and Cox neighbors: *Thirteenth Census of the United States [1910], Schedule I: Population*, City of West Hartford, ED 206, Sheet 13A. Cox's history: letter from J. F. Cox to F.S. Cate, 12 June 1908, reproduced in Zordich, "A.B.C's of the Pope Manufacturing Company," 40.

25. "Interview with Norman A. Clarke," 2; letter from Norman A. Clarke to Bruce Epperson, 29 December 1997, appended to the transcript of the Norman Clarke interview.

26. "Frank W. Schwinn's 1942 Personal Notes on the Bicycle Industry," 3–7, 16. This monograph was published by the now-defunct Bicycle Museum of America (also known as the Schwinn Museum) in Chicago in 1993.

27. "List of Bicycle Manufacturers Invited to Attend Meeting of November 8th," Box 5, File 1, Arthur Garford Papers, OHS; "1913 Bicycle Figures," *Motorcycling and Cycle Trades Review* (2 February 1914): 49. The eleven firms in 1913, in rough order of size, were: Davis Sewing Machine (later Huffy); Excelsior Cycle (bought by Rollfast in 1930); Pope (later Westfield); H.P. Snyder (a.k.a. Rollfast); Miami Cycle; Emblem; Reading Cycle (a.k.a. Great Western); Iver Johnson; Excelsior Motor and Mfg. (a.k.a. Schwinn); National Cycle. 1933 firms: "A Bicycle Rampant," *Fortune* 8, 3 (September 1933): 49–51ff. The seven were: Snyder; Westfield; Shelby Cycle; Schwinn; Emblem (who now owned Pierce); and Colson (later Evans Product Co.). In 1954 the firms were: Schwinn; Monarch; Huffman; Cleveland Welding (a.k.a. Roadmaster); Evans Product; Westfield (soon Columbia); Snyder (a.k.a. Rollfast); Shelby Cycle; Murray-Ohio; Excelsior Mfg.

28. Judith Crown and Glen Coleman, *No Hands: The Rise and Fall of the Schwinn Bicycle Company* (New York: Henry Holt, 1996), 25–37; Jay Pridmore and Jim Hurd, *Schwinn Bicycles* (Osceola, WI: Motorbooks International, 1996), 34–38.

29. Letter from Norman A. Clarke to Bruce Epperson, 20 May 1998; appended to the transcript of the Norman Clarke interview.

30. "Interview with Norman A. Clarke," 34; "Incorporates to Makes Cycles," *Cycle Age and Trade Review* 23 (11 May 1899): 35; Charles Meinert, "Wheels along the Mohawk: The Snyder Bicycle Company," *The Wheelmen* 52 (May 1998): 2–9; Charles Meinert, "Notes from interview with Bill Snyder, Fall 1997" (unpublished). Many thanks to Charles Meinert, a talented and dedicated independent scholar. One of his Rollfast trips: *Motorcycling and Bicycling News* (23 October 1916).

31. "Interview with Norman A. Clarke," 34; *Phoenix State Bank v. Whitcomb*, 183 A. 5 (Conn. 1936); *Fifteenth Census of the United States [1930], Schedule I: Population*, West Hartford, ED 2-222, sheet 7A (Wilbur); ED 2-71, sheet 46A (Charles).

32. "A Bicycle Rampant," 51, 116; "Will Retire Stock," *New York Times*, 2 August 1929; "Westfield Manufacturing Company," *New York Times*, 2 April 1932; "Interview with Norman A. Clarke," 34;

33. "U.S. Bicycle Market Statistics, 1895 to 1977," *Schwinn Reporter* (February 1978): unpaginated. Many thanks to Frank Berto for this invaluable source.

34. "A Bicycle Rampant," 50.

35. "A Bicycle Rampant," 51, 116; "John P. Fogarty," *New York Times*, 2 March 1932; "Interview with Norman A. Clarke,": 1, 12, 34; State of Florida Death Certificate, File No. 4806, 3 March 1929. Florida Office of Vital Statistics, Tallahassee.

36. "Interview with Norman A. Clarke," *passim*; *Phoenix State Bank v. Whitcomb*, 183 A. 5 (Conn. 1936); "Miss Jane Walker Engaged to Marry," *New York Times*, 16 August 1953; "C. E. Walker Dies," *Hartford Courant*, 24 February 1950.

37. Schwinn, "Frank V. Schwinn's Personal Notes on the Bicycle Industry," 5.

38. Schwinn, "Frank V. Schwinn's Personal Notes on the Bicycle Industry," 19.

39. "Opinions of Dealers," *Cycle Age and Trade Review* 21 (1 September 1898): 498.

40. Crown and Coleman, *No Hands*, 30–55.

41. "Interview with Norman A, Clarke," *passim*; letters from Norman A. Clarke to Bruce Epperson, 25 April 1997; 7 May 1997; 29 December 1997; 20 May 1998; appended to the transcript of the Norman Clarke interview.

42. "Interview With Norman A, Clarke," 10–11.

43. "2 Plants Designated to Produce Bicycles," *New York Times*, 3 September 1942.

44. "Interview with Norman A. Clarke," 4, 32.

45. "Interview with Norman A. Clarke," 20

46. U.S. Department of Commerce, "Facts for Industry: Bicycles" (Series M49-1-6, 26 November 1946); Canadian Ministry of Trade and Commerce, *The Bicycle Manufacturing Industry: 1955* (Series A9-13-11-55): table 6.

47. The BMA was one of four divisions of the Bicycle Institute of America (BIA). The BIA, in turn, had been in existence since the early 1900s as the Cycle Trades Association. It changed its name in the closing days of World War II to BIA. It was the umbrella organization for the cycle trades, and also included associations for jobbers, parts makers and wholesalers. It discontinued operations about 1970, leaving only the BMA, the manufacturer's organization. Frank V. Schwinn withdrew his firm from the BMA at its 1969 mid-winter meeting in a dispute over the role mass merchandisers (principally Sears) should play in the revamped organization, but continued to work with it on areas of common concern. Interview with Bill Wilkinson, 17 July 2008, Interview with Jay Townley, 23 May 2009.

48. "Interview with Norman A. Clarke," 16–17; "Bicycle Makers Seek Tariff Help," *New York Times*, 22 August 1954.

49. Pridmore and Hurd, *Schwinn Bicycles*, 101, 105; "Interview with Norman A. Clarke," 10–11, 28–29; Roger Lloyd-Jones and M.J. Lewis, "Culture as Metaphor: Company Culture and Business Strategy at Raleigh Industries, 1945–60," *Business History* 41, 3 (July, 1999): 93.

50. "Interview with Norman A. Clarke," 23–24.

51. "Interview with Norman A. Clarke," 9; Frank J. Berto, "The Great American Bicycle Boom" *Cycle History 10: Proceedings of the 10th International Cycle History Conference*, ed. Hans-Erhard Lessing and Andrew Ritchie (San Francisco: Van der Plas Publications, 2000): 133–48.

52. Arthur M. Louis, "How the Customers Thrust Unexpected Prosperity on the Bicycle Industry," *Fortune* 89; 3 (March 1974): 117–24.

53. "Interview with Norman A. Clarke," 23.

54. Peter M. Kerr, "Demographic and Energy Effects on the U.S. Demand for Bicycles," *Transportation Research Record* 1141 (1987): 37–42; Berto, "The Great American Bicycle Boom," 143.

55. Crown and Coleman, *No Hands*, 50–53; 142–43; "Interview with Norman A. Clarke," 23.

56. "Interview with Norman A. Clarke," 9.

57. "Interview with Norman A. Clarke," 26; Gregory Houston Bowdin, *The Story of the Raleigh Cycle* (London: W. H. Allen, 1975), 170; Berto, *The Dancing Chain*, 186.

58. Many thanks to Ross Petty for bringing the Booz, Allen report to my attention.

59. "Interview with Norman A. Clarke," 25–26.

60. "Interview with Norman A. Clarke," 17–18.

61. The exact date of Clark's trip to Japan is difficult to pin down. Twice, he said it was 1961. Bowdin's *The Story of the Raleigh Cycle* dates the Booz, Allen and Hamilton report to 1964, pushing the Western Auto incident back to 1964 or early 1965. Frank Berto's *The Dancing Chain*, probably the most reliable of the sources, states that the Raleigh decision was made in 1963. Crown and Coleman's *No Hands* presents virtually the same story that Clarke related, but misidentifies the Columbia president as Ben Harding. It gives a general date of 1962–1964. I conclude that it probably took place in 1963.

62. "Interview with Norman A. Clarke," 27.

63. Louis, "How the Customers Thrust Unexpected Prosperity on the Bicycle Industry," 119–120; "Two-Wheel Drive: Bicycle Makers Are Headed for Another Record Year," *Barron's* 47, 50 (11 December 1967): 11.

64. Griff Witte, "A Rough Ride for Schwinn Bicycle," *Washington Post*, 3 December 2004.

65. "500 Strike Columbia Bike Plant in Westfield," *Boston Globe*, 10 July 1984; "Bicycle Firm Seeks Chapter 11," *Boston Globe*, 2 September 1993.

66. Bill Zajac, "Columbia Recycles '41 Cruiser," *Springfield Republican*, 19 October 1997; Pridmore and Hurd, *Schwinn Bicycles*, 152.

67. "A Memory Reborn," *Bicycle Rider* 3, 1 (January/February 1987): 18–19.

68. Berto, *The Dancing Chain*, 280–320; Rosen, *Framing Production*: Appendix C; Witte, "A Rough Ride for Schwinn Bicycle."

## Chapter 13

1. Letter from Arthur L. Garford to C.L. Mosher of *Bicycling World*, 15 July 1914, Box 18, File 8, Arthur Garford Papers (MSS 6), Ohio Historical Society, Columbus.

2. *Greer's Hartford Directory* for years 1900–01 through 1906–07; Bettye H. Pruitt and Jeffrey R. Yost, *Timken: From Missouri to Mars* (Boston: Harvard Business School Press, 1998), 54; 57; 62; *Chicago Tribune*, 13 November 1950.

3. Henry Cave, "Hartford, Incubator of the Automotive Industry" *Old Timers News* 2, 2 (April 1944): 30–31; "Milton J. Budlong, 72, of Newport Is Dead," *New York Times*, 7 July 1941.

4. *Thirteenth Census of the United States [1910], Schedule I: Population*, Virginia, Orange County, SD 8, ED 91, Sheet 12B.

5. Carole Nichols and Joyce Pendery, "Pro Bono Publico: Voices of Connecticut's Political Women, 1915–1945," *Oral History* 11 (1983) 48–74; Jimmy Elaine Wilkinson Meyer, *Any Friend of the Movement: Networking for Birth Control 1920–1940* (Columbus: Ohio State University Press, 2004), 37–38.

6. Hermann Cuntz, "A Sketch of the Life of Harold Hayden Eames, October 12, 1940." Box 3, File 1, Henry Cave Collection, National Automotive History Collection, Detroit Public Library; "Hayden Eames, 74, an Industrialist," *New York Times*, 25 November 1938.

7. Ellsworth S. Grant, *Yankee Dreamers and Doers: The Story of Connecticut Manufacturing* (Hartford: Connecticut Historical Society, n.d. [1996?]), 252; *Boston Globe*, 10 November 1908.

8. "Charles R. Flint Dies," *New York Times*, 14 February 1934.

9. Old Colonel: Letter from Arthur L. Garford to Hart O. Berg, 6 October 1904, Arthur Garford Papers,

OHS; "Quits the Cycle Trade," *Bicycling World* 49, 9 (28 May 1904): 123; "Garford, Arthur Lovett," *The Automobile Industry, 1896–1920*, ed. George S. May (New York: Facts on File, 1990).

10. "H.A. Lozier Dead," *Bicycling World* 47, 9 (30 May 1903): 285–86; Percy J. Boore, *The Seamless Story* (Los Angeles: Commonwealth, 1951), 210–212.

11. "Pope, Abby Linden [sic]," *The Biographical Cyclopedia of American Women*, Mabel Ward Cameron, ed. (New York: Halvord Publishing Company, 1924): I, 357–58; *Boston City Directory* (Boston: Sampson, Davenport and Co.) for 1930.

12. "Albert Linder Pope Dies, Pioneer in Auto Industry," *Hartford Courant*, 11 August 1955; "Albert L. Pope Dies, Retired Industrialist," *Hartford Times*, 10 August 1955; "Pope, William," *Hartford Courant*, 4 January 2003.

13. "Edward W. Pope Dead in Newton," *Boston Globe*, 15 December 1936; "Edward W. Pope, 91," *New York Times*, 15 December 1936.

14. Letter from Emily F. Pope to Margaret Noyes Kleinert, 11 January 1928, Box 9, Folder 34, New England Hospital Collection, Sophia Smith Collection, Smith College; Letter from Harry Pope, 5 March 1928, excerpted in Gerald O. Kelver, *Respectfully Yours—H. M. Pope*. (Fort Collins: Robinson Press, 1976), 102; "Dr. C. Augusta Pope," *Boston Globe*, 29 March 1931; "Dr. C. Augusta Pope," *New York Times*, 29 March 1931.

15. "Death Comes to Col. George Pope," *Hartford Courant*, 20 April 1918; "George Pope Wants Employers' Union," *New York Times*, 13 August 1916; let us help him: Andrea Tone, *The Business of Benevolence: Industrial Paternalism in Progressive America* (Ithaca: Cornell University Press, 1997), 36.

16. "Aeronautics: First Stock Scandal," *Time* 14, 9 (26 August 1929): 4; "Pope, Harold L." *National Cyclopedia of American Biography* (New York: Scribner's, 1958): IV, 51; *Pope v. United States*, 296 F.Supp. 17 (S.D. Cal. 1968).

17. Kelver, *Respectfully Yours—H. M. Pope*, Chapter 25; Ray M. Smith, *The Story of Pope's Barrels*. (Harrisburg: Stackpole Books, 1960), Chapter 8.

18. *Boston City Directory*, 1911–35.

19. "Frank V. Schwinn, Sr.," *Chicago Tribune*, 22 April 1963; Judith Crown and Glenn Coleman, *No Hands: The Rise and Fall of the Schwinn Bicycle Company* (New York: Henry Holt, 1996): 51, 71, 251.

20. "Death Comes to Henry Souther," *Hartford Courant*, 17 August 1917; Electronic mail transmission from William A. G. Mackey to the author, 11 December 2007.

21. Peter Levine, *A. G. Spalding and the Rise of Baseball* (New York: Oxford University Press, 1985), 123–50.

22. Charles Wrege and Ronald Greenwood, *Frederick W. Taylor: The Father of Scientific Management* (Homewood, IL, Business One Irvin, 1991), 179–80; 229–31; 235–41.

23. *Phoenix State Bank & Trust Co. v. Whitcomb*, 183 A. 5 (Conn. 1936); "Miss L. Higginson to Wed John Gould," "Marie Abbie Walker to Be Married Nov. 14," *New York Times*, 15 October 1950; "C. E. Walker Dies, Former Official of Pope Company," *Harford Courant*, 24 February 1950.

24. Mark D. Hirsch, *William C. Whitney: Modern Warwick* (Hamden, CT: Archon Books, 1969 [1948]), 556–61.

25. *New York Times*, 8 December 1938.

## Chapter 14

1. Fred H. Colvin, *60 Years with Men and Machines: An Autobiography* (New York: McGraw-Hill, 1947), 83; 86.

2. David A. Hounshell, *From the American System to Mass Production, 1800–1932: The Development of Manufacturing Technology in the United States* (Baltimore: Johns Hopkins University, 1984), Chapter 5.

3. Glen Norcliffe, "Popeism and Fordism: Examining the Roots of Mass Production," *Regional Studies* 31, 3 (1997): 267–280. See also: Glen Norcliffe, *The Ride to Modernity: The Bicycle in Canada, 1869–1900* (Toronto: University of Toronto Press, 2001). If I interpret the latter work correctly, Norcliffe attempts to soften the conclusions in his earlier *Regional Studies* article by substituting the more ambiguous "modern production methods" for "mass production," a shift that, in my opinion, does not improve his case.

4. Ross D. Petty, "Peddling the Bicycle in the 1890s: Mass Marketing Shifts into High Gear," *Journal of Macromarketing* (Spring 1995): 32–46.

5. Phillip S. Scranton, *Endless Novelty: Specialty Production and American Industrialization, 1865–1925* (Princeton: Princeton University Press, 1997), 282.

6. Letter from H. B. Smith to G. W. Pressey, 17 April 1882, *Transcript of Witnesses, 23 January 1888*, *Pressey v. H. B. Smith Mfg. Co.*, 19 A. 618 (N.J. App. 1889), Hagley Museum and Library, Wilmington, Delaware, 124 (hereafter "*Pressey v. Smith* Case File").

7. Scranton, *Endless Novelty*, 10–11. I have somewhat modified Scranton's definitions. He looked at a wide variety of manufacturers, from textiles to locomotives, where I have examined a much narrower cross-section of firms, those in specialty metalworking, such as sewing machines and machine tools.

8. Lindy Biggs, *The Rational Factory: Architecture, Technology and Work in America's Age of Mass Production* (Baltimore: Johns Hopkins University Press, 1996), 10–29; Paul Rosen, *Framing Production: Technology, Culture and Change in the British Bicycle Industry* (Cambridge: MIT Press, 2002), 58–65; Harold Roth, *Bicycle Factory* (New York: Pantheon, 1985).

9. Rosen, *Framing Production*, 55–70.

10. Roth, *Bicycle Factory*, 16.

11. "Huffy Corporation," *International Directory of Company Histories* (New York: St. James Press, 2000): 231.

12. *Ibid.*, 153.

13. Samuel Vauclain of the Baldwin Locomotive Works in his book *Steaming Up!* (New York: Macmillan, 1930), 146.

14. "History of the American Bicycle," *American Athlete and Cycle Trades Review* 7, 11 (20 March 1891): 240.

15. Duncan's article was reproduced in the United States as "Exhibitions and Foreign Competition," *The American Athlete* 4, 5 (7 November 1888): 60.

16. "Comparative Study of the Bicycle, Parts 1–4," *Bicycling World* 2 (31 December 1880): 118–119; (7 January 1881): 131–134; (28 January 1881): 181–182; (7 February 1881): 195–197.

17. Carl F. Burgwardt, "A Landscape of Early Bicycle History: From the Lips of George R. Bidwell, an Exraordinary Pioneer Wheelman from Buffalo, N.Y.," *Cycle History 7: Proceedings of the 7th International Cycle History Conference*, ed Rob van der Plas (San Francisco: Van der Plas Publications, 1997): 92.

18. Julius Wilcox, "The Cost of It," *The Wheelman* 3, 5 (February 1884): 379–380.

19. Charles E. Pratt, "A Sketch of American Bicycling and Its Founder," *Outing* 18, 4 (July 1891): 342–349.

20. Letter from George Pope to David J. Post, 4 March 1891, Pope/Hartford Papers, History and Genealogy Division, Connecticut State Library, Hartford. The weight of an 1891 Hartford was 51 pounds; in 1896 this was down to 26 pounds with guards and brake, 23 stripped. *Hartford Cycle Catalog for 1891*; *Columbia and Hartford Bicycle Catalog for 1896*.

21. *Scientific American*, July 1899, reprinted as "Effect of the Guarantee: Bicycles Growing Heavier," *Cycle Age and Trade Review* 23 (1 September 1899): 509.

22. Letter from Arthur L. Patrick to Arthur L. Garford, 5 September 1898, Box 1, File 10, Arthur Garford Papers (MSS 6), Ohio Historical Society, Columbus.

23. "Local Builder's Risks," *Cycle Age and Trade Review* 21 (27 October 1898): 755.

24. "Buying Late Stock," *Cycle Age and Trade Review*, 21 (13 October 1898): 692.

25. George F. Parker, "American Bicycles in England," *The North American Review* 163, 481 (December 1896): 688–95.

26. "Bisons Are Bouyant," *Cycle Age and Trade Review*, 23 (1 June 1899): 113.

27. Willard S. Mattox, "American Bicycle Fittings and Machinery in England," *Iron Age* 62 (3 November 1898): 8.

28. "Affidavit of Mr. George Pope, 20 May 1901," *Report of the Industrial Commission on Trusts and Industrial Combinations* (57th Cong., 1st Session, House Document No. 182) (Washington, D.C.: Government Printing Office, 1901) XIII: 688–691.

29. "Figures of the Industry," *Cycle Age and Trade Review* 20 (17 February 1898): 571.

30. "The Industry: How It Grew Up," *Bicycling World* 46 (18 December 1902): 325.

31. "Assemblers or Manufacturers?" *Cycle Age and Trade Review* 23 (22 June 1899): 189.

32. *Ibid.*, In the 1990s the American component maker SRAM sued the dominant supplier, Shimano, who sold its original equipment manufacture (OEM) parts to cyclemakers at a significant discount when purchased as a complete package. SRAM used the same argument: that at least one component in each group was inferior, and given a choice, makers and their customers would rather have options other than an all-Shimano bicycle. *SRAM Corp. v. Shimano*, unpublished opinion 00–55626 (9th Cir., 14 January 2002). See also *SRAM Corp. v. Shimano*, unpublished opinion CV-96-0028-GLT (N.D. California, 2001).

33. "Importance of the Assemblers," *Cycle Age and Trade Review* 23 (29 June 1899): 211.

34. *Ibid.*, 211.

35. "Local Builders' Risks," 755.

36. Petty, "Peddling the Bicycle in the 1890s," 33–35. Petty attributes the $4–$6 million per year to a 1978 conference paper by Robert Steiner, while the $100 million figure is from a 1948 magazine article by Hannibal Coons. The billion dollar number is from Charles Austin Bates, "The Rise and Fall of Bicycle Advertising," *The Art and Science of Business* (4 vols.) (New York: Bates Advertising, 1902): IV, 240. In fairness, it should be noted that Petty also rejects many of these figures as improbable. It appears that many were concocted by the bicycle trust to try to coerce trade journals away from bad publicity through threats to withhold advertising from a single journal or even the entire trade. See "Refused to Be Coerced," *Cycle Age and Trade Review* 24 (25 January 1900): 5, and, "Allegations and the Facts," *Cycle Age and Trade Review* 25 (3 May 1900): 5. Blasting a claim by one factory owner that the big firms each spent five to six million dollars a year, *Cycle Age* estimated that "the aggregate amount paid to the trade press since the inception of the industry, with compound interest at 7 percent, would not reach the figures mentioned." "General Notes and Information," *Cycle Age* 23 (25 May 1899): 88.

37. Pope advertising: Charles Austin Bates, *Good Advertising* (New York: Holmes Publishing, 1896), 16; Sterling advertising, Petty, "Peddling the Bicycle in the 1890s," 34, citing Frank S. Presbrey, *The History and Development of Advertising* (New York: Doubleday, 1927); "Lessons of Cycle History," *Cycle Age and Trade Review* 23 (21 August 1899): 518.

38. *Ibid.*, 121.

39. "Blackmail Advertising," *American Athlete and Cycle Trades Review* 11, 15 (14 April 1893): 334. Karl Kron [Lyman Hotchkiss Bagg], *Ten Thousand Miles on a Bicycle* (New York: Karl Kron, 1887), 665–798; Steven Goddard, *Colonel Albert Pope and His American Dream Machines* (Jefferson: McFarland, 2000), 10–11. Author Chris Wheeler's real name was Arthur MacOwen: see Kron.

40. "Testimony of C. H. Chickering," *Pressey v. Smith* Case File, 124.

41. "Figures of the Industry," 571.

42. "Assemblers or Manufacturers?" 189.

43. "Blackmail Advertising," 334.

44. Letter from George Pope to David J. Post, 9 January 1892, Pope/Hartford Papers, CHS.

45. Susan Strasser, *Satisfaction Guaranteed: The Making of the American Mass Market* (Washington, D.C.: Smithsonian Institution Press, 1989), 82–83.

46. Cash on Delivery, a service offered by the railway express agencies; "The Manufacture of Sewing Machines," *Scientific American* 42, 12 (20 March 1880): 181.

47. Wilcox, "The Cost of It," 380.

48. Pratt, "A Sketch of American Cycling and Its Founder," 347.

49. Strasser, *Satisfaction Guaranteed* 83.

50. "Combine Cannot Control the Trade," *Cycle Age and Trade Review* 23 (8 June 1899): 137–39; "Survival of the Fittest, Part 1," *Cycle Age and Trade Review* 26 (8 November 1900): 25–27; "Survival of the Fittest, Part 2," *Cycle Age and Trade Review* 26 (15 November 1900): 53.

51. 1903: List of Manufacturers Invited to Attend [Bicycle Manufacturers' Association] meeting of November 8 [1902], Box 5, File 1, Arthur L. Garford Papers, OHS; 1909: "Bicycles (paragraph 193)," *Tariff Hearings Before the Committee on Ways and Means of the House of Representatives, 1908–1909* (60th Cong., 2nd Session, Document No. 1505): III: 2718–2725; 1913: "1913 Bicycle Figures," *Motorcycling* (2 February 1914): 49; 1946: U.S. Bureau of the Census, "Facts for Industry: Bicycles" (Series M49-1-96, September 1946).

52. "Interview with Norman A. Clarke, April 5, 1998, North Chatham, MA," 5–6.

53. U.S. Bureau of the Census, "Facts for Industry: Bicycles" (Series M49-1-6, 26 November 1946); Canadian Ministry of Trade and Commerce, *The Bicycle*

*Manufacturing Industry: 1955* (Series A9-13-11-55): table 6. U.S. Bureau of the Census, "Facts for Industry: Bicycles" (Series M49-1-6, 26 November 1946); Canadian Ministry of Trade and Commerce, *The Bicycle Manufacturing Industry: 1955* (Series A9-13-11-55): table 6. Judith Crown and Glen Coleman, *No Hands: The Rise and Fall of the Schwinn Bicycle Company* (New York: Henry Holt, 1996), 142.

54. "Interview with Norman A. Clarke," 21.

55. Letter from George Pope to David J. Post, 5 January 1895, Pope/Hartford Papers, CHS.

# *Bibliography*

## Archival and Primary Source Material

In Hartford, the Connecticut Historical Society (CHS) is the repository for the microfilm copy of the Pope Scrapbooks, a series of bound newspaper articles assembled by a commercial clipping service for the Pope firm between 1890 and 1899, with some gaps due to missing volumes. The microforms also include copies of Col. Pope's letterbooks from the same period. The latter are horribly difficult to read, but the material that can be deciphered is often enlightening. These microforms are the property of the Pope family, and when I used them in the mid–1990s it was necessary to secure the advance permission of the family, although I have been informed by subsequent users that any researcher who registers in advance to use the Society's reading room may now use them. The Society also holds the Lindley Hubbell collection of notebooks, kept in the early years of the twentieth century by the chief engineer of the Pope-Hartford motor factory. These mostly cover technical details, but some administrative issues are also touched upon. The Ellsworth Grant collection contains information pertaining to the Henry Souther Engineering Company and the Veeder Manufacturing Co., where David J. Post worked in his late years. Down the street, the History and Genealogy and Archives Unit at the Connecticut State Library holds the vital Pope/Hartford Papers, a series of about 50 letters written by George Pope to David J. Post discussing the day-to-day affairs of the Hartford Cycle Co. between 1890 and 1895. Other resources include the papers and notebooks of Hiram Maxim, which others have found highly valuable, but that I found less so. Other resources include Sanborn fire maps of the various Pope factories and, in Archival Record Group #6, the original articles of incorporation for the Pope firm. Elsewhere in Hartford, the Stowe-Day Foundation maintains records relating to the activities of the Hartford Real Estate Improvement Company.

The Ohio Historical Society in Columbus contains the massive Arthur Garford Collection (MSS 6), composed of correspondence, letterbooks, accounting day books and other documents commencing about the time Garford first embarked in the bicycle saddle business in 1890 until well after he had left the bicycle and automobile businesses about 1914. Although the entire collection comprises over 135 boxes of material, papers from Garford's bicycle years are mostly contained in the first eleven. This is the largest collection of primary source material pertaining to the early American bicycle industry currently known in the United States.

In and around Washington, D.C., the Smithsonian Institution has three separate documentary sources under the one roof of the National Museum of American History (NMAH). The Warshaw Business History Collection, administered by the archives division, has an extensive collection of catalogs, advertisements, correspondence and other literature filed under the subject heading "bicycles." The transportation library at NMAH, administered by the Smithsonian Libraries, has a vertical file with several unpublished documents pertaining to the early history of the auto industry in Hartford, including the 1947 exhibit catalog "Hartford's Golden Automobile Jubilee," probably written by Henry Cave, who was working for Hartford's Fuller Brush Co. at the time. The NMAH transportation division itself holds the Charles E. Pratt scrapbook, a complete run of pre–World War I Columbia bicycle catalogs, and bound copies of *Bicycle World* magazine. In nearby College Park, Maryland, the National Archives and Record Administration's Archives II facility contains the Patent Office's "Digest of Patent Assignments" for the years 1864–80 in bound volumes in Records Group NC-147, and the early records of the Bureau of Public Roads in Record Groups 30.1 and 30.2.

In Boston, the Henry L. Higginson collection in the Baker Library contains several letters between the Popes and banker Higginson. These are in the general correspondence files, alphabetically by sender/recipient. The archives of the Supreme Judicial Court of Massachusetts in downtown Boston are normally closed, but archivist Elizabeth Bouvier granted me sufficient access to their garret to transcribe Albert Pope's will and codicil, and to flesh out the details of the *Pope v. Winkey* probate dispute that do not appear in the published opinion. In Northampton, Massachusetts, the New England Hospital Collection of the Sophia Smith Collection at Smith College contains limited information about Drs. Emily and C. Augusta Pope, and the establishment of the Pope memorial dispensary in 1896 and its subsequent operation, primarily in the form of annual reports.

In Detroit, the National Automotive History Collection at the Detroit Public Library has the Henry Cave Collection, containing information that Cave collected while researching his 1944 article "Hartford, Incubator of the Automobile Industry." The Charles B. King and David Becroft collections similarly have letters and sketches from Pope employees, including Hermann Cuntz and Henry Souther. The NAHC also has a bound, multi-volume set of the case record (No. 8566) of the Selden patent case (*Electric Vehicle Co. v. C.A. Duerr & Co. et. al.*). It is not inconceivable that the case record exists on microform (which I used for the *Pope v. Gormully* patent suit), but not being a Supreme Court Case (as was *Pope v. Gormully*), that may not be so. Finally, the NAHC's collection of bound early automobile journals is unmatched. At the Benson Ford Research Center, part of the Henry Ford Museum, the Frank C. Armstrong Collection (MS 1750) contains information relating to the early days of the Electric Vehicle Company.

Additional primary source material pertaining to the Electric Vehicle Company is in the William F.D. Crane Collection (MS 1092) at the New Jersey Historical Society in Newark. In nearby Hoboken, the Stevens Institute of Technology maintains the Frederick W. Taylor manuscript collection, the source of the material related to industrial espionage in the bicycle industry appearing in Chapter 7.

In Delaware, the Hagley Museum and Library holds, in microform, the case record file for *Pressey v. H. B. Smith Mfg. Co.*, and the records of many small, now defunct, manufacturing and distribution firms, of which those of the Soo Hardware Co. proved helpful. Bicycle scholars have not yet begun to mine the wealth of resources that lies within the Hagley.

In Ottawa, the Canadian National Museum of Science and Technology was just starting to process the material that now comprises the Lorne Shields collection when I visited their library in 1999, but even then the collection of bound early cycling journals was extremely helpful, and by now it is undoubtedly a fruitful source of primary source material of all types.

## Books and Book Chapters

*Accuracy for Seventy Years.* Hartford: Pratt and Whitney Company, 1930.
Adams, G. Donald. *Collecting and Restoring Antique Bicycles.* Orchard Park: Pedaling History Museum, 2nd ed., 1996.
Alderson, Frederick. *Bicycling: A History.* New York: Praeger, 1972.
Anderson, Frederick, ed. *Mark Twain's Notebooks and Journals, Volume III, 1883–1891.* Berkeley: University of California Press, 1979.
Bates, Charles Austin. *Good Advertising.* New York: Holmes Publishing, 1896.
_____. "The Rise and Fall of Bicycle Advertising." In *The Art and Science of Business.* 4 vols. New York: Bates Advertising, 1902.
Beeley, Serena. *A History of Bicycles.* Secaucus, NJ: Wellfleet Books, 1992.
Berto, Frank, et al. *The Dancing Chain: History and Development of the Derailleur Bicycle.* San Francisco: Van der Plas Publications, 2000.
Bijker, Wiebe. *Of Bicycles, Bakelites and Bulbs: Toward a theory of Sociotechnical Change.* Cambridge: MIT Press, 1997.
Blanke, David. *Hell on Wheels: The Promise and Peril of America's Car Culture, 1900–1940.* Lawrence: University Press of Kansas, 2007.
Boore, P. J. *The Seamless Story.* Los Angeles: Commonwealth, 1951.
*Boston City Directory.* Boston: Sampson, Davenport and Company, 1880–1910.

Bourne, Francis G. "American Sewing Machines." In *One Hundred Years of American Commerce*, edited by Chauncey Depew, II, 525–39. New York: D. O. Haynes, 1895.
Bowden, Gregory Houston. *The Story of the Raleigh Bicycle.* London: W. H. Allen, 1975.
Bunting, Bainbridge. *Houses of Boston's Back Bay, 1840–1917.* Cambridge: Belknap Press, 1967.
Braverman, Harry. *Labor and Monopoly Capital.* New York: Monthly Review Press, 1974.
Burgwardt, Carl F. *The Story of Buffalo's Bicycles.* Orchard Park: Pedaling History Museum, 2001.
Burton, Walter E. *The Story of Tire Beads and Tires.* New York: National-Standard Co., 1954.
Cadin, Martin, and Jay Barbee. *Bicycles in War.* New York: Hawthorne Books, 1974.
Chandler, Alfred D. *The Visible Hand: The Managerial Revolution in American Business.* Cambridge: Belknap, 1977.
Chernow, Ron. *Titan: The Life of John D. Rockefeller, Sr.* New York: Random House, 1988.
Clark, Victor. *The History of Manufacturers in the United States, 2 Vols.* Cleveland: Carnegie Institution, 1929.
Colvin, Fred H. *60 Years with Men and Machines.* New York: McGraw-Hill, 1947.
Crawford, Margaret. *Building the Workingman's Paradise: The Design of American Company Towns.* New York: Verso, 1995.
Crown, Judith, and Glenn Coleman. *No Hands: The Rise and Fall of the Schwinn Bicycle Company.* New York: Henry Holt, 1996.
Cudahy, Brian J. *Cash, Tokens, and Transfers: A History of Mass Transit in America.* New York: Fordham University Press, 1990.
Davis, Donald. *Conspicuous Production: Automobiles and Elites in Detroit, 1899–1933.* Philadelphia: Temple University Press, 1988.
Dewing, Arthur. "The American Bicycle Company." Chapter 10 in *Corporate Promotions and Reorganizations.* Cambridge: Harvard University Press, 1914.
Dodge, Pryor. *The Bicycle.* Paris: Flammarion, 1996.
Doolittle, James Rood, ed. *The Romance of the Automobile Industry.* New York: Klebold, 1916.
Downey, Gregory J. *Telegraph Messenger Boys: Labor, Technology and Geography, 1850–1950.* New York: Routledge, 2002.
Drachman, Virginia G. *Hospital with a Heart: Women Doctors and the Paradox of Separatism at the New England Hospital, 1862–1969.* Ithaca: Cornell University Press, 1984.
Drucker, Peter. *The Practice of Management.* New York: Perennial Library, 1986 [1954].
Du Cros, Arthur Roy. *Wheels of Fortune.* London: Chapman & Hall, 1938.
Earle, Horatio S. *The Autobiography of "By Gum" Earle.* Lansing: State Review Publishing, 1929.
Flink, James J. *America Adopts the Automobile, 1895–1910.* Cambridge: MIT Press, 1970.
_____. *The Automobile Age.* Cambridge: MIT Press, 1990.

Flint, Charles R. *Memories of an Active Life.* New York: G.P. Putnam's Sons, 1923.

Giddings, Howard A. *Manual for Cyclists for the Use of the Regular Army, Organized Militia, and Volunteer Troops of the United States.* Kansas City: no publisher, 1898.

Goddard, Stephen B. *Getting There: The Epic Struggle Between Road and Rail in the American Century.* New York: Basic Books, 1994.

_____. *Colonel Albert Pope and His American Dream Machines.* Jefferson, NC: McFarland, 2000.

Goodman, Cary. *Choosing Sides: Playground and Street Life on the Lower East Side.* New York: Schocken, 1979.

Graham, Hugh David, and Nancy Diamond. *The Rise of American Research Universities.* Baltimore: Johns Hopkins University Press, 1997.

Grant, Ellsworth. *Yankee Dreamers and Doers: The Story of Connecticut Manufacturing.* Hartford: Connecticut Historical Society, no date [ca. 1996].

Greenleaf, William. *Monopoly on Wheels: Henry Ford and the Selden Automobile Patent.* Detroit: Wayne State University Press, 1961.

*Greer's Hartford Directory.* Hartford: Greer Commercial Publishing, 1876–1910.

Groenewold, John. *Quackenbush Guns.* Mundelein, IL: John Groenewold, 2000.

Hager, Louis P. *History of the West End Street Railway Company.* Boston: Louis P. Hager, 1892.

Hayes, Kevin J. *An American Cycling Odyssey, 1887.* Lincoln : University of Nebraska Press, 2002.

Heine, Jan, and Jean-Pierre Praderes. *The Golden Age of Handbuilt Bicycles.* New York: Rizzoli, 2009 [2005].

Herlihy, David V. *Bicycle: The History.* New Haven: Yale University Press, 2004.

Hewett, Janet B., ed. *Supplement to the Official Records of the Union and Confederate Armies, Part II: Record of Events.* Wilmington: Broadfoot, 1996.

Hirsch, Mark D. *William C. Whitney: Modern Warwick.* Hamden, CT: Archon, 1969 [1948].

Hoke, Donald R. *Ingenious Yankees: The Rise of the American System of Manufacturers.* New York: Columbia University Press, 1990.

Holt, William Stull. *The Bureau of Public Roads: Its History, Activities, and Organization.* Baltimore: Institute for Government Research, 1923. Service Monographs of the U.S. Government No. 26.

Hounshell, David A. *From the American System to Mass Production.* Baltimore: Johns Hopkins University Press, 1984.

*An Industrial Achievement: The Pope Manufacturing Company.* Hartford: Pope Mfg. Co., 1907.

Kanigel, Robert. *The One Best Way: Frederick Winslow Taylor and the Enigma of Efficiency.* New York: Viking, 1997.

Kelver, Gerald O. *Respectfully Yours—H. M. Pope.* Fort Collins: Robinson, 1976.

Kirsch, David A. *The Electric Vehicle and the Burden of History.* New Brunswick: Rutgers University Press, 2000.

Kron, Karl [Lyman H. Bagg]. *Ten Thousand Miles on a Bicycle.* New York: Karl Kron, 1887.

Lacy, Robert. *Ford: The Men and the Machine.* Boston: Little, Brown, 1986.

Laird, Pamela Walker. *Advertising Progress: American Business and the Rise of Consumer Marketing.* Baltimore: Johns Hopkins University Press, 1998.

Lamoreaux, Naomi R. *The Great Merger Movement in American Business, 1895–1904.* Cambridge: Cambridge University Press, 1985.

Lawton, Frederick L. "The Servant in the House: A Brief History of the Sewing Machine." In *Annual Report of the Board of Regents of the Smithsonian Institution for 1929*, 559–83. Washington D.C., Smithsonian Institution, 1930.

Lay, M. G. *Ways of the World: A History of the World's Roads and of the Vehicles that Used Them.* New Brunswick: Rutgers University Press, 1992.

Leavitt, Emily Wilder. *A Genealogy of the Bogman Family.* No location [Boston]: Moses Conant Warren, 1890.

Levine, Lawrence W. *Highbrow, Lowbrow: The Emergence of Cultural Hierarchy in America.* Cambridge: Harvard University Press, 1988.

Levine, Peter. *A. G. Spalding and the Rise of Baseball.* New York: Oxford University Press, 1985.

Lloyd-Jones, Roger, and M. J. Lewis. *Raleigh and the British Bicycle Industry: An Economic and Industrial History, 1870–1960.* Aldershot: Ashgate, 2000.

Lyon, Peter. *Success Story: The Life and Times of S. S. McClure.* New York, Charles Scribner's Sons, 1963.

May, George S. *A Most Unique Machine: The Michigan Origins of the American Automobile Industry.* No location: William B. Eerdmans, 1975.

Maxim, Hiram Percy. *A Genius in the Family.* New York: Harper & Brothers, 1936.

_____. *Horseless Carriage Days.* New York: Harper & Brothers, 1962 [1936].

McClure, S. S. *My Autobiography.* New York: Frederick A. Stokes, 1914.

McShane, Clay. *Down the Asphalt Path: The Automobile and the American City.* New York: Columbia University Press, 1994.

Meyer, Jimmy Elaine Wilkinson. *Any Friend of the Movement: Networking for Birth Control 1920–1940.* Columbus: Ohio State University Press, 2004.

Mom, Gijs. *Electric Vehicle: Technology and Expectations in the Automobile Age.* Baltimore: Johns Hopkins University Press, 2004.

Morantz-Sanchez, Regina Markell. *Sympathy and Science: Women Physicians in American Medicine.* New York: Oxford University Press, 1985.

Nankivell, John H., ed. *History of the 25th Regiment United States Infantry from 1869 to 1926.* Denver: no publisher, 1927.

Nevins, Allan. *Ford: The Times, The Man, The Company.* New York: Scribner's, 1954.

Norcliffe, Glen. *The Ride to Modernity: The Bicycle in Canada, 1869–1900.* Toronto: University of Toronto Press, 2001.

Nye, Peter. *Hearts of Lions: The History of American Bicycle Racing*. New York: W. W. Norton, 1988.
_____. *The Six-Day Bicycle Races*. San Francisco: Van der Plas, 2006.
Oliver, Smith Hempstone, and Donald H. Berkebile. *The Smithsonian Collection of Automobiles and Motorcycles*. Washington, D.C.: Smithsonian Institution Press, 1968.
_____, and _____. *Wheels and Wheeling: The Smithsonian Cycle Collection*. Washington, D.C.: Smithsonian Institution Press, 1974.
Ordway, Brig. Gen. Albert. *Cycle-Infantry Drill Regulations*. Boston: Pope Mfg. Co., 1892.
Pope, Albert A. *Highway Improvement: An Address*. Boston: Pope Mfg. Co., 1889.
_____. *The Relation of Good Street to the Prosperity of a City: An Address*. Boston: Pope Mfg. Co., 1892.
_____. "The Bicycle Industry." In *One Hundred Years of American Commerce*, edited by Chauncy M. Depew, I, 548–553. New York: D.O. Haynes, 1895.
Pope, Charles Henry. *A History of the Dorchester Pope Family*. Boston: Charles Henry Pope, 1888.
Pope, Emily F., C. Augusta Pope and Emma Call. *The Practice of Medicine by Women in the United States*. Boston: Wright and Potter, 1881.
Pridmore, Jay, and Jim Hurd. *The American Bicycle*. Osceola: Motorbooks International, 1995.
_____. *Schwinn Bicycles*. Osceola: Motorbooks International, 1996.
Pruitt, Bettye. *Timken: From Missouri to Mars*. Boston: Harvard Business School Press, 1998.
Rae, John B. *American Automobile Manufacturers: The First Forty Years*. Philadelphia: Chilton, 1959.
Ransom, David F. *George Keller, Architect*. Hartford: Stowe-Day Foundation, 1978.
Rezneck, Samuel. *Business Depressions and Financial Panics*. Westport, CT: Greenwood, 1971.
Riess, Stephen A. *City Games: the Evolution of American Urban Society and the Rise of Sports*. Champaign: University of Illinois Press, 1989.
Ritchie, Andrew. *King of the Road: An Illustrated History of the Bicycle*. Berkeley: Ten Speed, 1975.
_____. *Major Taylor: The Extraordinary Career of a Champion Bicycle Racer*. San Francisco: Bicycle Books, 1988.
Rose, Mark H. *Interstate: Express Highway Politics, 1939–1990*. 2nd ed. Knoxville: University of Tennessee Press, 1990.
Rosen, Paul. *Framing Production: Technology, Culture and Change in the British Bicycle Industry*. Cambridge: MIT Press, 2002.
Roth, Harold. *Bike Factory*. New York: Pantheon, 1985.
Roy, William G. *Socializing Capital: The Rise of the Large Industrial Corporation in America*. Princeton: Princeton University Press, 1977.
Rybczynski, Witold. *A Clearing in the Distance: Frederick Law Olmsted and America in the Nineteenth Century*. New York: Scribner's, 1999.
Schiffer, Michael B. *Taking Charge: The Electric Automobile in America*. Washington, D.C.: Smithsonian Institution Press, 1994.
Scranton, Philip. *Endless Novelty: Specialty Production and American Industrialization, 1865–1925*. Princeton: Princeton University Press, 1997.
Seasholes, Nancy S. *Gaining Ground: A History of Landmaking in Boston*. Cambridge: MIT Press, 2003.
Seltzer, Lawrence H. *A Financial History of the American Automobile Industry*. Boston: Houghton Mifflin, 1928.
Shlakman, Vera. *Economic History of a Factory Town: A Study of Chicopee, Massachusetts*. New York: Octagon, 1969 [1934].
Sharp, Archibold. *Bicycles and Tricycles: An Elementary Treatise on Their Design and Construction*. Cambridge: MIT Press, 1977 [1896].
Shuey, Edwin L. *Factory People and Their Employees*. New York: Lentilhon and Co., 1900.
Smith, Philip Hillyer. *Wheels within Wheels: A Short History of American Motor Car Manufacturing*. New York: Funk and Wagnalls, 1968.
Smith, Ray M. *The Story of Pope's Barrels*. Harrisburg, PA: Stackpole, 1960.
Smith, Robert A. *The Social History of the Bicycle*. New York: American Heritage Press, 1972.
Smith, W. H. B. *Smith's Standard Encyclopedia of Gas, Air and Spring Guns*. New York: Castle, 1957.
Stevens, Thomas. *Around the World on a Bicycle*. Mechanicsburg, PA: Stackpole, 2001 [1887].
Strasser, Susan. *Satisfaction Guaranteed: The Making of the American Mass Market*. Washington, D.C.: Smithsonian Institution Press, 1989.
Street, Roger. *The Pedestrian Hobby-Horse*. Christchurch: Artesius, 1998.
Sucher, Harry V. *The Iron Redskin*. Newbury Park, CA: Haynes, 1988.
Taylor, Marshall W. *The Fastest Bicycle Rider in the World*. North Stratford: Ayer, 1977 [1928].
Tone, Andrea. *The Business of Benevolence: Industrial Paternalism in Progressive America*. Ithaca: Cornell University Press, 1997.
Twain, Mark. "Taming the Bicycle." In *Collected Tales, Sketches, Speeches & Essays, 1852–1890*, 892–99. New York: Library of America.
Vauclain, Samuel. *Steaming Up!* New York: Macmillan, 1930.
Warner, Sam Bass. *Streetcar Suburbs: The Process of Growth in Boston, 1879–1900*. Cambridge: Harvard University Press, 1978.
Wermiel, Sara E. *The Fireproof Building: Technology and Public Safety in the Nineteenth Century American City*. Baltimore: Johns Hopkins University Press, 2000.
Williamson, Geoffrey. *Wheels within Wheels: The Story of the Starleys of Coventry*. London: Goeffrey Bles, 1966.
Wilson, David Gordon. *Bicycling Science*. 3rd ed. Cambridge: MIT Press, 2004.
Wolman, Paul. *Most Favored Nation: The Republican Revisionists and U. S. Tariff Policy, 1897–1912*. Chapel Hill: University of North Carolina Press, 1992.
Woodforde, John. *The Story of the Bicycle*. New York: Universe Books, 1971.

Woodward, Henry P. "Weed Sewing Machine Company." In *Hartford in History*, 112–16. Hartford: Board of Trade, 1889.
Wrege, Charles D., and Ronald G. Greenwood. *Frederick W. Taylor: The Father of Scientific Management*. Homewood, IL: Business One Irwin, 1991.

## Unpublished Monographs and Manuscripts

Capless, Robert T. *Historical Compendium: City of Newton Legislative Branch, 1874–1997*. Clerk of the Board of Aldermen, City of Newton, MA., no date [ca. 1998].
Herlihy, David V. *Pierre Lallement and His Bicycle*. Boston: privately printed by David V. Herlihy, 1992.
Petty, Ross D. *Raleigh vs. Schwinn: The Post–World War II Battle for the U.S. Bicycle Market*. 39-page manuscript, no date [ca. 2002].
Schwinn, Frank V. *1942 Personal Notes on the Bicycle Industry*. 42-page manuscript, Chicago: Bicycle Museum of America, 1993.
Weingroff, Richard F. *Portrait of a General: General Roy Stone*. Federal Highway Administration, U.S. Department of Transportation, 2003.

## Theses and Dissertations

Burr, Thomas C. *Markets as Producers and Consumers: The French and U.S. National Bicycle Markets, 1875–1910*. Ph.D. dissertation, University of California at Davis, 2005.
Dunham, Norman Leslie. *The Bicycle Era in America*. Ph.D. dissertation, Harvard University, 1957.
Harrison, Anthony Edward. *Growth, Entrepreneurship and Capital Formation in the United Kingdom's Cycle and Related Industries, 1870–1914*. Doctoral thesis, University of York (UK), 1977.
Mason, Philip P. *The League of American Wheelmen and the Good-Roads Movement, 1880–1905*. Ph.D. dissertation, University of Michigan, 1957.
Millward, Andrew. *Factors Contributing to the Sustained Success of the U.K. Cycle Industry, 1870–1939*. Doctoral thesis, University of Birmingham (UK), 1999.

## Encyclopedia Entries and Other Reference Works

*Appleton's Cyclopaedia of American Biography*. James Grant Wilson and John Fisk, eds. New York: D. Appleton and Co., 1888. s.v. "Pope, Albert Augustus."
*The Automobile Industry 1896–1920*. George S. May, ed. New York: Facts of File, 1990. s.v. "Day, George S."
_____. "Garford, Arthur Lovett."
_____. "Jeffery, Thomas."
_____. "Maxim, Hiram Percy."
_____. "Pope, Albert Augustus."
The *Biographical Cyclopaedia of American Women*. New York: Halvord, 1924. s.v. "Pope, Abby Linden [sic]."
*Dictionary of American Biography*. Dumas Malone, ed. New York: Charles Scribner's Sons. s.v. "Miles, Nelson Appleton."
*International Directory of Company Histories*. New York: St. James Press, 2000. s.v. "Huffy Corporation."
*National Cyclopedia of American Biography*. New York: Scribner's, 1958. s.v. " Pope, Harold Linder."

## Magazine and Journal Articles

(For journals in the cycle and hardware trades, only the most significant articles are included.)
"A.B.C. Affairs Come to a Climax." *Bicycling World* 55, no. 23 (4 September 1902): 580.
"Advertising the Columbia." *Profitable Advertising* 7, no. 8 (1897): 275–78.
"Aeronautics: First Stock Scandal." *Time* 14, no. 9 (26 August 1929): 4.
"Albert A. Pope: His Place in History." *Bicycling World* 46, no. 12 (18 December 1902): 313–20.
"An American Bicycle Manufactory, Part 1." *Engineering* 64 (16 July 1897): 65–69.
"An American Bicycle Manufactory, Part 2." *Engineering* 64 (30 July 1897): 131–33.
Bahma, Donald G. "The Pope-Toledo Strike: Part 1." *Northwest Ohio Quarterly* 35 (Summer 1963): 106–121.
_____. "The Pope-Toledo Strike: Part 2." *Northwest Ohio Quarterly* 35 (Autumn 1963): 172–187.
Balf, Todd. "The Great Debate." *Bicycling* 36, no. 5 (May 1998): 71–74.
Batchelder, A. G. "The Story of the Bicycle." *Harper's Weekly* 60 (11 April 1896): 359.
"Bicycle Engineering." *American Machinist* 9 (4 September 1886): 8.
"Bicycle Making." *Frank Leslie's Illustrated Monthly* 5 (1882): 641–44.
"Bicycle Manufacturing." *Bicycle World* 1, no. 13 (1 May 1880): 204–05.
"A Bicycle Rampant." *Fortune* 8, no. 3 (September 1933): 49–51*ff.*
Bijker, Wiebe, and Trevor J. Pinch. "SCOT Answers, Other Questions: A Reply to Nick Clayton." *Technology and Culture* 43, no. 2 (April 2002): 361–90.
Buttrick, John. "Inside the Contract System." *Journal of Economic History* 12, no. 3 (Summer 1952): 201–221.
"Canadian News: More Protection for the Bicycle Industry," *Iron Age*, 61 (3 February 1898): 17.
Cave, Henry. "Hartford, the Incubator of the Automobile Industry." *Old Timers News* 2, no. 2 (April 1944): 24–33.
"Central Station of the Electric Vehicle Company." *Horseless Age* 3 (September 1898): 9–17.
"The Chicago Motorcycle Contest." *American Machinist* 18 (19 December 1895): 1009–11.

Clayton, Nick. "SCOT: Does it Answer?" *Technology and Culture* 43, no. 2 (April 2002): 351–60.

"Col. Pope's Response to the Toast, 'The Wheel' at the L.O.W. Banquet." *The Wheelman* 1, no. 1 (October 1882): 69–72.

"The Combine and *Cycle Age*." *Cycle Age and Trade Review* 23 (1 June 1899): 111–112.

"Combine Cannot Control the Trade." *Cycle Age and Trade Review* 23 (8 June 1899): 137–139.

"A Comparative Study of the Bicycle" (4-part series). *Bicycling World* 2, no. 8 (31 December 1880): 118–19; no. 9 (7 January 1881): 131–34; 3 no. 2 (28 January 1882): 181–82; no. 3 (4 February 1882): 195–97.

Dolnar, Hugh [probably Horace L. Arnold]. "Bicycle Tools" (a 31-part series from October 1895 to September 1896). *American Machinist* 18 (1895): 781–82; 801–02; 821–22; 842–44; 863–64; 909–11; 924–25; 941–42; 963–64; 1001–02; 1021–22. *American Machinist* 19 (1896): 1–2; 50–52; 79–81; 104–05; 152–54; 182–84; 205–07; 231–33; 252–55; 275–76; 325–26; 348–50; 474–76; 495–97; 517–19; 617–19; 657–60; 677–79; 736–39; 871–73; 894–97.

———. "Bicycle Brazing." *American Machinist* 19 (1896): 1077–81.

———. "Cycle Stampings." *American Machinist* 19 (1896): 1063–67.

"Electric Automobiles in Boston." *Electrical World and Engineer* 35, no. 24 (16 June 1900): 895–896.

"Electrical Automobiles in New England." *Electrical World and Engineer* 37, no. 5 (19 January 1901): 136–137.

"Electric Motor-Cab Service in New York, Part I." *Electrical World* 30 no. 7 (14 August 1897): 183–186.

"Electric Motor-Cab Service in New York, Part II." *Electrical World* 30, no. 8 (21 August 1897): 213–216

"The Electric Wagon: Address Delivered by Hayden Eames Before the Association of Electric Vehicle Manufacturers." *Power Wagon* 2 (April 1907): 11–12.

Elliott, Sterling. "The League of American Wheelmen: Its Origin, Growth, and Prospects." *Harper's Weekly* 39 (March 1895): 284–286.

Epperson, Bruce. "Failed Colossus: Strategic Error at the Pope Manufacturing Company, 1878–1900." *Technology and Culture* 41, no. 2 (April 2000): 300–20.

———. "Does SCOT Answer? A Comment." *Technology and Culture* 43, no. 2 (April 2002): 371–73.

"Errors in School Books." *The Manufacturer and Builder* 25, no. 2 (February 1893): 41.

"Exports of Bicycles and Bicycle Materials." *Iron Age* 59 (24 June 1897): 35.

Felding, Lawrence W. and Lori K. Miller. "The ABC Trust: A Chapter in the History of Capitalism in the Sporting Goods Industry." *Sport History Review* 29 (1998): 44–58.

"Figures of the Industry." *Cycle Age and Trade Review* 20 (17 February 1898): 571.

Foreman-Peck, James. "Diversification and Growth of the Firm: The Rover Company to 1914." *Business History* 25, no. 2 (July 1983): 179–92.

"Frank W. Weston: The Man and His Work." *Bicycling World* 46, 12 (18 December 1902): 309–12.

Galvin, Peter, and Andre Morkel. "The Effect of Product Modularity on Industry Structure: The Case of the World Bicycle Industry." *Industry and Innovation* 8, no. 1 (April 2000): 31–47.

"A Great American Manufacture." *Bicycling World* 2, no. 21 (1 April 1881): 326–31.

"The Greatest Gathering of Cyclists Since Cycling Ceased to Be a Craze." *Bicycling World* 49, 6 (7 May 1904): 204–08.

Harmond, Richard. "Progress and Flight: An Interpretation of the American Cycle Craze of the 1890s." *Journal of Social History* 5 (1971): 235.

Harrison, A. E. "The Competitiveness of the British Cycle Industry, 1890–1914." *Economic History Review* 22, no. 2 (August 1969): 287–303.

———. "Joint-Stock Company Flotation in the Cycle, Motor-Vehicle and Related Industries, 1882–1914." *Business History* 23, no. 3 (July 1981): 165–189.

———. "The Origins and Growth of the UK Cycle Industry to 1900." *Journal of Transport History* 6, no. 1 (1985) 41–69.

Haupt, Louis M. "Colonel Pope and Good Roads." *Lippencott's Monthly* 6 (May 1893): 646–47.

Herlihy, David V. "The Velocipede Craze in Maine." *Maine History* 38, nos. 3/4 (1999): 186–209.

Hill, R. G. "The Capabilities and Limitations of the Bicycle as a Military Machine." *Journal of the Military Service Institution of the United States* 17 (1895): 312–22.

"History of the American Bicycle." *American Athlete and Cycle Trades Review* 7, no. 11 (20 March 1891): 240.

"History of the Sewing Machine." *Atlantic Monthly* 19 (May 1897): 529–544.

"Horseshoe for Col. Pope." *Bicycling World* 48, no. 3 (17 October 1903): 61–62.

Howland, Edward. "A Bicycle Era," *Harper's Monthly* 63 (July 1881): 282.

Hubbard, Guy. "Development of Machine Tools in New England: Part 11." *American Machinist* 60, no. 5 (31 January 1924): 171–73.

Hubert, Philip G. "The Wheel of To-Day." *Scribner's Magazine* 17 no. 6 (18 June 1895): 692–702.

"The Industry: How It Grew Up." *Bicycling World* 46, no. 12 (18 December 1902): 323–30.

Kerr, Peter M. "Demographic and Energy Effects on the U.S. Demand for Bicycles." *Transportation Research Record* 1141 (1987): 37–42.

Kimes, Beverly Rae. "A Family in Kenosha: The Story of the Rambler and the Jeffery." *Automobile Quarterly* 16, no. 2 (1978): 3–21.

Kirsch, David A., and Gijs P. A. Mom. "Visions of Transportation: The EVC and the Transition from Service- to Product-Based Mobility." *Business History Review* 76, no. 1 (Spring 2002): 75–110.

Lawton, E. P. "The Bicycle in Military Use." *Jour-

*nal of the Military Service Institution of the United States* 21 (1897): 449–61.

"Lead Cab Activity in Boston." *Horseless Age* 5, no. 17 (24 January 1900): 13.

"Lessons of Cycle History." *Cycle Age and Trade Review* 23 (21 September 1899): 518.

Lisa, Gregory C. "Bicyclists and Bureaucrats: The League of American Wheelmen and the Public Choice Theory Applied." *Georgetown Law Review* 84 (1995): 373–98.

Lloyd-Jones, Roger, M. J. Lewis and Mark Eason. "Culture as Metaphor: Company Culture and Business Strategy at Raleigh Industries, c. 1945–60." *Business History* 41, no. 3 (July 1999): 93–134.

"Looking Backward Twenty-Five Years and Beyond." *Bicycling World* 46, no. 12 (18 December 1902): 303–309.

Louis, Arthur M. "How the Customers Thrust Unexpected Prosperity on the Bicycle Industry." *Fortune* 89, no. 3 (March 1974): 117–24.

"Making a Bicycle." *Iron Age* 49 (2 June 1892): 1070–72.

"The Manufacture of Bicycle Tubing, Part 2." *Iron Age* 54 (14 January 1897): 1–5.

"The Manufacture of Electric Automobiles." *Electrical World and Engineer* 35, no. 2 (13 January 1900): 53–56.

"The Manufacture of Sewing Machines." *Scientific American* 42, no. 12 (20 March 1880): 181–82.

Mattox, Willard S. "American Bicycle Fittings and Machinery in England." *Iron Age* 62 (3 November 1898): 8.

Meinert, Charles. "Wheels Along the Mohawk: The Snyder Bicycle Company." *The Wheelmen* 52 (May 1998): 2–9.

"A Memory Reborn." *Bicycle Rider* 3, no. 1 (January/February 1987): 18–19.

Moss, James A. "Report of a Bicycle Trip from Fort Missoula, Montana, to St. Louis, Missouri." *Army and Navy Journal* 34 (1 September, 1897): 954.

"New York's Electric Cab Service." *American Electrician* 10, no. 9 (September 1898): 409–18.

Nichols, Carole, and Joyce Pendery. "Pro Bono Publico: Voices of Connecticut's Political Women, 1915–1945." *Oral History* 11 (1983): 48–74.

"1913 Bicycle Figures." *Motorcycling and Cycle Trades Review* (2 February 1914): 49.

Norcliffe, Glen. "Popeism and Fordism: Examining the Roots of Mass Production." *Regional Studies* 31, no. 3 (1997): 267–80.

Norton, Peter D. "Street Rivals: Jaywalking and the Invention of the Motor Age Street." *Technology and Culture* 48, No. 2 (April 2007): 331–59.

"Papa Weston Thumbs Back Numbers." *Bicycling World* 46, no. 12 (18 December 1902): 311–13.

Parker, George F. "American Bicycles in England." *North American Review* 163, no. 481 (December 1896): 688–95.

Parsons, Albert S. "The Massachusetts Bicycle Club." *The Wheelman* 2, no. 3 (June 1883): 161–72.

"Personnel of Management of A.B.C." *Cycle Age and Trade Review* 23 (7 September 1899): 463.

Petty, Ross D. "Peddling the Bicycle in the 1890's: Mass Marketing Shifts into High Gear." *Journal of Macromarketing* 15, no. 1 (Spring 1995): 32–46.

_____. "The Impact of the Sport of Bicycle Riding on Safety Law." *American Business Law Journal* 35, no. 2 (Winter 1998): 185–224.

"The Pioneers of the Retail Trade." *Bicycling World* 46, no. 12 (18 December 1902): 335–37.

"Pope Gets Majority." *Bicycling World* 45, no. 5 (1 May 1902): 173.

Pratt, Charles E. "A Wheel Around the Hub." *Scribner's Monthly* 19, no. 4 (February 1880): 481–99.

_____. "The Tariff Question." *The Wheelman* 1, no. 1 (October 1882): 60–69.

_____. "Our First Bicycle Club." *The Wheelman* 1, no. 6 (March 1883): 401–12.

_____. "Pierre Lallement and His Bicycle." *The Wheelman* 4, no. 1 (October 1883): 4–13.

_____. "The L.A.W. and Legal Rights." *Outing* 7, no. 3 (January 1886): 454–56.

_____. "A Sketch of American Cycling and Its Founder." *Outing* 18, no. 4 (July 1891): 342–49.

"Racing Rules." *American Athlete and Cycle Trades Review* 11, no. 16 (21 April 1893): 356.

Rae, John B. "The Electric Vehicle Company: A Monopoly That Missed." *Business History Review* 29 (December 1955): 298–311.

Rezneck, Samuel. "Unemployment, Unrest and Relief in the United States during the Depression of 1893–1897." *Journal of Political Economy* 4 (August 1953): 324–345.

Rosenberg, Nathan. "Technological Change in the Machine Tool Industry, 1840–1910." *Journal of Economic History* 23 (1963): 414–443.

Saal, Thomas F. "Pope-Hartford: Too Good to Fail." *Automobile Quarterly* 36, no. 1 (December 1996): 93–109.

"Six Months of the Trust." *The Cycle Age and Trade Review* 25 (3 May 1900): 5.

"The Storage Battery in the Commercial Operation of Electric Automotives." *Electrical World* 39 (12 April 1902): 646.

"Survival of the Fittest" (4-part series). *The Cycle Age and Trade Review* 26, no. 1 (1 November 1900): 1; no. 2 (8 November 1900): 25–26; no. 3 (15 November 1900): 49–50; no. 4 (22 November 1900): 77–78.

"Testing the Parts of a Modern Bicycle." *Scientific American* 75, no. 2 (11 July 1896): 1; 22.

"Thomas B. Jeffery Dead." *Horseless Age* 25, no. 14 (6 April 1910): 521.

Tobin, Gary Allen. "The Bicycle Boom of the 1980's: The Development of Private Transportation and the Birth of the Tourist." *Journal of Popular Culture* 7 (1974): 838–49.

"Two-Wheel Drive: Bicycle Makers Are Headed for Another Record Year." *Barron's* 47, no. 50 (11 December 1967): 11.

"U.S. Bicycle Market Statistics, 1895 to 1977." *Schwinn Reporter* (February 1978): n.p.

"Victor Bicycles." *Scientific American* 64, no 18 (2 May 1891): 1.

Waldo, Leonard. "The American Bicycle: Its Theory and Construction." *Engineering* 64 (3 December 1897): 679–80.

"Wheeling and Dealing: Bicycle Makers Can Scarcely Keep Up with Demand." *Barron's* 53, no. 24 (11 June 1973): 11.

Whitney, Henry H. "The Adaptation of the Bicycle to Military Uses." *Journal of the Military Service Institution of the United States* 17 (1895): 542–63.

"Wild-Cat Agencies for Bicycles." *Iron Age* 59 (25 March 1897): 37.

Willoughby, William Franklin. "Employers' Associations for Dealing with Labor in the United States." *Quarterly Journal of Economics* 20, no. 1 (November 1905): 110–50.

Zordich, James. "The A. B.C.'s of the Pope Manufacturing Company." *Horseless Carriage Gazette* 46, no. 4 (July–August 1984): 27–45.

## Newspaper Articles

"Albert Linder Pope Dies, Pioneer in Auto Industry." *Hartford Courant*, 11 August 1955.

"Albert Linder Pope Dies, Retired Industrialist." *Hartford Times*, 10 August 1955.

"Auto Dispute Settled: Pope-Toledo Withdraws." *New York Times*, 4 October 1906.

"Bicycle Firm Seeks Chapter 11." *Boston Globe*, 2 September 1993.

"The Bicycle Industry." *Hartford Courant*, 2 April 1899.

"Bicycle Makers Seek Tariff Help." *New York Times*, 22 August 1954.

"Big Pope Concern in Receiver's Hands." *New York Times*, 15 August 1907.

"Col. A. A. Pope Dies at Summer Home." *New York Times*, 11 August 1909.

"Col. Albert Pope Dies of Pneumonia," *Hartford Courant*, 11 August 1955.

"Colonel George Pope Wants Employers' Union." *New York Times*, 13 August 1916.

"Col. Pope Passes Away at Cohasset." *Boston Post*, 11 August 1909.

Cuntz, Hermann. "Hartford, Birthplace of the Automobile." *Hartford Times*, 16 September; 17 September; 18 September 1947.

"Death Comes to Col. Albert A. Pope: Was Leader in Good Roads Movement." *Boston Globe*, 11 August 1909.

"Exchange Expels Member: Unusual Punishment for J. W. Ritchie." *New York Times*, 21 December 1904.

"Fire Loss, $275,000." *Boston Globe*, 13 March 1896.

"500 Strike Columbia Bike Plant in Westfield." *Boston Globe*, 10 August 1984.

"Lytle's Car Barred from Big Auto Race." *New York Times*, 26 September 1906: 2.

"Pope Building Not a Ruin." *Boston Transcript*, 13 March 1896.

"Pope Manufacturing Company Goes Into a Receivership." *Wall Street Journal*, 29 August 1913.

"Social Science Studies." *New York Times*, 8 September 1881.

"Strike Costly to Pope's." *Toledo Blade*, 25 February 1907.

"Welcome to Pope." *Hartford Courant*, 3 July 1903.

## Published Conference Proceedings

Berto, Frank. "The Great American Bicycle Boom." In *Cycle History 10: Proceedings of the 10th International Cycle History Conference, Nijmegen*, edited by Hans-Erhard Lessing and Andrew Ritchie, 133–48. San Francisco: Van der Plas Publications, 2000.

Burgwardt, Carl F. "A Landscape of Early Bicycle History: From the Lips of George R. Bidwell, an Extraordinary Pioneer Wheelman from Buffalo, N.Y." In *Cycle History: Proceedings of the 7th International Cycle History Conference, Buffalo* edited by Rob van der Plas, 87–93. Osceola: Motorbooks International, 1997.

Burr, Thomas. "French Expansion, American Collapse, 1890–1910." In *Cycle History 16: Proceedings of the 16th International Cycle History Conference, Davis*, edited by Andrew Ritchie, 120–42. San Francisco: Van der Plas Publications, 2006.

Clayton, Nick. "Who Invented the Penny-Farthing?" In *Cycle History: Proceedings of the 7th International Cycle History Conference, Buffalo*, edited by Rob van der Plas, 31–40. San Francisco: Bicycle Books, 1997.

_____. "The Quest for Safety: What Took So Long?" In *Cycle History 8: Proceedings of the 8th International Cycle History Conference, Glasgow*, edited by Nicholas Oddy and Rob van der Plas, 15–20. San Francisco: Van der Plas Publications, 1998.

_____. "Of Bicycles, Bijker and Bunkum." In *Cycle History 10: Proceedings of the 10th International Cycle History Conference, Nijmegen*, edited by Hans-Erhard Lessing and Andrew Ritchie, 11–24. San Francisco: Van der Plas Publications, 2000.

Epperson, Bruce. "Failed Colossus: Albert A. Pope and the Pope Manufacturing Company, 1876–1900." In *Cycle History 9: Proceedings of the 9th International Cycle History Conference, Ottawa*, edited by Glen Norcliffe and Rob van der Plas, 93–108. San Francisco: Van der Plas Publications, 2001.

_____. "After Pope: the Pope Manufacturing Company and the American Bicycle Industry, 1899–1990." In *Cycle History 10: Proceedings of the 10th International Cycle History Conference, Nijmegen*, edited by Hans-Erhard Lessing and Andrew Ritchie, 32–42. San Francisco: Van der Plas Publications, 2000.

_____. "How Many Bikes: An Investigation into the Quantification of Bicycling, 1878–1914." In *Cycle History 11: Proceedings of the 11th International Cycle History Conference, Osaka*, edited by Andrew Ritchie and Rob van der Plas, 42–50. San Francisco: Van der Plas Publications, 2001.

_____. "The Monopoly Machine: The Lallement

Patent and the Attempted Monopolization of the American Bicycle Industry, 1880–86." In *Cycle History 15: Proceedings of the 15th International Cycle History Conference, Vienna,* edited by Rob van der Plas, 102–20. San Francisco: Van der Plas Publications, 2005.

\_\_\_\_\_. "It Cannot Be That They Have Made No Profit: The Great Bicycle Trust, 1899–1903." In *Cycle History 16: Proceedings of the 16th International Cycle History Conference, Davis,* edited by Andrew Ritchie, 98–110. San Francisco: Van der Plas Publications, 2006.

Hadland, Tony. "Raleigh UK in the Last Quarter of the Twentieth Century." In *Cycle History 11: Proceedings of the 11th International Cycle History Conference, Osaka,* edited by Andrew Ritchie and Rob van der Plas, 63–71. San Francisco: Van der Plas Publications, 2001.

Herlihy, David V. "Who Invented the Bicycle?" In *Cycle History 4: Proceedings of the 4th International Cycle History Conference, Boston,* edited by Rob van der Plas, 11–26. San Francisco: Bicycle Books, 1994.

\_\_\_\_\_. "The Velocipede Craze in Maine." In *Cycle History: Proceedings of the 8th International Cycle History Conference, Glasgow,* edited by Nicholas Oddy and Rob van der Plas, 9–14. San Francisco: Van der Plas Publications, 1998.

Hounshell, David A. "The Bicycle and Technology in late Nineteenth Century America." In *Tekniska Museet Symposia: Transport Technology and Social Change,* 172–85. Stockholm: Tekniska Museet Symposia, 1980.

Millward, Andrew. "UK and Japanese Competition in the Inter-War Period." In *Cycle History 11: Proceedings of the 11th International Cycle History Conference, Osaka,* edited by Andrew Ritchie and Rob van der Plas, 147–59. San Francisco: Van der Plas Publications, 2001.

Norcliffe, Glen. "Colonel Albert Pope." In *Cycle History: Proceedings of the 7th International Cycle History Conference, Buffalo,* edited by Rob van der Plas, 74–86. San Francisco: Bicycle Books, 1997.

\_\_\_\_\_. "The Rise of the Coventry Bicycle Industry and the Geographical Construction of Technology." In *Cycle History 15: Proceedings of the 15th International Cycle History Conference, Vienna,* edited by Rob van der Plas, 41–58. San Francisco: Van der Plas Publications, 2005.

Oddy, Nicholas. "An Insight into Cycle Purchases during the Post-Boom Period, 1897–1899." In *Cycle History 12: Proceedings of the 12th International Cycle History Conference, San Remo,* edited by Andrew Ritchie and Rob van der Plas, 146–59. San Francisco: Van der Plas Publications, 2002.

\_\_\_\_\_. "Cycling's Dark Age? The Period 1900–20 in Cycling History." In *Cycle History 15: Proceedings of the 15th International Cycle History Conference, Vienna,* edited by Rob van der Plas, 79–86. San Francisco: Van der Plas Publications, 2005.

Petty, Ross. "The Bicycle's Role in the Development of Safety Law." In *Cycle History 4: Proceedings of the 4th International Cycle History Conference, Boston,* edited by Rob van der Plas, 125–41. San Francisco: Bicycle Books, 1994.

\_\_\_\_\_. "Peddling the Bicycle and the Development of Mass Marketing." *Cycle History 5: Proceedings of the 5th International Cycle History Conference, Cambridge (UK),* edited by Rob van der Plas, 107–16. San Francisco: Bicycle Books, 1995.

\_\_\_\_\_. "The Rise of the Asian Bicycle Business." In *Cycle History 11: Proceedings of the 11th International Cycle History Conference, Osaka,* edited by Andrew Ritchie and Rob van der Plas, 189–204. San Francisco: Van der Plas Publications, 2001.

\_\_\_\_\_. "The Bicycle as a Communications Medium: A Comparison of Bicycle Use by the U.S. Postal Service and Western Union Telegraph Company." *Cycle History 16: Proceedings of the 16th International Cycle History Conference, Davis,* edited by Andrew Ritchie, 147–59. San Francisco: Van der Plas Publications, 2006.

Rubenson, Paul. "Patents, Profits & Perceptions: The Single-Tube Tire and the Failure of the American Bicycle, 1897–1933." In *Cycle History 15: Proceedings of the 15th International Cycle History Conference, Vienna,* edited by Rob van der Plas, 87–97. San Francisco: Van der Plas Publications, 2005.

\_\_\_\_\_. "Missing Link: The Case for Bicycle Transportation in the United States in the Early 20th Century." In *Cycle History 16: Proceedings of the 16th International Cycle History Conference, Davis,* edited by Andrew Ritchie, 72–84. San Francisco: Van der Plas Publications, 2006.

Trescott, Martha Moore. "The Bicycle: a Technical Precursor to the Automobile." In *Business and Economic History: Papers Presented at the Twenty-Second Annual Meeting of the Business History Conference,* 51–75. Champaign: University of Illinois, 1976.

Wild, Ari De. "Norman Duncan: A Pioneer Academic Cycling Historian and His Dissertation." In *Cycle History 17: Proceedings of the 17th International Cycle History Conference, York (Canada),* edited by Glen Norcliffe, 72–84. San Francisco: Van der Plas Publications, 2007.

Wrenge, Charles D., and Ronald Greenwood. "Frederick W. Taylor and Industrial Espionage, 1895–1897." *Business and Economic History: Papers Presented at the Thirty-Second Annual Meeting of the Business History Conference,* edited by Jeremy Atack, 181–96 (Champaign-Urbana, University of Illinois Press, 1987).

## *Government Reports and Records*

Canadian Department of Trade and Commerce. *The Bicycle Manufacturing Industry: 1935.* Ottawa, 1936. Series No. 31-7-36.

Canadian Department of Trade and Commerce. *The Bicycle Manufacturing Industry: 1940.* Ottawa, 1940. Series No. 19-30-41.

Canadian Department of Trade and Commerce. *The*

*Bicycle Manufacturing Industry: 1945.* Ottawa, 1946. Series No. A9-13-11-46.

Cohen, Harry. *See* U.S. Bureau of the Census [1914].

Colorado Department of Labor. *Seventh Biennial Report of the Bureau of Labor Statistics of the State of Colorado, 1899–1900,* by James Smith. Denver, 1901.

Josephsson, Axel. *See* U.S. Bureau of the Census [1900].

Massachusetts Adjutant General. *Record of the Massachusetts Volunteers, 1861–1865.* Boston: Wright & Potter, 1898.

Massachusetts, Offices of Health and Human Services. *Return of a Death: Albert Augustus Pope, August 10, 1909* (No. A667322). Registry of Vital Records, Boston.

Merriam, Robert. *See* U.S. Bureau of the Census [1905].

Ohio State Board of Arbitration. *Fourteenth Annual Report to the Governor of the State of Ohio for the Year Ending December 31, 1906.* Columbus, 1907.

Smith, James. *See* Colorado Dept. of Labor.

U.S. Adjutant General. *Official Army Register of the Volunteer Force of the United States Army for the Years 1861–65, Part 1 (New England).* Washington, D.C.: U.S. Army, Adjutant General's Office, 1865.

U.S. Adjutant General. *Official Army Register of the Volunteer Force of the United States Army for the Years 1861–65, Volume 8: Colored Infantry.* (Washington, D.C.: U.S. Army, Adjutant General's Office, 1865).

U.S. Bureau of the Census [1850]. *Sixth Census of the United States* [1850], *Schedule I, Population: Inhabitants in Brookline, Massachusetts.*

U.S. Bureau of the Census [1880]. *Tenth Census of the United States, Schedule I, Population: Inhabitants in Middlesex, Massachusetts.*

U.S. Bureau of the Census [1880]. *Compendium of the Tenth Census: Statistics of Manufacturers.* Table 3: General statistics for specified industries by state and territory.

U.S. Bureau of the Census. [1890] *Special Census of Union Veterans and their Widows, June 1, 1890, Schedule I, Veterans in Boston, Massachusetts.*

U.S. Bureau of the Census. [1890] *Compendium of the Eleventh Census: Statistics of Manufacturers.* Table 5: specified industries by states and territories.

U.S. Bureau of the Census. [1900] *Twelfth Census of the United States.* Schedule I: Population, Commonwealth of Massachusetts, Norfolk County, Enumeration District 1829, p. 22.

U.S. Bureau of the Census. [1900] *Compendium of the Twelfth Census: Manufacturing Industries.* Table 4: specified industries by states and territories.

U.S. Bureau of the Census. [1900] *Compendium of the Twelfth Census: Part 3, Special Reports: Bicycles and Tricycles,* by Axel Josephsson.

U.S. Bureau of the Census [1905] *Census of Manufacturers: 1905. Bicycles and Tricycles: Special Report,* by Robert Merriam. (Washington, D.C.: Government Printing Office 1907). Bulletin 66.

U.S. Bureau of the Census. [1910] *Thirteenth Census of the United States.* Schedule I: Population, State of Connecticut, City of West Hartford, Enumeration District 206, Sheet 13A.

U.S. Bureau of the Census. [1910] *Compendium of the Thirteenth Census: Part 3, manufacturing Industries, Special Reports: Bicycles, Motorcycles and Parts.*

U.S. Bureau of the Census [1915] *Census of Manufacturers: 1915. Volume II: Special Reports, Bicycles and Tricycles,* by Harry B. Cohen.

U.S. Bureau of the Census. [1930] *Fifteenth Census of the United States.* Schedule I: Population, State of Connecticut, City of West Hartford, Enumeration District 2-222, Sheet 7A; Enumeration District 2-71, Sheet 46A.

U.S. Bureau of the Census, "Facts for Industry: Bicycles." October 16, 1946 (Series M49-1-66); October 30, 1946 (Series M49-1-86); November 26, 1946 (Series M49-1-6,). These were the only three reports produced in this series.

U.S. House of Representatives. "Affidavit of George Pope, May 20, 1901." In *Report of the Industrial Commission on Trusts and Combinations, Volume XII.* 57th Congress, 1st Session, Document No. 182.

U.S. House of Representatives. *Tariff Hearings Before the House Committee on Ways and Means, 1908–1909, Vol. III, Paragraph 193: Bicycles.* 60th Congress, 2nd Session, Document No. 1505.

U.S. Senate. *United States Strike Commission's Report on the Chicago Strike of June–July, 1894.* 53rd Congress, 3rd Session, Senate Executive Document No. 7.

U.S. Strike Commission. See U.S. Senate.

U.S. Tariff Commission. See U.S. House of Representatives.

## Legal Cases

*Ashley v. Winkley,* 95 N.E. 932 (Mass. 1911)

*Burr v. Redhead, Norton, Lathrop Co.,* 72 N.W. 1058 (Neb. 1897)

*Eisenstadt v. Baird,* 405 U.S. 438 (1972)

*Griswold v. Connecticut,* 381 U.S. 479 (1965)

*In re Wright et. al.,* 63 How. 345 (S.C.N.Y.C. 1882)

*In re Wright, Foster & Walker,* 65 How. 119, (S.C.N.Y.C. 1883)

*Kirkpatrick v. Pope Mfg. Co.,* 64 F. 369 (1894)

*Miller v. Bridgeport Brass Co.,* 17 F. Cass. 309 (D. Conn. 1877)

*Miller v. Bridgeport Brass Co.,* 104 U.S. 350 (1881)

*National Typewriter Co. v. Pope Mfg. Co.,* 56 F. 849 (D. Mass. 1893)

*Overman Wheel Co. v. Pope Mfg. Co.,* 46 F. 577 (D. Conn. 1891)

*Phoenix State Bank v. Whitcomb,* 183 A. 5 (Conn. 1936)

*Pierce v. Merrill,* 61 P. 64 (Cal. 1900)

*Pope v. Hinkley,* 905 N.E. 798 (S.J.C. Mass., 1911)

*Pope v. Pope,* 95 N.E. 864 (Mass. 1911)

*Pope v. United States,* 296 F.Supp. 17 (S.D. Cal. 1968)

*Pope Mfg. Co. v. Arnold, Schwinn & Co.,* 193 F. 649 (7th Cir. 1911)

*Pope Mfg. Co. v. Clark,* 46 F. 768 (D. Conn. 1891)

*Pope Mfg. Co. v. Fairchild*, 133 A. 886 (N.Y.S. 1909)
*Pope Mfg. Co. v. Gormully*, 34 F. 877 (N.D. Ill. 1888)
*Pope Mfg. Co. v. Gormully*, 144 U.S. 224 (1892)
*Pope Mfg. Co. v. Gormully & Jeffery Mfg. Co. (No. 1)*, 144 U.S. 238 (1892)
*Pope Mfg. Co. v. Gormully & Jeffery Mfg. Co. (No. 2)*, 144 U.S. 243 (1892)
*Pope Mfg. Co. v. Gormully & Jeffery Mfg. Co. (No. 3)*, 144 U.S. 248 (1892)
*Pope Mfg. Co. v. Gormully & Jeffery Mfg. Co. (No. 4)*, 144 U.S. 254 (1892)
*Pope Mfg. Co. v. H. P. Snyder Mfg. Co.*, 139 F. 49 (N.D.N.Y 1905)
*Pope Mfg. Co. v. Koop*, Docket No. D-1814 (S.D.N.Y. 1881)
*Pope Mfg. Co. v. Marqua*, 15 Fed. R. 400 (1883)
*Pope Mfg. Co. v. Owsley*, 27 F. 100 (N.D. Ill. 1886)
*Pope Mfg. Co. v. Rubber Goods Mfg. Co.*, 110 A. 341 (S.C.N.Y. 1905)
*Pope Mfg. Co. v. Rubber Goods Mfg. Co.*, 100 A. 353 (S.C.N.Y. 1905)
*Pope Mfg. Co. Warwick Cycle Mfg. Co.*, 50 F. 321 (D. Mass. 1892)
*Pope Mfg. Co. v. Welch*, 37 S.E. 20 (S.C., 1900)
*Pope Motor Car Co. v. Keegan*, 150 F. 148 (N.D. Ohio 1906)
*Pressey v. H. B. Smith Mfg. Co.*, 19 A. 618 (N.J. App. 1889)
*Simonds Rolling Machine Co. v. Pope Mfg. Co.*, 62 N.E. 467 (Mass. 1902)
*SRAM Corp. v. Shimano*, CV-96-0028-GLT (N.D. California, 2001, unpublished)
*SRAM Corp. v. Shimano* (9th Cir.,14 January 2002, unpublished)
*Stevens-Davis Co. v. Mather & Co.*, 230 Ill. App. 45 (Ill. App. 1923)
*Swift v. City of Topeka*, 23 P. 1075 (Kan. 1890)
*Teichner v. Pope Mfg. Co.*, 83 N.W. 1031 (Mich. 1900)
*Turner v. Pope Motor Car Co.*, 86 N.E. 651 (Ohio Cir. 1908)
*United States v. Arnold, Schwinn & Co.* 388 U.S. 365 (1967)
*Williams et. al. v. Pope Mfg. Co.*, 27 So. 851 (La. 1900)

## Patent Documents

No. 36,161. "Improvement in Cantering Propellers." 12 August 1862, to P. W. Mackenzie of Jersey City, New Jersey. Reissued to Stephen W. Smith of New York, as assignee of P. W. Mackenzie. Reissue No. 3,319, dated March 2, 1869.

No. 41,310. "Improvement in Auto-Propelling Horses and Vehicles." 19 January 1864, to P. W. Mackenzie of Jersey City, New Jersey. Reissued to the Montpelier Manufacturing Co. as assignees of Philip W. Mackenzie. Reissue No. 7,818, dated July 31, 1877.

No. 46,705. "Improvement in Velocipede Trotting or Pacing Horse." 7 March 1865, to Harvey A. Reynolds, of New York. Reissued to Harvey A. Reynolds, as assignor to Henry M. Richardson and George McKee. Reissue No. 8,252, dated 28 May 1878.

No. 59,915. "Improvement in Velocipedes." 20 November 1866, to Pierre Lallement of Paris, France, assignor to himself and James Carroll, of New Haven. Reissued to Henry M. Richardson and George McKee, as assignees of Pierre Lallement. Reissue No. 7,972, dated November 27, 1877.

Patent No. 86,834. "Improvement in Velocipedes." 7 February 1874, to William Hanlon of New York, New York.

No. 156,890. "Improvement in Air Pistols." 17 November 1874, to Henry M. Quackenbush of Herkimer, New York, assignor to Albert A. Pope of Boston.

No. 350,981. "Die for Forging Bicycle-Head Blanks." December 13, 1881, to Henry T. Russell, of Hartford, Connecticut, as assignor to the Pope Mfg. Co. of Boston.

# Index

Advertising, bicycle 58–61, 241–244
Agencies, bicycle *see* Bicycle agents and repair shops
Air guns 21–22
Alden, Herbert 129, 194, 229
Alexander & Green 172, 173
Allyn House Hotel (Hartford) 7–11, 188
American Bicycle Company (bicycle trust) 7, 8, 138, 143–144, 146, 163–164, 165, 171–188, 191, 202, 206, 245
*American Bicycling Journal* 28, 57, 59, 197, 242
"American Champion" bicycle 51, 52
"American Ideal" bicycle 49, 50
*American Machinist* 5, 109, 121, 122, 123, 124, 126, 136
Ames, J.T. 50
Ames & Frost Cycle Co. 158
Ames Mfg. Co. 46, 50
Apperson Motor Car Co. 205
"Arab" bicycle 28
"Ariel" bicycle 24
Armsmere (Hartford) 7
Arnold, Schwinn & Co. *see* Schwinn Bicycle Co.
Ashley, Eleanor 209
Association of Licensed Automobile Manufacturers (ALAM) 132, 146–147
Aston, William 151
Atkins, Arthur L. 186, 191, 192
Atwell, William S. ("Billy") 28, 197
Auerbach, Joseph 175
Automobile & Cycle Parts Mfg. Co. *see* Federal Mfg. Co.
Automobile racing *see* Racing, automobile

Back Bay (Boston) 19, 20–21
Bagg, Lymon H *see* Kron, Karl
Bartholomew farm 111, 152, 155
Beach, J. Watson 31, 80
Beach, Katherine *see* Day, Katherine Beach
Beers, Lon 150
Belden, Frank 80, 87, 112
Bell & Richards 14
Berg, Hart O. 136
Bethlehem Steel Corp. 115
Berto, Frank 2, 225
Bicycle agents and repair shops 63–70, 159, 161–162, 166–167, 198, 221, 241–243, 245
Bicycle commuting in cities 55, 199
Bicycle Manufacturers' Association *see* Cycle Trades Associations and Organizations
Bicycle production: industry-wide 57–58, 75, 107, 178, 185, 190, 197, 198, 210, 219, 222, 224; at Pope's 8–9, 31, 57–58, 75, 106, 107, 108, 197, 199, 210–211, 221, 222
Bicycle racing *see* Racing, bicycle
*Bicycling World* 29, 45, 46, 49, 59, 60, 66, 96, 171, 184, 192, 197, 198, 239
Bidwell, George 21, 26–27, 31, 56, 65, 68, 84, 106, 107, 112, 239, 244
Billings & Spencer Co. 7, 30
Blackwell, Elizabeth 18
Bogman, George 14
Boothroyd, I.W. 119
Boston Bicycle Club 29, 55, 92
Boston fire of 1872 20, 42
Bowditch, Alfred 125, 127–128
Bowdon, Frank 110, 200

Branch houses *see* Bicycle agents and repair shops
Brandon, David 40, 43
Broadwell, Edward ("Ned") 220
Bromley, J.E. 186
Brooks & Mecuen 15
Brown & Sharpe Co. 80, 122
"BSA" bicycles 46
Budlong, Milton 147, 229
Burdett, Charles 98
Bureau of Public Roads 89, 99, 101–104
Burke, Betty 14, 16

Carroll, James 25, 27, 40
Central Park bicycle ban 71–72, 141
Century Road Club 197
Chandler, Alfred 28, 197
Charles L. Pope Memorial Church *see* Pope Memorial Church
*Chicago Times Herald* auto race (1895) 131, 134
Chicago World's Fair (1893) 95, 99, 101, 152
Clarke, Norman 168, 199, 216, 217, 219, 220, 221, 222–228, 229, 245
Clarke, Russell 216, 219, 220, 229
Clemente, Adolphe 172
"Cleveland" bicycle 111, 191
Cleveland Machine Screw Co. 126
"Clipper" bicycle 177–178
Coburn, L.L. 51–52
Cockley, D.L. 111, 112, 113
Coleman, R. Lindsay 67, 143, 154, 159, 165, 172, 175, 177–182, 184–188, 191, 229
Collamore, John 15
"Color Bar" in L.A.W. 96–97

Colt, Elizabeth 7
Colt, Samuel 7, 30, 80
Colt's Armory 7, 30, 79–80, 112, 235, 237
Colt's Patent Firearms Co. *see* Colt's Armory
Columbia & Electric Vehicle Co. *see* Electric Vehicle Co.
Columbia cash register 11
Columbia Century (Safety) 121
Columbia Expert (Ordinary) 61, 66, 76
Columbia Light Roadster (Ordinary) 122
Columbia Light Roadster (Safety) 121
Columbia Mfg. Co. 199, 226–228, 229, 237, 245
Columbia Mustang (Ordinary) 48
Columbia Road Racer (Safety) 121
Columbia Shaft-Drive (Safety) 9, 168
Columbia Special (Ordinary) 32–33, 50, 76
Columbia Standard (Ordinary) 33, 61, 239
Columbia Street homes *see* Hartford Real Estate Improvement Co.
Columbia Typewriter *see* World Typewriter
Columbia Veloce (Safety) 85, 106, 122
Colvin, Fred H. 121
Comstock Law 156, 230
Condict, Herbert 139–140
Connecticut National Guard 85–86
Copely Square Hotel (Boston) 20, 77, 209
Costello, John 149–150
Cox, Charles M. 57
Cox, Joseph F. 216
Credenda bicycle 88, 157
Credenda Cold Drawn Tube Co. 110, 111
Cunningham, Heath & Co. (Cunningham & Co.) 23, 28–29, 42, 43, 44, 48–49, 59, 68, 88, 197, 238
Cuntz, Hermann 5, 112–113, 130, 133, 136, 137, 141, 145–147, 229
Custer City, CO 182–184
*Cycle Age* 159, 169, 174, 177, 179, 242, 245
Cycle shows 134, 157, 160, 181, 189–191, 210
Cycle trades associations and organizations 107, 109, 158–159, 161, 189–191, 218, 223, 229

Davis, Peter 225, 245
Day, George 11, 31, 32, 33, 64–65, 68, 80–81, 87–88, 109, 111, 112, 114, 118, 119, 120, 127, 130, 131, 135, 137, 141 145–147, 152, 153, 155, 156, 167, 179, 216, 230
Day, Katherine Beach 31, 81, 156, 230
Department of Tests 112–113, 230
Dimock, Henry 141
Dimock, Susan 141
Dingley, Bert 212–213
Dock Square (Boston) 14, 18
Dodge, Charles 95
Dodge, Philip T. 145
Dorner, Otto 94, 102
Dow, L.S. 154
Drais, Karl von 25
Draisiane 25
Duncan, H.O. 238
Dunlop tires 68, 118, 119, 120, 161, 175, 221
Dunn, James 93, 95, 97
Duplex Excelsior Bicycle 29, 30, 31, 32, 56 65

Eames, Harold Hayden 112, 129, 130, 131, 132, 133, 135, 136, 141, 145, 167, 179, 230
Earle, Horatio 92–93, 97
Eisenhower, Dwight D. 104, 224
Electric Carriage & Wagon Co. *see* Electric Vehicle Co.
Electric Storage Battery Co. *see* Exide Battery Co.
Electric Vehicle Co. 4, 5, 9, 11, 131–148, 174, 179
Elliot, Sterling 96, 97, 101
Emery Hydraulic Testing Machine 113, 117
Employment, at Pope's 7, 57, 75, 83
Exide Battery Co. 131, 134, 136, 140, 144
Exports of American bicycles 161, 165, 166, 167, 191, 198, 211

Fairfield, George A. 30, 31, 32, 33, 42, 56–57, 64–65, 79, 80, 118, 230, 239
Fairfield, John 118
Federal Mfg. Co. 181, 193–194, 205
Ferodowill Cycle Co. 69, 70
Firestone Tire Co. 216, 221, 237
Flint, Charles R. 144, 146, 174–176, 179, 184, 191, 230
Fogarty, John P. 216–217, 220
Ford, Henry 9, 132, 147, 199, 231, 235, 237

Forest Hills Cemetery (Boston) 4, 77, 169
Franco-Prussian War 28

"G&J" tire 118–119, 120
Garford, Arthur L. 12, 13, 24, 123, 143, 146, 157, 159, 162–165, 166, 168, 171–188, 189–191, 193, 202, 217, 229, 230, 240
Gibbs, W.W. 140
Gillette, Charles H. 155, 194
Gillette, Marion Pope 155, 194, 208
Goddard, Stephen 16–17, 207
Gooch, A.M. 29
*Good Roads* magazine 93
Goodman, Harry 117
Goodrich, B.F. Tire Co. 120
Gormully, R. Philip 45, 46, 48, 49, 50, 51, 52, 53, 67, 177, 230
Gormully & Jeffery Mfg. Co. 49, 50, 51, 52, 55, 67, 85, 118–119, 120, 122, 175, 179, 230
Grand Rapids Cycle Co. 64, 177–178
Graves, John A.S. 20–21
Gray, John W. 119, 120, 176
Greenleaf, William 132, 141, 147
Gregory, Samuel 18
Griffins, John Cycle Co. 68, 110, 161
Gross, Charles 22, 88
Gunn, George 67

Hall, James 14
Hanlon brothers 26
*Harper's* 26, 242
Harrington, Andrew 15
Harrington, Charles F. 44
Harrington, John 28, 152, 197
Harris, DeLancy P. 218, 219
Harris, D.P. Hardware and Mfg. Co. 218, 219, 220
Hartford Cycle Co. 9, 65, 87–88, 106–107, 108, 109, 110, 127, 134, 137–138, 153, 154, 157, 174
Hartford Real Estate Improvement Co. 4, 80–81, 82, 111, 152, 153, 156, 230
Hartford Rubber Works Co. 119–121, 154, 155, 166, 174–176, 221
Hartford Typewriter Co. 117–118
Hauge, Gabriel 223
Hawley, Charles E. 168
Herlihy, David V. 2, 3, 27, 40
Higginson, Henry L. 136, 162, 169, 177
Hillman, William 24, 28

## Index

Hinkley, Freeman 189, 208, 231, 233
Hinkley, Margaret Pope 19, 152–153, 189, 207, 233
Hodges, E.C. ("Ned") 59, 60, 197
Hodgson, R.H. 29, 44, 241
Hooley, E. Terah 140, 174
Horsman, E.I. 56, 68
"Hosepipe" tire *see* Single-tube tire
Hounshell, David 1, 2 63, 64, 80, 235
House, E.W. 80
Howard, E.L. 20
Howe, Elias 33
Howe, Oliver 207
Howland, W.B. 60
Hoyt, Colgate 186
Hubbell, Lindley 194
Huffman, Horace 224, 237
Huffman Mfg. Co. 219, 222, 227, 228, 237
Hyde, Henry 151

Ickes, Harold 223
Indiana Bicycle Co. 143, 163–164, 179
Inside contractors 79–80
International Association of Machinists 203–206, 227
International Union of Bicycle Workers 202
*Iron Age* 5, 159, 161

Jaynes, Amy *see* Pope, Amy Jaynes
Jeep *see* Willys-Overland
Jeffery, Thomas B. 44, 45, 49, 50, 51, 52, 53, 118, 147, 158, 179, 230–231
Jobbers, bicycle 9, 64, 67, 158, 189–191
Johnson, Hiram 164
Joy, Charles F. 57, 80, 154
Joy, Henry 147

Kaiser, J.W. 163, 240
Keating, Robert 157, 166, 170
Keating Cycle Co. 157, 161, 163, 166, 170, 239
Keller, George 4, 80–81, 152, 156–157, 214
Kellogg steel tube process 115
Kendall, Ernest 127–128
Kingsbury, Jeffery 220, 234
Kirsch, David 136, 138, 141
Knaus, John 80
Kron, Karl 25, 26, 27, 31, 56, 60, 61, 65, 84, 91, 152, 243

Labor relations, at Pope factories 80–81, 83, 185, 202–206

Lallement, Pierre 25, 26, 35, 36, 37, 41, 42, 44, 54, 132
Lamb Knitting Machine Co. 88, 157–158
Latta Bros. Cycle Co. 241–242, 243
Law, Fred 134, 147, 231
L.A.W. *see* League of American Wheelmen
Lawson, Henry John 140, 174
Lawson, Iver 195
League Cycle Co. 127, 134, 167, 168, 201
League of American Wheelmen (L.A.W.) 51, 61–62, 72, 84, 90–104, 159, 182; *Bulletin* 93, 96, 101
Lear, Oscar 240
Lee, Roswell 30
Leland, Henry F. 168
Lenz, Frank 62
Levine, Judith 55
Linder, George 19
Linder, Matilda 19
Lindermere (Cohasset) 4, 74–75, 166, 178, 207, 208
Lobdell, Eugene 214
Lozier, Henry A. 111, 113–114, 175, 177, 184, 186, 231
Lozier Mfg. Co. 111, 124, 179
Lytle, Herb 194

MacDermot, Bridget 14, 16
Machinists' Union *see* International Assn. of Machinists
MacKenzie, Philip 36, 38–39, 40, 42
MacWaugh, Joseph 151–152
Manderson, Charles 95, 97, 98, 99
Mannesmann Steel Tube Co. 110, 113, 114–115
Margins, price (dealer markups) 65–68
Maschin, Harold 224, 226
Mason, Elliot 65, 68, 182, 231
Massachusetts Bicycle Club 29, 45, 60, 77, 92
Matlack, J.C. 186
Maxim, Hiram P. 9, 112, 118, 129–148, 201, 214, 229, 231
Maxim, Hiram S. 112, 118, 129
McClure, John 61
McClure, S.S. ("Sam") 58, 59, 60, 61, 166, 243
*McClure's* 58, 61, 166, 243
McCurdy, A.A. 91
McFarland, Floyd 195–196
McKee, George 42, 44
McKee, Joseph 42, 44
McKee & Harrington 42, 44, 45
McKinley Act *see* Tariffs and import duties

McManus-Kelly Co. 204
Merceles, Theodore 184, 186
Metropole "L'Acatene" bicycle 167–168
Metropolitan Traction Co. 9, 134, 140
Meyer, Eugene 28
Michaux, Pierre 26
Miles, Nelson 15, 59, 86, 87, 89, 103, 136, 156, 173, 197
Military bicycles 85–87
Miller, William E. 112, 113, 114, 115
*Miller v. Bridgeport Brass Co.* (1881) 47, 54
Millett, Stephen C. ("Scotty") 214, 216, 219
Mines 162, 182–184
Modern Tool & Design Co. (MTD) 227
Mom, Gijs 136, 138, 141, 142
"Monarch" bicycle 163, 191, 242
"Monster" good roads petition (1893) 98–100
Montpelier Mfg. Co. 36, 42, 43
Morgan & Wright Tire Co. 120, 123, 174
Morris, Henry 131, 134, 136, 139, 141
Morton, J. Sterling 99, 101
Moss, James A. 87
Motorcycles 200–202, 210
Murray-Ohio Co. 222, 227, 228

National Association of Manufacturers 156, 215
National Metal Trades Association 203–206
Nelson, Elizabeth Bogman 14
Nelson, James 14
Nelson, Parley Bogman 14
Nevins, Allan 132, 147
New England Vehicle Transportation Co. 132, 138, 142–143, 146
New England Women's and Children's Hospital 4, 18–19, 141, 232
New England Women's Medical College 18
"Newton Challenge" bicycle 44
Newton Common Council 23, 89
Norcliffe, Glen 2, 63–64, 91, 235

Office of Road Inquiry *see* Bureau of Public Roads
Olivier brothers 26
Olmstead, Frederic Law 156
Ordway, Albert 86

# Index

Orient Cycle Co. 201
*Outing* 60, 61, 62, 95
Overman, Albert H. 46, 47, 49, 50, 51, 80, 88, 231
Overman Wheel Co. 46, 49, 51, 62, 80, 85, 87, 118–119, 120–121, 128, 157–158

Paris Universal Exhibition (1867) 26, 30
Park River (Hartford) 7, 111, 155, 156
Park Terrace homes *see* Hartford Real Estate Improvement Co.
Parker, Felton 141
Parker, Louis 120, 176
Parrish, Maxfield 63
Pattison, Arthur E. 80, 87, 105, 154, 155, 167
Peck, Alonzo 150, 196
Peekskill Military Academy 78, 169, 173
Petty, Ross 2, 236
Philadelphia Centennial Exhibition (1876) 23, 24, 28, 64, 144
Phillips Exeter Academy 78
"Pioneer" steel tube 116
Pittman, Will 71
Pope, Abby Linder (AAP's wife) 19, 77, 152, 186, 207, 208, 209, 231
Pope, Ada 19
Pope, Adelaide Leonora (AAP's sister) 16, 19, 207, 231
Pope, Albert Augustus: benefactor to family 18–19; birth 13; builds first Columbias 31–32; childhood and youth 15; Civil War service 16–18; colonel's rank questioned 17–18, 47; death of 207; early business enterprises 18–21; estate involved in litigation 209–210; imports first bicycles 29; incorporates Pope Mfg. Co. 22; love of publicity 58; marriage and children 19, 154–155, 169–170, 189; mining speculations 162; real estate investor 19–20, 182–184; sees first bicycle in Philadelphia, 23; sells cigarette rollers and air pistols, 21–22; serves as Newton alderman 23, 89; treasurer of bicycle trust 171–188
Pope, Albert A. & Co. (shoefindings firm) 19, 20, 21, 22, 214
Pope, Albert Linder (AAP's son) 11, 19, 77, 78, 49, 151, 152, 153, 155, 167, 176, 189, 192–193, 194–195, 205, 213, 215–216, 231
Pope, Allen 10, 231
Pope, Amy Jaynes 153, 231
Pope, Annie 14
Pope, Arthur (AAP's brother) 20, 77, 213, 214
Pope, Augusta *see* Pope, Caroline Augusta
Pope, Carolina Augusta (AAP's sister) 18–19, 60, 79, 141, 207, 231
Pope, Charles (AAP's father) 13, 14, 15, 16, 20, 22, 43, 79, 209
Pope, Charles Allen (AAP's brother) 16, 19
Pope, Charles H. 19
Pope, Charles Linder (AAP's son) 77, 169–170
Pope, Clara Hinkley 189, 231
Pope, Edward (AAP's cousin) 22, 23, 77, 80, 87–88, 105, 151, 154, 157, 197, 231
Pope, Elizabeth Bogman (AAP's mother) 13, 14, 79, 141
Pope, Emily F. (AAP's sister) 18–19, 60, 79, 141, 207, 231
Pope, Fred (architect) *see* Pope, Frederick C
Pope, Frederick 13
Pope, Frederick C. ("Fred") 20, 209–210
Pope, George (AAP's cousin) 5, 17, 23, 44, 60, 65, 67, 77, 80, 83, 87–88, 106, 107, 108, 109, 112, 119, 122, 122, 127, 137, 154, 156, 157, 162, 174–175, 181, 184, 186, 197, 192, 204, 205, 211, 213, 215, 231, 239, 241, 243, 245
Pope, Harold Linder (AAP's son) 8, 77, 173, 189, 194, 207, 213, 215, 231
Pope, Harry (AAP's nephew) 10, 16, 21, 65, 77, 78, 88, 107, 112, 137, 167, 202, 231
Pope, Julia Mellish 16
Pope, "Linder" *see* Pope, Ralph
Pope, Louis (AAP's brother) 19, 77, 78, 209
Pope Luella ("Ella") 19, 209
Pope, Margaret Roberts (AAP's daughter) *see* Hinkley, Margaret Pope
Pope, Marion *see* Gillette, Marion Pope
Pope, Mary (AAP's sister) 14, 23
Pope, Mary Bogman (AAP's aunt) 14
Pope, Mary Linder (AAP's daughter) 77
Pope, Ralph (AAP's son) 79, 207, 233
Pope, Walter 44
Pope, William (AAP's uncle) 14, 15, 23
Pope, William ("Col. William") 13
Pope & Talbot Lumber Co. 13, 182
Pope & Waldron 14, 15
Pope Building (Boston) 105, 149–152
Pope Building (Hartford) 11, 152–153, 165–166, 209
Pope-Hartford automobile 10, 194, 199, 212, 213
Pope-Mannesman Co. *see* Mannesman Steel Tube Co.
Pope Memorial Church 4, 173, 208
Pope motorcycles 201–202, 210
Pope Park 155, 156
Pope-Robinson Automobile 189
Pope-Toledo automobile 10, 194–195, 199, 202, 212
Pope-Tribune automobile 10, 189, 193, 199
Pope Tube Co. 109–118, 155, 166, 174–176, 213
*Pope v. Gormully* 6, 51–54
*Pope v. Marqua* 48
Pope's Bicycle Club 197
Pope's Hill (Dorchester) 13
"Pope's Messenger Special" bicycle 212, 222
Pope's Military Band and Orchestra 82
Pope's Mutual Benefit Society 82
"Pope's Row" homes *see* Hartford Real Estate Improvement Co.
Post, David J. 65, 67, 80, 83, 87, 107, 108, 120, 127, 154, 167, 214
Potter, Asa 74
Potter, Isaac 94, 95, 98, 103
Potter, Orlando 33, 54
Pratt, Charles E. 5, 27, 29, 30, 42, 43, 48–54, 60, 61, 63, 66, 75–76, 141, 243, 244
Pratt, Elmer 64
Pratt & Whitney Tool Co. 7, 30, 80, 112, 122, 214
Pressy, George 46
Pueblo, CO 182–183
Pullman, IL 4, 155–156, 204

Quackenbush, Henry 21, 22, 28

Racing, automobile 194–195, 212–213
Racing, bicycle 90–93, 195–196

## Index

Rae, John B. 129, 132, 139, 141, 147
Raleigh Cycle Co. 80, 82–83, 110, 200, 224, 226, 228, 237
"Rambler" bicycle and automobile 147, 159, 179, 191
Redding, William 172
Redhead, Norton & Lathrop Co. 66
Reynolds, Harvey 40, 41, 42
Rice, Charles D. 119, 168
Rice, H.H. 10, 179, 193, 206
Rice, Isaac 136, 139
Richardson, Henry M. 42
Richardson & McKee 36, 42, 43 44, 54
Ritchie, John W. 193
Robinson, John T. Co. 189
Rockefeller, John D. 61, 162, 184–185, 186
"Rollfast" bicycles 3, 189–190, 218–219
Roosevelt, Theodore 61, 165
Rosen, Paul 80
Rosewald, Lessing 222
"Rover" bicycle 84, 200
Rowe, William 45
Rubber Goods Mfg. Co. 174–175, 184, 191
Rudolphe & Krummel Co. 122, 237
Rural Free Delivery 101–102, 244
Russell, Eugene 139
Russell, Henry 121

Sachtelben, W.L. 62
Safety bicycle 84–85
"Safety" Ordinaries 84
St. Nicholas Bicycle Co. 43, 44, 48, 123
Salom, Pedro 131, 134, 136, 139, 141
Schaaf, Albert E. 202, 205, 206
Schwinn, Edward R. 225
Schwinn, Frank, Jr. 225, 233, 245
Schwinn, Frank, Sr. 119, 120, 216–218, 220–221, 222, 233
Schwinn, Ignatz 216, 218
Schwinn Bicycle Co. 69–70, 218, 220, 221, 222, 223–224, 225, 228, 245
Scott, Frederick 96
*Scribner's* 60, 61, 103, 133, 159, 242
Sears, Roebuck & Co. 218, 222
Selden, George 132, 144–146
Sellers, Coleman 127–128
Sewing Machines 30, 33, 63, 111, 244
Shadbolt, H.S. 127–128
Shaft-drive bicycles 127, 167, 168

Sharps Rifle Co. 10, 30
Shaw's Regiment 16–17, 162
Shelby Steel Tube Co. 111, 112, 113–114, 174–176
Shimano Corp. 3, 226, 227
Simmonds Rolling Ball Co. 125–128
Singer, I.M. 33
"Singer Challenge" bicycle 28
Singer Sewing Machine Co. 33, 63, 65, 80, 244
Single-tube tire 119–121, 161, 221
Smith, Charles F. 143, 163, 175, 240
Smith, Frederic 147
Smith, H.B. Machine Co. 46, 76, 80, 84, 236
Smith, Steven 40
Snyder, Bill 219
Snyder, Homer P. 189, 218–219
Society of Automobile Engineers 147
Souther, Henry 10, 112, 113, 135, 147, 167, 194, 233
Spalding, Albert G. 8, 88, 143, 144, 146, 167, 171–178, 233
Spalding Bros. Sporting Goods Co. 87, 157, 158, 159
Spanish-American War 7, 87, 141, 169, 173
Sprague, Frank 133
Springfield Armory 30
Stanley Club Show 238–239
"Star" bicycle 46, 76, 84, 91, 236, 243
Starley, James 83
Starley, James Kemp 24, 28, 84
"Sterling" bicycle 122, 163, 231, 240
Sterns Cycle Co. 180
Stevens, Thomas 61, 62, 152
Stevens, J.P. Arms Co. 10, 138, 182, 202
Stiefel, Ralph 114–115
"Sting-Ray" bicycle 225
Stone, Roy 95, 98–104
Stowe, Harriet Beecher 4
Strohmeyer 25
Studebaker, Clem 98, 140, 141
*Sturmey's Indispensable Handbook* 238–239
Sweeting Cycle Co. 108
*Swift v. City of Topeka* 72

Taplan Mfg. Co. 216, 231
Tarbell, Ida 61
"Target" air pistol 21, 22
Tariffs and import policy 29, 106–107, 109, 115, 167–168, 223–224
Taylor, Frederick W. 4, 124–128, 233–234, 235

Taylor, Marshall W. ("Major") 195
Teall, Edward 218, 219
Tillinghast, P.W. 119
Tillinghast tire *see* Single-tube tire
Timms & Lawford 24
Toledo strike of 1906–7 156, 202–206
Torrington Co. 216, 220, 225, 237
Traveler's Insurance Co. 46
Treaty of Springfield 51, 88
Troy, Bill 149, 151
"Tuttle" shaft-drive bicycle 4
Twain, Mark 4, 56

"Union" bicycle 44
Unzicker, Otto 67, 184

Vanderbilt Cup 194–195, 212–213
Varrecke, Monsieur 44
"Velocity" bicycle 44, 241
"Victor" bicycles and tricycles 46, 49, 85, 121, 159, 197
Vinal, James 14

Waldorf-Astoria Hotel (New York) 63, 173–174, 190
Walker, Charles 12, 154, 187, 191, 192, 213, 214, 216, 219, 220, 234
Walker, Wilbur 154, 192, 213, 214, 216, 219, 220, 234
Walthour, Bobby 195
Wanamaker's Department Store 102, 212
Warner, Sam Bass 12
Warren, Francis Bogman 14
Warren, Moses 14
Warren & Bogman 14
Watts, William 96–97
"Waverly" bicycle 9, 163
"Waverly" electric automobile 9, 179, 187, 193, 194, 206
Weed, T.E. 30
Weed Sewing Machine Co. 7, 11, 30, 31, 49, 54, 75, 80, 87, 154, 230, 244
Weldless Steel Tube Co. 110, 111
West End Street Railway Co. 78, 133, 169
Western Auto stores 69, 226
Western Toy Co. *see* Western Wheel Works
Western Union 211, 212
Western Wheel Works 43, 48, 66–67, 121, 123, 143, 154, 165, 172, 175, 182, 184, 191
Westfield ("Lozierville") factory 3, 192, 206
Westfield Mfg. Co. 214, 216–217, 219, 220, 222, 224,

255–228; *see also* Columbia Mfg. Co.
Weston, Frank  28, 29, 59, 197
Wetmore, Edmund  52, 53, 98
Weymouth, Edmund  125
"Wheel Around the Hub" tour  59–60
*The Wheelman*  50, 51, 60, 61, 62, 166, 243
Whitehouse, Harold  173
Whitlock, Brand  203, 204
Whitney, Henry M.  74, 78, 131, 133, 142

Whitney, William C.  9, 11, 131, 132, 133–134, 138, 140–146, 234
Wilcox, Julius  66, 84, 244
Williams, Emily  69
Williams, Florence  69
Williard, W.A.  126–128
Willys, John  205
Willys-Overland  10, 205–206, 213
Wilson Cycle Co.  158
Winchester Arms Co.  79–80
Winkley, Robert  63, 149, 151, 177, 187, 209, 234

Winton Motor Carriage Co.  146
Witty, Calvin  21, 26, 27, 40, 42, 234
"World" typewriter  11, 117
World's Columbian Exposition *see* Chicago world's fair

Yates, Ritchie & Pope  192–193
Yost, Joseph A.  111

Zakrzewska, Marie  18

www.ingramcontent.com/pod-product-compliance
Lightning Source LLC
Chambersburg PA
CBHW081541300426
44116CB00015B/2715